APPROACHES TO THE QUR'AN IN CONTEMPORARY IRAN

Approaches to the Qur'an in Contemporary Iran explores the importance of the reception of the Qur'an in the religious, intellectual, political and artistic discourses in modern and contemporary Iran, from the nineteenth century to the present.

The chapters included in the volume have been written by some of the most authoritative specialists in the modern history of Iran. Their contributions span a wide range of subjects and themes, covering such varied ground as the examination of the trends in Qur'anic exegesis that are currently prominent in Iran, the use of Qur'anic themes in contemporary Iranian cinema, the concept of revelation as the basis of diverse political trends in the Islamic Republic of Iran, Sufi mystical interpretations of the Qur'an, the use of the Qur'an in the arts, the Qur'an as a living scripture in specific intellectual and social circles, and case studies of individual intellectuals.

Through this wide-ranging survey, the book aims to become a reference for anyone interested in the Qur'an's imprint on the religious, political, cultural and anthropological history of modern and contemporary Iranian society.

Alessandro Cancian is a Research Associate in the Qur'anic Studies unit at the Institute of Ismaili Studies, London. Dr Cancian's areas of interest and expertise are the intellectual history of Shiʿism, Shiʿi Sufism in early modern times and the anthropology of Islam, Shiʿism and modern Iran. His monograph *Sufism, Shiʿism and Qur'anic Exegesis in Early Modern Iran: Sulṭān ʿAlī Shāh Gunābādī and his Tafsīr Bayān al-Saʿāda* (Qur'anic Studies Series) is due to be published soon. He is co-editing (with Nuha Alshaar) a volume on ethics for *An Anthology of Qur'anic Commentaries* (Qur'anic Studies Series). He holds a PhD in Anthropology, with a concentration on the Cultural Anthropology of Muslim Societies and the Anthropology of Religion, from the University of Siena. His dissertation was on the Shiʿi theological colleges (*hawza ʿilmiyya*) in Syria. Among his recent publications is the monograph *Alla scuola dell'Imam: Storia dell'educazione religiosa nell'Islam sciita* (*At the Imam's School: History of Religious Education in Shiʿi Islam*; Rome, 2016).

The Institute of Ismaili Studies

Qur'anic Studies Series 18

Series editor, Omar Alí-de-Unzaga

Previously published titles:

1. Suha Taji-Farouki, editor, *Modern Muslim Intellectuals and the Qur'an* (2004; Paperback 2006)
2. Abdullah Saeed, editor, *Approaches to the Qur'an in Contemporary Indonesia* (2005)
3. Annabel Keeler *Sufi Hermeneutics: The Qur'an Commentary of Rashīd al-Dīn Maybudī* (2006; Paperback 2017)
4. Fahmida Suleman, editor, *Word of God, Art of Man: The Qur'an and its Creative Expressions* (2007; Paperback 2010)
5. Feras Hamza and Sajjad Rizvi, editors, with Farhana Mayer, *An Anthology of Qur'anic Commentaries, Volume I: On the Nature of the Divine* (2008; Paperback 2010)
6. Toby Mayer, translator, *Keys to the Arcana: Shahrastānī's Esoteric Commentary on the Qur'an* (2009; Paperback 2019)
7. Travis Zadeh *The Vernacular Qur'an: Translation and the Rise of Persian Exegesis* (2012)
8. Martin Nguyen *Sufi Master and Qur'an Scholar: Abū'l-Qāsim al-Qushayrī and the Laṭā'if al-ishārāt* (2012)
9. Karen Bauer, editor *Aims, Methods and Contexts of Qur'anic Exegesis (2nd/8th–9th/15th C.)* (2013)
10. Angelika Neuwirth *Scripture, Poetry and the Making of a Community: Reading the Qur'an as a Literary Text* (2014)
11. M. Brett Wilson *Translating the Qur'an in an Age of Nationalism: Print Culture and Modern Islam in Turkey* (2014)
12. Andreas Görke and Johanna Pink, editors, *Tafsīr and Islamic Intellectual History: Exploring the Boundaries of a Genre* (2014)
13. S.R. Burge, editor, *The Meaning of the Word: Lexicology and Qur'anic Exegesis* (2015)

14. Suha Taji-Farouki, editor, *The Qur'an and Its Readers Worldwide: Contemporary Commentaries and Translations* (2015)

15. Annabel Keeler and Sajjad Rizvi, editors, *The Spirit and the Letter: Approaches to the Esoteric Interpretation of the Qur'an* (2016)

16. Nuha Alshaar, editor, *The Qur'an and Adab: The Shaping of Literary Traditions in Classical Islam* (2017)

17. Asma Hilali *The Sanaa Palimpsest: The Transmission of the Qur'an in the First Centuries AH* (2017)

Approaches to the Qur'an in Contemporary Iran

EDITED BY

Alessandro Cancian

OXFORD
UNIVERSITY PRESS

in association with

THE INSTITUTE OF ISMAILI STUDIES
LONDON

OXFORD
UNIVERSITY PRESS

Great Clarendon Street, Oxford OX2 6DP
Oxford University Press is a department of the University of Oxford.
It furthers the University's objective of excellence in research, scholarship,
and education by publishing worldwide in
Oxford New York
Auckland Cape Town Dar es Salaam Hong Kong Karachi
Kuala Lumpur Madrid Melbourne Mexico City Nairobi
New Delhi Shanghai Taipei Toronto

With offices in

Argentina Austria Brazil Chile Czech Republic France Greece
Guatemala Hungary Italy Japan Poland Portugal Singapore
South Korea Switzerland Thailand Turkey Ukraine Vietnam

Oxford is a registered trade mark of Oxford University Press
in the UK and in certain other countries

Published in the United States
by Oxford University Press Inc., New York

First published 2019

British Library Cataloguing in Publication Data
Data available

Library of Congress Cataloging in Publication Data
Data available

Cover photograph: Tiles and Calligraphy, Sheikh Lotfollah Mosque,
Isfahan, Iran. © LOK KokWah.
Cover design: RefineCatch Limited
Map illustration: Oxford Designers & Illustrators

Index by Jacqueline Pitchford, Professional Member of the Society of Indexers
Typeset by RefineCatch Limited, Bungay, Suffolk
Printed in Great Britain on acid-free paper by
TJ International, Padstow, Cornwall

ISBN 978-0-19-884076-3

The Institute of Ismaili Studies

The Institute of Ismaili Studies was established in 1977 with the objectives of promoting scholarship and learning on Islam, in historical as well as contemporary contexts, and fostering better understanding of Islam's relationship with other societies and faiths.

The Institute's programmes encourage a perspective which is not confined to the theological and religious heritage of Islam, but seeks to explore the relationship of religious ideas to broader dimensions of society and culture. The programmes thus *encourage* an interdisciplinary approach to Islamic history and thought. Particular attention is given to the issues of modernity that arise as Muslims seek to relate their heritage to the contemporary situation.

Within the Islamic tradition, the Institute promotes research on those areas which have, to date, received relatively little attention from scholars. These include the intellectual and literary expressions of Shiʿism in general and Ismailism in particular.

The Institute's objectives are realised through concrete programmes and activities organised by various departments of the Institute, at times in collaboration with other institutions of learning. These programmes and activities are informed by the full range of cultures in which Islam is practised today. From the Middle East, South and Central Asia, and Africa to the industrialised societies in the West, they consider the variety of contexts which shape the ideals, beliefs and practices of the faith.

In facilitating the *Qur'anic Studies Series* and other publications, the Institute's sole purpose is to encourage original research and analysis of relevant issues, which often leads to diverse views and interpretations. While every effort is made to ensure that the publications are of a high academic standard, the opinions expressed in these publications must be understood as belonging to their authors alone.

QUR'ANIC STUDIES SERIES

THE QUR'AN has been an inexhaustible source of intellectual and spiritual reflection in Islamic history, giving rise to ever-proliferating commentaries and interpretations. Many of these have remained a realm for specialists due to their scholarly demands. Others, more widely read, remain untranslated from the primary language of their composition. This series aims to make some of these materials from a broad chronological range – the formative centuries of Islam to the present day – available to a wider readership through translation and publication in English, accompanied where necessary by introductory or explanatory materials. The series will also include contextual-analytical and survey studies of these primary materials.

Throughout this series and others like it which may appear in the future, the aim is to allow the materials to speak for themselves. Not surprisingly, in the Muslim world where its scriptural sources continue to command passionate interest and commitment, the Qur'an has been subject to contending, often antithetical ideas and interpretations. The series takes no sides in these debates. The aim rather is to place on the record the rich diversity and plurality of approaches and opinions which have appealed to the Qur'an throughout history (and even more so today). The breadth of this range, however partisan or controversial individual presentations within it may be, is instructive in itself. While there is always room in such matters for personal preferences, commitment to particular traditions of belief, and scholarly evaluations, much is to be gained by a simple appreciation, not always evident today, of the enormous wealth of intellectual effort that has been devoted to the Qur'an from the earliest times. It is hoped that through this objective, this series will prove of use to scholars and students in Qur'anic Studies as well as other allied and relevant fields.

Contents

Section II: Alternative Approaches: Between Marginality and Legitimacy

Section III: The Arts, Material Culture and Everyday Life

Notes on Contributors

Alice Bombardier is a Research Associate at the Centre d'Analyse et d'Intervention Sociologiques (CNRS–EHESS Paris). In 2012, she received her PhD in Persian-Arabic Studies from Geneva University and in Sociology from EHESS-Paris. She holds an 'agrégation' in Geography and is a specialist in modern and contemporary Iranian painting. Her latest publications include *Les pionniers de la Nouvelle peinture en Iran: Oeuvres méconnues, activités novatrices et scandales au tournant des années 1940* (Bern, 2017).

Nicholas Boylston is currently College Fellow of the Committee on the Study of Religion at Harvard University. He received his PhD in Theological and Religious Studies from Georgetown University in 2017, his MA in Islamic Philosophy from the University of Tehran in 2011, and his BA from Harvard College in 2007. His research focuses on literary and philosophical approaches to pluralism in pre-modern Islam.

Rainer Brunner has been Directeur de Recherche at the Centre National de la Recherche Scientifique (CNRS), Paris, since 2005. Before that he was Assistant Professor at the Orientalisches Seminar of Freiburg University (1998–2004), Directeur d'Études Invité at the École Pratique des Hautes Études, Section Sciences Religieuses at the Sorbonne (2002), Fellow at the Institute for Advanced Studies of the Hebrew University of Jerusalem (2002–2003), and was a member of the Institute for Advanced Study in Princeton (2004/2005 and 2013/2014). His main research interests are modern Muslim intellectual history, especially the history and theology of the Shiʿa, the relationship between the Sunni and the Shiʿa, Muslim modernism since the nineteenth century, and the history of Oriental Studies.

Alessandro Cancian is a Research Associate in the Qur'anic Studies unit at the Institute of Ismaili Studies, London. Dr Cancian's areas of interest and expertise are the intellectual history of Shiʿism, Shiʿi

Sufism in early modern times and the anthropology of Islam, Shiʿism and modern Iran. His monograph *Sufism, Shiʿism and Qur'anic Exegesis in Early Modern Iran: Sulṭān ʿAlī Shāh Gunābādī and his Tafsīr Bayān al-Saʿāda* (Qur'anic Studies Series) is due to be published soon. He is co-editing (with Nuha Alshaar) a volume on ethics for *An Anthology of Qur'anic Commentaries* (Qur'anic Studies Series). He holds a PhD in Anthropology, with a concentration on the Cultural Anthropology of Muslim Societies and the Anthropology of Religion, from the University of Siena. His dissertation was on the Shiʿi theological colleges (*hawza ʿilmiyya*) in Syria. Among his recent publications is the monograph *Alla scuola dell'Imam: Storia dell'educazione religiosa nell'Islam sciita* (*At the Imam's School: History of Religious Education in Shiʿi Islam*; Rome, 2016).

Giovanni De Zorzi is Associate Professor of Ethnomusicology at the Ca' Foscari University of Venice (https://www.unive.it/data/persone/5590760). His main research areas are the Ottoman and Central Asian traditions of classical and Sufi music. Among his many publications is his monograph *Musiche di Turchia: Tradizioni e Transiti tra Oriente ed Occidente* (Milan, 2010). He is also a musician (*ney* flute player), and performs both as a soloist and with his Ensemble Marâghî (http://www.ensemblemaraghi.it/).

Ingvild Flaskerud is Assistant Professor at the Faculty of Theology, University of Oslo. Holding a PhD in Religious Studies from the University of Bergen, her field of speciality is ethnographic research into Twelver Shiʿism in Iran and Norway. Her work focuses on the visual and material culture of Twelver Shiʿism in Iran (*Visualizing Belief and Piety in Iranian Shiism*; London, 2010), women and ritual performance, the religious theatre, local pilgrimage, the transfer of religion and cultural formation in Western migrancy, religious authority and the vernacular production of contextual theology. Among her latest publications is the co-edited anthology *Muslim Pilgrimage in Europe* (London, 2017). In 2018 she was a guest editor (with Oddbjørn Leirvik) for the journal *Islam and Christian–Muslim Relations*, on the topic *The Study of Islam between University Theology and Lived Religion*. She has also produced an ethnographic film about women as ritual performers in Iran (2005).

Niloofar Haeri is Professor and Chair of the Department of Anthropology at Johns Hopkins University and the Director of the Program in Islamic Studies. Her first book examined the roles of gender and class as causes of language change in Egypt. Her second major project on Egypt examined the layered ramifications of the ambiguity of classical Arabic as the sacred language of the Qur'an and as the official state language used in almost all non-religious domains. The examination of that ambiguity also entailed a historical analysis of the reasons for the rejection of vernacular Arabic as the language of writing by almost all strands of Islamist and (secular) nationalist movements. More recently, she has been doing research in Iran on how classical poetry and different kinds of prayer serve as grounds for debate on what is true Islam. Her forthcoming book is tentatively titled *In the Presence of the Divine: Women, Prayer and Poetry in Iran*.

Seyfeddin Kara is an Assistant Professor of Shi'i Studies and Relations between Islamic Schools of Thought and Holder of the Imam Ali Chair for Shi'i Studies and Dialogue among Islamic Legal Schools at Hartford Seminary. He is the author of *In Search of Ali Ibn Abi Talib's Codex: History and Traditions of the Earliest Copy of the Qur'an* (Berlin, 2018).

Leonard Lewisohn was a Senior Lecturer in Persian and Iran Heritage Foundation Fellow in Classical Persian and Sufi Literature at the Institute of Arab and Islamic Studies of the University of Exeter, where he taught Persian language, Sufism, the history of Iran, as well as courses on Persian texts and Persian poetry in translation. He specialised in the translation of Persian Sufi poetry and prose. He was the author of *Beyond Faith and Infidelity: The Sufi Poetry and Teachings of Mahmud Shabistari* (London, 1995) and the editor of three volumes on *The Heritage of Sufism* (Oxford, 1999). He was editor of the *Mawlana Rumi Review*, an annual journal devoted to Jalāl al-Dīn Rūmī. He was also editor (with Christopher Shackle) of *'Aṭṭār and the Persian Sufi Tradition: The Art of Spiritual Flight* (London, 2006), co-translator with Robert Bly of *The Angels Knocking on the Tavern Door: Thirty Poems of Hafez* (New York, 2008), and editor of *Hafiz and the Religion of Love in*

Classical Persian Poetry (London, 2010). He had contributed articles to several encyclopaedias and journals. Dr Lewisohn sadly passed away on 6 August 2018.

Banafsheh Madaninejad is a Visiting Assistant Professor of Philosophy at Southwestern University where she focuses on critical race theory, feminist ethics and activism. She has written about Islamic New Theology and racialisation of Muslims, and is currently working on a collection of phenomenological essays about solidarity in the age of Donald Trump. She is also in the process of translating Mohsen Kadivar's *Ḥukūmat-i wilāʾī* (*Governance by Guardianship*) into English.

Yaser Mirdamadi is currently a PhD candidate in Islamic Studies at the University of Edinburgh and is the current recipient of the IIS Mohammad Arkoun Doctoral Scholarship. He spent eight years in an Islamic seminary. His main areas of research are modern Islam and the philosophy of religion. He is a Visiting Teaching Fellow at al-Maktoum College, Dundee, and a Research Assistant at the Institute of Ismaili Studies, London.

Nacim Pak-Shiraz is the Head of Islamic and Middle Eastern Studies and Senior Lecturer in Film and Persian Studies at the University of Edinburgh. She has published widely on Iranian visual culture, particularly on Iranian cinema. These include her monograph, *Shiʿi Islam in Iranian Cinema: Religion and Spirituality in Film* (London, 2011), and *Visualizing Iran: From Antiquity to the Present* (2017), a special issue edition of the *Iranian Studies* journal. Dr Pak-Shiraz is also active on the cultural scene and engages with international film festivals both within and outside the UK.

Sajjad Rizvi is an Associate Professor of Islamic Intellectual History at the University of Exeter. Trained as a historian at Oxford and then Cambridge, he specialises in Islamic thought in the post-classical period and has published on the philosophers of the Safavid and Qajar periods in particular. His other main interest lies in exegesis and Qur'anic hermeneutics. He is the co-editor with Feras Hamza (and Farhana Mayer) of *An Anthology of Qur'anic Commentaries, Volume One: The Nature of the Divine* (Oxford,

2008; Qur'anic Studies Series 5), and co-editor with Annabel Keeler of *The Spirit and the Letter: Approaches to the Esoteric Interpretation of the Qur'an* (Oxford, 2016; Qur'anic Studies Series 15). He is currently writing a number of studies on Muḥammad Ḥusayn Ṭabāṭabā'ī, investigating the nature of hermeneutics and metaphysics in contemporary Islamic thought in the Twelver Shiʿi context.

Reza Tabandeh holds a PhD in Islamic Studies from the Institute of Arab and Islamic Studies at the University of Exeter, with a specialisation in the revival of Niʿmatullāhī Sufism in Iran. His research interest lies in Islamic mystical philosophies in contemporary Iran. His doctoral work focused on the second generation of Niʿmatullāhī masters, during the period following the return of the order to Iran from India. He is currently undertaking post-doctoral research at Brock University, Canada, on the interaction between the Sufis and the *ʿulamāʾ* in the Persianate World.

Liyakat Takim is the Sharjah Chair in Global Islam at McMaster University, Canada. A native of Zanzibar, Tanzania, he has spoken at more than eighty academic conferences and authored 100 scholarly works on diverse topics such as reformation in the Islamic world, the treatment of women in Islamic law, Islam in America, the indigenisation of the Muslim community in America, dialogue in post-9/11 America, war and peace in the Islamic tradition, Islamic law, Islamic biographical literature, the charisma of the holy man and shrine culture, and Islamic mystical traditions. He teaches a wide range of courses on Islam and offers a course on comparative religions. Professor Takim's publications include *Shiʿism in America* (New York, 2009) and *The Heirs of the Prophet: Charisma and Religious Authority in Shiʿite Islam* (Albany, NY, 2006). He is working on his third book, 'Ijtihad and Reformation in Islam'. Professor Takim has taught at several American and Canadian universities and is actively engaged in dialogue with different faith communities.

Anna Vanzan teaches History and Culture of the Middle East at the University of Pavia. She holds a PhD in Near Eastern Studies from New York University and works on gender studies with a particular focus on Asian Muslim societies. Her latest book, *L'Islam Visuale. Immagini e potere dagli Omayyadi ai giorni nostri* (Rome, 2018), is a reflection on how the rhetoric of image has been used for political purposes by many leaders in the Muslim Middle East.

Neguin Yavari studied medieval history at Columbia University and is currently a Senior Research Fellow at The Humanities Centre for Advanced Studies "Multiple Secularities – Beyond the West, Beyond Modernities", University of Leipzig. Her book on the rhetoric of advice in medieval political thought, *Advice for the Sultan: Prophetic Voices and Secular Politics in Medieval Islam* (London, 2014), is a comparative study of mirrors for princes from the European and Islamic worlds. Mirrors for princes across political and spatial divides is the subject of her co-edited volume, *Global Medieval: Mirrors for Princes Reconsidered* (Cambridge, MA, 2015). Her latest book, entitled *The Future of Iran's Past: Nizam al-Mulk Remembered* (London, 2018), is a biography of Niẓām al-Mulk, the prominent eleventh-century Seljuk vizier.

Note on Transliteration, Conventions and Abbreviations

Arabic and Persian transliterations follow a modified system based on the standard of the *International Journal of Middle East Studies*. Names, terms and toponyms from non-Latin alphabets are transliterated unless common to English. The genealogical sequence Muḥammad ibn Qāsim, etc., is abbreviated with 'b.' for ibn (son) and 'bt.' for bint (daughter); the definite article on the *nisba* and the *laqab* is generally dropped after its first appearance, that is, from 'al-Khargūshī' to 'Khargūshī' or 'al-Jāḥiẓ' to 'Jāḥiẓ', and so forth. Definite articles, however, are by and large maintained for formal titles, that is, al-Ḥakīm. The various forms of spelling for the toponymics Iṣbahānī and Naysāpūrī, etc., have been standardised throughout to Iṣfahānī and Nīshābūrī. Dates pertaining to Islamic history are indicated both in *hijrī* and Common Era forms before the nineteenth century CE, and in Common Era forms from the twentieth century onwards. Dates marked with the abbreviation 'Sh.' in the bibliographical material correspond to the modern solar *hijrī* calendar used in Iran. All translations are the relevant author's unless otherwise indicated.

Abbreviations

EI[2]	*Encyclopaedia of Islam*, 2nd edition, ed. H.A.R. Gibb *et al.* Leiden, Brill, 1960–2004
EI THREE	*Encyclopaedia of Islam THREE*, 3rd edition, ed. Kate Fleet *et al.* Leiden, Brill, 2010–
EIr	*Encyclopaedia Iranica*, ed. Ehsan Yarshater. London, Routledge and K. Paul; New York, Encyclopaedia Iranica Foundation, 1982–
EQ	*Encyclopaedia of the Qur'ān*, ed., Jane Dammen McAuliffe. Leiden, Brill, 2001–6

Preface and Acknowledgements

This volume is the final outcome of an effort commenced in August 2012, with two panels which I convened at the Ninth Biennial Iranian Studies Conference in Istanbul, and continued one year later with an International Colloquium which I organised at the Institute of Ismaili Studies (IIS) in London (2–4 September 2013). Most of the chapters in this book were developed from the papers presented at these two events, and although not all of the participants have contributed to this volume (and others have joined us along the way), this work encapsulates the spirit of all the discussions both within the panels and during the informal conversations that punctuated the events.

Throughout this project I have benefited from the support and generosity of a number of colleagues and friends. Many people have helped bring this book to light, and I will probably fail to mention them all. I would, therefore, like to express my gratitude to those who are not mentioned here, but who have supported me directly or indirectly.

First and foremost, I would like to thank the authors whose chapters appear in this book. It has been a privilege to work with such a diverse, brilliant, insightful and stimulating group of scholars. I would also like to thank the participants whose work for various reasons does not appear in this volume: Aun Hasan Ali, Mohammad Hadi Gerami, Omid Ghaemmaghami, Denis Hermann, Mirjam Künkler, Todd Lawson, Mohammad Mesbahi and Daryoush Mohammad Poor. At the Institute of Ismaili Studies, I would like to thank our editor Lisa Morgan, who scrupulously went through every section of this book and undertook the not-easy task of working with each author with competence, insight and respect. She also helped me deal with particularly complicated conundrums that I would not have been able to solve on my own. I would like to specially thank the academic coordinator of the Qur'anic Studies Unit at the IIS, Dr Omar Ali-de-Unzaga. Not only was Omar the intellectual father of the Approaches to the Qur'an project and the person who entrusted me with the task of preparing this volume on Iran, he has also been a guiding presence over the years and a continuous source of support and friendship. A great deal of the merit of this book lies with him, not least because he closely followed every phase of this project, from the original idea to the editing. I would also like to thank the Co-Director of the IIS, Dr Farhad Daftary, who always let his support be felt; Hena Miah, who helped with the practical and logistical issues of the Istanbul panels and the London Colloquium; Naushin Sharif, who took over from Hena and never failed to help with practicalities; Julia Kolb for her assistance at various phases of the project; my colleagues at the Qur'anic Studies Unit for their support and advice; Dr Dagi Dagiev, with whom I shared an office during this project, and who was always ready to provide welcome diversionary conversation, whether on serious or less serious matters. I would also like to thank Reza, Mahdi Platone, Virginia and Gioia, for their love, support and patience; my mother Barbara, my father Beniamino and my sister Francesca; also Reza Fazeli, who managed to arrange access for me to places I would not have been able to access without him: this is my way of repaying him.

To end on a sombre note, while the editing process of this volume was already in its final stages, and at the exact moment Omar and I were discussing his chapter, we received the terrible news of Leonard Lewisohn's premature return to the mercy of the One. Lenny was an erudite and sensitive scholar, a lively intellectual stimulus at every phase of this project, a tough nut to crack when it came to editing his chapter, but, first and foremost, a true friend and mentor. I am sure that I convey the sentiments of all the authors in considering this volume a heartfelt, collective homage to him and his passion for our field of research.

Alessandro Cancian
19 December 2018

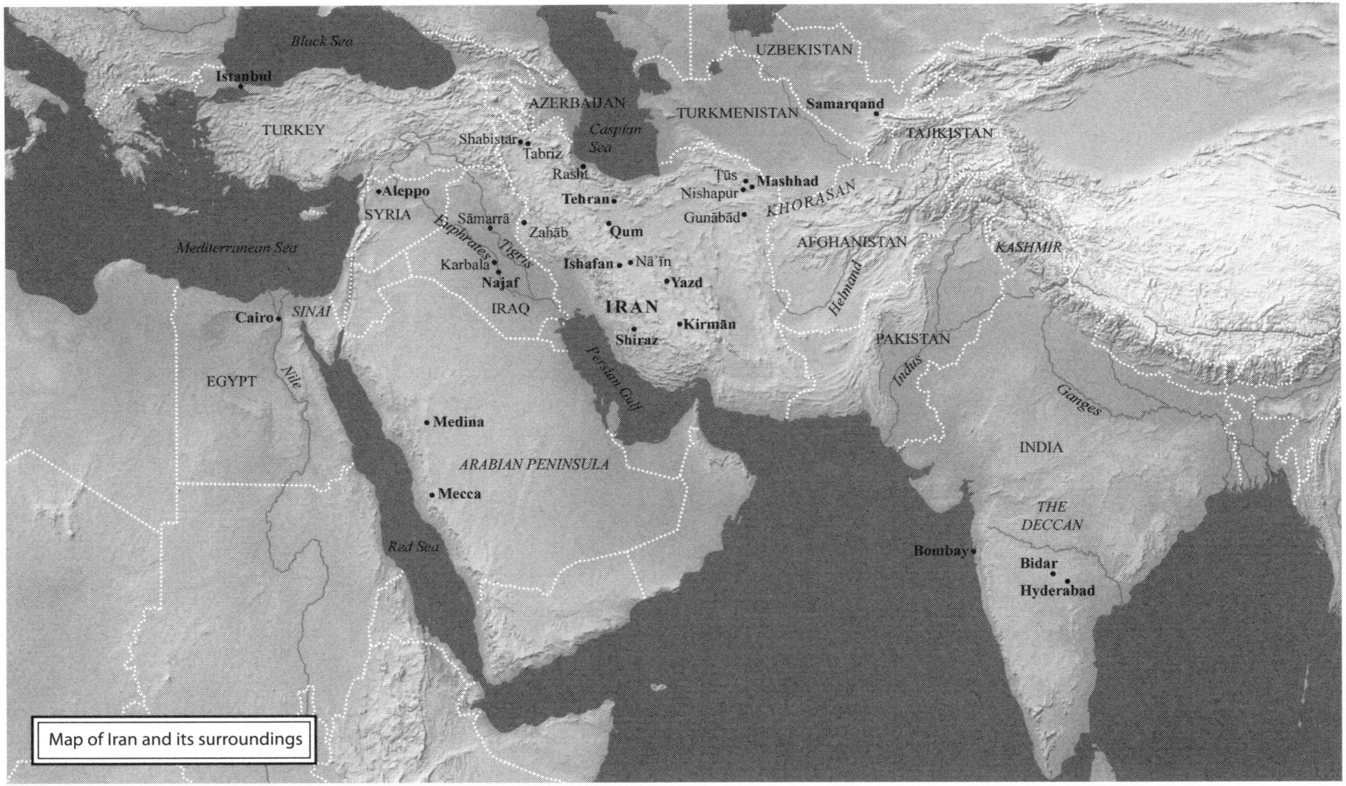

Map of Iran and its surroundings

Introduction

ALESSANDRO CANCIAN

THE ENGAGEMENT of Persianate culture with the Qur'an is as long as Islamic Persia's history. This historical interaction can be pinpointed from as early as classical times. It is visible, for example, in Persian poetry. Such foundational poets as Abū'l-Majd Ṣanā'ī (d. 525/1131) and Farīd al-Dīn al-ʿAṭṭār (d. 617/1220) incorporated Qur'anic phrases as standard rhetorical devices in their works; Firdawsī (d. 411/1020 or 416/1025) is argued to have adapted Qur'anic rhythms in his epic poem *Shāh-nāma*;[1] and Jalāl al-Dīn Rūmī (d. 672/1273) elaborated on Qur'anic material throughout his *Mathnawī*, to the extent that he himself deemed his work to have originated from the same prophetic source as the Book, and the *Mathnawī* in Iran came to be widely referred to as a 'Qur'an in Persian'.[2] Apart from poetry, many other forms of art in the Persianate cultures have been inspired by the Qur'an and keep drawing on the Book for their sustainment; calligraphy is emblematic in this respect. Other areas which bear testimony to the Persianate culture's engagement with the Qur'an are, of course, Qur'anic exegesis – where large numbers of works produced by Persian scholars, both in Arabic and in Persian, draw on the Book or parts of it – and Persian translations of the Qur'an, exegetical or otherwise.[3] In premodern times, roughly up until the mid-nineteenth century, Persian-language commentaries were meant to make the Qur'anic legacy known to as wide as possible an audience in the Persian-speaking milieu so that they could increase their interaction with it. These two elements of accessibility and interplay are the basis of the studies offered in the present volume.

During the nineteenth and twentieth centuries, the wide availability of the Qur'anic discourses in Persian was facilitated by the new publication technologies which made it easier to disseminate information. This made it possible for a field that once was only accessible to a closed circle of learned clerics to reach a larger pool of intellectuals who occupied the middle ground between the traditional intellectual circles and a nascent civil society. This pool of intellectuals started to produce a less technical range of Qur'anic exegeses, or at least of Qur'an-inspired thought, that made its way into the political discourse in the form of debates on constitutional rights in the years preceding and following the Constitutional Revolution in Iran (1905–11). Long a domain of the clerical classes, exegesis became more and more politicised and embedded in the public discourse under the nationalist regimes of Reza Shah Pahlavi (1925–41) and his son Mohammad Reza Shah (1941–79). This was a time when influential intellectuals who operated outside of the clerical milieu, for example Jalāl Āl-i Aḥmad (d. 1969), ʿAlī Sharīʿatī (d. 1977) and Mahdī Bāzārgān (d. 1995), emerged in the public arena, and in different ways and measures took inspiration from the Qur'an. Other names that populated the exegetical landscape are well known, and constitute some of the intellectual pivots of the Islamic republic: Maḥmūd Ṭāliqānī (d. 1979), Murtaḍā Muṭahharī (d. 1979), ʿAllāma Ṭabāṭabāʾī (d. 1981) and Ruhollah Khomeini (d. 1989) to name a few; they all engaged with the Qur'an in different ways and with different approaches. Some of the works that define Shiʿi Iran's understanding of scripture in modern times were produced in these years as a result of religious scholars' and intellectuals' engagement with the challenges posed by the social and political transformations occurring in the country during this period of revolution. One of the works worth noting here is the *Tafsīr-i namūna*, which makes available in Persian a number of classical commentaries, both Shiʿi and Sunni, and which has been republished innumerable times in Iran. A result of the collective effort of a number of scholars working over several years prior to the revolution under the direction of the ayatollah Makārim Shīrāzī, the twenty-seven-volume undertaking shows the social and political concerns of the editing committee: it interprets the Qur'an through reference to a number of influential reformist and modernist thinkers of the nineteenth and twentieth centuries, regardless of their denomination.[4]

No matter how much the Qur'an has informed Iranian culture through the ages, in the centuries preceding the revolution the

Qur'an was not as central to public life as it was in Sunni-majority countries. This was probably due to the prominence of the extensive corpus of the sayings of the imams, which represents within Shiʿism an expansion of the notion of scripture. The richness and articulation of that corpus allowed a monumental set of other authoritative voices to exist alongside the Qur'an, within the category of scripture. Besides this element, the Pahlavi dynasty contributed to the marginalisation of the Qur'anic element by promoting a supposedly pure national culture which viewed the Arab elements as alien and imposed. The establishment of the Islamic Republic of Iran has changed this trend, however, predictably triggering an unprecedented host of Qur'an-related activities at every level of society. Describing the entirety of these is beyond the scope and capability of this introduction, but it suffices to say that a number of state agencies – like the state television (IRIB), the Iranian Qur'an News Agency (IQNA) and many others – alongside the more traditional institutions of learning, are active in the promotion, dissemination and elaboration of Qur'anic materials.[5] A number of government ministries have their own special unit for the promotion of Qur'anic activities, including the Ministry of Culture and Islamic Guidance; the Ministry of Education; and the Ministry of Science, Research and Technology.[6] As a result, the promotion of what we may define as 'Qur'anic culture' received a powerful impetus at every level of Iranian society, from the more traditional activities of recitation and memorisation[7] to software production, exhibitions, and productions of the audiovisual and film industry.

This Volume

The chapters of this volume explore the developments in the conversation between Iran and the Qur'an over roughly the last two centuries. The first section (Power, Authority and Exegesis) covers the understanding, reading and interpretation of the Qur'an in the contemporary era. Exegesis, here, is intended in its wider delineation and not only in the sense of the highly formalised, technically codified genre of *tafsīr*.[8] It goes without saying that traditional *tafsīr*s, as historically transmitted within the scholarly circle of the *ḥawza* (the Shiʿi religious seminaries), represent an unavoidable reference even for those scholars who, whether or not they were *ḥawza*-educated at some point in their lives, have moved away from the codified genre of scholarly exegesis *stricto sensu*. The influence, to be sure, is mutual: even *ḥawza*-based *tafsīr*s in modern times, particularly in the twentieth and twenty-first centuries, bear the signs of an intense conversation with the western hermeneutical studies and Qur'anic studies of scholars within the academic environments of Europe. The three main streams of effort in understanding the Qur'an (i.e. Shiʿi exegesis; Sunni classical and modernist *tafsīr*; and Western research on the Qur'an) are to be found in varying combinations and ratios within most contemporary Iranian exegetical undertakings. The state's effort to bring about communication between religious and secular intellectuals has been enhanced even further in post-revolutionary Iran, as the Islamic Republic's policy of positively integrating the *ḥawza* and the universities has increasingly blurred the boundaries between the two: today, it is not unusual to have *ḥawza*-educated scholars teaching in universities, and for subjects traditionally taught in universities to be offered in the *ḥawza* curriculum. The media, as well, have been involved in the propagation of exegetical knowledge. The television show 'Dars-hāʾī az Qurʾān', hosted by Muḥsin Qarāʾatī, has been aired for the past thirty years with the aim of popularising and disseminating Qur'anic exegesis. Iranian radio broadcasts the ayatollah Jawādī Āmulī's daily lessons on the Qur'an, from which his *Tasnīm* has been extracted. These are only two examples among the most remarkable, but many others would fit the picture.

The discourse on the interpretation of the Qur'an and on who has the authority to interpret its true meaning has a clear political bearing on today's Iran. This is probably more so now than it was in the past due to the embedding of the doctrine of the *wilāyat-i faqīh* in the Constitution of Iran. This doctrine posits that religious scholars are the sole class who have the authority to interpret the Qur'an, and that the governance of the country should be based on their interpretation. It is for this reason that the first section of this book refers to power and authority. Connected with issues of religious authority are the developments in the areas of classical hermeneutics and jurisprudence, both of which have informed, and continue to inform, the practice of Qur'anic exegesis. Seyfeddin Kara's chapter (chapter 1) illustrates this. He points out that the success of Uṣūlism in the late eighteenth century, with its rational-analytical method of jurisprudence, resulted in the adoption of a parallel method of exegesis. This method of exegesis utilised elements borrowed from jurisprudence. Though this was not an exclusively modern phenomenon, it gained momentum in the twentieth century, as exemplified by the *tafsīr* works of two of the most prominent Iranian exegetes of the period, namely *al-Mīzān* by Muḥammad Ḥusayn Ṭabāṭabā'ī (d. 1981) and *Tasnīm* by 'Abd Allāh Jawādī Āmulī (b. 1933). These highly influential and popular works are partly the product of the success of neo-Uṣūlism and its enshrinement as the unchallenged leading juridical/ideological school of revolutionary Iran.[9]

The theme of the permeability of the *tafsīr* genre and of its function in imbuing the exegete with authority is present in Sajjad Rizvi's chapter (chapter 2). Rizvi reviews the exegetical works of Ṭabāṭabā'ī, though not his celebrated *tafsīr*, *al-Mīzān*. His close scrutiny of the extant literature by the great scholar and some of those associated with his informal, non-Sufi mystical *ṭarīqa* (order), allows one to better understand how the ideas circulating among those who subscribed to Ṭabāṭabā'ī's apparatus shaped a diffuse interpretation of the Qur'an. It also allows one to better appreciate the strategies adopted by these intellectuals, and Ṭabāṭabā'ī *in primis*, which enabled them to propose an approach to the Qur'an that stayed true to the school's *weltanschauung* while obviating accusations that such a method involved 'interpreting the Qur'an according to one's own ideas'. The mystical and philosophical reading of the Qur'an, against which Ṭabāṭabā'ī himself warns the reader in his introduction to the *Mīzān*, comes back to the interpretation of the Book in other works of exegesis without technically being *tafsīr*. In addressing these strategies, Rizvi argues that the *ṭarīqa* in question works as a *dispositif*, or apparatus, in the Foucaultian sense; that is, it encapsulates a given set of structures, modes of comportment, discourses and relationships that govern the projection of self by a specific group, community or sodality. The main point made by Rizvi is that the exegetical use of the Qur'an in some of the staple works of the apparatus, such as the *Risāla-yi sayr wa sulūk* attributed to Sayyid Baḥr al-ʿUlūm (d. 1212/1797), the *Tadhkirat al-muttaqīn* by Shaykh Muḥammad Bahārī Hamadānī (d. 1907) and the *Risālat al-walāya* by Ṭabāṭabāʾī, was part of a strategy by the apparatus to present elements of Sufi theory and practice to a Twelver Shiʿi audience that was opposed to Sufism. They accomplished this by deploying authoritative readings of the Qurʾan carried out by charismatic figures.

A number of hermeneutical strategies have been triggered by the establishment of the Islamic Republic. How jurisprudence negotiated its way through the practical needs of a modern state and developed hermeneutical strategies to that end is at the heart of Liyakat Takim's essay on Yūsuf Ṣāniʿī (b. 1937) and his juridical thought and practice (chapter 3). Takim's essay explores the theme of the new jurisprudence. He places the idea of revelation at the centre by looking at a specific case of the ruling on the *khulʿ* form of divorce *apud* the outspoken reformist cleric Ṣāniʿī. Takim argues that through an egalitarian and progressive reading of the Qurʾan, Ṣāniʿī challenges the preexisting rulings on the matter and shows how privileging the revelation and its interpretation is key to the development of a flexible jurisprudence.

The negotiability of the meaning, social significance and political clout of the Qurʾanic text is made clear in the next chapter. Interpretative efforts to wrest back from the opposing camp religious ideas, concepts or even characters is nothing new in contemporary Iran – for example, one can think of the politically oriented struggle over the meaning of the tragedy of Karbala in the decade preceding the revolution,[10] or the reformist claim to Khomeini's legacy.[11] Neguin Yavari (chapter 4) explores further the theme of the negotiability of the meaning of scripture. She analyses the rereading of the Qurʾanic precept of *amr biʾl-maʿrūf wa naḥy ʿan al-munkar* (commanding right and forbidding wrong) by one of Iran's most prominent theoreticians of political reform, Muṣṭafā Tājzāda (b. 1956). Yavari argues that Tājzāda's treatment of the subject represented an attempt 'to appropriate the mantle of doctrinal orthodoxy and legitimacy for Reformist politics' and to wrest from the conservatives a concept crucial to the understanding of Muslims' ethical engagement with society. Pointing out the programmatic centrality of the Qurʾan, as opposed to the Sunna, as the arbiter of the practice of political Islam in the Muslim world in the twentieth century, Yavari compares Tājzāda's views with those of Khomeini and other religious intellectuals. Her aim in doing so is to study the role of Qur'anic sanction in the political discourse of the Islamic Republic.

It is interesting to note how momentous the notion of the flexibility of the meaning of the revelation is in this context: the meaning here generates authority and is susceptible to being accommodated to a specific political agenda. It is within this same framework that religious intellectuals in contemporary Iran have sought to provide a Qur'anic basis for their political position and criticism of the state of affairs in the Islamic Republic. This theme is tackled in the two following chapters, through the analysis of two case studies whose common denominator is that they both gravitate around the milieu of the Iranian Religious Intellectual Movement, albeit with different characteristics. In the first (chapter 5), Banafsheh Madaninejad examines the intellectual trajectory of Abū'l-Qāsim Fanā'ī (b. 1959), one of the 'rising stars' of the current Iranian religious intelligentsia, in the context of the wider debates on secularism, religiosity, rationality and commitment that were occurring in Iran in the late twentieth and early twenty-first centuries. Well versed in both the Twelver Shi'i religious tradition and Western philosophy,[12] Fanā'ī works within the non-radical (he is still considered as operating from 'within the orthodoxy') end of the ideological spectrum of the religious intellectual movement. He develops an innovative approach to jurisprudence (*fiqh*) in order to argue for a 'more adaptable Qur'an', one whose hermeneutics would allow the basis of the exegetical undertaking to be updated. Along with Fanā'ī, Madaninejad highlights the case of other Iranian religious intellectuals well known to the Western public interested in the debate, namely Mohsen Kadivar (b. 1959) and Abdolkarim Soroush (b. 1945), showing how they share some of their hermeneutical strategies with Western Muslim feminist intellectuals. The case is different for Soroush, the established star of the pleiad of Iranian religious intellectuals, whose approach to the Islamic revelation is addressed in detail and from another perspective in the chapter authored by Yaser Mirdamadi (chapter 6). In inverting the terms traditionally ascribed to the 'orthodox dogma', by affirming that the revelation is human and accidental (*ʿaraḍī*) in nature rather than divine and essential (*dhātī*), Soroush challenges the very core of the idea of 'holiness' in Islam. Mirdamadi assesses Soroush's thought on the Qur'anic revelation against the history of theology, namely by comparing it to similar ideas found among Muʿtazilī theologians and looking at its implications for pressing contemporary issues, such as the relationship between religion and science and the broadening of the juridical horizon of today's Shiʿi jurists. Mirdamadi's analysis of the Soroushian theory of revelation shows that attempts have been made throughout history to desacralise the letter of the Qur'an while preserving the sacrality of its inspirational source. This desacralisation perhaps helps to explain why Soroush's ideas have been met with criticism by the religious authorities in the Islamic Republic and have been scarcely influential in precipitating a substantial change within juridical practice in a religious, Twelver Shiʿi environment where the sacrality of the very form of the imam is so dear both in theology and in popular devotion. If one thinks of the imam as the Perfect Man and as the iconic 'proof of God', statuses traditionally attributed to him by theologians and mystics, it is easy to understand why the sacrality of the form is often jealously preserved.

In forms and ways different to those deployed by theologians and jurists, the centrality of the imam as the holy guide of the faithful is a theme frequented by the mystics. The latter's diverse approaches to the Book, which can be considered non-mainstream for reasons ranging from their beliefs to their intellectual outlook, are reflected in the second section of this volume (Alternative Approaches: Between Marginality and Legitimacy). The personalities on which the contributions in this section focus are only tangential, in different ways, to the universe of formal Shiʿi religious education. A number of these personalities are responsible for some of the most original and influential pieces of work that deal with the Qur'an, interpreting, revisiting and even defending it. One such defence comes from a master of the Niʿmatullāhī order, Muḥammad Ḥusayn Iṣfahānī (d. 1818), known by the *ṭarīqa* sobriquet Ḥusayn ʿAlī Shāh. He was requested by the Qajar ruler of Persia, Fatḥ ʿAlī Shāh (r. 1797–1834), to compose a response to a refutation of Islam and the Qur'an written in Persian by the Anglican missionary Henry Martyn (d. 1812), as discussed by Reza Tabandeh (chapter 7). Martyn's contentious work, the *Mīzān al-ḥaqq*, was influential in the early eighteenth century, to the extent that the court, unable to take direct action against the missionary for diplomatic reasons, found it necessary to appoint Shiʿi scholars to respond in kind by writing rebuttals of the treatise. The sovereign's initiative gave rise to the *radd-i pādrī* (refutations of the priest), which can be considered a sort of literary genre in its own right, of which the Sufi master Ḥusayn ʿAlī Shāh's work is the first written example. Tabandeh contends that Ḥusayn ʿAlī Shāh's rebuttal of Martyn is important not only because it served as a model for the subsequent responses to Martyn's attack on the Qur'an and Islam, but also because it gives us a sample of the dialectical strategies of a resurgent Sufism jostling for position within the wider context of Shiʿi orthodoxy. Tabandeh shows how Ḥusayn ʿAlī Shāh's *Radd-i pādrī* is more theological than mystical, though Sufi elements are interspersed throughout the pages in a veiled fashion. Ḥusayn ʿAlī Shāh, it is worth noting, was the first *quṭb* (grand master) of the Niʿmatullāhī renaissance to be an Iranian and, for good measure, a trained jurist. His defence of the Qur'an – his only written work – is an appropriate specimen of the cautious way the Sufi masters negotiated the transition from charismatic and somehow antinomian characters to a more mature Twelver Shiʿi religious identity.

Religious identity from both within and without one's own denomination is a major theme in this second section of the book, and the next chapter addresses it from the dogmatically crucial standpoint of the authenticity, integrity and inalterability of the Qur'anic text. With regard to this, the contribution of Rainer Brunner (chapter 8) is essential in our overview because it offers a glimpse of the most important contemporary Shiʿi contributions on the issue of whether the Qur'an that came down to us is the authentic one that God entrusted to Muslims or whether it is inauthentic because it had been subject to degrees of falsification (*taḥrīf*). By looking at the works of some of the most influential Shiʿi *ʿulamāʾ* of the nineteenth and twentieth centuries, Brunner unveils a picture of problematicity, where the diplomatic necessity to discard *taḥrīf* as a fancy theory of some maverick scholar of the past clashes with the abundance of hints from the past and the sometimes ambiguous references by contemporary theologians which suggest otherwise. *Taḥrīf* may have well been a marginal topic in the history of Shiʿi theology, but contemporary Shiʿi scholars, from Ḥusayn Taqī al-Nūrī al-Ṭabrisī (d. 1902) to Khomeini, cannot ignore that the corpus of the sayings of the imams is evidence that the problem cannot be entirely discarded. The sensitivity of the matter, however, as Brunner points out, is attested by the fact that apart from Nūrī in his *Faṣl al-khiṭāb fī taḥrīf Kitāb Rabb al-arbāb*, no Twelver Shiʿi scholar after him has publicly endorsed the thesis that the Qur'an was falsified or altered. Nūrī's stance, therefore, can to some extent be considered 'marginal', at least concerning the last century.

In the chapter authored by Nicholas Boylston (chapter 9), a different kind of marginality is analysed, one which stems from a mystical and poetical approach to the understanding of the Qur'an. In his exploration of the *tafsīr* by the Niʿmatullāhī master Ṣafī ʿAlī Shāh (d. 1898), the singularity of the work under scrutiny is highlighted. The *Tafsīr-i Ṣafī* is the first known translation-cum-commentary of the entire Qur'an in the Persian language. While the use of the vernacular in Qur'anic exegesis has a long and, at times, noble history,[13] this is the first significant commentary written entirely in Persian rhyming couplets by a charismatic Sufi master after the resurgence of the Niʿmatullāhī order and its return from India to Iran in the late eighteenth century. Ṣafī ʿAlī Shāh's *tafsīr* was completed in 1890, but its literary value and exegetical significance had been long overlooked in both Western and Iranian scholarship. Boylston's examination of it, therefore, is a valuable attempt to do justice to a work too long absent from the histories of literature and of exegesis. The author of the *tafsīr*, as shown by Boylston, does not aim to situate his work within the scholarly madrasa-centred tradition. For Ṣafī ʿAlī Shāh, writing a poetic commentary on the Qur'an was an act of worship fully within the framework of his role as a Sufi master, and he drew more upon the tradition of mystical Persian poetry than that of highly technical Qur'anic exegesis (although he sought, through the intercession of the Qajar ruler Nāṣir al-Dīn Shāh [r. 1848–96], a fatwa on the legitimacy of translating the Qur'an into poetry, which was granted by the celebrated Mīrzā Muḥammad Ḥasan Shīrāzī [d. 1896]).

The variety of approaches to the Qur'an in Iran in the late nineteenth century, as well as the creativity of the protagonists, is attested by Ṣafī ʿAlī Shāh's coeval Sufi master Sulṭān ʿAlī Shāh Gunābādī (d. 1909). Head of another branch of the Niʿmatullāhī Sufi order, Sulṭān ʿAlī Shāh composed, among many other mystical works, a hitherto understudied Qur'anic commentary, the *Tafsīr Bayān al-saʿāda fī maqāmāt al-ʿibāda*, which stands at the opposite end of the spectrum to the *Ṭafsīr-i Ṣafī* in terms of its formal aspects and intended audience. The commentary, presented in my contribution (chapter 10), was penned according to the entirety of the formal codes of the *tafsīr* genre: it is written in Arabic, it covers different aspects of each verse (semantic, lexicological, historical, etc.), it comments on the whole of the Qur'an, and it is in conversation with the exegetical tradition. Its specificity lies, however, in the fact that the focus of the discussion is evidently the esoteric meaning of the Book, which is expounded by referring to and conflating three sources of inspiration: the mystical, stemming from classical Sufism; the philosophical/theosophical, stemming from the legacy of Sulṭān ʿAlī Shāh's long-standing and fruitful studentship with the most important philosophers of the school of Ibn ʿArabī in Iran and the 'School of Isfahan'; and the Twelver Shiʿi Hadith-based juridical and theological tradition. The result has been monumental and hugely influential in Iran throughout the twentieth century and into the twenty-first century, despite a long period of ostracism due to the Shiʿi *ʿulamā*''s disparagement of Sufism. The chapter offers an overview of the main themes of the commentary and contextualises it within the intellectual history of contemporary Iran. It illustrates how Sulṭān ʿAlī Shāh's reading of the Qur'an had been crucial to his positioning of himself and his order within the mainstream landscape of Twelver Shiʿism.

The next chapter brings the second section to a close with a temporal leap of about one century. It offers an analysis of a unique work by one of the most renowned public intellectuals in Iran today, Muḥyī al-Dīn Ilāhī Ghomshei (b. 1940). In his contribution (chapter 11), Leonard Lewisohn discusses Ghomshei's work *365 Days in the Company of the Qur'an*. Although not a *tafsīr* in the technical sense, the book is a commentary on 365 passages of the Book – one for each day of the year; the result is a voluminous work of exegesis *sui generis*. Lewisohn, with a fine sensibility for things poetical, allows us to appreciate in the English language Ghomshei's novel yet traditional approach to the scripture, and situates the work within the spiritual, social and political context of twentieth-century Iran. Lewisohn points out that Ghomshei's lyrical reading of the Qur'an draws on the wealth of Persian mystical literature to shed light on the meaning of the Book. This allows him to bring it alive and simultaneously make it comprehensible to a general public not versed in the subtleties of the language of the *ḥawza* while leaving its interpretation open to the creative imagination of classical Persian mysticism.

The Qur'an, as we have seen, continues to be a source of inspiration for Iranians at the spiritual, religious, political and intellectual levels, but it has also been inspirational at the level of material culture. This is the theme of the contributions in the third section of this volume (The Arts, Material Culture and Everyday Life). There is little surprise, therefore, in the fact that the artistic vanguards have continued to engage with the Qur'an in the twentieth and twenty-first centuries. The Saqqākhāna movement stands out as one of the most significant and successful popular artistic movements in Iran that encapsulated the Qur'anic fabric of that country. Alice Bombardier (chapter 12) offers an overview of a very important yet little-known work by one of the most successful artists associated with this particular form of 'spiritual pop art', Charles-Hossein Zenderoudi (b. 1937), who illustrated the French translation of the Qur'an by Jean Grosjean (d. 2006). This work was published, under Bombardier's direction, in 1972, and her article contributes to the rediscovery of an important chapter in the reception of the Qur'an in a milieu close to an Iranian artistic vanguard. Bombardier's outline shows us how the conflation of modern artistic inspiration and traditional forms of Qur'anic art (from Sufi symbolism to miniature painting and Qur'anic illumination) can generate an outstanding 'visual companion' to the Qur'an. Bombardier's analysis of Zenderoudi's illustrations shows how, in a contemporary Iranian context, the Qur'an can function as the fulcrum where a number of streams of inspiration come together in a coherent unicum, visually representing the Book and reinventing traditions.

Continuing this focus on the visual aspect of the reception of the Qur'an, the contribution by Anna Vanzan (chapter 13) looks at calligraphy in contemporary Iran from a new perspective. It specifically discusses calligraphy as a space for the expression of the female self within religion. Vanzan argues the translating the Qur'an into visuals through the traditional medium of calligraphic script is a means through which women can transcend the limitations imposed on them by the patriarchal Iranian society. Placing interviews with a number of women calligraphers within a historical perspective, the author of the chapter shows that calligraphy is envisaged by women as an interpretive practice and a devotional act; it is also a powerful means for them to rediscover the emancipatory force of Islam and challenge the top-down version of religion sub-ministered by the state – a state which, it is worth noting, has acted as a generous supporter of the Qur'anic arts since its inception, triggering a movement that reached as far as the entertainment industry.

In the chapter that follows (chapter 14), Nacim Pak-Shiraz persuasively argues that the cinematic genre of the Iranian 'religious epic' offers a Qur'anic version of Biblical stories already explored in Western cinema and provides at the same time a new development in the genre of Biblical films. The phenomenon of the Muslim religious epic in the film industry in Iran is a telling example of how the Qur'an is considered central to the promotion of a national religious culture and how it is credited with the potential to offer a counter-narrative of the highest quality to the dominant cultural artefacts of the Western film industry. Pak-Shiraz looks at Shahriar Bahrani's 2010 film *The Kingdom of Solomon* to illustrate the way a collaborative work between the film industry and the clergy could bring about highly polished results in the genre in Iran. Cinema, which earlier in the twentieth century had been looked at with suspicion as a 'Western medium', has now taken on a religious and political function in Iran.

The next two chapters of this volume are ethnographical accounts of the everyday Qur'an-related religious practices and rituals of Iranian women. Niloofar Haeri's contribution (chapter 15) is based on fieldwork that the author undertook in Tehran between 2008 and 2013. During that time, Haeri interacted with a group of middle-class women in their sixties, sitting in on their Qur'an classes as well as their classes on Rūmī's mystical poetry. Based on her observations and interviews with these students, Haeri draws a lively portrait of the way they negotiate their place within the Twelver Shiʿi community at large and within the hermeneutical tradition. The rituals and performances of the women in these groups, Haeri argues, have an impact on the way they read the Qur'an, recite it in prayers and understand it; not only is their understanding of the Qur'an – aided by the commentary provided by Rūmī's mystical poetry – informed by the way they perform the prayer, but their performance of the prayer is in turn modified by the elements introduced within the classes.

Ingvild Flaskerud's chapter (chapter 16), on the other hand, discusses the engagement of a network of pious women in Shiraz with the Qur'an. This chapter, too, is the result of field research. Flaskerud, between 1999 and 2003, had the opportunity to attend a number of Qur'anic classes and other Twelver Shiʿi rituals frequented by pious women. Using the ethnographic data she gathered, she reflects on how the 'everyday' Qur'an experiences of the subjects of her study represent a form of living exegesis, where typically Shiʿi elements such as the imam's proximity to the Book, the concept of the imam as the 'speaking Qur'an' and others, are incorporated in the devotional performance. Flaskerud argues that the Qur'an becomes, in practice, a living text whose spiritual, protective and miraculous efficacy is granted through the faithful's devotion to the *ahl al-bayt* (the People of the House). In the settings observed, everyday needs are addressed in the context of ritual, which in turn affects the behavioural patterns in everyday life. The centrality of the Book in the lives of a section (albeit circumscribed) of today's Iranian society is thus reinstated.

It goes without saying that the Qur'an, as much as it is positively placed centre stage in the lives of the most religious segments of society, is also marginalised, ignored by or even removed from the lives of other segments of the same society. The offering of different approaches to the Book in this volume is an attempt to reflect this diversity, which resonates in the last contribution of this volume. Giovanni De Zorzi (chapter 17) offers a fascinating examination of the oral/aural universe represented by the strong connection between the Qur'an and music in twentieth- and twenty-first-century Iran, as he illustrates how most classical musicians in contemporary Iran have a background in one of the sciences of Qur'anic recitation. Without going as far as equating it with the fate that befell Mushtāq ʿĀlī Shāh (d. 1791),[14] De Zorzi's essay is an apt testimony of the consequence of the Qur'an in religious, political, social and cultural life in contemporary Iran.

NOTES

1 See Badīʿ al-Zamān Furūzānfar, *Sukhan wa sukhanwarān* (Tehran, 1387 Sh./2008–9), pp. 51–2.

2 Rūmī's *Mathnawī* was first dubbed a 'Qur'an in Persian' by the Persian poet and scholar Jāmī (d. 849/1492), and that reference became embedded in the popular Iranian conception of the work.

3 See Travis Zadeh, *The Vernacular Qur'an: Translation and the Rise of Persian Exegesis* (Oxford, 2012) and idem, 'Persian Qur'anic Networks and the Writings of "an Iranian Lady", Nusrat Amin Khanum', in Suha Taji-Farouki, ed., *The Qur'an and its Readers Worldwide: Contemporary Commentaries and Translations* (Oxford, 2015), pp. 275–323 (in particular the opening section).

4 *Tafsīr-i namūna*, under the direction of Nāṣir Makārim Shīrāzī (Tehran, 1362–74 Sh./1983–95).

5 The IQNA is reported to publish articles and news on the Qur'an in thirty-five languages. See the excellent overview in Morteza Karimi-Nia, 'Contemporary Qur'anic Studies in Iran and its Relationship with Qur'anic Studies in the West', *Journal of Qur'anic Studies* 14, no. 1 (2012), pp. 45–72, esp. pp. 46–9.

6 Ibid., p. 46.

7 For example, the Ministry of Culture and Islamic Guidance tests biannually the memorisation, translation and understanding of the Qur'an. Those who pass are awarded the equivalent of a Bachelor's degree in Qur'anic Studies, without their having to gain a university education. Ibid., p. 47.

8 On the issue of *tafsīr* as a genre in the context of Islamic intellectual history, an issue clearly relevant to our approach here, see Andreas Görke and Johanna Pink, eds, *Tafsīr and Islamic Intellectual History: Exploring the Boundaries of a Genre* (London, 2014).

9 For more on 'neo-Uṣūlism', see Zackery Heern, *The Emergence of Modern Shiʿism: Islamic Reform in Iraq and Iran* (London, 2015).

10 The context of the debate is reported in Roy P. Mottahedeh, *The Mantle of the Prophet: Religion and Politics in Iran* (New York, 1985), p. 353.

11 See Daniel Brumberg, *Reinventing Khomeini: The Struggle for Reform in Iran* (Chicago, 2001).

12 Fanā'ī is a qualified mujtahid who was educated in the Iranian religious seminary (*ḥawza ʿilmiyya*). He also has a degree in philosophy, which he earned in the United Kingdom, where he lived for fifteen years.

13 See Zadeh, *The Vernacular Qur'an*.

14 Mushtāq ʿAlī Shāh was a charismatic Niʿmatullāhī dervish who was killed by a mob in Kirmān. The killing was instigated by a fanatical cleric who could not tolerate the mystic wandering around his town declaiming ecstatic poetry and the Qur'an accompanied by music. Muḥammad Maʿṣūm Shīrāzī (Maʿṣūm ʿAlī Shāh), *Ṭarā'iq al-ḥaqā'iq* (Tehran, 1382 Sh./2003–4), vol. III, pp. 188–92.

SECTION I
Power, Authority and Exegesis

1

Rational-analytical *Tafsīr* in Modern Iran: The Influence of the Uṣūlī School of Jurisprudence on the Interpretation of the Qur'an*

SEYFEDDIN KARA

In memory of Mohammad Jafar Elmi

As far as traditional/orthodox Muslim scholarship is concerned, there have always been strict prerequisites in place for Muslims before they could undertake the interpretation of the verses of the Qur'an.[1] Even for those equipped with the necessary knowledge of relevant Islamic sciences, such as a deep knowledge of the Arabic language, the life and the sayings of the Prophet, and Islamic history and Islamic law, interpreting 'the word of God' has been an arduous undertaking for sincere believers, since the consequences of committing an error during this process could potentially endanger one's own faith and lead others to wrong beliefs and practices. In this regard, Prophetic traditions like 'Whoever interprets the Qur'an according to his own opinion has prepared a place for himself in the fire'[2] have discouraged many faithful from undertaking an interpretation of the Qur'an. Nevertheless, despite the harsh cautioning, various schools of thought have tried to impose their own teachings or understanding on the text of the Qur'an. The various schools of thought, such as those of the Muʿtazilī, Ashʿarī,

* I would like to thank Mohammad Jafar Elmi for patiently teaching me Muḥammad Ḥusayn Ṭabāṭabāʾī's *tafsīr* method and *ʿilm al-ʿuṣūl* (principles of Islamic jurisprudence), which enabled me to put together this paper. I am also grateful to Mohammad Saeed Bahmanpour for his comments and corrections.

Shi'i and Sufi, produced exegeses that championed the tenets of their own schools. Further, various other exegetes examined the verses of the Qur'an from 'scientific', 'philosophical' or 'jurisprudential' perspectives, and some others merely relied on the Hadith to interpret the verses of the Qur'an. As a result, they have come under scrutiny due to their inclination to exploit the Qur'an to support the teachings of their respective schools of thought, and consequently for being exposed to a great many methodological issues.[3]

In the case of the Twelver Shi'i, there are two prominent rival juridical schools, namely the Uṣūlīs and the Akhbārīs, whose intellectual approach generated different approaches to the science of *tafsīr*. These two schools have been the two major juridical actors in Shi'i Islam, and their proponents put up a long-lived intellectual conflict, the consequences of which can be observed well into modern times.

It is generally believed that the Uṣūlī legal school emerged after the occultation of the twelfth Shi'i imam. Shaykh al-Mufīd (d. 413/1022) is known as the founder of the school who advocated the implementation of *ijtihād* (independent reasoning). The process included the use of *'aql* (reasoning) and *ijmā'* (consensus) in addition to the Qur'an and the Sunna (deeds and sayings) of the Prophet.[4] However, there is no consensus regarding the origins of the Akhbārī school, and scholars are divided into two camps on the issue. Wilferd Madelung, Etan Kohlberg, Devin Stewart[5] and Andrew Newman[6] maintain that Akhbārism predated Muḥammad Amīn al-Astarābādī (d. 1036/1626–7), who is usually known as the founder of the Akhbārī school.[7] However, Robert Gleave argues that such a thesis is not tenable and concurs with the generally accepted view within Shi'ism that it was Astarābādī who had established the Akhbārī school.[8]

Andrew Newman, in his PhD dissertation, mentions thirty-nine points of difference between the Uṣūlī and the Akhbārī schools based on *Munyat al-mumārisīn* by the Akhbārī scholar 'Abd Allāh b. Ṣāliḥ al-Samāhījī (d. 1135/1722).[9] The main difference between the two schools[10] is that while Uṣūlīs use *ijtihād*, Akhbārīs reject it, instead relying on the *akhbār* (narrations) of the Prophet and the imams. Further, Uṣūlīs accept four sources (the Qur'an, the Sunna, reasoning and consensus), but Akhbārīs only accept the Qur'an and the Sunna as valid sources of Islamic law.[11]

Whether he was the founder of the Akhbārīs or merely revived it, Astarābādī played a significant role in the history of the Akhbārī school, and because of his attacks on the Uṣūlīs, Akhbārīs became the dominant force within Shi'i Islam until the period of the influential Uṣūlī scholar Muḥammad Bāqir al-Bihbahānī (d. 1205/1790–91).[12] Bihbahānī defeated the Akhbārīs in most of the Shi'i world towards the end of the eighteenth century through intellectual efforts and aggressive practices such as the excommunication (*takfīr*) of Akhbārīs.[13] Since then, the Uṣūlī school has been the dominant faction within Shi'i Islam.

In brief, the clash revolved around the two schools' differences in views about what constituted a source of Islamic law. Their differing views, as we have mentioned above, gave rise to the schools' distinctive approaches to *tafsīr*, with the Uṣūlīs adopting reasoning in the interpretation of the Qur'an and the Akhbārīs categorically rejecting its use in the interpretation of the Qur'an; for the latter, the only accepted form of interpretation was through relevant traditions. Towards the end of the Safavid period in the eighteenth century, Uṣūlism emerged as the dominant school of thought and influenced most of the Shi'i centres.[14]

The present chapter will examine the influence of the Uṣūlī school on the exegesis of the Qur'an in modern Iran through an examination of the works of two prominent Twelver Shi'i scholars who were educated as Uṣūlī clerics, Muḥammad Ḥusayn Ṭabāṭabā'ī (d. 1981) and 'Abd Allāh Jawādī Āmulī (b. 1933). The chapter will first give an overview of their method and then focus on their use of jurisprudential concepts in establishing methodological principles in *tafsīr*.

Ṭabāṭabā'ī's Hermeneutics and Āmulī's Uṣūlī Influences

The publication of *al-Mīzān fī tafsīr al-Qur'ān* by Ṭabāṭabā'ī led scholars to believe that a new era in the field of *tafsīr* had arrived. Ṭabāṭabā'ī is known to have been one of the greatest Shi'i scholars and to have deeply influenced the intellectual and religious landscape of modern Iran. Mahmoud Ayoub considers Ṭabāṭabāʾī the foremost representative of the modern Shiʿi *tafsīr*, and offers these words of praise about the influence and acuity of his *tafsīr*: '*Al-Mizan fi Tafsir al-Qur'an* by Sayyid Muhammad Husayn al-Tabataba'i is meant to speak to the young intellectuals of the Shiʿi Muslim community and often approaches the verses of the Qur'an from philosophical, sociological, and traditional viewpoints. It reflects the wide and profound learning of one of the most respected recent religious scholars of the Shiʿi community.'[15]

Ṭabāṭabāʾī wrote his masterpiece *al-Mīzān*, a commentary of the Qur'an, between 1954 and 1972 in the Arabic language. Spanning twenty volumes, the book is arguably the most influential Shiʿi commentary written in the twentieth century, thanks to its approach to the interpretation of the Qur'an and also to Ṭabāṭabāʾī's fame and standing among the Shiʿi *ʿulamāʾ*.

The first attempt to translate the work into the English language was undertaken by Tehran-based World Organization for Islamic Services, when the well-known Shiʿi scholar Sayyid Saeed Akhtar Rizvi translated six Arabic volumes into twelve English volumes. When he passed away in 2002, his son Sayyid Akhtar Rizvi continued with the work and translated Arabic volumes 7 to 12 into English volumes 13 to 24. The Tawheed Institute Australia then undertook the translation of *al-Mīzān*, with Tawus Raja translating Arabic volume 13 into English volume 27.

Despite its significance, there has been a dearth of research on *al-Mīzān* in Western academia. Aside from scattered references,[16] I have come across only two unpublished PhD theses on the subject. The first is 'An Objective Approach to Revelation: S.M.Ḥ. Ṭabāṭabāʾī's Method of Interpreting the Qur'ān' by Mohammad Jafar Elmi.[17] One may understand from the title of the work that it is dedicated solely to the methodology of Ṭabāṭabāʾī. The work is perhaps the most comprehensive study of Ṭabāṭabāʾī's method of *tafsīr* and provides an excellent understanding of how Ṭabāṭabāʾī implemented his method in *al-Mīzān*. The second doctoral work is authored by Mohammad Hossein Mokhtari, under the title 'The Exegesis of Tabatabaei and the Hermeneutics of Hirsch: A Comparative Study'.[18]

The dissertation compares Ṭabāṭabāʾī's and Eric Donald Hirsch's methods of interpretation, and in doing so provides a brilliant review of the development of Shiʿi exegesis throughout history; however, it does this without mentioning the roots of the methodology of Ṭabāṭabāʾī, which I will show are Uṣūlī based.

Ṭabāṭabāʾī's heavy reliance on the rational-analytical method of interpretation is thought to differentiate *al-Mīzān* from previous exegesis of the Qur'an. In this method, Ṭabāṭabāʾī refers to other relevant verses of the Qur'an in order to unveil mainly the inner meaning of the Qur'anic verse at hand; this approach is also called 'interpreting the Qur'an through the Qur'an'. As justification for this method, Ṭabāṭabāʾī points not only to the teachings of the Prophet and the imams, but also to the verse from the Qur'an itself: *We have revealed the Book to you explaining everything clearly* (Q. 16:89),[19] which for him indicates the self-explanatory nature of the Qur'an.[20]

Aside from his chosen method, Ṭabāṭabāʾī comments on a second type of interpretation of the Qur'an, which entails imposing one's own opinion or worldview on the Qur'an. He notes that followers of this method, be they academics or theologians, possess preconceived ideas/worldviews and interpret the Qur'an in a way that provides legitimacy for those ideas/worldviews. Ṭabāṭabāʾī argues that this has been the common approach to interpretation of the Qur'an by Muslim scholars, and criticises it for being an approach which is not sanctioned by the Qur'an.[21] His work in this regard gives the impression that one of his main goals in writing *al-Mīzān* was to discredit this type of interpretation of the Qur'an. He proclaims that his approach in *al-Mīzān* is free from any presupposition,[22] and declares the Qur'an to be the main source that he relied on for the interpretation found in his *tafsīr*. He presents this method as rather a new method, not used previously.[23]

In another work entitled *Qurʾān dar islām* (*The Qur'an in Islam*),[24] Ṭabāṭabāʾī further examines the different ways of interpreting the Qur'an. He narrows these down to three methods. The first is based on human speculative knowledge; however, he notes that this method is not acceptable, as the Prophet ordained that one cannot interpret the Qur'an according to one's own opinion. The second is based on the traditions; yet, he says, this method is limited since there are not many reliable traditions that can be employed for this purpose. The third is through 'a combination of methods: by reflection and analysis, or by allowing the verse to become clarified by comparing it to other verses, or by use of the sayings of the Prophet and the imams, whenever possible'.[25] He clearly favours the third method, as he believes that this is the method taught in the sayings of the Prophet and the imams. In this regard, he quotes a saying of the Prophet: 'The verses were revealed to confirm each other',[26] and a saying of ʿAlī b. Abī Ṭālib (r. 36–41/656–61): 'One part of the Qur'an explains another and one part witnesses to the other.'[27] Ṭabāṭabāʾī stresses the significance of this approach in *al-Mīzān* by stating that the Prophet and the imams always preferred to interpret the Qur'an through the Qur'an and never relied on any philosophical or academic theory during the process.[28]

Although Ṭabāṭabāʾī rejects the use of reasoning alone in interpreting the Qur'an, he does strongly advocate its use in aiding his method. Thus, one of the most prominent features of *al-Mīzān* is its reliance on reasoning. The work constantly demonstrates that the Qur'an calls humankind to reasoning and contemplation in order to ascertain the truth. He maintains that religion and reason are firmly linked and that reason leads people to religiousness. While he undertakes an analytical study of Qur'anic verses in order to interpret other verses, he claims to be relying on rational thinking to establish connections between groups of verses. Therefore, in the work of Ṭabāṭabāʾī, the reader witnesses a combination of analysis of Qur'anic verses and the presentation of rational arguments.

Ṭabāṭabāʾī's treatment of the story of Moses, which is referred to in various places in the Qur'an, is a good example of the implementation of this combination. The following story of Moses appears in Q. 7:143:

> *And when Moses arrived at Our appointed time and his Lord spoke to him, he said, 'My Lord, show me [Yourself] that I may look at You.' [God] said, 'You will not see Me, but look at the mountain; if it should remain in place, then you will see Me.' But when his Lord appeared to the mountain, He rendered it level,*

and Moses fell unconscious. And when he awoke, he said, 'Exalted are You! I have repented to You, and I am the first of the believers.'

The verse describes the conversation between God and Moses and the latter's request to see God (*anẓuru ilayk*). Ṭabāṭabā'ī comments on the verse in volume 8 of *al-Mīzān*. He first gives the definition of *naẓar* as seeing something that has a physical existence with the eye. However, he goes on to state that according to the knowledge and reasoning that one can gather from the Qur'an (Q. 6:73, Q. 23:91, Q. 37:159 and Q. 42:11), this is impossible since God has no physical existence. He is beyond the concepts of time and place and has no image or likeness either in or outside of the minds of people.[29] Ṭabāṭabā'ī then examines the verses of the Qur'an that mention or imply sightings of God (Q. 18:110, Q. 29:5, Q. 41:53–4, Q. 53:11 and Q. 75:22–3), and, extrapolating from these two sets of verses, concludes that what Moses requested was not a vision of God but rather to attain a special type of knowledge (*tajallī*) of Him.[30]

The method used by Ṭabāṭabā'ī was later adopted by Āmulī, the second person whose method is under scrutiny here. Āmulī is one of the most prominent students of Ṭabāṭabā'ī, and was allowed to attend his private lectures for twenty-five years. He is now one of the most revered Shi'i scholars living in Iran and has considerable influence in the Shi'i seminaries located in the city of Qum. He is also an influential political figure, as he led the Friday prayers in Qum until his resignation in 2009. Āmulī has been lecturing in nationally famous *tafsīr* classes for the past decade. The lessons are delivered to seminary students in Qum and are compiled as a written commentary on the Qur'an, entitled *Tasnīm*.[31] Like his teacher Ṭabāṭabā'ī, Āmulī employed the rational-analytical methodology in his twenty-four volumes (more volumes are still being published) of Persian language exegesis of the Qur'an.

In his *Tasnīm*, and another *tafsīr* work entitled *Qur'ān dar Qur'ān*[32] (The Qur'an in the Qur'an), Āmulī explains that interpreting the Qur'an by the Qur'an means understanding the core verses of the Qur'an and explaining the subsidiary verses of the Qur'an through the core verses. Similar to Ṭabāṭabā'ī, Āmulī maintains that the Prophet and the imams used this method to explain the Qur'an; therefore, it remains the best method in the interpretation of the Qur'an.[33] One of Āmulī's main priorities is to legitimise the method that he inherited from his teacher. In this regard, he mentions a rule from Islamic law which states that if a person is just in the eye of the public, his testimony is acceptable in court; this is self-evident and no further evidence is needed regarding his truthfulness. He views the Qur'an from a similar perspective – because the Qur'an is the word of God, and he believes God to be the most just, the Qur'an is thus perfectly able to validate and interpret itself.[34]

Āmulī ostensibly uses a rational argument, but his argument is rather theological because he takes it for granted that the Qur'an in its current form is the true word of God, and therefore he does not attempt to establish its authenticity. Further, his jurist background is dominant in his arguments and is noticeable throughout his work.[35] He then refers to other arguments that he derives from the verses of the Qur'an, to attest that the Qur'an legitimises the method. These include Q. 5:15 and Q. 7:157, which refer to the Qur'an as *nūr* (light), which he considers the Qur'an's attribute of both enlightening and explaining itself.[36] Like Ṭabāṭabā'ī, Āmulī also refers to Q. 16:89. The verse, according to Āmulī, confirms the authority of the Qur'an to explain everything to mankind, thus indicating that it is also capable of explaining itself; some verses clarify the meaning of the other verses.[37] Āmulī concedes that the method is not a recent invention, noting that jurists have used the method to identify jurisprudential concepts such as 'unconditional' (*'ām* or *muṭlaq*), 'conditional' (*makhṣūṣ* or *muqayyad*), and 'abrogated' (*nāsikh*) verses to extract rulings.[38] He clearly links his method of interpreting the Qur'an to the method that has been used by jurists.

Āmulī also allocates a significant number of chapters to the discussion of the use of reasoning in *tafsīr*. In terms of its functioning, he considers *tafsīr* to be a social science and thus argues that, in keeping with other social sciences, *tafsīr* should come up with a systematic methodology, in this case for extracting the meaning of the verses, which he believes can be achieved by the use of reasoning.[39] Further, he claims that the rational-analytical method that relies on the use of rational tools in interpreting the verses of the Qur'an by the Qur'an, is holistic, so the utmost precaution must be taken to avoid any inconsistency in the interpretation of the Qur'an when a particular verse is treated. In this regard, verses of the Qur'an need to be read in harmony with, and with the aid of, other verses in order to refute any allegation regarding contradiction in the Qur'an. Āmulī holds the firm conviction that such contradiction would be incompatible with the 'miraculous nature' of the Qur'an.[40] Āmulī further explains the main criteria of the method by elaborating on how Ṭabāṭabāʾī implemented it. According to Āmulī, Ṭabāṭabāʾī did not exclude traditions, but made use of 'authentic traditions' where available. Thus, Ṭabāṭabāʾī relied on the traditions of the infallible imams to explain the verses of the Qur'an. If there was any reliable evidence in the sayings of the imams regarding interpretation of the verses, he would incorporate it into his interpretation. Even if there was no evidence about the verse, he would still make sure that his interpretation did not contradict the traditions of the imams in general. This was due to Ṭabāṭabāʾī's belief that there is no discrepancy between the word of God and the traditions of the infallible imams.[41]

Āmulī continues with his elaboration on Ṭabāṭabāʾī's method, noting that Ṭabāṭabāʾī extensively searched for rational arguments. However, if there was no rational evidence, he would then make sure that the interpretation was not in conflict with absolute rational principles. Ṭabāṭabāʾī's belief was that whatever is in conflict with absolute rational principles is void. He therefore maintained that reasoning and the revelation must be in harmony, and they should support each other in guiding humankind; hence it is not acceptable for the two to be in conflict.[42]

Āmulī provides caveats to the method of interpreting the Qur'an through the Qur'an. For instance, he stipulates that verses of the Qur'an should never be interpreted in a way that would put them into apparent contradiction with other verses of the Qur'an. For example, on the issue of seeing God, there are apparently contradictory verses; some of them suggest that God has a corporeal presence and might be seen (Q. 75:22–3 and Q. 89:22) whereas some other verses rule out this possibility and affirm the invisibility of God to human eyes (Q. 7:143). Āmulī notes that some might want to use these verses to argue the 'inconsistency' of the Qur'an instead of coming up with a plausible explanation for it. The issue here seems to come down to the intention of the interpreter, whose interpretation depends on whether he is searching for consistency or inconsistency in the Qur'an. Quoting a tradition from Jaʿfar al-Ṣādiq (d. 148/765), Āmulī states that only unbelievers provide clashing interpretations of the verses of the Qur'an, and they do so in order to discredit the Qur'an.

Āmulī then gives his definition of the interpretation of the Qur'an through the Qur'an, which he says means establishing relations between verses such as *nāsikh* (abrogated) and *mansūkh* (abrogating), *ʿāmm* (general) and *khāṣṣ* (specific), *muṭlaq* (all encompassing) and *muqayyad* (conditional). He believes that through making these relations one can reveal the true meaning of individual verses and avoid the trap of interpreting the Qur'an according to one's own opinion and views.[43]

Āmulī's definition of the method makes use of many terms that have been borrowed from Islamic jurisprudence and reveals that he sees no difference between the interpretation of the Qur'an and *ijtihād* (the process of extracting rulings from the sources). An examination of all these concepts is not possible in this chapter, but we may be able to touch upon some key concepts to understand the implementation of the method.

The Use of the Apparent Meaning in the Interpretation of the Qur'an

The key component of the discussion on the apparent meaning of the Qur'an for both Ṭabāṭabā'ī and Āmulī is the acceptance of the Qur'an as the communication between God and human beings. For them, therefore, customary understanding of the language in which God communicates his message should be taken into consideration when the Qur'an is interpreted. Their assumption is that God's message is inherently intelligible because He is the creator and knows how to communicate His message to people in a way that they will understand. Nevertheless, they argue that understanding God's message in its entirety is not an unqualified right, and the interpreter ought, in general terms, to be 'sensible'; thus, Ṭabāṭabā'ī says, finding apparent meaning should be the domain of 'sensible people' (*sīrat al-'uqalā'* or *banā al-'uqalā'*).[44]

As Āmulī points out in his *Tasnīm*, exegetes did not invent this criterion for the accurate interpretation of the Qur'an; it was devised, along with other guidelines, by jurists for deducing principles of Islamic law from the sources. A brief study of Shi'i *uṣūl* works would testify to this. Jurists who have undertaken the work of extracting rules from the Islamic sources needed to devise principles by which they could interpret the word of God and the sayings of the Prophet and the imams. The pressing need of the society to live according to Islamic law seems to have pushed the jurists to come up with a sophisticated methodology that would enable them to issue verdicts on a mass scale from very early times. As Elmi notes, Ṭabāṭabā'ī makes use of the methods that jurists employed to arrive at the principles of Islamic jurisprudence (*uṣūl al-fiqh*).[45] In this regard, therefore, a quick glance at the *Uṣūl al-fiqh*[46] of the jurist Muḥammad Riḍā al-Muẓaffar (d. 1998) would be very useful in order to note the similarities between jurists and Ṭabāṭabā'ī in terms of their approach to interpretation. This work by Muẓaffar is highly esteemed in the Shi'i seminaries and has been used as a textbook for many decades. He discusses the concept of apparent meaning in great detail in the section entitled 'The Authority of the Apparent Meaning' (*Hujjiyat al-ẓuhūr*). Muẓaffar, like many other jurists, and also like Ṭabāṭabā'ī and Āmulī, as already noted above, considers the Qur'an a form of communication between God and people. God is the creator and it is expected that He, better than anyone/anything else, would thus know how to communicate His message to people in a way that they can understand.[47] Consequently, Muẓaffar assumes that God communicates with people in the language they use in their day-to-day lives.

Therefore, in order to understand 'the word of God' one should interpret the meaning of the Qur'an according to the vernacular usage of the language by 'sensible people', unless there is valid evidence that suggests otherwise.[48] Ṭabāṭabā'ī elaborates on the *banā al-'uqalā'* in volumes 2, 13 and 18 of his *tafsīr*, and he provides the most pertinent discussion on the *banā al-'uqalā'* in his commentary on Q. 49:6. There, he makes his case for the use of the common understanding of the Arabic language held by the *banā al-'uqalā'*. This particular verse is often quoted by jurists in discussions of *uṣūl al-fiqh* to justify the use of *khabar al-wāḥid* (isolated traditions)[49] in religious verdicts. According to jurists, the verse ostensibly cautions believers not to rely on significant information provided by a mortal sinner (an unreliable informant) without first investigating it, but it is tacitly sanctioning the converse, that is, the acceptance and use of information provided by reliable informants; this is what the verse implies and what a commonly-held understanding would suggest.

Therefore, Ṭabāṭabā'ī notes, the majority of Shi'i jurists feel comfortable in making use of *khabar al-wāḥid* to help them in the process of extracting law from the sources.[50] Ṭabāṭabā'ī believes that people manage their social affairs according to information that they gather from other people, who base it on their experiences and on things they have witnessed. According to him, the reliability of this received information is established through the common understanding held by the *banā al-'uqalā'*.[51] Therefore, the use of apparent meaning is a legitimate tool in the interpretation of the verses of the Qur'an if there is no other evidence to establish the meaning of the verses. In the case of a consensus among the sensible people, a valid meaning of the words is established. His justification of the method is that since it is implemented in Islamic law, there is no reason for it not to be used in interpreting the Qur'an. In other words, since the statements of sensible people, who have integrity of character, can be accepted for their apparent meaning, then there is no reason not to apply the same principle to the Qur'an. Thus, apparent meanings of the Quran should have a similar authority over other meanings.

Both Ṭabāṭabā'ī and Āmulī refer to other similar evidence from the Qur'an to justify the use of apparent meaning, and there is no need to go through them all. Instead, crucial questions need to be answered when we define 'apparent meaning of the Qur'an'. Who are the 'sensible people' that are interpreting the apparent meaning? And how do they decide what is apparent? The 'sensible people', according to Ṭabāṭabāʾī, are not the Companions of the Prophet, but rather the people who exist in every time. However, this does not mean that a particular verse can be interpreted differently according to the understanding of people at different times. Rather, the applicability of the verses is infinite and finds different 'instances' (*maṣādiq*) at different times. An example of Ṭabāṭabāʾī's implementation of this can be seen in his treatment of Q. 4:36 in his book *The Qur'an in Islam*.[52] In reference to the first part of Q. 4:36: *Worship God, and associate* (*tushrikū*) *nothing with Him*, he asserts that idol worship is not limited to worshipping physical idols.[53] Instead, he argues that there are many forms of it, and that even pursuing one's own desire can be considered idol worship. In order to back up his point, Ṭabāṭabāʾī refers to Q. 36:60, which reads: *O children of Adam, did I not enjoin upon you that you not worship Satan*. He points out that submission to Satan through giving in to one's desires is tantamount to worshipping Satan; thus, even submission to desires can be considered idol worship. His further proof is Q. 45:23, which reads: *him who makes his desire his God* . . . According to Ṭabāṭabāʾī, this is a clear example of how one can take one's desire as one's god and worship it.

If this is accepted, the meaning of *shirk* expands to include everyone who has succumbed to their desires,[54] which would include a great majority of people, including Muslims. However, there is no explicit mention in the Qur'an of one's submission to one's own desire being considered idol worship. Further, as Elizabeth Sirriyeh states, 'at the advent of Islam *shirk* is normally to be understood in a specific and strictly limited sense as meaning association with God of various deities, and it is principally the belief in tribal gods of pre-Islamic Arabia that is under attack'.[55] Therefore, such an argument seems to be inconsistent with Ṭabāṭabāʾī's methodology. As we see from Sirriyeh's statement, *shirk* was understood by the first Muslims only as the 'association with God of various deities'; therefore, the vernacular use of the language does not give the meaning that Ṭabāṭabāʾī suggests, which is that submission to one's desires can be considered idol worship.

Al-Muḥkam and al-Mutashābihāt

Ṭabāṭabā'ī's entire theory of interpreting the Qur'an through the Qur'an is based on categorising the verses as either unequivocal (*muḥkam*) or equivocal (*mutashābih*) and analysing them accordingly. *Tafsīr* scholars have associated each term with the other since the very early periods, but have struggled to definitively identify the verses that may be included in either category. In general, early scholars tended to identify verses that produce certain rulings, especially rulings pertaining to things which are *ḥalāl* (permissible) and *ḥarām* (forbidden), as *muḥkam*. On the other hand, they identified verses that 'resemble one another or confirm the truth of one another' as *mutashābih*.[56] Among the early exegetes, Abū Ja'far b. Jarīr al-Ṭabarī (d. 310/923) came up with the most limited definition of *mutashābih* and only considered *fawātiḥ* or *muqaṭṭa'āt* (the mysterious letters) to be *mutashābih*; he considered the remaining verses *muḥkam*. After Ṭabarī 'a shift of perspective' took place and attention turned 'from the taxonomic to the hermeneutic'.[57] However, owing to this hermeneutic perspective, a distinction emerged between the Shi'i and Sunni approach to the *mutashābih*. Shi'i exegetes, by and large, maintained that it was possible to interpret the *mutashābih* verses, while Sunni exegetes maintained that *mutashābih* verses were inherently dubious and ambiguous and thus could not be fully interpreted.[58]

Ṭabāṭabā'ī's lengthiest discussion on the subject takes place in the analysis of Q. 3:7 (which talks about clarity and ambiguity in the Qur'an) and Q. 3:9 (which refers to the certainty of the Day of Judgement). In his discussion, he conceptually divides the Qur'an into equivocal and unequivocal verses and considers the interpretation of the Qur'an to involve the unveiling of the meaning of the equivocal verses through the unequivocal verses. Unequivocal verses are the set of verses whose meaning is clear and leave no room for ambiguity, while equivocal verses are those which have no clear meaning and need to be further explained. Ṭabāṭabā'ī referred to the unequivocal verses as *umm al-kitāb* (mother of the book), defined as a base to which all things return; in other words, one can make equivocal verses unambiguous by interpreting them with the help of unequivocal verses.[59]

Ṭabāṭabā'ī elaborates upon how this mechanism works using Q. 20:5, which reads: *The most Merciful (God) sat firmly on the throne*. The verse itself does not indicate if it should be read in the literal sense, which casts anthropomorphic attributes on God.[60] Therefore, Ṭabāṭabā'ī considers the verse equivocal, needing to be interpreted according to relevant unequivocal verses. He turns to Q. 42:11, which unequivocally states: *there is no likeness of Him*, affirming that God has no physical form and cannot sit on a throne. Therefore, he concludes that Q. 20:5 is allegorical and refers to God's power and dominance over the affairs of the universe and its creatures.[61] Ṭabāṭabā'ī does not depart from the view of traditional Shi'i exegetes, such as 'Alī b. Ibrāhīm al-Qummī (d. after 307/919), Muḥammad b. al-Ḥasan al-Ṭūsī (d. 460/1067 or 458/1065) and al-Faḍl b. al-Ḥasan al-Ṭabarsī (d. 548/1153), who also maintained that equivocal verses are 'ultimately intelligible' and 'they may require supporting demonstration and their significations may be multiplex but they are not, finally, inexplicable'.[62]

In another example, Ṭabāṭabā'ī looks at Q. 75:23, which reads: *Looking at their Lord*, which similarly implies that God is a physical entity and can be seen. However, he then refers to a relevant verse, Q. 6:103, which reads: *vision does not comprehend Him, but He comprehends (all) visions*. In light of the latter verse, Ṭabāṭabā'ī believes that Q. 75:23 does not suggest God is seen with one's eyes since Q. 6:103 unequivocally states that God is invisible. This is exactly the same stand that Āmulī takes on the issue as he describes the concepts in a similar way in volume 13 of his *Tasnīm*.[63] His description of the concepts of equivocal and unequivocal verses is the same as those of Ṭabāṭabā'ī.[64] He, too, divides the Qur'an into equivocal and unequivocal verses;[65] however, his terminology is different as he describes unequivocal verses as *uṣūl* (pillars) and equivocal verses as *furu'ī* (branches).[66] Despite the differences in terminology the concepts are the same; he maintains that the 'branches' or equivocal verses can only be understood by referring back to the 'pillars' or unequivocal verses.

Furthermore, Ṭabāṭabā'ī elaborates on the reason that the Qur'an contains equivocal verses in the first place. He argues that there are very complex spiritual concepts that not everyone can grasp, as people have different levels of understanding. Since the Qur'an is a form of communication between God and people, God tries to explain those complex concepts in the Qur'an. The Qur'an does not exclude those who are only able to grasp material concepts and thus it contains equivocal verses to address those people. Therefore, God expresses his attributes through metaphors such as 'hand', 'throne', 'face', and so on.

On the other hand, Ṭabāṭabā'ī continues, those who have elevated their spiritual station can easily grasp complicated spiritual concepts.[67] For these people, the Qur'an contains unequivocal verses. Of course, this is the case in every spiritual work and is not peculiar to the Qur'an.[68] This is a systematic approach to resolving the 'problem of contradiction' in the Qur'an that has been pointed out by some Western scholars. However, another problem arises in this process: how to identify the equivocal verses? Ṭabāṭabā'ī admits that this identification process has been arbitrary, and that it has been up to individuals to decide which verses are equivocal and which ones are unequivocal.[69] This seems to be a noteworthy problem in interpreting the Qur'an and may potentially lead to interpretation according to personal opinions. There is no indication in the Qur'an as to which individual verses are defined as either equivocal or unequivocal, nor is there an accepted list by exegetes that differentiates the equivocal from the unequivocal verses.

At this point, Āmulī comes to the aid of his teacher and introduces a rule to identify the equivocal verses of the Qur'an: the content of the unequivocal verses must relate to the principles of religion (*uṣūl al-dīn*)[70] and the equivocal verses must refer to the branches of the religion (*furūʿ al-dīn*).[71] For example, he considers Q. 48:10 (*the hand of Allah is over their hands*) an equivocal verse and states that it can only be understood through relevant unequivocal verses of the Qur'an that clearly explain the attributes of God and the concept of *tawḥīd* (the unity of God).[72] If the verse is interpreted through Q. 42:11, he notes, it becomes clear that the verse refers to the omnipotence of God and not to a physical hand, as it is clear from the verse that the word 'hand' is used metaphorically.[73] He then stresses that the most important principles of the religion are the attributes of God and among them is the unity of God;

therefore, the equivocal verses should contain the characteristics of these principles.[74] This attempt seems to solve some of the problems as it at least provides some guidance regarding the identification of the unequivocal and equivocal verses; yet, there are still nebulous areas in this method. The concept of the principles of religion is not a clear-cut subject for Muslims and the lack of unity on the issue has given rise to the various theological schools that have advocated their principles.

For example, the Ashʿarīs have a different understanding of the attributes of God. They maintain that God may be visible, and therefore for them the principles of religion are different than those of the Shiʿi and they may interpret relevant verses differently. To a certain extent, Abū Ḥasan al-Ashʿarī (d. 324/936) concurred with the literalists in interpreting verses pertaining to the 'vision of God', but he was cautious not to attribute any physical material sense to these descriptions of God (such as the 'face' or 'hand' of God). As Henry Corbin says, 'In his view, the Muslim must believe that God really does possess hands, face and so on, but without "asking how". This is the famous *bi-lā kayfa*, in which faith attests that it can dispense with reason.'[75] Ashʿarī's position on the issue is considered to be of the 'middle path', as he maintained that God's 'hand' or 'face' in verses refers to neither corporeal entities nor metaphors.[76] As Nader El-Bizri writes, he was 'against excess in literal exegesis, while being suspicious of allegorical hermeneutics'.[77] In this regard, Ashʿarī interprets the 'face of God' as an attribute that God ascribed to himself and maintains that its real significance can only be known by God.[78] Such an interpretation is certainly different from the Shiʿi point of view, which rejects the attribution of physical features to God, and therefore indicates the arbitrary nature of the method. Moreover, one can easily define a verse as unequivocal and determine the meanings of relevant equivocal verses accordingly. In such a scenario, there remains only a slight difference between interpreting the Qur'an with the Qur'an and interpreting the Qur'an according to one's own opinion.

The rational-analytical method is clear evidence of the influence of the method of Uṣūlī jurisprudence on current Shiʿi *tafsīr*. As we have observed, both Ṭabāṭabā'ī and Āmulī have adopted the method and implemented it in the interpretation of the Qur'an with considerable success. But as we have noted above, it is difficult to consider the method as entirely new; the method in general represents the traditional Shi'i perspective through a method that Shi'i Uṣūlī jurists have employed. Having said that, the method combines *tafsīr* and Uṣūlī jurisprudence and comes up with a systematic *tafsīr* method, thus it may still be considered an innovative approach to the interpretation of the Qur'an.

This is perhaps a sign of the growing success of Uṣūlī jurisprudence, which throughout the centuries has provided practical solutions for the problems of the Shi'i community. They apply the same practicality to the interpretation of the Qur'an through the use of concepts such as that of 'sensible people' to understand the apparent meaning of verses and identify 'equivocal' and 'unequivocal' verses through the principles of religion. Consequently, it remains an effective method for approaching the interpretation of the Qur'an systematically. However, the method is not foolproof. For instance, in the case of distinguishing between 'equivocal' and 'unequivocal' verses the criteria is not very clear and depends on the exegetes' intention and/or theological adherence. Thus, there is room for subjectivity. Owing to its structured approach, the method reduces the possibility of subjective interpretation of the Qur'an, but does not remove it altogether.

NOTES

1 Some modernist scholars such as Mohammed Arkoun vociferously opposed such criteria established by the 'orthodox' Muslim scholars. He argued that this creates privileged access to the Qur'an which results in the limited and rigid interpretation of the Qur'an, and imposes the understanding of the early Muslim orthodoxy on the Qur'an. See Mohammed Arkoun, 'Introduction: An Assessment of and Perspectives on the Study of the Qur'an', in Andrew Rippin, ed., *The Qur'an: Style and Contents* (Aldershot, 2001), pp. 297–332.

2 Abū 'Īsā Muḥammad Ibn 'Īsā al-Tirmidhī, *Jāmi' al-Tirmidhī*, ed. Ḥāfiẓ Abū Ṭāhir Zubayr 'Alī Za'ī (Riyadh, 2007), vol. V, p. 275.

3 On this, see Muḥammad Ḥusayn Ṭabāṭabā'ī, *al-Mīzān fī tafsīr al-Qur'ān*, 2nd edn (Qum, 1993), vol. I.

4 Todd Lawson, 'Akhbārī Shī'ī Approaches to *Tafsīr*', in Gerald R. Hawting and Abdul-Kader A. Shareef, eds., *Approaches to the Qur'ān* (London, 1993), pp. 173–4.

5 Devin J. Stewart, *Islamic Legal Orthodoxy: Twelver Shiite Responses to the Sunni Legal System* (Salt Lake City, UT, 1998), p. 205. Madelung and Kohlberg are cited in Stewart.

6 Andrew Newman, 'The Development of Political Significance of the Rationalist (Uṣūlī) and Traditionalist (Akhbārī) Schools in Imāmī Shi'ī History from the Third/Ninth to the Tenth/Sixteenth Century A.D.' (Unpublished PhD dissertation, University of California, Los Angeles, 1986), p. 10 and *passim*.

7 Robert Gleave, *Scripturalist Islam: The History and Doctrines of the Akhbārī Shī'ī School* (Leiden, 2007), pp. 16–17.

8 Ibid., p. 10 and *passim*.

9 Newman, 'The Development of Political Significance of the Rationalist (Uṣūlī) and Traditionalist (Akhbārī) Schools', pp. 26–37.

10 See Gleave, *Scripturalist Islam*, pp. 179–215.

11 Newman, 'The Development of Political Significance of the Rationalist (Uṣūlī) and Traditionalist (Akhbārī) Schools', pp. 26–7.

12 Gleave, *Scripturalist Islam*, p. 8. On Bihbahānī, see Zackery M. Heern, *The Emergence of Modern Shi'ism: Islamic Reform in Iraq and Iran* (London, 2015), chapter 4.

13 Ibid., p. 156.

14 Colin Turner, *Islam without Allah? The Rise of Religious Externalism in Safavid Iran* (Richmond, 2000).

15 Mahmoud Ayoub, *The Qur'an and its Interpreters, Volume I* (Albany, NY, 1984), p. 7.

16 See ibid.; Mahmoud Ayoub, 'The Speaking Qur'ān and the Silent Qur'ān: A Study of the Principles and Development of Imāmī Shī'ī Tafsīr', in Andrew Rippin, ed., *Approaches to the History of the Interpretation of the Qur'ān* (Oxford, 1988), pp. 177–98; Diana Steigerwald, 'Twelver Shī'ī Ta'wīl', in Andrew Rippin, ed., *The Blackwell Companion to the Qur'ān* (Malden, MA, 2006), pp. 373–85; Mohd Najib Abdul Kadir *et al.*, '*Al-Mizan Fi Tafsir Al-Quran*: A Review on Al-Tabataba'i's Philosophical Exegesis', *The Social Sciences* (*Medwell Journals*) 10, no. 3 (2015), pp. 325–32.

17 Mohammad Jafar Elmi, 'An Objective Approach to Revelation: S.M.Ḥ. Ṭabāṭabā'ī's Method of Interpreting the Qur'ān' (Unpublished PhD dissertation, University of Birmingham, 2002).

18 Mohammad Hossein Mokhtari, 'The Exegesis of Tabatabaei and the Hermeneutics of Hirsch: A Comparative Study' (Unpublished PhD dissertation, Durham University, 2007). Available at Durham e-Theses Online, http://etheses.dur.ac.uk/2569/.

19 All Qur'an translations are my own.

20 Ṭabāṭabā'ī, *al-Mīzān*, vol. I, p. 11.

21 Ibid.

22 Ibid., p. 8.

23 Ṭabāṭabā'ī's claim that his method of interpretation was a new one might be challenged, however, as there were earlier attempts that considered the Qur'an itself to be the utmost authority in the interpretation of the Qur'an. One of the most prominent examples of the method is found in Fakhr al-Dīn al-Rāzī's *Mafātīh al-ghayb*, where Rāzī (d. 606/1209) explains many verses of the Qur'an

with the help of other verses. However, it needs to be acknowledged that his undertaking was not on the scale found in Ṭabāṭabā'ī's *al-Mīzān*.

24 Muḥammad Ḥusayn Ṭabāṭabā'ī, *Qur'ān dar islām* (Tehran, 1974); edited and translated into English by Seyyed Hossein Nasr as *The Qur'an in Islam* (London, 1987). According to Nasr, although Ṭabāṭabā'ī wrote the book in Persian, its 'express purpose' was to be translated into English (*The Qur'an in Islam*, p. 9).

25 Ṭabāṭabā'ī, *The Qur'an in Islam*, pp. 87–8.

26 Ibid., p. 53.

27 Ṭabāṭabā'ī, *al-Mīzān*, vol. I, p. 12.

28 Ibid.

29 Ibid., vol. VIII, p. 237.

30 Ibid., pp. 238–40.

31 'Abd Allāh Jawādī Āmulī, *Tasnīm*, 8th edn (Qum, 2009).

32 'Abd Allāh Jawādī Āmulī, *Qur'ān dar Qur'ān*, 10th edn (Qum, 2011).

33 Jawādī Āmulī, *Tasnīm*, vol. I. p. 61; idem, *Qur'ān dar Qur'ān*, vol. I, p. 395.

34 Jawādī Āmulī, *Tasnīm*, vol. I, pp. 63–4.

35 Ibid., p. 64.

36 Ibid., p. 65.

37 Ibid., p. 66.

38 Jawādī Āmulī, *Qur'ān dar Qur'ān*, vol. I, p. 396.

39 Jawādī Āmulī, *Tasnīm*, vol. I, p. 176.

40 Jawādī Āmulī, *Qur'ān dar Qur'ān*, vol. I, p. 397.

41 Ibid.

42 Ibid., pp. 397–8.

43 Ibid., p. 394.

44 Ṭabāṭabā'ī, *al-Mīzān*, vol. XIII, pp. 93–4.

45 Elmi, 'An Objective Approach to Revelation', p. 57.

46 Muḥammad Riḍā al-Muẓaffar, *Uṣūl al-fiqh*, 2 vols (Beirut, 1990).

47 Ibid., vol. II, pp. 121–3.

48 Ibid., pp. 123–4.

49 Traditions that were transmitted through only one chain of narration.

50 Ṭabāṭabā'ī, *al-Mīzān*, vol. XVIII, p. 311.

51 Ibid., pp. 311–12.

52 Ṭabāṭabā'ī, *The Qur'an in Islam*, p. 29.

53 In his treatment of the verse in *al-Mīzān*, he relates *shirk* (associating someone or something with God) to the actions of the people. See Ṭabāṭabā'ī, *al-Mīzān*, vol. IV, p. 354.

54 The subject of the definition and scope of *shirk* has been one of the most disputed among the Muʿtazilīs, Ashʿarīs, Shiʿas, Sufis and Ḥanbalīs. For detailed studies on the issue, see Elizabeth Sirriyeh, 'Modern Muslim Interpretations of *Shirk*', *Religion* 20, no. 2 (1990), pp. 139–59; Gerald R. Hawting, *The Idea of Idolatry and the Emergence of Islam: From Polemic to History* (Cambridge, 1999).

55 Sirriyeh, 'Modern Muslim Interpretations of *Shirk*', pp. 139–40.

56 Jane Dammen McAuliffe, 'Text and Textuality: Q. 3:7 as a Point of Intersection', in Issa J. Boullata, ed., *Literary Structures of Religious Meaning in the Qur'ān* (Richmond, 2000), pp. 58–9.

57 Ibid., p. 59.
58 Ibid.
59 Ṭabāṭabā'ī, *al-Mīzān*, vol. III, pp. 20–22.
60 Shi'i and Mu'tazilī exegetes have opposed the idea of attributing physical qualities to God, thus they have considered relevant verses allegorical and have interpreted them accordingly. Conversely Ash'arī, Ḥanbalī and Ẓāhirī exegetes believed in attributing physical qualities to God and thus provided anthropomorphic and literary interpretations of the relevant verses. See Mahmoud M. Ayoub, 'Literary Exegesis of the Qur'ān: The Case of al-Sharīf al-Raḍī', in Issa J. Boullata, ed., *Literary Structures of Religious Meaning in the Qur'ān* (Richmond, 2000), pp. 297–9.
61 Ṭabāṭabā'ī, *al-Mīzān*, vol. III, p. 21.
62 McAuliffe, 'Text and Textuality', p. 59.
63 Jawādī Āmulī, *Tasnīm*, vol. XIII, p. 176.
64 Ibid., pp. 101–4.
65 Ibid., p. 104.
66 Ibid., pp. 114–17.
67 Long before Ṭabāṭabā'ī, Rāzī used the same argument to justify the existence of *mutashābihāt*. See McAuliffe, 'Text and Textuality', p. 65.
68 Ṭabāṭabā'ī, *al-Mīzān*, vol. III, p. 22.
69 Ibid.
70 Jawādī Āmulī, *Tasnīm*, vol. XIII, p. 114.
71 Jawādī Āmulī, *Qur'ān dar Qur'ān*, vol. I, p. 404.
72 Jawādī Āmulī, *Tasnīm*, vol. XIII, pp. 114–15.
73 Ibid., p. 117.
74 Ibid., p. 115.
75 Henry Corbin, *History of Islamic Philosophy* (Abingdon, 2014), p. 116.
76 Binyāmîn Abrahamov, ed. and tr., *Anthropomorphism and Interpretation of the Qur'ān in the Theology of al-Qāsim Ibn Ibrāhīm: Kitāb al-Mustarshid* (Leiden, 1996), pp. 6–7.
77 Nader El-Bizri, 'God: Essence and Attributes', in Tim Winter, ed., *The Cambridge Companion to Classical Islamic Theology* (Cambridge, 2008), p. 129.
78 El-Bizri, 'God: Essence and Attributes', p. 130.

2

Striving beyond the Balance (*al-Mīzān*): Spiritual Practice and the Qur'an in the Ṭabāṭabā'ī *Ṭarīqa*

SAJJAD RIZVI

WHILE THE major exegesis *al-Mīzān* by Muḥammad Ḥusayn Ṭabāṭabā'ī (d. 1981) has been much lauded as perhaps the best comprehensive Shi'i exegesis of the twentieth century, in which his skills as philosopher, theologian and exegete are clearly on display, a more careful analysis of the text should seek to problematise the ways in which he mediates the Qur'an through his own person, his circle of fellow travellers in the seminary and for his readership.[1] An appreciation of the exegetical strategies of Ṭabāṭabā'ī and his circle, beyond formal scholastic exegesis, will help to illuminate the uses and receptions of the Qur'an in modern Iran.[2] For those of us interested in what the Qur'an is and can mean for contemporary (Shi'i) Iran, it is tempting to revert to the famous account of the exegesis, understanding and experience of the text located in the words of the early imams. This relationship between manifest exegesis and esoteric experience, between the privileged knowledge of the elite and the popular dissemination of the Truth to believers, is expressed clearly in the second hadith in the relevant chapter on this issue in *Baṣā'ir al-darajāt*, one of the earliest of the Shi'i hadith collections compiled by Abū Ja'far al-Ṣaffār al-Qummī (d. 290/903):

> [Muḥammad] al-Bāqir [d. 114/733] was asked about the narration: every verse has a manifest (*ẓāhir*) and a hidden (*bāṭin*) aspect, and then an expression (*ḥarf*) that has a scope (*ḥadd*) and a point of rising (*muṭṭala'*). Manifest is clear and the hidden is its

> *ta'wīl* and what has happened and what will not, and the course of the sun and the moon, and the *ta'wīl* of all that will happen to the dead just as it will happen to the living. As God says, *No one knows its interpretation except God and those firmly grounded in knowledge* (Q. 3:7).[3]

The second is the idea expressed in a hadith narrated also from al-Bāqir, the fifth imam, which states that each verse of the Qur'an has an apparent (*ẓāhir*) and a hidden (*bāṭin*) aspect, and that even the hidden aspect has further aspects which suggests a hierarchy or multiplicity of esoteric meanings.[4]

In this paper, I will juxtapose the notion of Islam as a discursive tradition and as a lived practice predicated on the notion of the 'walking Qur'an' (as articulated by Rudolph T. Ware) with four levels of interrelated exegetical practice within the wider circle of Ṭabāṭabā'ī and his legacy or apparatus which, for all intents and purposes, looks and functions like a Sufi order or *ṭarīqa* (pl. *ṭuruq*) without the name. I will then attempt to examine the uses of the Qur'an in his circle, focusing upon some key texts associated with his teaching in Qum from 1949. I intend to uncover what this might tell us about modern attempts at holistic exegesis articulated to evince mystical truths about the nature of reality within our phenomenologically embodied experiences in this world. I hope to demonstrate that a careful textual examination allows us to offer a reading of the discourse of mysticism and exegesis within the context of the Shi'i seminary in Iran that is differentiated from the study of Sufi orders and other expressions of the occult. It also forces us to think more creatively about the very processes of what we term 'exegesis' and the living, walking Qur'an in the contemporary Muslim world, in order to further the debate conducted in recent years about what constitutes living the authentic Muslim life and what significations and meanings can be ascribed when we use the term 'Islamic'.

Senses of Exegesis

The process of exegesis revolves around four levels through which the Qur'an may be encountered and lived. The first level is through the Qur'an as a textual artefact, a book, a scripture, an object of veneration or recitation and contemplation, a collection of inscribed words that have a structure and syntactical arrangement, and strings of meanings as expressed in narrations that stress the importance of a venerable treatment of the artefact and reading the scripture in a book (*muṣḥaf*).[5] We normally understand exegesis at this level as a learned, scholastic discourse intended to reveal layers of meaning, from the lexical to the narratological to the experiential.[6] The process of exegesis, of the dialectics of engaging with the text and the many intellectual contexts that constitute the text's semiosphere (that is, the field in which sign processes operate within a context), is an expression of the art of living, the cultivation of values, the dissemination of correct comportment (*adab*) and the civilising mission.[7] But this level of encountering the Qur'an can include the role that the artefact plays as a talisman, as a purveyor of spiritual power, as a source of augury (*istikhāra*) and geomancy (*raml*), a magical book by which one protects or casts aspersions upon another or heals.[8] The plenitude of meaning, which, as we saw above, embraces the exoteric and esoteric and much beyond, and the polyvalency of the text should not require much further argument.

The second level is through the Qur'an as a signifier within the intertextual weaving and production of cultural, intellectual and aesthetic capital that we all experience and consume. Exegesis at this level articulates and elucidates elements of the logosphere of the Qur'an (that is, the field in which it is articulated, uttered and expressed linguistically). In this sense, while believers often stand in awe of the text, they have already experienced the architectonics of the Qur'an in the very fabric of Muslim life. As the famous saying goes, God is beautiful and loves beauty, and the very expression of the Qur'an in its different articulations and presentations follows that maxim in which the contingencies of aesthetic harmony and form act as homologies for the Divine.[9] Discerning and perceiving the beauty of the Qur'an is not simply an act of textual reception but of aesthetic perception of life imbued with 'Qur'anicity'; appreciation of that art rests on cultural literacy – though someone may be functionally illiterate, he or she can still recognise the calligraphic tokens, the melodies and intonation of recitation, the motifs in the plastic arts, and the signatures and citations in music.[10] The beauty of the Divine, manifest in the cosmos, is remade and reshaped in the aesthetics of human craft; that mimesis of the Divine must contain elements of imperfection and human error in order not to fall into idolatry by considering the Qur'an as either shibboleth or an idol.[11] It is here that Henry Corbin's famous admonition about the distinction between an idol and icon is salutary.[12] The former entails a contraction of the Divine, a location of theophany and power within an object that in itself becomes the focus of veneration and does not allow one to see beyond, while the latter retains its role as a *symbolon* that propels the perceiver to use their imagination to go beyond the physical artefact and contemplate the 'theophanic form'.[13] Or to use another analogy drawn by Corbin, it is like the distinction between 'existents', which can act as a veil that ushers in phenomenal multiplicity, and 'Being', that is the True One that underlines all that exists: one can marvel at the multiplicity and stop there, indulging in idolatry, or one can look at the underlying reality and recognise that each 'existent' is an icon that reveals Being. It is also encountering the Qur'an in an indexical manner, in the way in which much Islamic literature bears the hallmarks of Qur'anicity, by merely citing, acknowledging or referencing the scripture without deriving or marking out its meaning in the production of a new text. This attraction to what is familiar is that same inclination that inspires love for the original signifier, both the Qur'an and its revelator, by evoking the human faculties of the external senses as well as the internal senses of the intellect, insight and intuition, and divine inspiration and illumination in the heart.[14]

The third level is through the Qur'an as a primordial, timeless reality revealing the nature of the cosmos, the light and the guide that requires rehearsal and teaching among people, and as a mediating reality.[15] Exegesis of this kind is the archosphere of the Qur'an, that is, it pursues the origins and the principle from whence the scripture came. This is partly what the tradition understands by the teaching or revelation in its first instance, in which it exists on the heavenly, pre-eternal 'Preserved tablet' (*al-lawḥ al-maḥfūẓ*), as well as by the pre-eternal 'Muhammadan Light' (*al-nūr al-muḥammadī*) in the form of the Prophet (and the imams, according to Shiʿi traditions), who was the first beloved made to stand apart from the first Lover.[16] Allied to this notion, albeit in a more historically contingent sense, is Shahab Ahmed's notion of the 'pre-text'.[17]

The fourth level is through the Qur'an as a recitation (*qirā'a*, *tartīl*) and cantillation (*tajwīd*), the power of the uttered word of God, doubled in its potency when articulated on the tongue of the imam.[18] Exegesis of this kind concerns the phonosphere of the Qur'an, that is, the aural field in which the scripture is encountered. Recitation becomes a means not only of internalising the text and the Divine, of meeting the imam, but also of aesthetic embellishment and achieving healing and therapy of the self and one's immediate context within conventional modes and registers.[19] Alongside the rational exhortation to those listening, the poetic register evinces similar stylistic responses in the reciter and in the listener.[20] Evoking imagery (*takhyīl*) and provoking poetical argumentation and rhetoric is central to the notion of what is beautiful in the language of revelation.[21] These processes of cultural production from the phonosphere remained efficaciously imaginary whether the articulation was in Arabic or the vernacular.[22]

Do these preliminary points amount to considering the Islam of the exegetical practices a 'discursive tradition' *apud* Talal Asad?[23] This approach is often contrasted with a cultural-anthropological affirmation of the idea of many Islams that cohere around established symbols – particularly with regard to their uses in differing spaces and times – and the constructed nature of traditions. The former insists upon techniques of world-making, of self-emergence and of argumentations that pivot on texts. But our notion of exegesis goes beyond, without lapsing into the varying constructions and symbol manipulations of the anthropological approach. It embraces modes of transmission and character formation that address not only the what, why and how of the encounter with the Qur'an but also the techniques that are used to disseminate an understanding of Islam, an Islam which Rudolph T. Ware describes as the 'walking Qur'an', one that reconciles our rational souls with their material and temporal embodiment, the oral and the textual, the male and the female, the public and the private, and the culturally particular with the 'religiously universal'.[24] Embracing this more 'expansive' sense of Islam as a discursive tradition can allow for a more integrative approach to the analysis and hermeneutics of both text and practice, and to the whole religious person engaged with the Qur'an on the horizons of their experience, within their various embodied contexts. Religions are indeed collectivities of arguments, doctrines, values and worldviews, but they are also frameworks for narrative, myth-making and myth-evoking, imagery and imagination, sounds, colours, smells and the whole range of human agency.

Apparatus

Before continuing to the analysis of the modes of exegesis, it is critical to present the central figure, Ṭabāṭabā'ī, and his wider apparatus. First, let us consider the term 'apparatus'. Michel Foucault seems to have been the first to use the term 'apparatus' or *dispositif* in relation to the *souci de soi* (care of the self) and governance of the self, indeed selves, in an interview in 1977. He said:

> What I'm trying to pick out with this term is, firstly, a thoroughly heterogeneous ensemble consisting of discourses, institutions, architectural forms, regulatory decisions, laws, administrative measures, scientific statements, philosophical, moral and philanthropic propositions – in short, the said as much as the unsaid. Such are the elements of the apparatus. The apparatus itself is the system of relations that can be established between these elements.
>
> Secondly, what I am trying to identify in this apparatus is precisely the nature of the connection that can exist between these heterogeneous elements. Thus, a particular discourse can figure at one time as the programme of an institution, and at another it can function as a means of justifying or masking a practice which itself remains silent, or as a secondary re-interpretation of this practice, opening out for it a new field of rationality.

> In short, between these elements, whether discursive or non-discursive, there is a sort of interplay of shifts of position and modifications of function, which can also vary very widely.
>
> Thirdly, I understand by the term 'apparatus' a sort of – shall we say – formation which has as its major function at a given historical moment that of responding to an *urgent need*. The apparatus thus has a dominant strategic function. This may have been, for example, the assimilation of a floating population found to be burdensome for an essentially mercantilist economy: there was a strategic imperative acting here as the matrix for an apparatus which gradually undertook the control or subjection of madness, sexual illness and neurosis . . .
>
> I said that the apparatus is essentially of a *strategic* nature, which means assuming that it is a matter of a certain manipulation of relations of forces, either developing them in a particular direction, blocking them, stabilizing them, utilizing them, etc. The apparatus is thus always inscribed in a play of power, but it is also always linked to certain coordinates of knowledge which issue from it but, to an equal degree, condition it. This is what the apparatus consists in: strategies of relations of forces supporting, and supported by, types of knowledge.[25]

Giorgio Agamben further elaborates on the role of the apparatus in the 'plays' of power, in the human and the historical role in the management of politics, as well as in the formulation of knowledge.[26] The apparatus creates its subject – and, indulging in some political theological reasoning, Agamben insists upon the theological genealogy of the term – and hence produces the process of subjectivisation, whereby the pure activity of governance may be realised.[27]

Nevertheless, Agamben's rather paradoxical conceptualisation of agency – already present in his *Homo Sacer* series – goes even further by dividing all entities into living beings and apparatuses, between the ontology of selves and the governance of apparatuses that 'seek to guide them towards the good'. According to Agamben, an apparatus is thus

> literally anything that has in some way the capacity to capture, orient, determine, intercept, model, control, or secure the

> gestures, behaviors, opinions, or discourses of living beings. Not only, therefore, prisons, madhouses, the panopticon, schools, confession, factories, disciplines, juridical measures, and so forth (whose connection with power is in a certain sense evident), but also the pen, writing, literature, philosophy, agriculture, cigarettes, navigation, computers, cellular telephones and – why not – language itself, which is perhaps the most ancient of apparatuses – one in which thousands and thousands of years ago a primate inadvertently let himself be captured, probably without realizing the consequences that he was about to face.[28]

For Agamben, the apparatus is a fundamental feature of modern life, one that we do not escape, nor do we escape its ability to make us its subjects. The term apparatus actually allows us to place together the totality of structures, modes of comportment, exchanges, discourses and many other rules that govern selves and interpersonal relationships in Iran, especially since the 1978 revolution. But given the focus on the governance of the self and the direction that takes, it seems a highly appropriate way of talking about the regulation of selves within the wider network of *ʿirfān* (practical mysticism) associated with Ṭabāṭabāʾī.[29] Given the reluctance of members to define themselves as a *ṭarīqa* because of its association with Sufism (*taṣawwuf*), which is anathema in the *ḥawza*s (the Shiʿi theological seminaries), and given the fact that we are not talking about a singular lineage but multiple and parallel transmissions from the early thirteenth/nineteenth century down to the present, 'apparatus' strikes me as a highly useful term to encapsulate all of these phenomena associated with Ṭabāṭabāʾī.[30] 'Apparatus' encompasses the techniques of disciplining selves, the multiple lineages and trends, the hermeneutics of text and social practice, and the emphases on particular spiritual practices and ritual configurations. It allows us to include different lineages and legacies of Ṭabāṭabāʾī's impact as a spiritual master.

In terms of authority, much has been written about the applicability of Max Weber's tripartite conception – not least by Hamid Dabashi; however, the modern question of authority relates to legitimacy and the manufacturing of consent.[31] Recent, more sociological works concern the ways in which authority is derived, constructed and manifested. In our context, we are concerned with the way in which the Ṭabāṭabāʾī apparatus, from the projection of the moral psychology of the persons subjectified, establishes the discourses and modes of practice that inform a hegemonic path to God, guided by exegetical strategies of the Qurʾan, and concomitantly a political conceptualisation of interpersonal relationships and claims to power within them. *ʿIrfān* in this sense locates legitimacy and the power to make subjects of its apparatus in the figure of the mystical seeker (*ʿārif*), whether that seeker exercises executive power or not. As in the medieval Sufi discourse, the *ʿārif* is the true sultan, privileged over and above the jurist because of the ability to see beyond the ephemeral and the apparent, which are the domains of jurisprudence.

Ṭabāṭabāʾī: An Exegesis of a Philosophical Life

Muḥammad Ḥusayn Ṭabāṭabāʾī was born in Shādābād, a village near Tabriz, in 1904 into a *sayyid* family of prominent scholars, judges and spiritual guides.[32] As his parents died when he was still very young, his uncle Sayyid Muḥammad ʿAlī took charge of him and his younger brother Sayyid Muḥammad Ḥasan (d. 1968) who later became known as Ilāhī and was himself a spiritual master in Tabriz.[33] Being an orphan is an important trope in hagiography. After his elementary studies in Tabriz, where he learned Arabic and Persian language and literature, Ṭabāṭabāʾī moved in 1925 to Najaf where he studied for ten years with major jurists and Uṣūlīs including Mīrzā Ḥusayn Nāʾīnī (d. 1936),[34] and Sayyid Abūʾl-Ḥasan Iṣfahānī (d. 1946), the leading juristic source of emulation (*marjaʿ*) of the time.[35] Ṭabāṭabāʾī was particularly attached to the philosophically minded jurist Shaykh Muḥammad Ḥusayn Gharawī Iṣfahānī (d. 1942), and indeed later he edited and glossed a famous correspondence between him and Sayyid Aḥmad Ṭihrānī Karbalāʾī (d. 1914) on the nature of being – a debate between a philosopher and a mystic.[36] In 1935, Ṭabāṭabāʾī's juristic formation was complete and he was recognised in Najaf as a mujtahid.

Even more significant for Ṭabāṭabāʾī's formation were his studies in philosophy with Sayyid Ḥusayn Bādkubaʾī (d. 1939), himself a student of Sayyid Abū'l-Ḥasan Jilwa (d. 1896), an Avicennan critic of Mullā Ṣadrā (d. 1045/1636);[37] and with his relative Sayyid ʿAlī Qāḍī (d. 1947), a renowned teacher of *ʿirfān*, in the guise of 'ethical instruction' (*akhlāq*).[38] Ṭabāṭabāʾī in his own account says that he studied with Bādkubaʾī for six years, reading the *Sharḥ-i manẓūma* of Mullā Hādī Sabzawārī (d. 1873); the *Asfār* and *al-Mashāʿir* of Mullā Ṣadrā; the complete *Shifāʾ* of Avicenna, as well as the *Uthūlūjiyā* [Theology of Aristotle] – the famous paraphrase of sections of Plotinus' *Enneads* IV–VI classically attributed to Aristotle; and the *Tamhīd* [*al-qawāʿid*] of Ibn Turka (d. 835/1432).[39] Qāḍī had been a prominent student and even teacher of jurisprudence. In recent works, he has been described as a *faqīh-i mutaʾallih* (a mystically inclined jurist) for bringing together *ʿirfān* and law in a new fusion; he stressed a spiritual path through prayer vigils, extensive prostrations and the methods of *dhikr* (the invocation and remembrance of God) including the Yūnusiyya (*There is no God but You, glory is Yours but I am merely one of those who wrong*; *lā ilāha illā anta subḥānaka innī kuntu min al-ẓālimīn*, Q. 21:87) that can be traced back through his own spiritual master Karbalāʾī and to Karbalāʾī's master in turn, Āqā Ḥusayn-qulī Hamadānī (d. 1893), and beyond.[40] (I shall return to the lineage later.) Qāḍī also taught Ṭabāṭabāʾī the works of Ibn ʿArabī (d. 638/1240), not least *al-Futūḥāt al-Makkiyya* (the Meccan Revelations).[41] This was a central aspect of the *ʿirfān* curriculum from the nineteenth century, but perhaps significantly Ṭabāṭabāʾī himself never taught the works of Ibn ʿArabī back in Iran, especially in Qum; instead, he focused on mysticism arising from Qur'anic exegesis and the supplications and spiritual practices taught by the imams.[42] This seems clearly another aspect of the influence of Qāḍī on Ṭabāṭabāʾī, as he was known for promoting *tafsīr al-Qurʾān biʾl-Qurʾān*, a method of exegesis which was supposedly the foundation of Ṭabāṭabāʾī's method in *al-Mīzān*, and also authored a commentary on a famous supplication *Duʿāʾ al-simāt*.[43] It is mentioned that Qāḍī wrote a *tafsīr* from the beginning until verse 92 of *Sūrat al-Anʿām* (Q. 6:92) using this method, but it has not been published.[44] He was also embraced as a clerical activist by the revolutionary ideology after 1979.[45] About Qāḍī, Muḥammad Ḥusayn Ḥusaynī Ṭihrānī (d. 1995) writes: 'Qāḍī was the Salmān of his times, the expositor of the Qur'an and the outstanding figure of his age, in disciplining his soul, and manifesting excellent character traits and mastery of divine sciences and revelations and unveilings of the heart. He was a great repository and font of divine secrets.'[46]

Ṭabāṭabā'ī returned with his brother to Tabriz in 1935 and taught and earned a basic living working the family lands. It was only in March 1946 that he moved to Qum, perhaps due to major land reforms initiated by the nationalists who had been installed in power under Soviet protection.[47] In Qum, he struggled to make ends meet. Not recognised as a jurist there, he did not receive *khums* (obligatory religious taxes collected by a *marja'*) that would allow him to establish a patronage network and sustain students. He instead focused on teaching philosophy and exegesis, both disciplines being marginal to the curriculum of the *ḥawza*, and the former considered with some suspicion. Ṭabāṭabā'ī wrote about his conflict with the prominent *marja'* Sayyid Ḥusayn Burūjirdī (d. 1962) precisely on this point.[48] This conflict was not only about the legitimacy of philosophy and *'irfān* but also of authority. His class on the *Asfār* was apparently quite popular, attracting around a hundred students, which might also have been a factor in his dispute with Burūjirdī.[49] Given his recent arrival in Qum and his relatively junior status, Ṭabāṭabā'ī obliged by discontinuing his public classes by 1947 while continuing to teach in private classes.[50] The paramountcy of jurisprudence was thus preserved; clearly Burūjirdī was at the height of his influence and his closeness to the monarchy further bolstered his authority in Qum.

Nevertheless, Ṭabāṭabā'ī considered philosophy alongside exegesis to play a major social role in providing a dual critique of the materialism and secularism that had arisen with the advent of communism in Shi'i Iran and Iraq. For Ṭabāṭabā'ī, these two disciplines, along with the more reflective and spiritually exercised practice of *'irfān*, constituted a means for purifying the self and elevating the intellect as a basis for an individual active in society. Additionally, they also pointed to one of Ṭabāṭabā'ī's key insights, which is that there were only two possible ways of understanding and decoding the nature of reality: through revelation mediated by an infallible imam or prophet, or through inner revelation (*kashf*) and vision (*shuhūd*) in the process of *ʿirfān*.[51] He taught a small group of students who had earlier begun studying with Mīrzā Mahdī Āshtiyānī (d. 1952) the works of Avicenna and Mullā Ṣadrā. From 1949, he began to hold classes in Tehran on *ʿirfān* and *akhlāq*, taking as base texts the work *Risāla-yi sayr wa sulūk* attributed to Sayyid Mahdī Ṭabāṭabāʾī 'Baḥr al-ʿUlūm' (d. 1212/1797) and the correspondence mentioned above between Iṣfahānī and Karbalāʾī.[52] Some of the transcripts of these classes were published as *Lubb al-lubāb* by his student Ṭihrānī.[53] This included the spiritual exercises of the Ṭabāṭabāʾī apparatus, to which we will return. Ṭihrānī, writing after the death of Ṭabāṭabāʾī, and no doubt furthering his own holistic approach, suggests that he believed in the complete homology between philosophy, mysticism and the law, and that he was a master in all because of the concomitance of law and ethics: in fact, in Ṭihrānī's words, for Ṭabāṭabāʾī, *ʿirfān* and philosophy were the two foundations of the law.[54] On the more theoretical aspects of mysticism, Ṭabāṭabāʾī was familiar with the works of Ibn ʿArabī. While there is no strong evidence indicating that he taught the works of the master himself, he does seem to have taught the *Tamhīd al-qawāʿid* of Ibn Turka.[55]

Ṭabāṭabāʾī's major project was his exegesis, *al-Mīzān fī tafsīr al-Qurʾān*, which he commenced in 1954 and completed in 1972.[56] His student Jawādī Āmulī argues that Ṭabāṭabāʾī undertook the project not only to recentre the focus of the seminary on the Qur'an and demonstrate the significance of a Qur'anocentric and exegetical *ʿirfān*, but also because he believed that in his role as the vicegerent of God (*khalīfat Allāh*) he was authorised to comment upon the scripture.[57] Any act of exegesis, and especially one that claims to be comprehensive in its rational and scriptural discussions like this one, is ultimately a claim to authority, an assertion that the exegete is a spokesman for the Divine and can define what the scripture means for us in our time. Exegesis is thus not just the appropriation of the divine word for the disciplines that form the exegete, it is an arrogation of authority. Most of the accounts of Ṭabāṭabāʾī's life are hagiographical and were posthumously compiled by his students, but it is clear that no one lives such a neat narrative life in the way that biographers conceive of it after the fact. Ṭihrānī's biography of Ṭabāṭabāʾī in particular revels in the supernatural in order to construct the life of a saint. There, he reflects on Ṭabāṭabāʾī as someone who was tried and tested and had to overcome obstacles before becoming recognised in later life, gathering disciples and performing miracles; in recounting his last moments, he portrays him as dying in adversity, but with contentment in his heart, after an illness on 17 Muḥarram 1402/November 1981.[58]

The *Ṭarīqa*: Texts and Practices

To date, hardly anything concrete has been published in European languages on the modern networks of mysticism and informal Sufi brotherhoods in the Shiʿi seminary, while the last couple of decades have witnessed a plethora of sources published in Persian (and Arabic) on the *ʿirfān* of the seminary. These have focused on the various branches of the Shūshtariyya or the apparatus *ṭarīqa-yi maʿrifat-i nafs* (path of self-knowledge), the idea of formal lineages often in rival branches with differing methods stemming from the teachings of Sayyid ʿAlī Shūshtarī (d. 1866) in Najaf in the Qajar period (1794–1925).[59] The apparatus is sometimes also called the 'mystical-ethical school of Najaf' (*madrasa-yi akhlāqī-yi ʿirfānī-yi Najaf*) because of the centrality of the shrine city to the teaching and dissemination of the apparatus from the later nineteenth century. This is what I mean by the Ṭabāṭabāʾī apparatus, which is the dominant mystical tendency in the Shiʿi seminary. Much has been written on the role of Ruhollah Khomeini (d. 1989) and his encouragement of the study of *ʿirfān* and its discourse in the modern sphere in Iran. There has also recently been published, and even translated, some of the key works of those in the circles around Ṭabāṭabāʾī, who was perhaps the key figure of the Shūshtariyya since the Second World War up until his death.[60]

What is the main lineage down to Ṭabāṭabāʾī and how might it relate to other more established *ṭuruq*, not least the branch of the Niʿmatullāhī known as the Ṣafī-ʿAlī-Shāhī? What relationship was there between the rise of Sufi-like networks and relationships in the seminary with the formal Sufi brotherhoods?[61] The following lineage is given in a number of sources: 12th Imam → Mullā[-qulī]

Jūlā/Juhlā [Indian in Karbalā'?] → [Sayyid Ṣadr al-Dīn Dizfūlī (d. 1843)] → Sayyid 'Alī Shūshtarī (d. 1866) Karbalā'/Najaf → Āqā Ḥusayn-qulī Hamadānī (d. 1893) Karbalā'/Najaf → Sayyid Aḥmad Iṣfahānī Ṭihrānī Karbalā'ī (d. 1914) Karbalā'/Najaf → Sayyid 'Alī Qāḍī Ṭabāṭabā'ī (d. 1947) Najaf → 'Allāma Ṭabāṭabā'ī (d. 1981) Najaf/Qum.[62] Significant is the claim of *uwaysī* origins for this lineage of spiritual direction beginning with the imam of the time (i.e. that the progenitor did not have a spiritual master physically present and knowable to others), indicating not only the need to insist upon a properly Shi'i transmission of spiritual guidance but also, no doubt, occluding the relationship with existing orders like the Dhahabiyya (a Shi'i Sufi order) and even the Naqshbandiyya (a Sunni Sufi order), links that are clear in the forms of litanies and *dhikr* practised.[63] I have placed Dizfūlī in brackets because the Dhahabiyya indicate this link, but that could equally be down to Sufis appropriating a major figure into their tradition, which they often did – a good example of this imagined and constructed history of Sufism in Iran into modern times is the famous biographical dictionary *Ṭarā'iq al-ḥaqā'iq* of Nā'ib al-Ṣadr Shīrāzī, also known as Ma'ṣūm 'Alī Shāh (d. 1926).[64] In terms of the numbers of disciples and teachings transmitted from them, the two key figures are Ḥusayn-qulī Hamadānī and Sayyid 'Alī Qāḍī. Since there is very little on these figures and I have commented on Qāḍī above, it might be worth discussing the 'eponymous' founder and the key common link: Shūshtarī and Hamadānī.

Sayyid 'Alī Shūshtarī was a mystically inclined figure in the shrine city of Najaf and a fifth-generation descendant of the theologian Sayyid Ni'matullāh al-Jazā'irī (d. 1112/1701) of the Safavid era (1501–1736).[65] After training as a jurist, he became a judge and prayer leader in his hometown of Shūshtar, much like his ancestors. However, as the hagiographies mention, dissatisfied, he turned towards Najaf and, arriving there, encountered Mullā Jūlā sitting on the ground in the famed cemetery of Wādī al-Salām, and inspired by him, became his disciple. The hagiographies also mention that despite his fame as a jurist and being the appropriate heir to Shaykh Murtaḍā Anṣārī (d. 1864), an Imāmī *marja' al-taqlīd* (model for emulation), he was more inclined to the spiritual path and trained his disciples accordingly in his classes on ethics (*akhlāq*). Though he was famed for performing miracles, the only written works he left behind were on juristic theory and not on philosophy, exegesis or *ʿirfān*.

Ḥusayn-qulī Hamadānī was perhaps Shūshtarī's most important disciple. Born in Shavand, he first studied in Iran, including with the famed philosopher Sabzawārī, and then moved to Najaf where he became a student of Anṣārī in legal theory. He was a favoured disciple of Anṣārī's, and taught his classes after he died.[66] He then quickly attached himself to Shūshtarī and became the main conduit for his teachings in ethics and the spiritual path. In turn, he trained a number of disciples, including Karbalāʾī, whom we met above, and Shaykh Muhammad Bahārī Hamadānī (d. 1907).[67] His stress upon the disciplining of the soul and the importance of spiritual exercises was critical; one major mystic of the wider apparatus and himself a disciple, Mīrzā Jawād Malakī Tabrīzī (d. 1924), spoke of the 'alchemical effect' that his spiritual master Ḥusayn-qulī Hamadānī had in transforming disciples.[68] Because of his role as the 'common link' in the spiritual lineage, the apparatus is also sometimes associated with the school of Hamadānī.

Hagiographies mention various significant themes taught by Ḥusayn-qulī Hamadānī that impinge upon the exegesis of the Qur'an. First, he stressed the importance of maintaining a watchful state over the self in remembrance of death, coupled, most importantly, with the practice of the prayer of Jonah (*dhikr al-Yūnusiyya*) to be performed in the state of prostration.[69] This included a range of spiritual exercises and the purification of the soul (*tazkiyat al-nafs*). The watchful state involved the constant remembrance and invocation of the Divine, so that the heart of the seeker might become the sanctuary of God.[70] Second, he insisted upon walking in the steps of the friends of God, and a particular attachment to ʿAlī – always referred to as the pole of the mystics (*Quṭb al-ʿārifīn*) and the imam of the wayfarers (*Imām al-sālikīn*) – and to the collection of his sayings and sermons, *Nahj al-balāgha*.[71] Part of the process was invoking the hagiographies of saints as exemplary narratives. Third, he taught that the mystical path through its spiritual exercises was concerned with invoking the attraction of the

Divine and effecting the ecstasy of the encounter with God (*liqā' Allāh*), hence so many of his disciples, including Ḥusayn-qulī Hamadānī and Tabrīzī, wrote treatises on this subject. Fourth, he distanced himself from the practice of the Sufis, of formal initiations and the institutional aspects of orders and their nomenclature, and tied the spiritual path to an ethical understanding of the law, rooted in prayer and the contemplation of the Qur'an.[72] Fifth, he stressed the way of sanctity (*walāya*) by following the friends of God in the quest for godlikeness (*theosis*, *ta'alluh*) and encountering the Divine.[73] This marks out the method as Shi'i in particular: sanctity involves three levels – the most general (*'āmm*) is the absolute sanctity of God and the availability of His intimacy to all; the specific (*khāṣṣ*) relates to the believers and what they owe the imams, God and themselves; and the most specific (*akhaṣṣ*) refers to the proper status of the imams as intimates of the Divine and of the believers.[74] In particular, there is a stress upon imitating the way of Salmān al-Fārisī (d. 35/655–6 or 36/656–7), the close Companion of the Prophet – and we saw above the praise of Qāḍī as being 'like Salmān'.[75] Along with these themes and practices, Ḥusayn-qulī Hamadānī seems to have directed his disciples to inculcate the teachings and practices in certain texts, such as the *Minhāj al-najāt* of Muḥsin Fayḍ Kāshānī (d. 1090/1680), the *Miftāḥ al-falāḥ* of Shaykh Bahā' al-Dīn al-'Āmilī (d. 1030/1621) and the *Kashf al-ghiṭā' 'an wujūh marāsim al-ihtidā' fī 'ilm al-akhlāq* of Mullā Muḥammad Ḥasan Qazwīnī (d. 1825).[76]

A number of other significant figures are associated with this apparatus: Āqā Muḥammad Bīdābādī (d. 1783), the philosopher whose links to the Dhahabī Sufi order are known;[77] Baḥr al-'Ulūm, whereby a text attributed to him, entitled *Risāla-yi Sayr wa sulūk*, is popular in the apparatus; 'Abd al-Ṣamad Hamadānī (d. 1802), who died during the Wahhābī assault on Karbala and is the author of *Baḥr al-ma'ārif*, which was adopted as the teachings of the apparatus;[78] Bahārī Hamadānī, a close disciple of Ḥusayn-qulī Hamadānī and author of *Tadhkirat al-muttaqīn*;[79] the illiterate sage Rajab 'Alī Khayyāṭ (d. 1961);[80] Sayyid Hāshim Ḥaddād (d. 1986), on whose life a number of those within the apparatus have written and who himself was associated with Ṭabāṭabā'ī, but especially with his spiritual master Qāḍī;[81] Sayyid Murtaḍā Raḍawī Kashmīrī (d. 1932), who was known for his miracles and work with the occult and his stress upon invoking the *dhikr al-Yūnusiyya* in long acts of prostration; Sayyid ʿAbd al-Karīm Raḍawī Kashmīrī (d. 1999), who was a disciple of Qāḍī and a close friend of Shaykh Muḥammad Taqī Bahjat (d. 2009; more on him below) – his teaching followed Hamadānī in its stress upon the *walāya* of the imams, including devotion due to them and pilgrimage to their shrines, as well as the path of self-purification that involves the watchfulness over the self and striving to annihilate the self to subsist in God;[82] Sayyid Ḥasan Masqaṭī (d. 1931), who was a close disciple of Qāḍī and taught philosophy and mysticism in Najaf before returning to Oman and then to India on the invitation of the Nizam of Hyderabad;[83] Ḥusaynī Ṭihrānī, a disciple of Ḥaddād and Ṭabāṭabāʾī and perhaps the one who did the most to promote the view of Ṭabāṭabāʾī as both a mystic and juristic source of emulation (*ʿārif-marjaʿ*);[84] and the late *marjaʿ*, Bahjat, yet another disciple of Qāḍī. In one recent work, Matthijs van den Bos, drawing upon Maʿṣūm ʿAlī Shāh via Richard Gramlich, has argued that this apparatus is actually known as the Ḥujjat ʿAlī Shāh branch of the Niʿmatullāhī order, named after Sayyid ʿAbd al-Ḥujjat Balāghī, also known as Ḥujjat ʿAlī Shāh.[85] However, this is difficult to verify, not least because those within the apparatus would not admit such a linkage because of the suppression of the Sufi orders still active in Iran. Some within the apparatus prefer the term the Shūshtariyya to indicate the origins through Shūshtarī, but this seems to be a very recent phenomenon, and particularly among non-Iranian adherents who do not have the same psychological and intellectual restrictions that arise from internalising the contested history of Sufi orders and their reputations in post-revolutionary Iran.

While there is very little information on many of the figures in terms of the details of their taking on the mantle of Ṭabāṭabāʾī and the way in which ethics, the spiritual path and the practical necessities of jurisprudence converged within them and their works, one can examine the case of Bahjat. In recent years, many works have been published on Bahjat, no doubt because of his popularity as a *marjaʿ*.[86] His intellectual biography is similar to that of Ṭabāṭabāʾī.

Like the latter he studied in Najaf with Nāʾīnī and Iṣfahānī, and in matters of *ʿirfān* was closely associated with Qāḍī.[87] Similarly, he moved back to Qum in 1944 (a bit earlier than Ṭabāṭabāʾī), where he began to teach jurisprudence. Apart from his growing fame as a jurist, which resulted in his recognition as a *marja*ʿ, he was admired for his piety and character, and even his miracles.[88] In his teachings in the area of jurisprudence he stressed many of the features of the school of Ḥusayn-qulī Hamadānī. First, the spiritual path is located within the Shiʿi path of the imams and the contemplation of the Qur'an.[89] Second, the spiritual path involves spiritual exercises, and these must be directed by a master;[90] the central practice on the path is *dhikr* – not least the Qur'anically taught one of Jonah.[91] Third, companionship along the path is critical, and through the narratives of saints' lives one learns how to comport oneself.[92] Fourth, the goal of the path is the encounter with God, fleeing to God from the vicissitudes of this embodied existence and becoming godlike.[93] Bahjat, unlike Ṭihrānī or Ḥasanzāda Āmulī, was known for his more scripturally founded Qur'anic ethics, a distancing from the formal aspects of an order, and the avoidance of the formal language of both the Ibn ʿArabī school and of mystical philosophy.

The apparatus uses several key texts: *Risāla-yi sayr wa sulūk*, *Lubb al-lubāb* as well as various treatises on encountering God, and the scriptural and practical *Risālat al-walāya*. The latter has become the more cerebral and theoretical expression of the apparatus and spawned a number of translations, paraphrases and commentaries in Persian.[94] While the texts discuss techniques and provide a conscious construction of the history of the apparatus, the main conduit for the dissemination of ideas is biographical, through works in the style of *Tadhkirat al-muttaqīn* and indeed the biographies of Hamadānī, Qāḍī, Ḥaddād and Ṭabāṭabāʾī himself;[95] this is also clear in *Lubb al-lubāb*. His method fits the approach of the apparatus, which stresses the importance of narrative and storytelling to convey and perpetuate doctrine and spiritual practice; as such, it is continuous with the Sufi methods that one finds from the earliest period, which combine hagiography with spiritual guidance and exhortation. These texts primarily concern the mystical governance of the self and the process through which the moral psychology of the individual is attuned to the path to God; they aim to bestow authority upon the individual, an authority that may extend into the political realm of the governance of the state. All these convergences do not preclude the variety of approaches and methods in the apparatus – some are more textual and exegetical, some are more focused on Ibn ʿArabī, some are focused on the occult, while others are focused on the socio-political significance of ethics and spiritual practice.[96]

Before analysing the exegetical aspects of these texts, some analytic points about ʿAbd al-Ṣamad Hamadānī's *Baḥr al-maʿārif* (a work that somewhat predates the apparatus) are worth making. He presents one of the many examples of the apparatus intersecting with formal Sufi orders, since he was probably a disciple of the Niʿmatullāhī Sufi Ḥusayn ʿAlī Shāh (d. 1818) and an associate of Muḥammad Jaʿfar Kabūdarāhangī known as Majdhūb ʿAlī Shāh (d. 1824).[97] The *Baḥr al-maʿārif* shares a number of features with other esoteric, even Sufi, works of the Qajar period: a focus on *walāya* and the cosmic role of the imams, the exegesis of some key texts such as the famous *Khuṭbat al-bayān* and the recognition of the imam through his luminous reality (*al-maʿrifa biʾl-nūrāniyya*).[98] The Shiʿi particularity, perhaps in the polemic age of the late Safavid and early Qajar periods, is expressed through a strong emphasis on dissociation from the enemies of the imams (*tabarrāʾ*).[99] This theological concern marks the second half of the text. The first half primarily deals with the importance of *dhikr* as part of a process of watchfulness over one's soul and the purification of the soul (*riyāḍat al-nafs*, *tazkiyat al-nafs*) on the path to the encounter with God.[100] Companionship on the path is critical. Like another classic text of the apparatus, *Rūḥ-i mujarrad*, *Baḥr al-maʿārif* spends much time on the need for a spiritual master or guide and the correct comportment of the disciple; it also underscores the need to frequent the friends of God, the living saints, and the shrines and sacred spaces of those who have passed.[101] ʿAbd al-Ṣamad Hamadānī's own practice expressed this, as he spent most of his life in the shrine cities of Karbala and Mashhad. Throughout, one notices the complementarity of doctrine and practice, the integration of the exoteric and the esoteric, and a deep scriptural contemplation, especially on hadith as is the practice of Ṭabāṭabā'ī in *Lubb al-lubāb*. In many ways, *Baḥr al-ma'ārif* is a summa of the Shi'i Sufism of the late eighteenth century, and it anticipates many of the concerns of works of the Qajar period.

The first text that will be discussed here is the treatise on the spiritual path, *Risāla-yi sayr wa sulūk*, attributed to Baḥr al-'Ulūm. Like *Lubb al-lubāb*, which was composed of the transcripts of Ṭihrānī, this text contains the core of Ṭabāṭabā'ī's classes in ethics from 1949. It begins with the exhortation of the initiate on the path to imitate Moses' response to the theophany on Sinai (as recorded in Q. 20:10, Q. 27:7, Q. 28:29).[102] At the heart of the path is the turn away from multiplicity towards sincere immersion in God (*ikhlāṣ*), which is extensively glossed from Qur'anic verses.[103] The aim of purifying the soul for God is to allow the divine light to dwell within and for wisdom to issue forth.[104] This involves a process of moving away from the prison of one's embodiment and freeing the soul *apud* Plotinus. The middle section of the text entails twelve (not an accidental number) stages predicated on four key concepts.[105] The first key concept is *islām*, the simple act of the initial submission to the message of the Prophet; the second is faith (*īmān*) that takes one beyond actions to inner sincerity and realisation of the Truth; the third is fleeing with the Prophet (*hijrat*); the fourth is struggling for God (*jihād*). The stages are as follows: first, the lesser *islām* that merely involves acquiescence to the two testimonies of faith (*shahādatayn*); second, the lesser faith, which is the acceptance of the two professions in the heart; third is the greater *islām* that involves complete submission to acts of the religion; fourth is the greater faith that involves all that the Qur'an invokes; fifth is the great struggle whereby one flees from evil; sixth is the greater struggle, which is fighting along with the forces of good and the intellect against those of Satan (alluding to the famous hadith on the forces of intellect); seventh is vanquishing the forces of Satan; resulting in the eighth, which is the greatest *islām*; followed by the ninth, the greatest faith; the tenth, the greatest fleeing; and the eleventh, the greatest struggle. The twelfth, the culmination, is entering into a state of pure sincerity (*khulūṣ*) and union with the Divine. One particular practice that seems to stem from Central

Asian Sufis, and the Naqshbandiyya in particular, is the stages of focus upon the invocation given by the master: first upon the master, then upon the Prophet and finally upon God.[106] The most efficacious times stressed for invocation, as expected from other texts, is the dawn, before sunrise.[107]

The author continues with various prescriptions. The key to the path lies with disciplining the soul and body, elevating the former while perfecting it through the invocations that allow God to dwell in the heart.[108] He then describes forty stages and levels, moving away from embodiment, using companionship on the path, towards greater spiritual exercises to free the soul. Two themes within the text are worth stressing. The first is the necessity to safeguard the secret (*kitmān al-sirr*), the cause of the imams in the Hadith.[109] The other is the importance of the relationship between the disciple and the master, and the necessity of the latter to guide the disciple along the path.[110] The text ends with a practical list of invocations and spiritual exercises carried out, one supposes, by Baḥr al-ʿUlūm and followed by Ṭabāṭabāʾī. This includes various litanies involving the Qur'anic names of God, but also critically includes the famous *dhikr al-Yūnusiyya* and the repetition of the chapter on divine unity from the Qur'an – all of which had become the hallmarks of the apparatus.[111]

The second text is the *Tadhkirat al-muttaqīn* of Bahārī Hamadānī. This mixes various formulae and advice on how to traverse the spiritual path with the advice of famous masters of Najaf, such as Karbalāʾī. Like other works, it is perhaps apologetically Shiʿi and predicated upon the absolute homology and complementarity between what spiritual masters do and what the Qur'an and Hadith profess and guide. It refers to the significance of disciples making a pilgrimage to the saints who are alive (citing Q. 3:169–70), which it says is critical for providing the former with the company and help they need on the path, as is the obligatory ritual of the Ḥajj, which it explains in a deeply Qur'anic manner.[112] The spiritual path comprises four steps: a repentance and turning away from sin, such that one realises oneself; an ever-watchful state of disciplining the soul; seeking good companionship on the path with spiritual masters and true friends; and good comportment with the family to make sure one's private space is conducive to the path.[113] In one letter, Karbalāʾī stresses a kind of repentance in which the individual forgoes reprehensible acts, and even those things allowed, in order to turn completely away from all that is not God.[114] Particular practices that bring together the themes of the apparatus also appear in some of the correspondence. For example, Karbalāʾī advises that after the morning ritual prayer, one should seek forgiveness continuously and recite *Sūrat al-Tawḥīd* (also known as *Sūrat al-Ikhlāṣ*, Q. 112) eleven times and blessings upon the Prophet and his family (*ṣalawāt*) one hundred times: these inculcate within the self three aspects of the path – continuous seeking of forgiveness from the sin of pride and selfhood; stressing the uniqueness of God such that naught exists save him; and the attachment to the true friends of God, the Shiʿi imams.[115] In other letters, Karbalāʾī also stresses two major features of the apparatus that are rooted in the Shiʿi tradition: the absorption in the esoteric (even occult) sciences that results from the watchfulness over the self, and the importance of *kitmān al-sirr*,[116] which, according to many hadiths, the imams urge their followers to do, since their very cause is the most secret doctrine to be heavily guarded from the uninitiated.[117]

Lubb al-lubāb is based on the teachings of Ṭabāṭabāʾī and manifests his character and his style of mastership. It demonstrates a spiritual and Sufi practice that is not only deeply Qurʾanic but, consistent with his apparatus, explicitly Shiʿi.[118] In this regard – and on many issues such as the stages of the path it outlines in chapters three and four – the text follows the work attributed to Baḥr al-ʿUlūm closely and is clearly a gloss upon it. At the same time, Ṭabāṭabāʾī's other works, including his formal exegesis, display his learning in philosophy and mysticism such that one reads his exegesis through the lens of his philosophical method.[119] The final section of the *Lubb* that draws upon hadiths recalls the importance of the approach of Bahāʾ al-Dīn al-ʿĀmilī in his *Miftāḥ al-falāḥ*.[120] Consistent with his other work, Ṭabāṭabāʾī sees the spiritual path as a Qurʾanic spiritual exercise that brings out the non-material nature of the human and resists the rampant materialism of the post-war period.[121] The main addition to the earlier work of Baḥr al-ʿUlūm concerns the explicit methods of the apparatus that he names after

Ḥusayn-qulī Hamadānī and what one can learn from them. He describes the apparatus as the true revival of the spiritual path of ʿAlī b. Abī Ṭālib (d. 40/661) by Sayyid ʿAlī Shūshtarī.[122] The example set by these forebears and the martyrs whose shrines are places of pilgrimage serves as a critical guide along the path towards singularity of the Divine and true sincerity resulting from the annihilation of the self.[123] Many of these themes are not peculiar to Shiʿi mysticism, and the influence of the school of Ibn ʿArabī on the monistic theory expressed is clear.

The final text is Ṭabāṭabāʾī's *Risālat al-walāya*, first published within six months or so of his death.[124] It is prefaced with a short paragraph or two by his student Ḥasanzāda Āmulī, who explains that the treatise is a result of Ṭabāṭabāʾī's insight drawn from his mystical experiences and contemplation of the Qurʾan; it is thus an act of exegesis. The text is divided into five chapters (the fifth is rather cursory) and a conclusion. Throughout, it is scripturally contemplative, citing authorities and providing glosses; overall, it concerns *walāya* as a path to God, of those who successfully traversed the four journeys of the rational soul set out in the magnum opus of Mullā Ṣadrā.

The pithy opening sermon (*khuṭba*) makes it clear how Ṭabāṭabāʾī sees the status of *walāya*: it is the culmination of what it means to be human and is, in fact, the final goal of the dispensation of religious law, supported and attested by both the clear sight of rational proof and the text of scripture. *Walāya* is thus a superior stage of jurisprudence – ethics is thus the result of the law – and directly associated with a hermeneutics of the scripture and of philosophy. This constitutes a rather holistic approach to the human and its becoming.[125]

The first chapter of *Risālat al-walāya* builds on this by establishing the hermeneutics of the exoteric and the esoteric, and it is clear that Ṭabāṭabāʾī privileges the esoteric (*bāṭin*) based on his selection of hadiths. He expounds on one of his key philosophical contributions: all entities are either those that exist in themselves with a referent in extra-mental reality (*yakūn lahu muṭābiq fīʾl-khārij mawjūd fī nafsih*) or conceivables which are pure beings of reason that do not correspond to any extra-mental reality.[126] Since life is true and everlasting, one needs to understand how to arrive there and hence requires a deeper understanding of the secrets within the scripture. The remainder of the chapter is taken up with the citation of hadiths on why the Shiʿi path is an esoteric one of decoding the true, underlying reality of the world that we inhabit in order to discern how we arrive at God – safeguarding the secret once again, recalling one of the most important themes of Shiʿi esotericism. The first chapter is thus a methodological propaedeutic, and the role of politics in it is clear as a first step on the path to sanctity.

Chapter two moves on to how one might discern the true nature of reality through the dual approach of contemplation of the scripture and of metaphysical truths – indeed, philosophical insights such as the essential nature of causality are hidden within the secrets of the text.[127] Ṭabāṭabāʾī argues that every divine faith understands this and the need to use these two means to arrive at God. Then, consistent with such schema, he states that there are three classes of people.[128] The first comprises people of perfect certainty who are capable of receiving truth, understanding divine realities, transcending this world and devoting themselves sincerely to God. They are the friends and intimates of God, including the prophets and the imams. The second class includes those who have certainty about the true nature of this world and the afterlife, but do not have a perfect ability to detach themselves from the carnal. They sincerely worship God, though from behind a veil (unlike the first class of people who are not veiled from God). The third comprises everyone else and includes both those who are contented with their faith and lack of understanding and those who are obstinate (*al-muʿānid*) in rejecting faith and reality; both remain attached to the carnality of this world. It is not just the Neoplatonic desire to forgo the body that separates these groups but also, concomitantly, their intellectual ability and hence their capacity to act morally; it is possible to move between these groups.

Chapter three discusses the means and necessity of transcending the mundane, the worldly, the profane; this is of critical importance for spiritual exercises and practices that are ultimately rooted in the Neoplatonic distrust of the body (and no doubt inspired by the famous doffing metaphor in Plotinus' *Enneads* IV.8.1, transmitted into Arabic through the *Theology of Aristotle*, *mīmar* I). One needs the body and the accoutrements of the apparent, but reality rests with the soul, which is eternal, and that which is hidden. Sensory perception is the gate to the intellect and it is reason that differentiates people. The epistemological hierarchy is clear, and follows in ascending order: the senses, the intellect, inner revelation (*kashf*) and vision (*shuhūd*). Ṭabāṭabā'ī then cites numerous Qur'anic verses and hadiths that support his contention.

The penultimate chapter considers how to achieve human perfection on this path. This is the longest chapter, and half of it is taken up with proof texts. Perfection, it says, lies in the ability to recognise the pure being – that is the goal of creation, meeting the One. Everything searches for its perfection and recognises that that process requires it to connect to higher entities.[129] Perfection strives towards that which has no imperfections and limitations; hence, it entails the seeker's quest to arrive at God, the everlasting and self-subsistent, in whom there is no suspicion of the contamination of non-existence.[130] This process involves the extinction of the independent identity and being of the seeker so that he or she may achieve everlasting survival in God. For humans, this means dissolving one's existence in the perfect human (the *walī*) as a first step.[131] Ṭabāṭabā'ī refers us back to the first chapter in which he stated that the process of perfecting is through the intellect; thus, he locates the transformation in the soul (*nafs*). Happiness (*sa'āda*) and success in this life and the hereafter is predicated on understanding this; wretchedness (*shaqāwa*) and failure lie in the neglect or ignorance of the process of perfecting. Ṭabāṭabā'ī then cites a series of scriptural texts on these issues, including the Shi'i philosophy in which recognition of the imams is as essential as a proper understanding of one's self: there is a special gate of paradise for the followers of the imams.[132] God is the true *walī* and, hence, must be the goal of everyone on the path of *walāya*.[133]

The final chapter on the nature of the goal is very brief and refers back to chapter two: it is mystical union, pure and simple, and through traversing the divine names and attributes (*asmā' wa'l-ṣifāt*), acts (*af'āl*) and the very divine essence (*dhāt*), the *walī* realises the true unity of these three aspects (of the *ṣifāt*, *af'āl* and *dhāt*).[134] This more essential understanding of *tawḥīd* stems from the Ibn 'Arabī tradition and is explicitly cited in the work of Sayyid Ḥaydar Āmulī (d. after 787/1385). It ends with a reference to the state and stations of the friends of God, the authority of those who have completed the journey and become the intimates and friends of God (*awliyā'*), who are discussed in the conclusion. Special knowledge – a central theme in Shi'i doctrine – as well as piety and certainty are some of the features of the friends of God.[135] Once again, one finds a series of scriptural texts and glosses, including a brief commentary on the famous light verse (Q. 24:35) as well as part of the longest narrative about the Prophet's heavenly ascension (*mi'rāj*) in *al-Irshād* of Daylamī, cited through Majlisī's *Biḥār*.[136] From contemplation comes the determination and understanding of how we should act in this world.

The treatise is short and rich. It is an expression of the school of Ibn 'Arabī's approach to *walāya* as the path of human perfection located within a Shi'i idiom, and as such is different to the early period. It constitutes a conscious echo of the works of the Safavid period, including those of Kāshānī on *walāya*, such as his *Kalimāt-i maknūna*. (Ṭabāṭabā'ī respected Kāshānī greatly; his apparatus used works such as *Najāt al-sālikīn* and *Qurrat al-'uyūn* of the Safavid sage.) Politics remains a necessity, but because its method is flexible one finds a range of legacies of Ṭabāṭabā'ī in those terms. Nevertheless, read alongside his *'irfān* works and his *tafsīr*, one can discern some major themes of how he envisaged the spiritual path of this elite, whose selves are governed by spiritual masters and who master themselves and others. Since he is instructing people on the path of *walāya*, the text has an implicit claim that Ṭabāṭabā'ī is a *walī* himself; only one who has seen the goal for humanity's path can best advise them on how to proceed, guided further by the scripture from the perfected friends of God, the imams. While not given explicitly, it is clear that people on the path of *walāya*, who pursue *'irfān* and *akhlāq*, are best placed to govern people administratively, because they share in the *walāya* of the imams. In this way, the theory that placed the representation of the imam with the generality of the scholars during the occultation is applied particularly to the people of *ʿirfān* and *walāya*. Ṭabāṭabāʾī clearly acted as a spiritual guide directly in the governance of the self, as did his forebears and his disciples in the apparatus, and this comes through in *Lubb al-lubāb* but especially in Ṭihrānī's *Rūḥ-i mujarrad* on the life of Ḥaddād.[137]

Concluding Remarks

The exegetical uses of the Qur'an form part of the strategy produced by the Ṭabāṭabāʾī apparatus of rather apologetically presenting their spiritual exercises to their (mainly Iranian) Shiʿi audience in the context of modern Iran, where both Sufism and elements of mysticism and philosophy are highly contested. The borrowings from established Sufi orders and thinkers (including, of course, those normally considered to be Sunni) are clear enough to observers. But so too are the borrowings from the heart of the best seat of Shiʿi jurisprudence, particularly regarding the idea that a path to God predicated upon a simple adherence to rules was insufficient, and that an ethical reintegration of why humans need religion required the spiritual path without jettisoning the key element of identity and the confessional affiliation that was established by the late Safavid period. The various legacies of the Ṭabāṭabāʾī apparatus still require inquiry, and that process in itself is not easy given the politicisation of the mystical path in the contemporary seminary and the contestations of the 'true legacy'. Nevertheless, some key questions remain. Why do some stress the Qur'an more than others whilst others still focus on the occult, and others further emphasise the teachings of Ibn ʿArabī? Does it make sense to talk of a Qur'anic mysticism that is independent of the more gnostic elements of Ibn ʿArabī? How will the apparatus survive in a context in which there are so many more demands made in the market of spirituality that leads to a cacophony in the semiosphere?

NOTES

1 There is a large body of literature in praise of the qualities of Ṭabāṭabāʾī's formal exegesis. See, for example, Hamid Algar, "Allāma Sayyid Muḥammad Ḥusayn

Ṭabāṭabāʾī: Philosopher, Exegete, and Gnostic', *Journal of Islamic Studies* 17, no. 3 (2006), pp. 326–51; Louis Medoff, 'Ijtihad and Renewal in Qur'anic Hermeneutics: An Analysis of Muḥammad Ḥusayn al-Ṭabāṭabāʾī's *al-Mīzān fī tafsīr al-Qurʾān*' (Unpublished PhD dissertation, University of California, Berkeley, 2007); ʿAlī Awsī, *al-Ṭabāṭabāʾī wa manhajuhu fī tafsīrihi al-Mīzān* (Tehran, 1986); Shubbar Faqīh, *al-Dalāla al-qurʾāniyya fī fikr Muḥammad Ḥusayn Ṭabāṭabāʾī* (Beirut, 2008); Sayyid Kamāl al-Ḥaydarī, *Uṣūl al-tafsīr wa'l-taʾwīl: Muqārana manhajiyya bayn ārāʾ al-Ṭabāṭabāʾī wa-abraz al-mufassirīn* (Beirut, 2006).

2 I do not address *al-Mīzān* directly here – for that, see my article written with Amin Ehteshami, 'Beyond the Letter: Explanation (*tafsīr*) versus Adaptation (*taṭbīq*) in Ṭabāṭabāʾī's *al-Mīzān*', in Annabel Keeler and Sajjad Rizvi, eds, *The Spirit and the Letter: Approaches to the Esoteric Interpretation of the Qur'an* (Oxford, 2016), pp. 443–73.

3 Abū Jaʿfar al-Ṣaffār al-Qummī, *Baṣāʾir al-darajāt*, edited under the supervision of Sayyid Muḥammad Abṭaḥī (Qum, 2010), vol. I, p. 365. All Qur'an translations are my own.

4 Abū Nāḍr al-Samarqandī al-ʿAyyāshī, *Tafsīr*, ed. Muḥammad al-Kāẓim (Beirut, 1991), vol. I, p. 12; Sahl al-Tustarī, *Tafsīr al-Qurʾān al-ʿaẓīm*, ed. M. Jīrat Allāh (Cairo, 2002), p. 16. Only the imams know the totality of the Qur'an, its exoteric and esoteric aspects – see Abū Jaʿfar al-Kulaynī Muḥammad b. Ya'qūb, *al-Kāfī* (Qum, 2005), hadith no. 611, *k. al-ḥujja* Ch. XXV, no. 2, vol. II, pp. 566–7.

5 Kulaynī, *al-Kāfī*, hadith no. 3519, *k. faḍl al-Qurʾān* Ch. VII, no. 1, vol. IV, p. 626.

6 Michael M.J. Fischer and Mehdi Abedi, *Debating Muslims: Cultural Dialogues in Postmodernity and Tradition* (Madison, WI, 1990), pp. 95–102. On the formal, scholastic disciplines of exegesis, see Jane Dammen McAuliffe, Barry D. Walfish and Joseph W. Goering, eds, *With Reverence for the Word: Medieval Scriptural Exegesis in Judaism, Christianity, and Islam* (Oxford, 2003); Karen Bauer, ed., *Aims, Methods, and Contexts of Qur'anic Exegesis (2nd/8th–9th/15th C.)* (Oxford, 2013); Feras Hamza and Sajjad Rizvi, with Farhana Mayer, eds, *An Anthology of Qur'anic Commentaries, Volume I: On the Nature of the Divine* (Oxford, 2008).

7 I borrow the term 'semiosphere' from Yuri Lotman, *Universe of the Mind: A Semiotic Theory of Culture* (Bloomington, IN, 1990), pp. 123–7 via Shahab Ahmed, *What is Islam? The Importance of Being Islamic* (Princeton, NJ, 2015), pp. 359–60. On agonistic and Socratic dialectics of textual study, see Alexander Nehamas, *The Art of Living: Socratic Reflections from Plato to Foucault* (Berkeley, CA, 1998); on the Qur'an, the interplay of the authority of the scripture and its authoritative exegesis, and practices of *adab*, see Barbara Metcalf, ed., *Moral Conduct and Authority: The Place of* adab *in South Asian Islam* (Berkeley, CA, 1984); and on discursive practices, alongside manners and customs, as civilising, Norbert Elias, *The Civilizing Process*, tr. Benjamin Jephcott (Oxford, 1994).

8 Reinhold Loeffler, *Islam in Practice: Religious Beliefs in a Persian Village* (Albany, NY, 1988), pp. 26, 84, 113, 274–86. There is a huge prescriptive literature on 'efficacious' supplications/spells (*mujarrabāt*) from the Qur'an;

see, for example, Muḥammad Bāqir Nāṣirī, *al-Durūʿ al-ḥaṣīna wa'l-kunūz al-dafīna* (Beirut, 2004).

9 See Valerie Gonzalez, *Beauty and Islam: Aesthetics in Islamic Art and Architecture* (London, 2001), pp. 26–41; Jamal Elias, *Aisha's Cushion: Religious Art, Perception, and Practice in Islam* (Cambridge, MA, 2012), pp. 150ff.

10 On musical expressions in Qawwali (ecstatic celebration and dirges in South Asia), see Barbara Metcalf, ed., *Islam in South Asia in Practice* (Princeton, NJ, 2009), pp. 93–119.

11 See, for example, Elias, *Aisha's Cushion*, p. 147.

12 *Inter alia*, Henry Corbin, *La philosophie iranienne islamique aux XVIIe et XVIIIe siècles* (Paris, 1981), pp. 358–64.

13 It is perhaps the Qur'an as idol, as authority in itself, to which one unreflectively genuflects that was best exemplified in the *topos* of 'raising the text on lances' at the Battle of Ṣiffīn in 37/657. In this role as idol, the Qur'an challenged the authority and person of the imam, considered by Shiʿi Muslims to be the living Qur'an; see Fischer and Abedi, *Debating Muslims*, p. 106. See also Mohammad Ali Amir-Moezzi, *Le Coran silencieux et le Coran parlant: Sources scripturaires de l'islam entre histoire et ferveur* (Paris, 2011).

14 Following the formulation of Abū Ḥāmid al-Ghazālī (d. 505/1111) in his *Kīmīya-yi saʿādat*, ed. Ḥusayn Khadīw-jām (Tehran, 1975), vol. II, pp. 572–3, cited in Elias, *Aisha's Cushion*, pp. 164–5.

15 Kulaynī, *al-Kāfī*, hadith no. 3519, *k. faḍl al-Qurʾān*, vol. IV, pp. 596–606.

16 On the notion of the heavenly Ur-text or exemplar, see Friedrich Heiler, *Erscheinungsformen und Wesen der Religion* (Stuttgart, 1961), pp. 351–2.

17 Ahmed, *What is Islam?*, pp. 346ff.

18 Kulaynī, *al-Kāfī*, hadith no. 3524, *k. faḍl al-Qurʾān*, vol. IV, pp. 614–19.

19 On these processes, see Kristina Nelson, *The Art of Reciting the Qur'an* (Cairo, 2001). On healing, *inter alia*, see Rudolph T. Ware, *The Walking Qur'an: Islamic Education, Embodied Knowledge, and History in West Africa* (Chapel Hill, NC, 2014), pp. 62–7.

20 Kai Kresse, *Philosophising in Mombasa: Knowledge, Islam and Intellectual Practice on the Swahili Coast* (Edinburgh, 2007), pp. 107–8; Fischer and Abedi, *Debating Muslims*, pp. 107–11.

21 Navid Kermani, *God is Beautiful: The Aesthetic Experience of the Quran*, tr. Tony Crawford (Cambridge, 2015), pp. 133–84; Geert Jan van Gelder and Marlé Hammond, eds, *Takhyīl: The Imaginary in Classical Arabic Poetics* (Cambridge, 2009).

22 See the very interesting study of Travis Zadeh, *The Vernacular Qur'an: Translation and the Rise of Persian Exegesis* (Oxford, 2012).

23 Talal Asad, *On the Idea of an Anthropology of Islam*. (Washington, DC, 1986), p. 14: 'An Islamic discursive tradition is simply a tradition of Muslim discourse that addresses itself to conceptions of the Islamic past and future, with reference to a particular Islamic practice in the present.'

24 Ware, *The Walking Qur'an*.

25 Michel Foucault, *Power/Knowledge: Selected Interviews and Other Writings, 1972–1977*, ed. Colin Gordon, tr. Colin Gordon *et al.* (New York, 1980), pp. 194–5, 196.

26 Giorgio Agamben, *What is an Apparatus and Other Essays*, tr. David Kishik and Stefan Pedatella (Stanford, 2009), pp. 8–10.

27 Ibid., p. 10.
28 Ibid., p. 14.
29 This group is rather neglected, even if their literary output is growing rather extensively especially through a series of hagiographies of the key figures through the efforts of the Mu'assasa-yi Shams al-Shumūs located in the area around the Bazaar in Tehran. One study that does mention them within a wider examination of magic and the occult in Iran is Alireza Doostdar's 'Fantasies of Reason: Science, Superstition, and the Supernatural in Iran' (Unpublished PhD dissertation, Harvard University, 2012), pp. 214–16, 232–50.
30 On the shifting discourse, from the late Safavid period, from Sufism to *ʿirfān* and the anathemisation of Sufism in Shiʿi learned culture, see Ata Anzali, 'Safavid Shiʿism, the Eclipse of Sufism and the Emergence of ʿIrfān' (Unpublished PhD dissertation, Rice University, 2012).
31 Hamid Dabashi, *Authority in Islam: From the Rise of Muhammad to the Establishment of the Umayyads* (New York, 1989).
32 There are numerous biographies (and hagiographies) of Ṭabāṭabā'ī, but these are the most useful: Sayyid Muḥammad Ḥusayn Ḥusaynī Ṭihrānī, *Mihr-i tābān: Yādnāma wa muṣāḥibāt-i tilmīdh wa ʿallāma* (Mashhad, 1418/1997), pp. 11–136; Ghulām-Riḍā Gulī Zawwāra, *Jurʿa-hā-yi jānbakhsh: Farāz-hā-yi az zindagī-yi ʿAllāma Ṭabāṭabā'ī wa asātīd wa shāgirdān-i ān mufassir-i ʿālī-qadr* (Qum, 1375 Sh./1996); ʿAbd Allāh Jawādī Āmulī, *Shams al-waḥī-yi Tabrīzī: Sīra-yi ʿilmī-yi ʿAllāma Ṭabāṭabā'ī* (Qum, 1386 Sh./2007); Algar, "Allāma Sayyid Muḥammad Ḥusayn Ṭabāṭabā'ī', pp. 326–51. His autobiography has finally been published: 'Zindagī-yi man', *Marzubān-i waḥī wa khirad: Yādnāma-yi marḥūm ʿallāma-yi Sayyid Muḥammad Ḥusayn Ṭabāṭabā'ī* (Qum, 1381 Sh./2002), pp. 39–47.
33 For a hagiography of this important figure in the Ṭabāṭabā'ī apparatus, see *Ilāhiyya: Sharḥ-i aḥwāl-i ʿārif-i ilāhī Āyatullāh Sayyid Muḥammad Ḥasan Ilāhī Ṭabāṭabā'ī* (Tehran, 1386 Sh./2007).
34 Gulī Zawwāra, *Jurʿa-hā-yi jānbakhsh*, pp. 73–8.
35 Ibid., pp. 79–81.
36 Sayyid Muḥammad Ḥusayn Ḥusaynī Ṭihrānī, ed, *Tawḥīd-i ʿilmī wa ʿaynī dar makātib-i ḥikmī wa ʿirfānī-yi Ḥājj Sayyid Aḥmad Karbalā'ī wa Ḥājj Shaykh Muḥammad Ḥusayn Iṣfahānī Kumpānī bā ḍamīma-yi tadhyīlāt wa muḥākamāt-i Ḥājj Sayyid Muḥammad Ḥusayn Ṭabāṭabā'ī* (Tehran, 1410/1989).
37 Bādkuba'ī had also studied with Mīrzā Hāshim Ashkiwarī (d. 1332/1914), the *ʿirfān*-inclined, Tehrani teacher at the Madrasa-yi Sipahsālār, and hence one can see the coming together of Avicennism and *ʿirfān* in Bādkuba'ī's teaching, which in turn influenced Ṭabāṭabā'ī. His other, lesser teacher was the Ṣadrian thinker Āqā ʿAlī Mudarris-i Zunūzī (d. 1307/1889). Bādkuba'ī wrote a gloss on Mullā Ṣadra's *Asfār* and also on the theological summa *Shawāriq al-ilhām* of Mullā Ṣadrā's student ʿAbd al-Razzāq Lāhījī. His other famous student was Sayyid Jalāl al-Dīn Āshtiyānī (d. 2005). See Manūchihr Ṣadūqī Suhā, *Tārīkh-i ḥukamā' wa ʿurafā'-yi muta'akhkhir az Ṣadr al-muta'allihīn* (Tehran, 1980), pp. 71–2; Gulī Zawwāra, *Jurʿa-hā-yi jānbakhsh*, pp. 65–6.
38 There is a growing (hagiographical) literature on Qāḍī – and there was even a conference dedicated to him in Tehran in 2012. Three rather hagiographical places to start are *ʿAṭash: Nā-gufta-hā-yi az sayr-i tawḥīdī-yi kāmil-i ʿaẓīm*

ḥaḍrat-i Āyatullāh Sayyid ʿAlī Qāḍī Ṭabāṭabāʾī (Tehran, 1383 Sh./2004); Hādī Hāshimiyān and Sayyid Muḥammad Ṣafavī, *Daryā-yi ʿirfān: Sharḥ-i ḥāl-i Āyatullāh Sayyid ʿAlī Qāḍī Ṭabāṭabāʾī* (Qum, 1382 Sh./2003); Sayyid Muḥammad Ḥusayn Ḥusaynī Ṭihrānī, *Mihr-i tābnāk* (Mashhad, 1375 Sh./1996).

39 Jaʿfar Subḥānī, 'Naẓarī wa gudharī bar zindagānī-yi ustād', in *Yādnāma-yi ustad ʿAllāma Ṭabāṭabāʾī* (Qum, 1361 Sh./1982), p. 56. Given the amount covered in the time, he was either a very precocious student or complete texts were not studied.

40 On Ḥusayn-qulī Hamadānī, who in philosophy had been a student of the most prominent Qajar thinker Sabzawārī, see, among other sources, Aḥmad Nithārī, *Shamʿ-yi jamʿ: Sharḥ-i ḥāl-i Āyatullāh Mullā Ḥusayn Qulī Hamadānī* (Tehran, 1375 Sh./1996). The origins of the form of the invocation probably come from a branch of the Niʿmatullāhī order and its influence by Qādirī Sufi practice in the Kurdish borderlands.

41 On his teaching of the works of the school of Ibn ʿArabī, see Ḥusaynī Ṭihrānī, *Mihr-i tābnāk*, pp. 265–73.

42 We still lack a clear account of how the modern *ʿirfān* curriculum came about. Modern accounts tell us that the texts studied include the *Mafātīḥ al-ghayb* of Ṣadr al-Dīn Qūnawī (d. 673/1274), the *Sharḥ Fuṣūṣ al-ḥikam* of Dāwūd al-Qayṣarī (d. 751/1350), the *Miṣbāḥ al-uns* of Ibn Ḥamza Fanārī (d. 834/1431) and the *Tamhīd al-qawāʿid* of Ibn Turka. One suspects that this was established later in the nineteenth century, especially in the circle of *ʿirfān* associated with Muḥammad Riḍā 'Sahbā' Qumshihī (d. 1889), whence it was disseminated into the shrine cities of Iraq and Iran. The contemporary Ḥasanzāda Āmulī is quoted as stating that it was Qumshihī who established the study of the *Tamhīd al-qawāʿid*, replacing the *Miṣbāḥ al-uns* that was the main focus text before; see Gulī Zawwāra, *Jurʿa-hā-yi jānbakhsh*, p. 149.

43 See the website dedicated to him: http://www.seiedalighazi.ir/main/ (accessed 27 August 2013; link no longer available). For the commentary, see Sayyid ʿAlī Qāḍī, *Sharḥ-i duʿāʾ-yi simāt* (Tehran, 1387 Sh./2008).

44 Subḥānī, 'Naẓarī', p. 60.

45 See, for example, Raḥīm Nīkbakht and Ṣamad Ismāʿīlzāda, *Zindagānī wa mubārizāt-i Āyatullāh Qāḍī Ṭabāṭabāʾī* (Tehran, 1380 Sh./2001).

46 Ḥusaynī Ṭihrānī, *Mihr-i tābān*, p. 27.

47 Nāṣir Bāqirī Bīd-i Hindī, 'Mufassir wa ḥakīm-i ilāhī', *Nūr al-ʿIlm* 3, no. 9 (Āzar 1368 Sh./1989), p. 48.

48 Ḥusaynī Ṭihrānī, *Mihr-i tābān*, pp. 104–6, cited and translated in Algar, 'ʿAllāma Sayyid Muḥammad Ḥusayn Ṭabāṭabāʾī', pp. 334–5; see also Hamid Dabashi, *Theology of Discontent: The Ideological Foundations of the Islamic Revolution in Iran* (New York, 1993), pp. 274–5, 281–4.

49 Gulī Zawwāra, *Jurʿa-hā-yi jānbakhsh*, p. 98.

50 Jawādī Āmulī, *Shams al-waḥī-yi Tabrīzī*, p. 223.

51 Ibid., pp. 25–6.

52 Sayyid Mahdī Ṭabāṭabāʾī 'Baḥr al-ʿUlūm' (attrib.), *Risāla-yi sayr wa sulūk* with commentary by Muḥammad Ḥusayn Ṭabāṭabāʾī, ed. Sayyid Muḥammad Ḥusayn Ḥusaynī Ṭihrānī (Mashhad, 1416/1995); tr. Tawus Raja as *Treatise on Spiritual Journeying and Wayfaring* (Chicago, IL, 2013). See Ṭihrānī on the use of this text, *Mihr-i tābān*, pp. 107–12.

53 Sayyid Muḥammad Ḥusayn Ḥusaynī Ṭihrānī, ed., *Risāla-yi Lubb al-lubāb dar sayr wa sulūk-i uli'l-albāb* (Mashhad, 1375 Sh./1996); tr. Mohammad H. Faghfoory as *Kernel of the Kernel: Concerning the Wayfaring and Spiritual Journey of the People of Intellect* (Albany, NY, 2003).
54 Ḥusaynī Ṭihrānī, *Mihr-i tābān*, pp. 122–4.
55 Gulī Zawwāra, *Jur'a-hā-yi jānbakhsh*, p. 150.
56 Ḥusaynī Ṭihrānī, *Mihr-i tābān*, p. 63.
57 Jawādī Āmulī, *Shams al-waḥī-yi Tabrīzī*, pp. 54–7.
58 Ḥusaynī Ṭihrānī, *Mihr-i tābān*, pp. 128–31.
59 On the naming of the apparatus as the *ṭarīqa-yi ma'rifat-i nafs*, see Muḥammad Bahārī Hamadānī, *Tadhkira al-muttaqīn* (Tehran, 1361 Sh./1982), p. 177. There are some collective hagiographies on Shūshtarī: Ḥasanzāda Āmulī, *Dar āsimān-i ma'rifat: Tadhkira-yi awḥadī az 'ālimān-i rabbānī* (Qum, 1375 Sh./1996); Ṣādiq Ḥasanzāda, *Uswat al-'urafā'* (Qum, 1424/2003); Muḥammad Ṭihrānī, *Sarguzasht-i 'ārifān* (Tehran, 1393 Sh./2014); Ḥāṭim Ibrāhīm, *Qiṣaṣ al-'urafā'* (Beirut, 2008); Ibrāhīm Surūr, *Sīrat al-'urafā'* (Beirut, 2008); Ḥusayn Najīb Muḥammad, *Waṣāyā al-'urafā'* (Beirut, 2011); Maḥmūd Shaykh, *Maktab-i akhlāqī-yi 'irfānī-yi Najaf: Maktab-i 'irfānī-yi Mullā Ḥusayn-qulī Hamadānī* (Tehran, 1395 Sh./2016); Sayyid Muḥammad Muḥsin Ḥusaynī Ṭihrānī, *Nafahāt-i uns: Insān-i kāmil dar farhang-i shī'a* (Tehran, 1395 Sh./2016).
60 On Khomeini and *'irfān*, see Christian Bonaud, *L'Imam Khomeyni, un gnostique méconnu du XXe siècle: Métaphysique et théologie dans les oeuvres philosophiques et spirituelles de l'Imam Khomeyni* (Beirut, 1997); Vanessa Martin, *Creating an Islamic State: Khomeini and the Making of a New Iran* (London, 2003), pp. 29–47; Ruhollah Khomeini, *The Mystery of Prayer: The Ascension of the Wayfarers and the Prayer of the Gnostics*, tr. Sayyid Amjad Naqawi (Leiden, 2015); idem, *Islam and Revolution: Writings and Declarations of Imam Khomeini (1941–1980)*, tr. and ed. Hamid Algar (Berkeley, CA, 1981), pp. 351–434 (this latter text includes his lectures glossing the opening chapter of the Qur'an in which he cites his teachers in *'irfān*, including Muḥammad 'Alī Shāhābādī [d. 1949] and 'Alī Akbar Ḥakamī Yazdī [d. 1926] as well as those in the Ṭabāṭabā'ī apparatus, like Bahārī Hamadānī [d. 1907]).
61 For a brief discussion of the rise of the practice of *'irfān* in the Qajar period in the seminary, see 'Abd al-Rafī' Ḥaqīqat, *Tārīkh-i 'irfān wa 'urafā'-yi Īrānī* (Tehran, 1370 Sh./1991), pp. 222–7.
62 Ḥasanzāda Āmulī, 'Nigarishī-yi kūtāh bih zindagī-yi ustād', in *Yādnāma-yi ustad 'Allāma-yi Ṭabāṭabā'ī* (Qum, 1361 Sh./1982), p. 97. Āmulī provides one of the first accounts of Shūshtarī meeting Mullā-qulī Jūlā. See Ḥusaynī Ṭihrānī, *Lubb al-lubāb*, pp. 146–50; 'Azīz Mikā'īlī, "Urafā'-yi mu'āṣir-i silsila-yi Jūlā', *Furūgh-i andīsha* 1 (1380 Sh./2001), pp. 47–54.
63 'Abd al-Laṭīf al-Ḥirz, *Min al-'irfān ilā'l-dawla: Al-taṣawwuf fī fikr al-imām al-Khumaynī wa'l-shahīd al-Ṣadr* (Beirut, 2011), pp. 221–2.
64 One good source that explicitly mentions Shūshtarī as a disciple of Dizfūlī is Sayyid 'Abbās Qā'im-maqāmī, 'Āthār wa afkār-i Ṣadr al-Dīn Kāshif Dizfūlī', *Kayhān-i andīsha* 38 (1992), pp. 77–93.
65 Nithārī, *Sham'-yi jam'*, p. 19; I'timād al-Salṭana, *al-Ma'āthir wa'l-āthār*, ed. Īraj Afshār (Tehran, 1363 Sh./1984), p. 145; Sayyid Muḥsin al-Amīn, *A'yān al-shī'a*

(Beirut, 1986), vol. VIII, p. 8; Mīrzā Muḥammad Kashmīrī, *Takmilat Nujūm al-samā'* (Qum, 1979), vol. I, p. 336; Ḥusaynī Ṭihrānī, *Lubb al-lubāb*, pp. 154–8; Ma'ṣūm 'Alī Shāh, *Ṭarā'iq al-ḥaqā'iq*, ed. Muḥammad Ja'far Maḥjūb (Tehran, 1966), vol. III, pp. 466–7; Āqā Buzurg Ṭihrānī, *Ṭabaqāt a'lām al-shī'a* (Beirut, 2009), vol. XIV, pp. 674–6; Sayyid al-Ḥasan al-Ṣadr, *Takmilat Amal al-āmil*, ed. 'Abd al-Karīm Dabbāgh (Beirut, 2008), vol. IV, p. 93, vol. VI, p. 45.

66 Nithārī, *Sham'-yi jam'*, pp. 17–23.

67 On Ḥusayn-qulī Hamadānī's disciples, see Āmulī, *Dar āsimān-i ma'rifat*, pp. 128–30; Nithārī, *Sham'-yi jam'*, pp. 27–30.

68 Mīrzā Jawād Malakī Tabrīzī, *Risāla-yi liqā' Allāh*, ed. Sayyid Aḥmad Fihrī (Tehran, 1360 Sh./1981), p. 89. There are a number of works by Tabrīzī that disseminate the spiritual teachings of Ḥusayn-qulī Hamadānī, such as *Sulūk al-'ārifīn* and *al-Murāqabāt*.

69 Nithārī, *Sham'-yi jam'*, pp. 36, 42.

70 Ibid., pp. 65, 72, drawing upon the saying of Imam al-Ṣādiq: 'The heart is the sanctuary of God' (*al-qalbu ḥaram allāh*), cited in Muḥammad Bāqir Majlisī, *Biḥār al-anwār* (Beirut, 1983), vol. LXVII, p. 25.

71 Nithārī, *Sham'-yi jam'*, pp. 38, 45–9.

72 Ibid., pp. 51–5, 60–61.

73 Ibid., p. 103.

74 Ibid., pp. 86–90.

75 Ibid., pp. 113–14.

76 Ibid., p. 99. See Muḥsin Fayḍ Kāshānī's *Minhāj al-najāt*, ed. Ghālib Ḥasan Shābandar (Beirut, 1987), a text divided into a first section on beliefs and doctrines, a second on practices that make the body and the heart conform to God, and an epilogue on the importance of good comportment, where salvation is deemed a matter of the tongue, the soul, the heart and the body; Bahā' al-Dīn al-'Āmilī, *Miftāḥ al-falāḥ*, ed. Ḥasanzāda Āmulī (Tehran, 1366 Sh./1987) – his edition of this text marks Āmilī's affiliation to the apparatus, with the text itself being a popular prayer manual; Muḥammad Ḥasan Qazwīnī, *Kashf al-ghiṭā' 'an wujūh marāsim al-ihtidā' fī 'ilm al-akhlāq*, ed. Muḥsin Aḥmadī (Qum, 1380 Sh./2001) – this text has much in common with its near contemporary *Jāmi' al-sa'ādāt* by Mahdī Narāqī (d. 1795), and after a first section on virtues that inhere in the soul and how to cultivate them and forgo the vices, Qazwīnī discusses useful knowledge, the spiritual significance of one's acts and the necessity of loving God.

77 'Alī Karbāsīzāda Iṣfahānī, *Ḥakīm-i muta'allih Bīdābādī* (Tehran, 1381 Sh./2002).

78 'Abd al-Ṣamad Hamadānī, *Baḥr al-ma'ārif*, ed. Ḥasan Ustād-Walī (Tehran, 1416/1995).

79 Muḥammad Bahārī Hamadānī, *Tadhkirat al-muttaqīn* (Qum, 2006); see Āqā Buzurg Ṭihrānī, *al-Dharī'a ilā taṣānīf al-shī'a* (Najaf, 1978), vol. VI, p. 64.

80 Muḥammadī Rayshahrī, *Kīmiyā-yi muḥabbat: Yādnāma-yi marḥūm shaykh Rajab 'Alī Khayyāṭ* (Qum, 1385 Sh./2006).

81 The most important work on him is Ḥusaynī Ṭihrānī's *Rūḥ-i mujarrad* (Mashhad, 1416/1995); see also the work by his grandson Sayyid 'Alī al-Ḥaddād, *al-'Ārif fī riḥāb al-qudsiyya* (Beirut, 2007); there is also a pure hagiography – *Dilshuda* (Tehran, 1386 Sh./2007).

82 *Shaydā* (Tehran, 1389 Sh./2010).

83 See the hagiography by his nephew, Sayyid Taqī Mūsawī Masqaṭī, *Qudwat al-ʿārifīn* (Beirut, 2007).

84 See the extensive two-volume hagiography by his son, Sayyid Muḥammad Ṣādiq Ḥusaynī Ṭihrānī, *Nūr-i mujarrad* (Mashhad, 2015).

85 Matthijs van den Bos, *Mystic Regimes: Sufism and the State in Iran, from the Late Qajar Era to the Islamic Republic* (Leiden, 2002); Richard Gramlich, *Die schiitischen Derwischorden Persiens. Erster Teil: Die Affiliationen* (Wiesbaden, 1965), pp. 38–59; Maʿṣūm ʿAlī Shāh, *Ṭarāʾiq al-ḥaqāʾiq*, vol. III, p. 90.

86 See, for example, *al-ʿAbd: ʿAbd-i khudā Muḥammad Taqī Bahjat* (Tehran, 1390 Sh./2011); Ibrāhīm ʿĀmilī, *Bahjat al-ʿārifīn* (Beirut, 2007); Maḥmūd Badrī, *Uswat al-ʿārifīn* (Qum, 1382 Sh./2003).

87 *Fī madrasat al-Shaykh al-Bahjat* (Beirut, 2005), vol. I, pp. 19–20.

88 Ibid., pp. 33–8.

89 Ibid., pp. 141–202.

90 Ibid., pp. 45–66.

91 Ibid., pp. 121–9.

92 *Fī madrasat al-Shaykh al-Bahjat*, vol. II, pp. 11–118.

93 Ibid., vol. I, pp. 66–99.

94 For example, this work by the son of Ḥasan Ḥasanzāda Āmulī: Ṣādiq Ḥasanzāda, *Ṭarīq-i ʿirfān: Tarjuma wa sharḥ-i risālat al-walāya* (Qum, 1383 Sh./2004).

95 For example, the collection that includes the work of Shaykh Muḥammad Bahārī Hamadānī, *Tadhkirat al-muttaqīn fī ādāb al-sayr waʾl-sulūk*, tr. Ḥusayn Kūrānī (Qum, 2006).

96 Ḥirz, *Min al-ʿirfān*, p. 223.

97 Gramlich, *Die schiitischen Derwischorden Persiens*, pp. 40–42. Nūr al-Dīn Mudarrissī Chahārdihī noticed this connection with the Kawthar ʿAlī Shāh branch of the Niʿmatullāhiyya in his article, ʻSilsila-yi kawthariyyaʼ, *Wahīd* 243 (1357 Sh./1978), pp. 41–2.

98 Hamadānī, *Baḥr al-maʿārif*, vol. II, pp. 469–74, 557–72 and the whole of vol. III.

99 Ibid., vol. I, pp. 441–512.

100 Ibid., pp. 21–63, 135–71, 207–81.

101 Ibid., vol. II, pp. 39–59, 63–79, vol. III, pp. 11–172; Ḥusaynī Ṭihrānī, *Rūḥ-i mujarrad*, pp. 45–66.

102 Baḥr al-ʿUlūm, *Risāla-yi sayr wa sulūk*, p. 27.

103 Ibid., pp. 51–68.

104 Ibid., pp. 205–7.

105 Ibid., pp. 76–110.

106 Ibid., pp. 194–6.

107 Ibid., p. 200.

108 Ibid., pp. 139, 171–80.

109 Ibid., pp. 163–6.

110 Ibid., pp. 166–72.

111 Ibid., p. 215.

112 Bahārī Hamadānī, *Tadhkirat al-muttaqīn*, pp. 42–9.

113 Ibid., pp. 3–36.

114 Ibid., pp. 87–9.
115 Ibid., p. 95.
116 Ibid., pp. 70, 98.
117 See, for example, Qummī, *Baṣāʾir al-darajāt, juzʾ* 1, *bāb* 17, vol. I, pp. 70–72 [variants of the following text are found across these pages]: 'Our cause is a secret lying in a secret, a secret that is covered and can only be uncovered by a secret, secret upon secret, and a secret veiled by a secret.' The polyvalency of the term '*sirr*' is critical to this: it is something hidden, it is the very essence of the human soul and spirit, and it is the hidden reality of the imam and his light that follows one after the other.
118 Ḥirz, *Min al-ʿirfān*, pp. 268–71.
119 Ibid., pp. 228–9.
120 Ibid., p. 273.
121 Ḥusaynī Ṭihrānī, *Lubb al-lubāb*, pp. 23–4.
122 Ibid. p. 146.
123 Ibid., p. 28.
124 Sayyid Muḥammad Ḥusayn Ṭabāṭabāʾī, *Risālat al-walāya*, in *Yādnāma-yi mufassir-i kabīr ustād ʿallāma-yi sayyid Muḥammad Ḥusayn Ṭabāṭabāʾī* (Qum, 1361 Sh./1982), pp. 251–305. The text has been printed and glossed. There are at least two English translations as well. For a discussion of the contents of the text, see Jawādī Āmulī, *Shams al-waḥī-yi Tabrīzī*, pp. 271–99.
125 Ṭabāṭabāʾī, *Risālat al-walāya*, p. 251.
126 Ibid., pp. 251–2. Ṭabāṭabāʾī refers to an extended discussion in his work *al-Iʿtibārāt* in *Majmūʿat al-rasāʾil* (Qum, 1387 Sh./2008).
127 Ṭabāṭabāʾī, *Risālat al-walāya*, p. 257.
128 Ibid., pp. 261–2.
129 Ibid., p. 271.
130 Ibid., p. 272.
131 Ibid., p. 273.
132 Ibid., p. 275.
133 Ibid., p. 288.
134 Ibid., p. 294.
135 Ibid., p. 295.
136 Ibid., pp. 299, 303–4.
137 Ḥusaynī Ṭihrānī, *Lubb al-lubāb*, pp. 133–4.

3

Privileging the Qur'an: Divorce and the Hermeneutics of Yūsuf Ṣāniʿī

LIYAKAT TAKIM

THE ESTABLISHMENT of an Islamic republic in Iran in 1979 and the consequent calls to apply Islamic law in that country have given Shiʿi jurists fresh impetus to re-examine their sacred literature and to engage with Qur'anic hermeneutics in a new way. For the first time, Shiʿi jurists have had to respond to the challenges and practical needs of a modern Shiʿi state. In response, reformist scholars such as ayatollahs Yūsuf Ṣāniʿī (b. 1937), Ibrāhīm Jannātī (b. 1932) and Muḥammad al-Mūsawī Bujnūrdī (b. 1942) have argued that what is essential to a proper understanding of Islam is not the sanctification of Prophetic traditions (hadiths) and exegetical literature but the deciphering and application of the spirit or basic *élan* of the Qur'an and Prophetic traditions. They also claim that there is no single valid interpretation of the Qur'an and that previous interpretations can be challenged or revised according to the needs of the time. It is important for them that Muslims continue to review and revise the law in keeping with the dictates of their changing circumstances. Hence, reform-minded scholars have developed various genres of hermeneutical stratagems in reinterpreting and applying the Qur'anic injunctions and traditions reported from the Prophet and imams.

This chapter will initially discuss the question of reformation in Islamic laws as enunciated by some reformist Shiʿi scholars. The chapter will then discuss Ṣāniʿī's legal ruling on *khulʿ* in Twelver Shiʿism as a specific example of this. *Khulʿ* is a form of divorce (*ṭalāq*) in which a wife can divorce her husband by returning or forfeiting her claim to the dowry (*mahr*) he had given her upon their marriage. As will be demonstrated, jurists like Ṣāniʿī accentuate the ethical and egalitarian undertones of the Qur'an, challenging, in the process, the validity of previous legal rulings and the methodologies utilised by erstwhile scholars.

Reformation in the Shiʿi World

One of the most important voices for reformation in recent times has been Ruhollah Khomeini (d. 1989). In the statement below, he outlined a range of issues which he believed Islamic jurisprudence should be concerned with updating or addressing:

> It is important that contemporary juridical discourse be engaged in issues such as ownership and its boundaries; land and its division into spoils and public wealth; farming and collaboration (*mudāriba*), renting and mortgage; penance and blood money; civil laws; cultural issues and various arts such as photography, painting, sculpture, music, theatre, movies, calligraphy, etc. Islamic jurisprudence should also be concerned with discussions regarding the preservation of the environment, expanding or nullifying some decrees at various times and places; legal and international issues and their adaptation with the precepts of Islam; the limits of individual and social liberties; the manner of observing religiously prescribed acts in space travel and movement against or along the earth's rotation etc.

If some of these issues had not been discussed in the past, because they were specifically modern-day issues, Khomeini believed that jurists should now make provisions for them through the application of personal reasoning (*ijtihād*): 'If, in the past, some issues were not set forth or were irrelevant, the *fuqahā'* [jurists] should now speculate about them.'[1]

Other jurists in Iran have also argued for a re-examination and reformulation of previous juridical rulings. As an example of the possible reinterpretation of the law regarding the rights of married women, the contemporary jurist Mostafa Mohaghegh Damad (b. 1942) looks at Q. 4:19, which tells husbands: *And live with them* [their wives] *in kindness. For if you dislike them – perhaps you dislike a thing and Allah makes therein much good* (*al-maʿrūf*).[2] According to

Damad, the Qur'anic proclamation to cohabit in what is perceived as 'good'

> is the foundation of Islamic family law and the foundation of individual laws pertaining to the rights of married women. In past times, when social and economic lives were much different and women were housewives, essentially consumers confined to the home without economic responsibility or the need to earn a living, this Qur'ānic phrase had a particular meaning.

But Damad asks, 'Does cohabitation "in accordance with that which is recognized as good' have the same meaning today? In the past, maintenance (*nafaqah*) due to a wife after divorce was calculated by the jurists at a very low rate.'[3] For Damad, this rate is contingent on the needs of the time. He continues:

> If, for instance, one of the imāms had been asked a thousand years ago about the maintenance due to a woman after divorce, he might have mentioned clothes, a dwelling, or food, indicating that according to the external standard of the social life of those times maintenance consisted of something like the fixed payment mentioned above [i.e. the low payment calculated by a jurist]. Neither the education of women nor means of transportation was as important as it is today. Thus maintenance is an external and not an objective standard. On the other hand, 'marriage in accordance with that which is recognized as good' is a general legal rule (*ḥukm*) of the *sharīʿah*, and since times always change and social and economic conditions evolve, the Qur'ān here lays down a standard whose criteria are subject to change.[4]

Damad is arguing that the maintenance of a wife should no longer be restricted to household items like accommodation, clothes and food. Transportation and the other necessities of life should also be included in the costs of maintenance.

In another example of a previous law in need of re-examination, Damad turns to the law pertaining to slavery, which he maintains must be radically reformed. He writes:

> [T]he international community has agreed to abolish slavery; the institution of slavery has disappeared. It is now necessary

to conclude that slavery is also forbidden by Islamic law, for the basis of application of the law of slavery has changed. The jurist cannot claim that since in the past prisoners of war were enslaved, they must be enslaved today. Islamic countries have readily signed the international conventions on slavery, and the abolition of slavery is not in any way inconsistent with Islamic law.[5]

Other jurists in Iran have also come up with novel formulations of traditional understandings of Islamic law. Ṣāniʿī, for example, holds progressive views on women's equality with men based on his unique perspective on the sacred and other sources. He also contends that women should be allowed to stand as *marājiʿ*, that is, religious authorities who serve as points of reference for emulation by their community of followers. Traditionally, *marājiʿ* have always been men. In a private conversation I had with Ṣāniʿī in Qum in 2004, he told me that women should even be allowed to lead men in prayers. During this conversation I asked him several questions. Some of the more salient ones follow below.[6]

Question: What is your view on women's rights?

Answer: Women do have equality in all rights except inheritance, which is half as much as men, but I consider it fair, and I have given elaborate explanation on this issue.

Question: Are they regarded as equals in giving testimony?

Answer: They have equality. In 'The Cow', the second chapter of the Qur'an [*Sūrat al-Baqara*], two women are found necessary to testify in the court of law where one man suffices. The reason is [so that] one of them can serve as a reminder to help vivid remembrance. There, we come to understand that women are more likely to forget a past event in this special case. Now, this Qur'anic verse [Q. 2:282] was revealed with relevance to commercial affairs. Having few social associations, women mostly did not know much about financial and commercial subjects. To guarantee a fair judgement, two women would testify. Similarly, to provide assurance, the testimony of two men is essential when they are more likely to forget a past event than women are. The criterion is knowledge and awareness. Both men and women can be of equal number when they have equal knowledge.

Question: What is your verdict on blood money for women?

Answer: I regard men and women equals in the following cases: blood money, retaliatory punishment, appointment as a judge, and even being an expert on jurisprudence.

Ṣāniʿī's erudition in the Islamic sciences and forthright views have made him a leading figure in the call for the reinterpretation of Islamic laws in modern times. It is to his view on *khulʿ ṭalāq* that I turn to next.

Ṣāniʿī on *Khulʿ* Divorce

Before discussing the reformation of Islamic law, specifically the revisions to *khulʿ* divorce, I want to briefly introduce Yūsuf Ṣāniʿī, who has not received the attention that he deserves among Western scholars. In fact, very little has been written about him. I will then go on to examine his views on *khulʿ*, his engagement with the Qur'an and traditions, and his ruling on the subject.

Ṣāniʿī was born in 1937 into a family of prominent scholars. According to his website, he started lecturing in the Qum seminary in 1975, which says:

> His lectures, compiled by two of his pupils at the School, are testimony of his command of the subject and the clarity of his teaching. When he began to teach the *dars-i khārij* (an advanced level of classes at a seminary school, equivalent to post graduate studies at any given university independent of any text or prescribed text) courses, a number of seminary students and lecturers attended his classes, among whom are a number of distinguished seminary researchers and *mujtahids* of our time who are active either at the seminaries or serve in governmental agencies.[7]

The website continues:

> For hundreds of seminary students and researchers who attend his classes, the lucidity of the argument and the critical and incisive view, deep reverence for his righteous predecessors, respect for the canonical method of the seminaries, accompanied by an

> exceptional profundity of views and principles bestowed on lessons given by this illustrious teacher all of which characterize his teaching approach mean that he imparts to his students a wealth of invaluable and potent methods to be used in solving contemporary social problems and brings a clarity of elucidation to the main topics in the canon.[8]

Ṣāniʿī is also seen by many as a source of reference (*marjaʿ*), although this status has been disputed by some in the Qum seminary due to his political views and radically different juristic opinions. Currently, Ṣāniʿī is seen as politically suspect, and he is a largely peripheral figure in Qum.[9]

In the past ten years, Ṣāniʿī's office has published a series of booklets that pronounce his rulings (fatwas) on some important and controversial juridical points. The following section will look at one of these booklets which demonstrates his engagement with Islamic sacred literature and exhibits his hermeneutical strategies. This will give us an insight into how he deduced some of his controversial rulings on divorce.

Divorce, according to Islamic law, is the prerogative of men. A woman cannot unilaterally divorce her husband, and, if she wants to initiate a divorce, she must petition an Islamic judge for one. A judge only pronounces divorce on her behalf under certain circumstances, such as if she is abandoned by her husband or he fails to provide maintenance for her. The Shiʿi legal tradition recognises three types of divorce: *rujūʿ* – a divorce initiated by the husband, which is revocable; *mubarāt* – a divorce where both parties wish to end the marriage; and *khulʿ* – a divorce initiated by the wife.[10] It is the *khulʿ* form of divorce that we will be concerned with in this chapter.

Ṣāniʿī's views on the need to change the Islamic laws pertaining to women can be gleaned from his discussions with Ziba Mir-Hosseini. He says, 'since the subject [women's situation] has changed, the framework of civil laws must change too. Our current laws are in line with the traditional society of the past, whereas these civil laws should be in line with contemporary realities and relations in our own society.'[11] Speaking to Mir-Hosseini more specifically about women and divorce, Ṣāniʿī states that, even without a marriage contract, a woman can unilaterally annul a marriage if she feels she cannot live with a man, although he indicates it is better for her if the *ṭalāq* is recited. He reiterates that 'Islam does not say that a woman must stay and put up with her marriage if it is causing her harm – never.' The problem, Ṣāniʿī states, is that the laws are still in the process of evolution.[12] Statements such as these clearly represent a major departure from the views held by most previous and contemporary jurists. Indeed, Ṣāniʿī indicates there is juridical tension in Qum when he paraphrases an imam who expressed the caustic view that within the seminaries there are petrified, fossilised devout ignoramuses who prevent such reforms in the law from taking place.[13]

Ṣāniʿī starts his discourse on divorce, *Wujūb ṭalāq al-khulʿ ʿalā al-rajul*, with a caveat: although allowed, according to a well-known Prophetic tradition, *ṭalāq* is considered the most detestable acceptable act in the eyes of God.[14] To understand Ṣāniʿī's views on divorce, it is important, at the outset, to note the Qur'anic perspective on the subject. While it allows divorce, the Qur'an states that it should be conducted based on commonly accepted standards of behaviour, as described here:

> *O Prophet, when you [Muslims] divorce women, divorce them for [the commencement of] their waiting period and keep count of the waiting period, and fear Allah, your Lord. Do not turn them out of their [husbands'] houses, nor should they [themselves] leave [during that period] unless they are committing a clear immorality. And those are the limits [set by] Allah. And whoever transgresses the limits of Allah has certainly wronged himself. You know not; perhaps Allah will bring about after that a [different] matter. And when they have [nearly] fulfilled their term, either retain them according to acceptable terms or part with them according to acceptable terms. And bring to witness two just men from among you and establish the testimony for [the acceptance of] Allah. That is instructed to whoever should believe in Allah and the Last day. And whoever fears Allah – He will make for him a way out.* (Q. 65:1–2)

In examining this verse and before engaging in an in-depth discussion of the subject of *khulʿ ṭalāq*, Ṣāniʿī first tackles the tradition which states that the right to divorce has not been given to women because they are more likely to resort to divorce. The rationale behind this is that women were thought to become emotional at the most trivial provocation or when they encounter slight difficulties; thus the belief that granting them the right to divorce would destabilise the family. Ṣāniʿī dismisses this tradition, stating there is no proof to substantiate the claim that women are more disposed to divorce. Moreover, he argues, the chain of transmission (*isnād*) of the tradition is weak.[15] Having rejected the tradition, he proposes a new reading of the texts, as I will demonstrate. By engaging different genres of sacred literature, employing various hermeneutical strategies, and arguing based on reasoning and on the principle of divine justice, he provides vindication for his juridical opinions.

The central thesis in Ṣāniʿī's tract is that a woman should have the same rights as a man to annul a marriage. He thus questions the ruling maintained by several jurists that allows a man to walk out of a marriage at will but not a woman. For Ṣāniʿī, this ruling is in conflict with not only reason but the important Qur'anic principle of justness. He then considers the main condition for a wife to be legally able to seek *khulʿ ṭalāq*, which is that her hatred for her spouse has reached such a degree that she is neither able nor willing to continue living with him. For Ṣāniʿī, this is untenable, as he believes there should be no conditions attached to, or restrictions imposed on, the degree of her aversion. He insists that when a relationship deteriorates to a level whereby the wife detests her husband, he is obliged to divorce his wife should she ask for it. This would apply even if the reason for her seeking the annulment of the marital relationship is to marry another man. The only condition which he maintains should be stipulated is that the wife should return the *mahr* that had been given to her by her husband. In essence, he believes that just as a husband can divorce his wife by giving her the *mahr* agreed upon at the time of the marriage, so too should she be able to divorce him by simply returning his *mahr*. This would ensure that both parties had equal rights to divorce. As we shall see further on, Ṣāni'ī's teacher Khomeini shared a similar opinion on the subject. However, the contemporary mujtahid 'Alī al-Hussaynī Sīstānī (b. 1930), who is considered by many to be the most widely emulated and learned jurist in the Shi'i world, espouses a different view on *khul'* divorce. For him, the wife has the right to *khul'* if 'the hatred [has] reached a proportion where she would not allow [her husband] conjugal rights'.[16]

In the process of articulating the rationale for his ruling, Ṣāni'ī examines the history of *ṭalāq* to show how women's rights were embedded within it from the earliest days of Islam. He explains that *ṭalāq* is among the *aḥkām-i imazī'*, that is, rulings that were present in pre-Islamic Arabia which Islam endorsed. Islam had adopted and then revised many pre-Islamic customs and laws, such as those concerning slavery, blood money (*diyya*), *mahr*, temporary marriage (*mut'a*) and many others. Ṣāni'ī notes that in the case of permanent marriage, pre-Islamic Arabs observed two types of marriage – *ṣadiqa* marriage, which was 'based on the mutual consent of the man and woman involved', and *ba'l* marriage, which 'was either imposed by the man on female war captives, or arranged between the would-be husband and the bride's family'[17] – and indicates that Islam adopted aspects of both forms of marriage. But key to his position on divorce, Ṣāni'ī notes that while Islam endorsed many pre-Islamic laws on *ṭalāq*, it also revised them by granting women the right to seek divorce.

For many jurists, the right of women to undertake *khul' ṭalāq* and the principles undergirding this type of divorce are outlined in the following Qur'anic verse:

> *Divorce is [to be done] twice. Then, either keep [her] in an acceptable manner or release [her] with good treatment. And it is not lawful for you to take anything of what you have given them unless both [parties] fear that they will not be able to keep [within] the limits of Allah. But if you fear that they will not keep [within] the limits of Allah, then there is no blame upon either of them concerning that by which she expiates herself. These are the limits of Allah, so do not transgress them. And whoever transgresses the limits of Allah – it is those who are the wrongdoers.* (Q. 2:229)

The statement in the verse *then there is no blame upon either of them concerning that by which she expiates herself* indicates, according to Muslim jurists, that the wife can free herself from the relationship by compensating her husband for the divorce. Importantly, the verse does not impose any condition or set any restriction on the grounds for her seeking a divorce, nor does it stipulate a figure that would be considered appropriate remuneration for the divorce. For Ṣāniʿī, this Qur'anic verse serves as the basis for his ruling that the wife does have the right to remove her husband from her life,[18] and that any degree of hatred or aversion on her part is sufficient to warrant the divorce.

There are many traditions that have been successively transmitted (*mutawāṭir*) in both Shiʿi and Sunni books which substantiate that this form of divorce has been legislated in Islam. Ṣāniʿī states that *khulʿ ṭalāq* becomes mandatory if there is a possibility that the wife might sleep with someone else. However, he assiduously maintains that there should be no distinction between the couple regarding the grounds on which the wife can get a divorce. Stated differently, for Ṣāniʿī, the wife has the same grounds for divorce as her husband.[19] The principle of equivalent right to divorce represents a juridical innovation, one which is not shared by most jurists.

Ṣāniʿī's rebuttal of jurists' arguments against *khulʿ ṭalāq*

For Ṣāniʿī, even if a wife's hatred of her husband is minimal or she is seeking divorce because she wants to marry someone else, she is entitled to a divorce.[20] He proceeds to examine the proofs that have been deduced which refute his position. Most scholars, he points out, have ruled that the husband is not required to grant a wife *khulʿ ṭalāq*, even if she insists on it, though scholars like Muḥammad b. Jaʿfar al-Ṭūsī (d. 459/1067) and ʿAbd al-ʿAzīz Ibn Barrāj (d. 480/1088) have ruled differently, arguing that it is compulsory for the husband to agree to *khulʿ ṭalāq* if his wife asks for it.[21]

Ṣāniʿī critically analyses whether it is valid for scholars to use the principle of absolvement (*aṣl al-barāʾa*) as a basis for their argument that it is not obligatory for a man to agree to divorce his wife.

Basically, this means that when an act has not been mentioned in the revelatory sources, then by default, it is presumed to be permissible. Stated differently, as long as an act has not been explicitly prohibited, it is assumed to be permissible. Thus, this principle, which is also rooted in Sunni legal theory, decrees that a jurist cannot rule that an act is required or prohibited unless it is explicitly mentioned in the sacred sources.[22] Scholars therefore argue that since there is no clear injunction on the matter in the Qur'an or the traditions, a husband is not obliged to divorce his wife. Ṣāniʿī objects to this argument and endeavours to show that it is mandatory for a husband to agree to *ṭalāq*. He contends that, due to other proofs that are available, the principle of absolvement cannot be deployed in this case.

The section of the above-cited Qur'anic verse which reads *And it is not lawful for you to take anything of what you have given them* (Q. 2:229) is also advanced to support the view that a husband is not obliged to divorce his wife. However, Ṣāniʿī argues that the verse specifies that the wife is not to be censured for compensating her husband for her freedom: *there is no blame upon either of them concerning that by which she ransoms herself* (Q. 2:229). He further points out that this segment of the verse is conjoined to the previous segment which states that the husband should not insist on taking back what he gave to his wife. In other words, the part of the verse which addresses the issue of the redemption that the wife offers her husband in exchange for her release from the marriage is an exception to the previously stated rule that the husband cannot take back what he gave her. Ṣāniʿī contends that since the verse mentions the conditions by which *khulʿ* can be executed (i.e. through compensation), Q. 2:229 cannot be utilised to argue that it is not obligatory for a husband to concede to a divorce.[23] His interpretation of the verse is supported by the great Shiʿi exegete of the last century, ʿAllāma Muḥammad Ḥusayn Ṭabāṭabāʾī (d. 1981). In the commentary of this section of Q. 2:229, Ṭabāṭabāʾī states:

> 'There is no blame on them': Before that, the husband was prohibited from taking any part of what he had given the wife. It means that the wife, on her part, was prohibited from giving

> him anything back, because if she gave him anything while he was not allowed to take it, she would be cooperating with him in a sin and transgression. Now, this verse gives an exception to that general rule: In *al-khulʿ* form of divorce they are allowed to agree on an amount which the wife pays to the husband to get herself free. In this situation, there is no blame on the husband for taking it, nor on the wife in giving it. Hence the expression, 'there is no blame on them'.[24]

Ṣāniʿī cites a tradition along the same lines, that is, a woman can give back her *mahr* to obtain her freedom. It states that 'what he [the husband] takes [back] from her is *ḥalāl* for him'. Ṣāniʿī insists that the tradition and Q. 2:229 do not state whether it is mandatory or not for a husband to agree to *khulʿ ṭalāq*, rather, it merely enunciates it is *ḥalāl* for him to take what she offers him *in lieu* of the divorce.[25] It does not say that it is not obligatory for him to divorce her.

Ṣāniʿī next goes on to examine the reasoning advanced in favour of mandating that the husband divorce his wife if she asks it. In the first case, he notes that some jurists (whom he does not mention) contend that it is compulsory for the husband to grant his wife *ṭalāq* if it is conceivable that, in not divorcing her, she might commit a sin by not performing her marital duty of having sexual relations with him because of her hatred for him. Though Ṣāniʿī agrees that the husband should grant his wife a divorce, he argues that this obligation, based on the reasoning given by the jurists in this instance, would wrongfully penalise the husband because it would force him to dissolve a marriage due to his wife's wrongdoing (of not providing him with sex). For Ṣāniʿī, it is unfair to penalise him for her sins or acts of transgression.[26]

Ṣāniʿī's application of the 'conduct of reasonable people'

As mentioned earlier, for Ṣāniʿī, both parties must have identical rights to nullify a marriage if they so choose. To substantiate his argument, he invokes various methodological tools that go beyond the textual sources. In this instance, he uses, as a tool, a concept that is rooted in Shiʿi legal theory: the conduct of reasonable people (*sīra al-ʿuqalāʾ*).

In Shiʿi legal theory, the concept of the conduct of reasonable people replaces the need for a written text and becomes a binding sunna if there are no textual proofs that repudiate a particular mode of behaviour. Although no reported text is essential for *sīra*, the continuous practice of a certain mode of behaviour by rational people is a sufficient proof for a jurist to rule that the imams approved the demeanour, and that the demeanour is therefore acceptable. It is assumed that all reasonable beings accept and behave according to commonly held norms and values. This being the case, a particular principle can be established by arguing that the pattern of behaviour was common to all rational beings, whether they lived in the times of the imams or not, and that no objection had been raised by the Lawgiver.[27]

In proving the validity of this genre of *sīra*, the Shiʿi jurist Muḥammad Bāqir al-Ṣadr (d. 1980) cites the example of the tendency of all reasonable people to accept the apparent meaning of a person's speech. This must have also been the practice of the imams, he says. If they understood the locution of people in a different way, one would have expected this demeanour to be reflected in the reports that have been transmitted, especially as this behaviour would have been contrary to the accepted praxis established for understanding people's speech. As no report of this type of behaviour has reached us, it can be established that the *sīra* of the imams was the same as that of reasonable beings.[28] Thus, a practice that is based on reason and is not opposed by the imams is regarded as authoritatively binding (*ḥujja*).

Based on this principle, Ṣāniʿī maintains that reasonable people would opine that since a wife cannot unilaterally undertake a divorce, it falls to the Lawgiver to legislate rules that will compel her husband to annul the relationship, even if he does not wish to do so. This opinion can be established based on the views of rational beings, and is in line with the ethos of Islam, which upholds the dignity (*ikrām*) and inalienable rights of all human beings.[29]

Furthermore, Ṣāniʿī argues, there is nothing in the sharia that rejects this rational principle. This intrinsicality (*mulāzama*) – that both parties have equal rights to divorce – is in accordance with Islamic principles and laws; it is also premised on another principle that undergirds Islamic law, that of justice. Ṣāniʿī quotes verses from the Qur'an that underline God's commitment to justice, for example, Q. 41:46: *And your Lord is not ever unjust to [His] servants*, to substantiate his argument. Furthermore, the *ʿuqalāʾ* (reasonable people) would rule that what is against this *mulāzama* (that both parties have equal rights to divorce) is unjust and would be tantamount to oppressing the woman. Basing his argument on the Qur'anic principle of God's justice and the reasoning of all rational beings, Ṣāniʿī states that the *mulāzama* is valid and applicable.[30]

Ṣāniʿī further argues that it is both rationally and morally wrong that authority should be bestowed on someone of one gender yet denied to someone of another gender, since individuals have no choice over their sex. He concludes that, from a rational point of view, gender should not be a factor in determining who can and who cannot give *ṭalāq*.[31] Ṣāniʿī also argues that reason (*ʿaql*) would suggest that it is wrong and unjust for the husband to be able to divorce his wife by giving her the *mahr*, even if she does not desire the divorce, without her being able to do the same to him. *ʿAql* also rules that it is oppression (*ẓulm*) to deny the right of *ṭalāq* to the wife.[32] This is because reason does not construe gender to be a basis for denying a woman her rights. To prove this, Ṣāniʿī resorts to the normal legal argument; that is, he points out that there is nothing in the texts to invalidate the ruling of *ʿaql*. He states that if the Lawgiver wanted to repudiate what *ʿaql* rules or what is in the human conscience on this issue, then it would have been necessary for him to do so with clear textual proofs, not with isolated reports.[33] Stated differently, it is obligatory for the Lawgiver to pronounce, in clear and unequivocal terms, that what reason has ruled on the issue is either evil or wrong.

A single tradition which repudiates what *ʿaql* had ruled is not authoritatively binding. This is because the Lawgiver, who has given us the capacity to reason and think, is obliged to interject when *ʿaql* has reached a wrong conclusion. He should intervene based on clear and multitudinous traditions. The invalidation of what *ʿaql* has perceived cannot be established in any tradition that has been reported nor is there any text on this, let alone many clear traditions. Ṣāniʿī states that he has demonstrated that traditions which oppose proofs based on *ʿaql* are not legally binding. Similarly, traditions which oppose the principles of *ʿadl* (justice) and claim that there is no injustice in Islamic law are not legally binding either. Based on this, Ṣāniʿī argues that there is no other alternative but to rule that it is obligatory (*wājib*) for the husband to grant *khulʿ ṭalāq* if his wife insists on it.[34]

Ṣāniʿī's examination of the traditions on *ṭalāq*

As is the custom in demonstrative jurisprudence (*al-fiqh al-istidlālī*), Ṣāniʿī then examines various traditions which contradict his ruling on the topic. His purpose is to spot the flaws in them and formulate a rebuttal.

Tradition 1: Divorce is in the hands of the man

In the first of these, he looks at an important Prophetic tradition from a Sunni source which states that divorce is in the hands of the man. Roughly translated, the tradition states '*ṭalāq* is for the one who took the [wife's] leg' (*al-ṭalāq li-man akhadha bi'l-sāq*). Ṣāniʿī identifies three areas of weakness. First, he maintains that the *isnād* of this Sunni hadith is flawed since the report has not been authenticated, thus making it an unreliable source. Second, he argues that this tradition was not meant to be a general declaration that gave men exclusive rights to divorce. If we look at the context in which the Prophet allegedly made the statement, he says, we will see that he was reportedly addressing the practice of a master who allowed a slave man and woman to marry each other and then insisted on separating them. Third, Ṣāniʿī argues that the tradition refers to divorce in general, as it does not mention the special case of *khulʿ ṭalāq* where the wife petitions the husband for a divorce. The tradition of a general proclamation of *ṭalāq*, in which the man has the right of divorce, does not apply to *khulʿ*, which is a special type of *ṭalāq*.[35]

Tradition 2: Husbands should not be forced to consent to divorce

Ṣāniʿī then focuses his analysis on another tradition, which is opposed to the husband being forced to consent to divorce his wife. According to Ṣāniʿī, the tradition merely states that it is the husband who gives the *ṭalāq* and not the other way around. He thus argues that, in itself, the tradition does not contradict the obligatoriness (*wujūb*) of the husband to grant his wife *khulʿ ṭalāq*.[36] The tradition also states that the woman does not have the right to insist that her husband should divorce her anytime she wants. Without mentioning why, Ṣāniʿī maintains that the tradition is not relevant to the point of contention. As a matter of fact, he argues that some jurists have even ruled there is no need to pronounce the formula of *ṭalāq* (*sīgha*) in *khulʿ*. They believe that a wife's demonstration of hatred for her husband and her desire to seek divorce is enough to annul the marriage.[37]

Tradition 3: Husbands can demand unlimited payment for divorce

Ṣāniʿī next turns his attention to traditions which state that a man can demand any amount of *mahr* he wants from his wife. He argues that such traditions are unjust and cannot be accepted because they are contrary to the rationally derived principle of justice, which is ingrained in the Qur'an. He quotes Murtaḍā Muṭahharī (d. 1979), who said, 'justice is one of the standards of Islam; whatever justice decides, religion rules likewise'.[38] By appealing to the central principle of *ʿadl* in the Qur'an, Ṣāniʿī suggests that God's laws cannot violate this principle. He states that even the Lawgiver is bound (*muḍṭarr*) to legislate a law that will diffuse justice throughout society and remove injustice and discrimination.[39]

It is notable that other jurists have not stipulated the amount that a husband can demand of his wife in exchange for his divorcing her. According to Sīstānī, '[t]he property which the husband takes in *mubarat* divorce should not exceed the *mahr* of his wife. But in the case of *khulʿ* divorce, there is no harm if it exceeds her *mahr*.'[40] The fact that there is no restriction in Islamic law as to how much a husband can demand in *khulʿ ṭalāq* has meant that many women are not financially able to annul their marriages.

In Ṣāniʿī's opinion, contemporary jurists have often sacrificed the principles of equality and justice when faced with the pronouncements of erstwhile jurists, regardless of the sociocultural contexts of the earlier statements. The juridical proclamation that a man can demand as much as he wishes for *khul' ṭalāq* is against the Qur'anic ethos, especially of Q. 41:46 (*And your Lord is not ever unjust to [His] servants*). Based on this important Qur'anic principle, Ṣāni'ī questions why the amount of *mahr* that a man can pay to divorce his wife can be capped at no more than what he paid when he married her while she can be compelled to give more than the *mahr* she received when she seeks a divorce? He cites other verses from the Qur'an where God promises to be just to all human beings, and thereby shows that a judgement which states that a wife has to give back more than the *mahr* to obtain a divorce violates Qur'anic principles. By privileging the Qur'an and invoking its principles, he invalidates traditions which state that the husband can demand any amount he wishes from his wife and in that way deny her enjoying a decent lifestyle after the divorce.[41]

For Ṣāni'ī, there is a clear conflict between the message found in traditions that have been deemed to be sound and the message conveyed in the Qur'anic verses. He argues that such traditions must be rejected. He adds that in the realm of theology, there are many reliable and sound traditions that speak of alteration (*taḥrīf*) in the Qur'an and claim that the Prophet had committed acts of inadvertence (*sahw*) in his prayers. Jurists have rejected these traditions due to their belief in the infallibility (*'iṣma*) of the Prophet. As a matter of fact, there are eighteen *riwāya* (narrations) transmitted from thirteen major Companions on such principles, but Shi'i jurists, apart from Shaykh Ṣadūq (d. 381/991), have rejected them, as they conflict with the principle of the *'iṣma* of the prophets.[42] Hence, the mere existence of *ṣaḥīḥ* (sound) traditions does not justify issuing a fatwa in support of an issue, since even reliable traditions have to be measured by Qur'anic injunctions and rational principles.[43]

In support of his stance, Ṣāni'ī cites the case of Muqaddas Ardabīlī (d. 993/1585), who also deployed this strategy many times. For example, on the question of *diyya* (blood money), Ardabīlī stated that a ruling that fixes the *diyya* to be paid in compensation for the murder of a woman at only half the *diyya* for the murder of a man is against what has been transmitted and what is rational.[44] Thus, a jurist cannot give a fatwa based on a tradition that goes against *ʿaql*, even if it is a *ṣaḥīḥ* tradition. The only exception to this rule, according to Ṣāniʿī, is if the traditions pertain to devotional or pious acts (*taʿābudī*), since reason cannot perceive what is rationally correct on such issues.[45]

At this point Ṣāniʿī cites another possible argument. Traditions which state the husband can demand any amount over and above the *mahr* he gave his wife contravene what reason rules under the circumstance and are unjust to the woman. According to this argument, this discrepancy can be resolved by requiring the wife to state in the marital contract that if she wishes to divorce her husband, she will return the *mahr* only, and that he cannot compel her to give back more than that. Such a stipulation, the argument continues, would resolve the incongruity since it would not infringe the traditions which state that the husband can take as much as he wants from his wife; at the same time it resolves the problem of the injustice committed against the wife. Ṣāniʿī maintains that this argument is still problematic, because it indicates that the Lawgiver has, in the first instance, legislated something which is against His justice.[46]

According to Ṣāniʿī, laws are not only supposed to be fair and just but must also be general (*ʿāmm*) in their application. This means that justice should be extended to those who observe the law and those who do not. Since justice is universal and applicable to all human beings, no restrictions can be imposed on it. Thus, it is improper to insist that justice will be done only if the wife inserts certain conditions in her contract. The concept of a universal system of justice means that no condition or restriction can be imposed to remove the oppression or wrongdoing that is pervasive in an injunction in the first place.[47]

Those who maintain that the husband can take property without any conditions or restrictions in *khulʿ ṭalāq* also claim that there is a consensus (*ijmāʿ*) regarding the ruling. They also cite Q. 2:229 and traditions to justify their ruling on this issue. As stated above, Ṣāniʿī argues that the traditions cannot be accepted, nor are they valid. As for the Qurʾanic verse, its signification is not general, that is, it does not imply that the husband has the prerogative to demand as much as a condition to granting the *ṭalāq*. Ṣāniʿī says that the context of the verse indicates that it is merely making a declaration (*maqām bayān*) of the right of the husband to demand compensation without stipulating how much.

Secondly, the statement from Q. 2:229, *that by which she ransoms herself* . . ., is a general proclamation informing the believers that the husband is allowed to accept the compensation; it does not state that he can demand as much as he likes. Ṣāniʿī argues that if the verse signifies that the husband can demand as much compensation as he wishes, then it would be defeating the ruling that it pronounces (that the wife can obtain her release through payment), since it would grant the husband the power to ask for an exorbitant sum that the wife might not be able to afford.

Ṣāniʿī concludes by ruling that if the wife detests her husband and returns the *mahr* or pays him a sum in compensation which is mutually agreed upon, then he is obliged to divorce her. If he refuses, then the matter should go to court where the divorce could be issued.[48]

Ṣāniʿī's Methodology

Compared to other jurists, Ṣāniʿī's approach is very different. In contrast to others who rely heavily on traditions, Ṣāniʿī invokes Qur'anic principles like justice and equality in his juridical rulings. He often relies on reason to discern the underlying spirit of the Qur'anic verses that he cites in the derivation of legal rulings. Furthermore, Ṣāniʿī contextualises Qur'anic verses and hadiths by considering them within the time (*zamān*) and space (*makān*) in which they were revealed or uttered, respectively. As we shall see in the example cited below, Ṣāniʿī rejects traditions that conflict with core Qur'anic values, human reason and the understanding of what makes a just society.[49]

As mentioned, when deducing legal rulings from textual sources Ṣāniʿī applies certain principles which are rooted in the Qur'an. One of these principles is that religion should be easy to follow and should not engender difficulties for its adherents. This is premised on the Qur'anic verse which states: *Allah intends for you ease and does not intend for you hardship* (Q. 2:185). As we have seen, Ṣāniʿī also insists that any legal ruling must accord with the Qur'an's vision of a just social order, since God cannot impose a duty or law that is unjust. He also appeals to the reasoning of rational beings and, like other jurists, invokes, at times, secondary rulings (*al-aḥkām al-thanawiyya*), since a kind and merciful deity would provide dispensation (*rukhṣa*) if the implementation of a ruling would entail hardships that could be seen as excessive in the view of rational beings.[50]

The Views of Other Jurists on Women's Rights to Divorce

Given the restrictions surrounding a woman's judicial capacity to divorce her husband, other jurists have sought to empower women in this sphere of legal rulings. Jurists like Jannātī posit that a wife can insert a clause in her marital contract that she should have the authority (*wikāla*) to pronounce the *ṭalāq* if she so chooses. Based on this condition, she can recite the *ṭalāq* at any time she wishes. She can also insert a clause in the contract stating that she has the right to recite the *ṭalāq* if she finds it difficult to live with her husband.[51] However, Ṣāni'ī is more circumspect than Jannātī, as the former does not require the inclusion of any restriction or condition in the marital contract.

With respect to a woman's right to divorce her husband, Ṣāni'ī's views are closely aligned with Khomeini's. When asked his opinion on this matter, Ṣāni'ī responded by reiterating what Khomeini had stated, which is that a husband should be persuaded to grant a divorce if his wife seeks it; if he refuses that request, then the divorce can be implemented with the permission of a judge.[52]

Another prominent contemporary jurist, Bujnūrdī, has issued radical fatwas in favour of women on issues relating to women's testimony in court, inheritance matters, child custody, the age of puberty, and so on.[53] Like Ṣāni'ī, Bujnūrdī rules that a wife can petition a court for divorce if she finds that living with her husband is causing her great distress.[54]

Another Iranian jurist, Muḥsin Sa'īdzāda (b. 1958), argues that laws in which women lack equality with men are products of the Islamic hermeneutical tradition that has favoured men. For Sa'īdzāda, such laws are amenable to change.[55] He also insists that the protection of people, especially women, is an important duty of a society:

> Islam accepted the Principle of protection, but the form it took in the Islamic society of that era was only one instance. We cannot assume that only this instance among many other instances of protection is sanctioned by a religion which is based on revelation and absolute reason! Our explanation and analysis, therefore, is: since that instance was accepted by the people of that era and was useful for them, it was left as it was.[56]

Saʿīdzāda goes on to argue that 'eternity, immutability and unchangeability all pertain to principles and rulings, not to details and forms'. He argues, 'We too consider the Rulings of Islam to be eternal, immutable, and unchangeable, but distinguish Principles from forms.'[57] He further argues:

> since we made it clear that the cause of the Ruling [on divorce] was the theory of protection, it follows that the forms of marriage and divorce are relative and subordinate to the will of the people. The known form of this theory cannot be the concern and cause of a ruling.
>
> The law sanctions marriage and divorce (as based on the Principle of protection) and the prevailing practices (as among the useful and accepted forms of the time), but never considers them to be eternal.[58]

According to Mir-Hosseini, Saʿīdzāda 'sees gender inequality in the shariʿa not as a manifestation of divine justice, but as a mistaken construction by male jurists; and he argues that it goes contrary to the very essence of the divine Will as revealed in the Koran'.[59]

Conclusion

Ṣāniʿī challenges normative textual readings which have been sacralised and treated as immutable and eternal. For him, the fact that erstwhile Muslim jurists differed widely on what they believed constituted the divine will and often issued a wide range of rulings on a single topic suggests there is a need to differentiate divine pronouncements from the hermeneutics of later scholars. For Ṣāniʿī, Muslims need to distinguish between the voice of God and the human voice and be aware that while the former is authoritative, the latter is clearly not.

Ṣāniʿī is among the few contemporary jurists who accentuate the egalitarian ethos of the Qur'an. While exhibiting the breadth and depth of his scholarship, Ṣāniʿī utilises other methodological devices such as reason and justice as important criteria for inferring juridical rulings. He refuses to accept some of the discriminatory rulings that permeate the juridical literature. Based on the principles of justice, equality and reasoning acknowledged by all rational beings, he argues that a woman has the same right to divorce as a man. Contrary to the thinking of most jurists, he argues that upon receiving the *mahr* that he gave her, a husband is obliged to divorce his wife even if that is against his wishes.

NOTES

1 The quotes from Khomeini are taken from an email I received from Muhammad al-Hijazi in September 2008.

2 All translations of the Qur'an in this chapter are from Saheeh International, with minor modifications.

3 Seyyed Mostafa Muhaghegh-Damad, 'The Role of Time and Social Welfare in the Modification of Legal Rulings', in Lynda Clarke, ed., *Shīʿite Heritage: Essays on Classical and Modern Traditions* (Binghamton, NY, 2001), p. 218. See also Liyakat Takim, *Shiʿism in America* (New York, 2009), pp. 156–7; idem, 'Maqāṣid al-Sharīʿa in Contemporary Shīʿī Jurisprudence', in Adis Duderija, ed., *Maqasid al-Shariʿa and Contemporary Reformist Muslim Thought: An Examination* (New York, 2014), pp. 120–21.

4 Muhaghegh-Damad, 'The Role of Time and Social Welfare', p. 219.

5 Ibid.

6 These and other points that I discussed with Ṣāniʿī were documented on his website, http://saanei.xyz/. Unfortunately, the interview is no longer available there.

7 See 'Biographical Note', http://saanei.xyz/?view=02,00,00,00,0#02,01,14,23,0 (accessed 18 May 2015; text in link has been amended).

8 http://saanei.xyz/undefined?view=02,01,14,20,0 (accessed 12 October 2018; link no longer available).

9 Naser Ghobadzadeh, *Religious Secularity: A Theological Challenge to the Islamic State* (New York, 2014), pp. 196–7. See also the Wikipedia entry on Ṣāniʿī, https://en.wikipedia.org/wiki/Yousef_Saanei.

10 Syed Ali al-Husaini Seestani, *Islamic Laws: English Version of Taudhihul Masae'l* (London, 1994), pp. 468–70.

11 Ziba Mir-Hosseini, *Islam and Gender: The Religious Debate in Contemporary Iran* (Princeton, NJ, 1999), p. 160.
12 Ibid., p. 162
13 Ibid., p. 160.
14 Yūsuf Ṣāniʿī, *Wujūb ṭalāq al-khulʿ ʿalā al-rajul* (Qum, n.d.), p. 20.
15 Ibid., p. 15.
16 Seestani, *Islamic Laws*, p. 469.
17 For details on the differences between the two types of marriages, see Mahmoud Ayoub, *Islam: Faith and History* (London, 2012), p. 180.
18 Ṣāniʿī draws on the literal meaning of the term '*khul*ʿ' – 'to remove' or 'take off', akin to the act of removing an item of clothing – when talking about the divorce. He writes that when a wife detests her husband, she 'removes him' from her life. Ṣāniʿī, *Wujūb ṭalāq al-khul*ʿ, p. 24.
19 Ibid. p. 33.
20 Ibid.
21 Ibid., p. 35.
22 On this, see Robert Gleave, *Inevitable Doubt: Two Theories of Shīʿī Jurisprudence* (Leiden, 2000), chapter three.
23 Ṣāniʿī, *Wujūb ṭalāq al-khul*ʿ, pp. 36–7.
24 Muḥammad Ḥusayn Ṭabāṭabāʾī, *Tafsīr al-Mīzān*, Q. 2:229, p. 21, http://www.almizan.org/.
25 Ṣāniʿī, *Wujūb ṭalāq al-khul*ʿ, pp. 37–8.
26 Ibid., pp. 43–5.
27 See Liyakat Takim, *The Heirs of the Prophet: Charisma and Religious Authority in Shiʿite Islam* (Albany, NY, 2006), pp. 132–3.
28 Muḥammad Bāqir al-Ṣadr, *Durūs fī ʿilm al-uṣūl* (Beirut, 1978), vol. II, p. 182; Takim, *The Heirs of the Prophet*, pp. 132–3.
29 Ṣāniʿī, *Wujūb ṭalāq al-khul*ʿ, pp. 50–51; Liyakat Takim, 'Customary Law as a Source of Legislation for Shiʿi Law', *Studies in Religion/Sciences Religieuses* 47, no. 4 (2018), pp. 488–9.
30 Ṣāniʿī, *Wujūb ṭalāq al-khul*ʿ, p. 51; Liyakat Takim, 'Customary Law', p. 489.
31 Ibid., p. 52.
32 Ibid.
33 Ibid.
34 Ibid., pp. 53–4.
35 See his arguments in ibid., pp. 55–9.
36 Ibid., pp. 62–3.
37 Ibid., p. 65.
38 Ibid., p. 76.
39 Ibid., p. 77.
40 Seestani, *Islamic Laws*, p. 471.
41 Ṣāniʿī, *Wujūb ṭalāq al-khul*ʿ, pp. 77–8.
42 Martin McDermott, *The Theology of Shaikh al-Mufīd* (Beirut, 1978), p. 358.
43 Ṣāniʿī, *Wujūb ṭalāq al-khul*ʿ, p. 80.
44 Ibid., pp. 80–81.
45 Ibid., pp. 82–3.
46 Ibid., p. 83.
47 Ibid., pp. 84–5.

48 Ibid., p. 88.

49 See Hamid Mavani's discussion on Ṣāni'ī's methodology in 'Paradigm Shift in Twelver Shi'i Legal Theory (*uṣūl al-fiqh*): Ayatullah Yusef Saanei, *Muslim World* 99, no. 2 (2009), pp. 342–5.

50 Secondary rulings are those which are enforced under circumstances when the primary rulings create difficulties or when there is extreme need. An example of this would be inter-gender handshaking. Men and women are not, under normal circumstances, allowed to shake hands. However, when they are required to, they may do so.

51 See also Mahdī Mahrīzī, *Mas'alat al-mar'a: Dirāsāt fī tajdīd al-fikr al-dīnī* (Beirut, 2008), p. 102.

52 Mir-Hosseini, *Islam and Gender*, p. 165. See also Mahrīzī, *Mas'alat al-mar'a*, pp. 137 and 271.

53 Liyakat Takim, '*Ijtihad* and the Derivation of New Jurisprudence in Contemporary Shi'ism: The Rulings of Ayatollah Bujnurdi', in Carool Kersten and Susanne Olsson, eds, *Alternative Islamic Discourses and Religious Authority* (Farnham, 2013), pp. 17–34.

54 Muḥammad Mūsawī Bujnūrdī, *Majmū'a-yi maqālāt-i fiqhī, ḥuqūqī wa ijtimā'ī* (Tehran, 2002), vol. I, pp. 37–8.

55 Muhammad Qasim Zaman, *The Ulama in Contemporary Islam: Custodians of Change* (Princeton, NJ, 2002), p. 186.

56 Sa'īdzāda quoted in Ziba Mir-Hosseini, *Islam and Gender*, pp. 270–71.

57 Ibid., p. 271.

58 Ibid., pp. 271–2.

59 Ibid., p. 272.

4

Al-Amr bi'l-ma'rūf and the Semiotics of Sovereignty in Contemporary Iran

NEGUIN YAVARI

IN APRIL 2003 when the Reformists (*iṣlāḥṭalabān*) were in government in Iran, Muṣṭafā Tājzāda (b. 1956), a prominent reformist politician and public intellectual,[1] published a short article entitled 'Amr bi ma'rūf, ta'āwun wa taḥazzub' ('Commanding right, association and party formation'; see Appendix), calling for the revival of this salient religious duty as the solution to Iran's contemporary political woes.[2] Long considered the purview of theological debates, the concept of *al-amr bi'l-ma'rūf wa nahy 'an al-munkar* (or *amr bi ma'rūf wa nahy az munkar* in Persian, 'commanding right and forbidding wrong') is of Qur'anic origin and enjoys Qur'anic sanction (Q. 3:104 and 110; Q. 7:157; Q. 9:67, 71 and 112; Q. 22:41; Q. 31:17). Its deployment by Tājzāda is an important strategic move to appropriate the mantle of doctrinal orthodoxy and legitimacy for Reformist politics.

The Reformists came to power with the victory of Mohammad Khatami (b. 1943) in the presidential elections of 1997.[3] In opposition since 2005, Reformist ideology has played a crucial role in defining one end of the political spectrum in contemporary Iran. In choosing *al-amr bi'l-ma'rūf wa nahy 'an al-munkar* as a cornerstone of their oppositional language, Tājzāda and his fellow Reformists paradoxically followed in the footsteps of Ruhollah Khomeini (d. 1989), whose ingenious manipulation of tradition and authoritative discourse was instrumental in birthing modern Islamic politics. By reinterpreting past discourse to legitimate new doctrines, as for instance in his redefinition of the guardianship of the jurist (*wilāyat al-faqīh*) discussed below, Khomeini bound the past together with the present. From the vantage point of intellectual history, Khomeini's deliberate strategy of bringing old questions and concepts to bear on new conditions redefined the political public in Iran and crafted a proper ideational context for modern Islamic politics, which had far-reaching ramifications around the globe.[4] The Iranian revolution of 1979 is but one example of the many consequences of that auspicious vision.

Promoting political change by emphasising Qur'anic doctrine also corroborates Reinhard Schulze's claim that the Qur'an has emerged in the twenty-first century as the arbiter par excellence of the practice of politics in the Islamic world, overshadowing the Hadith and the Sunna.[5] Considered a constitution of the sovereign Islamic state, the Qur'an functions as the *lex scripta* (written law) of the Islamic world, and in this manner, works to supplant the sharia itself, a vast, unwritten corpus of knowledge on Islamic conceptions of law, theology and political legitimacy which is primarily the work of experts in Islamic law (*fuqahā'*) and theologians, and accessible, almost exclusively, to them alone.[6] This chapter places Tājzāda's elaborations on *al-amr bi'l-maʿrūf* in a comparative framework, against the views of Khomeini and other Islamic intellectuals on the same subject, to study the use of Qur'anic sanction in Iran's contemporary political lexicon.

The long history of the invocation to command right and forbid wrong as a religious justification for rebellion against injustice and tyranny, and concomitant efforts to suppress that instinct to forestall anarchy, is the subject of Michael Cook's celebrated study, *Commanding Right and Forbidding Wrong in Islamic Thought*.[7] For the most part, and throughout Islamic history, the religious establishment has sought to carefully delimit the applicability of the injunction by limiting access to it. A good majority of theologians subscribe to calibrating the duty so that invoking it remains a privilege of the leaders of a community. In addition, the medieval scholastic establishment imposed a danger condition, mandating that the potential good that may accrue from invoking the command outweigh its adverse consequences. Against that quietist current, Khomeini, for example, famously resorted to commanding right to incite rebellion against the Pahlavi regime that ruled Iran from

1924 until its downfall in 1979. In the midst of a generally unremarkable scholastic discussion of the doctrine, Khomeini argued that 'there is a category of wrongs of such relative weight (*ahammiyya*) that the obligation to right them overrides the danger condition, particularly for the clergy; and, typically, such wrongs involve some threat to the very basis of Islam.'[8] The Pahlavi regime, and its capitulation to Western designs, was deemed such a threat.

With Khomeini on that point stood Muḥammad Ḥusayn Bihishtī (d. 1981), another revolutionary ayatollah and an astute student of politics. Like Khomeini, Bihishtī had a long history of public disagreements with more traditionally inclined theologians. His opposition to the views of the conservative cleric Muḥammad Taqī Miṣbāḥ Yazdī (b. 1935) in crafting a curriculum for the Ḥaqqānī school (a seminary founded in Qum in the 1960s whose politicised and activist graduates were instrumental in the success of the Islamic revolution in 1979) is the stuff of legend in contemporary political debates.[9] On several occasions, Bihishtī is reported to have denounced Miṣbāḥ Yazdī's intransigence and bombastic rhetoric.[10] Tellingly, Bihishtī's understanding of *al-amr bi'l-maʿrūf* has little to do with the conventional applications of that Qur'anic injunction in Iranian history, be it the observance of Islamic guidelines in public behaviour and attire in classical debates or the normalisation of party politics in the contemporary period. He considered *al-amr bi'l-maʿrūf* as a religious duty relevant to a widely defined array of political and social topics, most important of all, the right to speak truth to power. Punishing individual wrongdoers, especially on accusations of moral laxity, is wrong, he argued, since there is always a limit to how much individuals, especially young people, may succeed in suppressing desire and lust. Instead, Bihishtī notes, *al-amr bi'l-maʿrūf*, as articulated in the Qur'an and in the teachings of ʿAlī b. Abī Ṭālib (d. 40/661), mandates the critique of power and the fighting of corruption at the governmental level.[11]

Al-amr bi'l-maʿrūf enjoys particular prominence in modern Shiʿi scholarship. Cook observes that while the Sunni scholastic tradition on *al-amr bi'l-maʿrūf* has shaped it into a hallowed though ossified dictum: 'rather like a revered monument, it is cherished by people who no longer really inhabit it. The Imāmī scholastic tradition, by contrast, can still be described as a living one, owing its continuity and adaptation to scholars who operate within it.'[12] Furthermore, while Sunni laypersons comprise the majority of the participants in debates on *al-amr bi'l-ma'rūf*, in the Shi'i world, reshaping and modernising the concept has fallen to the clergy.[13] Cook's stated method is to canvass major Shi'i positions on the conditions and requisites of performing this religious duty, with the following caveat, that he 'has not looked through the newspapers from the Islamic world, and he has not conducted any field work'.[14] Cook has made here, willy-nilly, an uncharacteristically radical choice: he has fixed the boundary of what passes as historical record in the same way a medievalist would do, and in doing so fails to address some of the challenges of writing contemporary history. We will return to this point later in the discussion.

Having demonstrated the centrality of the injunction of *al-amr bi'l-ma'rūf* to modern Islamist theories of state – the Constitution of the Islamic Republic, for example, referring to Q. 9:71, states that 'the duty [of *amr bi'l-ma'rūf*] is one that must be fulfilled by the people with respect to one another, by the government with respect to the people, and by the people with respect to the government'[15] – Cook notes that in present-day Iran, the principle is most readily invoked by Shi'i authorities against liberalism and individualism.[16] Cook also identifies an ascendant counter-current that puts *al-amr bi'l-ma'rūf* at the service of neoliberal precepts (my reading not Cook's) of civil society; by way of example, he notes the writings of Ḥasan Islāmī Ardakānī (b. 1960), a junior cleric and professor of ethics resident in Qum. Islāmī Ardakānī not only decries intrusion into the private lives of other Muslims, but is also ecumenical in his approach, relying frequently on Sunni doctrine to argue his thesis. In Cook's estimation,

> Islāmī's ideas are certainly not representative of the prevailing religious culture in Iran. But they are likely to have considerable resonance for a significant part of the educated population. What this means for the future could perhaps be expressed in a highly conditional sentence. If civil society is fated to remain a globally relevant notion, if Iran – and other Islamic countries – are to

> become recognisably civil societies, and if they are timed to do so under an Islamic aegis, then Islāmī's thinking about forbidding wrong can help us to imagine what such a development may look like.[17]

Contra Cook, who sees an ascendant liberalising current in Islamist thought based on radical reinterpretations of well-established doctrine, the present chapter argues – based primarily on a close reading of public debates in Iran – that the duty to do right and prevent wrong is invoked in the Islamic Republic not to promote liberal values, but to energise political life, and democratise the political process, without necessarily liberalising it. This is not to deny that the liberalisation of the Islamic social order – often in contravention of the will of the clerical establishment – is in evidence in Iran (and elsewhere in the Islamic world) and laxer modes of social interaction and individual attire have been regnant at least since the coming to power of Khatami in 1997. However, an increasing sense of the importance of being organised, which is among the major innovations in modern Iranian thought on *al-amr bi'l-maʿrūf* that Cook notes,[18] has also become a staple of calls for the formal establishment of political parties. In a lecture delivered in 1960, Murtaḍā Muṭahharī (d. 1979), argued that without proper organisation, commanding wrong cannot be effective, as one individual accomplishes little in the way of societal change.[19] And, in a later speech, he equated commanding right with empathy and, in a macro sense, with boosting comity (*ʿaṣabiyya*) in society. Another theologian, Ḥusayn ʿAlī Muntaẓirī (d. 2009), at one point groomed as successor to Khomeini as *walī-yi faqīh* (custodian jurist), the highest office in Iran's government, has written on the importance of *al-amr bi'l-maʿrūf* in the formation of political parties.[20]

Tājzāda, a prominent disciple of Muntaẓirī, in his short article mentioned at the beginning, sought to justify the deployment of *al-amr bi'l-maʿrūf* as an instrument for the promotion of civility and communal bonds, the fostering of *ʿaṣabiyya*. To that end, he endows the injunction with a long genealogy. In legal discussions, he writes, it is mentioned with equal frequency as sister duties such as prayer, fasting, hajj and jihad. In contrast to Cook's assertion regarding the vibrancy of contemporary Imāmī debates on *al-amr bi'l-ma'rūf*, Tājzāda laments the exclusion of the subject matter from manuals of practice (*risāla 'amaliyya*) over the past century.[21] According to Tājzāda, *al-amr bi'l-ma'rūf* mandates a collective or public responsibility: each individual is accountable to his family and society. This responsibility entails aptitude, and the exigency of that aptitude has two elements: expertise and social vision on the one hand, and temperance (*ta'ādul*), collegiality (*hamkārī*) and seeking power (*taḥṣīl-i qudrat*) on the other. One element entails knowledge and prudence and the second one, power. From the vantage point of knowledge, it requires psychology and sociology, and on the power front, collaboration, institutionalisation, and the accumulation of tools and strategies for penetrating society. Association is an Islamic principle, Tājzāda continues, and it is the practical application of *al-amr bi'l-ma'rūf*. The correct implementation of *al-amr bi'l-ma'rūf* stipulates interaction among various strata of society. The lay public may perceive *al-amr bi'l-ma'rūf* as a religious teaching preoccupied with the way people dress or observe Islamic decorum in public; those aspects of life, however, fall within the purview of the freedom of individuals, he adds, and he claims much injustice has been committed in the name of the injunction of *al-amr bi'l-ma'rūf* on this front.

Tājzāda crafts his argument by drawing on past authorities that enjoy widespread legitimacy among contemporary Shi'i jurists. He cites the late Muṭahharī, who argued that unlike other religious duties such as prayer, fasting, hajj and almsgiving (*zakāt*), which are compulsory, *al-amr bi'l-ma'rūf* is a voluntary act that must therefore entail some enlightenment, for the commanding individual must have an understanding of the long-term consequences of his or her exhortations, otherwise they may outweigh the benefits to society in the long run. To Muṭahharī, *al-amr bi'l-ma'rūf* is about association and requires collective action. According to Tājzāda, Muṭahharī called for systemic action, organised activity and a division of labour for the proper execution of *al-amr bi'l-ma'rūf*, and further refined the intellectual pedigree of his claim by casting the formation of political parties as the quintessence of the famous Qur'anic exhortation in Q. 5:2: *Help ye one another in righteousness and piety* (*ta'āwanū*

ʿalā'l-barr wa'l-taqwā).[22] With careful programming, Tājzāda thinks it is possible to fight corruption and transgressions against the law through the implementation of the injunction to command right. In the modern world, Tājzāda concludes, political parties alone are capable of drafting comprehensive and cohesive political and social agendas since they bring together individuals with variegated skills and interests. Should they be elected to office, these individuals will be able to execute their carefully honed agendas, policies which have been made well-known to the electorate.

Political life in Iran, Tājzāda asserts in his closing paragraph, is plagued by apathy and widespread disinterest. Should this new interpretation of *al-amr bi'l-maʿrūf* as a call for collective participation in public life and an invitation to the formation of political parties be propagated, the public (*shahrwandān*) will benefit from an impressive arsenal of skills deployed to improve the quality of social life and promote good governance.[23]

Crucially, the Reformists are not alone in advocating for political change legitimised through the injunction *al-amr bi'l-maʿrūf*. From the opposite end of the ideological spectrum,[24] *Panjara*, a weekly news magazine of the conservative faction Jamʿiyyat-i Rahpūyān-i Inqilāb (Society of Adherents of the Revolution),[25] carried an interview with ʿAlī-Riḍā Zākānī (b. 1965), a conservative MP, in June 2011. Zākānī posited *nahy az munkar* as the most effective tool for fighting perdition and vice in government, and as the most trenchant critique of power.[26] The airing of concerns by public figures, he suggested, would help curb the excesses of then-president Mahmoud Ahmadinejad (b. 1956), whose rise to power had been supported by influential conservative political actors.

The reinstatement of Ahmadinejad as president for a second term in the 2009 elections united Iranian politicos from competing camps in their demand for political parties as the antidote to populism. Political analysts, academics, journalists and those based in think-tanks – the entire gamut of people who have made politics their business – converge on the necessity of political organisation, published platforms, and national reach to prevent the possibility of a corrupt demagogue ascending to the presidency. Among the better-known advocates of this demand was Ali Akbar Hashemi

Rafsanjani (d. 2017), speaker of parliament and former president of Iran (1989–97), whose call for political party formation gained momentum after the election of his erstwhile protégé Hasan Rouhani (b. 1948) to the presidency in 2013.[27] Articles debating the pros and cons of party formation are splashed across newspapers affiliated with Rafsanjani, prime among them *Armān-i imrūz* (Today's Ideal)[28] as well as more liberal news outlets. The daily newspaper *Etemad* (Confidence), under the general editorship of Elias Hazrati,[29] who was formerly commander of the Revolutionary Guards of the northern province of Gilan, a prominent Reformist and member of parliament (1990–2003), for example, carries a whole page on political parties in every issue.[30]

The invocation of the duty to command right and prohibit wrong to justify the establishment of political parties may reverse their fortunes in modern Iran, where parties have tended to coalesce around political personalities rather than platforms or ideological agendas, and most have been sponsored by the state.[31] The Islamic Revolution of 1979 brought a brief interlude of free political association, and the right to form political parties was recognised by the Iranian constitution of 1981.[32] However, the idyllic political pluralism of the early years of the Islamic Republic was short-lived. The pathology of that history is the subject of raging debate.[33] The Islamic Republican Party (Ḥizb-i Jumhūrī-yi Islāmī), established in 1979, enlisted most of Khomeini's supporters. It was led by Bihishtī who had been instrumental in organising opposition to the Pahlavi monarchy in the two decades prior to the revolution. Longstanding leftist parties, including the pro-Soviet Tudeh Party,[34] established in 1921, initially joined ranks with the Islamist *ʿulamāʾ* to overthrow the Pahlavi regime, convinced that the left could not incite a popular uprising. Nūr al-Dīn Kiyānūrī (d. 1999), first secretary of the central committee of the Tudeh Party since 1978, credited the vigilance of the Iranian people and the firm leadership of Khomeini with safeguarding the achievements of the revolution.[35] The compact of sorts, however, one in which the left was entrusted with rule and the *ʿulamāʾ* were to deliver the votes, proved to be a figment of the former's imagination. As the Soviet Union threw its weight behind Saddam Hussein in the war he had launched in 1980 against the Islamic Republic, the regime intensified its crackdown on the Tudeh Party. Its leaders were executed or jailed, and Iran's political spectrum was closed to non-Islamist ideologies for the foreseeable future.[36]

Unbridgeable differences, however, prevailed as well among the Islamists, leading to the official dissolution of Bihishtī's Islamic Republican Party in 1987. Almost two decades later, in a series of articles commemorating the 1981 assassination of Bihishtī, the liberal-leaning monthly journal *Mihrnāma* carried an interview with the late ayatollah's son, Muḥammad Riḍā Bihishtī (b. 1958–9). The party failed, according to him, because its leadership failed to chart a platform capable of gaining traction among the high-ranking jurists.[37] Students of Iranian history will also recognise in this skeletal outline the manifold resonances with pre-revolutionary Iran, where independent political parties were a rarity. Especially poignant are the parallels, not with the Rastākhīz Party of Muhammad Reza Shah Pahlavi (r. 1941–79), but rather with the mid-twentieth-century Democrat Party of Iran. Founded by Qawām al-Salṭana (d. 1955), the Democrat Party was also famously unsuccessful, as the leadership failed to arrive at a minimalist platform that could represent their collective wills.[38] The same fate befell Bihishtī's Islamic Republican Party. Even the formidable authority of Khomeini, who was at that point the uncontested leader of the Islamic world, and his strong support of the party failed to carry the day among the patricians of the religious establishment, all of them his closest allies and long-standing fellow revolutionaries. Internally, the party was split between right-wing conservatives who, led by Rafsanjani, were strictly pro-market forces, and the left-leaning faction under Mīr Ḥusayn Mūsawī (b. 1942), who was once prime minister, then presidential candidate, and is now under house arrest for contesting the elections of 2009 that brought Ahmadinejad a second term as Iran's president. The rift was deemed serious enough for Rafsanjani, who headed the parliament, and Ali Khamenei (b. 1939), then president of Iran and currently its *walī-yi faqīh*, to write to Khomeini to ask that the party be dissolved.[39]

There is another, less obvious and more consequential component to the story of political parties in modern Iran. The rift inside the

Islamic Republican Party went deeper than economic policy and touched on the definition and scope of *wilāyat-i faqīh*, the cornerstone of Khomeini's blueprint for Islamic governance that mandated that there be an executor charged with implementing the laws of Islam and managing the affairs of Muslims.[40] An Islamic government, Khomeini had written from exile in Najaf in 1971, could not be reduced to the imposition of Islamic law, for '[a] body of laws alone is insufficient for a society to be reformed'.[41] In addition to laws, Khomeini continues, Islam has established executive power, and the person who holds this executive power must be a religious jurist (*faqīh*, pl. *fuqahā'*), for jurists are 'the legatees, at one remove, of the Most Noble Messenger . . . and . . . all the tasks He entrusted to the Imams . . . are also incumbent on the *fuqaha*; all the tasks that the Messenger performed, they too must perform, just as the Commander of the Faithful . . . did'.[42] In their squabbles with Mūsawī and other supporters of centralised economic policy, Rafsanjani and Khamenei turned to the doctrine of *wilāyat-i faqīh* to argue that the very existence of a *walī-yi faqīh* obviates the need for legislation. The mandate of the parliament and representatives of the people in such a system of government must be restricted to implementing the laws of Islam (*aḥkām-i awwaliyya*).[43] In their defence, Mūsawī's faction relied on the concept of making secondary or derivative laws to supplement the primary laws of Islam in order to accommodate the exigencies of governance.[44] The unresolved conflict between Islamism and republicanism, as reflected in institutions of governance formed through elections and parallel ones that are conceived through appointment, is a perennial feature of politics in the Islamic Republic.[45] The similarly unresolved tension between popular and divine (read Islamic state) sovereignty is an avatar of the same ideological edifice.

The dissolution of the Islamic Republican Party did not put an end to dissent and fissure within the Islamist establishment,[46] although fronts or factions rather than fully fledged parties dominate the landscape with mixed results.[47] It did, however, militate against the public articulation of genuine political difference. In the very same year that the Islamic Republican Party was shut down at the behest of sectors of its leadership, members of the Jāmiʿa-yi Rawḥāniyyat-i Mubāriz (formed in 1977),[48] including Mūsawī and several left-leaning clerics, gained Khomeini's approval to declare an official political organisation if not a fully fledged political party. Their sphere of influence, however, was limited to Tehran. Khomeini's publicised endorsement of the left-leaning faction brought it to victory in the parliamentary elections of January 1988. In the first decade of the life of the Islamic Republic, Rafsanjani and Khamenei were united against Mūsawī, whose allies included two-term president Mohammad Khatami; Muḥammad Riḍā Mahdawī-Kanī (d. 2014), once prime minister and minister of interior; and the infamous Ṣādiq Khalkhālī (d. 2003), chief justice of the revolutionary courts in the early days of the Islamic Republic, whose readiness for the swift extermination of political foes was seen as emblematic of the character of Islamic governance.

That political line-up is history already. Rafsanjani and Khamenei have sparred publicly, especially in the wake of the 2009 elections and after the presidential bid of the twice-former president Rafsanjani was blocked in 2013 by the Guardian Council.[49] Among the supra-governmental institutions that mitigate republican governance in the Islamic Republic by overriding the political process when necessary, the Guardian Council, overseen by the supreme leader and accountable to that office, is also charged with vetting candidates for elected office. In an interview, ʿAlī-Riḍā Bihishtī (b. 1962–3), another son of Bihishtī, points to the centrality of historical context for understanding politics in contemporary Iran. He justifies his father's failed pet project by pointing to the dire realities of Iran in the 1980s, when the Islamic Republic was faced with armed insurrection at home and Iraqi aggression and international isolation.[50] The Islamic Republican Party, Bihishtī claims, did not wish to be the only party permitted to operate, but the government could not afford political fragmentation on the domestic front at that time.[51] Bihishtī also points out that many of the staunchest defenders of political parties today are its erstwhile opponents. In other words, political precepts are contingent and unstable formulations that are regularly reconfigured in response to changes in historical context.

Shifting alliances and frequent political volte-faces are the very currency of politics in the Islamic Republic, so much so that it is no longer open to decoding via a simple archaeology of classical debates without regard for historical change. Paradoxically, classical concepts are at the heart of the new political language, as we have seen with contemporary debates on *al-amr bi'l-maʿrūf* and other Qur'anic precepts, such as that of the false idol (*ṭāghūt*), invoked frequently to discredit Westernised or secular rulers.[52] The aim of this chapter has been to point to shortcomings in the academy's understanding of Iranian politics, by demonstrating the rather sizeable cleavage that separates 'the newsworthy' in the West from that which attracts energy and thought in the Islamic world. Cook's excellent study sees in modern Iran a proclivity to espouse liberalism, and presents innovative thought as thought that meticulously traces the trajectory of modern intellectual developments in the West. What is in evidence in present-day Iran is the very secularisation of the sacral when Tājzāda and Khomeini turn to the Qur'an to resolve contemporary political issues. In this instance, religion in political life is not antithetical to politics but an innovative articulation of it.[53] In fact, the lineage of sovereignty as political concept in the eastern Islamic world – today's Iran, India and Pakistan – goes back to debates in the late eighteenth century. That history is thoroughly ignored in conventional iterations of modern Islamic intellectual history, which rely, for reasons unclear, exclusively on Sunni thought.[54] If we concede, with Schulze[55] and Armando Salvatore[56] among others, that the modern world unfolded across the globe, but in an era of Western hegemony, accompanied by a political vocabulary that is thoroughly bound by history and geography, then it will be possible to consider an Islamic debate for the establishment of political parties as an instance of sovereignty, pure and simple. As a claim to authority,[57] sovereignty is on display when the ruling elite transforms itself in response to changing circumstances, and when those shifting alliances and conceptual manipulations are scrutinised by the political public.

Furthermore, the Iranian state has adopted a revised understanding of *al-amr bi'l-m'aruf*,[58] insofar as the doctrine has bearing on individual conduct and the private sphere, one that closely approximates what Michael Cook had characterised as an oppositional and minority view. In the context of a commemorative conference held in honour of Khomeini's late wife in 2015, for example, Iran's president, Hasan Rouhani, said that forbidding wrong is not limited to issues related to women. In present-day Iran, the president noted, the most important right command (*maʿrūf*) is the nation's development, and the biggest wrong (*munkar*) is the water crisis that plagues the country.[59]

A recent and extremely popular television show, aired in summer 2015 on Iran's state-owned Channel 3,[60] is also instructive in this regard. 'Tanhāʾī-yi Laylā' tells the story of a rich Iranian expat who returns from an unnamed Western country to claim her property. Laylā falls in love with and marries the deeply devout Muḥammad, a shrine keeper in a small town in the vicinity of Tehran. Unfortunately, he suffers from congenital heart disease and dies early. In one episode,[61] the newly widowed Laylā is accused of adultery by her neighbours. The imam of the local mosque chides the accusers, claiming that the good name of a Muslim is more sacrosanct than God's abode, pointing to his own mosque. The heated exchange between the shaykh and his parishioners caused an uproar within conservative circles.[62] These circles, however, failed to exert enough pressure to have the show cancelled. The argument put forward by the local imam in 'Tanhāʾī-yi Laylā' had previously appeared in a number of interviews and reports collected in the conservative monthly magazine *Hamshahri Ayeh*,[63] published by the Tehran Municipality, a few months earlier.[64] In one interview, ʿAlī Sarlak (b. 1971), a mid-ranking cleric, upholds the sanctity of the private sphere, evidenced by a long string of hadiths and opinions issued by past authorities.[65] In another interview, Ḥasan Iskandarī, a mid-ranking cleric who teaches in Qum, elaborates on the noble genealogy of upholding the private sphere in Islamic thought, drawing on numerous examples from the Prophet's life and textual references culled from the Qur'an, including Q. 24:27: *O ye who believe! enter not houses other than your own, until ye have asked permission and saluted those in them . . .* [66] In a separate interview, Mohsen Imani, a sociologist at Tarbiat Modares University in Tehran, decries the defamation of individuals in public outings of private lives, a trend that has benefited significantly from the growing presence of social media. Citing the writings of Mūsā Ghaḍanfarābādī (b. 1966), a mid-ranking cleric, member of the legal committee of the Iranian parliament and currently president of the Tehran Revolutionary Court, Imani argues that prying into the private has become a global disease (*bīmārī-i jahānī*) that must be addressed through education.[67]

What is in evidence in contemporary Iran is the emergence of a public sphere, which, although severely delimited and by no means pluralistic, cannot be ignored. Ideological cleavages are not evaluated or resolved on a theoretical register alone. Competing ideologies govern political acts, and precepts are translated into concrete instantiations of governance. Elaborate knots twine doctrine, practice and institution to such a degree that it is no longer possible to interpret political acts without regard for internal ideological debates. Concepts are contingent and unstable, and in tandem with changing material contexts. J. G. A. Pocock has written that history (that is, all written historiography which may be understood as conservative or liberal in its intention and effect) can be written 'only in political societies with the capacity to manage their history in the present and, as a necessary accompaniment, to review and renew it in the perceived past'.[68] That political thought is fully contextualised in post-revolutionary Iran is an articulation of sovereignty, of which process the debate presented here is emblematic.

APPENDIX

Commanding Right, Association and Party Formation*

MUṢTAFĀ TĀJZĀDA

Commanding right and forbidding wrong, which is fostering a type of commitment and responsibility among individuals toward their society . . . is an Islamic principle. It is an integral part of Islamic teachings . . . and in the field of jurisprudence, it is regularly invoked on a par with prayer, fasting, pilgrimage and *jihād*, commercial law, personal status law, surrogacy law, representation, judgement, testimony, divine punishment and retribution (although, unfortunately, it is now a hundred years that it has been dropped from manuals of practice).[1] According to this principle, every individual bears a degree of responsibility vis-à-vis his/her family and society. The commitment is a grave one on both the practical and conceptual fronts, as it requires a certain competency, which, in turn, demands two important requisites. The first is awareness, expertise and social insight, so that one may be excluded from those for whom 'what corrupts them is greater than what redeems them'. The second is temperance, collaboration and efficacy. The first regards knowledge and insight and the second power.

Knowledge, the first requisite, expects psychological and sociological insight, and the second, power, demands association,

* Translation from the Persian by Daryoush Mohammad Poor, Senior Research Associate, Institute of Ismaili Studies.

[1] In juridical writings, the *risāla ʿamaliyya* (manual of practice), is a distinct genre distinguished by its lay audience. It provides instruction on quotidian matters for ordinary believers, and emphasises the need to emulate a living guide (*marjaʿ al-taqlīd*). The *risāla ʿamaliyya* is also distinguished by its relatively late (nineteenth-century) origin, that is, coeval with the rise of the office of *marjaʿ al-taqlīd*. As such, it is an integral component of the formalisation of hierarchical authority among Shiʿi *ʿulamā*'; see Devin J. Stewart, 'Islamic Juridical Hierarchies and the Office of *Marjaʿ al-taqlīd*', in Lynda Clarke, ed., *Shīʿite Heritage: Essays on Classical and Modern Traditions* (Binghamton, NY, 2001), pp. 154–5.

institutionalisation, amassing means and tools, and influence at the highest levels of society . . . Insight must be social, group-oriented, cooperative and associational; institutionalisation, organisation and division of labour are necessary; and on another front, decisiveness, determination, efficacy and resolution are in order. Like the regard for insight, the practical regard of this social objective demands association and cooperation. In general, association (*taʿāwun*) is a valorised principle in Islam. This principle is the justification for commanding right, both in terms of its knowledge requirement and its practical implementation.

The popular perception of the duty of commanding right is that we indulge in nitpicking regarding people's attire, appearance, clothing and hairstyle. However, these fall within the domain of individual liberties, which is separate and distinct from the societal zone. 'May God curse the Khawārij for inflicting such hardship upon themselves' . . . O forbidding wrong! How many wrongs have been committed in your name!

Combating wrong requires a practicable plan. Just as politics and economics are governed by their own rules that must be observed, so too combating corruption . . . Commanding right is not compulsory (*taʿabudī*) because every ailment has a remedy that must be implemented judiciously. And anyway, we cannot proceed blindly on this matter: attention must be paid to [the relationship between] action and reaction.[2]

According to Muṭahharī, unlike almost all secondary rules of Islam that relate to worship and are compulsory (such as prayer, fasting, pilgrimage, alms-giving, etc), commanding right and forbidding wrong, which demands social responsibility and engagement for Muslims, is a voluntary and liberating obligation that rests on knowledge. [B]ut unfortunately, too many crimes have been committed in the name of this injunction in the course of history. Muṭahharī has expressed these ideas on various occasions. Moreover, he has repeatedly explained that the necessary condition and requirement for the person performing the duty of commanding right and forbidding wrong is to have knowledge and insight so that the likelihood of

[2] Murtaḍā Muṭahharī, *Yāddāsht-hāyi Ustād Muṭahharī, Vol. I* (Tehran, Ṣadrā, 1998), pp. 247–52.

having a positive impact and circumventing wrongdoing and corruption will be higher when resorting to this religious/rational duty.

The important point in his recently published writings is that, firstly, he considers the acquisition of knowledge for the purpose of commanding right, a 'social, collective, association and party-based' issue and maintains that drawing from different disciplines of knowledge such as sociology and psychology is necessary in these matters. Moreover, he believes that acting upon the duty is also dependent upon and conditioned by collective, associative and party-based action. That is, he believes that the performance of the duty will be enhanced with organisation, regimentation and division of labour – the quintessence of association. In other words, the foundation of his argument is that one of the greatest illustrations of *Help ye one another in righteousness and piety* (Q. 5:2) is the forming of political parties. Muṭahharī rightly believed that, armed with a comprehensive and well-conceived plan, one can propagate the good and prevent corruption and wrongdoing. In very clear terms, in the contemporary world, institutions such as political parties are capable of bringing together experts from a variety of fields, to collaborate and produce a master plan and implement it upon election to office. This is the most rational and efficacious path to commanding right and forbidding wrong.

Moreover, respected readers know that due to a myriad of reasons, including political obstacles, governmental opposition, the high costs of party activity and the lack of commensurate reward, poor management in political parties and, finally, legislative shortcomings and a legal framework unconducive to a party-based electoral system, a very small percentage of the citizenry – even among the political elite – are prepared to join political parties and play an active role in them. Now, if the attention of Muslims is diverted to the fact that one of the best venues for commanding right in our time is party activity – as Āyat Allāh Muntadhirī has also emphasised in his recent fatwas – then a significant transformation in that structure may become possible. That is, a proper drive among a sizeable portion of the citizenry for membership in existing political parties, or for forming new ones, may be realised. As commanding right is obligatory (*wājib*), then its prerequisite (creating organisations and groups for making known the good and the wrong, and for promoting one and discouraging the other) may also be considered obligatory.

NOTES

1 Tājzāda began his political career as a student activist in the 1970s. Following the revolution of 1979, he held several government posts, including special adviser to Iran's president, Mohammad Khatami, from 2004 to 2009. He was imprisoned for contesting the election of 2009, and remained in Evin Prison until 2016. For his political biography, see Muhammad Sahimi, 'Patriots and Reformists: Behzad Nabavi and Mostafa Tajzadeh', *Tehran Bureau*, 11 August 2009, https://www.pbs.org/wgbh/pages/frontline/tehranbureau/2009/08/patriots-and-reformists-behzad-nabavi-and-mostafa-tajzadeh.html.

2 Muṣṭafā Tājzāda, 'Amr bi maʿrūf, taʿāwun wa taḥazzub', *Yās-i naw* (8 Tīr 1382 Sh./30 June 2003); reprinted in Muṣṭafā Tājzāda, *Jawāmiʿ-i musalmān, dimukrāsī wa Bin Lādin*, ed. Muḥammad Turkamān (Tehran, 2004), pp. 200–202.

3 For English language sources on Reformist ideology, see Daniel Brumberg, *Reinventing Khomeini: The Struggle for Reform in Iran* (Chicago, IL, 2003), pp. 152–252; Eskandar Sadeghi-Boroujerdi, *Revolution and its Discontents: Political Thought and Reform in Iran* (Cambridge, 2019).

4 For more on Khomeini's innovative take on Qur'anic exegesis and his transformative role in modern Islamic political thought, see Neguin Yavari, '*Tafsīr* and the Mythology of Islamic Fundamentalism', in Andreas Görke and Johanna Pink, eds, *Tafsīr and Islamic Intellectual History: Exploring the Boundaries of a Genre* (Oxford, 2014), pp. 289–319.

5 Reinhard Schulze, *A Modern History of the Islamic World*, tr. Azizeh Azodi (New York, 2002), p. 292.

6 For an insightful discussion of the tug of war between sharia and constitution in modern Islamic states, see Knut S. Vikør, 'The Shariʿa and the Nation State: Who Can Codify Islamic Law', in Bjørn Olav Utvik and Knut S. Vikør, eds, *The Middle East in a Globalized World: Papers from the Fourth Nordic Conference on Middle Eastern Studies, Oslo, 1998* (London, 2000), pp. 220–50.

7 Michael Cook, *Commanding Right and Forbidding Wrong in Islamic Thought* (Cambridge, 2000).

8 Ibid., p. 534, paraphrasing Ruhollah Khomeini, *Taḥrīr al-wasīla* (Beirut, 1981), vol. I, pp. 472–6.

9 Miṣbāḥ Yazdī later gained fame as an arch-conservative hardliner, and the clerical rock behind the bellicose rhetoric and radical politics of Mahmoud Ahmadinejad (president from 2005 to 2013), as well as a staunch supporter of Iran's current *walī-yi faqīh* Khamenei. For a sample of his views, see Muḥammad Taqī Miṣbāḥ Yazdī, *Jān-hā fadā-yi dīn*, ed. Muḥammad Mahdī Nādirī Qumī (Qum, 2004); Neguin Yavari, 'Ayatollah Mohammad Taqi Mesbah Yazdi', in Michael R. Fischbach, ed., *Biographical Encyclopedia of the Modern Middle East and North Africa* (New York, 2007), vol. 2, pp. 532–4.

10 Bahman Shaʿbānzāda, *Tārīkh-i shafāhī-yi Madrasa-yi Ḥaqqānī* (Tehran, 2005), pp. 153–64; and Maḥmūd Riḍā Dāvarī, 'Intiqādāt-i Shahīd Bihishtī az Miṣbāḥ Yazdī', *Khabar* Online, 9 Tīr 1393 Sh./30 June 2014, https://www.khabaronline.ir/detail/362959/Politics/parties.

11 Muḥammad Ḥusayn Bihishtī, 'Bakhshī az sukhanrānī-yi shahīd Dr. Bihishtī dar bāra-yi ahammiyyat-i amr-i bi maʿrūf wa nahy az munkar: Masʾūliyyat-i

mutaqābil dar jāmiʿa-yi Islāmī', *Mardumsālārī*, Thursday, 27 June 2013, pp. 10–11.

12 Cook, *Commanding Right*, p. 505.

13 Ibid., pp. 532–3.

14 Ibid., p. 506.

15 Ibid. p. 545; see also Article 8 of the Iranian constitution, *Qānūn-i asāsī-i Jumhūrī-i Islāmī-i Īrān* (Tehran, 1990), p. 16 (for the English translation, see http://fis-iran.org/en/resources/legaldoc/constitutionislamic).

16 Cook, *Commanding Right*, p. 515.

17 Ibid., p. 560.

18 For the same trend in the Sunni world, see, for example, Frank E. Vogel, 'The Public and Private in Saudi Arabia: Restrictions on the Powers of Committees for Ordering the Good and Forbidding the Evil', *Social Research: An International Quarterly of Social Sciences* 70, no. 3 (2003), pp. 749–68.

19 Cook, *Commanding Right*, p. 542.

20 Ibid., p. 532; Shahrough Akhavi, 'The Thought and Role of Ayatollah Hossein'ali Montazeri in the Politics of Post-1979 Iran', *Iranian Studies* 41, no. 5 (2008), pp. 645–66, reference is from pp. 654–5; Sussan Siavoshi, *Montazeri: The Life and Times of Iran's Revolutionary Ayatollah* (Cambridge, 2017), p. 218.

21 Tājzāda, 'Amr bi maʿrūf, taʿāwun wa taḥazzub', p. 200.

22 Throughout, I use Abdullah Yusuf Ali's translation of the Qur'an, *The Holy Qur'an* (Ware, 2000); also available online at http://www.islam101.com/quran/yusufAli/.

23 Tājzāda, 'Amr bi maʿrūf, taʿāwun wa taḥazzub', p. 202.

24 For the current political line-up in Iran, see Farzan Sabet, 'The Islamic Republic's Political Elite and Syria: Understanding What they Think through Iranian Media Narratives', *IranPolitik* blog, June 2013, pp. 7–8, http://www.iranmediaresearch.org/en/research/download/1422 (link no longer available).

25 This faction is headed by Farīd al-Dīn Ḥaddād ʿĀdil. His sister is the daughter-in-law of Ali Khamenei, leader of the Islamic Republic. His better-known father, Ghulām ʿAlī, was speaker of parliament from 2004 to 2008; he has served as advisor to Khamenei since 2008.

26 ʿAlī Rajabī and ʿAbd al-Muṭahhar Muḥammadkhānī, 'Naqd ba mathāba-yi nahy az munkar', *Panjara* 3, no. 96 (June 2011), p. 20.

27 Rafsanjani's own party, Ḥizb-i Kārguzārān-i Sāzandigī, generally referred to as the Constructionists, celebrated its twentieth anniversary in 2015. An entire issue of the weekly news magazine *Ṣidā* was devoted to the genesis and development of Ḥizb-i Kārguzārān-i Sāzandigī. (*Ṣidā*'s editor, Muḥammad Qūchānī, vice chair of the party's political committee, broke with the Reformists following Ahmadinejad's election to office in 2004.) See *Ṣidā* 47 (24 Murdād 1394 Sh./15 August 2015), pp. 16–34.

28 The newspaper *Armān-i imrūz* is published by the Arman Public Relations Institute. See http://armanpr.com/#.

29 For more on him, see 'Elias Hazrati', Wikipedia Farsi, http://fa.wikipedia.org/; Fayyāẓ Zāhid, 'Iliyās Haẓratī dar yik nigāh', *Aftab*, http://www.aftabir.com.

30 http://www.etemad.ir/ (p. 11 in most issues).

31 See Murād Thaqafī, 'Aḥzāb wa junbish-hāyi Islāmī: Yik bastar wa dū rūyā'?' *Goft-o-gū* 67 (Tīr 1394 Sh./July 2015), pp. 105–25, http://goftogu.com/; Ṣādiq

Zībā-Kalām, 'Chirā ḥizb nadārīm: Raddiyya-yi bar ingāra-hāyi ma'mūl dar bāb-i taḥazzub dar Iran', *Mihrnāma* 23 (1394 Sh./2015), pp. 68–72.

32 Freedom to associate and to form political parties is guaranteed by Article 26 of the Iranian constitution: 'It shall be allowed to form parties, societies, political or professional associations and Islamic or other religious societies of the recognized minorities, provided that they do not violate the principles of freedom, independence, national unity, Islamic standards and essentials of the Islamic Republic. No one may be stopped from participating in them or forced to participate in one of them', http://fis-iran.org/en/resources/legaldoc/constitutionislamic. For the Persian original see *Qānūn-i asāsī-i Jumhūrī-i Islāmī-i Īrān*, p. 24.

33 For a comprehensive survey of differing views on political parties in Iran and explanations for the parties' instability, see the articles and interviews collected in a forum in *Mihrnāma*, Iran's premier political and current affairs monthly, 'Nāpāydārī-i aḥzāb', *Mihrnāma* 3, no. 23 (1391 Sh./2012), pp. 67–92; and for an alternative view, see Editorial Staff, 'Hizb-i rūḥāniyūn-i inqilābī: Ḥizb-i Jumhūrī-yi Islāmī chi naqshī dar siyāsat-i Īrān dāsht?' *Muthallath* 5, no. 224 (1393 Sh./2014), pp. 44–5.

34 The Tudeh Party remains active, if rather ineffectively, in exile; see http://www.tudehpartyiran.org/.

35 The literature on the left in Iranian politics is vast. Ervand Abrahamian's *Iran: Between Two Revolutions* (Princeton, NJ, 1982) offers a perceptive history of leftist politics in the twentieth century, and Stephanie Cronin's edited volume *Reformers and Revolutionaries in Modern Iran: New Perspectives on the Iranian Left* (London, 2004) covers the later period. I have chosen here to focus on the perspective on offer in Farhang Jahanpour's short article, mainly because of its contemporaneity with the events under discussion; see Farhang Jahanpour, 'Iran: The Rise and Fall of the Tudeh Party', *The World Today* 40, no. 4 (1984), pp. 152–9, reference is from p. 153.

36 See chapter 2 ('The Nature of the Party System') of Hassan Rezaei's 'The Politics in Post-Revolution Iran: With Special Reference to Khatami's Presidency' (PhD dissertation, University of Pune, 2011), http://hdl.handle.net/10603/2024.

37 Muḥammad Jawād Rūḥ, 'Tajruba-yi Ḥizb-i Jumhūrī-yi Islāmī dar guft wa gū bā Muḥammad Riḍā Bihishtī', *Mihrnāma* 23 (2012), pp. 88–92.

38 Muḥammad Jawād Rūḥ, 'Ra'īs jumhūr-i mashrūṭah-khwāh yā mashrūṭah-khwāhī-i ra'īs jumhūr?' *Ṣidā* (7 Shahrīwar 1394 Sh./29 August 2015), pp. 49–51; and for more on the history of the Democrat Party, see Ralph Kauz, *Politische Parteien und Bevölkerung in Iran: Die Ḥezb-e Demukrāt-e Īrān und ihr Führer Qavāmo s-Salṭanä* (Berlin, 1995), pp. 154–95.

39 The fall of the Islamic Republican Party has been the subject of countless debates for the past two decades. For a succinct summary, see Muḥammad Ḥusayn Mihrzād, 'Sarniwishtī ki bā Ḥizb-i Jumhūrī wa Jāmi'a-yi Rawhāniyyat-i Mubāriz nasākht', *Etemad*, no. 3255, 28 May 2015, p. 11, http://www.etemadnewspaper.ir/Default.aspx?NPN_Id=159&PageNO=11.

40 The competing views of Iran's political elite on the authority and definition of *wilāyat-i faqīh* and their corresponding positions on political parties is discussed in detail in Ḥamīd Riḍā Ẓarīfīniyā's *Kālbudshikāfī-i jināh-hā-yi*

siyāsī-yi Iran, 135–78, intro. Muṣṭafā Tājzāda (Tehran, 1999), pp. 173–206, esp. pp. 182–6.

41 Ruhollah Khomeini, *Islam and Revolution: Writings and Declarations of Imam Khomeini (1941–1980)*, tr. and annot. Hamid Algar (Berkeley, CA, 1981), p. 40.

42 Ibid., pp. 40–149, reference is from p. 83.

43 Mihrzād, 'Sarniwishtī'.

44 Ibid.

45 Ibrahim Moussawi, *Shi'ism and the Democratisation Process in Iran: With a Focus on Wilayat-i Faqih* (London, 2011), pp. 141–64.

46 For the current line-up of parties see Mohammad Hassan Khani, 'Political Parties in the Islamic Republic of Iran: A Short Review', *Iran Review* (17 July 2012), http://www.iranreview.org/content/Iran_Spectrum/Political-Parties-in-the-Islamic-Republic-of-Iran-A-Short-Review.htm.

47 Rezaei, 'The Politics in Post-Revolution Iran', chapter 2.

48 For background on the organisation, see 'Jame'e-ye Ruhaniyyat-e Mobarez-e Tehran: The Society of the Militant Clergy of Tehran (JRM)', Iran Data Portal Online, http://irandataportal.syr.edu/the-society-of-the-militant-clergy-of-tehran-jrm. Importantly, the Society was formed by Rafsanjani and Khamenei before the revolution of 1979. For more on its timeline until the present, see Ḥāmid Ṭabībī, 'Shaykh-hāyi siyāsat pisha', *Shargh*, no. 2404, 22 September 2015, pp. 6–7.

49 Explanations for Rafsanjani's volte-face are plentiful. Examples include Firishta Sādāt Ittifāghfar and Ṣādiq Zībākalām, *Hāshimi bidūn-i rūtūsh: Panj sāl guftugū bā Hāshimī Rafsanjānī* (Tehran, 2008); Riḍā Ṣan'atī, *Hāshimī dar sāl-i 88* (Tehran, 2011); Umīd Adīb, 'Siyāsat warzī-hā-yi Hāshimī', *Tarāz* 7 (Mordad 1392 Sh./July 2013), pp. 10–11; articles collected in Editorial Staff, 'Amalgarā'ī ba jāy-i dīplumāsī-yi inqilābī', *Muthallath* 86 (2011), pp. 66–8; Yūsuf Sayfī, 'Hāshimī wa Facebook', *Muthallath* 129 (20 Khordad 1391 Sh./10 June 2012), pp. 37–8; and Muṣṭafā Ṣādiqī, 'Rūzigār-i jadīd-i Āyat Allāh', *Muthallath* 178 (10 Tir 1392 Sh./2 July 2013), pp. 29–31.

50 Muḥsin Āzmūda, 'Interview with 'Alī-Riḍā Bihishtī', *Etemad*, no. 3279, 28 June 2015, pp. 8–9, http://www.etemadnewspaper.ir/Default.aspx?NPN_Id=183&PageNO=8.

51 Ibid.

52 Khomeini, *Islam and Revolution*, pp. 48, 92–3.

53 On the Christian sediment in modern political language as it relates to the concept of sovereignty, see Martti Koskenniemi, 'Conclusion: Vocabularies of Sovereignty – Powers of a Paradox', in Hent Kalmo and Quentin Skinner, eds, *Sovereignty in Fragments: The Past, Present and Future of a Contested Concept* (Cambridge, 2010), pp. 222–42, esp. pp. 223–5.

54 One recent example is Muhammad Qasim Zaman, 'The Sovereignty of God in Modern Islamic Thought', *Journal of the Royal Asiatic Society* 25, no. 3 (2015), pp. 389–418. Peter Mandaville notes the same in his review of *Islamic Political Thought: An Introduction*, edited by Gerhard Bowering, *Journal of Islamic Studies* 29, no. 3 (2018), pp. 476–8. For one example of Shi'i thought on popular sovereignty, see 'Alī Akbar Hāshimī Rafsanjānī, *Mardumsālārī az dīdgāh-i Hāshimī*, ed. Mihrdād Siyāwushī-Far (Tehran, 2015).

55 Schulze, *A Modern History of the Islamic World*, pp. 1–13.
56 Armando Salvatore, 'The Sociology of Islam: Precedents and Perspectives', *Sociology of Islam* 1 (2013), pp. 7–13. See, as well, Muhammad Khalid Masud and Armando Salvatore, 'Western Scholars of Islam on the Issue of Modernity', in Muhammad Khalid Masud, Armando Salvatore and Martin van Bruinessen, eds, *Islam and Modernity: Key Issues and Debates* (Edinburgh, 2009), pp. 36–53.
57 That definition of sovereignty belongs to Hent Kalmo and Quentin Skinner. See their 'Introduction: A Concept in Fragments', in *Sovereignty in Fragments*, pp. 1–25; the reference is from p. 7.
58 Muḥammad ʿAlī Bahmanī Qājār, 'Ḥuqūq, āzādī, wa amniyyat-i shakhṣī', *Gofto-gu* 62 (Azar 1392 Sh./December 2013), pp. 33–47.
59 Hasan Rouhani, 'Nahy az munkar tanhā ʿalayh-i zanān nīst', *Aftab*, no. 4302, 13 April 2015, p. 3.
60 http://www.iranianlivetv.com/tanhai-leila.php (link no longer available).
61 'Tanhāʾī-yi Laylā', Episode 24, minutes 20–24, http://www.iranianlivetv.com/videomotion.php?tv=k23ZzTfQLmQY1DcCyeK (link no longer available).
62 'Tanhāʾī-yi Laylā' was discussed extensively in journals and newspapers from across the political spectrum: Editorial Staff, 'Bumbī ki tarraqa shud: Parwanda-yi barāyi siryāl-i Tanhāʾī-yi Laylā', *Hamshahri Jawan* 11, no. 517 (31 Murdād 1394 Sh./22 August 2015), pp. 40–45; Nasrin Sharif, 'Suqūṭ-i āzād: Dar ḥāshiya-i siryāl-i Tanhāʾī-yi Laylā', *Ṣidā* 48 (31 Murdād 1394 Sh./22 August 2015), p. 113; interviews with the show's actors in the weekly tabloid, *Bi sūy-i iftikhār* 314 (9 Shahrīvar 1394 Sh./31 August 2015), p. 10; and Editorial Staff, 'Tanhāʾī-yi Laylā', *Panjara* 7, no. 246 (31 Murdād 1394 Sh./22 August 2015), p. 78; Amīn Mīrzāʾī, 'Hama-yi gāf-hāyi yik siryāl-i bi ẓāhir madhhabī: Dar naqd-i Tanhāʾī-yi Laylā', *Alef* (2 Shahrīvar 1394 Sh./24 August 2015), http://alef.ir/vdcjiye8yuqehmz.fsfu.html?290650; Editorial Staff, 'Sarguzasht-i Laylā-yi badbakht-tar az Sitāyish', *Tabnak* (8 Shahrīvar 1394 Sh./30 August 2015), http://www.tabnak.ir/fa/news/527823.
63 *Hamshahri Ayeh*, http://ayeh.hmg.ir5.
64 Editorial Staff, 'Ḥarīm-i khuṣūṣī, nigāh mamnūʿ', *Hamshahri Ayeh* 35 (Isfand 1393 Sh./March 2015), pp. 50–60.
65 Ḥasan Ḥasanzāda, 'Interview with Ḥujjat al-Islām ʿAlī Sarlak: Ābirū-yi mardum khaṭṭ-i qirmiz ast', ibid., pp. 52–3.
66 Ḥasan Ḥasanzāda, 'Interview with Ḥujjat al-Islām Ḥasan Iskandarī: Lā tajassasū', ibid., pp. 50–51.
67 Amīn Yigānah, 'Interview with Dr. Muḥsin Īmānī: Abirū-yi mardum zang-i tafrīḥ nīst', ibid., pp. 56–7; Mohsen Imani also has a webpage: http://www.modares.ac.ir/~eimanim.
68 J.G.A. Pocock, Review of *The History of Politics and the Politics of History*, by Quentin Skinner, *Common Knowledge* 10, no. 3 (2004), pp. 532–50; the quote is from p. 549.

5

The Limits of a 'Fixed' Qur'an: The Iranian Religious Intellectual Movement and Islamic New Theology*

BANAFSHEH MADANINEJAD

DESPITE THE details that differentiate the main thinkers in the Iranian Religious Intellectual Movement,[1] an important unifying characteristic is their interest in creating the epistemological category of a historically situated Qur'an. This is primarily done by employing a series of hermeneutic strategies similar to the group of strategies used in Western Muslim feminist exegesis. The feminist toolbox is populated by the historical contextualisation method, the intra-textual method and the *tawḥīdic* paradigm.[2] Not surprisingly, the push to understand the historical circumstances of Qur'anic revelation is a concern that the three Iranian religious intellectuals covered in this chapter – Abdolkarim Soroush (b. 1945), Mohsen Kadivar (b. 1959) and Abū'l-Qāsim Fanā'ī (b. 1959) – share with Western Muslim feminist scholars. In works of Western feminist exegesis, Aysha Hidayatullah sees the historical contextualisation method as comprising the following series of hermeneutic strategies:

> researching the occasion of a verse's revelation (*sabab al-nuzūl*);[3] distinguishing between prescriptive and descriptive verses of the

* I wish to extend my gratitude to Kamran Aghaie, Roy Casagranda, Abū'l-Qāsim Fanā'ī, Hanan Hammad, Shehnaz Haqqani, Phil Hopkins, Mohsen Kadivar and Omar Rivera for their invaluable help in reading various versions of this chapter, providing forums where the contents of the paper could be presented and for being tirelessly available as a sounding board.

> Qur'an; ... distinguishing between universal and particular verses; and identifying historical situations that shaped the context of revelation in seventh-century Arabic and subsequent exegesis of the Qur'an.[4]

I will call this last strategy 'the historical situating of the *tanzīl* process (i.e. of the sending down of the Qur'an)'. The Iranian religious intellectuals not only use some of the same strategies utilised by the feminists, but have added a few more to the greater Muslim reformist toolkit. Unlike their feminist counterparts, however, the Iranian intellectuals have gone a step further and tackled the theological consequences which result from using unorthodox Qur'anic hermeneutics. The least problematic and most promising theological consequence results from the strategy they share with the feminists: the historical situating of the *tanzīl* process.

At least a certain wing of Muslim feminist scholars (Amina Wadud, Kecia Ali and Aysha Hidayatullah, to name a few) are no longer sure if the Qur'an can deliver the gender justice they have been seeking. Hidayatullah senses that 'no amount of interpretation [can] make the text definitively cohere with [the feminist's] contemporary sense of justice'.[5] What does it mean, she contemplates, 'when we seek a standard of justice that is "beyond" the Qur'anic text?' Hidayatullah's particular choice is to embrace a 'radical uncertainty'.[6] For the Iranian Religious Intellectual Movement, when certain Qur'anic verses create what Khaled Abou El-Fadl calls a 'conscientious-pause', when a crisis of conscience results from a moral impasse in the Qur'anic text,[7] the choice is not uncertainty, but to 'abide by the dictates of [one's] conscience'.[8] When hermeneutic acrobatics have reached the limits of their usefulness in explaining away, for instance, the sexist parts of the Qur'an, choosing to bring one's conscience to bear on the matter can lead to theological contradictions. In other words, the epistemological source of the radical uncertainty Hidayatullah points to can at least partially be traced back to theological contradictions. One of the most pronounced theological contradictions appears when subsequent downgrading of the importance of certain verses threatens to contradict the universally held belief about the Qur'an's 'fixedness'. How are we to square this new way of reading with the Qur'an's self-referential claims to completeness and perfection? Soroush, Kadivar and Fanāʾī have envisioned different theological innovations to smooth out the ensuing inconsistencies. In other words, new hermeneutic strategies have solicited what the religious intellectuals have coined a New Theology. Although the thinkers seldom engage directly with issues of gender justice, acceptance of religious difference, lack of religious belief, or more comprehensively an appreciation for alterity to ground their work, these scholars' hermeneutics has the potential to pave the way for a new, inclusive imaginary and possibly a more progressive Islamic theology.

Before we discuss hermeneutic strategies and ensuing new theologies, we should perhaps not only spend some time pondering the methodology but also the efficacy of the Iranian Religious Intellectual Movement. One could argue that this convergence of the religious and the intellectual in a movement could be considered oxymoronic, especially in light of the widely available secular alternatives and the ongoing discussion around whether or not secularity should be considered a precondition for critical thinking.[9] One could also argue that even if we allow that secularity ought not be considered a precondition for critical thinking and that being religious does not exclude one from serious intellectual work,[10] the Iranian Religious Intellectual Movement should still be considered a failure because it 'is taking its practitioners to a place they did not initially intend to go to'.[11] Yet another possible critique of the movement could be that it has failed to yield much in the way of tangible, on the ground, democratic political change. Considering these possible objections to the movement, this chapter will spend some time describing what the movement has accomplished so far, arguing that one of its great achievements is the expansion of what Charles Taylor calls an Immanent Frame – a space where diversity and what Taylor calls the 'mutual fragilisation' of different kinds of religiosity can be discussed.[12]

Methodology: The Overriding Question

Classifying the thinkers within a movement is a methodological challenge. How do we begin to identify competing traditions within a movement? One approach could focus on individual thinkers, assessing their work by considering the strengths and weaknesses of the arguments they make. Basing the analysis of a movement on a study of the works of several great thinkers is instructive, but it may be repetitive if two or more of the thinkers advance similar lines of reasoning. An added issue could be the lack of an overriding thread that ties the thinkers together.

Another approach could focus on traditions of thought and assess the weaknesses and strengths of particular traditions or groups of thinkers who have trends in common. For instance, Fanāʾī can be placed alongside Kadivar, as part of a faction that still operates within the confines of orthodoxy, even if from the margins. Early Soroush and early Mujtahid Shabestari (b. 1936) could be placed in the same marginally orthodox category for the work they conducted during the early to mid-1990s. However, on the other side of the spectrum, since later Soroush and later Shabestari are understood by many to have exited the realms of orthodoxy altogether,[13] they could be placed in a more radical category. As we can see, this second approach is also problematic. It relies heavily on being able to identify who is a member of a tradition and who is not. Also, the method makes the most sense if members of a tradition speak with one voice on issues. As is evident in the case of Soroush and Shabestari, the categorisation is only complicated by the fact that thresholds are murky and multiple, and thinkers might decide to move across them.

A third possible option for the study of the Religious Intellectual Movement – the one adopted in this chapter – could focus on each thinker's response to a particular question while not excluding the conjunctive use of the two approaches delineated above. The question we focus on in this chapter can be summarised as follows: given that the Religious Intellectual Movement in Iran has taken to using some unorthodox hermeneutic strategies to jump over the wall of revelation, and given that some of these strategies have created theological inconsistencies that the movement has subsequently tried to resolve with a New Theology, how has this process pushed the boundaries of what is universally understood to be a 'fixed' Qur'an?

The Iranian Religious Intellectual Movement's Legacy: Expanding the Immanent Frame

The Religious Intellectual Movement is composed of an array of thinkers who may individually resist common affiliation. What unites them, however, is a critical mindset and the set of hermeneutic strategies and rhetorical practices they use in their commitment to both rationality and religion. To varying degrees, the thinkers employ binary concepts – such as minimal versus maximal religion, accidentals or essentials versus non-essentials of religion – or categories like the 'heart/main message/*lubb-i kalām*/*maqāṣid*' of the religion. They believe in the need for a transcendent life, they employ Gadamerian philosophical hermeneutics which question presuppositions and biases, and they champion ethical intuitionism. All these they use to destabilise other concepts, such as the idea of a static Qur'an, epistemic certainty, *taʿābud* (blind religious commitment), univocity of meaning and the universal applicability of non-essential Qur'anic verses.

The movement's simultaneous pledge to religious and intellectual commitments could be construed as a possible epistemological contradiction. In fact, I argue that it is exactly this defining characteristic of the movement – its unwavering commitment to wedding the transcendent and the immanent – that clues us in to why it has been successful. Western secularism rejects the idea of a reconciliation between religious commitment (*taʿābud*) and rational commitment (*taʿaqqul*), where religious commitment is defined as 'obedience' to divine law (*aḥkām*) and rational commitment as intellectual activity. Secularism considers the coming together of the two paradoxical. Mostafa Malekian (b. 1956), a well-known former member of the movement, claims that it is exactly the impossibility of internally reconciling these two commitments that caused his exodus.[14] Taking an evidentialist position towards religion, Malekian argues that since religion occasionally requires the shutting down of rational faculties, a compromise between our rational and religious commitments are at best questionable.[15] The idea that one can either be rational or religious but that a liminal, in-between position is either not valid or at best not well understood would not encounter much resistance. But what if this reconciliation was less about a resolution with definitive, clear-cut answers and more about the dialogic nature of stepping into our own histories and identities in a post-secular world. What if it is not as much about moving in-between religious, secular, post-secular sensibilities? When we ask about the legacy of the Iranian Religious Intellectual Movement, perhaps the object of study should not be so much the corpus of the work itself but the Immanent Frame the work has affected. What is being suggested here is this: that when we think of the impact of the movement, perhaps we should not be focusing on what the movement has achieved in terms of actual liberation from tyrannical institutions and structures, but on its cultural impact.

The Immanent Frame, Taylor argues, is 'not usually, or even mainly a set of *beliefs* which we entertain about our predicament . . . rather it is the sensed context in which we develop our beliefs'.[16] 'The sensed context or immanent frame for a secularist and a person who adheres to one orthodoxy or another is constricted, closed – there is limited room for entertaining what the world looks like through the other side's lens'. We are told that the choices are clear: religious commitment (*taʿābud*) or rational commitment (*taʿaqqul*). Members of the religious intellectual movement perceive themselves as being caught between two poles, pulled at once towards the opening of transcendence and 'the closure of immanence'; they feel 'cross-pressured,' pulled in both directions, caught up somewhere between an 'open' and a 'closed' perspective of the world – and pushed to choose one over the other.[17] The movement's goals can be summarised as a reconciling of these two sensibilities. We spend most of our lives immersed in what Taylor calls the 'immanence of ordinary life'.[18] But there are moments of 'fullness'. 'Fullness' to Taylor is the sense that something larger or more deeply meaningful is out there.

> [T]o most moderns this sense of fullness of the world is a strong sense of wonder that goes beyond everyday concerns about health, material prosperity, politics, even justice . . . [I]t is typically episodic, available only for moments, perhaps aided by ritual but sometimes just surprising us . . . [I]t is less available now than

> it used to be, when it seemed routinely the case that the material world was not all that there was.[19]

But this affirmation of ordinary life has not led to the disappearance of the need for transcendence. Given Iran's rich and long-running culture of internal transformation (think Sufi poetry), it seems that in spite of new social imaginaries like the market, democracy and the public sphere, the members of the movement are still not ready to limit the good to human flourishing.[20] But must religious commitment and rational commitment be reconciled through a formulised, 'mapped-out' solution? The end result of this complex and expanded immanent frame (what I argue the movement has created in the Iranian public sphere) is what Taylor calls the 'mutual fragilization' of both options.

> [N]o matter how we might differently resolve the issues for ourselves of faith or belief, living in pure immanence or reorienting ourselves to some understanding of transcendent being, we still cannot escape the fact that we live with others who resolve it [the problem of rational vs. religious commitment] differently; and this fact has significance for the quality of our own convictions, no matter how securely we might think we hold them. The options . . . have been mutually 'fragilized'.[21]

Through this growing mutual fragilization, what the Iranian Religious Intellectual Movement has made possible is a move, not towards consensus and uniformity (that we must either choose *taʿaqqul* or *taʿābud*) but a respectful coexistence through a better theorisation and understanding of the possible choices. The Iranian Religious Intellectual Movement has introduced the option of living with ambiguity and liminality.

The members of the movement, in the very act of being in conversation with each other and traversing the margins of orthodoxy, sometimes even crossing the boundaries altogether, are allowing themselves, their students and the thinking public to grow into new Islams. In this space, the orthodoxies, heterodoxies and the secular are subject to what Taylor calls 'social and ethical cross-pressures'.[22] To speak of moving beyond the religious into the secular – as so many secular intellectuals within Iran and abroad have yearned for – is to miss a large part of this complex formation altogether. What is of utmost importance here is the complexity and expansive nature of the immanent frame. This immanent frame is a necessary backdrop to growth and the resolution of different ways of being and coexistence. In this space, each thinking person who is searching gets to choose between rational and religious commitment and all of the liminal choices in-between, even if they are not able rationally to convince others of that choice.

The Qur'an as a 'Fixed' Text

What can be so problematic about 'downgrading' a handful of Qur'anic verses? The issue is this: among Muslims, there is an almost universal belief that the Qur'an, as a whole, is not only sacred but also 'fixed'; having divine origins, the Qur'an is understood to be forever applicable and its message eternally relevant. This universally held belief of a 'fixed' Qur'an means that 'rejecting any part of the Qur'an is tantamount to rejecting Islam'.[23] This belief is the reason why even 'scholars of feminist exegesis have remained unable to account for the existence of certain Qur'anic statements that appear to be neglectful or harmful to women'.[24] It is for this reason that Muslim feminist hermeneutics 'has predominantly attributed problematic meanings of the text to the interpretive errors or linguistic difficulties of human beings rather than the divine text itself'.[25] As such, downgrading certain parts of the Qur'an is considered problematic if not outright blasphemous. Although this 'fixedness' is one of the most defining features of the Qur'an in the popular imaginary, resistance to what seems, at first glance, to be a rigid and steadfast position has been a defining characteristic of reformist Islam.

In line with Hidayatullah's position, a recent work by Wadud 'openly confronts the possibility that that the Qur'an *itself* may cause violent readings', suggesting that the only choice left to the unapologetic Muslim feminist is to grapple with the Qur'an's 'textual inadequacies'.[26] What does one do with the 'fixedness' of the Qur'anic text when Q. 4:34 advises, through use of the word '*ḍaraba*', that the husband beat his wife? The current Muslim feminist toolbox of hermeneutic strategies have all fallen short of rescuing this particular Qur'anic text from its sexist and male-centred meaning. Wadud admits that 'there is no way to get around this one, even though I have tried for two decades'.[27] She finally suggests 'an intervention opposing the literal application' of sexist verses in the Qur'an.[28] This is not something strange or disruptive, since 'the collective community has always manipulated the text in concert with civilizational . . . development. We must now acknowledge that it has always been done and accept the responsibility of . . . doing so openly.'[29] And this is what the Iranian Religious Intellectual Movement has also attempted to do. What sets the Religious Intellectual Movement's work apart from that of feminists like Wadud is that the former attempt to work through the theological issues that downgrading Qur'anic verses can cause.

Hidayatullah suggests that it might be time to recognise that 'feminist interpretation may very well be inappropriate to the Qur'an'.[30] It might just be, she muses, that 'our demands [on the Qur'an] might be anachronistic and incommensurate with Qur'anic statements'.[31] 'The Qur'an perhaps cannot in the end be fully reconciled with our understandings of sexual equality and justice' and a significant reason behind this is that the standard of sexuality we demand from the Qur'an is 'specific to us and not reflected in the Qur'an'.[32] Is Hidayatullah proposing that the Qur'an is better read according to the meaning it had for its initial audience? She cannot suggest that the Qur'an (in its entirety) ought to be read 'historically' and understood according to the meaning it had for its first-/seventh-century Hijazi audience because this would have disastrous theological consequences. But she could suggest that certain verses in the Qur'an – and this is the important detail – ought to be read historically and understood according to the meaning those specific verses had for their first-/seventh-century Hijazi audience.

Consider, for instance, the case of Egyptian literary scholars, most notably Muhammad Ahmad Khalafallah (d. 1991) in the early twentieth century.[33] Khalafallah argued that authorship of texts (scripture included) bears the mark of the historical environment of its authorship, that all texts become encoded by their historical context. This goes beyond the Muʿtazilite view of the createdness of the Qur'an, which argued for the creation of the Qur'an in time. The argument here was that the Qur'an in its entirety was not only created in time but also in history.[34] What Kadivar and Fanā'ī highlight here is that we don't have to throw the baby out with the bathwater; it is possible to have a reformed reading of the Qur'an without reading the whole text historically – all we have to do is pinpoint the problematic verses and target them alone.

Reading the whole Qur'an as if it were a historical text, mimicking what Friedrich Schleiermacher (d. 1834) proposed for the Bible,[35] has unacceptable theological consequences for the Qur'an. This, however, does not keep us from reading a subset historically. But what effect does downgrading even a few verses have on the Qur'an's 'fixedness'? We will return to this question at the end of the chapter. The next few pages are dedicated to the movement's strategies and their ensuing theological innovations.

The Religious Intellectual Movement's Hermeneutic Strategies and the Resulting New Theology

Kadivar and how the time of certain verses has come to an end

To see how those from the Religious Intellectual Movement have dealt with the consequences of the historical situating of the *tanzīl* process, we turn to the works of Kadivar. According to Fazlur Rahman, someone whose methodology Kadivar holds in high esteem,[36] 'one must understand the import or meaning of a given statement by studying the historical situation or problem to which it was an answer'.[37] This study of each verse's sociohistorical context is the first step of what Fazlur Rahman called the 'twofold movement'. According to the twofold movement model, 'first one must move from the concrete case treatments of the Qur'an – taking the necessary and relevant social conditions of that time into account – to the general principles upon which the entire teaching converges'.[38] Like Rahman, Kadivar's first movement is to pinpoint the 'meaning of the Qur'an as a whole'. For Kadivar, the aim of the Qur'an, it's meaning as a whole, is to communicate the importance of compassion. Kadivar encapsulates this Qur'anic message, the spirit of the Book, in what he calls 'Compassionate Islam' (*Islām-i raḥmānī*).[39] After extracting the meaning of the Qur'an as a whole, Kadivar then applies this general message of compassion to our present-day sociohistorical context. To apply this intended message of compassion across time and space, Kadivar proposes his theological innovation. In his breakthrough 2001 essay 'Az Islām-i Tārīkhī ba Islām-i Maʿnawī' (Moving from an Historical Islam towards a Spiritual One), which he claims 'represented a turning point in his academic career',[40] Kadivar suggests we have no choice but to consider that the time of some Qur'anic verses has come to an end (*zamān-i [īn āyāt] bi pāyān risīdah ast*).[41] Anticipating the theological contradiction of the Qur'an's 'fixedness', he adds that

> if we read secondary discussions about the Sunna and the Qur'an, we see that the scholars are not referring to permanence (*thubāt*) and staying power (*dawām*) of the divine word. That is because certain divine laws are not fair (*ʿādilāna nīstand*), are not compatible with modern rationality (*ʿaqlānīyyat-i fiʿlī*) and are not ethical (*akhlāqī nīstand*).[42]

Although issues of faith and creed (*umūr-i īmānī wa ʿitiqādī*), ethical values, jurisprudence that is related to rules of worship, and some rules in the jurisprudence of interpersonal relations and transactions (*fiqh-i muʿāmilāt*) need to be left untouched because they are commandments or precepts that are beyond time and space and are perpetually relevant, much of the jurisprudence of interpersonal relations and transactions, constituting the non-creedal legal decisions, can be deemed adaptable. This includes all of the legal decisions that fall under the purview of the penal/disciplinary/civil (*jazāʾī/kayfarī/madanī*) codes, international relations and fundamental human rights laws (*ḥuqūq-i asāsī*).[43]

According to Kadivar, the incompatibility of rational and religious commitment have resulted because the social domain and the conventions of human societies have undeniably changed. As a result, many of the issues that were considered 'just, reasonable and appropriate' in the past are today considered 'unjust, inappropriate and in contravention of the way of the men of reason (*sīra-yi ʿuqalāʾ*)'.[44] Some might wonder, Kadivar suggests, why God allowed what are now considered unjust laws to enter the Qur'an; his response is that if God had not allowed the less than ideal laws to be enacted, 'he would have been remiss in taking care of the needs of the people.'[45] Kadivar then adds that 'if some folk today go so far as to consider rulings that are so dependent on the exigencies of time and place – as is the case with the *mu'āmilāt* – as still valid, then they have not understood the "meaning" of religion, the goal of the Prophet's mission or, in short, the spirit of Islam'.[46] Because the spirit of Islam dictates a compassionate cosmology, we have no choice but to consider that the time of certain verses in the Qur'an has come to an end.

According to Kadivar, the two criteria for whether or not a legal ruling passes the test of permanence, validity, legal force and authenticity is if it is 'just and in tune with the opinion of reasonable people'.[47] He suggests that if a legal decision does not pass the two criteria mentioned above, it should be considered a '*mutaghayyir* law', that is, a law which is subject to change depending on specific exigencies.[48] Interestingly enough, Kadivar believes that updating the rulings is not the responsibility of the jurists or the *walī-yi faqīh* (the guardian jurist) because lawgiving (*tashrī'*) is the sole responsibility of God and his messenger.[49] For Kadivar, these divine rulings, 'whose time has come to an end', will then be replaced by 'new secular rules created by a community of reasonable people, rules that will under no circumstance have any relation to religion'.[50] In essence, we have 'no new religious laws'. According to Kadivar's thought, religious lawgiving is left in the hands of God and God alone and time shrinks the realm and jurisdiction of *fiqh*.[51]

Kadivar not only applies the intended message of the Qur'an to the present but also questions the 'fixedness' of the Qur'an. Kadivar's argument for the controversial statement which suggests that some verses are no longer relevant is based on the claim that the Qur'an was presented to a first-/seventh-century Hijazi audience and, as such, certain parts might no longer reflect current sensibilities. In essence, Kadivar is taking one of the most important hermeneutic strategies which is also used by feminist scholars – the historical situating of the *tanzīl* process – and pushing it to its logical conclusion.

Note that what Kadivar does is a nuanced version of what the Egyptian literary theorist Khalafallah had suggested in the early twentieth century. The idea that only a small subset of the Qur'an needs to be read and understood according to the meaning it had for its first audience satisfies the undeniable situatedness of the *tanzīl* process, without detracting from the divinity of the Qur'an.

Recognising that certain Qur'anic verses are problematic is the first step. But suggesting that the time of those verses has passed introduces an actual solution to the problem of revelation that Western feminist scholars face. Furthermore, signifying that a verse's time has passed is tantamount to allowing its importance to be downgraded. This is perhaps the single most important contribution the Iranian Religious Intellectual Movement has made to the reformist hermeneutic toolbox.

Soroush's first theory: The 'Theory of the Expansion and Contraction of Religious Knowledge'

When first presented in the early 1990s, Soroush's reception theory for scripture, 'Theory of Expansion and Contraction of Religious Knowledge', laid the foundation for the Iranian reformist movement. Presented in the book entitled *Qabḍ wa basṭ-i tiʾūrīkī-yi sharīʿat* (Theory of Expansion and Contraction of Religious Knowledge) in 1994, the theory essentially highlights the difference between religious knowledge and religion *qua* religion.[52] Using philosophical hermeneutics, Soroush exposes the role of presuppositions in religious knowledge and understanding.[53] He suggests that scriptural interpretations (our 'understandings' of the Qur'an) are developed within a cultural context, that interpretations are not natural, or essential and thus do not exist universally beyond time and space. Soroush argues that, just like all human understanding, our understanding of the Qur'an and Islam today, our reception of scripture, is coloured by cultural and historical lenses. Affected by our ever-expanding extra-religious knowledge which comprises the natural and human sciences and the arts, human beings' understanding of religion will, as a result, never be complete and always remain in the process of 'becoming'. Today, just as it was in every age since it was received, the Qur'an is understood by a mind that is imbued with cultural presumptions. Even for something as foundational and undisputed as prayer, we may not question the fact that prayer is obligatory, but the 'depth of our understanding' of the concept evolves with each generation.[54]

At this point in his career, Soroush is still a steadfast supporter of a 'fixed' Qur'an. He argues that although our knowledge of the Qur'an is in a state of flux, the Qur'an itself 'is complete', 'free of contradictions', and that 'it contains all the information God felt was necessary for human guidance'.[55] What is incomplete is human perception and understanding. In line with orthodoxy, Soroush argues that 'what is in the Qur'an, what our religious leaders (The Prophet and the imams) have said is unchanging, we have received them without alteration and no one has the right to add to or subtract from them.'[56] 'Religion is Truth, all its parts are truth.'[57]

Soroush's second theory: The Qur'an as the Prophet's speech

Less than ten years after the presentation of his first theory, Soroush put forth a second theory in his book *Expansion of the Prophetic Experience*. In it, he suggests that 1) the prophetic experience continues forever and did not end, as orthodoxy holds, with the Prophet Muhammad; and 2) the Qur'an, although inspired by God, was written by the Prophet. In this scenario, certain verses of the Qur'an are once again allowed to be downplayed, but mostly because, as the author, the Prophet's understanding of God's purely divine message cannot but be tainted with first-/seventh-century contexts.[58]

So, Soroush's second theory is based on two major principles.[59] Principle 1: 'revelation' or the 'prophetic experience' can be expanded and perfected (by non-prophets). To suggest that the prophetic mission can be extended to include individuals not directly chosen by God to be prophets, especially after the Qur'an explicitly states that Muhammad is the person with whom prophecy ends, and, furthermore, to suggest that perfection has not already been reached in the Qur'an looks suspicious if not outright blasphemous to the common believer. Principle 2: the Prophet was instrumental in actually 'creating' the Qur'an. For Soroush, the role of an impersonal God in the framework of revelation is restricted to the creation of someone who is able to speak in the particular way that the Prophet did. To further elucidate his points, Soroush uses the metaphor of a honeybee. Q. 16:68–9 states: *And thy Lord taught the Bee to build its cells in hills, on trees, and in (men's) habitations; Then to eat of all the produce (of the earth), and find with skill the spacious paths of its Lord: there issues from within their bodies a drink of varying colours, wherein is healing for men: verily in this is a Sign for those who give thought.*[60] Even though God is the one who wills the honey into being made, He has made it accessible to us by creating the honeybee. The same goes for the Prophet. God has created the Prophet in such a way as to make it possible for him to create the Qur'an for us. 'Instead of speaking about a parrot, the Qur'an speaks about a bee and considers the latter, not the former, to be the symbol of receiving revelation.'[61] The role of God in the creation of the Qur'an ended with the creation of the Prophet: 'Muhammad was the book that God wrote and when Muhammad read the book of his being it became the Qur'an.'[62]

The second principle is even harder for believers to digest. Orthodox Islam sees the Prophet as a conduit. Muhammad was given the ability to memorise the verses relayed to him by Gabriel, word for word, without corruption. Those verses were then either memorised or written down by reliable members of the community. To suggest that the Prophet's character, his likes, dislikes, his understanding of the world and, indirectly, the culture within which he was reared had any sort of imprint on what is considered the unadulterated word of God has since made a pariah of Soroush in certain circles.[63]

The response by Abdolali Bazargan[64] to Soroush's theory that the Qur'an is the Prophet's speech is typical of the more nuanced critiques Soroush received. Bazargan points out that there is not one verse in the Qur'an where the Prophet addresses his audience with his own words.[65] The Qur'an has made sure to inform us that Muhammad did not know what a book was or what faith was (Q. 42:52), that he had in fact never before read a book in his life or written a single line (Q. 29:48), and that he was only 'given' revelation as pointed out in Q. 7:203: *If thou bring them not a revelation they say: 'Why hast thou not got it together?' Say: 'I but follow what is revealed to me from my Lord: this is (nothing but) lights from your Lord, and Guidance and Mercy, for any who have faith.'* Bazargan further elaborates the Prophet's status as conduit:

> The Prophet was given the command *qul* (say), 332 times, and so he used *qul* in the Qur'an in the form presented to him. We also have in the Qur'an not just a praise and glorification of the prophets but at the same time an admonitory tone (nineteen times they warned him against hasty judgements), and at least four times he had been asked to ask for forgiveness in relation to topics like his judgement among the people, his tolerance of his adversaries, *tawḥīd* (oneness of God) and *qiyāma* (afterlife), and sometimes he even adopted a threatening tone, nine times he had been warned against obeying the non-believers (*lā taṭiʿ al-kāfirīn*), the hypocrites (*al-munāfiqīn*), the unaware and the straying majority (*al-ghāfilīn*).[66]

Of course, there are instances where we see the phrase '*qāla rasūl Allāh*' (said the Prophet of God), but the speaker is God and not the Prophet. Bazargan calls the Qur'an '*khodā-nāmeh*' (God's letter),[67] 'which is scattered throughout with pronouns such as "I" and "We", where sometimes the angels speak, sometimes the prophets become the speakers and sometimes even Iblīs (Satan). So the orator is not unitary.'[68]

Soroush's use of this radical theory is curious because he incorporates historicity into the revelation process by also introducing the historical situating of the Qur'an in the same book. Soroush divides Qur'anic verses into two ontological categories: essential and non-essential. He suggests that the contextually and historically determined non-essential, non-divine, all-too-human parts of the Qur'an (e.g. the superficial mentioning of the black eye-colour of the *ḥūrī*s in paradise as opposed to blue-eyed *ḥūrī*s, or treating women's legal status as secondary), while advantageous or perhaps even necessary at the time, are nothing but accidentals now and are in fact sometimes detrimental to the religion. The Qur'an contains these cultural details because first-/seventh-century audiences might have otherwise found the text too abstract and unintelligible, or too revolutionary, especially around issues like the legal status of women and the cost of becoming a Muslim. Culturally situated from the start, the Word had to be brought down to the limited level of its human audience.[69]

Fanāʾī's correction of a theological inconsistency

Less well-known than Soroush and Kadivar, Fanāʾī is a promising contemporary Iranian Shiʿi mujtahid and philosopher – specifically ethicist – who identifies with the Religious Intellectual Movement. He spent seventeen years as a seminarian in Qum, then another fifteen years in the United Kingdom acquiring a philosophy degree and teaching. Fanāʾī has written two influential books in the last few years,[70] both of which have caught the attention of reformist thinkers within and outside the movement.[71] He moved back to Iran in 2015 to take up a teaching position in Qum.

The cornerstone of Fanāʾī's hermeneutics is also the historical situating of the *tanzīl* process. Following in the footsteps of Soroush and Kadivar, Fanāʾī suggests that the divine message which is revealed in the Qur'an is not always 'ahistorical' or 'absolute', but is also situated in the cultural context of the period in which it was revealed. As such, the message is a combination of ahistorical/absolute religion and historical/applied religion. While the former is context-free and therefore applicable to all circumstances, the latter is not. In Fanāʾī's view, this ontological analysis of the nature of revelation has some important consequences for how the Qur'an is interpreted. The literal method of interpretation is still valid and suitable for understanding those verses of the Qur'an that contain ahistorical or absolute religion, but the same method leads to the misunderstanding of those verses that are historically bound. For the historically situated verses, we need another method that Fanāʾī calls the 'contextual method' of interpretation.[72] 'Once the ahistorical verses have been distinguished from the historical ones, what we need to do is to try to understand those verses of the Qur'an that are tainted by historicity in light of the context-free verses, and not the other way around.'[73] Fanāʾī suggests that 'orthodox Islam went wrong exactly because it failed to recognise the distinction between absolute and applied religion, treating the Qur'an as always talking about the former'.[74] For Fanā'ī, applied religion is the realm within which reform takes place.

What is innovative about Fanā'ī's theological perspective is that he claims to be catching an additional theological inconsistency that results from the hermeneutic strategy of historically situating the *tanzīl* process. Going against orthodoxy, Fanā'ī claims that as our understanding of the relevant verses of the Qur'an changes, as humanity evolves, God updates the Well-Preserved Tablet (*al-lawḥ al-maḥfūẓ*) in the heavens.[75] How else would the tablet be able to count as the eternal divine blueprint of the Qur'an?

According to Q. 85:21–2 – *this is a Glorious Qur'an, (Inscribed) in a Tablet Preserved (lawḥ al-maḥfūẓ)!* – the location of the *lawḥ al-maḥfūẓ* is traditionally understood to be in God's presence. The *lawḥ* is often identified with a heavenly book through the Qur'anic terms 'mother of the scripture' (*umm al-kitāb*, in Q. 3:7; Q. 13:39; Q. 43:4) and 'hidden writing' (*kitāb maknūn*, in Q. 56:78). As *umm al-kitāb*, it is understood to be the source (*aṣl*), the divine blueprint, not only of the Qur'an but also of the other scriptures (*kutub*), meaning that as God's writing, it contains all the divine decrees.[76]

Fanā'ī agrees with Soroush that the prophetic experience continues but the 'expansion, prior to, and more than being an expression of the truth of the Prophetic experience, is a result of the expansion of religion in the *lawḥ al-maḥfūẓ*'.[77] As far as I know, no one else has talked about what happens to the *lawḥ* when certain parts of the Qur'an begin to get downgraded due to the historicity of the *tanzīl* process.

As a critique of Soroush, Fanā'ī suggests that the theory that the Qur'an is the Prophet's speech is unnecessary. He thinks it is reasonable to suggest that while the Qur'an is divine speech it also contains ethical prescriptions we might consider unacceptable today, relying solely on the hermeneutic strategy of the historical situating of the *tanzīl* process. The problematic divine speech is there because it was necessary to make the text palatable to medieval Arabs. The explanation afforded by the historical situating of the *tanzīl* process suffices for both Kadivar and Fanā'ī, and neither agrees with Soroush's 'Qur'an as the Prophet's speech' theory.

What proves problematic for Fanā'ī, but seems to fall below both Soroush's and Kadivar's radar, however, is what happens to the *lawḥ* when certain parts of the Qur'an come to an end. How is it possible to accept the existence of the *lawḥ* as the ultimate eternal divine blueprint but simultaneously accept that parts of it are becoming less and less relevant? How can we assume that the *lawḥ*, which is the blueprint, stays unchanged while certain parts of the Qur'an seem to be losing their authoritative thrust? For Fanā'ī, the solution to this dilemma is to suggest that the *lawḥ al-maḥfūẓ* is also changing – as the Qur'an's useful parts shrink, so too do the same parts in the *lawḥ*. In other words, Fanā'ī proposes that not only is our reception/understanding of the Qur'an changing (early Soroush) and we are choosing to highlight certain parts and downgrade others due to the situatedness of the revelation process (late Soroush and Kadivar), but that the eternal Qur'an, *al-lawḥ al-maḥfūẓ* as imagined by God, and as it exists in the heavens, is also changing. 'This *lawḥ*', he contends, 'is the subject of expansion and contraction (*qabḍ wa basṭ*) and this change originates from the change in the *tashrī'ī* (suppositional/legislative) will of God, the lawmaker (*shāri'*). The way this change happens is through a ruling (*ḥukm*) being either added or removed from the collection of *'itibārī* rulings.'[78] This way, part of the Qur'an can safely be considered the cultural product of the time of its appearance – a mere copy of a self-renewing original – and divine speech can consistently remain the error-free and perfect object that the Qur'an tells us it is. This sort of updating of the divine will should not be surprising, Fanā'ī argues, since it is what was practised during the process of *nuzūl* (the sending down of the Qur'an) when the principle of abrogation was a sign that God was updating the *lawḥ* in the heavens.[79] In other words, Fanā'ī is suggesting that the abrogation process is being extended into the future in the *lawḥ*, even if we cannot see it happening in the codex we have in hand. As humanity evolves, so too does God's vision of what will lead humankind to Islam. What is important to note is that, as was the case in the era of abrogation, the impetus for change – even in the heavens – is initiated by the needs of the people.

The 'Fixed' Qur'an Revisited

Even though Kadivar and Fanā'ī seem to have relieved us of some theological inconsistencies, the problem resulting from allowing certain verses to be downgraded and the Qur'an referencing itself as complete still persist; see Q. 6:59: *There is not a grain* [*buried*] *in the darkness (or depths) of the earth, nor anything fresh or dry (green or withered), but is (inscribed) in a record clear (to those who can read)*; Q. 18:49: *And the Book (of Deeds) will be placed (before you); and thou wilt see the sinful in great terror because of what is (recorded) therein; they will say, 'Ah! woe to us! what a Book is this! It leaves out nothing small or great, but takes account thereof.'* With His complete message contained in the Qur'an, God also informs the believers that He has perfected their religion and approved it for them: Q. 5:3: *This day have I perfected your religion for you, completed my Favor upon you, and have chosen for you Islam as your religion.* These self-referential characteristics of completeness and perfection in the Qur'an have led to an understanding that everything contained therein is 'essential'.

The following quote from Fakhr al-Dīn al-Rāzī (d. 606/1209), which redefines what the Qur'an means by 'complete' and 'perfect' in Q. 5:3, aligns with Soroush's views on the issue:

> Those who accept the validity of analogy have said that what is meant here by 'religion being perfected by God' is that He has made known specific precepts about some actions in the Text while discussing precepts about some other actions by providing us with the instruments of analogy. It is as if God has divided things into two categories: those that have direct precepts and those for which the precepts must be derived from the first category by analogy. And since God has commanded the use of analogy and made it incumbent on believers to apply it, He has in fact made his precepts clear about all things in advance. Hence, religion is perfect/complete.[80]

The above discussion about the completeness of Islam demonstrates that there is no contradiction between simultaneously assuming a minimal definition for religion and considering Islam to be perfect. Soroush argues that it is the aim and mission of religion[81] to provide only minimums – whether in the realm of precepts or in the realm of ethics. He suggests that a 'religion that has provided these minimums has performed completely and is in no way lacking'.[82] The message of finality in fact points to the necessity of understanding religion and the purpose of religion in such a way, says Soroush, 'as to leave the door open to its dynamism and vitality. And the very minimum that we can do to make religion dynamic is to see it as minimal.'[83] A minimal definition of religion allows us to assume a 'perfect' religion within which God has truly provided the believer with the blueprint needed for salvation in this world and the next. This conception of completeness and perfection as contained in the Qur'an is more likely to allow for a less strict understanding of 'fixedness'.

Conclusion

I was recently struck by a message about the importance of language in Toi Derricotte's book *The Black Notebooks: An Interior Journey*. She calls her work in critical race theory, 'the search for a home, a safe home for all our complexities, our beauty, and our abhorred life'. She defines her mission as not about 'finding that home in the world' but as 'having to invent that home in language'.[84] I have thought long and hard about why I hear echoes of Derricotte's message about the importance of language in the works of the reformist Muslim scholars. I think it is because to create a home, to create an Islam that fits, one must be able to define oneself in a language that is familiar and narrates one's existence with the kind of prophetic power both Soroush and Cornel West (the American public intellectual and scholar) talk about. The orthodox understanding of Qur'anic 'fixedness' is the death of such an endeavour. If we trust that at least Kadivar has the authority to take the leap he has as a mujtahid, if we can sit squarely with the pronouncement that 'fixedness' applies only to certain creedal parts of the divine text, then we can also believe that this theological innovation can give Muslims the language they need to finally define Islam as they imagine it today and not as it was imagined in first-/seventh-century Arabia.

Downgrading certain non-creedal verses can also allow Islamic legal systems to circumvent haphazard, tweak-driven, unregulated legal gymnastics and surmount the challenges posed by the revelation when rationality dictates they should do so.

NOTES

1 Disappointed with the political and social results of the 1979 revolution, a group of Iranian intellectuals began working towards slowly changing the Islamic political system (*niẓām*) from within in the early 1990s. They were following in the footsteps of religious intellectuals like ʿAlī Sharīʿātī (d. 1977), Mehdi Bazargan (d. 1995) and Maḥmūd Ṭāliqānī (d. 1979), who reached their heyday in the pre-revolutionary period. This post-revolutionary religious intellectual movement, Rawshanfikrī-yi Dīnī, has involved philosophers, sociologists, political scientists and cultural theorists. An important characteristic of the post-revolutionary Iranian religious intellectuals is that they criticise tradition, and some even go so far as to criticise modernity. Most of them consciously adopt and apply contemporary Western discourses and methods in the academic study of Islam. For more on the Religious Intellectual Movement, see Lloyd Ridgeon, 'Introduction: Iranian Intellectuals (1997–2007)', *British Journal of Middle Eastern Studies* 34, no. 3 (2007), pp. 261–5; Shahra Razavi, 'Islamic Politics, Human Rights and Women's Claims for Equality in Iran', *Third World Quarterly* 27, no. 7 (2006), pp. 1223–37; Farzin Vahdat, 'Religious Modernity in Iran: Dilemmas of Islamic Democracy in the Discourse of Mohammad Khatami', *Comparative Studies of South Asia, Africa and the Middle East* 25, no. 3 (2005), pp. 650–64; Bahman Bakhtiari and Augustus Richard Norton, 'Voices within Islam: Four Perspectives on Tolerance and Diversity', *Current History* (2005), pp. 37–45; Farhad Khosrokhavar, 'The New Intellectuals in Iran', *Social Compass* 51, no. 2 (2004), pp. 191–202; Mahmoud Sadri, 'Sacral Defense of Secularism: The Political Theologies of Soroush, Shabestari and Kadivar', *International Journal of Politics, Culture and Society* 15, no. 2 (2001), pp. 257–70.

2 For more on these methods, see Aysha Hidayatullah, *Feminist Edges of the Qur'an* (New York, 2013).

3 A long-used hermeneutic strategy that predates modernity, *asbāb al-nuzūl* (sing. *sabab al-nuzūl*; literally, 'causes' or 'occasions of revelation') is the science devoted to identifying the specific historical moment that prompted the revelation of a particular verse. This literature records the historical context in which particular verses were revealed and identifies the problems to which a verse might have been responding.

4 Hidayatullah, *Feminist Edges*, pp. 65–6.

5 Ibid., p. 153.
6 Ibid., pp. 65–6.
7 Khaled Abou El-Fadl, *Speaking in God's Name: Islamic Law, Authority and Women* (Oxford, 2001), p. 93.
8 Ibid., p. 94.
9 For more on the preconditions of critique, see Talal Asad *et al.*, *Is Critique Secular? Blasphemy, Injury, and Free Speech* (New York, 2013).
10 For more on Islam and secularity, see Michael Warner, Jonathan VanAntwerpen and Craig Calhoun, eds, *Varieties of Secularism in a Secular Age* (Cambridge, MA, 2013); Philip Gorski *et al.*, *The Post-Secular in Question: Religion in Contemporary Society* (New York, 2012); and Charles Hirschkind and David Scott, eds, *Powers of the Secular Modern: Talal Asad and His Interlocutors* (Redwood, CA, 2006).
11 Soroush Dabbagh, Abdolkarim Soroush's son, argues against those who claim the Religious Intellectual Movement has already failed because 'it is taking its practitioners to a place they did not initially intend to go to'. See Soroush Dabbagh's chapter entitled 'Rawshanfikrī-yi Dīnī wa Sikūlārīsm', in his *Dar Bāb-i Rawshanfikrī-yi Dīnī wa Akhlāq* (Tehran, 2009), p. 31. The chapter was originally published in the July/August 2009 supplement of the daily newspaper *Iʿtimād*.
12 Mutual fragilisation refers to the belief that competing religious and nonreligious, believing and nonbelieving options are equally open to epistemological and ethical questioning.
13 This happened after they claimed that, although inspired by the Divine, the Qur'an was in fact the Prophet's own speech.
14 Mostafa Malekian is one of the most prominent reformist philosophers still living in Iran, who lost his professorship at Tehran University during Mahmoud Ahmadinejad's university purges. Malekian began his university career in mechanical engineering. In an interview conducted by Zahra Soleimani in the December 2013 edition of *Mehrnamah Quarterly*, Malekian reveals that studying engineering felt like following the wrong path, so he transferred to the philosophy department at Tehran University. After a while, he says, 'I saw that what I was looking for couldn't be found there either. I realised that I needed to go to "the source", and at that point in my life, Ḥawza-yi ʿIlmīya-yi Qum [Qum Seminary] represented "the source". I went to the Ḥawza in order to learn philosophy and *ʿirfān* [gnostic knowledge] and had no interest, whatsoever, in *fiqh* [jurisprudence].' In the same interview, Malekian reveals that, so far, his intellectual life had undergone four stages. In stage one (1979–84), he considered himself a 'non-violent Islamic fundamentalist' (*bunyādgarā-yi Islāmī minhā-yi khushūnat*). During the second stage (1984–8), he said he became 'a Muslim perennialist, like René Guénon and Seyyed Hossein Nasr, while simultaneously paying attention to non-Muslim perennialists as well'. In the third stage of his intellectual development (1988–95), he joined what promised to be the panacea for reconciling Islam and democracy: the Religious Intellectual Movement. This movement was spearheaded by the likes of Sharīʿātī, Bazargan, Ṭāliqānī, Yadullāh Sahabī (d. 2002), Shabestari, Aḥmad Qabīl (d. 2012), Kadivar and especially Soroush. Malekian admits that he finally relinquished that position because he 'found it and still find[s] it unsuccessful'. The fourth stage (1995–2001) he categorises as his existentialist years 'of course of the religious type'; he

continues, 'I soon came to realise that it was hard to defend that position also.' Malekian finally comes into his own upon creating the Rationality and Spirituality project in 2001. See Zahra Soleimani, 'The Fifth Malekian', *Mehrnamah Quarterly*, year 4, no. 32, December 2013, pp. 50–56.

15 Mostafa Malekian, *Rāhī ba Rahā'ī: Jastārhā-yī dar 'aqlānīyyat wa ma'nawīyyat* [Path of Deliverance: Queries into Rationality and Spirituality], 2nd edn (Tehran, 2002–3), p. 364.

16 Charles Taylor, *A Secular Age* (Cambridge, MA, 2007), p. 549.

17 Ibid.

18 Ibid., p. 550.

19 Taylor paraphrased in Warner, VanAntwerpen and Calhoun, *Varieties of Secularism*, p. 12.

20 Ibid., p. 18.

21 Ibid., p. 23.

22 Taylor, *A Secular Age*, p. 550.

23 Azizah al-Hibri, 'Muslim Women's Rights in the Global Village: Challenges and Opportunities', *Journal of Law and Religion* 15, nos. 1–2 (2000–2001), p. 40, n. 12.

24 Hidayatullah, *Feminist Edges*, p. 132.

25 Ibid.

26 Amina Wadud, *Inside the Gender Jihad: Women's Reform in Islam* (London, 2006), p. 199.

27 Ibid., p. 200.

28 Ibid., p. 98.

29 Ibid., p. 99.

30 Hidayatullah, *Feminist Edges*, p. 150.

31 Ibid.

32 Hidayatullah, *Feminist Edges*, p. 152.

33 See Ebrahim Moosa, 'Arabic and Islamic Hermeneutics', in Jeff Malpas and Hans-Helmuth Gander, eds, *The Routledge Companion to Hermeneutics* (London, 2015), p. 718. Moosa points out how Khalafallah created an uproar with his dissertation (and later book) 'al-Fann al-qaṣaṣī fi'l-Qur'ān al-karīm' [Art of Story-telling in the Noble Qur'an]. Khalafallah's non-literal hermeneutics highlighted the moral narrative behind the Qur'anic stories and downplayed their literalness, historical accuracy and factual veracity. The structured plot of the stories in the Qur'an, he argued, were shaped by the goals of the storytelling, influenced by the German Romantics.

34 Ibid.

35 See Friedrich Schleiermacher, 'The Hermeneutics: Outline of the 1819 Lectures', *New Literary History* 10, no. 1, Literary Hermeneutics (Autumn 1978), pp. 1–16.

36 In a personal conversation I had with Kadivar on 16 July 2015, he suggested that his hermeneutic methodology is closest to that of Fazlur Rahman.

37 Fazlur Rahman, *Islam and Modernity: Transformation of an Intellectual Tradition* (Chicago, IL, 1982), p. 6.

38 Ibid., p. 20.

39 Mohsen Kadivar, 'Compassionate Islam' (*Islām-i rahmānī*), talk given at Texas A and M University, College Station, TX, 2 July 2009.

40 Yasuyuki Matsunaga, 'Mohsen Kadivar: An Advocate of Postrevivalist Islam in Iran', *British Journal of Middle Eastern Studies* 34, no. 3 (2007), p. 323.
41 The exact wording and context is as follows: 'Instead of these legal rulings whose time has come to an end, the community of reasonable people will get together and devise new secular rules which will, under no circumstance, have any relation to religion.' Mohsen Kadivar, 'Az Islām-i tārikhī ba Islām-i maʿnawī' [From Historical Islam to Spiritual Islam] in *Ḥaqq al-nās: Islām wa huqūq-i bashar* [Rights of the People: Islam and Human Rights] (Tehran, 2008), p. 32.
42 Mohsen Kadivar, 'Sharia: A Legal Regime or Ethical Value System' [*Sharīʿat: Niẓām-i ḥuqūqī yā arzish-hā-i akhlāqī*], lecture delivered at the University of California, Los Angeles, School of Law, 10 October 2013; http://kadivar.com/?p=12859.
43 Kadivar, 'Az Islām-i tārikhī', p. 30.
44 Ibid.
45 Ibid.
46 Ibid.
47 Ibid.
48 Ibid.
49 Ibid.
50 Ibid., p. 32.
51 Ibid.
52 Abdolkarim Soroush, *Qabḍ wa basṭ-i ti'ūrīkī-yi sharīʿat: Naẓarīya-yi takāmul-i dīnī* [Theory of Expansion and Contraction of Religious Knowledge: The Theory of Religious Evolution] (Tehran, 1994). An earlier incarnation of this book was first presented from May 1988 to March 1990 in a four-part essay in *Kayhān-i Farhangī* (a cutting-edge cultural publication at the time). See Behrooz Ghamari-Tabrizi, *Islam and Dissent in Postrevolutionary Iran: Abdolkarim Soroush, Religious Politics and Democratic Reform* (London, 2008), p. 192.
53 Soroush claims that he had not read Hans-Georg Gadamer before coming up with his theory of the expansion and contraction of religious knowledge. Abdolkarim Soroush, *Reason, Freedom, and Democracy in Islam: Essential Writings of Abdolkarim Soroush*, tr. Mahmoud Sadri and Ahmad Sadri (Oxford, 2002), p. iv.
54 Soroush, *Qabḍ wa basṭ*, p. 523.
55 Ibid., p. 502.
56 Ibid., p. 503.
57 Ibid., p. 502.
58 Abdolkarim Soroush, *Expansion of the Prophetic Experience: Essays on Historicity, Contingency and Plurality in Religion* (Leiden, 2009), p. xvii.
59 The insight that Soroush's second theory can be condensed into the two principles presented here was borrowed from Arash Naraghi (Ārash Narāqī), 'Bazkhānī-yi naẓarīyah-i Soroush darbāra-yi tajruba-yi nabawī wa basṭ-i ān' [A Re-evaluation of Soroush's Views on the Prophetic Experience and its Expansion], 8 March 2005, http://arashnaraghi.org/wp/?p=352.
60 All Qur'anic translations are from Yusuf Ali.
61 Soroush, *Expansion of the Prophetic Experience*, p. 330.

62 Ibid., p. 329.

63 Soroush's views about revelation in his book *Expansion of the Prophetic Experience* and the now famous interview in Holland with Radio Netherlands Worldwide in 2007, later published in *Zemzem*, a leading Dutch magazine on the Middle East, North Africa and Islam, generated more than thirty newspaper and scholarly articles in late 2007 and early 2008. It also inspired a conference and at least one protest against his claims.

64 Abdolali Bazargan (b. 1943 in Tehran, Iran), son of Mehdi Bazargan, Iran's first post-revolutionary prime minister, is a liberal politician, writer and intellectual. He was elected leader of the Freedom Movement of Iran on 24 March 2011, succeeding Ebrahim Yazdi, who resigned on 20 March 2011. Bazargan is one of five major figures in the Green Movement who authored a manifesto calling for the resignation of Iranian president Ahmadinejad.

65 Abdolali Bazargan, 'Havā yā hudā' dar Kkalām-e vaḥy' [Whim or Guidance in Revelatory Speech], February 2008, http://www.drsoroush.com.

66 Bazargan, 'Havā yā hudā'', pp. 5–6.

67 Ibid., p. 2.

68 Ibid., p. 3.

69 Soroush, *Expansion of the Prophetic Experience*, pp. 63–93.

70 The two books by Fanā'ī are *Akhlāq-i dīnshināsī* [The Ethics of Religious Studies] (Tehran, 1392 Sh./2013–14) and *Dīn dar tarāzū-yi akhlāq* [Contemplating Religion on an Ethical Scale] (Tehran, 2013–14).

71 Jalā'īpūr, a reformist insider, calls Fanā'ī an up-and-coming star. See Muḥammad Riḍā Jalā'īpūr, 'Marḥala-yi ba'dī-yi rawshanfikrī-yi dīnī', *Mehrnamah Quarterly*, November 2011.

72 Fanā'ī, *Akhlāq-i dīnshināsī*, p. 309.

73 From a discussion with Fanā'ī on 9 May 2015.

74 Ibid.

75 Fanā'ī, *Akhlāq-i dīnshināsī*, p. 310.

76 Daniel Madigan, 'Preserved Tablet', *EQ*, vol. IV, pp. 261–3.

77 Fanā'ī, *Akhlāq-i dīnshināsī*, p. 399.

78 I'm indebted to Roy Mottahedeh for this clarification: an *'itibārī* ruling is any kind of judgement or ruling based on non-physical aspects of understanding. For example, mathematical and logical judgements are *'itibārī* but not tangible in the physical world. They are basically the rules by which the world operates. See Fanā'ī, *Akhlāq-i dīnshināsī*, notes at the back of the book, p. 579.

79 Ibid., p. 579.

80 Fakhr al-Dīn al-Rāzī, *Mafātīḥ al-ghayb* (Beirut, 1978), vol. III, p. 358, cited in Soroush, *Expansion of the Prophetic Experience*, p. 53.

81 This use of the word 'religion' here is different from its uses as 'religion *qua* religion' and as a concept with an essence. 'Religion' in this context means all things related directly to the sciences of the Qur'an, like *fiqh*, exegesis, theology, ethics, and so on, including religious experience.

82 Soroush, *Expansion of the Prophetic Experience*, p. 113.

83 Ibid.

84 Toi Derricotte, *The Black Notebooks: An Interior Journey* (New York, 1997), p. 19.

6

Soroush's Theory of Qur'anic Revelation: A Historical–Philosophical Appraisal

YASER MIRDAMADI

Introduction

WHAT IS taken to be 'revelation' (*tanzīl*) and 'divine communication' (*waḥy*) are central to the way Islam has been conceived doctrinally throughout its history. Although there are varied views about the nature of the Muslim revelation, its doctrinal centrality to Muslim religious thought cannot be denied. In Muslim theology, a prophet/messenger is someone who receives divine revelation and is obliged to convey it to other people in order to guide them;[1] thereby, understanding the nature of revelation is also vital to the comprehension of Muslim prophetology. From the early development of the theological debates within the Muslim communities, the idea of the 'Word of God' turned out to be highly debatable and controversial. Whether the Qur'an is 'created' or 'eternal' has been just one significant aspect of this heated discussion.[2]

In post-revolutionary Iran, especially after the death of Ruhollah Khomeini (d. 1989), those who are commonly described as 'religious intellectuals' (*rawshanfikrān-i dīnī*)[3] have called into question the traditional understanding of Islamic thought that is supported by the ruling Shi'i clerics in Iran. Not surprisingly, one of the main topics under scrutiny has been the nature of revelation and prophethood.[4] One prominent religious intellectual who has addressed these subjects is Abdolkarim Soroush (b. 1945).[5]

In this chapter I shall first sketch the intellectual biography of Soroush and then elucidate his theory of revelation; I shall then argue that his conception of revelation has a forerunner in the positions of some Muʿtazilī theologians. This will be followed by my brief philosophical critique of his theory of revelation. Finally, I shall outline some of the implications of this theory of revelation for secular law and science, as well as its implications for prophetology.

Soroush: An Intellectual Biography

Soroush is considered one of the foremost contemporary Muslim thinkers defending the radical reform of Islamic thought.[6] *Time* magazine named him one of the world's hundred most influential people in 2005,[7] and in a poll conducted in 2008 by *Prospect* magazine and *Foreign Policy*, in which over half a million people all over the world voted, he was named the world's seventh top public intellectual.[8] Soroush, as we will see, has also played a central, if controversial, role in the Iranian post-revolutionary intellectual discourse, to the extent that if one were to name one intellectual that stands out in the intellectual panorama of post-revolutionary Iran, it would be him, very much the same way ʿAlī Sharīʿatī (d. 1977)[9] would be the obvious name associated with the intellectual discourse of pre-revolutionary Iran.[10]

Soroush was born in 1945 in southern Tehran into a devoted Twelver Shiʿi, lower middle-class family. He underwent primary schooling at the Qāʾimiyya School,[11] then pursued his higher education at ʿAlawī School, a private foundation designated to promulgate Islamic teachings and ethics which was founded by a clergyman called ʿAlī Aṣghar Karbāschīyān in 1955. Soroush attended extracurricular classes on the exegeses of the Qur'an run by the lay teacher and director of the school Riḍā Rūzbih (d. 1973), where Rūzbih attempted to justify the Qur'anic verses on the basis of science in order to reconcile science and religion. Soroush, however, was rarely persuaded by Rūzbih's arguments and had great difficulty convincing himself of their coherency.[12] These classes and arguments regarding the relationship between religion and science were landmarks in Soroush's academic and intellectual career. He then sat the entry exam for university and was awarded a place at the University of Tehran to study pharmacology.

Along with pharmacology, he also studied philosophy and Islamic studies. His motivation to study philosophy came from reading the work by Muḥammad Ḥusayn Ṭabāṭabā'ī (d. 1981), *Uṣūl-i falsafa wa rawish-i ri'ālīsm* (The Principles of Philosophy and the Method of Realism),[13] annotated by his famed pupil and a religious intellectual heavyweight of the Islamic Republic in his own right, Murtaḍā Muṭahharī (d. 1979).[14] This was an introductory book to Muslim philosophy which attacked the popular Marxist literature of that time. The work made an impression on Soroush, especially since his period of study coincided with the power struggles and upheavals of, and Iranians' increasing protest against, the monarchical regime of Muḥammad-Reza Pahlavi (r. 1949–79). The events of this period served as another milestone in Soroush's academic life, for it led him to reflect on the correlation between politics and religion.[15]

Soroush then, in 1973, moved to London where he first studied analytical chemistry at the University of London (gaining an MSc), and then philosophy and the history of science at Chelsea College, although he left London for Iran a few months after the 1979 revolution without finalising his PhD. This academic move marked a noticeable and informative change in his intellectual career. He says, 'I was grappling with the questions of the relationship between science and philosophy, that is, science and metaphysics. No single waking minute would pass, whether walking, riding on the subway, sitting at home, or working in the library, unless I was struggling with some serious and grand problem.'[16] Moreover, the aforementioned period in his thought was noteworthy in another respect, and that was his close study of the thought of Jalāl al-Dīn Rūmī (d. 672/1273), the Persian poet and mystic. This encounter came to have strong and lasting effects on his controversial theory that became known as the 'Theory of the Contraction and Expansion of Religious Knowledge'.[17]

The period of Soroush's academic study in London laid the foundation for a series of books which he would publish in Iran with the intention of introducing the disciplines of the philosophy of science that were not taught there at that time. One of these works, *Nahād-i nā-ārām-i jahān* (The Dynamic Nature of the Universe) was written during that period in London.[18] Another book that he wrote at this time, and which was first published in 1978, was *Taḍādd-i diyāliktīkī* (Dialectical Antagonism).[19] Marxist thought was widespread and may be regarded as having been a prevailing discourse of that time,[20] and this prompted Soroush to provide an intellectual response to the Marxist challenge to Muslim thought. To these ends, he wrote this book, which was a critique of some of the Marxist arguments. Influenced by Popperian philosophy of science, especially Karl Popper's demarcation criterion between science and pseudo-science, Soroush criticised the Marxist theory of dialectical materialism and showed it to be non-scientific, contrary to the claim of its advocates.

Just over a year after the revolution, in the spring of 1980, universities in Iran were closed due to political reasons. A notorious council, the Advisory Committee on Cultural Revolution, was then formed to revise the curricula and reopen the universities. Soroush was one of the seven members of this committee appointed by Khomeini.[21] In 1983, after the reopening of the universities, he resigned at the time when the committee was about to increase its membership and transform itself into the Council of the Cultural Revolution. He joined the Academy of Philosophy and the Institute for Cultural Research and Studies in 1983, and immersed himself in teaching and introducing Iranian academia to the history and philosophy of science, philosophy of social sciences, philosophy of religion, philosophy of history and Islamic mysticism (especially Rūmī's thought). His lectures on the interpretation and explanation of Rūmī were broadcast on television on a weekly basis at the time and received tremendous positive feedback.

Having studied philosophy and history of science and considered them critical prerequisites for the interpretation of religion, he founded the faculty of history and philosophy of science at the Institute for Cultural Research and Studies in 1992. He then published a series of articles in *Kayhān Farhangī*, a journal devoted to the social and human sciences, and later in *Kiyān*, an influential monthly journal devoted to religious intellectuals, especially those who held similar ideas as Soroush. He wrote these articles in order to acquaint readers with the philosophy of science, religion and sociology; to defend the social sciences, which were denigrated as atheistic fields in the revolutionary atmosphere of Iran; and to criticise the official reading of Islam propagated by the ruling clerics.[22]

Soroush's Theory of the Contraction and Expansion of Religious Knowledge

In order to understand Soroush's position on the Qur'anic revelation, one needs to understand the cornerstone of his theorisation, his Theory of the Contraction and Expansion of Religious Knowledge. In it, he tried to find an explanation for the diversity of interpretations of the Qur'anic verses and Sunna. Soroush asked why no unanimous and definitive understanding of the same verse could be arrived at when interpreted by scholars from different schools of thought, and even by individuals.[23] The Theory of the Contraction and Expansion of Religious Knowledge is usually characterised by its epistemological approach towards religious texts. Simply put, in this theory, Soroush distinguishes between religion *per se* and religious knowledge. According to the theory, interpretations of religious texts are contingent upon the conceptual frameworks within which interpreters interpret the texts; hence their interpretations are time-bound and temporal. In addition, the theory holds that the final interpretation of religious texts is not attainable, leaving us only with contingent interpretations of the text. The Theory of the Contraction and Expansion of Religious Knowledge became a cause célèbre for a long time among Iranian intellectual circles inside and outside of Iran, and had a colossal impact on them. The major principles of Soroush's theory, which has a significant bearing on his discussion of the nature of a democratic religious state, among other issues, may be summarised as follows:

1. From an epistemological and historical point of view, 'religion' is different from 'the understanding of religion' (although, later, Soroush denied, or at least significantly modified, this distinction in his Theory of the Expansion of Prophetic Experience).
2. Religion *per se* is divine, eternal, immutable and sacred.
3. An understanding of religion is a human endeavour like any other human endeavour, such as the scientific attempt to

understand nature. Thus, religious knowledge, like any other kind of knowledge, is secular and not sacred.

4. Similarly, inasmuch as it is a human endeavour, an understanding of religion and religious knowledge is certainly affected by, and in constant exchange with, all other fields of human knowledge.
5. This being the case, religious knowledge is dynamic, diverse and time-bound.

Soroush's Theory of the Qur'anic Revelation

One of the main questions concerning the nature of Islamic revelation can be formulated as follows: What is the relationship between Muhammad, considered by Muslims to be the prophet of God, and the divine revelation? More specifically, what is the role of Muhammad in the process of revelation? According to the dominant understanding of revelation in Muslim theologies, Muhammad is regarded as the recipient of the divine message that had been passed faultlessly to him through, among other ways, the archangel Gabriel. One of the implications of this account is that, in the process of receiving the revelation, Muhammad is nothing but a faithful and mainly passive recipient.

Soroush criticises this dominant view, trying to provide a radically different account of the relationship between Muhammad as the prophet of God and the phenomenon of revelation.[24] For Soroush, the role of Muhammad in the process of revelation is by no means that of a passive recipient. Instead of conceiving of Muhammad as the recipient of the revelation, Soroush considers him the originator of the revelation. To make it more understandable, he draws an analogy between revelation and poetry: 'The metaphor of poetry helps me to explain this. Just like a poet, the Prophet feels that he is captured by an external force. But in fact – or better: at the same time – the Prophet himself is everything: the creator and the producer.'[25] Therefore, for him, it is Muhammad rather than God that is central to the process of revelation.

If, according to this theory, Muhammad is central in the process of revelation, then what is the role of God? For Soroush, God's role is to spark Muhammad's inspiration; Muhammad underwent a spiritual experience in which he was overwhelmed by the ubiquitous presence of the Divine. The Muhammadan revelation of God, thus, is the consequence and outcome of Muhammad's encounter with God. The content of the revelation, therefore, cannot be literally ascribed to God, because it is not directly the word of God. Rather, it is directly the word of Muhammad himself. However, since what Muhammad said was the result of his esoteric encounter with God, one is entitled to ascribe Muhammad's words, which are canonically recorded as the current Qur'an, to the God of Islam, but only in an indirect and figurative way: 'The one who is speaking is, in fact, Muhammad whose word has become identical to the word of God because of his closeness to Him. The attribution of speech to God, like the attributions of other human characteristics to Him, is to be taken metaphorically. They are not anthropomorphical.'[26]

In the prevalent understanding of revelation, on the contrary, God reveals to Muhammad His own words, in the Arabic language, that contain eternal truths. According to this conception, Muhammad does not play any determining role in shaping the content of the revelation. He only receives the revelation and conveys it as it is to people. The disagreement between these two theories about the nature of revelation is very deep.

One of the key questions that can be raised about the Soroushian theory of revelation is, why would God not speak the language of human beings? Soroush's answer is that God cannot speak in a human way because He is beyond and above anything related to human characteristics, and consequently He is free from the attribute of speech in an anthropomorphic sense. God, as Soroush describes Him in mystical terms, is beyond form (*bī-ṣūrat*) and hence every human form and attribute that is ascribed to Him must be interpreted and understood only figuratively.

The underlying idea that God has no form, which can be called 'the beyond formness of God', is, at least theoretically, commonly agreed upon by the majority of Muslim theologians, philosophers and jurists.[27] God is considered transcendent, which, *inter alia*, means He is transcendent of and beyond any forms including human form. Their dispute, however, seems to be over the extent to which they are prepared to apply the beyond formness of God to theological issues, such as the issue of the revelation. For example, although some Qur'anic verses have apparently attributed some corporeal aspects to God, such as His having hands (Q. 38:75, Q. 39:67, Q. 48:10) or eyes (Q. 6:103) or His sitting on the throne (Q. 7:54), the overwhelming majority of Muslim theologians and philosophers deny any corporeal attribution to God and consequently interpret those verses metaphorically.[28] But, again, the majority of Muslim theologians (if not philosophers) are not ready to take some other divine attributes such as God's speech metaphorically, whereas Soroush explicitly and wholeheartedly takes the attribution of speech to God completely metaphorically.

Contrary to God, whom he characterises as being beyond any form, for Soroush, revelation is not beyond any form. It takes a specific form, that is, the Arabic language, and was arguably influenced by the particular time and place in which Muhammad was born and lived, as well as by what happened to him, as a matter of chance or otherwise, during the time of his prophethood, such as the wars he experienced, the incidents that occurred and the questions that were put to him. According to Soroush, everything that occurs in this world has a natural cause, and the revelation is no exception to this rule.[29] To justify this claim, he appeals to a principle set by Mullā Ṣadrā Shīrāzī (d. 1050/1640). According to this principle every hadith, originated or emergent, or accidental (*ʿaraḍ*), is preceded by time and material potentiality (*kull ḥādith masbūq bi mādda wa mudda*). This means that in order for every temporal being (*ḥādith zamānī*) to come into being, it needs to actualise its potentialities; in order for that temporal being to actualise its potentialities, it requires material prerequisites.[30] This principle can be called 'the principle of materiality and temporality of every accidental being'. Since for Soroush revelation, even though it has something to do with divinity, is an accident and temporally originated like other events in history, the principle is instantiated, and consequently revelation requires natural explanation.

Because, on the one hand, God is beyond form, including human forms and attributes, and on the other hand, God's divine revelation is temporal and is expressed in human language, it follows that it is impossible to ascribe the letters of the Qur'anic revelation literally to God. However, since Muhammad was supposed to have undergone a mystical encounter with God, revelation is to be figuratively rather than literally ascribed to God. It is because Muhammad's encounter inspired him to utter what he said that it was recorded as divine revelation in the form of the current Qur'an. Consequently, Muhammad's words can be taken as God's words, though the content of the revelation belongs to Muhammad himself.

One can summarise Soroush's argument for his theory of revelation as follows (P stands for Premise; R stands for Result):

P 1: Revelation is an accident (event),
P 2: Every event has a natural explanation,
R 1: Revelation has a natural explanation.
P 3: God is beyond all human forms and attributes,
P 4: Speech is a human form,
R 2: Speech cannot be literally ascribed to God.
P 5: Muhammad is the prophet of God,
P 6: Revelation is a kind of speech,
P 7: Muhammad as a prophet of God underwent an encounter with God, as a result of which revelation emerged.
R 3: Revelation is to be literally ascribed to Muhammad and figuratively to God (R 1 and R 2).

Objections to the Soroushian theory of revelation

It is worth noting that the above argument is an *a priori* argument. In this argument Soroush only relies on philosophical principles (such as the principle of 'the beyond formness of God' and the principle of 'the materiality and temporality of every accidental being') to justify his position. He does not support his theory by *a posteriori* justification. However, in his earlier works, Soroush strove to provide us with an *a posteriori* argument for his theory of revelation. He argued that, as the biography of Muhammad witnesses, his prophetic experience was subject to contraction, ups and downs, expansion and development. He concluded that it was revelation that complied with the Prophet, not the Prophet who complied with revelation.[31]

Since Soroush did not pursue this line of argument in the above-mentioned formulation of his theory, one may conclude that he is no longer inclined to support his theory by an *a posteriori* argument. If this is the case, then this may be due to some criticisms that were levelled against it. For instance, Arash Naraghi (Ārash Narāqī, b. 1966), an Iranian-American philosopher of religion, criticised this kind of argument by contending that the expansion and development of Muhammad's prophetic experience during the time of his prophethood is compatible with the traditional conception of revelation, and therefore the developmental feature of revelation cannot necessarily be taken as a justification for the Soroushian theory.[32] According to Naraghi, during the process of revelation Muhammad gradually obtained a greater capacity for receiving revelation. This increasing capacity meant his prophetic experience was subject to development. However, the mere fact that the prophetic experience of Muhammad was subject to development does not necessary entail, Naraghi argues, that it was revelation that complied with Muhammad, because this fact is also compatible with the prevalent account of revelation, according to which, the content of the Qur'an was literally revealed by the God of Islam to Muhammad and his capacity gradually developed on receiving the revelation.

Although it appears that Soroush has abandoned or at least has no longer relied on this *a posteriori* argument, others tried to defend his theory by presenting a revised version of this kind of argument. For example, Muḥammad Mubāshirī, an Iranian philosopher of science,[33] attempted to support this version of the theory through 'inference to the best explanation' ('hypothetical deduction' or 'abduction'), a scientific method of explanation used in modern philosophy of science.

Briefly speaking, 'inference to the best explanation' (in short, ITBE) means if there are rival explanations A, B and C for a set of evidence or data S, then A is more likely to be true if it explains S better than the alternative hypotheses, B and C. From a philosophical point of view, the main question of ITBE is, what criteria are to be satisfied for a theory to be considered the best explanation? Two criteria that are usually proposed are 'simplicity' and 'explanatory power'. Meeting the criterion of simplicity means 'postulating the existence of fewer entities'. If a theory can explain the given data by postulating the existence of only one entity, then this theory is simpler than those alternative theories that explain the same data by postulating the existence of two or more entities. The second criterion, the criterion of explanatory power, is achieved if a theory, compared with other rival theories, can explain more phenomena with fewer or an equal number of hypotheses; that theory, then, has more explanatory power than its rivals.[34]

Without illustrating its criteria in detail, Mubāshirī relies on ITBE to show that Soroush's theory of revelation and that of some of his advocates, such as the self-exiled Iranian investigative journalist and writer Akbar Ganji (b. 1960) who had a role in supporting and expanding this theory of revelation,[35] can explain the phenomenon of revelation with more explanatory power than the traditional theory. This is because Soroush's theory does not postulate the existence of God to explain the content of the Qur'an and its origin, whereas the traditional theory does. Consequently, Soroush's theory is simpler and therefore it is the best explanation of the phenomenon of revelation.

Both of these *a posteriori* and *a priori* arguments have faced a number of challenges. For instance, distinguishing between two divergent conceptions of God in Muslim thought (the God of philosophy and the God of mysticism), Abolghasem Fanaei (Abū'l-Qāsim Fanā'ī, b. 1960), an Iranian-British scholar of ethics and religion, has tried to reinterpret the principle of 'the formlessness of God' in a way that allows us to literally ascribe the attribute of speech to God.[36] He explains that in Muslim philosophy, rather than mysticism, this principle is conceived in such a way that God cannot take any human form or attribute, including the attribute of speaking. This is because, according to the philosophical understanding of God, 'beyond formness' is an exclusive qualifier that qualifies God and thereby prevents Him from taking any forms.

The mystical conception of God, on the other hand, Fanaei argues, portrays God as being absolutely free from any quality and limitation, including (and not excluding) the quality of being beyond form. Therefore, the God of mysticism who is beyond form in His nature is able to take any form, including the form of being a speaker; at the same time, since He is not confined to any form He might have taken, He remains transcendent and beyond form. Thus, according to Fanaei's account, He is beyond form simply because He is not limited to any specific form, not because being beyond form is His exclusive form. Therefore, Fanaei concludes, God can manifest Himself as a speaker and can really talk to prophets. This requires that God is both beyond any form and takes some form. In this view, it is God who literally speaks in the Qur'an and not the Prophet.

Other critics have tried to show that Soroush's theory of revelation is not consistent with the way the Qur'an itself describes the phenomenon of the Qur'anic revelation. Abdolali Bazargan (ʿAbdolʿalī Bāzargān, b. 1943), an Iranian-American religious intellectual and Qur'anic exegete, for instance, mentioned in his critique of the Soroushian theory of revelation a number of the Qur'anic verses, arguing 'we cannot find even one verse [in the Qur'an] in which the Prophet addresses people in his own words and not in the words conveyed to him by God'.[37] Soroush answers this objection by formulating a methodological principle which stipulates that when talking philosophically about the nature of revelation, no theory about the nature of revelation should be taken for granted, even if it seems to be supported by the apparent meanings of the Qur'an; in other words, we should talk about the revelation from the outside and not from within the scripture:

> You cannot appeal to this or that verse that was uttered by the Prophet or say that this or that verse is inconsistent with that theory. The theory offered from the outside of the revelation would apply equally to all the verses, as long as the theory is correct. Then, if it is correct, we have to annotate the verses on the basis of the theory and annotate them in a way that does not alter the theory.[38]

The Historical Roots of the Theory

Although it seems apt to label the Soroushian theory of revelation as a modern theory of Muslim revelation, this by no means implies that it is not rooted in the history of Muslim theology. In fact, it is reasonable to claim that this theory is influenced by the tradition of negative theology (apophaticism) in Muslim thought at the epistemological level and is affected by the theology of the Muʿtazilīs at the ontological and metaphysical level. In this section I shall elaborate on these points.

The extent to which human beings can know God (if at all) is the subject of a long-standing debate in the history of theology and philosophy in Judaism, Christianity and Islam. According to negative or apophatic theologians, such as Philo of Alexandria (d. *c.* 50), Clement of Alexandria (d. *c.* 215), Moses Maimonides (d. 1204) and Meister Eckhart (d. *c.* 1328), God is beyond the reach of human knowledge. They conclude that human language (words, concepts, theories and so on) cannot be used in a literal way to describe God. Religious language is taken to be 'non-cognitive',[39] or at least not literally cognitive. Negative theologians emphasise that we, as finite beings, are not able to know God and talk about Him literally and positively. In other words, God is unimaginable, incomprehensible, ineffable and irreducibly other.[40]

On the other hand, proponents of positive or affirmative (cataphatic) theology accept that God transcends all human forms and attributes. Nevertheless, they hold that every term that refers to 'good' and 'beauty' in ordinary language can be analogously applied to God, such as 'God is good' and 'God is love'.[41] Consequently, for affirmative theologians, the language of religion turns out to be 'positively cognitive'. Generally speaking, the main distinction between these two trends in theology lies in their claim about the incapacity or capacity of human cognitive faculties to know and describe God.

It seems plausible to claim that the banner of the tradition of negative theology in the history of Muslim thought was raised by the Muʿtazilīs, although they were not alone in this. For example, Ḍirār b. ʿAmr (d. 200/815), an important Muʿtazilī theologian, tried to justify negative theology by drawing an analogy between self-knowledge and knowledge of God. He says, 'we know from ourselves that an outsider is never able to explore the hidden sides of our nature to the same extent that we are aware of them ourselves. This is why we must be satisfied with negative theology.'[42] According to this apophatic position, all attributes of God should be read negatively. God, for instance, is omniscient, and in this tradition this merely means he is not ignorant. Hence the language of religion has only a negative status, that is, it cannot describe God literally and in a positive manner.

The way Soroush makes use of negative theology to support his position, however, differs from the predominant direction it takes in apophatic Muslim theology. While Muslim theologians, especially Muʿtazilīs, readily admit that the human capacity to comprehend God is limited,[43] it appears that the majority of them are not inclined to develop this principle in such a way as to fully include Muhammad's own capacity to comprehend God. Rather, it seems that they are inclined to fully or partially exclude Muhammad's capacity to comprehend God from having any such kind of limitation because of his unique status as the prophet of God. But Soroush explicitly states that the limitation of the human mind in comprehending and describing God has no exception and hence this includes Muhammad's own mind as well. According to him, 'what Muhammad brought into play were his own limitations in existential and historical terms, in terms of his learning and his character, and so on and so forth; limitations that no being can avoid or escape'.[44] If one does not exclude Muhammad from having these human limitations, it implies that the content of the Qur'an is not divine in the prevalent sense of the term, due to the fact that Muhammad's capacity to comprehend and describe God is subject to the cognitive limitations inherent in all human beings, without any exception.

As I said earlier, Soroush seems to be epistemologically influenced by the tradition of negative theology, and as we have seen he utilises this tradition in a radical manner. I also said he is metaphysically affected by the Muʿtazilīs who, unlike some Ashaʿrīs and all Ḥanbalīs, believe that the Qur'an is created, which in the last analysis partially means it is humanly constructed. Muʿtazilīs deny the existence of an eternal and uncreated Qur'an because they consider this doctrine contradictory to the unity of God.

According to Muʿtazilīs, there is no difference between those Muslims who believe in the eternity of the Qur'an and those

Christians who believe that Jesus is eternal and not created based on the doctrine that he is the Word of God.[45] However, most Muʿtazilīs also believe that the Qur'an is created in the Preserved Tablet (*lawḥ maḥfūẓ*). The Preserved Tablet itself is believed to have been created before the world. The important question arising here is, what is the relationship between the Qur'an that exists on earth among human beings (i.e. the available copies of the Qur'an) and the Qur'an in the Preserved Tablet? Some theologians, such as Ibn Kullāb (d. *c.* 240/854–5), who believed that the Qur'an was eternal and uncreated, believed that the existent Qur'an was an expression (*ʿibāra*) and imitation (*ḥikāya*) of the uncreated Qur'an. This implies that the meanings of the Qur'an are uncreated but its wording is created.

However, those Muʿtazilīs, either Baghdādī or Baṣrī Muʿtazilīs, who believed that the Qur'an was created did not imply that it was humanly constructed. Rather, they thought that the Qur'an was created in the Preserved Tablet before the creation of the world and was revealed to Muhammad from that place in the course of Muhammad's life.[46]

There exists, however, a controversy among Muʿtazilīs regarding the relationship between the earthly Qur'an and the preexistent Qur'an in the Preserved Tablet. It appears that Baṣrī Muʿtazilīs believed that the preexistent Qur'an was inlibrated in (i.e. transformed into) the earthly Qur'an, whereas Baghdādī Muʿtazilīs maintained that the earthly Qur'an was an expression and imitation of the preexistent Qur'an in the Preserved Tablet but not its inlibration.

Although the majority of Muʿtazilīs held that the Qur'an was created by God in the Preserved Tablet, some of them denied the existence of the preexistent Qur'an in the Preserved Tablet. Ibrāhīm al-Naẓẓām (d. *c.* 220/836), a prominent Muʿtazilī theologian, for example, is reported to have believed that the revelation was created in the air at the time it was being revealed to Muhammad, not prior to it, in the form of sounds, although it was beyond a specific language. It is the reader, including Muhammad in the case of Islam, who chooses the language by which that body of revelation is read. This means the existent Qur'an is not even an imitation of the

Word of God. Rather, it is something that is paraphrased by the language chosen by the reader of the Qur'an.[47]

A question worthy of asking now is, what is the relationship between these accounts and Soroush's theory of revelation? Soroush describes himself as a 'neo-Muʿtazilite',[48] thus it is not surprising that his theory of revelation is incompatible with that of at least some Ashʿarīs and all Ḥanbalīs. However, it seems that his theory is incompatible with the position of the majority of Muʿtazilīs as well.

As we have seen, the standard Muʿtazilī position is that the Qur'an was created by God in the Preserved Tablet before the creation of the world. Soroush, on the other hand, does not seem to feel any need to postulate the existence of the Preserved Tablet to explain the Qur'anic revelation. Although his theory is closer to Naẓẓām's theory of revelation, especially when Naẓẓām assumes an active role for Muhammad and all other readers of the Qur'an, Soroush diverges from him by supposing that revelation is created by Muhammad rather than God. Soroush is aware of this divergence when he says,

> I believe that the Qur'an is God's creation [*makhlūq*]. The Muʿtazilites said this. But we can take one step further and say that the fact that the Qur'an is God's creation means that the Qur'an is the Prophet's creation. The Muʿtazilites didn't explicitly take this step but I believe it is a necessary corollary of their creed and school of thought.[49]

However, it seems that his historical judgement of Muʿtazilīs is not accurate, because there is, at least, one Muʿtazilī theologian who took this step: Muʿammar Ibn ʿAbbād al-Sulamī (d. 215/830), a leading Muʿtazilī theologian from Basra, believed that the Word of God 'is only a capacity created by God in man enabling him to produce a word which expresses the will and design of God'.[50] For him, the Qur'an is not directly the work of God, but the work of nature. The Qur'an, he believed, is an accident, and God does not create accidents. God only created substances; accidents are voluntary creations of substances rather than of God.[51]

For Muʿammar this distinction between substances, which are created by God, and accidents, which are created by nature, is necessary, because if substances and accidents were both created by God then there would remain no room for the free will of human beings. Therefore, according to Muʿammar, God only created the entity (substance) of the Prophet Muhammad, and the Qur'an as an accident of his entity was created by Muhammad himself rather than directly by God. However, because God created Muhammad in order to communicate through him to humankind, Muhammad's words are, in a figurative sense, the Word of God.

The similarity between the two theories seems striking. As we have seen, Soroush also says, 'I am not saying: God does not speak; I am saying in order for God to speak, a Prophet speaks and his words are considered to be God's words.'[52] Both theories ascribe the content of revelation literally to Muhammad and figuratively to God. To put the matter another way, in both theories the content of the Qur'an is a humanly constructed work, but a person who was created by God to convey the will of God produces it, and this allows us to ascribe the words of that person figuratively to God.

The debate over the nature of the Qur'anic revelation in the early history of Muslim theologies can be, by and large, classified as shown in Figure 6.1.[53]

The Philosophical Assessment of the Soroushian Theory of Revelation

We have shown how, for Soroush, the Qur'anic revelation is literally taken to be the word of Muhammad himself and only metaphorically the word of God. This position places his theory of revelation a far cry away from dominant theories of revelation, such as the Ḥanbalī theory.

The Qur'anic revelation is, for Soroush, the result of a religious experience, which, like other kinds of human experience, is bounded by the inherent limitations of humanity. Therefore, from this perspective, what is divine is that which inspired Muhammad to say what he said. This means it is the process of the revelation that is considered divine, while the Qur'an – the product of the process – is not regarded per se as divine, sacred and absolute, but human, historical and conditioned.

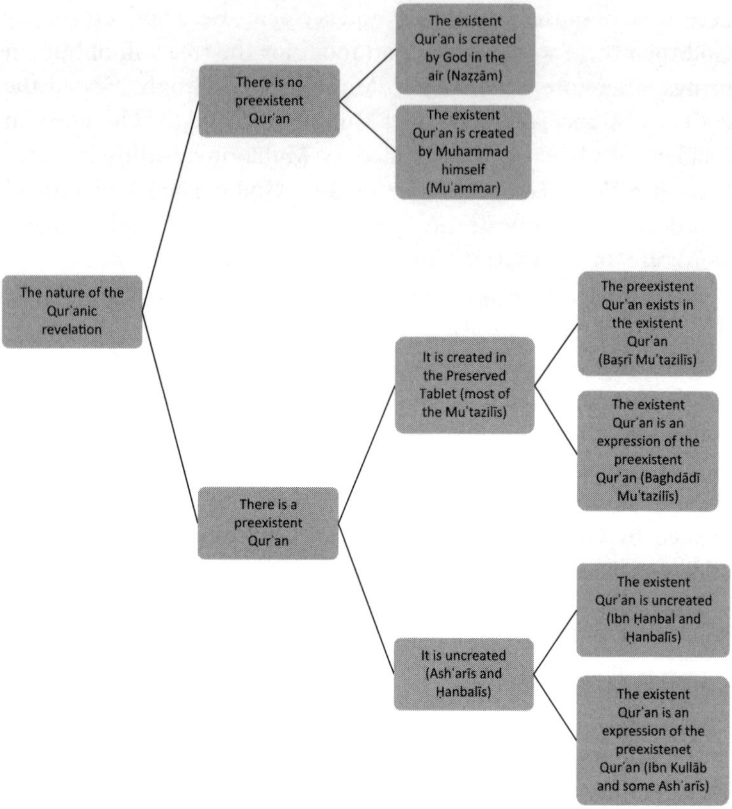

Figure 6.1. Schematic diagram outlining the various views about the nature of the Qur'anic revelation.

By taking into account direct realism, critical realism and non-realism – the triad of conceptions prevalent in modern epistemology and the philosophy of science – and applying them to the philosophical study of religion, the main philosophical question regarding the Soroushian theory of revelation is, what categories in question can best explain his theory of revelation: religious direct realism, religious critical realism or religious non-realism? However philosophically categorised, another question is whether his theory of revelation can be defended against epistemological criticisms that are (or can be) levelled at that category to which it belongs. One might ask why this question of realism/non-realism is important in the evaluation of Soroush's theory of revelation. The significance of the realism/non-realism issue lies in the fact that every theory of revelation is faced with the question of what the relationship (if any) is between historical reality (as reflected in the Qur'an) and divine reality (which is taken to be the source of the Qur'an).

Briefly put, according to direct realism, sometimes called naïve realism, human beings' understanding of an independent reality is essentially dependent upon reality itself and is not significantly shaped by our cognitive apparatus. But according to non-realism, sometimes called anti-realism, one cannot talk of an independent reality; rather, what is characterised as reality is, in one way or another, fully contingent upon us human beings. Critical realism, sometimes called indirect realism, however, takes a middle position, according to which there is an independent reality (unlike non-realism) that we as cognitive agents have an understanding of, but our understanding of reality is directly shaped by elements independent of reality and dependent upon us (unlike direct realism).[54]

In what follows, I will argue that the Soroushian theory of revelation can be properly categorised and classified as a critical realistic interpretation of the Qur'anic revelation. Then, I will show that Soroushian critical realistic interpretation of the Muslim revelation is confronted with the same problem that the British philosopher of religion and theologian John Hick (d. 2012) faced in his critical realistic interpretation of religion. The problem is that Soroush's theory of revelation seemingly turns out to be inconsistent, since it is in danger of lapsing into a relativistic position, though it is supposed to be non-relativistic due to its critical realistic position. The way Hick endeavoured to defend his position against this problem is beyond the scope of this article, but I will argue that Soroush's theory has not been able to rebut the above-mentioned objection.

Soroushian critical realistic interpretation of revelation

First of all, it seems clear that Soroush's interpretation of revelation cannot be taken as a direct (naïve) realistic interpretation. Religious direct realism, like philosophical direct realism, makes the assumption that we can perceive, in principle, things as they are. This is a theological and philosophical position regarding the nature of religious knowledge, to the effect that religious language can and sometimes does reflect, as it is, the transcendental reality, namely God and His attributes. Consequently, religious language ought to be interpreted, in principle, literally and not metaphorically.

Soroush proposed his theory of revelation to counter the prevalent understanding of revelation held by the majority of both Sunni and Shi'i Muslims, past and present, which is rooted in a direct realistic interpretation of religion. Moreover, Soroush makes the distinction between 'essentials and accidentals in religion' and 'maximalist and minimalist views of religion', and delineates between the divine aspects and human aspects of revelation in order to show that religious direct realism cannot account for the complexity of the formation of Islam. Soroush defines accidentals of religion counterfactually, namely in terms of what could have been rather than what currently is. He takes almost all traits of religions, including Islam, as accidental. He considers, among other things, Arabic language and culture, reactions of the Qur'an to questions put to Muhammad and oppositions against him, and terms, concepts and theories used by Muhammad as accidentals of Islam.[55] He further criticised what he calls a 'maximalist view of religion', by which he means a position according to which 'all the necessary and sufficient measures, instructions and rules for economics, governance, commerce, law, ethics, knowledge of God and so on for any kind of mentality or life, whether simple or complex, have been included in Islamic law'.[56] Furthermore, his emphasis on the inherent limitations of human understanding of the divine and on the historicity of all aspects of religion can be taken as his fundamental departure from religious direct realism.

However, my argument here is that there still remains, to a slight degree, an apparent similarity between his theory of revelation and religious direct realism in the interpretation of religion. Irrespective of that apparent similarity, it seems reasonable to claim that his analysis of revelation cannot be taken as reflecting direct realistic interpretation of revelation.

Does the position of Soroush also have something to do with non-realism? Religious non-realism (sometimes called religious anti-realism) is primarily a position regarding the analysis of the nature of religious language. It is a position that takes 'God', which is a key term in the Semitic religions (and also in Zoroastrianism and some branches of Hinduism), to be a word that does not refer to anything beyond the domain of language and/or states of mind. According to this position, there is nothing out there (or up there) that can be labelled in language as God or anything similar to it. For religious non-realists, however, what is to be denied is the realistic interpretation of religion and not its subjective interpretation. Therefore, they are not anti-religious but they are against the realistic interpretation of religion.

Can Soroush's theory be categorised as, and analysed according to, a non-realistic interpretation of religion? His epistemological position, at least as far as he himself has explained it, does not seem to deny all kinds of realism. For instance, he writes, 'the Theory of Contraction and Expansion of Religious Knowledge is a realistic theory, that is to say, it intentionally makes a distinction between the object and the perception of the object'.[57] But all non-realist/anti-realist theories try to blur or eliminate the underlying distinctions between the object and the subject of knowledge. However, in some of his recent lectures, Soroush has described God in a way that verges on a non-realistic way of talking about God. For instance, in one of his lectures he speaks about the centrality of love to make sense of God, and goes further to implicitly claim that love as God means God is nothing but love, and thereby seems to be blurring the distinction between the subject and object when talking about God.[58]

Although a few of his recent lectures seem to point to a shift towards religious non-realism, there is not yet any unambiguous evidence showing that his position has completely changed to this. Even if this shift has recently taken place, it is beyond reasonable doubt that Soroush had tried to base his religious epistemology on the tradition of critical realism. His critical realistic stance in analysing religion can be seen in his debates regarding religious pluralism. In order to defend religious pluralism, he draws some conclusions from his earlier debates about his Theory of the Contraction and Expansion of Religious Knowledge:

> The main theme in the Theory of the Contraction and Expansion of Religious Knowledge, roughly speaking, is that our understanding of religious texts is necessarily diverse and divergent and cannot be reduced to a single understanding, and that not only is religious knowledge diverse and divergent but it is also fluid. This is because religious text is speechless, and our expectations, questions and presuppositions contribute to the understanding of the religious text and its interpretation – this is the case in the fields of law, tradition (Sunna) or Qur'anic exegesis. Since no interpretation is possible without its being based on an expectation, question and presupposition, and owing to the fact that these expectations, questions and presuppositions stem from outside of religion, and because that which is outside of religion is changeable and fluid, and science, philosophy and human production are continually increasing, accumulating, changing and evolving, the interpretations which are made in the light of those expectations, questions and presuppositions become diverse and changeable.[59]

Upon this epistemological–hermeneutical foundation Soroush builds his definition of religious pluralism. Soroush argues that it is not only the way in which religious text is read and understood that is inevitably diverse and changeable, but also that religious experiences, upon which religion is essentially built, are inevitably diverse and changeable. According to his philosophical anthropology, no human experience, including prophetic experience, can be perfect. We are therefore presented with pluralism in understanding and interpreting religious texts (hermeneutical pluralism) as well as pluralism in religious experience (existential pluralism). There are different and irreducible readings and interpretations of religious texts and also there are different, divergent and irreducible experiences of what is taken to be the object of all these experiences (God or the Divine). For Soroush, religious experience is 'an encounter with the Absolute and the Transcendent' (*muwājiha bā amr-i muṭlaq wa mutaʿālī*).[60]

Soroush, who translated into Persian some of Hick's articles on religious pluralism, takes inspiration from Hick, and other philosophers of religion and theologians, to formulate his theory explained above. Soroush takes, *à la* Hick, religious experiences to be various experiences of the Transcendent, or to put it another way, he believes the Transcendent is experienced in every culture and religion in a different way, and even within a specific religion it is experienced differently from one person to another. As can be seen, Soroush's defence of religious pluralism takes what he calls the transcendent to be an independent object that all religions strive to make sense of. That is why his position is realistic. According to him, however, every experience needs to be conceptualised and there is no pure and meta-linguistic experience. In order to make an experience understandable, he argues, one utilises one's cultural and linguistic possibilities. In his analysis, this explicates the historical aspects of religions, the aspects that differ from one context to another. He explicitly claims that his religious epistemology is based on critical realism and not other epistemological rivals, that is, direct realism or non-realism:

> My position is actually that of complex and critical realism, in the sense that the real world, whether the world of religion, philosophy or nature, is more complex than one can capture in simple-minded rational judgements . . . One of the distinct consequences of critical realism is that the majority of people's certainties are no more than conjectures; this is not to say that human beings can never attain reality, but it means that the discovery of reality has no distinct criterion. Those criteria that are mentioned in traditional philosophy, such as certainty and self-evidence, are all flawed.[61]

Now, let us ask what critically can be said about this position: Can religious critical realism remain faithful to its middle-of-the-road position between direct realism and non-realism? Or will it be, in the final analysis, reduced to either direct realism or non-realism? If this position reduces to non-realism or direct realism, what factor makes it turn out to be so? In what follows I will briefly address these questions.

Religious critical realism has encountered the following problem: it makes God inaccessible or, as the American philosopher of religion and epistemologist William Alston (d. 2009) puts it, religious critical realism attributes 'transcendence to God so radical as to rule out the possibility of using any human concepts to make realistically true statements about Him, and to rule out the possibility of knowing some of them to be true'.[62] It seems Alston is right in his description of Hick's apophatic theology. Hick characterises the Real as something which

> cannot be said to be one or many, person or thing, conscious or unconscious, purposive or non-purposive, substance or process, good or evil, loving or hating. None of the descriptive terms that apply within the realm of human experience can apply literally to the unexperienceable reality that underlies that realm. All that we can say is that we postulate the Real *an sich* as the ultimate ground of the intentional objects of the different forms of religious thought-and-experience.[63]

It is a radical affirmation of divine ineffability. Hick goes further to claim, as just quoted, that the existence of the Real can only be postulated but cannot be proved or justified. In an interview with Soroush, Hick clearly says, 'I have not found the theistic arguments persuasive. I cannot prove religious realism and I think realistic interpretation of the world is merely a possible interpretation.'[64] Soroush agrees with him, and Hick continues, 'I would think one can interpret the world religiously or not. In other words, one can interpret the world in a religiously or non-religiously realistic way.'[65] Don Cupitt (b. 1934), a British philosopher of religion, and himself a religion non-realist, criticises Hick at this point:

> Hick has given no reason, and has admitted that he *can* give no reason, for describing it [i.e. the Real] as the 'Real,' rather than as merely an ideal focus of inspiration. All he can say is that in using religious language *he intends* it to have real reference, and he thinks that most ordinary people have always intended realism. [brackets added, emphases original][66]

Cupitt is therefore criticising Hick's realistic interpretation of the 'Real' as nothing but an arbitrary interpretation. Consequently, religious critical realism is theoretically no more defensible than religious direct realism. Based on this criticism, one might ask why the idea of the 'Real' has been preserved in Hick's religious epistemology given the fact that he concedes that he cannot prove or justify religious realism and the reality of the 'Real' vis-à-vis religious non-realism.

Here, influenced by the German philosopher Immanuel Kant (d. 1804), Hick has a practical answer, which is that all the ultimate realities in all the great world religions, which he called the Real, play an existential role; that is to say, they transform the human condition: 'the personal deities and non-personal absolutes have a common effect . . . in the transformation of human existence from self-centeredness to a new centeredness'.[67] This new centeredness is 'Reality-centeredness' and reality here belongs to practical reason, that is, it has a moral meaning, such as 'becoming an unselfish moral agent'.[68] Therefore, the 'Real' is the name of a being that is understood in different religions and cultures (in Islam, Allah; in Judaism, Jehovah; in Christianity, the triune God; and so on) and the 'Real' is taken in Hick's thought to be the source of existential and moral manifestation.

Hick also talks about 'transformational parity'. It means that since all great world religions can transform their believers from self-orientedness to reality-orientedness, all religions are equally true. But 'true' here does not mean theoretical truth in the prevalent sense of correspondence to reality. Hick's religious pluralism is not pluralism of truth, namely, he does not claim that the doctrine of all the great world religions are epistemically equally true; rather, it is a salvific pluralism: 'each of the great traditions constitutes a context and, so far as human judgment can at present discern, a more or less equally effective context, for the transformation of human existence from self-centredness to Reality-centeredness'.[69]

It might be contended that it is far from clear why one needs to take for granted the reality of the 'Real' in order to account for what Hick describes as 'the transformation of human existence from self-centeredness to Reality-centeredness'. It seems that Hick's pluralism is a kind of exclusivism, though it is a moderate exclusivism compared with the exclusivist approaches of the mainstream of almost all the great world religions. For it confines salvation to the great world religions and only excludes purely secularists and humanists (those who do not believe in the 'Real' in its broad sense) from salvific transformation. If the sign of the truth with regard to religions is the ability of religious traditions to transform their believers from self-orientedness to reality-orientedness, and if all the great world religions more or less have the same ability to bring about transformational parity, then

> Transformational parity can also be used as an argument against salvific pluralism. The basis for this claim is the fact that people making a 'secular' (non-religious) commitment to some goal, value, or metaphysical perspective – be it concern for the environment or world hunger or emotional health – often appear to have their lives transformed in ways quite similar to the ways in which the lives of religious believers are transformed. They, too, appear to have changed from self-centeredness to a focus on reality outside of self.[70]

To sum up, the main criticism raised against the religious critical realism of Hick is that if nothing can be presented to justify the proposition that 'the Real exists independent of us' and also that 'transformational parity' can in principle be applied to non-religious commitments (such as some humanitarian philanthropies), then Ockham's razor (which states that plurality should not be posited without necessity) must be utilised to eliminate the 'Real' as constituting a part of the explanation of religious language. If this criticism is defensible, then religious critical realism thus formulated is untenable.

So far, I have critically sketched Hick's account of religious critical realism and its application to his religious pluralism, due to the fact that his philosophical and theological position is much the same as that of Soroush. Both Hick and Soroush themselves have also endorsed this similarity.[71] Moreover, considering the fact that the religious epistemology of Soroush has not hitherto been elaborated as much as that of Hick, one can make use of Hick's epistemology to have a better comprehension of the Soroushian religious epistemology.

It seems reasonable to claim that the Soroushian religious critical realism and, specifically, his theory of revelation suffer from the same problem with which Hick's religious epistemology has been faced. It appears that, ultimately, the idea of God plays no substantial role in the Soroushian theory of the Qur'anic revelation. For Soroush, what is central in making sense of the phenomenon of the revelation is Muhammad, a man with all the limitations and shortcomings of a human being: 'God simply sent the "teacher"; everything else revolved around his experiences and his reactions.'[72]

It might be said, in rebuttal of my analysis, that although Soroush's theory takes the person of Muhammad and not the divine intervention to be central to the revelation, he frequently qualifies this by commenting that the revelation spoken by Muhammad occurred only with God's permission, for He had sent him as His prophet. But, everything considered, this addendum does not add anything to his account of the revelation because, according to apophatic theology, to which Soroush also subscribes, nothing literal can be said about God. Therefore, when Soroush writes that Muhammad was 'permitted' by God or God 'sent' him as a prophet, this is to be read metaphorically: 'the attribution of speech to God, like the attributions of other human characteristics to Him, is to be taken metaphorically. They are not anthropomorphical.'[73] If the idea of God and His attributes is to be interpreted metaphorically, one might wonder why we need the metaphor of God's chosen one or the one endorsed by God to elucidate the phenomenon of revelation. It might be because we have good reason to believe in God. But Soroush has conceded in his dialogue with Hick that he has not found the theistic arguments persuasive.[74]

If this is so, why then does Soroush still utilise the idea of God and prefer religious critical realism to religious non-realism or relativism? His answer is that one can believe in the being beyond form (*amr-i bī-ṣūrat*) even if it is reasonless (*bī-dalīl*), since, according to him, rationality itself is not rational but a fundamental, that is, irrational, choice. Rational people have faith (acceptance without reason) in rationality: 'when you decide to be rational and to trust in rationality, this decision itself is not based on rational proof, because if it were so, it would become a circular argument: to use rationality in order to justify itself'.[75] Soroush suggests that if trust in rationality is a fundamental and reasonless decision, one can also make another equally fundamental and reasonless decision: to opt for love. This decision to opt for love paves the way for believing in the being beyond form. The objectionable point here, however, is that Soroush is suggesting something that leads to relativism: believing in God (or in his mystical terminology 'the being beyond form') is epistemologically equal to not believing in Him, and there is no theoretical way to prefer one over the other. That is because both sides are finally and fundamentally non-rational, and we are left only with making a fundamental decision as to whether we would like to commit ourselves to theistic or atheistic (or non-theistic) beliefs.

If his epistemology, in the final analysis, is relativistic, then it is inconsistent. When asked whether his religious epistemology is relativistic, he replied that he works within the tradition of critical realism, which is non-relativistic,[76] but I have shown that his position does not remain faithful to critical realism.

Some Implications of the Soroushian Theory of Revelation

Due to limitations of space I cannot dwell on the implication of the Soroushian theory of revelation, but a quick glance is in order. In the prevalent understanding of Islamic revelation, the Qur'an is taken as the eternal Word of God for the guidance of humanity. Believing that the Qur'an is the direct and verbatim manifestation of the Word of God (inlibration) paves the way for – although it does not entail – the idea of the eternality of the content of the Qur'an, including the eternality of Qur'anic laws, since it is theologically widespread to think that as God is eternal and God's words are not separable from Him then the content of the Qur'an, His Word, is eternal too.

The Soroushian theory of revelation paves the way for demystifying and de-sacralising the content of the Qur'an without allegedly compromising its divine roots by analysing it in terms of a respectable human effort to discover and disclose the will of God. Accordingly, as the human aspect of the Qur'an is pivotal in this analysis, one cannot take the Qur'anic content, especially the

Qur'anic legislation (*tashrīʿ*) as eternal. Rather, the implication of this theory is that, due to the significant differences between the modus vivendi in the era of Muhammad (as reflected in the Qur'an) and that of modern-day life, the content of the Qur'an is temporal until proven otherwise. Soroush's theory of revelation implies that Muslims can embrace modern legal systems, especially the Declaration of Human Rights, because Qur'anic legislation was nothing but a human effort to organise Arabic society in accordance with the contingencies of the period (the first/seventh century) in which the Qur'an was revealed.

This theory of revelation has also far-reaching implications for prophetology. Compared with prevalent prophetology, according to which the Prophet is regarded as the person chosen by God to convey the divine truth, Soroushian prophetology depicts the Prophet as a mystic who presents his divine discoveries for people's guidance. The main difference between these two prophetologies is not only that in the former the Prophet is a recipient while in the latter he is a discoverer, but also that in the latter the Prophet is not infallible in his discoveries:

> In the traditional view, the revelation is infallible. But nowadays there are more and more interpreters who think that the revelation is infallible only in purely religious matters such as the attributes of God, life after death and the rules for worship. They accept that the revelation may be wrong in matters that relate to the material world and human society. What the Koran says about historical events, other religious traditions and all kinds of practical earthly matters does not necessarily have to be true.[77]

We should not take the phrase 'the revelation is infallible only in purely religious matters' as an expression of Soroush's own position, because his position, as illustrated above, entails the fallibility of revelation even in purely religious matters.

By the same token, the Soroushian theory of revelation can be looked upon as an answer to the seeming conflicts between some Qur'anic verses and the established findings of modern sciences. It takes the Qur'anic verses as reflecting, in principle, the level of knowledge available to Muhammad and people in his era; hence these verses can be overlooked without damaging the main message of the Qur'an.

NOTES

1 Uri Rubin, 'Prophets and Prophethood', *EQ*, vol. IV, pp. 290–91.

2 See Arent J. Wensinck and Andrew Rippin, 'Waḥy', *EI*², vol. XI, pp. 55–6; Yahya Michot, 'Revelation', in Tim Winter, ed., *The Cambridge Companion to Classical Islamic Theology* (Cambridge, 2008), pp. 180–96.

3 What unifies these religious intellectuals, despite their differences, are their theorisation and promotion of a reformist Islam and their critique of revolutionary Islam. They reject, most importantly, the intermingling of religion and politics in the form of the 'guardianship of the jurist' (*wilāyat-i faqīh*) or any other form. Therefore, they reject the very idea of a religious government backed by revolutionary rulers of Iran. See Farhad Khosrokhavar, 'The New Intellectuals in Iran', *Social Compass* 51, no. 2 (2004), pp. 191–202.

4 Some other issues widely discussed by religious intellectuals are whether and to what extent Islamic jurisprudence (*fiqh*) can find answers to modern social and scientific problems, and whether it is compatible with human rights; whether Islam is compatible with a parliamentary democracy; whether the advancement of secularism can be halted; and whether salvation can be found in other religions. See Eva Rakel, *Power, Islam, and Political Elite in Iran: A Study on the Iranian Political Elite from Khomeini to Ahmadinejad* (Leiden, 2008), chapter 4.

5 Some other religious intellectuals are Muḥammad Mujtahid Shabistarī (b. 1936) and Muḥsin Kadīwar (b. 1959). For an overview of their thought, see Mahmoud Sadri, 'Sacral Defense of Secularism: The Political Theologies of Soroush, Shabestari, and Kadivar', *International Journal of Politics, Culture, and Society* 15, no. 2 (2001), pp. 257–70.

6 By 'radical reform' I mean a kind of reform that does not confine itself to the hermeneutical realm (i.e. only suggesting new interpretations of the Qur'an and/or Sunna), but reconsiders critically the underlying philosophical and theological tenets of Islamic thought.

7 Scott Macleod, 'The 2005 TIME 100: Abdolkarim Soroush', *Time*, 18 April 2005, http://content.time.com/time/specials/packages/article/0,28804,1972656_1972712_1974251,00.html.

8 'Intellectuals—the Results | Prospect Magazine', http://www.prospectmagazine.co.uk/magazine/100-top-public-intellectuals.

9 For an excellent book about Sharīʿatī's life and thought, see Ali Rahnema, *An Islamic Utopian: A Political Biography of Ali Shariʿati* (London, 2000).

10 Forough Jahanbakhsh, *Islam, Democracy and Religious Modernism in Iran, 1953–2000: From Bazargan to Soroush* (Leiden, 2001), p. 140.

11 Kristian P. Alexander, 'Soroush, Abdolkarim (1945–)', in Michael R. Fischbach, ed., *Biographical Encyclopedia of the Modern Middle East and North Africa* (New York, 2008), vol. II, p. 777.

12 Abdolkarim Soroush, *Reason, Freedom, and Democracy in Islam: Essential Writings of Abdolkarim Soroush*, ed. Mahmoud Sadri and Ahmad Sadri (Oxford, 2000), p. 25.

13 Muḥammad Ḥusayn Ṭabāṭabāʾī and Murtaḍā Muṭahharī, *Uṣūl-i falsafa wa rawish-i riʾālīsm* (Tehran, n.d.).
14 Soroush, *Reason, Freedom, and Democracy in Islam*, p. 27.
15 Jahanbakhsh, *Islam, Democracy and Religious Modernism in Iran, 1953–2000*, p. 143.
16 Soroush, *Reason, Freedom, and Democracy in Islam*, p. 10.
17 Ibid., pp. 15–17.
18 Abdolkarim Soroush, *Nahād-i nā-ārām-i jahān* (Tehran, 1379 Sh./2000). It was read and praised by great and influential scholars such as Ṭabāṭabāʾī, Muṭahharī and Khomeini.
19 Abdolkarim Soroush, *Naqdī wa dar-āmadī bar taḍādd-i diyāliktīkī: Bi ḍamīma: Naqdī bar rawish-i shinākht* (Tehran, 1357 Sh./1978).
20 See Vali Nasr and Ali Gheissari, *Democracy in Iran: History and the Quest for Liberty* (Oxford, 2006), p. 18: 'In the 1960s and 1970s, a Marxist notion of liberation paraded as demand for freedom, a movement that defined the objective spirit of the Islamic revolution of 1979.'
21 Jahanbakhsh, *Islam, Democracy and Religious Modernism in Iran, 1953–2000*, p. 144.
22 Ray Takeyh, *Guardians of the Revolution: Iran and the World in the Age of the Ayatollahs* (Oxford, 2009), p. 183.
23 Soroush, *Reason, Freedom, and Democracy in Islam*, p. 35.
24 It is worth mentioning that Soroush has more recently suggested a slightly different theory of revelation. Due to the limitations of space, I shall completely confine myself to the early version of his theory here. For the later version of his theory of revelation, see his recent sequential articles that begin with this essay: Abdolkarim Soroush, 'Muḥammad Rāwī-yi Ruʾyā-hā-yi Rasūlāna' [Muhammad as the Narrator of Prophetic Dreams], 2013, http://www.rahesabz.net/story/71738/.
25 Abdolkarim Soroush, *The Expansion of Prophetic Experience: Essays on Historicity, Contingency and Plurality in Religion*, tr. Nilou Mobasser (Leiden, 2009), p. 272.
26 Ibid., p. 329.
27 Nevertheless, an apophatic theology is woven into a cataphatic theology in Islam, and that is rooted in the Qur'an itself. Ian Richard Netton articulates this point in this way: 'the Qur'ān conceives of God in both an apophatic and cataphatic or positive sense, a transcendent and an immanent way: on the one hand, it proclaims that there is nothing and no one like Him; on the other, God tells mankind that he is closer to man than his own jugular vein'. Ian Richard Netton, *Islam, Christianity and the Mystic Journey: A Comparative Exploration* (Edinburgh, 2011), p. 58.
28 For a typical Ashʿarī rejection of the attribution of corporeality to God, see 'Abd Allāh Bayḍāwī and Maḥmūd Iṣfahānī, *Nature, Man and God in Medieval Islam: 'Abd Allah Baydawi's Text, Tawaliʿ al-Anwar min Mataliʿ al-Anzar, along with Mahmud Isfahani's Commentary, Mataliʿ al-Anzar, Sharh Tawaliʿ al-Anwar*, tr. Edwin Elliott Calverley and James W. Pollock (Leiden, 2002), vol. II, pp. 755–61.
29 Soroush, *The Expansion of Prophetic Experience*, p. 338.
30 For Ibn Sīnā's formulation of this principle and his defence of it, see Abū 'Alī Ibn Sīnā, *al-Najāt fī'l-manṭiq wa'l-ilāhiyyāt* [The Book of Salvation on Logic

and Theology], ed. 'Abd al-Raḥmān 'Umayara (Beirut, 1992), vol. II, pp. 71–3. For Mullā Ṣadrā's formulation and defence of this principle, see Mullā Ṣadrā, *al-Ḥikmat al-muta'āliyya fi'l-asfār al-'aqliyya al-arba'a* [The Transcendent Theosophy in the Four Journeys of the Intellect], annotated by Muḥammad Ḥusayn Ṭabāṭabā'ī (Beirut, 1990), vol. III, pp. 49–56.

31 Soroush, *The Expansion of Prophetic Experience*, pp. 3–23.

32 Ārash Narāqī, 'Bāzkhānī-yi nazarīyya-yi Surūsh Darbāra-yi tajruba-yi nabawī wa basṭ-i ān' [The Rereading of Soroush's Theory of Prophetic Experience and Its Expansion], 2005, http://www.arashnaraghi.org/articles/revelation.pdf.

33 Muḥammad Mubāshirī, 'Naqdī bar "Naqd-i Narāqī" wa Defā' az Naẓar-i Ganjī dar bāb-i Qur'ān' [A Critique of Naraghi's Critique and a Defence of Ganji's Theory of the Qur'an], 2009, http://zamaaneh.com/idea/2009/02/post_490.html.

34 Kwame Anthony Appiah, *Thinking It Through: An Introduction to Contemporary Philosophy* (Oxford, 2003), p. 169.

35 Ganji wrote a twenty-one part article, which became highly controversial, to expand and defend this theory of revelation. See Akbar Ganji, 'Qur'ān Muḥammadī' [The Muhammadan Qur'an], *Radio Zamaneh*, 2008–9, https://mamnoe.files.wordpress.com/2009/06/quran-mohammadi.pdf. It is to be mentioned that Ganji later on radically changed his view and wrote another series of articles criticising the Soroushian theory of the Qur'anic revelation.

36 Abū'l-Qāsim Fanā'ī [Abolghasem Fanaei], 'Kalam-i bāri, ṣifāt-i bārī: Dar bāb-i imkān-i sukhan guftan-i Khudāwand' [Speech of God, Attributes of God: On the Possibility of God's Speaking], *Ayeen* 17 (2008), pp. 57–63.

37 'Abdol'alī Bāzargān, 'Hawā yā hudā dar kalām-i waḥy' [The Whim or the Guidance in the Language of Revelation], 2008, http://www.drsoroush.com/Persian/On_DrSoroush/P-CMO-Bazargan.html.

38 Abdolkarim Soroush, 'Islam, Revelation and Prophethood: An Interview with Abdulkarim Soroush about the Expansion of Prophetic Experience', 2008, http://www.drsoroush.com/English/Interviews/E-INT-Islam,%20Revelation%20and%20Prophethood.html.

39 'Negative Theology', in Nicholas Bunnin and Jiyuan Yu, eds., *Blackwell Dictionary of Western Philosophy* (Malden, 2004), p. 466.

40 David Braine, 'Negative Theology', in Edward Craig, ed., *The Shorter Routledge Encyclopedia of Philosophy* (Abingdon, 2005), p. 723.

41 Veselin Kesich, 'Via Negativa', in Lindsay Jones, ed., *Encyclopedia of Religion* (New York, 2005), p. 9587.

42 Jan Van Ess, 'Ḍirār b. 'Amr', *EI*², vol. XII, p. 226.

43 Abū'l-Ḥasan al-Ash'arī describes the Mu'tazilī apophatic position as follows: 'The Mu'tazilites are unanimous that God is unlike anything else and that He hears and sees and is neither body, ghost, corpse, form, flesh, blood, substance, nor accident and that He is devoid of color, taste, smell, tactual traits, heat, cold, moistness, dryness, height, width, or depth . . ., and that He is indivisible . . . and is not circumscribed by place or subject to time . . . and that none of the attributes of the creature which involve contingency can be applied to Him . . ., and that He cannot be perceived by the senses or assimilated to mankind at all', quoted in Majid Fakhry, *A History of Islamic Philosophy*, 3rd edn (New York, 2004), p. 58.

44 Soroush, *The Expansion of Prophetic Experience*, p. 296.
45 Harry Austryn Wolfson, *The Philosophy of the Kalam* (Cambridge, MA, 1976), pp. 240–41.
46 Ibid., p. 268.
47 Ibid., p. 275.
48 Matin Ghaffarian, 'I'm a Neo-Muʿtazilite: An Interview with Abdulkarim Soroush', 2008, http://www.drsoroush.com/English/Interviews/E-INT-Neo-Mutazilite_July2008.html.
49 Ibid.
50 Wolfson, *The Philosophy of the Kalam*, p. 276.
51 Hans Daiber, 'Muʿammar b. ʿAbbād', *EI*[2], vol. VII, p. 259. See also Anwar G. Chejne, 'Muʿammar Ibn ʿAbbād al-Sulamī, a Leading Muʿtazilite of the Eighth–Ninth Centuries', *Muslim World* 51, no. 4 (1961), pp. 314–15.
52 Soroush, *The Expansion of Prophetic Experience*, p. 295.
53 Wolfson, *The Philosophy of the Kalam*, pp. 235–80.
54 For an illuminating and diverse collection of articles which applies the realism/non-realism debate in philosophy to religion, see Joseph Runzo, ed., *Is God Real?* (New York, 1993).
55 Soroush, *The Expansion of Prophetic Experience*, pp. 63–91.
56 Ibid., pp. 93–4.
57 Abdolkarim Soroush, *Basṭ-i tajruba-yi nabawī* [The Expansion of Prophetic Experience] (Tehran, 1999), p. 341.
58 Abdolkarim Soroush, "Ishq hamchūn Khudā' [Love as God], 2007, http://lectures.drsoroush.com/Persian/Lectures/Eshgh%20hamchon%20khoda%2017,%2012,%2085.mp3.
59 Abdolkarim Soroush, *Ṣirāṭhā-yi mustaqīm* [Straight Paths] (Tehran, 1999), p. 4.
60 Ibid., p. 7.
61 Ibid., p. 59.
62 William P. Alston, 'Realism and the Christian Faith', *International Journal for Philosophy of Religion* 38, no. 1/3 (1995), p. 53.
63 John Hick, *An Interpretation of Religion: Human Responses to the Transcendent*, 2nd edn (New Haven, CT, 2004), p. 350.
64 Abdolkarim Soroush and John Hick, 'Ṣūrat bar bī-ṣūratī: Guft-u-gūy-i Jān Hīk wa ʿAbd al-Karīm Surūsh' [A Form upon Formless: A Dialogue between John Hick and Abdolkarim Soroush], 2005, http://www.drsoroush.com/Persian/Interviews/P-INT-138409-John&Soroush.html.
65 Ibid.
66 Don Cupitt, *Mysticism after Modernity* (Malden, 1998), p. 40.
67 Hick, *An Interpretation of Religion*, p. 278.
68 Ibid., p. 39.
69 Ibid., p. 369.
70 David Basinger, 'Religious Diversity (Pluralism)', in Edward N. Zalta, ed., *The Stanford Encyclopedia of Philosophy*, http://plato.stanford.edu/archives/fall2014/entries/religious-pluralism/.
71 Soroush and Hick, 'Ṣūrat bar bī-ṣūratī'.
72 Soroush, *The Expansion of Prophetic Experience*, p. 338.
73 Ibid., p. 329.

74 Soroush and Hick, 'Ṣūrat bar bī-ṣūratī'.
75 Abdolkarim Soroush, 'Ḥikmat-i īmānīyyān, ḥikmat-i yūnānīyyān' [The Wisdom of the People of Faith, the Wisdom of the People of Greece], 2004, http://www.drsoroush.com/Persian/By_DrSoroush/F-CMB-13830605-meisami.html.
76 Soroush, *Ṣirāṭhā-yi mustaqīm*, pp. 59ff.
77 Soroush, *The Expansion of Prophetic Experience*, p. 273.

SECTION II

Alternative Approaches: Between Marginality and Legitimacy

7

A Sufi Defence of the Qur'an: Ḥusayn 'Alī Shāh's Rebuttal of Henry Martyn

REZA TABANDEH

THE EUROPEAN-CHRISTIAN missionaries' encounter with Iranian Muslims in the nineteenth century was a remarkable event in the cultural and religious history of Iran. An excerpt from this page of history may be seen in Henry Martyn's theological challenge of the Shi'i *'ulamā'*. Martyn (d. 1812), a young and zealous evangelical preacher, spent a relatively short time in Iran, but wrote a polemical treatise in refutation of the Prophet Muhammad and his message. The Shi'i *'ulamā'*, in turn, wrote treatises in refutation of Martyn, and from this there developed a whole theological genre known as *radd-i pādrī* (refutation of the priest). This chapter will examine the treatise by Ḥusayn 'Alī Shāh (d. 1818), a Shi'i *'ālim* (seminary scholar) and Sufi master, who wrote a refutation of Martyn. The *Radd-i pādrī* was the only treatise Ḥusayn 'Alī Shāh ever wrote, and in it he set out to prove both the inimitability of the Quran and the legitimacy of the Prophet Muhammad as a messenger of God. His work was also among the very first of these kinds of treatises and, as will be shown in this chapter, it became the basis and source for all the other treatises that followed. It is, therefore, of tremendous importance and deserving of further scrutiny.

Sufism in Persia

Sufism was an important element in the religious history of Qajar-era Persia (1796–1925) – a reality that was noted by many a contemporary Western observer at the time.[1] This was in contrast to the Safavid era (1501–1722), when the Sufi orders were gradually jettisoned out of the spectrum of acceptable religious standard.[2] The oppression they faced led to the migration of many Sufi orders from Persia (Iran) to other more welcoming and stable places. Many Sufi masters with Sunni tendencies migrated to the Ottoman Empire, but most of the masters and orders migrated to India. Despite this, some Sufis retained their identity as Persians and always anticipated a return. After the fall of the Safavids, Persia faced a chaotic period of social turmoil and political quarrels between the Afshārids, Zands and Qajars. The result was that only a few Sufi masters remained in Persia: the Nūrbakhshī masters in Mashhad and the Dhahabī masters in Shiraz.[3]

The revival of Sufism started during the Zand dynasty (1750–1794) and continued through the Qajar era. During this time, the mystical philosophy of Sufism was brought into alignment with the theological standards of Twelver Shiʿism, the ruling theology of the land.[4] The two leading Sufi orders involved in this revival movement were the Niʿmatullāhīs and the Dhahabīs.[5] These two orders had much in common,[6] as both of them emphasised the importance of observing the sharia and conforming to mainstream Twelver creed, and were known to be among the propagators of the mysticism of Ibn ʿArabī (d. 638/1240).[7] These Sufi orders aimed for survival despite the inquisitional verve of Shiʿi clerics.[8] Besides the two orders, there were some minor activities by the Naqshbandīs, Qādirīs, Khāksārs and wandering dervishes, but these were not as influential as the Dhahabīs and Niʿmatullāhīs, as speculative Sufism (*taṣawwuf-i naẓarī*) predominated in these two orders.[9]

The Niʿmatullāhī order is named after the famous Sufi master of the eighth/fourteenth and ninth/fifteenth century, Shāh Niʿmatullāh Walī (d. 834/1431).[10] His successors migrated to the Deccan plateau in India in the ninth/fifteenth century, where they remained until their return to Persia in the late eighteenth century.[11] The last Niʿmatullāhī master to be resident in India was Riḍā ʿAlī Shāh (d. 1799). It was he who ignited the revival of the order in Persia after receiving complaints from Niʿmatullāhī Sufis there about not having a local master.[12] ʿAbd al-Ḥamīd Maʿṣūm ʿAlī Shāh (d. 1797), an Indian nobleman[13] and well-known disciple of Riḍā ʿAlī Shāh,[14] was eventually appointed as a spiritual guide and was enjoined to travel to Persia in order to revive the order in its motherland.[15]

Maʿṣūm set out for Persia to accomplish his spiritual mission in 1776.[16] There, he generated a wave of momentum that allowed the Niʿmatullāhī masters to gain considerable popularity,[17] and Sufism spread rapidly among the Persians,[18] largely due to the enthusiasm and charisma of the disciples that Maʿṣūm had gathered around him; though they were small in number, they were extremely active in propagating the order's mysticism.[19] Maʿṣūm's own charisma and enthusiasm served to attract many disciples in Shiraz – among them Mullā ʿAbd al-Ḥusayn Ṭabasī Fayḍ ʿAlī Shāh (d. 1785), his son Mullā Muḥammad ʿAlī Nūr ʿAlī Shāh I (d. 1797)[20] and Mullā Mahdī Mushtāq ʿAlī Shāh (d. 1792), all of whom were initiated into the order during this period[21] and constituted the backbone of the Niʿmatullāhī Sufi order (*silsila*) in the early nineteenth century.

The Niʿmatullāhiyya's charismatic personality, their poetry, as well as their emphasis on direct mystical experiences and the love of God were palatable to Persians because their philosophy reinterpreted and articulated classical Sufi teachings in light of Persian Shiʿi mystical theology. However, the Niʿmatullāhiyya did sometimes challenge the Shiʿi clerics. The poetry of Nūr ʿAlī Shāh is just one example of this. In a poem he says, 'And from the command of the Mahdī, I will revive the universe with my breath.'[22] The Shiʿi *ʿulamāʾ* saw this as an outrageous utterance and a direct challenge to their authority because they considered themselves to be the sole deputies of the twelfth imam (the Mahdī). In their view, anyone else claiming to have direct contact (spiritual or physical) with the twelfth imam was guilty of blasphemy. This was much more dangerous than not following Islamic laws; in extreme cases, it could end in the execution of the claimant.

Mīrzā Muḥammad Taqī Muẓaffar ʿAlī Shāh (d. 1800) was another influential master in the history of the Niʿmatullāhī order who antagonised the Shiʿi clerics. In praise of Mushtāq, he said:

Swear to God that in this cycle,
I am the deputy to the Mahdī of the ʿAskarī faith.

I am the sun of Truth, I am the one,
who was taught the art of fostering the inferiors.[23]

Such beliefs constituted challenges to the authority of the Shiʿi seminary scholars. Muẓaffar insinuates, here, that Shiʿi clerics' understanding of the traditions of the Shiʿi imams was limited and lacked true understanding of their in-depth meaning, but that the real Sufis, through the blessings of the Shiʿi imams, had gained the gnosis that is the true understanding of religion.[24]

Most Shiʿi clerics opposed the Niʿmatullāhī masters, and the few who were openly sympathetic to them were excommunicated. Muẓaffar ʿAlī Shāh and Fayḍ ʿAlī Shāh are just two examples of Niʿmatullāhī masters, Shiʿi clerics, philosophers who were excommunicated from Shiʿi seminaries due to their mystical activities.

As a result of the Niʿmatullāhī challenge to their authority, Shiʿi clerics set out to persuade the Zand ruler Karīm Khān (r. 1750–79) that Maʿṣūm ʿAlī Shāh's beliefs were corrupt and dangerous. Considering societal attitudes towards dervishes, this proved easy.[25] Shiʿi clerics also managed to convince Karīm Khān that not only were the Sufis heretical, they were also eroding his authority by claiming kingship, as demonstrated through their addition of the term 'Shāh' to their spiritual titles.[26] The Shiʿi clerics were successful in damaging the relationship between Karīm Khān and Maʿṣūm,[27] and the latter was banished from Shiraz.[28]

Maʿṣūm ʿAlī Shāh and Nūr ʿAlī Shāh were also banished from Isfahan by the Zand ruler ʿAlī Murād Khān (r. 1781–5).[29] However, the two Niʿmatullāhī masters received a warm welcome in Tehran from Āqā Muḥammad Khān Qājār (r. 1782–97),[30] the founder of the Qajar dynasty, who provided financial support for their pilgrimage to Mashhad.[31] His heir, Fatḥ ʿAlī Shāh Qājār (r. 1797–1834), was against Sufism, being more keen on the exoteric aspects of religion.[32] Fatḥ ʿAlī Shāh, who believed in astrological signs, talismans and magic,[33] needed the influential Shiʿi seminary scholars to provide religious legitimacy to the Qajar dynasty.[34] These scholars cultivated the monarch's superstitious beliefs, in which they were experts.[35]

Sufism in Persia was generally interpreted in light of the conduct of wandering dervishes. The wandering dervishes' food was provided through offerings from passers-by and tradesmen in the bazaar. Their earnings were based on begging. They did not identify with any particular Sufi order. The Niʿmatullāhī masters were well aware of the perception that people had of Sufism, and it dismayed them, leading them to stress the necessity of following Islamic laws.[36] The first *quṭb* (sole master) after Riḍā ʿAlī Shāh was Ḥusayn ʿAlī Shāh. Ḥusayn ʿAlī Shāh, who belonged to the clerical class of society and was known to be a good preacher in the mosque, managed to stabilise the Niʿmatullāhī order. He was well aware that the order's outward practices and manners had to be reformed in order to mitigate the persecution of the Sufis by the Shiʿi clerics. The *ʿulamāʾ* were anxious that the Sufis would try to infiltrate the royal palace and influence government officials, and thus upset their close relationships with the royal court.[37] They were also fearful that the mystical beliefs of the Sufis presented a challenge to their authority.[38] Although Ḥusayn ʿAlī Shāh was able to relatively reduce the level of persecution of the Niʿmatullāhīs, the Shiʿi clerics continued their opposition to the order. Due to their influence in Fatḥ ʿAlī Shāh's court, they were able to sustain the ruler's anxiety about Ḥusayn ʿAlī Shāh. As a result, Ḥusayn ʿAlī Shāh was summoned to the royal court. He was tormented and humiliated, but because of his seminary knowledge and his clerical background, he was able to win over Fatḥ ʿAlī Shāh.[39] Generally speaking, Ḥusayn ʿAlī Shāh was able to continue the Niʿmatullāhī Sufi tradition, despite the persecution faced by its followers. His mission during this chaotic period was therefore aimed less at furthering the propagation of the Niʿmatullāhī order and more at securing its continuity in early nineteenth-century Iran.

Ḥusayn ʿAlī Shāh: Preacher and Mystic

Ḥusayn ʿAlī Shāh became the master of the Niʿmatullāhī order at a critical period for Sufis in Persia. As noted above, during this time, Sufis were constantly harassed, attacked and criticised by various classes of society. It was common for members of the *ʿulamāʾ* – such as Āqā Muḥammad ʿAlī Bihbihānī (d. 1801), known as the Sufi-killer (*ṣūfī kush*),[40] and Mīrzā Abū'l-Qāsim Qummī (d. 1816), both of whom were contemporaries of Ḥusayn ʿAlī Shāh – to write treatises refuting Sufism. The Shiʿi *ʿulamāʾ* had a great deal of clout. They were allowed by Fatḥ ʿAlī Shāh to participate in matters of state,[41] and in this respect, it has been remarked that the Shiʿism of that age was characterised by a reassertion of the power of the mujtahid at both the judicial and social levels.[42] The *ʿulamāʾ* became powerful to the degree that they sometimes even challenged the state.[43]

In addition to being the master of the Niʿmatullāhī order, Ḥusayn ʿAlī Shāh was noted as a famous *ʿālim*, preacher and jurist.[44] Though there are conflicting reports about some aspects of his background – Zayn al-ʿĀbidīn Shīrwānī 'Mast ʿAlī Shāh' (d. 1837) maintained that he was from Khwānsār,[45] while Riḍā Qulī Khān Hidāyat believed that he came from Tabriz[46] – what is clear is that most of Ḥusayn ʿAlī Shāh's male family members belonged to the class of formally trained Shiʿi *ʿulamāʾ*.[47] In his early years, he was known as Ḥājj Muḥammad Ḥusayn Iṣfahānī, before he was conferred the spiritual title Ḥusayn ʿAlī Shāh. During his youth, Ḥusayn ʿAlī Shāh studied the traditional religious curriculum in Isfahan.[48] After he completed his studies, his spiritual thirst was still not quenched, so he travelled to various places in Persia and the Arabian Peninsula, seeking out religious scholars and spiritual masters.[49] At the end of his travels he met and became the disciple of the masters Maʿṣūm ʿAlī Shāh, Nūr ʿAlī Shāh and Fayḍ ʿAlī Shāh,[50] and through their guidance and instruction obtained the enlightenment and gnosis he sought.[51] These Niʿmatullāhī masters saw in Ḥusayn ʿAlī Shāh a person whose juridical background could be influential for the order. As Ḥusayn ʿAlī Shāh advanced on the spiritual path, Nūr ʿAlī Shāh appointed him as a spiritual master and told him to return to Isfahan to guide the seekers.[52] Maʿṣūm ʿAlī Shāh and Nūr ʿAlī Shāh also directed him to continue preaching and praying in the mosque and religious seminaries,[53] and to retain the clerical robes worn by the exoteric Shiʿi clerics. In this way, he would be able to continue his life as a cleric without anyone recognising him as a member of the Niʿmatullāhī Sufi order.[54]

Finally, in the year 1797, in the village of Zahāb in Kurdistān, Nūr ʿAlī Shāh appointed Ḥājj Muḥammad Ḥusayn Iṣfahānī as the sole master (*quṭb*) of the order and endowed upon him the spiritual title 'Ḥusayn ʿAlī Shāh'.[55] Ḥusayn ʿAlī Shāh became the first *quṭb* of the order who was a native of Persia, thus making the return of the Niʿmatullāhī order to Persia complete after a sojourn of nearly three hundred years on the Indian subcontinent. However, since the situation for the Sufis was one of extreme tribulation, Ḥusayn ʿAlī Shāh was careful to ensure that his conduct would not arouse the suspicions of Twelver Shiʿi clergymen; he always talked and behaved as if he were merely a jurist (*faqīh*) and preacher. During Ḥusayn ʿAlī Shāh's leadership, none of his disciples were tortured or arrested.[56] He was always open to dialogue with seminary scholars and adopted a conciliatory tone with Shiʿi clerics.[57]

Ḥusayn ʿAlī Shāh lived in a seminary school[58] – the Madrasa-i ʿAlī Qulī Āqā – in Isfahan, where he taught and preached. This allowed him to cultivate better relations with the exoteric *ʿulamā'*,[59] and led at times to the initiation of a number of jurists and philosophers into Sufism.[60] Nevertheless, he was not totally free and safe from the criticism, jealousy and attacks of the *ʿulamā'*. Mullā ʿAlī Nūrī (d. 1830), who was a great philosopher and had many students and disciples, was his greatest enemy. Mullā ʿAlī Nūrī's jealousy of Ḥusayn ʿAlī Shāh arose when some of his disciples left him and became devotees of Ḥusayn ʿAlī Shāh, to whom they confessed the deficiency of their past beliefs.[61] Mullā ʿAlī Nūrī requested the help of Ḥājj Muḥammad Ḥusayn Khān Marwī (an influential noble who, it is claimed, supported the jurists) to discredit Ḥusayn ʿAlī Shāh. Marwī accepted, and wrote a letter to Fatḥ ʿAlī Shāh accusing Ḥusayn ʿAlī Shāh of treason and of aspiring to become king. The shah summoned Ḥusayn ʿAlī Shāh to Tehran,[62] and ordered his arrest. However, Fatḥ ʿAlī Shāh changed his mind while Ḥusayn ʿAlī Shāh was on his way to Tehran, and instead ordered that he be escorted to his presence as a guest rather than as a convict.[63] Ḥusayn ʿAlī Shāh was able to win the shah's admiration during their meeting in Tehran, with the shah calling him a person of spirituality. During the interrogation of his beliefs, the shah was so impressed by Ḥusayn ʿAlī Shāh that he even asked to receive spiritual instruction from him. The shah eventually ordered Ḥusayn ʿAlī Shāh to return to Isfahan and to continue to lead prayers in the mosques there.[64]

By the end of his life, Ḥusayn ʿAlī Shāh had established a relatively stable relationship between the Shiʿi clerics and the Niʿmatullāhī masters, which allowed the order to thrive; the Shiʿi clerics no longer saw the order as competitors or challengers to their authority. In 1818, Ḥusayn ʿAlī Shāh went to Karbala on pilgrimage. Sensing that he had accomplished his spiritual mission, he gathered all his disciples and appointed Majdhūb ʿAlī Shāh (d. 1823) as his successor. During his stay in Karbala, on 10 November 1818 (11 Muḥarram 1234), he passed away.[65]

Arrival of the Christian Missionaries

One of the important social and religious events in the history of Qajar Persia began with the arrival in 1781 of the Christian missionary Henry Martyn, who eagerly commenced his religious mission to convert Shiʿi Muslims in Persia to Christianity. The extent of his influence was described by the late nineteenth-/early twentieth-century historian Muḥammad Maʿṣūm Shīrāzī (d. 1925) as a calamity (*fitna*)[66] for Persian society.[67]

Due to the sociopolitical circumstances in Qajar Persia, Protestant missionaries had opportunities to travel to Persia to pursue their proselytising agenda. As the Qajar monarchy was in debt to the great Western powers, the monarch usually kept silent and did not make public his objections to their presence. Although Fatḥ ʿAlī Shāh commissioned scholars to write refutations of missionaries' doctrines, he avoided direct personal engagement in these theological disputes.[68]

Christian missionaries were particularly influential in Azerbaijan and active in the fields of medicine and education.[69] As a consequence of the appearance of Christian missionaries like Joseph Sabastiani[70] and Henry Martyn in Persia, the Shiʿi *ʿulamāʾ* inaugurated a new religious and literary genre devoted to refutation of their doctrines.

Henry Martyn: Missionary

Henry Martyn[71] was an Anglican priest who grew up in a family of followers of John Wesley (d. 1791),[72] the founder of the English Methodist movement.[73] During his youth, Martyn was influenced by the beliefs of his spiritual master Charles Simeon (d. 1836).[74] In 1802, Martyn was hired by the Society for Missions to Africa and the

East, which was later renamed the Church Missionary Society.[75] In 1806, he set off for India to serve as a priest in the employment of the British East India Company. There, he translated the Bible into the local languages, as a result of which he gained the appellation 'the Holy Father' (*pādrī*).[76] His attitude towards Muslims and Hindus was aggressive and intolerant, such that he called them the 'enemies of God'.[77]

Around 1811, Martyn left India for Persia where he immediately continued his mission by essaying to revise an earlier translation of the Bible into Persian. Although Sir John Malcolm (a major-general and administrator of the East India Company in Persia) warned Martyn about the danger of stirring up theological controversies between Muslims and Christians,[78] Martyn ignored his warning and became involved in religious disputations with Shi'i scholars,[79] which soon led to a strong reaction from them. Martyn considered the Persians 'immoral' and saw it as his mission to spread the message of Christ to the 'devilish Mohammedans'.[80]

Out of political expediency, Fatḥ 'Alī Shāh and his followers did not publicly oppose Martyn, who was supported directly by the English royal court. Nevertheless, Fatḥ 'Alī Shāh sought to appease the *'ulamā'* by encouraging them to write treatises in refutation of the Christian missionaries. Indeed, in the prefaces to their treatises, many acknowledged the support and encouragement of the shah and his court.[81] Meanwhile, in Shiraz, between June 1811 and May 1812, Martyn completed his translation of the Bible into Persian and then prepared two more copies of it in order to dedicate one to Fatḥ 'Alī Shāh and one to the shah's son, Prince 'Abbās Mīrzā (d. 1833). Martyn wanted to hand these copies to them personally, and set out for Tehran with the aim of doing this.[82] However, Fatḥ 'Alī Shāh and 'Abbās Mīrzā found excuses not to meet with him,[83] so Martyn began his journey to England. He died en route, in Turkey, on 16 October 1812 from an illness he had developed during his journey.[84]

Martyn's Confrontation with the Shi'i *'Ulamā'*

Martyn's first encounter with religious scholars in Persia occurred when he debated the validity of Islam and Muhammad's prophecy with some students of Mīrzā Ibrāhīm Fasā'ī, the chief mujtahid of Shiraz.[85] These discussions resulted in an exchange of polemical tracts and the composition of written responses: Fasā'ī wrote a response to Martyn's verbal refutations and Martyn countered with his treatises. Martyn also had long debates with Sufi masters in Shiraz.[86] He wrote a more complete treatise called *Mīzān al-ḥaqq* (The Scale of the Truth),[87] in which he made use of the Qur'an and the Prophetic traditions, the two most important sources of Islam, to argue against Islam itself. Henry Martyn was well versed in Islamic theology, Shi'ism and the seminary sciences in general, and this was acknowledged even by his opponents. Ma'ṣūm Shīrāzī, himself a scholar of considerable repute, gave Martyn the title of 'Christian sage' (*ḥakīm-i naṣrānī*) to indicate his respect for Martyn's knowledge and understanding.[88] Martyn's *Mīzān al-ḥaqq* played a crucial role in the social and religious history of this period, and led to the establishment of a new genre in literature known as 'responses'.

A Summary of Martyn's *Mīzān al-ḥaqq*

Martyn's treatise was written in elegant and fluent Persian and displayed his extensive knowledge of the Hadith and the Qur'an. He was also well versed in the history of Islam, as is evident in his references to historical events. The *Mīzān al-ḥaqq* consists of an introduction and three chapters. One of the major themes of the treatise is the eternal quest of human beings for happiness. In the introduction, he states that material joys and worldly sciences cannot satisfy this need; rather, it is through the knowledge of God that one can attain happiness.[89] Martyn's exclusivist approach is evident in this treatise, as he asserts that there is only one religion of Truth.[90]

The first chapter is devoted to proving that the New Testament and Old Testament had been neither abrogated (*naskh*) nor falsified (*taḥrīf*), as Muslims often claimed. This chapter is divided into three subchapters. The first subchapter deals with the Qur'an's doctrine about the New Testament and the Old Testament having been divinely revealed by God.[91] The second subchapter is devoted to demonstrating that neither the Old nor the New Testament was abrogated by the Qur'an. Here, Martyn asserts that though the Qur'an and its interpreters state that the Bible is rescinded by the Qur'an, none of the divine inspirations abrogate the others. Rather, all divine revelations were the completion of prior messages.[92] The New Testament completed the Old Testament;[93] thus he contends that 'the claim of Muhammad' that they abrogated each other was unfounded.[94] The third subchapter asserts that there had been no falsification of the Old Testament or the New Testament.[95] Martyn turns the Muslim argument against the Bible around and contends that Christians should argue that the Qur'an had been altered, as it was collected by the third caliph 'Uthmān (r. 23–35/644–55), who, he says, was known by Shi'is to be an infidel.[96] He concludes that the doctrines of Islam as presented in the Qur'an have been proven false,[97] and he invites 'Muhammadans' to read the Bible without prejudice.[98]

The second chapter justifies Jesus's divinity and the unity of the Trinity.[99] There, Martyn covers the overall Christian views about Jesus and the Holy Trinity – that Jesus sacrificed himself for the sins of humanity and that the Holy Spirit was always with the disciples of Christ.[100] From this, he concludes that the Bible was the perfect instruction for the salvation of humanity.[101] Martyn states that the human intellect is not capable of comprehending the Word of God, but argues that one could gain this knowledge through Jesus Christ, the Saviour,[102] and he names various prophets through whom God had promised the coming of a saviour.[103] Martyn refers to verses from the New Testament to prove the divinity of Christ.[104] The grace from Christ, he expounds, enlightens the believer's heart with knowledge[105] and cures believers of spiritual diseases.[106] He offers the apologetic proposition that the Father, the Son and the Holy Spirit are all one Holy Essence and not different, and he uses metaphors and references from the New Testament to show that the concept of the Trinity does not contradict monotheism.[107] Martyn writes that the Bible is the word of God and concludes that all the correct predictions and the miracles of Jesus are proof that the New Testament is a work of divine inspiration.[108]

The third chapter, which consists of five parts, is a refutation of Muhammad's claim to prophecy and his transmission of the

Qur'an. According to Martyn, one could not trust Muhammad's claim that he was the prophet of God because many mendacious prophets had made the same assertion. He avows that his investigation is based on justice and not on bigotry, and concludes that the Qur'an could not be the Word of God as it did not conform to any of the prior divine revelations. He contends that there are many points in the Qur'an which are in contradiction to previous revelations.[109]

In the Qur'an, there is a verse that states, *Nay! he has come with the (very) Truth, and he confirms (the Message of) the messengers (before him)* (Q. 37:37).[110] Muslim scholars saw this as a confirmation of Muhammad's legitimacy as a prophet and a reference to the New Testament prophecy from previous prophets about his coming. In his mission to discredit Muhammad as prophet, Martyn tackles the section of the Qur'an which claims that Jesus told the Children of Israel that there would be a prophet by the name of Aḥmad (Aḥmad being another name for Muhammad): *And remember, Jesus, the son of Mary, said: 'O Children of Israel! I am the messenger of Allah (sent) to you, confirming the Law (which came) before me, and giving Glad Tidings of a Messenger to come after me, whose name shall be Ahmad'* (Q. 61:6). He refutes the truth of this verse by emphasising that nowhere in the New Testament did Jesus predict the coming of a prophet named Aḥmad. However, in the Gospel of John, Jesus says, 'And I will ask the Father, and he will give you another Helper (Paraclete), to be with you forever' (John 14:16). Another translation of 'Paraclete', the one used by Muslims, is the 'praised one', which is the exact translation of 'Aḥmad'. From a Muslim point of view, the Paraclete prophesied by Jesus does not refer to the the 'Helper' (i.e. the Holy Spirit) but to the Prophet Muhammad, that is, Aḥmad. The abovementioned verse of the Qur'an supports this. Nevertheless, Martyn condemns those Muslims who claimed that the words 'Paraclete' and 'Aḥmad' were the same.[111] In ending the first part of the third chapter, Martyn again calls on Muhammadans to read the Bible without any bigotry so that they might discover the invalidity of the Qur'an's claims.[112]

Next, Martyn confronts the Muslim claim that because no human being would have been capable of writing a book like the Qur'an, it was a sign that the Qur'an was from God. He asserts that this is not good enough proof. For him, the eloquence of a book does not prove that it is a miracle from God,[113] thus, the Qur'an's eloquence neither legitimises it as the Word of God nor validates the apostleship of Muhammad.[114] Martyn points out that the Qur'an contained verses that were in complete accordance with the Bible and states that it had therefore copied some of the commandments. In his view, this shows that the Qur'an was not the Word of God, and he makes the judgement that it was simply a very defective forgery of previous divine revelations.[115] He also asserts that, in the Qur'an, Muhammad left out anything he did not agree with in the Bible, and that many of the stories from the Bible that Muhammad did use had been distorted because he added some parts according to his imagination or from the Talmud and the Zohar, traditional Jewish texts.[116] Martyn then argues that Muhammad could not possibly be the saviour of humanity because he was not divine. He bolsters this contention by referring to various verses from the Qur'an that mention Muhammad having to repent. These verses, he claims, suggest that Muhammad had been sinful and not immaculate.[117] According to Martyn, the Qur'an contains many unethical commandments[118] which he stresses were based on Muhammad's carnal desires and permitted Muhammad to commit any form of oppression.[119] Martyn sees this as proof that the Qur'an is a man-made book.[120] He further accuses Muhammad of being a fraud by contending that he was not even able to create miracles, save one. In support of this declaration, he refers to several verses from the Qur'an stating that the only miracle attributed to Muhammad was the Qur'an.

Martyn argues that Muhammad used the verses of the Qur'an to justify his unethical lifestyle: the verses allowed him to create an idea of a heaven that would tempt lustful Arabs to convert to his religion and also enabled him to divorce his innocent wives, without any reason, and marry new ones out of lust.[121] Continuing in this vein, he turns to Muhammad's migration to Medina and his gathering of an army there; he asserts that Muhammad made up the verses on jihad to justify taking revenge on his enemies, and that he murdered those who were against him and forced others to convert.[122]

At the end of his treatise, Martyn claims to have successfully proven that the religion of the Muhammadans was not based on the Truth, and invites everyone to embrace the religion of Christ. The *Mīzān al-ḥaqq* promotes Martyn's belief that the soul of humanity thirsts for happiness and that this thirst can be satisfied only through the divine inspiration found in the Bible. Martyn also emphasises his conviction that the New Testament did not abrogate the Old Testament, but completed it. Therefore, he argues, the Qur'anic verses on its abrogation were null and void.[123]

Martyn's treatise, particularly his views that the Qur'an was invented by Muhammad to justify his carnal desires and that Islam had been spread through the sword and was, therefore, a false religion, incited a vehement reaction from the Shiʿi seminary scholars, who saw all of this as blasphemy. Doubtless, their ire was also fuelled by the Sufi undertones in the work, as is evident from Martyn's use of such Sufi terms as *maʿrifa* (gnosis) and *khāhish-hāyi nafsānī* (carnal desires). It is interesting that though Martyn was against Islam, he seemed to connect to Sufism, or at the very least, the language of Sufism made sense to him.

The Result of Martyn's Treatise: The *Radd-i pādrī* Genre

Henry Martyn's stay in Persia and his composition of *Mīzān al-ḥaqq* gave rise to the *radd-i pādrī*, which can be considered a sort of literary genre in its own right. By the end of Fatḥ ʿAlī Shāh's rule in 1834, twenty-eight responses to Martyn's work had been written by jurists, philosophers and Muslim scholars of all backgrounds.[124] Later on, it became routine for many laypersons to write refutations of Martyn, such as Mīrzā Muḥammad Hāshim Āṣif (d. 1874), who wrote *Rustam al-tawārikh*.[125] The Sufi masters who wrote refutations of Martyn's ideas followed the same path as jurists, while building on their own spiritual doctrines. Certainly, Ḥusayn ʿAlī Shāh's treatise was among the first of such treatises, and served as a model for the genre. Here is Maʿṣūm Shīrāzī's testimony of this:

> Truly [Ḥusayn ʿAlī Shāh] responded in a clever and pleasing manner with fascinating phrases. The rest of the responses are by

> the *'ulamā'*, such as the divine mystic Ḥājji Mullā Riḍā Hamadānī, with the spiritual title of Kawthar 'Alī Shāh, and the likes of 'Allāma Narāqī, each of whom wrote a detailed book devoted to the rebuttal of the *pādrī* [Henry Martyn's book]. The basis for all of these books is the book of Ḥājji Iṣfahānī [Ḥusayn 'Alī Shāh].[126]

Being the first written refutation of Martyn, it became the basis and source for all the other treatises that followed.[127] Before embarking on a detailed explanation of Ḥusayn 'Alī Shāh's response to Martyn, it will be helpful to review some of the other responses to Martyn's work by other contemporary *'ulamā'* and Sufi masters.

Among the rebuttals, the one by Mullā Muḥammad Riḍā Hamadānī (d. 1831) carries some weight, if anything because he was a Sufi himself. Known as Kawthar 'Alī Shāh, he was a Ni'matullāhī master who was well versed in the sciences of the Shi'i seminary.[128] Mullā Muḥammad Riḍā authored two treatises refuting Martyn. The first is called *Irshād al-muḍillīn fī ithbāt khātam al-nabiyyīn* (Guidance for the Misguided on the Proof of the Prophecy of the Seal of Prophethood), written with the encouragement of Fatḥ 'Alī Shāh and supported by the influential Mīrzā Buzurg Qā'im-Maqām Farāhānī (d. 1822), which was completed in 1812.[129] In this treatise, Mullā Muḥammad Riḍā critiques Martyn's quotations from the New Testament. He argues that the Christians had misinterpreted the word 'Paraclete' (*fāraqīlīṭ*) by translating it as 'Holy Spirit' whereas it really meant the Prophet Muhammad.[130] The second treatise is called *Miftāḥ al-nubuwwa* (The Key of Prophethood), which Muḥammad Riḍā wrote three years after *Irshād al-muḍillīn*. It is an updated, revised and more complete version of the former work which he wrote in six parts and presented to Fatḥ 'Alī Shāh.[131] In *Miftāḥ al-nubuwwa*, Muḥammad Riḍā accuses Martyn of following his 'ignorant carnal soul' (*nafs-i jāhil*) by denying the Qur'an. He also asserts that Martyn's claims were unjust and were meant to deceive the masses.[132]

Another noteworthy rebuttal of Martyn came from Sufi master Mīrzā Abū'l-Qāsim (d. 1823),[133] also known as Sukūt. He had met Nūr 'Alī Shāh in Isfahan[134] and subsequently became a disciple of Ḥājj 'Abd al-Wahāb Nā'īnī (d. 1797),[135] known as Pīr Nā'īn, who was a Nūrbakhshī master based in the city of Nāʾīn.[136] Sukūt did not refute Christianity and he interpreted the Christian faith through the philosophical Sufi doctrine of *waḥdat al-wujūd* (Unity of Being), which upholds the belief in the transcendental unity of religions. Sukūt maintained that the differences between prophets and other human beings had to do with how much they had evolved spiritually towards perfection.[137]

Another well-known scholar and philosopher of the time who wrote a rebuttal of Martyn was Mullā ʿAlī Nūrī.[138] His refutation of the *Mīzān al-ḥaqq*, called *Ḥujjat al-islām* (Proof of Islam), uses philosophical methods in responding to Martyn.[139] It was written at the request of Fatḥ ʿAlī Shāh and ʿAbbās Mīrzā.[140]

As testimony to the popularity of the genre, one can count the fact that the famous jurist Mullā Aḥmad Narāqī (d. 1829) too wrote a rebuttal. His *Sayf al-umma* (The Sword of the [Muslim] Community) is a perfect example of what came to be known as 'scriptural argumentation' (*iḥtijāj kitābī*). This was 'a new strategy in *uṣūl al-fiqh* devised by Shīʿī jurists in questioning the prophethood (*nubuwwa*) of Jesus'.[141] It was based on textual analysis of the Qur'an and the New Testament.[142]

Mīrzā Abū'l-Qāsim Qummī (d. 1816), another well-known jurist, wrote an incomplete response to Martyn. He had intended to write a fuller treatise, but died before its completion and before he could name it.[143] In many parts of his treatise, he based his exposition on the theory of scriptural argumentation, like Narāqī.[144] In it, Qummī maintains that Christians denied the soundness of the Qur'an and that it was therefore impossible to expect Muslims to believe in the past prophets, including Jesus.[145]

Ḥusayn ʿAlī Shāh's Response to Martyn's *Mīzān al-ḥaqq* (1833)

As an Islamic scholar, Ḥusayn ʿAlī Shāh set out to write a response grounded in his theology, and he challenged Martyn to submit to a *mubāhala*. *Mubāhala* literally means 'mutual prayer', and in Islamic tradition it refers to an ordalic form of resolving religious disputes. It has a Qur'anic basis in *Sūrat al-ʿImrān* (Q. 3), which states, *If any one disputes in this matter with thee, now after (full) knowledge Hath come to thee, say: 'Come! let us gather together,– our sons and your sons, our women and your women, ourselves and yourselves: Then let us earnestly pray, and invoke the curse of Allah on those who lie!'* (Q. 3:61). Thus when the argumentations from both sides fail to resolve a religious issue, the parties jointly pray to God asking Him to cast His curse on whichever of the two parties is false. In *mubāhala*, the call to the ordeal may be more important than the execution of it.[146] In calling Martyn to the *mubāhala*, Ḥusayn 'Alī Shāh said: 'You are a Christian and I am a follower of Muhammad. Come thou that we go to the fire; whoever does not burn, his religion is based on the Truth.'[147] Martyn responded: 'I must be persuaded with knowledge and not with action', indicating that he would be persuaded only by arguments based on reason.[148]

Ḥusayn 'Alī Shāh's *Radd-i pādrī* is his only written work, and he composed it at the request of a number of his companions. His treatise, following the style of other jurisprudential and theological treatises, starts by praising God and continues with a salutation to the Prophet and the People of the House (*ahl al-bayt*), before eulogising Fatḥ 'Alī Shāh and Abbās Mīrzā. He refers to 'the Abode of Peace' (*dār al-islām*, here meaning Persia), which was in a state of jihad with Russia under the leadership of the shah and his heir.[149] He then responds to what he considers the 'futile' objections of Martyn to the miracle of the Qur'an and other miracles from the Prophet Muhammad.[150] He proposes that Martyn was motivated by 'carnal desires and temptations from Satan'.[151]

Ḥusayn 'Alī Shāh then establishes the validity of the Pillars of Islam,[152] and asserts that he would not rely exclusively on Islamic sources, such as the Hadith or stories about the Prophet, to provide evidence for prophecy, but would employ rational ways of proving his ideas that would be acceptable to anyone from any religion. Ḥusayn 'Alī Shāh confirms his firm belief in Judgement Day;[153] contrary to the beliefs of philosophers and many Sufi masters, he advocates that the spiritual and corporeal resurrection would happen together.[154] His approach was to first summarise Henry Martyn's beliefs and then reject them all methodically and rationally, providing quotations from the *Mīzān al-ḥaqq* before adding his response to or rebuttal of each quotation. What follows is a thematic summary of his riposte to Henry Martyn's polemic.

The unity of religions

In his treatise, Martyn claims that because the Old Testament and the New Testament did not negate each other, one could not believe in one and reject the other. Ḥusayn ʿAlī Shāh extrapolates from this, saying that Islam rejects neither Judaism nor Christianity, and arguing that if one negates Islam, as Martyn did, then one negates all other religions, because the essence of all is divine light.[155] Ḥusayn ʿAlī Shāh uses this theme of divine light to defend the prophethood of Muhammad:

> Also, I say that he whose light was in Adam's forehead was transferred to Eve's forehead. And continuously, it was transferred from fathers to mothers until he [Muhammad] was born. Always and in all eras, prophets gave the good tidings of the manifestations of the light and they were proud of it. The priests of Judaism and Christianity have given the good tidings about his [Muhammad's] coming.[156]

Even though Ḥusayn ʿAlī Shāh notes the good tidings of the appearance of the 'Prophet at the end of time', he still maintains there was always a light which was transferred through the prophets and their spouses down to the next prophet. The concept of the 'Perfect Man' and the 'Divine Light of Guidance', also known as the 'Muhammadan Light' or the 'Light of the Imamate', are intertwined in the mystical philosophy of Islam. Although Ibn ʿArabī laid the foundation for this philosophy, it predates the formation of Ibn ʿArabī's school of thought.[157] Toshihiko Izutsu, in his definition of Ibn ʿArabī's philosophy of the Perfect Man, said 'The Absolute, in its self-revealing aspect, reaches perfection in the Perfect Man', and added that there could be no more perfect self-manifestation than this being.[158] This definition was adopted by the Shiʿi followers of Ibn ʿArabī and applied to mean the perfection of the Shiʿi imam. Ḥaydar Āmulī (d. *c.* 787/1385) claimed that the light of the imams (the Muhammadan Light) was the source for the manifestation of the rest of creation and the main purpose of creation.[159] A hadith from ʿAlī (d. 40/661) reported in *Ḥayāt al-qulūb* and *Jalāʾ al-ʿuyūn* by Muḥammad Taqī Majlisī states that the first emanation from God was the Muhammadan Light. From that light, twelve ranks of lights emanated, which were the lights of the twelve imams. From these twelve lights, according to their rank, the lights of the prophets and other creatures emanated.[160]

In the *Knowledge of Certainty* (*ʿIlm al-yaqīn*), the Shiʿi mystic and philosopher Mullā Muḥsin Fayḍ Kāshānī (d. 1090/1679) cites a tradition of Prophet Muhammad which states that ʿAlī and the Prophet were the light between the Hands of God before the existence of creation. He concludes that the lights of Shiʿi imams were the manifestation of the most Beautiful Names of God, which at the end of the day was called the Muhammadan Light (*Nūr-i Muḥammadī*) or Muhammadan Reality.[161] Therefore, this philosophy existed long before the time of Ḥusayn ʿAlī Shāh and he borrowed it from prior Shiʿi philosophers to respond to Martyn.

Miracles

The Hour (of Judgment) is nigh, and the moon is cleft asunder.
But if they see a sign, they turn away, and say: 'This is (but) transient magic.'
They reject (the warning) and follow their (own) lusts but every matter has its appointed time.

(Q. 54:1–3)

Miracles are the proof of prophethood, and for the Prophet Muhammad the Qur'an and Hadith have confirmed his miracles. In later traditions of Islam, there are a number of narrations about the performance of supernatural wonders by Muslim mystics. These wonders were deeply rooted in Sufi tradition. For these supernatural wonders, Sufis did not use the same terminology as they did for the miracles of the prophets. They used the term *karāmat*, which Ahmet Karamustafa translates as 'charismatic gift'.[162] If one questions the miracles of the Prophet and can disprove them, then his prophecy can be rejected. In the above-mentioned verses of the

Qur'an, Prophet Muhammad was accused of sorcery and many did not accept his miracles.

Henry Martyn follows a similar path; he proposes that a miracle, which is one sign of prophethood, should be defined as an extraordinary act that no human being could perform.[163] Ḥusayn ʿAlī Shāh does not see any problem with this part of Martyn's statement. He maintains that miracles (*muʿjiza*), wonders (*karāmat*) and sorcery (*siḥr*) were extraordinary acts,[164] but that there were differences between the first two and the last. Miracles and wonders can be performed only by one who is in a state of proximity to God, whereas sorcery arises from distance from God and proximity to Satan.[165] However, Ḥusayn ʿAlī Shāh criticises Martyn's full definition of 'miracle', calling it defective and nonsensical;[166] he states that he did not need to investigate the miracles of previous prophets because of the certitude he felt for the authenticity of Prophet Muhammad and all the prophets, whereas Martyn found it necessary to investigate these miracles before their truthfulness could be revealed to him.

Martyn challenges the assertion of Muslim historians that the miracles of the prophets must be appropriate to the common understanding of the people; he argues that this was a false belief because none of the prior Christian historians had written about this. Ḥusayn ʿAlī Shāh counters Martyn's claim by pointing out that many miracles, such as the miracle of Ṣāliḥ's camel,[167] were not in accordance with the accepted norms and manners of their respective ages. Ḥusayn ʿAlī Shāh comments, 'If the father [Martyn] believes in religion, he must be aware that the claim of prophethood from the immaculate Muhammad was proven many times.'[168] Only those who felt enmity towards the Prophet Muhammad denied his prophethood and did not become believers. Ḥusayn ʿAlī Shāh stresses that the Qur'an is the eternal miracle of the Prophet Muhammad.[169]

Ḥusayn ʿAlī Shāh also explains that prophecy is divided into 'general prophecy' (*nubuwwat-i ʿāmma*), which is divine inspiration from the divine realm, and 'specific prophecy' (*nubuwwat-i khāṣṣa*), which refers to the new laws and new way of life that the prophets brought to their followers; this is a rendering of the classical distinction between *nubuwwa* (prophethood) and *risāla* (being a messenger of God).[170] He writes:

> Our prophet . . . claimed to be a prophet during his own era and this is proved to be so for both those who agree and disagree with him, as there are a series of narrations about it. No one denies these narrations. Also, he performed miracles as a sign of his claim [to prophecy] and there are numerous narrations about the miracles among those who agree and also those who disagree and doubt the miracles of prophet.[171]

Ḥusayn ʿAlī Shāh points out that no one could deny the Prophet's extraordinary acts. He responds to those who accused the Prophet of being a sorcerer by saying that anyone who was aware of the virtue, good manners and acts of the Prophet would not have these doubts and make these claims.[172]

Ḥusayn ʿAlī Shāh then turns his attention to another point of contention with Martyn. Martyn comments that if the miracles of the Prophet of Islam were not rejected and Islam was the religion of Truth, then all the Jews, Christians and some Arabs would convert to Islam; he also questions why the Muslims felt it necessary to convert them by the sword. Ḥusayn ʿAlī Shāh counters the first point by maintaining that some of those Jews, Zoroastrians and Christians who did not convert to Islam and who continued in their beliefs did so because they were not able to distinguish between miracles and sorcery, while others did not convert because of their love of wealth and social status. Nevertheless, he points out, many did convert, otherwise who were the Muslims of the time?[173] Regarding Martyn's second point, Ḥusayn ʿAlī Shāh states that the early Muslim wars were all fought in self-defence.[174]

The Qur'an as miracle

The Qur'an, in many places, refers to its inimitability (*iʿjāz*) and lays down the challenge to its audience to try to produce verses like it. This inimitability led to the construction of the philosophy that the Qur'an is miraculous by nature. The foretelling of the future or revealing knowledge of the unknown are the other aspects of the

Qur'an which make it inimitable.[175] The Qur'an's inimitability is one of the major subjects Ḥusayn ʿAlī Shāh covers in his treatise, and he takes on Martyn's claim that in the future someone well-versed in the Arabic language might indeed succeed in writing such a book. He retorts: 'It is enough that the contemporaries of the Prophet were helpless to write a book like the Qur'an.'[176] He adds that those who do not have enough knowledge of the Arabic language should put their trust in the opinion of those who do.[177] He then claims that Martyn approached Jews and Christians who were well versed in Arabic and asked them to write a book like the Qur'an, and that their inability to do so was proof of the inimitability of the Qur'an.[178]

Ḥusayn ʿAlī Shāh maintains that the miracles of the former prophets were linked to the sensible world (i.e. they were readily perceivable). He remarks:

> Since the Qur'an is in written form, it is sensible to the eye, and since it is literal, it is sensible to the ear as well. Regarding other miracles, [there] was the utterance of the burning bush to Moses, which [was] audible to the sense of hearing, and Moses' cane [turning] into a giant snake, which was sensible to the eyes.[179]

He argues that 'the Qur'an is a superior type of miracle because it is intellectual as well as sensible'.[180] The 'Word' or Logos was manifested in a book (Qur'an) in Islam, whereas in Christianity, it was manifested in flesh (Jesus); this means that the bodily form has disappeared in the case of Christianity, whereas in Islam the living Logos, which is the inspired book, can still be perceived today.

Next, Ḥusayn ʿAlī Shāh comments on Martyn's view that there were not more than five or six secrets in the whole of the Qur'an; he dismisses this by arguing that Martyn was not trustworthy enough to be privy to the Qur'an's secrets, which only the imams could know.[181] The Qur'an, he said, was like a bride wearing a veil (*burqa*); those who were not trustworthy were not able to see its beauty.[182] For him, Martyn did not have a true understanding of the Qur'an: he was poisoned by 'the snake of death'.[183] He asserts, furthermore, that anyone who followed the possessor of sainthood (*wilāyat*) with veneration and held the love of the saints in his or her heart would not suffer from the 'poison of the snake of death'.[184] In Ḥusayn 'Alī Shāh's view, those who had become saints (*awliyā'*) had a true understanding of the Qur'an.[185] They were privy to the Qur'an's secret beauties, to the point where, as the tradition says, they 'have gnosis of the real meaning of the Qur'an'; this tradition has long been part of Sufi culture.[186] Thus, Sufis have the inner understanding of the reality of the Qur'an, gained through their moments of ecstasy (*wajd*).[187] On the other hand, Shi'i clerics believed that the Shi'i imams were the only ones who had the inner understanding, and therefore complete knowledge, of the Qur'an.[188] Ḥusayn 'Alī Shāh cautiously creates an amalgamation of both viewpoints, emphasising the superiority of the imams' knowledge of the Qur'an's inner meaning. Saints, he believed, also possessed certain knowledge, although limited in comparison to that of Shi'i imams.

Islamic law

> 'The gnostic is the soul of the Divine law and the soul of piety:
> Gnosis is the result of past asceticism.'[189]

From the very earliest development of Sufi theology, Sufi masters had emphasised that there were two dimensions of religion: the exoteric aspects, that is, the canon of Islamic law (the sharia) and the inner aspects, that is, those aspects which make up the mystical path (*ṭarīqa*).[190] This latter theological belief was developed and theorised by generations of mystical philosophers and Sufi theologians.[191] Abū Ḥāmid al-Ghazālī (d. 505/1111) was among the first great mystic theologians who spoke of this distinction between esoteric and exoteric forms of Islam in his *Revivification of the Sciences of Religion* (*Iḥyā' 'ulūm al-dīn*).[192] Mast 'Alī Shāh, in line with this mystical philosophy, asserted that there was a path beyond the sharia taught in seminary schools.[193]

Muslim theologians and jurists always railed against Sufis for their alleged 'libertinism' and for not following Islamic laws. This accusation was largely based on their distaste for wandering dervishes (known as *qalandar*s), many of whom did not follow Islamic law and were therefore called antinomian dervishes (*darwīshān-i bī-shar'*). These dervishes were not initiated into any specific Sufi order and therefore did not follow the traditions of an order.[194] However, most Sufi masters always urged the importance of abiding by the exterior aspects of religion, that is, Islamic law. Ḥusayn ʿAlī Shāh put great effort into following the sharia to ensure that he would not attract the censure of Shiʿi clerics.[195]

Martyn argues that many commandments in Islamic law (*aḥkām-i sharīʿat*) had been promulgated merely to satisfy the passion of the carnal soul (*nafs*).[196] He uses polygamy as an example, and asks why Muslims were permitted to have no more than four wives while the Prophet Muhammad was permitted to have nine.[197] Examining the stories of the marriage of the Prophet Muhammad to Zaynab, the wife of his adopted son,[198] he notes that the Prophet had also taken an oath that he would not have sexual intercourse with his Coptic female slave Māriyya,[199] but that this oath was apparently later removed by divine revelation.[200] In response to Martyn's question about why the wives of the Prophet Muhammad were prohibited from remarrying,[201] Ḥusayn ʿAlī Shāh provides a mystical interpretation: 'the Prophet was the spiritual father of the community ... thus, for any other Muslims to marry the Prophet's wives would be a shameful act'.[202]

By referring to these stories and the traditions of the Prophet Muhammad, Martyn tries to prove that the Qur'an was not a divine revelation but rather a book written by a human being, and to show that many of the Islamic laws in the Qur'an were based on the Prophet Muhammad's carnal desires. In response, Ḥusayn ʿAlī Shāh refers to the famous hadith where the Prophet is believed to have said, 'Three things have been made beloved to me in this world of yours: women, perfume, while the coolness of my eye was placed in ritual prayer' (*ḥabbib ilyya min dunyākum al-nisāʾ wa al-ṭīb wa jaʿltu qurrat ʿaynī fīʾl-ṣalāt*),[203] stressing that it indicates the perfection of the Prophet. According to Ḥusayn ʿAlī Shāh, the Prophet's love of women was in accordance with Islamic laws and his lust fell within the legal limits permitted by the sharia for the continuation of the human race.[204] He proposes that love of the three abovementioned things results in the acquisition of *maʿrifa*,[205] and then interprets the saying as meaning that the Prophet Muhammad's main consideration was for the ultimate fruition of these three beloved things. He argues that anyone who was wise would follow the Prophet's example because reproduction was necessary for the survival of humanity and was a basic principle of human life.[206]

Ḥusayn 'Alī Shāh then asks why Martyn did not condemn Solomon for having had a thousand wives and for having followed the temptations of his carnal soul. He contends that Martyn's criticisms were born out of enmity towards the Prophet and concludes that his research did not bring him to the truth of the situation.[207]

Intercession (*shafā'a*) in Christianity and Shi'ism

The concept of 'spiritual intercession' (*shafā'a*) was another important theological doctrine held by many Sufis as well as Shi'is. Shi'is believe that the imams and the higher-ranked followers of the imams can intercede for the salvation of their followers.[208] Sufis also accept the philosophy of spiritual intercession by the Prophet Muhammad and saints. For example, Rūmī wrote: 'He [Prophet Muhammad] is the intercessor in this world and in yonder world – in this world (for guidance) to the (true) religion, and yonder (for entrance) to Paradise.'[209] Ḥusayn 'Alī Shāh defends the Shi'is' and the Sufis' theological beliefs about intercession and rejects the idea of general intercession based on Christian principles. In Sufism and Shi'ism, intercession can only be made by imams, saints or pious servants of God, and they can only do this on behalf of people who faithfully ask for intercession and whose beliefs accord with that of their intercessors.

In response to Martyn's explanation of the Christian idea of spiritual intercession (i.e. of Jesus's sacrifice for the sins of humanity),[210] Ḥusayn 'Alī Shāh writes that spiritual intercession is possible only if it is done in accordance with wisdom (*ḥikmat*).[211] He challenges Martyn's claim that Jesus is the spiritual intercessor for all humanity, and maintains that the idea of general intercession is contrary to divine justice and religious law.[212] He writes that in order to receive spiritual blessings, when praising Jesus one should include all the prophets and the faithful.[213] Ḥusayn 'Alī Shāh postulates that if the sacrifice and blood of Jesus had served to achieve the purification of humanity, there would have been no need for exoteric religious laws or religious prohibitions for humanity after Jesus. Therefore, all religions, including Christianity, would be abrogated due to the abrogation of those laws. Ḥusayn ʿAlī Shāh's Sufi understanding of religion as consisting of interior and exoteric laws that are inseparable from each other[214] resulted in his belief that if one part is destroyed it brings about the destruction of the whole.

Ḥusayn ʿAlī Shāh uses the term 'physician' (*ṭabīb*) for intercessor, as had other Sufis before him. Rūmī, for instance, writes, 'Hail, O love that bringest us good gain – thou that art the physician of all our ills, the remedy of our pride and vainglory, our Plato and our Galen!'[215] Also, the title of one of Rūmī's stories in the *Mathnawī* is, 'The Meeting of the King with the Divine Physician Whose Coming had been Announced to Him in a Dream';[216] the phrase indicates that the saints are viewed as divine physicians. Ibn ʿArabī, too, compared apostleship (*risāla*) with the physicians' duty, and said, 'Know that, just as the physician is said to be a "servant of Nature" (*khādim al-ṭabīʿa*), so the apostles and their successors are commonly said to be the "servant of the Divine command".'[217] Ibn ʿArabī elucidated the superiority of the apostle as the physician of the soul, and defined him as a spiritual doctor.[218] For him, because physicians have limited control and knowledge of the physical body, their power is inferior to that of the spiritual doctors.

Ḥusayn ʿAlī Shāh maintains that sin is like rotten food. If a person were to eat it, he would need medicine to prevent sickness. If he were to become sick, he would need to go to a physician, and the physician would tell him that he could not eat any food other than the distasteful medicine.[219] In this metaphoric example, he points out that the medicine is repentance (*tawba*), and the physician is the intercessor or saint who prescribed self-mortification for the sinner to purify his soul; without this cleansing, the sinner would be worthy of hellfire, that is, death.[220] Ḥusayn ʿAlī Shāh's explanation here contains an indirect reference to the Sufi path. According to most Sufi masters, the spiritual physician is the Sufi saint, and repentance is his medication. Ḥusayn ʿAlī Shāh also maintains that recovery from affliction with the sickness of deviations and disobedience to a healthy spiritual state occurs through the guidance of the spiritual physician. In this regard, Abū'l-Qāsim al-Qushayrī

(d. 465/1072) proposed that repentance was a return to the Islamic law and spiritual codes;[221] likewise, Abū Naṣr al-Sarrāj al-Ṭūsī (d. 378/988) and Abū'l-Ḥasan ʿAlī b. ʿUthmān Hujwīrī (d. *c.* 469/1077) also considered repentance to be the first station (*maqām*) of the spiritual path.[222]

The People of the Book

Ḥusayn ʿAlī Shāh's conciliatory tone towards the People of the Book is clear when he comments that the Jews and Christians who lived in the environs of Mecca in the Prophet's day socialised with Muslims and that there was no antagonism between them.[223] His views about the wars between the People of the Book and Muslims during the time of the Prophet are crucial. He believed that these wars were fought by Muslims in defence of their territories and their faith, and not for conquest.[224] He admires Sunni Muslims for their relationship with the People of the Book, and remarks, 'Sunni people, who are the dignified people of Islam on account of their numerousness and wealth, maintained friendship, brotherhood and social interactions with Jews and Christians.'[225]

Ḥusayn ʿAlī Shāh, like Shiʿi theologians, believed that the disciples of Jesus had altered the Word of God, the New Testament (*injīl*), and that there were different narrations of the Gospel among various Christian sects. This led him to question how Muslims could validate the Bible if there was no consensus about the Bible among Christians.[226] In his view, the New Testament was the Divine Word, but since the text had been altered, it was now nearly impossible to distinguish truth from falsehood in it.[227] Ḥusayn ʿAlī Shāh uses this point to rebut Martyn's statement that there was no mention of the Prophet Muhammad in the books of former prophets. Ḥusayn ʿAlī Shāh argues that the leaders of the Christian community omitted the name and titles of the Prophet Muhammad from the Bible and attributed these titles to themselves because of their love of power and wealth.[228] He states:

> The Prophet Muhammad in both the Torah and the *Injīl* was described in appearance and name. Some people do not come across it or they do not recognise it, whilst others have said that

these signs that are in the Torah and the *Injīl* are for a saviour that will come in the future. The consensus [among Muslims] is that this was Qā'im Āl-i Muḥammad [Mahdī] who is the promised Messiah.[229]

Ḥusayn ʿAlī Shāh also takes on Martyn's defence of the Trinity. He rejects the Christian doctrine that God had created someone in his own likeness, a God-figure who was Jesus, stating that this belief was evidently untrue.[230] He refers to various verses of Qur'an which refute the idea of the Trinity, and argues that belief in the Trinity arose from Christians' lack of understanding and from their altering the sayings of the prophets. He calls the Trinity a 'foolish imitation' and apostasy, and asserts that those who believed in the Trinity would go to the lowest level of hell (*asfal al-sāfilīn*).[231] Ḥusayn ʿAlī Shāh concedes that Jesus was the true prophet of God, but adds that with the emergence of Islam the religion of Jesus had been abrogated.[232] In this regard, his views were closer to Shiʿi theology than to the mystical philosophy of Sufism.[233]

Martyn claims that the vast diffusion of Christianity and conversion of people to its faith was a miracle. However, Ḥusayn ʿAlī Shāh makes the counterclaim that these conversions had been to a false religion, so there had been no miracle at all.[234] He believed that the religion of Christ was the religion of Truth, whereas the religion of Christians had strayed from the straight path of Truth. Thus, his statement: 'The religion that the *pādrī* and his cohorts hold is not the religion of Christ.'[235] Though he thinks that the Christians of his time were not the true heirs of Jesus, he nevertheless has good things to say about them: 'Truly, Christians (*naṣāra*) are superior in knowledge, intelligence, truthfulness, serenity, chivalrousness and loyalty in comparison to the followers of other religions.'[236] He also asserts that the Jews and the Magians who had converted to Islam during the time of the Prophet Muhammad were not true Muslims, but the Christians who had converted to Islam were because they converted out of 'truthfulness, serenity and righteousness'.[237] He invites Christians to contemplate the truthfulness of the Qur'an and Islam, and reminds them that Islam abrogated all former religions.[238]

Conclusion

Ḥusayn ʿAlī Shāh was among the first scholars who contributed to, and laid the foundation for, the polemical genre known as the *radd-i pādrī*. His short treatise was written more from the stance of a scholar of theology and of jurisprudence rather than a mystic. However, there are some mystical points in his treatise, though this is veiled and not really elaborated upon. According to the social and religious context of his time, Ḥusayn ʿAlī Shāh was more moderate in his defence of Islam than the majority of his contemporaries. This moderation was the result of his Sufi beliefs. However, he lived during an era when Sufis were being persecuted, therefore he was careful not to provoke the wrath of his fundamentalist Uṣūlī enemies with any mystical interpretations of Christianity. His views about the unity of all religions and of their having a divine light in their essence is indicative of his moderate view. This is also related to his polemical writing, as one who rejects one religion rejects all other religions. He respected other religions, and this comes across in the sections of his treatise where he adopted a conciliatory tone towards Christians and expressed the sentiment that there should be interaction, amity and brotherhood between Muslims and the People of the Book.

Ḥusayn ʿAlī Shāh's comportment, as the first Persian Niʿmatullāhī master, was appropriate to the context of the religious seminary milieu and the wider sociopolitical situation of this period. His mission was to dissimulate his beliefs and to conform to mainstream Shiʿism.[239] Ḥusayn ʿAlī Shāh presented himself as a preacher and scholar, and wrote his only treatise as a Shiʿi theologian. This treatise generally defended the Qur'an, the Prophet Muhammad and Islamic law against Christian missionaries and specifically responded to Martyn's criticism of Islam with theological arguments. His treatise was an important contribution to the literary and religious genre of *radd-i pādrī*.

Ḥusayn ʿAlī Shāh did not distinguish himself from seminary scholars, and his treatise reads like a dry Shiʿi jurisprudential refutation of Martyn with some hints of his mystical thinking. Today, it is hardly recognisable as the work of a Sufi who was also the supreme master of the Niʿmatullāhī order. His contribution to the intellectual and literary legacy of his period can be found in his riposte to Martyn. Before Ḥusayn ʿAlī Shāh's direct response to Martyn's attack on the Qur'an and Prophet Muhammad, there was no written refutation of Martyn, although there were a number of polemical quarrels and debates in religious seminaries and public places. Martyn's encounters with the students of Fasā'ī constitute the most important debates between Shiʿi seminarians and a Christian. However, Ḥusayn ʿAlī Shāh founded an intellectual environment for clerics, seminarians, intellectuals and Sufis to respond to Martyn through rational means. To him, the Qur'an was a supreme miracle because it was spiritual as well as intellectual, and he defended it well.

NOTES

1 As Sir John Malcolm noted, 'The doctrines, or rather principles of the Soofees, or philosophical devotees, which have lately spread very widely in Persia, will also merit a portion of our attention.' John Malcolm, *The History of Persia: From the Most Early Period to the Present Time* (London, 1815), vol. II, p. 218.

2 Abbas Amanat, *Resurrection and Renewal: The Making of the Babi Movement in Iran, 1844–1850* (Ithaca, NY, 1989), p. 14.

3 Muḥammad Taqī Khū'ī, *Ādāb al-musāfirīn*, MS 2409, Kitābkhāna-yi Dānishgāh-i Tihrān (Library of Tehran University), Tehran, p. 372.

4 ʿAbd al-Ḥusayn Zarrīnkūb, *Dunbāla-yi justujū dar taṣawwuf-i Īrān* (Tehran, 1362 Sh./1983), p. 309.

5 Ibid.

6 However, the reader should consider the peculiarities of Dhahabī Sufism, as pointed out in Ata Anzali, 'Safavid Shiʿism, the Eclipse of Sufism and the Emergence of ʿIrfān' (Unpublished PhD dissertation, Rice University, 2012), *passim*.

7 Ibid., pp. 193–209; Leonard Lewisohn, 'An Introduction to the History of Modern Persian Sufism, Part II: A Socio-cultural Profile of Sufism, from the Dhahabī Revival to the Present Day', *Bulletin of the School of Oriental and African Studies* 62, no. 1 (1999), p. 47.

8 Lewisohn, 'An Introduction to the History of Modern Persian Sufism, Part II', p. 57.

9 Leonard Lewisohn, 'An Introduction to the History of Modern Persian Sufism, Part I: The Niʿmatullāhī Order. Persecution, Revival and Schism', *Bulletin of the School of Oriental and African Studies* 61, no. 3 (1999), p. 438; Zarrīnkūb, *Dunbāla*, p. 309.

10 For further information on him, see Ḥamīd Farzām, *Taḥqīq dar aḥwāl wa naqd-i athār wa afkār-i Shāh Niʿmatullāh Walī* (Tehran, 2000); Nasrollah Pourjavady and Peter Lamborn Wilson, *Kings of Love: The History and Poetry*

of the Niʿmatullāhī Sufi Order (Tehran, 1978), pp. 13–92; Sholeh A. Quinn, 'Rewriting Niʿmatu'llāhī History in Safavid Chronicles', in Leonard Lewisohn and David Morgan, eds, *Heritage of Sufism, Vol. III: Late Classical Persianate Sufism (1501–1750)* (Oxford, 1999), pp. 201–25; Muḥammad Maʿṣūm Shīrāzī, *Ṭarāʾiq al-ḥaqāʾiq* (Tehran, 1966), vol. III, pp. 1–63; Ḥājj Mīrzā Muḥammad Bāqir Sulṭānī, *Rahbarān-i ṭarīqat wa ʿirfān* (Tehran, 1371 Sh./1992), pp. 180–88.

11 Anzali, 'Safavid Shiʿism', p. 252; Terry Graham, 'Shāh Niʿmatullāh Walī: Founder of the Niʿmatullāhī Sufi Order', in Leonard Lewisohn, ed., *The Heritage of Sufism, Vol. II: The Legacy of Medieval Persian Sufism (1150–1500)*, p. 178; Oliver Scharbrodt, 'The *Quṭb* as Special Representative of the Hidden Imam: The Conflation of Shiʿi and Sufi *Vilāyat* in the Niʿmatullāhī Order', in Denis Hermann and Sabrina Mervin, eds, *Shiʿi Trends and Dynamics in Modern Times (XVIIIth–XXth Centuries)/Courants et dynamiques chiites à l'époque modern (XVIIIe–XXe siècles)* (Beirut, 2010), p. 37.

12 Amanat, *Resurrection and Renewal*, p. 71; Anzali, 'Safavid Shiʿism', p. 252; Aḥmad Dīwānbaygī Shīrāzī, *Ḥadīqat al-shuʿarā*, ed. ʿAbd al-Ḥusayn Nawāʾī (Tehran, 1364 Sh./1985), vol. II, p. 1036; Scharbrodt, 'The *Quṭb* as Special Representative of the Hidden Imam', p. 37.

13 Asadullāh Khāwarī, *Dhahabiyya: Taṣawwuf-i ʿamalī-āthāri adabī* (Tehran, 1362 Sh./1983), p. 357; Pourjavady and Wilson, *Kings of Love*, p. 94; Scharbrodt, 'The *Quṭb* as Special Representative of the Hidden Imam', p. 37; Zayn al-ʿĀbidīn Shīrwānī (Mast ʿAlī Shāh), *Bustān al-sīyāḥa* (Tehran, 2010), p. 660.

14 Khāwarī, *Dhahabiyya*, p. 357; Scharbrodt, 'The *Quṭb* as Special Representative of the Hidden Imam', p. 37.

15 Amanat, *Resurrection and Renewal*, p. 71; ʿAbd al-Rafiʾ Ḥaqīqat, *Tārīkh-i ʿirfān wa ʿārifān-i Īrānī* (Tehran, 1388 Sh./2009), p. 219; Riḍā Qulī Khān Hidāyat, *Uṣūl al-fuṣūl*, MS 22920, Kitābkhāna-yi Majlis Shūrā-yi Islāmī, Tehran, fol. 547; idem, *Uṣūl al-fuṣūl*, MS 57B, registration number 56326, Bū ʿAlī Sīnā University Library, Hamadān, fol. 352; idem, *Tadhkira-yi Rīyāḍ al-ʿārifīn* (Tehran, 1385 Sh./2007), p. 539; Asadullāh Īzadgushasb, *Risāla Nūr al-abṣār* (Tehran, 1325 Sh./1946), p. 11; Khūʾī, *Ādāb al-musāfirīn*, p. 352; Shahrām Pāzūkī, 'Taṣawwuf dar Īrān baʿd az qarn shishum', in *Tārīkh wa Jughrāfīyāy-i taṣawwuf* (Tehran, 1388 Sh./2009), p. 43; William Ronald Royce, 'Mīr Maʿṣūm ʿAlī Shāh and the Niʿmat Allāhī Revival, 1776–77 to 1796–97: A Study of Sufism and Its Opponents in Late Eighteenth Century Iran' (Unpublished PhD dissertation, Princeton University, 1979), p. 2; Scharbrodt, 'The *Quṭb* as Special Representative of the Hidden Imam', p. 37; Shīrāzī, *Ṭarāʾiq*, vol. III, pp. 170–71; Shīrwānī, *Bustān*, pp. 264, 661; Sulṭānī, *Rahbarān-i ṭarīqat wa ʿirfān*, p. 206.

16 Amanat, *Resurrection and Renewal*, p. 71; Anzali, 'Safavid Shiʿism', p. 252; Īzadgushasb, *Nūr al-abṣār*, p. 10; Khāwarī, *Dhahabiyya*, p. 357; Khūʾī, *Ādāb al-musāfirīn*, p. 342; Pāzūkī, 'Qarn shishum', p. 43; Royce, 'Mīr Maʿṣūm ʿAlī Shāh and the Niʿmat Allāhī Revival', p. 13; Shīrwānī, *Bustān*, p. 661; Sulṭānī, *Rahbarān-i ṭarīqat wa ʿirfān*, p. 206.

17 According to Sir John Malcolm, the number of Maʿṣūm ʿAlī Shāh's disciples amounted to 'thirty thousand', but this was probably exaggerated by him. See Malcolm, *The History of Persia*, vol. II, p. 295.

18 Ibid., p. 292.

19 Amanat, *Resurrection and Renewal*, p. 71; Scharbrodt, 'The *Quṭb* as Special Representative of the Hidden Imam', pp. 37–8.
20 Amanat, *Resurrection and Renewal*, p. 72; Dīwānbaygī Shīrāzī, *Ḥadīqat al-shuʿarā*, vol. II, p. 1037; Ḥaqīqat, *Tārīkh*, p. 230; Khūʾī, *Ādāb al-musāfirīn*, pp. 352–3; Javad Nurbakhsh, *Masters of the Path: A History of the Masters of the Nimatullahi Sufi Order* (New York, 1980), p. 76; Scharbrodt, 'The *Quṭb* as Special Representative of the Hidden Imam', pp. 37–8; Shīrāzī, *Ṭarāʾiq*, vol. II, p. 332 and vol. III, p. 171; Shīrwānī, *Bustān*, p. 661; Zayn al-ʿĀbidīn Shīrwānī (Mast ʿAlī Shāh), *Ḥadāʾiq al-siyāḥa* (Tehran, 1348 Sh./1969), p. 27; Sulṭānī, *Rahbarān-i ṭarīqat wa ʿirfān*, p. 206.
21 Anzali, 'Safavid Shiʿism', p. 253; Dīwānbaygī Shīrāzī, *Ḥadīqat al-shuʿarā*, vol. II, p. 1037; Ḥaqīqat, *Tārīkh*, p. 230; Scharbrodt, 'The *Quṭb* as Special Representative of the Hidden Imam', p. 38; Shīrāzī, *Ṭarāʾiq*, vol. II, p. 332; Shīrwānī, *Bustān*, p. 661.
22 Mullā Muḥammad ʿAlī Nūr ʿAlī Shāh I, *Dīwān*, ed. Jawād Nūrbakhsh (Tehran, 1381 Sh./2002), p. 122; Scharbrodt, 'The *Quṭb* as Special Representative of the Hidden Imam', p. 43.
23 Amanat, *Resurrection and Renewal*, p. 74.
24 Scharbrodt, 'The *Quṭb* as Special Representative of the Hidden Imam', p. 43; Shīrwānī, *Bustān*, p. 1497.
25 Karīm Khān had always believed that those dervishes who propagated magic and hashish smoking deserved punishment. See Muḥammad Hāshim Āṣif ('Rustam al-Ḥukamā''), *Rustam al-tawārikh* (Tehran, 1352 Sh./1973), p. 323.
26 Malcolm, *The History of Persia*, vol. II, p. 295.
27 Amanat, *Resurrection and Renewal*, p. 75; Malcolm, *The History of Persia*, vol. II, p. 295.
28 Īzadgushasb, *Nūr al-abṣār*, p. 76; Malcolm, *The History of Persia*, vol. II, p. 295; Shīrāzī, *Ṭarāʾiq*, vol. III, p. 172; Shīrwānī, *Bustān*, p. 661; Zarrīnkūb, *Dunbāla*, p. 320. Aḥmad Dīwānbaygī Shīrāzī claimed that it was due to Karīm Khān's generosity and humility that he only banished Maʿṣūm from Shiraz with no other punishment. See Dīwānbaygī Shīrāzī, *Ḥadīqat al-shuʿarā*, vol. II, p. 1037; Ḥaqīqat, *Tārīkh*, p. 230; Hidāyat, *Uṣūl* (Hamadān), p. 359.
29 Muḥsin Kīyānī, *Tārīkh-i khāniqāh dar Īrān* (Tehran, 1369 Sh./1990), p. 267.
30 Ḥaqīqat, *Tārīkh*, p. 231; Sulṭānī, *Rahbarān-i ṭarīqat wa ʿirfān*, p. 207.
31 Despite Āqā Muḥammad Khān Qājār's good relationship with Sufis, his interest in mysticism was perfunctory and he failed to establish any firm beliefs regarding Sufism. He was more focused on military activities and the consolidation of the Persian kingdom. See Īzadgushasb, *Nūr al-abṣār*, p. 38; Shīrāzī, *Ṭarāʾiq*, vol. III, p. 173; Sulṭānī, *Rahbarān-i ṭarīqat wa ʿirfān*, p. 207; Zarrīnkūb, *Dunbāla*, p. 320.
32 Kīyānī, *Tārīkh*, p. 269.
33 Saʿīd Nafīsī, *Tārīkh-i ijtimāʿī wa sīyāsī dar dawra-yi muāāṣir* (Tehran, 1354 Sh./1975), vol. I, p. 100.
34 The volume of correspondence between the Shiʿi seminary scholars and the monarchy is proof of their close relationship. See ʿAbd al-Hādī Ḥāʾirī, *Nakhustīn rūyārūyī-i andīshihgarān-i Īrān* (Tehran, 1367 Sh./1988), pp. 356 and 360.
35 Nafīsī, *Tārīkh-i ijtimāʿī wa sīyāsī*, vol. I, p. 107.

36 Amanat, *Resurrection and Renewal*, p. 72.
37 Ḥā'irī, *Nakhustīn*, p. 360.
38 Kaywān Samī'ī and Manūchihr Ṣadūqī, *Du Risāla dar Tārīkhi jadīd-i taṣawwuf* (Tehran, 1370 Sh./1991), p. 63.
39 Hamid Algar, *Religion and State in Iran* (Los Angeles, CA, 1969), p. 64; Lewisohn, 'An Introduction to the History of Modern Persian Sufism, Part I', p. 441; Samī'ī and Ṣadūqī, *Du Risāla*, p. 63; Khāwarī, *Dhahabiyya*, p. 362.
40 A group of Shi'i clerics, championed by Bihbihānī, believed that Sufis should be physically persecuted. They viewed themselves as the protectors of Islam and therefore believed themselves qualified to demand punishment for those who they saw as polluting the religion of God. Bihbihānī encouraged the Qajar rulers in this action, which resulted in the martyrdom of Ma'ṣūm 'Alī Shāh (Lewisohn, 'An Introduction to the History of Modern Persian Sufism, Part I', p. 441) and Mushtāq 'Alī Shāh, and the poisoning (twice) of Nūr 'Alī Shāh. For this reason, Bihbihānī gained the title of Sufi-killer. See Amanat, *Resurrection and Renewal*, p. 77; Anzali, 'Safavid Shi'ism', p. 255. Even John Malcolm, who had a close relationship with Bihbihānī, took a reproachful tone when talking about Bihbihānī's conduct towards the Sufis. He stated, 'Aga Mahomed Ali treats every Soofee sect with a severity that must detract from the credit due to his extensive knowledge.' See Malcolm, *The History of Persia*, vol. II, p. 287.
41 Khāwarī, *Dhahabiyya*, p. 63.
42 Algar, *Religion and State in Iran*, p. 72.
43 The monarch was sometimes forced to pay hush money (*ḥaqq al-sukūk*) to the jurists (*fuqahā*) and the *'ulamā'*. See Algar, *Religion and State*, p. 16. In many cases, their greed was justified, even glorified, by Shi'i historians and theologians such as Muḥammad b. Sulaymān Tunikābunī (d. 1885), who considered the blackmail of the sovereign a kind of miracle (*karāmāt*) that had been wrought by the *'ulamā'*. See Muḥammad b. Sulaymān Tunikābunī, *Qiṣaṣ al-'ulamā'* (Tehran, 1383 Sh./2004).
44 Shīrwānī, *Bustān*, p. 248; Zarrīnkūb, *Dunbāla*, p. 341.
45 Shīrwānī, *Bustān*, p. 249.
46 Hidāyat, *Uṣūl* (Tehran), p. 644.
47 Ma'ṣūm Shīrāzī indicated that there were some great Shi'i scholars (*'ālimān*) among Ḥusayn 'Alī Shāh's ancestors. His grandfather was Shaykh Zayn al-Dīn, a renowned jurist, whom Shīrwānī 'Mast 'Alī Shāh' called 'the one who had gained complete knowledge of the rational and traditional sciences (*jāmi' 'ulūm-i 'aqlī wa naqlī*)', who had migrated to Isfahan from Tabriz (Shīrāzī, *Ṭarā'iq*, vol. III, p. 221). See Amanat, *Resurrection and Renewal*, p. 78; Shīrwānī, *Bustān*, p. 249; Zarrīnkūb, *Dunbāla*, p. 341.
48 Shīrwānī, *Bustān*, p. 249.
49 Ibid.; Pourjavady and Wilson, *Kings of Love*, p. 140.
50 Shīrwānī, *Bustān*, p. 249; Shīrāzī, *Ṭarā'iq*, vol. III, p. 221.
51 Shīrāzī, *Ṭarā'iq*, vol. III, p. 221.
52 Shīrwānī, *Bustān*, p. 250.
53 Pourjavady and Wilson, *Kings of Love*, p. 140.
54 Shīrāzī, *Ṭarā'iq*, vol. III, p. 221; Hidāyat, *Uṣūl* (Tehran), p. 647.
55 Shīrwānī, *Bustān*, p. 250; Shīrāzī, *Ṭarā'iq*, vol. III, p. 222.
56 He himself was once arrested, but was never tortured or imprisoned.

57 Amanat, *Resurrection and Renewal*, p. 78.
58 Pourjavady and Wilson, *Kings of Love*, p. 141.
59 Shīrāzī, *Ṭarā'iq*, vol. III, p. 225.
60 Shīrwānī, *Bustān*, pp. 250–51.
61 See Muḥammad b. 'Abd Allāh Qaragūzluw, *Abḥāth'i 'ashara* (Tehran, 1385 Sh./2007), p. 129; Shīrāzī, *Ṭarā'iq*, vol. III, p. 223; Hidāyat, *Uṣūl* (Tehran), p. 649; Zarrīnkūb, *Dunbāla*, p. 341.
62 Ḥā'irī, *Nakhustīn*, p. 410.
63 Shīrāzī, *Ṭarā'iq*, vol. III, pp. 223–4; Hidāyat, *Uṣūl* (Tehran), p. 649; Shīrwānī, *Bustān*, p. 251.
64 Shīrāzī, *Ṭarā'iq*, vol. III, p. 224.
65 Shīrwānī, *Bustān*, pp. 251–2; Shīrāzī, *Ṭarā'iq*, vol. III, p. 232; Zarrīnkūb, *Dunbāla*, p. 341.
66 The term *fitna* literally means 'disturbance', 'riot' or 'trial', although in Islamic history it has been used to refer to revolutionary movements and civil wars within the Muslim community. See Marshall G.S. Hodgson, *The Venture of Islam, Vol. I: The Classical Age of Islam* (Chicago, IL, 1988), pp. 214–23, 273–5, 300–301 and 475–81.
67 Shīrāzī, *Ṭarā'iq*, vol. III, p. 227.
68 John Elder, *Tārīkh-i mīssiyūn Āmrīkā'ī dar Īrān*, tr. Suhayl Āzarī (Tehran, 1956), pp. 9–15; Robin Waterfield, *Christians in Persia: Assyrians, Armenians, Roman Catholics and Protestants* (London, 1973), pp. 79–84.
69 Florence Hellot, 'The Western Missionaries in Azerbaijani Society (1835–1914)', in Robert Gleave, ed., *Religion and Society in Qajar Iran* (London, 2005), p. 287.
70 For further information about Joseph Sabastiani, see Abbas Amanat, '*Mujtahids* and Missionaries: Shī'ī Responses to Christian Polemics in the Early Qajar Period', in Robert Gleave ed., *Religion and Society in Qajar Iran* (London, 2005), pp. 251–2.
71 For detailed information on his beliefs and life, see George Smith, *Henry Martyn, Saint and Scholar: First Modern Missionary to the Mohammedans, 1781–1812* (Grand Rapids, MI, n.d.).
72 See Stephen Tomkins, *John Wesley: A Biography* (Oxford, 2003).
73 Waterfield, *Christians in Persia*, pp. 454–71.
74 Amanat, '*Mujtahids* and Missionaries', p. 248.
75 One of the founders of the Church Missionary Society was Charles Simeon. Ibid.; Waterfield, *Christians in Persia*, pp. 22–5.
76 Waterfield, *Christians in Persia*, pp. 22–5; Amanat, '*Mujtahids* and Missionaries', p. 248; Wara Ardeli, *Henry Martyn*, tr. Soheil Azari (Tehran, 1962), p. 73.
77 Amanat, '*Mujtahids* and Missionaries', p. 249.
78 Ibid., p. 250.
79 Ibid.
80 Ibid.
81 Ḥasan Anūsha, 'Pādrī', in *Da'irat al-ma'ārif-i tashayu', Vol. VI* (Tehran, 1996), p. 598.
82 Ardeli, *Henry Martyn*, pp. 126–35.
83 Denis Wright, *The English amongst the Persians: Imperial Lives in Nineteenth-Century Iran* (London, 1977), pp. 113–14.

84 Amanat, '*Mujtahids* and Missionaries', p. 247.
85 Ibid., p. 251.
86 Ibid.
87 Henry Martyn, *Mīzān al-ḥaqq* (n.p., 1833).
88 Shīrāzī, *Ṭarā'iq*, vol. III, p. 227.
89 Martyn, *Mīzān*, pp. 1–8.
90 Ibid., p. 8.
91 Ibid., pp. 15–18.
92 Ibid., pp. 19 and 23–4.
93 Ibid., pp. 23–4 and 103–10.
94 Ibid., p. 26.
95 Ibid., p. 32.
96 Ibid. For further information about the compilation of the Qur'an, see W. Montgomery Watt and Richard Bell, *Introduction to the Qur'an* (Edinburgh, 2003), pp. 40–57.
97 Martyn, *Mīzān*, pp. 42–3.
98 Ibid., pp. 44–9.
99 Ibid., pp. 49–50.
100 Ibid., pp. 55–7.
101 Ibid., pp. 58–9.
102 Ibid., pp. 92–3.
103 Ibid., pp. 94–100.
104 Ibid., pp. 111–17.
105 Ibid., pp. 120–23.
106 Ibid., pp. 127–8.
107 Ibid., pp. 133–8.
108 Ibid., pp. 170–73.
109 Ibid., pp. 189–91.
110 All translations of the Qur'an have been taken from Yusuf Ali.
111 Martyn, *Mīzān*, pp. 194–9.
112 Ibid., pp. 200–201.
113 Ibid., pp. 201–6.
114 Ibid., pp. 204–6.
115 Ibid., p. 206.
116 Ibid., pp. 206–12.
117 Ibid., pp. 214–20.
118 Ibid., pp. 220–26.
119 Ibid., pp. 226–36.
120 Ibid., pp. 236–46.
121 Ibid., pp. 251–7.
122 Ibid., pp. 258–9.
123 Muslim scholars developed the doctrine of 'abrogation', which refers to certain rules in the Qur'an which had temporary application and were later changed, replaced or abrogated by other laws, commands or rules. See Watt and Bell, *Introduction to the Qur'an*, pp. 87–8. There are verses in the Quran, substituting or replacing the prior revelations. For example, Q. 16:101 states, *When we substitute one revelation for another, and Allah knows best what He reveals (in stages), they say, 'Thou art but a forger': but most of them understand not.*

124 Amanat, '*Mujtahids* and Missionaries', p. 256.
125 Ibid.
126 Shīrāzī, *Ṭarā'iq*, vol. III, p. 227.
127 Ibid.
128 Ibid., pp. 264–6. In the *Bustān al-sīyāḥa*, Mast 'Alī Shāh makes the following complimentary comments about Mullā Muḥammad Riḍā: '[he was] the most learned among learned men of his time and the most knowledgeable among the *'ulamā'* of the period. His high degree in respect to human virtues and his spiritual qualifications were greater than all the clergymen of his time.' Shīrwānī, *Bustān*, pp. 1914–15.
129 Amanat, '*Mujtahids* and Missionaries', p. 256.
130 Muḥammad Riḍā Hamadānī, *Irshād al-muḍillīn* (manuscript in the possession of the Ḥaqīqat publication archive), p. 77.
131 Muḥammad Riḍā Hamadānī, *Miftāḥ al-nubuwwa* (Tehran, 1961), p. 10.
132 Ibid., p. 89.
133 For further information on him, see Shīrāzī, *Ṭarā'iq*, vol. III, pp. 247–9. His treatise does not have any title other than *Radd-i pādrī*.
134 Āqā Buzurg Ṭihrānī, *al-Dharī'a ilā taṣānīf al-shī'a*, vol. II (Qum, 1408/1987), p. 454.
135 Shīrāzī, *Ṭarā'iq*, vol. III, p. 247.
136 Ibid., p. 96.
137 Amanat, '*Mujtahids* and Missionaries', p. 261.
138 Hidāyat referred to Nūrī as a divine philosopher (*ḥakīm-i ilāhī*) in his *Rīyāḍ al-'ārifīn*. See Hidāyat, *Rīyāḍ*, p. 696.
139 'Alī Nūrī, *Ḥujjat al-islām*, MS IR10-23243, Majlis Library, Tehran, p. 110.
140 Amanat, '*Mujtahids* and Missionaries', p. 256.
141 Ibid.
142 Ibid., pp. 256–7.
143 Moojan Momen, *An Introduction to Shi'i Islam: The History and Doctrines of Twelver Shi'ism* (New Haven, CT, 1985), p. 319.
144 Amanat, '*Mujtahids* and Missionaries', p. 257.
145 Ibid.
146 See Matti Moosa, *Extremist Shiites: The Ghulat Sects* (Syracuse, 1988), p. 78.
147 Shīrāzī, *Ṭarā'iq*, vol. III, p. 227.
148 Ibid.
149 Muḥammad Ḥusayn Ḥusayn 'Alī Shāh, *Radd-i pādrī* (Tehran, 1387 Sh./2008), pp. 43–5.
150 Ibid., p. 45.
151 Ibid.
152 In Shi'ism, unlike Sunnism, sainthood (*wilāya*) is considered one of the five Pillars of Islam. As Mohammad Amir-Moezzi says, 'In the economy of the sacred, *walāya* is essential and of such fundamental importance that it is considered one of the Pillars (*da'ā'im*) if not *the* Pillar of Islam. M.M. Bar-Asher's observation that for Shi'is the *walāya* of the imams is the most important of the canonical obligations and a precondition for all the rest is very pertinent. The many traditions describing the *walāya* as one of the Pillars as well as a number of differences among these traditions lead him (just as J. Eliash before him) to wonder whether one must count *walāya* among the

five Pillars or rather as a sixth one in itself. Indeed, to cite Abū Ja'far Muḥammad b. Ya'qūb al-Kulaynī (d. 329/940–941) as only one example, in a chapter of his *Uṣūl min al-Kāfī* dealing with the subject of the Pillars of Islam he reports fifteen traditions all going back to the fifth and sixth imams in which *walāya* is included separately as one of the five Pillars: "Islam is built upon five elements: canonical prayers, alms, the fast, pilgrimage to Mecca and *walāya*. More than the others, it is to the latter than people are called."' See Mohammad Ali Amir-Moezzi, *The Spirituality of Shi'i Islam* (London, 2011), pp. 241–2.

153 Ḥusayn 'Alī Shāh, *Radd-i pādrī*, pp. 50–51.

154 Ibid., p. 51.

155 Ibid., p. 54.

156 Ibid., p. 156.

157 For further information about the Light of Divine Guidance, see Mohammad Ali Amir-Moezzi, *The Divine Guide in Early Shi'ism: The Sources of Esotericism in Islam*, tr. David Streight (Albany, NY, 1994), pp. 29–59; idem, *The Spirituality of Shi'i Islam*, pp. 51–3.

158 Toshihiko Izutsu, *Sufism and Taoism: A Comparative Study of Key Philosophical Concepts* (Los Angeles, 1984), p. 238.

159 Ḥaydar Āmulī, *Jāmi' al-asrār wa manba' al-anwār*, ed. Henry Corbin and Osman Yahya (Tehran, 1384 Sh./2005), p. 541.

160 Muḥammad Ja'far Kabūdarāhangī, *Rasā'il-i Majdhūbīyya* (Tehran, 1377 Sh./1998), p. 57.

161 Ibid., p. 55.

162 Ahmet T. Karamustafa, *Sufism: The Formative Period* (Berkeley, CA, 2007), p. 42.

163 Ḥusayn 'Alī Shāh, *Radd-i pādrī*, p. 55.

164 For further information about the definition of miracles (*mu'jiza*) and wonders (*karāmat*) in classical Sufi texts, see Abū'l-Ḥasan 'Alī b. 'Uthmān Hujwīrī, *Kashf al-maḥjūb*, ed. Maḥmūd 'Ābidī (Tehran, 1384 Sh./2005), pp. 329–52.

165 Ḥusayn 'Alī Shāh, *Radd-i pādrī*, pp. 55–6. This theological dispute amongst Sufis about the difference between sorcery and miracles predated Ḥusayn 'Alī Shāh. Hujwīrī (d. *c.* 469/1077), one of the early Persian Sufis, wrote a detailed explanation of sorcery, wonders and miracles in his *Kashf al-maḥjūb*, the first important Sufi treatise written in Persian. In it, he indicated that only the sincere saints could perform wonders. See Hujwīrī, *Kashf al-maḥjūb*, p. 327. On the other hand, Ruzbihān Baqlī (d. 606/1209) did not distinguish between sorcery and wonders, and used the term *siḥr* for both. However, he indicated that 'shameful' (*mustaghbaḥāt*) *siḥr* was an obscene act, whereas the wonders performed by Ḥallāj (d. 309/922) were part of the tradition of God's martyrs. See Ruzbihān Baqlī, *Sharḥ-i shaṭḥiyyāt* (Tehran, 2003), p. 322. Hujwīrī indicated that although *siḥr* is permitted according to Sunni doctrine, the people of perfection (*ahl-i kamāl*) – the Sufis – prohibited it. Wonders (*karāmat*) performed by mystics are signs of gnosis and are a proof of their sincerity (Hujwīrī, *Kashf al-maḥjūb*, pp. 231 and 327 respectively).

166 Ḥusayn 'Alī Shāh, *Radd-i pādrī*, p. 59.

167 Ibid., p. 92.

168 Ibid., pp. 52–3.
169 Ibid.
170 ʿAlī Riḍā Masjid Jāmiʿī, *Pazhuhishī dar maʿārif imāmīyih* (Tehran, 1380 Sh./2001), p. 329. 'General prophecy' and 'specific prophecy' have been the subject of dispute between the various theological schools of Islam. For a contemporary insider discussion on this, see Muḥammad Taqī Miṣbāḥ Yazdī, *Maʿārif Qur'ān: Rāh wa rahnamāshināsī* (Qum, 1386 Sh./2007), vols. IV and V; Jaʿfar Subḥānī Tabrīzī, *Manshūr-i ʿaqāyid imāmiyya: Sharḥī gūyā wa mustadal az ʿaqāyid shīʿa; athnā ʿasharī dar yikṣad wa panjāh aṣl* (Qum, 1385 Sh./2006); Murtiḍā Muṭaharī, *Khatm nubuwat* (Tehran, 1388 Sh./2009).
171 Ḥusayn ʿAlī Shāh, *Radd-i pādrī*, pp. 65–6. Mīrzā Ibrāhīm Fasā'ī in his Arabic treatise, *Risāla*, composed in refutation of Martyn, wrote a detailed explanation of 'specific prophecy' and 'general prophecy'. See Amanat, '*Mujtahids* and Missionaries', p. 252.
172 Ḥusayn ʿAlī Shāh, *Radd-i pādrī*, pp. 66–7.
173 Ibid., pp. 93–8.
174 Ibid., pp. 98–9.
175 Mahmoud Ayoub, *The Qur'an and Its Interpreters, Volume I* (Albany, NY, 1984), p. 2.
176 Ḥusayn ʿAlī Shāh, *Radd-i pādrī*, pp. 68–70.
177 Ibid., pp. 76–80.
178 Ibid., p. 80.
179 Ibid., p. 120.
180 Ibid.
181 Ibid.
182 Ibid., pp. 120–21. Ḥusayn ʿAlī Shāh's metaphor echoes Abū'l-Majd Sanā'ī's verses, which read: 'The bride of the reverend Qur'an shall strip off her veil/ Once she sees the state government of Faith free from riot.' See Abū'l-Majd Sanā'ī, *Dīwān ḥakīm Abū'l-Majdūd b. Ādam Sanā'ī Ghaznawī*, ed. Muḥammad Taqī Mudarris Raḍawī (Tehran, 1380 Sh./2006), p. 52.
183 This expression was used in this context by a number of Sufi masters.
184 Ḥusayn ʿAlī Shāh, *Radd-i pādrī*, p. 187.
185 The tradition of knowing the inner meaning and having a true understanding of the Qur'an is deeply rooted in the philosophy of Sufism. It dates back to as early as Abū ʿAbd al-Raḥmān Sulamī (d. 412/1021), who first treated it in his *Ḥaqā'iq al-tafsīr* [Realities of Interpretation], a collection of sayings attributed to the sixth imam Jaʿfar al-Ṣādiq (d. 148/765). For further information about this text, see Michael A. Sells, tr., ed. and intro., *Early Islamic Mysticism: Sufi, Qur'an, Miʿraj, Poetic and Theological Writings* (Mawhah, NJ, 1996), pp. 29–47 and 75–89; Nasrollah Pourjavady, ed., *Majmūʿih athār-i Abū ʿAbd al-Raḥmān Sulamī* (Tehran, 1369 Sh./1990). This philosophy continued through generations of Sufis, 'like the Qur'an which is sevenfold in meaning, and in which there is food for the elect and the vulgar', as Rūmī says. See Jalāl al-Dīn Rūmī, *The Mathnawí of Jalálu'ddín Rúmí*, tr. Reynold A. Nicholson (Istanbul, 2004), vol. III, p. 1897.
186 Ḥusayn ʿAlī Shāh, *Radd-i pādrī*, p. 188.
187 Ibid., p. 34.

188 'Allāma Ṭabāṭabā'ī thus reasoned that people referred to in Q. 56:79, *none shall touch* [the Qur'an] *save those who are clean*, refers to the 'People of the House', that is, the Prophet's daughter Fāṭima and the Shi'i imams. Ṭabāṭabā'ī asserts that 'they are the People of the House who have the knowledge of the exegesis of the Qur'an'. See Ayoub, *The Qur'an and Its Interpreters, Volume I*, p. 35.
189 Rúmí, *Mathnawí*, vol. VI, p. 2090.
190 Annemarie Schimmel, *Mystical Dimensions of Islam* (Chapel Hill, NC, 1975), p. 43.
191 For more on *ṭarīqa*, see ibid., pp. 99–186.
192 For further information, see Marshall G.S. Hodgson, *The Venture of Islam, Vol. II: The Expansion of Islam in the Middle Periods* (Chicago, IL, 1977), pp. 188–92.
193 Shīrwānī, *Kashf*, p. 15.
194 Zarrīnkūb, *Dunbāla*, p. 244.
195 Amanat, *Resurrection and Renewal*, p. 78.
196 Ḥusayn 'Alī Shāh, *Radd-i pādrī*, pp. 255–6.
197 Ibid., p. 252.
198 Ibid., p. 256.
199 Māriyya, daughter of Shim'ūn, was born into a Coptic family. She was sent as a gift (a female slave) to the Prophet Muhammad by the Christian ruler of Egypt. See Bint al-Shati', *The Wives of the Prophet*, tr. Matti Moosa and D. Nicholas Ranson (New Jersey, 2006), pp. 203–4.
200 Ḥusayn 'Alī Shāh, *Radd-i pādrī*, pp. 255–6.
201 Ibid., p. 253.
202 Ibid., p. 177.
203 Prophet Muhammad, *The Sayings of Muhammad*, tr. Neal Robinson (London, 2003), pp. 18 and 153.
204 Ḥusayn 'Alī Shāh, *Radd-i pādrī*, pp. 173–4.
205 Ibid., p. 174.
206 Ibn 'Arabī's interpretation of this tradition differs from Ḥusayn 'Alī Shāh's. Ibn 'Arabī notes that the word 'perfume' is the only masculine term among the other two terms ('women' and 'prayer'). He notes that the masculine term is placed between the two feminine ones, just as the man is placed between the Divine Essence (a feminine noun) and the woman. For him, this specifies the governance of the feminine by the masculine. See Ralph J.W. Austin, 'The Sophianic Feminine in the Work of Ibn 'Arabī and Rumi', in Leonard Lewisohn, ed., *The Heritage of Sufism, Vol. II: The Legacy of Medieval Persian Sufism (1150–1500)* (Oxford, 1999), p. 240.
207 Ḥusayn 'Alī Shāh, *Radd-i pādrī*, pp. 175–6.
208 For further information on this idea, see Muḥammad Ḥusayn Ṭabāṭabā'ī, *Tafsīr al-Mīzān*, tr. Nāṣir Makārim Shīrāzī (Qum, 1364 Sh./1985); Murtaḍā Muṭahharī, *Āshnā'ī bā Qur'ān* (Tehran, 1381 Sh./2002). The early Shi'i theologian Muḥammad b. Ḥasan Ṭūsī (d. 460/1067) clearly explained that only the sin of infidelity could not be forgiven by intercession and that only God could forgive this sin. See Muḥammad b. Ḥasan Ṭūsī, *al-Tibyān fī tafsīr al-Qur'ān* (Beirut, n.d.), vol. X, p. 214.

209 Rúmí, *Mathnawí*, vol. VI, p. 167.
210 Ḥusayn ʿAlī Shāh, *Radd-i pādrī*, p. 207.
211 Ibid., p. 204.
212 Ibid., p. 205.
213 Ibid., pp. 210–11.
214 Ibid., pp. 219–20.
215 Rúmí, *Mathnawí*, vol. I, pp. 23–4.
216 Ibid., p. 30.
217 Cited by Izutsu, *Sufism and Taoism*, p. 173.
218 Ibid.
219 Ḥusayn ʿAlī Shāh, *Radd-i pādrī*, p. 204.
220 Ibid.
221 Abū'l-Qāsim al-Qushayrī, *Risāla Qushayriyya*, tr. Abū ʿAlī Aḥmad ʿUthmānī (Tehran, 1361 Sh./1982), pp. 136–45.
222 Abū Naṣr al-Sarrāj al-Ṭūsī, *Kitāb al-Lumaʿ fī'l-taṣawwuf*, tr. Mihdī Maḥabbatī (Tehran, 1383 Sh./2004), pp. 98–99; Hujwīrī, *Kashf al-maḥjūb*, p. 274.
223 Ḥusayn ʿAlī Shāh, *Radd-i pādrī*, pp. 97–8.
224 Ibid., pp. 98–9.
225 Ibid., p. 108.
226 Ibid., pp. 124–8.
227 Ibid., p. 158.
228 Ibid., pp. 158–9.
229 Ibid., pp. 155–6.
230 Ibid., p. 208.
231 Ibid., p. 209.
232 Ibid., p. 225.
233 Ibid., p. 221.
234 Ibid., p. 222.
235 Ibid.
236 Ibid., pp. 215–16.
237 Ibid.
238 Ibid., pp. 225–6 and 220.
239 Shīrwānī, *Bustān*, p. 81; Zarrīnkūb, *Dunbāla*, p. 341.

8

Abrogation and Falsification of Scripture According to Twelver Shi'i Authors in Iraq and Iran (19th–20th Centuries)

RAINER BRUNNER

Falsification (*taḥrīf*)

WHOEVER OPENS any Shiʿi book about the Qur'an, its textual history and its interpretation, will inevitably find a more or less lengthy chapter containing solemn declarations about the integrity of the scripture and its preservation from any kind of falsification. Usually, the authors will continue by stressing that this had always been the broad consensus of the Shiʿi religious scholars, except for a few eccentrics, and except for some traditions in the early collections which, however, were to be regarded as unreliable.[1] Occasionally, some writers would even go so far as to state that there are several cases in point to be found in Sunni sources as well, in which textual alterations of the Qur'anic text were affirmed.[2] These affirmations, however, would normally not be called by the usual name, *taḥrīf* (i.e. falsification), but by a different term, a misnomer indeed, and they would accordingly be classified in a different category. If, on the other hand, one opens any modern Sunni diatribe against Shiʿism, one will also inevitably find the accusation that the Shiʿa believe in the falsification of the text of the Qur'an, and that they, as a matter of fact, have always done so. Reality, as is usually the case, is more complicated.[3]

The conviction seems to have been widespread among the early Shiʿi exegetes that the present text of the Muslim holy scripture is incomplete and that a substantial number of references to the Shiʿi imams and the family of the Prophet (*ahl al-bayt*) in general had been deliberately removed by the (Sunni) collectors of the bits and pieces of the revelation. In the pre-*ghayba* period (i.e. until the first half of the fourth/tenth century), many traditions going back to the Shiʿi imams report this accusation, and several treatises on this subject were composed, the majority of which have regrettably been lost or preserved in later sources only in a fragmentary way.[4] Also in several classical Hadith collections, especially in *al-Kāfī* by Abū Jaʿfar Muḥammad b. Yaʿqūb al-Kulaynī (d. 328–9/939–41), one finds more or less open *taḥrīf* allegations, even though in a somewhat remote 'chapter on rare things' (or anecdotes: *bāb al-nawādir*).[5] One of the most common of these is the statement that the words 'on (behalf of) ʿAlī' (*fī ʿAlī*), that is ʿAlī b. Abī Ṭālib (d. 40/661), had been deleted in many verses which accordingly were said to have been revealed with special reference to the first imam. It was only after the occultation of the twelfth imam and the beginning of a Shiʿi theology proper that this attitude began to change. Starting with Abū Jaʿfar Muḥammad Ibn Bābūya (d. 381/991) in the second half of the fourth/tenth century and continuing with luminaries such as al-Shaykh al-Mufīd (d. 413/1022–3), Abū Jaʿfar al-Ṭūsī (d. 460/1067) or al-Faḍl b. al-Ḥasan al-Ṭabrisī (d. 548/1153–4), most significant Shiʿi jurists and exegetes now confirmed that these traditions were not to be taken at face value.[6] Rather, they were either unreliable because they were transmitted only by a single authority (so-called *akhbār āḥād*), or the passages they deemed omitted were only part of Qur'anic exegesis (*tafsīr*), but did not belong to the actual text of the Qur'an.

This, however, was not the end of the story. Starting in the eleventh/seventeenth century, in the context of the revival of the Akhbārī school of thought in Shiʿism,[7] the topic of *taḥrīf* witnessed a remarkable renaissance. This was so because the rather unconditional belief in the authority of the traditions of the imams which was not allowed to be filtered by the individual reasoning (*ijtihād*) of the Uṣūlīs was the hallmark of the Akhbārīs. And as basically all relevant traditions were attributed to the imams, they were prisoners of their own allegiance to the hadiths. In a great number of Akhbārī *tafsīr* works, the issue of *taḥrīf* was dealt with in a rather offensive way, and names such as Muḥsin Fayḍ al-Kāshānī (d. 1090/1679), Hāshim al-Baḥrānī (d. *c.* 1107/1695), Niʿmatullāh al-Jazāʾirī (d. 1112/1701), Abū'l-Ḥasan al-Sharīf al-ʿĀmilī (d. *c.* 1139/1727), or Yūsuf al-Baḥrānī (d. 1185/1772–3) bear witness to the relevance of *taḥrīf* in the Akhbārī doctrine.[8] The fact that it even managed to survive the final defeat of the Akhbārīs at the beginning of the nineteenth century proves that the importance of the topic transcended the actual dividing line between the two groups. On the contrary, in the writings of Uṣūlī figurehead jurists such as Jaʿfar Kāshif al-Ghiṭāʾ (d. 1812), Murtaḍā al-Anṣārī (d. 1864) and Muḥammad Kāẓim al-Khurāsānī (d. 1911) one finds – albeit somewhat between the lines – covert confirmation of the *taḥrīf* suspicion.[9] Characteristically, it was thus no longer in Qur'anic commentaries or Hadith compilations – both the key to Akhbārī scholarship – that the issue of *taḥrīf* was dealt with, but rather in theoretic legal works, that is, the hallmark genre of the Uṣūlīs. These brief remarks make it clear that the Shiʿi attitude towards the text of the Qur'an has remained a thorny issue in modern times.

In what follows, four rather characteristic voices will be presented: one scholar (in fact the only one, as far as I can judge) who composed a staunch defence of the classical *taḥrīf* theory, and three prominent critics who tried to undo the effect caused by their colleague, especially with regard to the wider inner-Islamic debate between the Sunnis and the Shiʿa. As we shall see, these critics even went so far as to question a commonly accepted method of exegesis in order to ward off the suspicion of the falsification of the Qur'an.

Ḥusayn Taqī al-Nūrī al-Ṭabrisī (d. 1902)

It was only at the end of the nineteenth century that Ḥusayn Taqī al-Nūrī al-Ṭabrisī – presumably against his own intention – contributed most to a thorough and lasting change of attitude within Shiʿism concerning the text of the Qur'an. Nūrī, who was of Iranian origin, was a student of Mīrzā Ḥasan al-Shīrāzī (d. 1895) and became later the teacher of Āqā Buzurg al-Ṭihrānī (d. 1970) and Muḥammad al-Ḥusayn Āl Kāshif al-Ghiṭāʾ (d. 1954). He largely divided his time between Iran and the Iraqi shrine cities (*'atabāt*), Sāmarrā' and Najaf; only towards the end of his life, in 1896/7, did he finally settle in Najaf, where he died in 1902.[10] His renown is above all based on his monumental hadith collection *Mustadrak al-wasā'il*, which is the continuation of the equally famous collection *Tafṣīl wasā'il al-shī'a* by Muḥammad b. al-Ḥasan al-Ḥurr al-'Āmilī (d. 1104/1693),[11] and he may justifiably be called the last great Akhbārī scholar of Shi'ism (his peers at the *ḥawza* in Najaf today do point-blank consider him to be an Akhbārī).[12] What is of greater interest in our context is a different compilation of his, namely his book *Faṣl al-khiṭāb fī taḥrīf Kitāb Rabb al-arbāb*, which was finished in 1876 and published in a lithograph edition in 1881; it is rather characteristic that this has remained the only available edition until today and that it was not published in Najaf but in Tehran, far away from the *'atabāt*.[13] Nūrī's book is considerably more than a mere collection of traditions about the *taḥrīf* allegations, and even as such it would have been of great significance, since he managed to unearth relevant references from the remotest sources, many of which had never before been accessible in print. But Nūrī went a step further and classified these traditions in twelve chapters, with the explicit purpose to prove once and for good that the existent text of the Qur'an had been tampered with and that the 'true' version of God's revelation was in the custody of the hidden twelfth imam who would bring it back on the occasion of his return at the end of days. Of particular interest is certainly the last chapter of his book, in which he gathered more than one thousand traditions, arranged according to the suras and verses of the Qur'an, reporting the seemingly 'correct' reading of the relevant passages. As a sort of preventive measure, he ended his book with a short but substantial critique of possible objections to the *taḥrīf* suspicion, such as those produced by many a classical scholar, above all by al-Sharīf al-Murtaḍā (d. 436/1044) and al-Faḍl b. al-Ḥasan al-Ṭabrisī, both of whom he severely criticised.

Nūrī's book caused quite a stir at the *'atabāt*, and he apparently became an outcast, particularly after the death of his teacher al-Shīrāzī in 1895.[14] It seems also that several polemical treatises and refutations were composed by other Shi'i scholars as Nūrī tried in vain to defend himself against their criticism; none of these treatises has been published so far, however. Beyond these immediate reactions, the long-term effect of his book proved to be of two kinds with respect to the Shiʿi religious literature on the one hand, and the Sunni on the other. Within Shiʿism it managed to produce a nearly unanimous closing of the ranks. The only distinguished scholar who was ready to protect Nūrī (without necessarily following his point of view) was his student Āqā Buzurg al-Ṭihrānī, but his fellow student Muḥammad al-Ḥusayn Āl Kāshif al-Ghiṭāʾ prohibited Āqā Buzurg from publishing his apologia, for fear of scoring points from the wrong side.[15] Apart from this solitary voice, I know of no prominent Shiʿi scholar who, in the course of the 130 years which have passed since the publication of Nūrī's book, has publicly endorsed the latter's main thesis that the Qur'an suffered from deliberate falsification.

Things look totally different, however, if one delves into the Sunni religious literature of the twentieth century, especially into the literature of a more polemical tinge. It took their authors a little while to discover what precious treasure Nūrī's collection constituted for their own purpose. Early authors such as Yūsuf b. Aḥmad al-Dijwī (d. 1946) or the indefatigable Muḥammad Rashīd Riḍā (d. 1935) mentioned the book,[16] but it was quite apparent that they knew little about it beyond its title, as they went hardly beyond quoting the usual suspects from bygone times, such as Kulaynī and Taqī al-Dīn Aḥmad Ibn Taymiyya (d. 728/1328). It was as late as the 1960s when, in the slipstream of cautious ecumenical activities between Sunni and Shiʿi institutions, the Wahhabi journalist Muḥibb al-Dīn al-Khaṭīb (d. 1969) published a short but snide pamphlet outlining the foundations on which Twelver Shiʿism is based.[17] There, he not only placed the question of *taḥrīf* and the person of Nūrī at the centre of his argumentation but also had the ingenious idea to combine *taḥrīf* and *taqiyya* (dissimulation) in such a way that he called any Shiʿi denial of *taḥrīf* allegations nothing but dissimulation. As short and superficial as Khaṭīb's diatribe may have been, it proved to have a lasting effect on the debate and became one of the most influential polemics against Shiʿism in modern times.[18]

Reading these polemics – and their counterparts on the Shiʿi side – is usually not very entertaining. More often than not, the tone is ugly, the arguments are foreseeable and the degree of innovative thinking is rather modest. There are, however, occasional exceptions to this rule. One of the topics where the mode of arguing is – at least sometimes – more sophisticated (although not always free of polemics) concerns the question of abrogation (*naskh*), that is, the problem of whether some verses of the Qur'an had been cancelled by others.[19] Addressed by the Qur'an itself (especially in Q. 2:106: *And for whatever verse We abrogate or cast into oblivion, We bring a better or the like of it*),[20] it is not only a crucial problem for Islamic law but also a highly sensitive issue of Qur'an interpretation. As such, it could take three distinct forms: the content of a verse was abrogated by a later revelation but its wording remained part of the existing text[21] (the so-called *naskh al-ḥukm dūn al-tilāwa*); the wording of a verse disappeared but its meaning remained to be effective (*naskh al-tilāwa dūn al-ḥukm*); both the wording and the meaning were considered to have been abrogated (*naskh al-tilāwa wa'l-ḥukm*). Of these three cases, the second and third ones (abrogation of the text but not of the content, as well as abrogation of both) are all the more tricky, as they presuppose a change of, possibly an encroachment on, the existing text of the scripture. What is more, reports to this effect are quoted in many classical Sunni sources as well. The best-known example of this kind is the so-called 'stoning verse' (*āyat al-rajm*) whose Qur'anic origin was allegedly confirmed by ʿUmar b. al-Khaṭṭāb (r. 13–23/634–44) and which stipulates that adulterers should be punished by stoning, contrary to the existing verse Q. 24:2 in which 'only' one hundred lashes are prescribed.[22] It comes as no surprise therefore that the issue of *naskh* formed part of the wider *taḥrīf* debate, the 'stoning verse' being, throughout the twentieth century, one of the central proof texts that Shiʿi authors in particular used to claim the existence of *taḥrīf* in Sunni works.[23]

Nūrī devotes some fifteen pages of his treatise to the question of abrogation,[24] and characteristically enough, he completely neglects the first form of *naskh* (inner-Qur'anic abrogation), which he accepts in passing elsewhere in the book.[25] Instead, he concentrates on those cases in which a disappearance of the Qur'anic wording is reported, and his judgement is as outspoken as it is simplistic: as neither ʿAlī nor any other imam certified such a category, it simply cannot have existed. On the contrary: ʿAlī explicitly stated that not a single word of the revelation had been dropped from his collection, and the imams who enumerated some sixty forms of verses knew of no genre called 'the abrogating and the abrogated' (*al-nāsikh wa'l-mansūkh*).[26] Rather, any form of *naskh al-tilāwa* is nothing but the invention of 'the evil imams' (*a'immat al-jawr*) who tried to camouflage their tampering with the Qur'anic text, especially by dropping all references to ʿAlī's claims to leadership and to their own disgrace. If, Nūrī concludes, some verses had been eliminated by *naskh al-tilāwa*, how could the remaining Qur'an then possibly tally with the one preserved by God on the 'guarded tablet' (*al-lawḥ al-maḥfūẓ*)?[27] Apparently, it suits him well in this context that there is one particular tradition – circulating also among Sunni exegetes such as Jalāl al-Dīn al-Suyūṭī (d. 911/1505) or Abū'l-Qāsim al-Zamakhsharī (d. 538/1144), whom he quotes extensively – according to which *Sūrat al-Aḥzāb* (Q. 33) had originally been much longer and even surpassed *Sūrat al-Baqara* (Q. 2). For Nūrī, this is the final proof of his thesis, and without giving further evidence, he identifies this as the spot where all the atrocities of the Sunnis is located.[28]

Hibat al-Dīn al-Shahrastānī (d. 1967) and Abū'l-Qāsim al-Khū'ī (d. 1992)

Nūrī's analytical shortcut – *naskh* equals *taḥrīf* – may be simplistic, but it is also slippery ground for all Shiʿi exegetes after him who affirm the completeness of the Qur'anic text. It is precisely for this reason that the topic is usually dealt with at more or less great length in all Shiʿi books and treatises on *taḥrīf*, and some of the conclusions the respective authors come up with are quite far-reaching, going as far as a complete rejection of any form of inner-Qur'anic abrogation. Several passages taken from the works of Shiʿi scholars of the twentieth century may well serve to illustrate this point. The first example is a long essay by the Iraqi Qur'anic scholar (*ʿālim*) and, for some time, minister of education, Hibat al-Dīn al-Shahrastānī (d. 1967).[29] As is already made clear by the title ('The noble Qur'an is beyond abrogation, faultiness and falsification'),[30]

Shahrastānī considers abrogation to be a sign of falsification, but contrary to Nūrī, he does not take it as proof of the existence of *taḥrīf*, but rather as proof of the inexistence of both *taḥrīf* and *naskh*. Further, he extends the discussion of abrogation to include also the inner-Qur'anic mode of one verse cancelling the prescriptions of other verses. For him, it is not acceptable that there is any verse in the Qur'an whose instruction (*ḥukm*) could have been abrogated. First of all, he asserts, *naskh* does not refer to replacing one verse with another, but to replacing the pre-Islamic religions of Judaism and Christianity with Islam, and it is in this way that the usual Qur'anic proof text in favour of abrogation, the above-mentioned Q. 2:106, has to be understood, for in the preceding verse, the *ahl al-kitāb* are explicitly addressed.[31] Moreover, he enumerates a number of other verses which he deems incompatible with the theory of abrogation, for example Q. 5:3 (*Today I have perfected your religion for you* – how could a religion be perfect if there were verses which were suspended or overruled?) or Q. 2:2 (*That is the Book, wherein is no doubt, a guidance to the godfearing* – and any kind of *naskh* would be tantamount to sowing doubt).[32] In addition to that, he links the problem of abrogation with another hermeneutic challenge within the Qur'an: that those traditions which seem to affirm the existence of abrogated verses actually bear a different meaning. In reality, he repeats several times, they refer to 'clear' (*muḥkam*, i.e. in the sense of abrogating) verses and 'ambiguous' (*mutashābih*, i.e. abrogated) ones, a concept which is alluded to in Q. 3:7 (*It is He who sent down upon thee the Book, wherein are verses clear that are the Essence of the Book, and others ambiguous*). This idea as such is not new, as the combination of the problem of abrogation and the ambiguous verses played a substantial role in classical commentaries. According to Shahrastānī, the purpose of this form of 'abrogation' is not to rescind some divine injunctions with others, but rather to extinguish all traces of imaginary exegesis: the whole Qur'an is *muḥkam*, only human beings with their narrow horizons render the message *mutashābih*.[33] And finally, he concludes, if there had been any necessity, strictly during the lifetime of the Prophet, to cancel any *ḥukm* of the revelation for the sake of humanity, surely the *tilāwa* would also have disappeared.[34]

Shahrastānī's severe rejection of the concept of abrogation in general is basically also the line of argument of our second example, written by Abū'l-Qāsim al-Khū'ī, who was commonly regarded as the most revered model for emulation (*marjaʿ al-taqlīd*) in Shiʿism during the 1970s and 1980s, following the death of Ayatollah Muḥsin al-Ḥakīm in 1970, and notwithstanding the rising star of Ruhollah Khomeini. Like Nūrī, Khū'ī was of Iranian origin (he was born in Iranian Azerbaijan in 1899), but came to Najaf at the age of thirteen. He spent all his life in that city, and died there in 1992.[35] In his book *al-Bayān fī tafsīr al-Qur'ān*, which he finished in the mid-1950s,[36] he deals with this question in two places. First, he includes it in his lengthy chapter on the *taḥrīf* suspicion, where he explicitly talks on *naskh al-tilāwa dūn al-ḥukm*, that is, abrogation of the wording but not of the content.[37] Like Nūrī before him, he readily identifies this as a view which was held by the majority of classical Sunni exegetes, and like Nūrī, he quotes a representative sample of Sunni traditions about, among other things, the 'stoning verse' and the alleged size of *Sūrat al-Aḥzāb*. From these, he draws two conclusions, namely, (a) that 'the belief in the abrogation of recitals (i.e. *naskh al-tilāwa*) is similar to the belief in alteration and omission', and (b) that 'it is possible to claim that the view that the Qur'an was altered is the doctrine of the majority of Sunni scholars, because they maintain the permissibility of abrogating the recitation of a verse regardless of whether the ordinance contained in it is abrogated or not'.[38] Contrary to Nūrī, however, and very much in line with Shahrastānī's deductions, Khū'ī does not take the fact that Sunni sources testify to alterations of the text of the Qur'an as positive evidence for the existence of *taḥrīf*. Rather, he proceeds by rejecting the reliability of all relevant traditions (both Sunni and Shiʿi), and by adducing other Qur'anic verses as well as the sayings of the Shiʿi imams to the effect that the existing text of the Qur'an is complete, unaltered and obligatory.[39]

Like Shahrastānī before him, he now goes one step further. In addition to his proclamation in the chapter on *taḥrīf*, he elaborates on the issue in a separate chapter, and the fact that this is the longest one in the book shows the importance he attached to the problem.[40] Having once more rejected the abrogation of the wording as synonymous with *taḥrīf*,[41] he now proceeds to categorically deny the possibility of any kind of abrogation within the text of the Qur'an, including that kind of *naskh* which is generally accepted in Islamic law: the abrogation of earlier verses by later ones (i.e. *naskh al-ḥukm dūn al-tilāwa*). He even goes so far as to deny those cases that are usually taken for granted in *tafsīr*, such as the prohibition of wine.[42] Not that Khū'ī is tempted to allow drinking, but he stresses that Q. 4:43 which admonishes the believer not to show up at prayer drunk does not constitute any permissibility to drink wine in the first place, and that therefore it could not have been abrogated by Q. 5:90, which prohibits wine in general.[43] In such a way, he singles out thirty-six verses (the alleged permission of temporary marriage in Q. 4:24 receiving the most detailed investigation) in order to 'prove' that basically the whole category of *al-nāsikh wa'l-mansūkh* is utterly wrong.[44] In the end, there remains only a single instance of *naskh* which Khū'ī, again like Shahrastānī, is ready to accept: the abrogation by Islam of all preceding religions, which is, in his eyes, confirmed by the fact that the New Testament 'abrogates' several injunctions of the Old Testament.[45] This last point takes us back to Nūrī, because he, too, uses Judaism and Christianity as a foil for his main thesis: in his very long first chapter, he takes pains to show that everything that happened to these two communities by necessity also happened to the Islamic community (*umma*) – and as their scriptures had been falsified (which is of course a well-known commonplace in Muslim theology), it surely is proof that the Qur'an also underwent *taḥrīf*.[46]

Both Shahrastānī and Khū'ī were ready to throw out the baby with the bathwater when they came to the conclusion that all forms of abrogation within the Qur'an have to be rejected. As far as modern Shi'ism is concerned, this radical stance seems to be somewhat exceptional, although some scholars – such as Hossein Modarressi[47] – come quite close to it. However, their categorical rejection of the possibility of *naskh al-tilāwa* by claiming that it would be tantamount to *taḥrīf* is more or less the standard line of argumentation in modern Shi'i *tafsīr* and beyond.[48] Especially in a great number of books and treatises that were published in Iran during the 1980s and 1990s, this assertion is defended with great vigour.[49] The background of these activities was provided by the initiative of the Iranian government to pose as the herald of Islamic unity and rapprochement with Sunni Islam by founding and sponsoring an ecumenical society, called Majmaʿ al-Taqrīb bayn al-Madhāhib al-Islāmiyya, in 1990 and organising a series of international conferences on this issue.[50] This seemed all the more necessary because the Iranian revolution was (and still is) widely perceived as an attempt to proselytise Sunni Muslims and undermine the neighbouring states and societies. What is more, Ruhollah Khomeini himself had included in his book *Kashf al-asrār*, which appeared in the 1940s (but was re-edited after 1979), a passage which could easily be read as an affirmation of the *taḥrīf* thesis, all the more so because he put great emphasis on the alleged violations of Abū Bakr (d. 13/634) and ʿUmar against the Qur'an. It goes without saying that these sentences were met with the utmost interest by Sunni polemicists, and the aforementioned publications (see note 49) were clearly intended to counter this devastating impression.[51]

Muḥammad Ḥusayn Ṭabāṭabāʾī (d. 1981)

The last Shiʿi scholar to be mentioned here who combined the rejection of *taḥrīf* allegations with a denial of the concept of *naskh* is the Iranian philosopher and exegete Muḥammad Ḥusayn Ṭabāṭabāʾī (d. 1981).[52] The expression *mansūkh al-tilāwa*, he states in his disquisition about Q. 15:9: *It is We who have sent down the Remembrance, and We watch over it* (which is universally regarded by Shiʿi writers as the scriptural guarantee against *taḥrīf*), is used by Sunni commentators in order to safeguard what is narrated by their traditions, for example, the injunction of stoning as punishment for adultery. There is no doubt, he continues, that this form of omitting the wording of the Qur'an is tantamount to nullification (*ibṭāl*), but how could that possibly go together with Q. 41:41–2, which explicitly declares *surely it is a Book Sublime; falsehood (al-bāṭil) comes not to it from before it nor from behind it*? It would run counter to all those honourable designations of the scripture as *al-lawḥ al-maḥfūẓ*, *dhikr*, *furqān*, and so on. Thus, according to him, both the *taḥrīf* traditions of the two sides and the narrations on *naskh al-tilāwa* decidedly run counter to the Qur'an itself. In general, it is completely unimaginable to him that anything in the Qur'an could have been 'cast into oblivion', as the generally accepted reading of Q. 2:106 (*And for whatever verse We abrogate or cast into oblivion* [*nunsīhā*], *We bring a better or the like of it*) implies. Ṭabāṭabā'ī argues that instead of reading *nunsīhā*, it ought to be *nansa'ahā*, in the sense of 'postponing (its appearance)', since Muhammad was immune to forgetting.[53] The verse, according to Ṭabāṭabā'ī, means that God cancelled both the wording and the content of a verse, yet at the same time kept them intact in *al-lawḥ al-maḥfūẓ*.[54] By this, however, it becomes clear that Ṭabāṭabā'ī, in comparison to Shahrastānī or Khū'ī, is considerably less radical as far as his judgement of the possibility of the ordinary form of abrogation, *naskh al-ḥukm dūn al-tilāwa*, is concerned. Indeed, in his exegesis of Q. 2:106, he readily admits the existence of abrogating and abrogated verses without further ado (and also refers to the reading *nansa'ahā* only in passing and without claiming it to be authoritative), as the last part of this very verse also gives an irrefutable explanation: *knowest thou not that God is powerful over everything?* Ṭabāṭabā'ī's only purely Shi'i reasoning in this regard is his rather casual remark that according to some Shi'i traditions (that go without concrete reference here) the death of an imam and the succession of another one also count as abrogation.[55] Ṭabāṭabā'ī could easily afford such a relaxed approach to the question of abrogation, as he had elsewhere refuted the whole idea of *taḥrīf* in the Qur'an as self-contradictory. According to him, the *akhbār āḥād*, on which the falsification theory usually rests, are dependent on the words of the imams, which, in turn, are dependent on the words of the Prophet (who appointed the imams) and on the conclusiveness of the Qur'an (upon which Muhammad's prophecy is based); thus, if one deprived the Qur'an of its conclusiveness by assuming any form of *taḥrīf*, this would mean that neither the Prophet's words nor those of the imams could be trusted – including the very traditions in which *taḥrīf* was stated. Corroborating the falsification of the Qur'an by adducing Prophetic or imamic traditions therefore automatically, and by necessity, amounts to the refutation of precisely these traditions.[56]

With regard to the question of abrogation, Ṭabāṭabā'ī seems to confirm his image as a maverick theologian.[57] This may be due to the fact that his approach to the Qur'an was a more philosophical one compared to that of Shahrastānī or Khū'ī who wrote from a more polemical angle, both with regard to Sunni authors and to Shi'i dissidents like Nūrī. As to the question of abrogation, the basic difference in the approach of the latter and his Shi'i critics may be summed up as follows: Nūrī denies the possibility of *naskh* because he believes in *taḥrīf*, Shahrastānī and Khū'ī deny it because ultimately it would mean that *taḥrīf* had happened – and this is an idea that is simply anathema to them.

Conclusion

Sunni critics normally do have a lot to say about Shi'ism in general and of Nūrī and his *taḥrīf* book in particular. With regard to abrogation and its relation to *taḥrīf*, they seem much more taciturn. Occasionally, there is severe criticism, especially of Khū'ī's thorough inquiry, and he is blamed for mixing up *naskh* (which, as a Qur'anic concept, is taken to be of divine origin) and *taḥrīf* (which is considered to be an entirely human device); one Wahhābī polemicist exclaims that the Shi'a had better declare those verses they claim to be missing as abrogated.[58] It is not up to a non-Muslim outsider to decide which side is right and which one is wrong. But it does go without saying that the entire debate about these points has always been and continues to be revealing with regard to the highly enigmatic character of the text of the Qur'an. Its own assertion that it is a 'book wherein is no doubt' notwithstanding, Islamic intellectual history time and again testifies to the contrary.

NOTES

1 See, for example, Ja'far Sobhani, *Doctrines of Shi'i Islam: A Compendium of Imami Beliefs and Practices*, tr. and ed. Reza Shah-Kazemi (London, 2001), pp. 93, 210–11.

2 Ja'far Murtaḍā al-'Āmilī, *Ḥaqā'iq hāmma ḥawl al-qur'ān al-karīm*, 2nd edn (Beirut, 1413/1992), pp. 32–3.

3 For a comprehensive treatment of the subject, see Rainer Brunner, *Die Schia und die Koranfälschung* (Würzburg, 2001).

4 The probably most important source that survived in a few manuscripts is the *Kitāb al-Qirā'āt* by Aḥmad b. Muḥammad al-Sayyārī (a contemporary of the eleventh imam, al-Ḥasan al-'Askarī [d. 260/873]), which was edited some years ago: *Revelation and Falsification: The Kitāb al-Qirā'āt of Aḥmad b. Muḥammad al-Sayyārī*, Critical Edition with an Introduction and Notes by Etan Kohlberg and Mohammad Ali Amir-Moezzi (Leiden, 2009).

5 See Ja'far b. Muḥammad b. Ya'qūb al-Kulaynī, *Uṣūl al-Kāfī*, ed. Muḥammad Jawād al-Faqīh and Yūsuf al-Biqā'ī (Beirut, 1413/1992), vol. II, p. 599 (no. 2), p. 602 (no. 16), p. 604 (no. 32), p. 605 (no. 28). On Kulaynī and his collection in general, see Mohammad Ali Amir-Moezzi and Hassan Ansari, 'Muḥammad b. Ya'qūb al-Kulaynī (m. 328 ou 329/939–40 ou 940–41) et son *Kitāb al-Kāfī*: Une introduction', *Studia Iranica* 38 (2009), pp. 191–247.

6 For the classical background of the debate, see Etan Kohlberg, 'Some Notes on the Imāmite Attitude to the Qur'ān', in Samuel M. Stern, Albert H. Hourani and Vivian Brown, eds, *Islamic Philosophy and the Classical Tradition: Essays Presented by His Friends and Pupils to Richard Walzer on His Seventieth Birthday* (Oxford, 1972), pp. 209–24; for Ibn Bābūya, see Saïd Amir Arjomand, 'The Consolation of Theology: Absence of the Imam and Tradition from Chiliasm to Law in Shi'ism', *Journal of Religion* 76 (1996), pp. 548–71 (esp. p. 554); for Mufīd, see Mohammad Ali Amir-Moezzi, 'Al-Šayḫ al-Mufīd (m. 413/1022) et la question de la falsification du Coran', in Daniel De Smet and Mohammad Ali Amir-Moezzi, eds, *Controverses sur les écritures canoniques de l'Islam* (Paris, 2014), pp. 199–229; for Ṭūsī, see Sarah Eltantawi, 'Ṭūsī Did Not "Opt Out": Shiite Jurisprudence and the Solidification of the Stoning Punishment in the Islamic Legal Tradition', in Alireza Korangy *et al.*, eds, *Essays in Islamic Philology, History, and Philosophy* (Berlin, 2016), pp. 312–32; for Ṭabrisī, see Etan Kohlberg, 'al-Ṭabrisī (Ṭabarsī)', EI^2, vol. X, pp. 40–41.

7 On the Akhbārīs, see in detail Robert Gleave, *Scripturalist Islam: The History and Doctrines of the Akhbārī Shī'ī School* (Leiden, 2007).

8 For all these scholars and their respective arguments, see in detail Brunner, *Die Schia und die Koranfälschung*, pp. 12–27.

9 Ibid., pp. 28–32.

10 On Nūrī, see ibid., pp. 39–42 and the literature given there; see also Omid Ghaemmaghami, 'Arresting the Eschaton: Mirza Husayn Tabarsi Nuri (d. 1902) and the Babi and Baha'i Religions', *Journal of Religious History* 36, no. 4 (2012), pp. 486–98.

11 On 'Āmilī, see Gianroberto Scarcia, 'al-Ḥurr al-'Āmilī', EI^2, vol. III, pp. 588–9 and Meir Bar-Asher, 'Ḥorr-e 'Āmeli', *EIr*, vol. XII, pp. 478–9; on his hadith collection, see Āqā Buzurg al-Ṭihrānī, *al-Dharī'a ilā taṣānīf al-Shī'a* (Beirut, 1983), vol. IV, pp. 352–5; on Nūrī's *Mustadrak* (which was published for the first time in Tehran 1311–21/1893–1903), see Ṭihrānī, *al-Dharī'a ilā taṣānīf al-Shī'a*, vol. XXI, pp. 7–8.

12 Personal communication, Najaf, July 2012.

13 On this book, see in detail Brunner, *Die Schia und die Koranfälschung*, pp. 42–69; a partial edition of the text (with no named editor) appeared in Cairo in 2010 (at a publishing house called Dār Nūn); another partial edition had been issued by the Pakistani Sunni polemicist Iḥsān Ilāhī Ẓahīr, *al-Shī'a wa'l-Qur'ān*, 3rd edn (Lahore, 1983), pp. 136–344.

14 Muḥammad Ḥasan al-Shīrāzī is famous beyond Shiʿi theology and law for his role in the so-called tobacco protest in 1891–2; for this incident, see Nikki R. Keddie, *Religion and Rebellion in Iran: The Iranian Tobacco Protest of 1891–1892* (London, 1966); on his religious leadership (*marjaʿiyya*), see Meir Litvak, *Shiʿi Scholars of Nineteenth-Century Iraq: The ʿulamaʾ of Najaf and Karbalaʾ* (Cambridge, 1998), pp. 83–90; for his biography, see Werner Ende, 'Der amtsmüde Ayatollah', in Gebhard J. Selz, ed., *Festschrift für Burkhart Kienast: Zu seinem 70. Geburtstage dargebracht von Freunden, Schülern und Kollegen* (Münster, 2003), pp. 51–63.

15 For Ṭihrānī's unpublished work *al-Naqd al-laṭīf fī nafy al-taḥrīf ʿan al-qurʾān al-sharīf*, see his *al-Dharīʿa ilā taṣānīf al-Shīʿa*, vol. XXIV, p. 278 and vol. III, pp. 312–13; for the fatwa by Kāshif al-Ghiṭāʾ, see ʿAbd al-Raḥīm Muḥammad ʿAlī, *Shaykh al-bāḥithīn Āqā Buzurg al-Ṭihrānī: Ḥayātuhu wa āthāruhu (1875–1970)* (Najaf, 1970), pp. 45–6; see also Brunner, *Die Schia und die Koranfälschung*, pp. 80–81.

16 Yūsuf b. Aḥmad al-Dijwī, *al-Jawāb al-munīf fīʾl-radd ʿalā muddaʿī ʾl-taḥrīf fīʾl-kitāb al-sharīf* (Cairo, 1913), pp. 164–87; Muḥammad Rashīd Riḍā, *al-Sunna waʾl-shīʿa aw al-wahhābiyya waʾl-rāfiḍa* (Cairo, 1928), pp. 12–13, 43–4, 74–5.

17 Muḥibb al-Dīn al-Khaṭīb, *al-Khuṭūṭ al-ʿarīḍa liʾl-usus allatī qāma ʿalayhā dīn al-shīʿa al-imāmiyya al-ithnā ʿashariyya*, 10th edn (Cairo, 1982); on this book and its author, see in detail, Rainer Brunner, *Islamic Ecumenism in the 20th Century: The Azhar and Shiism between Rapprochement and Restraint* (Leiden, 2004), pp. 255–75 and 331–7.

18 Brunner, *Die Schia und die Koranfälschung*, pp. 95–9.

19 On abrogation in general, see John Burton, 'Abrogation', *EQ*, vol. I, pp. 11–19; idem, *The Sources of Islamic Law: Islamic Theories of Abrogation* (Edinburgh, 1990); see also David S. Powers, 'The Exegetical Genre *nāsikh al-Qurʾān wa mansūkhuhu*', in Andrew Rippin, ed., *Approaches to the History of the Interpretation of the Qurʾān* (Oxford, 1988), pp. 117–38; Andrew Rippin, 'The Exegetical Literature of Abrogation: Form and Content', in Gerald R. Hawting, Jawid Ahmad Mojaddedi and Alexander Samely, eds, *Studies in Islamic and Middle Eastern Texts and Traditions in Memory of Norman Calder* (Oxford, 2000), pp. 213–31.

20 All Qur'anic translations are by Arthur J. Arberry, *The Koran Interpreted: A Translation* (New York, 1996).

21 One of the most obvious (and well-known) examples in this regard is the gradual Qur'anic prohibition of wine: Q. 16:67 praises wine as a divine gift; Q. 4:43 exhorts the believers not to drink and pray; and only Q. 5:90 outlaws wine as *an abomination, some of Satan's work*.

22 On the 'stoning verse' in general, see Burton, *The Sources of Islamic Law*, pp. 122–64; on the classical Shiʿi attitude, see Sarah Eltantawi, 'Ṭūsī Did Not "Opt Out"'.

23 See, for example, Muḥammad Jawād al-Balāghī al-Najafī, *Ālāʾ al-raḥmān fī tafsīr al-Qurʾān* (Ṣaydā, 1933), vol. I, pp. 21–3; Muḥsin al-Amīn, *Naqḍ al-washīʿa aw al-shīʿa bayn al-ḥaqāʾiq waʾl-awhām* (Beirut, 2001 [1st edn 1951]), pp. 203–6; Muḥammad Taqī al-Ḥakīm, *al-Uṣūl al-ʿāmma liʾl-fiqh al-muqāran*, 2nd edn (Beirut, 1979 [1st edn 1963]), pp. 107–8; Hāshim Maʿrūf al-Ḥasanī, *Dirāsāt fīʾl-kāfī liʾl-Kulaynī waʾl-ṣaḥīḥ liʾl-Bukhārī* (Ṣūr, 1388/1968),

p. 349; ʿAlī Āl Muḥsin, *Kashf al-ḥaqāʾiq: Radd ʿalā ʿHādhihi naṣīḥatī ilā kull shīʿīʾ* (Beirut, 1416/1995), pp. 75–7; Murtaḍā al-Raḍawī, *al-Burhān ʿalā ʿadam taḥrīf al-Qurʾān* (Beirut, 1411/1991), pp. 199–212; see also below, n. 49.

24 Mīrzā Ḥusayn b. Taqī al-Nūrī al-Ṭabrisī, *Faṣl al-khiṭāb fī taḥrīf Kitāb Rabb al-arbāb*, lithograph (Tehran, 1298/1881), pp. 105–20.

25 Ibid., pp. 5, 121 (in both places he writes that ʿAlī's collection comprised the abrogating [*nasikh*] and the abrogated [*mansūkh*] verses in their correct order, i.e. the abrogated ones first).

26 Ibid., p. 107. Nūrī does not elaborate on the apparent contradiction to those instances where he talks about ʿAlī's collection having both categories (see previous note).

27 Ibid., p. 109. The expression 'guarded tablet' (see Q: 85:22) denotes the location of the Qur'an in God's presence. See Daniel A. Madigan, 'Preserved Tablet', *EQ*, vol. IV, pp. 261–3 and Josef van Ess, *Theologie und Gesellschaft im 2. und 3. Jahrhundert Hidschra: Eine Geschichte des religiösen Denkens im frühen Islam* (Berlin, 1991–7), vol. IV, pp. 625–6.

28 Nūrī, *Faṣl al-khiṭāb*, pp. 109–15; on the reports about *Sūrat al-Aḥzāb*, see also John Burton, *The Collection of the Qurʾān* (Cambridge, 1977), pp. 80–82; idem, 'The Collection of the Qurʾān', *EQ*, vol. I, pp. 353 and 355.

29 On Hibat al-Dīn al-Shahrastānī, see Werner Ende, 'al-Shahrastānī', EI^2, vol. IX, pp. 216–17; Pierre-Jean Luizard, *La formation de l'Irak contemporain: Le rôle politique des ulémas chiites à la fin de la domination ottomane et au moment de la construction de l'état irakien* (Paris, 1991), index, s.v.

30 'Tanzīh-i muṣḥaf-i sharīf az naskh wa naqṣ wa taḥrīf', in Hibat al-Dīn al-Shahrastānī, *Kitāb Tanzīh al-tanzīl mushtamal bar sa bakhsh wa yak khātima* (Tehran, 1331 Sh./1951–2), pp. 5–79; this booklet seems to be the Persian translation of a treatise which was originally composed in Arabic but never published: 'Tanzīh al-tanzīl fī ithbāt ṣiyānat al-muṣḥaf al-sharīf min an-naskh wa'l-naqṣ wa'l-taḥrīf'.

31 Shahrastānī, 'Tanzīh-i muṣḥaf-i sharīf', pp. 16–19.

32 Ibid., pp. 32–3.

33 Ibid., pp. 28, 34–6; on 'clear' and 'ambiguous' verses, see Leah Kinberg, '*Muḥkamāt* and *Mutashābihāt* (Koran 3/7): Implication of a Koranic Pair of Terms in Medieval Exegesis', *Studia Islamica* 35 (1988), pp. 143–72 (esp. pp. 149–50 on abrogation).

34 Shahrastānī, 'Tanzīh-i muṣḥaf-i sharīf', p. 30.

35 On Khūʾī, see Elvire Corboz, *Guardians of Shiʿism: Sacred Authority and Transnational Networks* (Edinburgh, 2015), pp. 48–57, 94–100, 166–72; Abdulaziz A. Sachedina, 'Al-Khūʾī and the Twelver Shīʿites', in Abū al-Qāsim al-Mūsawī al-Khūʾī, *The Prolegomena to the Qurʾan*, tr. and intro. Abdulaziz A. Sachedina (Oxford, 1998), pp. 3–22; Robert Gleave, 'Political Aspects of Modern Shiʿi Legal Discussions: Khumayni and Khu'i on *ijtihâd* and *qada*'', *Mediterranean Politics* 7 (2002), pp. 96–116; Yousif al-Kho'i, 'Grand Ayatollah Abu al-Qassim al-Kho'i: Political Thought and Positions', in Faleh Abdul-Jabar, ed., *Ayatollahs, Sufis and Ideologues: State, Religion and Social Movements in Iraq* (London, 2002), pp. 223–30; Yūsuf al-Khoei, 'Abū'l-Qāsim al-Ḫūʾī', *Oriente Moderno* New Series, 18 (79), no. 2 (1999), pp. 491–500.

36 Abū'l-Qāsim al-Khū'ī, *al-Bayān fī tafsīr al-Qur'ān* (Najaf, 1375/1955–6); for the English translation see the previous note (*The Prolegomena to the Qur'an*). Contrary to what the title might indicate, the book is not a Qur'anic commentary per se, but rather a theoretical introduction to a *tafsīr*; Khū'ī never composed a fully fledged commentary.

37 Khū'ī, *al-Bayān*, pp. 136–81, esp. pp. 139–44 (English tr.: *The Prolegomena*, pp. 138–42); for his arguments against *taḥrīf*, see in detail Brunner, *Die Schia und die Koranfälschung*, pp. 88–92.

38 Khū'ī, *al-Bayān*, p. 143 (English tr.: *The Prolegomena*, p. 141).

39 Khū'ī, *al-Bayān*, pp. 175–81 (English tr.: *The Prolegomena*, pp. 156–61).

40 Khū'ī, *al-Bayān*, pp. 189–269 (English tr.: *The Prolegomena*, pp. 186–253).

41 Khū'ī, *al-Bayān*, pp. 195–6 (English tr.: *The Prolegomena*, pp. 191–2).

42 See above, n. 21.

43 Khū'ī, *al-Bayān*, pp. 233–5 (English tr.: *The Prolegomena*, pp. 221–3).

44 Khū'ī, *al-Bayān*, pp. 199–269 (English tr.: *The Prolegomena*, pp. 193–248); for classical Sunni lists of allegedly abrogated verses, see Powers, 'The Exegetical Genre', pp. 137–8.

45 Khū'ī, *al-Bayān*, pp. 190–95 (English tr.: *The Prolegomena*, pp. 188–91).

46 Nūrī, *Faṣl al-khiṭāb*, pp. 35–96, esp. pp. 92–6; see Brunner, *Die Schia und die Koranfälschung*, pp. 43–6; on the traditional Muslim view on the Jewish and Christian falsification of the scriptures, see Camilla Adang, *Muslim Writers on Judaism and the Hebrew Bible: From Ibn Rabban to Ibn Hazm* (Leiden, 1996); Hava Lazarus-Yafeh, 'Taḥrīf', *EI*², vol. X, pp. 111–12.

47 Hossein Modarressi, 'Early Debates on the Integrity of the Qur'ān: A Brief Survey', *Studia Islamica* 77 (1993), pp. 5–39, esp. the following quote on pp. 7–8 referring to Khū'ī: 'With a single possible exception, however, it is highly doubtful that the Qur'ān includes any abrogated verse.'

48 See, for example, al-Balāghī al-Najafī, *Ālā' al-raḥmān fī tafsīr al-Qur'ān*, vol. I, p. 115; Muḥammad Jawād Mughniyya, *al-Tafsīr al-kāshif* (Beirut, 1978), vol. I, pp. 169–70; Muḥammad Ḥusayn Faḍlallāh, *Min waḥy al-Qur'ān* (Beirut, 1998), vol. II, pp. 156–7; the latter avoids discussing the thorny issue in detail, but refers the reader to Khū'ī's *al-Bayān* instead.

49 See, for example, Rasūl Ja'fariyān, *Ukdhūbat taḥrīf al-Qur'ān bayn al-shī'a wa'l-sunna* (n.p., 1413/1992–3), pp. 46–59; idem, 'A Study of Sunnī and Shī'ī Traditions Concerning Taḥrīf', *al-Tawḥīd* 6, no. 4 (Rajab–Ramaḍān 1409/1988), pp. 34–42; Bahā' al-Dīn Khurramshāhī, *Qur'ān-pazhūhī: Haftād baḥth wa taḥqīq-i qur'ānī* (Tehran 1372 Sh./1994), pp. 106–7; 'Alī al-Ḥusainī Mīlānī, *al-Taḥqīq fī nafy al-taḥrīf 'an al-Qur'ān al-sharīf* (Qum, 1410/1990), pp. 272–92; Muḥammad Hādī Ma'rifat, *Ṣiyānat al-Qur'ān min al-taḥrīf* (Qum, 1410/1990), pp. 17–24; 'Izz al-Dīn Ibrāhīm, *Mawqif 'ulamā' al-muslimīn min al-shī'a wa'l-thawra al-islāmiyya* (Tehran 1406/1986), pp. 36–9; Riḍā Ḥusaynī Nasab, *Dar Tarīq-i waḥdat-i islāmī: Pāsukh ba 35 pursish ka pīrāmūn-i īn hadaf maṭraḥ mīkardand* (Qum, 1366 Sh./1988), pp. 52–60.

50 Brunner, *Islamic Ecumenism in the 20th Century*, pp. 382–3 and the references given there; the organisation was renamed al-Majma' al-'Ālamī li'l-Taqrīb bayn al-Madhāhib al-Islāmiyya in 2004; see also its website http://www.taghrib.org.

51 Ruhollah Khomeini, *Kashf al-asrār* (Qum, *c.* 1980), pp. 114–20; see in detail Brunner, *Die Schia und die Koranfälschung*, pp. 103–4.

52 On Ṭabāṭabā'ī, see Hamid Algar, "Allāma Sayyid Muḥammad Ḥusayn Ṭabāṭabā'ī: Philosopher, Exegete, and Gnostic', *Journal of Islamic Studies* 17 (2006), pp. 326–51 (which is of a heavily apologetic tendency); on some of his exegetical principles, see Mohammad Jafar Elmi, 'The Views of Ṭabāṭabā'ī on Traditions (*Aḥādīth*) and Occasions of Revelation (*Asbāb al-Nuzūl*) in Interpreting the Qur'an', *Journal of Shi'a Islamic Studies* 1 (2008), pp. 57–84; 'Alī al-Awsī, *al-Ṭabāṭabā'ī wa manhajuhu fī tafsīrihi al-Mīzān* (Tehran, 1405/1985).

53 This reading was already discussed by al-Faḍl b. al-Ḥasan al-Ṭabrisī (d. 548/1153–4), who remains one of the most important Shi'i commentators today; see his *Majma' al-bayān fī tafsīr al-Qur'ān* (Beirut, 2005), vol. I, p. 250; for references to the old codices, see Arthur Jeffery, *Materials for the History of the Text of the Qur'ān: The Old Codices* (Leiden, 1937), pp. 119, 195, 220, 246, 277, 285.

54 Muḥammad Ḥusayn Ṭabāṭabā'ī, *al-Mīzān fī tafsīr al-Qur'ān* (Beirut, 1411/1991), vol. XII, pp. 115–16 and 130–31; see also Brunner, *Die Schia und die Koranfälschung*, pp. 99–102.

55 Ṭabāṭabā'ī, *al-Mīzān*, vol. I, pp. 246–52 (esp. p. 252).

56 Quoted by Khurramshāhī, *Qur'ān-pazhūhī*, p. 112; see also Ṭabāṭabā'ī, *al-Mīzān*, vol. XII, p. 109; on the problem of *akhbār āḥād* in modern Shi'ism, see Robert Gleave, 'Modern Šī'ī Discussions of *Ḫabar al-wāḥid*: Ṣādr, Ḫumaynī and Ḫū'ī', *Oriente Moderno* New Series, 21 (82), no. 1 (2002), pp. 179–94.

57 See Hamid Dabashi, *Theology of Discontent: The Ideological Foundations of the Islamic Revolution in Iran* (New York, 1993), pp. 273–323.

58 Nāṣir b. 'Abdallāh b. 'Alī al-Qafārī, *Uṣūl madhhab al-shī'a al-imāmiyya al-ithnā 'ashariyya: 'Arḍ wa naqd* (Riyadh, 1414/1993), vol. I, pp. 247–8; see also 'Alī Aḥmad Sālūs, *Bayn al-shī'a wa'l-sunna: Dirāsa muqārina fī'l-tafsīr wa-uṣūlihi* (Cairo, 1989), pp. 160–61; idem, *Ma'a al-shī'a al-ithnā 'ashariyya fī'l-uṣūl wa'l-furū': Mawsū'a shāmila* (al-Dawḥa, 1417/1997), vol. II, pp. 158–519; for modern Sunni authors and their scepticism of the idea of abrogation, see Daniel Brown, 'The Triumph of Scripturalism: The Doctrine of Naskh and its Modern Critics', in Earle H. Waugh and Frederick M. Denny, eds, *The Shaping of an American Islamic Discourse: A Memorial to Fazlur Rahman* (Atlanta, GA, 1998), pp. 49–66.

9

Speaking the Secrets of Sanctity in the *Tafsīr* of Ṣafī ʿAlī Shāh

NICHOLAS BOYLSTON

THE *TAFSĪR* of Mīrzā Ḥasan Iṣfahānī (known as Ṣafī ʿAlī Shāh; d. 1899)[1] is a 32,000-verse translation and commentary on the entire Qur'an, written in Persian *mathnawī* verse (i.e. rhyming couplets).[2] This alone makes it a unique work in the history of Persian literature.[3] However, the *Tafsīr-i Ṣafī*, even from the point of view of content alone, is also a unique contribution to the genres of Sufi exegesis and Shiʿi-Sufi texts, providing both original insights into and a synopsis and synthesis of diverse elements of these traditions. The fact that this work has not received scholarly attention reveals an unfortunate lacuna in Western scholarship on the history of Persian literature, limiting our perception of the creativity of the tradition in what may be termed the 'post-classical' phase. This oversight is equally visible in Persian scholarship on its own tradition in the undervaluing of works produced in '*khānaqāhī*' circles (i.e. those produced in the cultural milieu of the Sufi lodges) and in the emphasis on stylistic originality alone as the yardstick of the worth of any work of literature.[4] A more multifaceted approach, which can situate the *Tafsīr-i Ṣafī* in its historical, literary and intellectual contexts, will be more adequate for revealing the qualities and significance of this work. By presenting an overview of the *Tafsīr-i Ṣafī* and its context, followed by a more detailed discussion of a few of the more remarkable particularities of this work, I aim here to introduce this remarkable text. It is also my hope that my multifaceted approach will sketch out a methodology that might allow us to re-envision the significance of similar literary works in Persian, leading to a new appreciation of the topology of a tradition that I consider to be even richer than is often recognised.

A Brief Biography of Ṣafī ʿAlī Shāh and the Context of Composition of the *Tafsīr*

As Ṣafī ʿAlī Shāh himself explains in the introduction to the *Tafsīr*, he was born in Isfahan on 3 Shaʿbān 1251 (24 November 1835) to a merchant father, who soon moved his family to the city of Yazd where they would stay for nearly twenty years.[5] Ṣafī[6] himself mentioned that from the age of fifteen he loved to frequent 'the possessors of spiritual states', despite the disapproval of his family, and in 1855–6, by his own account, an overwhelming spiritual state led him to set out from Isfahan for Shiraz on foot and without any provisions to seek initiation and spiritual guidance from the Niʿmatullāhī master Raḥmat ʿAlī Shāh (d. 1861), whom he followed to Kirmān (roughly corresponding to present-day Kerman province).[7]

Following the death of Raḥmat ʿAlī Shāh, Ṣafī lived in both Yazd and Kirmān again, before travelling to Bombay in 1864.[8] This journey was embarked upon on the instructions of Raḥmat ʿAlī Shāh's successor, Munawwar ʿAlī Shāh (d. 1884), who gave our author the name Ṣafī ʿAlī Shāh[9] and the task of making sure that the Niʿmatullāhī disciples in India received correct spiritual instruction.[10] From 1864 to 1871 Ṣafī remained in India, with the exception of two journeys. The first of these was a pilgrimage to Mecca in 1864, which he describes as full of tribulations, including nearly drowning after his ship capsized. The second followed the completion of the work that made him famous as a poet and spiritual authority, the *Zubdat al-asrār* (The Quintessence of Mysteries), printed in 1872, a work of spiritual instruction centred on the description of the events at Karbala, which Ṣafī had begun on Raḥmat ʿAlī Shāh's instruction while with him in Kirmān.[11] Though Ṣafī describes this journey as resulting from an irresistible desire to visit the holy sites in Iraq caused by the spiritual state that writing the *Zubdat al-asrār* had brought about in him, leading to a forty-day period of seclusion in Karbala, this journey also took him to Iran. He describes the confusion and dispute that he met with among the Niʿmatullāhīs there, and after some disagreement he decided to return to India,[12] though he does not himself here mention in this regard his break with Munawwar ʿAlī Shāh in 1877.[13] During this middle period of Ṣafī's life, in Bombay, he received the patronage of Aga Khan I and developed a close friendship with the future Aga Khan II which provided the most supportive environment for his spiritual and literary activities. As Nile Green has argued, the landscapes (and seascapes) over which Ṣafī travelled were indelibly shaped by the commercial geography of the period. Trade in the cities that Ṣafī inhabited from his childhood, particularly Yazd and Kirmān, was significantly affected by the influx of British textiles from India, and Ṣafī's own travels to India were facilitated by the mid-nineteenth-century steamship network.[14] Green also shows the importance of patronage and printing in this part of Ṣafī's career, for it was the support of the Aga Khans and their connections with the printing presses that made his stay in Bombay so successful and led to Ṣafī's works, of great significance to the development of his authority, being available in Iraq and Iran.[15] Ṣafī returned to Iran for good in 1871, settling in Tehran. Once again, Ṣafī describes the impetus for this journey as pilgrimage – this time to visit the eighth imam, Alī b. Mūsā al-Riḍā (d. 203/819) in Mashhad – though the famine in Iran at the time and his own poverty prevented him from completing the journey.[16] In 1877, the land upon which 'The Khānaqāh of Ṣafī ʿAlī Shāh' was built was donated by Muḥammad Mīrzā Sayf al-Dawla, a grandson of Fatḥ ʿAlī Shāh (r. 1772–1834); this building is still maintained today.

Between 1888 and 1890, while he was established at the Khānaqāh in Tehran, Ṣafī worked on and completed his *Tafsīr*. Given his travels in India and his residence in the capital of Qajar Iran ruled by Nāṣir al-Dīn Shāh (r. 1848–96), in whose court several of Ṣafī's closest disciples held important positions, undoubtedly Ṣafī was aware of the cultural, economic and technological upheavals that were occurring in his milieu as a result of both the British control of India and the attention that the Qajar court paid to Europe. As several scholars have observed, some of the effects of these upheavals were visible among the Ṣafī ʿAlī Shāh Niʿmatullāhīs (the Niʿmatullāhī branch that took Ṣafī's name) in the months that followed his passing: under the leadership of his foremost disciple Ẓahīr al-Dawla (the son-in-law of Nāsir al-Dīn Shāh [r. 1848–96] and his master of ceremonies), a group of Ṣafī's foremost disciples undertook an unprecedented transformation of the hierarchical structure of the order, establishing the committee-led Fraternal Society (Anjuman-i Ukhuwwat), the organisation of which may have been influenced by the secret societies of European origin that were by that time fairly common in Iran.[17]

Before studying the content of the *Tafsīr-i Ṣafī* itself, it is worth pausing to consider how the encroachment of modernity in late-nineteenth-century India and Iran are reflected within the *Tafsīr-i Ṣafī*. Considering the analogous question à propos the autobiographical recollections that Ṣafī recorded at the end of his life, Green rightly makes much of the fact that the author does not mention modernity or technology, even though he would have encountered striking examples of this during his years travelling and residing in British-ruled India:[18]

> For in his entire account of his travels in India we do not hear of a single encounter with a European. Nor is there any sense of his entering a domain governed by new political ideas, by a new power or by new forms of technology. Instead, his India remains a realm of white-bearded Sufi elders, venerable Muslim notables and contortionist yogis.[19]

Green reads into this silence a conscious yet tacit affirmation on Ṣafī's part that the correct response to the transformations of society was to assert truth of tradition in all its depth.[20]

The lack of attention to contemporary political circumstances is equally evident in the *Tafsīr-i Ṣafī*, despite the fact that the completion of this work was made possible through the intercession of Nāsir al-Dīn Shāh himself, who sought a fatwa on the legitimacy of translating the Qur'an into poetry from Mīrzā Muḥammad Ḥasan Shīrāzī (d. 1896). It is therefore possible to suggest, following Green, that Ṣafī wrote his *Tafsīr* with a studied separation from contemporary westernising trends and sought to consciously impress upon an audience of educated Persian speakers the vitality of the Qur'anic message and the highlights of centuries of exoteric and spiritual interpretation. It is difficult to be sure if this motivation was at the forefront of Ṣafī's mind as he composed the work, for he himself writes:

> It has been nearly two years that I have been occupied with composing my *tafsīr* on the Qur'an, which is an occupation, an act of worship, and an encouragement to Persian speakers to read and understand the glorious Word of God. Perhaps the reward of this one who is poor with God (*faqīr ʿinda'llāh*) shall not be lost and it shall be a means of guidance for the people for years and centuries.[21]

What is clear, however, is that the originality and freshness of the *Tafsīr-i Ṣafī*, both in its poetic form and its exemplary additions to the Islamic literary, exegetical, metaphysical, Shiʿi and Sufi traditions, do in fact mean that it is de facto proof of the vitality of these traditions in late nineteenth-century Iran, whether Ṣafī was aiming to make a point of this or not.

Content and Style of the Work

The endeavour to render the message of the Qur'an intelligible to those who do not understand Arabic is a task almost as old as the text itself.[22] The *Tafsīr-i Ṣafī* takes its place in a tradition of Persian translation of and commentary on the Qur'an that includes such works as the *Kashf al-asrār* of Rashīd al-Dīn Maybudī (fl. 517/1123)[23] and the *Minhaj al-ṣādiqīn* of Mullā Fatḥ Allāh Kāshānī (d. 988/1580),[24] which are among the most important examples of Sufi and Shiʿi *tafsīr* respectively. However, although the *Tafsīr-i Ṣafī* contains certain similarities to both of these works in content, and was directly influenced by the former if not also the latter, the uniqueness of its form sets it apart from them in the particular way in which it makes Qur'anic knowledge available to a Persian readership.

The importance of the verse form of the *Tafsīr-i Ṣafī* cannot be overstated, making it an unparalleled work in the history of Persian literature. Aside from the recent *Qur'ān-nāma* completed in 1997 by Umid Majd, I know of no other complete verse translation of the Qur'an in Persian.[25] However, there may be a partial precedent in the *Tafsīr-i manẓūm* attributed to the Niʿmatullāhī master Nūr ʿAlī Shāh I (d. 1798), which, though only a few pages long and including a simple commentary on the *basmala* and *alif-lām-mīm*, does show stylistic features that may have influenced Ṣafī, such as the intervening section of supplication (*munājāt*) that interrupts the commentary.[26]

Like Ṣafī ʿAlī Shāh's other magnum opus, the *Zubdat al-asrār*, the *Tafsīr-i Ṣafī* is written in *mathnawī* verse. As has been noted by other scholars,[27] both of these works are deeply influenced by Jalāl al-Dīn Rūmī's *Mathnawī-yi maʿnawī*, not simply in the choice of metre but in the style as a whole and through numerous references to famous verses of the latter text. There is in fact a profound inverse relationship between the *Tafsīr-i Ṣafī* and the *Mathnawī*, upon which Ṣafī ʿAlī Shāh must have contemplated deeply. Of roughly similar length,[28] *Tafsīr-i Ṣafī* is in one sense a mirror image of Rūmī's masterpiece: the *Mathnawī* is a spiritual discourse that constantly brings the reader back to the Qur'anic verses, which both crystallises the teachings of Rūmī and expounds on and reveals new significances within them in ways that are insightful and often surprising; the *Tafsīr-i Ṣafī* on the other hand does it the other way around, but achieves the same effect – it begins with the Qur'anic verses and then uses these as the occasion for spiritual teaching, which often but not always springs directly from the verse in question.

The enormous value of the *Tafsīr-i Ṣafī* as a work of Persian Sufi literature is not in the originality or genius of its style (though the work does bring eloquence to a peak at certain points, particularly in sections entitled 'mystical attraction' [*jadhba*], which we shall discuss later). Rather, it is what Ṣafī ʿAlī Shāh has been able to achieve within the *mathnawī* form that makes this work so significant. First of all, the very fact that Ṣafī ʿAlī Shāh was able to translate the entire Qur'an into Persian verse of a high quality is an unprecedented literary feat, and as we shall see Ṣafī was well aware of this. The effortlessness of the translation is easily sensed by the reader, and despite the fact that the Qur'anic text often echoes itself, the translation never becomes repetitive, a fact epitomised by Ṣafī's thirty-one different translations of the refrain of *Sūrat al-Raḥmān* (Q. 55): *So which of your Lord's boons do you two deny?*[29]

Indeed, the translation of the Qur'an into Persian poetry of such a high calibre is perhaps the most direct way that the aesthetic experience of reading the Qur'an can be reflected in another language. The rhythm of the Qur'an, which is of course not limited to any metre – but which, to adapt the terminology of Ibn 'Arabī (d. 638/1240), is in the 'metre of no metre' – is a crucial aspect of the aesthetics of the text.[30] Furthermore, the harmony between direct quotations from the Qur'an and the flow of the metric lines[31] joins the *Tafsīr-i Ṣafī* to the early tradition of didactic *mathnawī*s, particularly the *Ḥadīqat al-ḥaqīqa* of Abū'l-Majd Sanā'ī (d. 525/1131) and the *Mathnawī* by Rūmī,[32] in which direct quotations from the Qur'an are suggestive of a harmony between the sound and message of the poetry on the one hand and the Qur'an on the other.[33]

In parallel to its rhythmic dimension, the *mathnawī* form also has qualities that are perfectly suited to storytelling, both through its inherent characteristics and through the way the form has been crafted over the centuries. The literary attractiveness of the *Tafsīr-i Ṣafī* is nowhere as strong as when the author is recounting, and expanding upon, the Qur'anic tales of the prophets (*qiṣaṣ al-anbiyā'*). The literary heart of the work is in fact Ṣafī's extended retelling of the story of Joseph in his commentary on that 'most beautiful of tales' (*aḥsan al-qaṣaṣ*). The centrality of the theme of love in that particular story, in addition to the wealth of poetic tradition that has grown up around it, gives Ṣafī the opportunity to present a literary opus that at once contains a treasury of Sufi teachings and Ṣafī's own personal mystical responses to the tale, framed around the translation of this sura of the Qur'an. Viewed as a literary work, the *Tafsīr-i Ṣafī* achieves the task of making the message of the Qur'an accessible to the Persian reader in a form with which he or she is on intimate terms, in which the aesthetic experience of the poetic rendition would be intermingled for the believer with the sweetness of understanding the message of the Creator, such that the dimensions of mercy and love in the text come to the fore.

Complementing the verse form, which makes the Qur'anic message effortlessly and immediately available to the Persian reader, we must also note the concision of the text as a work of Qur'anic exegesis. The fact that the *Tafsīr-i Ṣafī* comprises over 32,000 *bayt*s (verses), which makes it one of the longest single works of Persian poetry, means that Ṣafī used on average around five *bayt*s per *āya* (Qur'anic verse) in both translation and commentary. Taken as a whole, a large proportion of the *Tafsīr-i Ṣafī* is constituted by his explanatory translation, which fills in the common Qur'anic ellipsis, completing the Qur'anic stories and showing many of the *āyas* in their historical context through a selective presentation of the material on the 'occasions of revelation' (*asbāb al-nuzūl*). The commentary proper is therefore selective, and the manner of selection, which maintains the impression that the most important points have been covered, should be considered a central feature of the artistry of the work.

The *Tafsīr-i Ṣafī* as Qur'anic Commentary

In addition to being a literary work, the *Tafsīr-i Ṣafī* is simultaneously a fully fledged *tafsīr* that includes both exoteric and esoteric exegesis. As mentioned, the work is by nature selective, but that does not prevent Ṣafī from including a surprisingly wide array of material. As befits his task of crafting an interpretive translation, Ṣafī pays a great deal of attention to the meaning of specific Qur'anic terms, a traditional exegetic practice that is further augmented by his Sufi sensitivity to the importance of clarifying terminology.[34] At those points where Ṣafī chooses to go into detail, he is apt to present several interpretations of the linguistic meaning of an *āya*, in which he relates common opinions of the *mufassirūn* (the classical commentators on the Qur'an), sometimes mentioning them by name.[35] This fact alone means that the *Tafsīr-i Ṣafī* is not simply a retelling of the Qur'an in Persian, but is a *tafsīr* proper.

However, the exoteric aspect of the commentary does not stop at the discussion of the linguistic complexities or the occasions of revelation of the *āyas*. Ṣafī also makes a point of mentioning – if fairly infrequently – certain legal, theological and historical debates surrounding particular Qur'anic texts. As far as the legal discussions are concerned, Ṣafī often mentions, fairly impartially, the views of the imams of the four schools of Sunni law as well as the prevailing Twelver Shi'i opinion, which of course he shows preference for. However, when it comes to typical theological issues such as free will and historical issues such as whether the Prophet's uncle Abū Ṭālib (d. 619) was a believer, Ṣafī invariably argues for the Shiʿi position and firmly rejects the alternatives.

As one might expect from the leader of a Sufi order, however, the genre of commentary that is most commonly used in the *Tafsīr-i Ṣafī* is mystical exegesis. The mystical material of the *Tafsīr-i Ṣafī* may be divided into several types. In addition to short insights about select aspects of many verses, which are consistent with the general contents of the tradition of Sufi commentary going back to the *tafsīr* of Abū ʿAbd al-Raḥmān al-Sulamī (d. 412/1021),[36] Ṣafī often uses certain verses as an opportunity to introduce lengthier discussions. It is these longer passages of mystical commentary that I consider to be worthier of our attention here.

Mystical Commentary in the *Tafsīr-i Ṣafī*

The ontological framework in which Ṣafī operates is undoubtedly that of the *waḥdat al-wujūd* ('the transcendent unity of being') of the school of Ibn ʿArabī,[37] and more particularly in the form in which this framework crystallised in the Persian literary texts from that school.[38] The work begins with an account of creation on the basis of this metaphysics and repeatedly makes use of the perspectives it offers to explain the Qur'anic teachings on unity (*tawḥīd*) and the signs (*āyāt*) in the natural world and within the soul.[39] In this respect, the *Tafsīr-i Ṣafī* is an important contribution to nineteenth-century Iranian intellectual and literary history, in the framework of the reception and development of Akbarian metaphysics in the Persian-speaking world; it continues a tradition that includes the literary masterpieces of figures such as Fakhr al-Dīn ʿIrāqī (d. 688/1289), Shīrīn Maghribī (d. 809/1406), ʿAbd al-Raḥmān Jāmī (d. 898/1492) and Ṣafī's own spiritual progenitor, Shāh Niʿmatullāh Walī (d. 834/1431). Indeed, Ṣafī follows both Jāmī and Shāh Niʿmatullāh in combining the literary styles of Rūmī with the metaphysics of the school of Ibn ʿArabī.[40] When considered beside these works, the *tafsīr* format of Ṣafī's work manifests its particular aptness for the exposition of the profound relation between the metaphysics of this school and the Qur'anic text, as was elaborated so thoroughly by Ibn ʿArabī himself.[41]

In addition to discussions of the doctrines of *waḥdat al-wujūd*, Ṣafī also makes use of what may be termed indirect commentary to discuss a wide range of Sufi themes. In fact, the *Tafsīr-i Ṣafī* is an encyclopaedic work on Sufism. Beginning from *Sūrat al-Baqara* (Q. 2), in which the author reveals the inner significance of each of the pillars of the religion as they are mentioned therein, Ṣafī seizes the opportunity throughout the commentary to explain all the major aspects of the Sufi tradition, from stories of the early masters to descriptions of the virtues and key spiritual practices. As one would expect from a Sufi *tafsīr*, Ṣafī is particularly sensitive to the importance of the word '*dhikr*' (invocation, remembrance) in the Qur'an, and in several places describes the different degrees of invocation leading to the 'invocation of the heart' (*dhikr-i khafī*).[42] Of particular interest are passages on the importance of meditation (*fikr*) and visualisation of the spiritual master.[43]

Viewed as a whole, the wealth of Sufi teachings presented succinctly throughout the *Tafsīr-i Ṣafī* means that its readers gain a well-rounded education in both the meaning of the Qur'an and all the major teachings of Sufism. The completeness of its teachings was no doubt one of the factors that led to the *Tafsīr-i Ṣafī* gaining liturgical significance among the Ṣafī ʿAlī Shāh Niʿmatullāhīs in much the same way that Rūmī's *Mathnawī* did for the Mevlevis. Furthermore, the fact that the *Tafsīr-i Ṣafī* not only gives the esoteric meanings of particular verses but also shows how these verses are the wellspring of all the fundamental aspects of Sufism makes it an important representative of those texts which demonstrate the Qur'anic basis of the Sufi tradition and, hence, the harmony of the esoteric and exoteric dimensions of Islam.

The *Tafsīr-i Ṣafī* at the Confluence of Sufism and Shiʿism

The harmonisation of the esoteric and the exoteric, which is a common feature in many of the important Sufi *tafsīr* works, is only one way in which the *Tafsīr-i Ṣafī* harmonises aspects of the Islamic tradition that might superficially seem to be incompatible. The *Tafsīr-i Ṣafī* is an important addition to a rich tradition of works going back to Ḥaydar Āmulī (d. 786/1385) and before, in which the two rivers of Sufi and Shiʿi spirituality and metaphysics converge into a single worldview. The nineteenth century was in fact one of the richest periods of this tradition, not least due to the activities of the Niʿmatullāhī order, as is seen in the history of the order written during the period, as well as in the important *tafsīr* of Ṣafī's contemporary, Sulṭān ʿAlī Shāh Gunābādī (d. 1909), the *Bayān al-saʿāda*.[44]

Several aspects of the Shiʿi-Sufi dimension of the *Tafsīr-i Ṣafī* should be remarked upon. Firstly, in addition to the presence of the Twelver Shiʿi theological and legal perspectives mentioned above, Shiʿi interpretations, specifically, take their place among the material drawn from previous commentators to elucidate the significance of particular Qur'anic verses and terms. The most noticeable of these are those interpretations in which particular verses are shown to be referring to ʿAlī b. Abī Ṭālib (d. 40/661) or the Family of the Prophet. But it is the way Ṣafī approaches these interpretations that mark him out from other Shiʿi commentators. To begin with, we see that Ṣafī makes use of the conceptual framework of the school of Ibn ʿArabī to uncover the hidden significance of some of these attributions. Rather than simply declaring ʿAlī's spiritual and temporal authority as other Shiʿi commentators had done, Ṣafī interprets the verse Q. 5:55 (*Your protector [walī] is only God, and His Messenger, and those who believe, who perform the prayer and give alms while bowing down* [the latter description being taken by Sunni and Shiʿi commentators, on the basis of the *asbāb al-nuzūl*, to refer to ʿAlī]) as expressing in particular ʿAlī's attainment of the highest possible spiritual station: while being utterly immersed in the contemplation of God, ʿAlī was nonetheless completely aware of God's creation around him.

However, in addition to using typically Sufi perspectives to reveal the depth of purely Shiʿi teachings, Ṣafī also uses these verses as part of a larger ecumenical project that resurfaces throughout the *Tafsīr*. When it comes to commenting on two of the verses that are interpreted as referring to ʿAlī,[45] Ṣafī explicitly states that he has taken this material from the Sunni commentators Fakhr al-Dīn al-Rāzī (606/1209) and Abū Isḥāq al-Thaʿlabī (d. 427/1035).[46] Although more polemical Shiʿi commentators used these same citations to refute the Sunnis' view using the Sunnis' own sources,[47]

Ṣafī's tone makes it clear that his point is ecumenical;[48] he is pointing out an element of a common Islamic heritage, one that is particularly important to him and to which his poetic legacy bears witness.[49]

In contrast to the genre just mentioned, the tone of the *Tafsīr-i Ṣafī* with respect to Sunnism is not polemical. In contrast to certain of the other Shiʿi-Sufi synthesisers, of whom Muḥsin Fayḍ Kāshānī (d. 1090/1680) is the clearest example, Ṣafī's attitude towards the Prophet's wife ʿĀʾisha (d. 58/678) and the first three caliphs is not at all critical. Rather, he manifests a form of moderation, showing his respect for the virtue of the first caliph Abū Bakr (r. 10–13/632–4) and his successor ʿUmar (r. 13–23/634–44) on several occasions, whilst also pointing out their mistakes. The contentious issue of the claim by Fāṭima (d. 11/632) to the Fadak garden as inheritance from her father the Prophet provides us with an excellent example of Ṣafī's approach. In interpreting Q. 17:26, *Give unto the kinsman his right, and unto the indigent and the traveler, but do not squander wastefully*, Ṣafī does affirm that upon receiving this verse the Prophet bequeathed Fadak to Fāṭima, and hence begins his interpretation by showing which party he sides with. But he follows that statement with these verses:

> 'Tis God who knows all the truth of the affair,
> To why t'was seized from Fāṭima.
> But not for Ṣiddīq or Fārūq, trustworthy,
> Is countenanced by the wise, oppression and enmity.
> After Aḥmad were they commanders then,
> Clear-sighted in the rule of God and in affairs of men.[50]

These verses epitomise Ṣafī's treatment of this event: he is certain of Fāṭima's infallibility but is unable to believe the unfavourable historical narrations about the behaviour of Abū Bakr, being also certain of his veracity and justice. Ultimately, he admits that only God knows the truth of the matter.

Ṣafī's approach to this incident is in conformity with other statements that he makes about the virtue of Abū Bakr, ʿUmar and ʿĀʾisha elsewhere in the *Tafsīr*.[51] In this respect we can see the similarity between Ṣafī and his predecessor in Shiʿi-Sufism, Ḥaydar

Āmulī; however, he may also be showing the influence here of his forefather in the *mathnawī* genre, Farīd al-Dīn ʿAṭṭār (d. 618/1221), whose masterpieces often contain censure of partisanship (*taʿaṣṣub*) and criticism of the caliphs in their introductory sections.[52]

The respectful indication of the attitudes that Ṣafī sees as most correct and praiseworthy (*aḥsan*) alongside the recognition of lower, partial, but nonetheless valuable, attitudes (*ḥusn*) is the cornerstone of his negotiation of the Sunni–Shiʿi divergence. This is most clearly seen in Ṣafī's innovative ecumenical interpretation of the 'Verse of Purification' (Q. 33:33): *God only desires to remove defilement from you, O People of the House, and to purify you completely.* The disagreement here turns on the identity of the 'People of the House' (*ahl al-bayt*): the context suggests that it indicates the Prophet's wives, while the *asbāb al-nuzūl*, Sunni and Shiʿi, and the major Shiʿi commentators, such as Abū ʿAlī al-Faḍl b. al-Ḥasan al-Tabrisī (d. 548/1154) and Fayḍ Kāshānī, state that it refers only to ʿAlī, Fātima, and their sons Ḥasan (d. 50/670) and Ḥusayn (60/680). Ṣafī affirms that the literal meaning of the 'People of the House' is general, and this indicates God's affirmation that He has kept them all pure from errors on the level of the sharia. However, the Shiʿi interpretation – that the five 'people of the mantle' were purified from all fault and given refuge in infallibility by God in pre-eternity – is the deeper one, addressed to the elite (*khawāṣṣ*); the former interpretation addresses the people at large (*ʿawāmm*).[53]

The theme of love of the Household of the Prophet looms large in the *Tafsīr-i Ṣafī*, as one would expect from a Shiʿa devoted to spirituality. Besides the more intellectual analyses that Ṣafī presents, as in his analysis of the 'Verse of Purification', he more often makes allusions to the Household as an opportunity to soar on the wings of love, in a manner that is well suited to the *mathnawī* poetic form crafted by ʿAṭṭār's and Rūmī's masterpieces. One of the most striking instances of this is Ṣafī's connection of this notion to the verse Q. 5:54 (. . . *whom He loves and who love Him* . . .), which has always been beloved by the Persian Sufis since Aḥmad al-Ghazālī (d. 517/1123 or 520/1126). This verse prompts Ṣafī to recall an occasion in which the Prophet prostrated five times when Gabriel had informed him of God's love for ʿAlī, for Fāṭima, for Ḥasan and Ḥusayn, for their Companions and for all those who love them. Ṣafī comments:

> Were the recipients (of this teaching) to have been more recipient,
> That Messenger would have would have made up to fifty prostrations.
> Nay, 'til the Resurrection he would have prostrated,
> From the Loving Lord's tidings, and never abated.[54]

As we have begun to see, the figure of ʿAlī reappears in the *Tafsīr-i Ṣafī* again and again, including particular Shiʿi interpretations of certain verses and references to ʿAlī as the embodiment of the fundamental virtues.[55]

It is apt that the figure of ʿAlī should play such a fundamental role in Ṣafī's harmonisation of Sufism and Shiʿism, and of course this was an extremely important element in post-Safavid Sufism in Iran in general. Given the role that ʿAlī plays in Shiʿi and Sufi spirituality in general, it is not so much his presence in the *Tafsīr-i Ṣafī* that attracts our attention as the nuances of Ṣafī's representation. His commentary on Q. 24:36 (*[It is] in houses that God has permitted to be raised and wherein His Name is remembered. He is therein glorified, morning and evening*) provides an important example of these nuances. Here, Ṣafī mentions a narration related to the revelation of the verse: Someone asked which houses these might be. The Prophet replied that these are the houses of the prophets, but Abū Bakr asked the Prophet, 'Surely, one of these houses must be the house of ʿAlī and Fātima.' To which the Prophet replied, 'Yes, 'tis among the best of them.'[56]

The inclusion of this verse has a subtle function. As with Ṣafī's other uses of Sunni *tafsīr* one is tempted to think that the purpose may be polemical. Though not polemical as such in this case, Ṣafī is nonetheless indicating the extreme reverence in which ʿAlī was held by the Companions, which both shows this aspect of Shiʿi spirituality to be praiseworthy from an external point of view and reminds us of the importance of showing love for the Household of the Prophet in Sunni Islam. Indeed, this is precisely the point that Ṣafī wants to remind us of in his commentary on Q. 42:23: *I* [the

Prophet] *ask not of you any reward for it, save affection among kinsfolk*. As he states, in both Sunni and Shiʿi commentaries we find the interpretation that this verse refers precisely to ʿAlī, Fāṭima, Ḥasan and Ḥusayn.[57]

However, although Ṣafī repeatedly reminds us that this central aspect of Shiʿi spirituality is a heritage shared with Sunnis, he is nonetheless uncompromising on the central Shiʿi doctrines that develop from it. Though he does not express animosity towards the first three caliphs, the extent of his hatred of the Umayyad rulers is revealed in several short interludes in the *Tafsīr*; there, Ṣafī laments the sufferings that the Household of the Prophet, and especially the imam Zayn al-ʿĀbidīn (d. 94/712 or 95/713), went through after the tragedy of Karbala. In this sense Ṣafī is directly participating in Shiʿi traditions of piety.[58] The tone of lamentation in these sections is encapsulated in the interpretation of Q. 17:59–60, in which the author narrates the Prophet's vision that his minbar would one day be ascended by monkeys, which Gabriel interprets for him as signifying the Umayyad rule. The poem closes with the lines:

Were I to write in continuity the whole,
The heart's blood from my eyes would flow,
My writing book would be washed clear,
And thus I pass on, listen to my *tafsīr*.[59]

Ṣafī's Shiʿi sense of the rightful place of the imams is most evident, as one might expect, in his treatment of the *wilāya/walāya* of ʿAlī. As taught by the fifth imam, Muḥammad al-Bāqir (d. 114/733), Ṣafī explains that the acceptance of this *wilāya* is the criterion that distinguishes between faith (*īmān*) and immorality (*fisq*), the latter being considered synonymous with unbelief/lack of faith, given the interpenetration of religious and ethical terms in the Qur'an and hadith.[60] For Ṣafī, this is precisely what is meant by the hadith in which ʿAlī identifies himself with the scales of judgement (*mīzān*) on the Day of Resurrection.[61]

As one might expect, Ṣafī's clearest expression of *wilāya* as the criterion for distinguishing between faith and immorality comes in his reflection on the events of Ghadīr Khumm, which the Shiʿa consider to be the moment when the Prophet, by divine command, invested ʿAlī with spiritual and temporal authority over the community after him. While commenting on verse 3 of *Sūrat al-Māʾida* (Q. 5), which begins with the prohibition, *Forbidden unto you are carrion and blood* . . . and later affirms, *This day I have perfected for you your religion, and completed My Blessing upon you, and have approved for you as religion, Submission (Islām)*, Ṣafī writes:

> The religion of Islam is completed with ʿAlī,
> Without his *wilāya* religion has no validity . . .
> This *wilāya* is the root of religion, a blessing
> For creation, from God a sign of exaltation.[62]

However, although this is a fundamental point of dispute among Muslims, Ṣafī only alludes to the conflict by providing an esoteric justification of the reason why the mentioned Qur'anic statement comes in the context of the prohibition of eating carrion (namely, that to abide by God's laws is precisely to seek perfection of the soul, which is the goal of *wilāya*, and that *wilāya* breathes life into religion, which, without it, would be as carrion).[63] Instead of focusing on the conflict, Ṣafī prefers to emphasise the great jubilation that this 'festival of sanctity' (*ʿīd-i wilāyat*) brought for the believers, as it continues to do among the Shiʿa today.

However, the most significant aspect of Ṣafī's treatment of *wilāya* is his indication of its esoteric reality, for this is indeed the heart of the Shiʿi-Sufi tradition. These indications are rarely explicit, and they are often associated with the dimension of Ṣafī's mystical ecstasies that interrupt the *tafsīr*, as we shall see shortly. Suffice it to say that when Ṣafī does speak directly about the mystery of *wilāya*, he speaks of the direct manifestation of the Absolute, of pure *tawḥīd*, through this reality. It is for this reason that Ṣafī identifies Ghadīr Khumm with the Day of Alast:[64] the open declaration of *wilāya* among mankind is equivalent to mankind's intimate communion with God in pre-eternity and their declaration of His Lordship.[65]

The Phenomenology of Mystical Exegesis

Ṣafī's treatment of *wilāya*, although it contains important elements of both Shiʿi and Sufi mystical doctrine, is not solely theoretical.

Rather, he makes full use of the possibilities of the poetic form for both emotive and mystical expression, just as had been done by his forebears in the genre. While commenting on Q. 3:125: *Yea, if you, are patient and reverent, and they come at you immediately, your Lord will support you with five thousand angels bearing marks*, Ṣafī turns his attention to the real battle facing the spiritual wayfarer, and this is the point from which his flight leaps skyward:

The adversary soul, the battlefield day,
Shall flee head held low, wounded, overcome.
Save the Friend of the Real on the field of battle,
When there settles the dust, no one shall remain.
The intellect judges that on this battleground
There is no man, no blade, save ʿAlī and Dhu'l-Faqār.
Be praised the invoker, who, save God, has expelled
Whatever there was upon the earth of intuition.
Along with the Prophet, Ḥaydar-i Karrār remained.
Beauty remained, and love remained, and the friend remained.
Beauty and love are but one in meaning,
If you know but a little of the secret of Truth.[66]

The battlefield image with which this passage begins serves as an opportunity for Ṣafī to expound on 'spiritual warfare', the battle with the lower soul. Just as in the Battle of Badr, it was ʿAlī, wielding the Prophet's sword (Dhu'l-Faqār) at Muhammad's command, who put the outward enemies to flight; in this inward battle it is the *wilāya* of ʿAlī which is the cause of victory, as the disciple finds that his ego has fled and only this *wilāya* remains. Through poetic association, Ṣafī then declares that if only the Prophet and ʿAlī remain then all that is present is beauty and love. However, since beauty and love are ultimately identical, Ṣafī realises that all that is left is a single Reality; hence his ardour turns into a metaphysical realisation:

In reality, save one Real, nothing exists.
Save being and existence absolute, nothing exists.
I have become drunk! The way slips from my hand once more,
Put aside the book, my love charming has come.[67]

There intervenes a subtitle: 'Mystical Attraction' (*jadhba*) and the poet continues, speaking of this realisation of unity as the visitation of the Beloved.

> Her missive hath come giving the madman tidings,
> Her missive was this, let the heart be overthrown.
> Not a mote of distinction shall remain in its place,
> So that you might distinguish reality from metaphor.
> Each moment from myself I become more estranged,
> From the desire of her tresses more insane I become.
> So much is it so that drunken she comes,
> When musky tresses come to hand, so much is it more.
> She sayeth the word my heart knows to my ear.
> See intellect and awareness, have they gone or remained?
> The one who was speaking of Badr and Uḥud
> I know not; if you know, tell me what has occurred.[68]

Having declared his own loss of consciousness in the face of the Beloved, Ṣafī begins to dwell on the paradox of the situation, for though he declares his lack of self-awareness, the poetry is still continuing. The elaboration of this paradox revolves around the question 'Who is speaking?' However, no definite answer is given as yet:

> If thou knowest 'Ṣafī', pray tell me where he is,
> The atoms of his being are nothing and naught.
> If thou do know him but even the slightest,
> Say but one word from his silent rubies.
> I have said but one, and died from self twice,
> She sayeth again, bring my word on thy lips.
> Stealing me from heart hath not yet been fulfilled,
> Before my rubies, she sayeth each moment, O thou die!
> Say from thy lips such speeches in death,
> Be revived after all of this stealing of hearts.
> Thy death before my rubies in inspirations,
> Is, every time, life within life.
> I die not indeed, for my essence is eternal,
> That of me which has died lives on by my life.[69]

Yet this paradoxical state of selfless speaking comes to an abrupt end, for there is work to do:

> That which thou hast said, say it now from my lips
> It is morning, seal thy lips of the secrets of my night.
> Tell the secret of night: 'Be veiled once more!
> Hide again reality in the veil of metaphor.'
> Speak again of Aḥmad and the resolute Companions,
> Of 'Alī, of Dhū'l-Faqār and the day of the battle.[70]

Flights of mystical ecstasy such as this, almost always entitled *jadhba*, punctuate the *Tafsīr-i Ṣafī*, becoming a characteristic element of this work that complements the exoteric and esoteric commentary of particular verses. These mystical interludes reveal a great deal about Ṣafī's inner responses to the Qur'an and about his attitude towards the *tafsīr* he is writing.

Much like other fine examples of Persian mystical poetry written after the formative period,[71] the twenty-five or so 'mystical attractions' of the *Tafsīr-i Ṣafī* take up the insights and symbols of the genre and recombine them in an original way, breathing into the clay of tradition the spirit of the poet's own genius.

From a metaphysical point of view, the 'attractions' are founded on the distinction between the conventional level of reality in which everyday events take place and the level of ultimate reality. As is common in Persian Sufi poetry, these two levels are characterised using different symbolic polarities: outward vs. inward, sobriety vs. drunkenness, day vs. night, and especially 'differentiation' (*farq*) vs. '(re)collection' (*jam'*). Of particular importance for the way these sections express Ṣafī's understanding of his own exegetical act – or what we might call the 'self-referentiality' of the *Tafsīr* – is the fact that human individuality, and in this case the existence of anyone who could be named 'Ṣafī', only exists on the first of these two planes.

The general structure of the 'attractions' is as follows. To begin with, a particular theme comes up, either in the Qur'anic verses being commented upon or in the exegesis that moves Ṣafī spiritually and emotionally. Examples include the concepts of 'love' (*'ishq*),[72] 'beauty' (*ḥusn*),[73] 'unity of the Essence' (*tawḥīd-i dhātī*),[74] the 'Night of Power' (*laylat al-qadr*),[75] or as we have seen, the *wilāya* of 'Alī.[76] These sections, therefore, represent a direct or indirect mystical response to the Qur'anic text. Ṣafī then announces that he has been taken from himself, that the tresses of the Beloved, which represent veiling in Sufi poetry – here, the veiling of ordinary consciousness and individuality – are pulling him uncontrollably. Ṣafī continues to speak despite the mystical ecstasy, engaging in a mystical discourse that could last anywhere from a few lines to a few pages, revealing secrets about the effects of divine love and unity. He is then called back to ordinary consciousness in order to complete the *Tafsīr*, the night of drunkenness and mystery having come to an end.[77]

Among the secrets that come to light during the 'attractions', several points directly concern us here. It becomes clear that it is not only the exegesis of the words of the Qur'an that belong to the level of multiplicity but even the words themselves in their particularity. The Reality that lies behind them is utterly One, and that which is of truest value is the Love that liberates us from multiplicity and returns us to this unity. Nevertheless, it is the external aspect of the Qur'an itself that is the inspiration of the 'attractions', it is the Qur'anic word that prompts the transformation of consciousness that is described in these passages. There is thus a tension in the text between the utmost reverence for the outward – for the sacred form which is a manifestation of the Essence – and the inward transcendence of this form. We see this tension in play when Ṣafī comments on Q. 6:160: *Whosoever brings a good deed shall have ten times the like thereof*. Ṣafī almost complains to the verse that the lover of God is not satisfied with ten rewards, for he wants the Beloved Himself, and even if he were to consider the divine gifts, these are innumerable, falling like drops of rain even upon the sinner.[78] Nonetheless, this verse prompts a state of mystical attraction.

The very act of writing about the transcendence of the individual plane involves a paradox, and Ṣafī plays on this point time and again during the 'attractions'. In the end it is impossible to say who is speaking, and it is precisely this point that creates the opportunity for Ṣafī to explain how it was that he was able to compose an entire Qur'anic commentary in verse in the space of two years. He approaches this theme from multiple angles: posing the question to the reader that if he is not speaking then whose speech is it;[79] hearing the Beloved whisper to him to repeat His words;[80] and declaring that an unseen voice warns that Ṣafī should be given less to drink so that he can return to ordinary consciousness. However, the result of all of these interludes is the same, that Ṣafī must return from the plane of unity, of night and of drunkenness to the world of multiplicity in order to complete his *Tafsīr*.[81]

Ṣafī's claim, therefore, is that his *Tafsīr* is inspired, that it is a gift from God to one who, like an ant facing a mountain, had not the slightest capability of his own to accomplish it. He compares the inimitability of his *tafsīr* to the inimitability of the Qur'an itself, which calls upon sceptics to produce a sura like it to defend their claim. Ṣafī's commentary on his own exegetical practice is that it is by virtue of his journey beyond the world of multiplicity, and indeed beyond his own individuality, that he was given the ability to produce a genuine *tafsīr* of the Qur'an.[82] As Ṣafī explains, it is through realising the secret of *wilāya* – which he finally reveals to be the voice he has heard accompanying him on his journey and drawing him back to the world below – the very same secret of *wilāya* that the Prophet discovered on his nocturnal ascent and which led him back to the world in order to guide humanity, that allows him to reveal the divine intention behind the speech of God.

> Who is this speaker? Our *pīr* and king,
> Who has been with us every step of the way.
> Wherever I have laid step, near and far,
> There was present the unique *pīr*.
> Likewise, when sweet-breathed Aḥmad came,
> Towards multiplicity from the unity of 'or nearer' (*'aw 'adnā*)[83]
> He saw the king of the spirit present in the heart.
> In the station of multiplicity unity was attained,
> This is unity in multiplicity, O *faqīr*,
> This is the characteristic of the hand-grasping saint.
> Were Mustafa not to have had this state,
> Living in the abode of body would have been impossible for him.

This is 'We have removed thy burden'
If you know anything of the station of the arrived.[84]

NOTES

1 For biographical and bibliographical information on Ṣafī ʿAlī Shāh, see Bihrūz Thirwatiyān, *Ṣafī ʿAlī Shāh wa tafsīr-ash* (Tehran, 1389 Sh./2010), pp. 1–52; Masʿūd Humayūnī, *Tārīkh-i silsila-yi ṭarīqa-yi Niʿmatullāhī* (Tehran, 1355 Sh./1976), pp. 162–78; Matthijs Van Den Bos, *Mystic Regimes: Sufism and the State in Iran, from the Late Qajar Era to the Islamic Republic* (Leiden, 2002), pp. 91–3; Nile Green, *Bombay Islam: The Religious Economy of the West Indian Ocean, 1840–1915* (Cambridge, 2011), pp. 137–50; Leonard Lewisohn, 'An Introduction to the History of Modern Persian Sufism, Part I: The Niʿmatullāhī Order: Persecution, Revival and Schism', *Bulletin of the School of Oriental and African Studies* 61, no. 3 (1998), pp. 453–6; Nile Green, 'A Persian Sufi in British India: The Travels of Mīrzā Ḥasan Ṣafī 'Alī Shāh (1251/1835–1316/1899)', *Iran* 42 (2004), pp. 201–18; and idem, intro. and tr., 'A Persian Sufi in the Age of Printing: Mirza Hasan Safi 'Ali Shah (1835–99)', in Lloyd Ridgeon, ed., *Religion and Politics in Modern Iran: A Reader* (London, 2005), pp. 99–112.

2 Notable editions of the *Tafsīr-i Ṣafī* include two lithographs (Tehran, 1308/1890 and Tehran, 1318 Sh./1939) and more recent editions by Ḥāmid Nājī Iṣfahānī (Isfahan, 1383 Sh./2004) and Bihrūz Thirwatiyān (Tehran, 1393 Sh./2014). However, the task of reading and interpreting the *Tafsīr-i Ṣafī* has now been made significantly easier by the publication of ʿAlī Riḍā Munajjimī's *Sharḥ-i jāmiʿ-i tafsīr-i ʿirfānī wa manẓūm-i Qur'ān-i Ṣafī* (Tehran, 1385 Sh./2006–7) [Abbreviated henceforth as *TS*]. Although not a critical edition, Munajjimī claims to have attempted to 'correct the mistakes in previous editions and manuscripts'. For this paper I use and provide references from this edition, while also giving the relevant Qur'anic verse number so that each passage can be located in any edition.

3 The importance of Ṣafī ʿAlī Shāh from a literary perspective alone is a matter of some disagreement amongst contemporary Iranian scholars. As Leonard Lewisohn ('An Introduction to the History of Modern Persian Sufism, Part I', pp. 453–4) has pointed out, although some literary historians have excluded him from the ranks of poets due to his *ṭarīqa* (Sufi order) affiliations, others have considered him to be 'the last great Sufi poet of Iran'; see, for example, ʿAṭā Karīm Barq, *Justujū dar aḥwāl wa āthār-i Ṣafī ʿAlī Shāh* (Tehran, 1352 Sh./1973), p. 3. A great deal of his fame is due to his *Zubdat al-asrār* [The Quintessence of Mysteries], which is a 6,000-line *mathnawī* consisting of a mystical exposition and interpretation of the events at Karbala and the afflictions of the prophetic household that followed them; see Ḥasan Iṣfahānī Ṣafī ʿAlī Shāh, *Zubdat al-asrār* (Tehran, 1341 Sh./1963). The *Tafsīr* is given a very short section in Alan Godlas' as yet unpublished article on 'Sufi Tafsīr' for *Encyclopaedia Iranica*, accessible online at http://islam.uga.edu/suftaf/tafsuftoc.html.

4 The first perspective in particular is discussed by Lewisohn in 'An Introduction to the History of Modern Persian Sufism, Part I', pp. 453–4.

5 Quoted in Thirwatiyān, *Ṣafī ʿAlī Shāh wa Tafsīr-ash*, p. 3.

6 'Ṣafī' is Ṣafī 'Alī Shāh's *takhallus* (nom de plume).
7 Ibid., p. 5.
8 Green, *Bombay Islam*, pp. 139–40.
9 See Lewisohn, 'An Introduction to the History of Modern Persian Sufism, Part I', p. 453.
10 Nile Green also mentions that this journey may have been made out of the necessity to quell some kind of rebellion among the Indian disciples. See Green, *Bombay Islam*, p. 140.
11 See Thirwatiyān, *Ṣafī 'Alī Shāh wa Tafsīr-ash*, p. 6; a slightly different account of this period is given in Green, *Bombay Islam*, p. 149.
12 Thirwatiyān, *Ṣafī 'Alī Shāh wa Tafsīr-ash*, pp. 6–7.
13 See Lewisohn, 'An Introduction to the History of Modern Persian Sufism, Part I', p. 453.
14 Green, *Bombay Islam*, pp. 138–9.
15 See ibid., pp. 142–3; Green, 'A Persian Sufi in British India', pp. 201–18.
16 Thirwatiyān, *Ṣafī 'Alī Shāh wa Tafsīr-ash*, p. 7; Green, 'A Persian Sufi in British India', p. 202.
17 See Lewisohn, 'An Introduction to the History of Modern Persian Sufism, Part I', p. 455.
18 See Green, 'A Persian Sufi in British India', pp. 210–14.
19 Ibid., p. 210.
20 Ibid., p. 214.
21 Quoted in Thirwatiyān, *Ṣafī 'Alī Shāh wa Tafsīr-ash*, p. 4.
22 See Travis Zadeh, *The Vernacular Qur'an: Translation and the Rise of Persian Exegesis* (Oxford, 2012).
23 See Annabel Keeler, *Sufi Hermeneutics: The Qur'an Commentary of Rashīd al-Dīn Maybudī* (Oxford, 2006); William C. Chittick, *Divine Love: Islamic Literature and the Path to God* (New Haven, CT, 2013), pp. xvi–xviii.
24 See, for example, Jane Dammen McAuliffe, *Qur'ānic Christians: An Analysis of Classical and Modern Exegesis* (Cambridge, 2007), pp. 76–8.
25 Umīd Majd, *Qur'ān-i Majīd yā Tarjuma-yi Manẓūm* (*Qur'ān-nāma*) (Tehran, 1376 Sh./[1997]).
26 The *Tafsīr-i manẓūm* attributed to Muḥammad 'Alī Iṣfahānī Nūr 'Alī Shāh is published on the website http://www.tasavof.ir/books/download/farsi/nouralishah-aval/tafsire-manzoom.pdf. More recently, Jawād Nūrbakhsh has published a collection of selected verse translations and commentaries of the Qur'an in Jawād Nūrbakhsh, *Tafsīr-i Manẓūm-i Ṣūra-hā-yi al-Ḥujurāt wa Qāf wa al-Ḥashr. Ba Inḍimām-i Sharḥ-i Manẓūm-i Khuṭba-hā-yi Mū'minīn wa Muttaqīn-i Ḥaḍrat-i 'Alī 'alayhi al-salām* (Tehran, 1994). Verse translations and commentaries of the Qur'an in other languages include: Muḥammad Ismā'īl Miyān, *Tafsīr-i Qur'ān Jān-i ilām nūr-i īmān manẓūm ba-zubān-e panjābī* (Gujarat, 1955) [Punjabi]; Ḥakīm Naẓīr Aḥmad Naẓīr, *Ṣūrah-i Kahf da Panjābī vich Tarjamah te Ohdi Manẓūm Tafsīr Aṣḥāb-i Kahf* (Sharqpur, 1992) [Punjabi]; Muḥammad Samī'ullāh Asad, *Qur'ān-i manẓūm ma' farhang wa tafsīr* (Calcutta, 2004) [Urdu]; Mīrzā Ghulām Ḥasan Beg 'Ārif and 'Abd al-Raḥmān Wār, *'Irfān-i Qur'ān: Tarjumah, Tafsīr o Manẓūm-i Jaqhar Rukū' ba-Zabān-i Kashmīrī* (Srīnagar, 2004) [Kashmiri]; and Ghaws Muhammad Gawhar, *Manẓūm Sindhī Tafsīr* (Kotli Kabir, 2005) [Sindhi]. On this topic, see

Abū'l-Qāsim Rādfar, 'Tarjuma-hā-yi Qur'ān-i Majīd bi Zabān-i Urdū', *Faṣl-nāma-yi Fadak* 1, no. 1 (1389 Sh./[2010], pp. 87–100.

27 See Lewisohn, 'An Introduction to the History of Modern Persian Sufism, Part I', p. 454.

28 Around 32,000 verses for the *Tafsīr-i Ṣafī* and around 26,000 verses for the *Mathnawī*.

29 All translations of the Qur'an are from *The Study Quran: A New Translation and Commentary*, ed. and tr. Seyyed Hossein Nasr et al. (New York, 2015).

30 The use of rhyme amidst phrases of differing metric value (hence, 'rhymed prose', *saj*ʿ) is of particular importance for the language of the Qur'an and may have been the origin of Arabic poetry. See T. Fahd, W.P. Heinrichs and A. Ben Abdesselem, 'Sad̲j̲ʿ', *EI*², vol. VIII, pp. 732–8.

31 That is to say, certain Qur'anic words fit the *fāʿilātun* (long-short-long-long) foot of the *ramal musaddas maḥdhūf* metre (long-short-long-long/long-short-long-long/long-short-long) used in the *Tafsīr-i Ṣafī* (and in Rūmī's *Mathnawī*), creating the possibility of direct quotation of the Qur'an in poetry or rhythmic simulation of certain Qur'anic passages.

32 As Jawid Mojaddedi points out, 'while 'Aṭṭār's *Asrārnāma* contains a citation from the Qur'ān approximately every 250 couplets and Abū'l-Majd Majdūd b. Ādam Sanā'ī's *Ḥadīqat al-ḥaqīqa* every 150 couplets, Rūmī's *Mathnawī* contains a Qur'ānic citation on average every 30 couplets'. Jawid Mojaddedi, 'Rūmī', in Andrew Rippin, ed., *The Blackwell Companion to the Qur'ān* (Malden, 2006), p. 367.

33 Seyyed Hossein Nasr sums up this relationship between the Qur'an and Persian poetry as follows: 'The rhyme and rhythm of Persian poetry reflects a "spiritual style" that relates it to the form of the Quran as the message of this poetry is related to the content of the Quranic revelation.' Seyyed Hossein Nasr, *Islamic Art and Spirituality* (Albany, NY, 1990), pp. 76–7.

34 Ṣafī compiled a work of Sufi terminology, *Baḥr al-ḥaqā'iq*, with which there is significant overlap in the terminological discussions of the *Tafsīr*. See Ṣafī ʿAlī Shāh, *Baḥr al-ḥaqā'iq; bi-inḍimām-i Mīzān al-maʿrifa* (Tehran, 1363 Sh./[1985]).

35 See, for example, Ṣafī's reference to Fakhr al-Dīn al-Rāzī (d. 606/1209) at *TS*, 5.2116 (Q. 13:7) and Abū Isḥāq al-Thaʿlabī (d. 427/1035) at *TS*, 7.3038 (Q. 27:20). The hallmark of Ṣafī's consideration of different interpretations is that the verses invariably begin with the words 'or that . . .' ('*yā ki* . . .').

36 I have not, however, been able to find any instances in which Ṣafī mentions one of these Sufi commentators by name.

37 See William C. Chittick, *Imaginal Worlds: Ibn al-ʿArabī and the Problem of Religious Diversity* (Albany, NY, 1994), pp. 15–30. However, Chittick points out that 'Ibn al-ʿArabī's name is associated with the expression *waḥdat al-wujūd*, the "oneness of being" or the "unity of existence" . . . [but that] to connect this expression to him is historically inaccurate, and doing so has led to gross over-simplifications and extreme misunderstandings of his writings'; see William Chittick, 'Time, Space, and the Objectivity of Ethical Norms: The Teachings of Ibn al-ʿArabī', *Islamic Studies* 39, no. 4 (2000), p. 581. *Waḥdat al-wujūd* is, however, of great importance in discussing the reception of his writings, both positive and negative, and was used both negatively (for example, by Taqī

al-Dīn Ibn Taymiyya [d. 728/1328]) and positively (for example, by ʿAbd al-Raḥmān Jāmī [d. 898/1492]); see William Chittick, 'Ibn Arabi', *The Stanford Encyclopedia of Philosophy* (Summer 2018 Edition), ed. Edward N. Zalta, https://plato.stanford.edu/archives/sum2018/entries/ibn-arabi/.

38 Ṣafī's preoccupation with the metaphysics of Being and, as we shall see, with sanctity (*wilāya/walāya*), is in harmony with the intellectual discourses of late nineteenth-century Iran, in which these were the most important issues in philosophical and mystical circles; see Sajjad Rizvi, 'Being (*wujūd*) and Sanctity (*wilāya*): Two Poles of Intellectual and Mystical Enquiry in Qajar Iran', in Robert Gleave, ed., *Religion and Society in Qajar Iran* (Abingdon, 2005), pp. 113–26.

39 Cf. Q. 41:53: *We shall show them Our signs upon the horizons and within themselves till it becomes clear to them that it is the truth. Does it not suffice that thy Lord is Witness over all things?*

40 On Shāh Niʿmatullāh Walī and his relationship to the thought of both Rūmī and Ibn ʿArabī, see Hamid Algar and J. Burton-Page, 'Niʿmat-Allāhiyya', *EI*[2], vol. VIII, pp. 44–8.

41 See Michel Chodkiewicz, *An Ocean without Shore: Ibn Arabī, the Book, and the Law* (Albany, NY, 1993). It is worth noting that the *Tafsīr-i Ṣafī* contains many passages that are poetic narrations of points made in the *Tafsīr Ibn al-ʿArabī*, most probably written by ʿAbd al-Razzāq Kāshānī (d. 736/1336). Compare, for example, their comments on *muḥkam* (clear) and *mutashābih* (ambiguous) verses referred to in Q. 3:7.

42 See, for example, *TS*, 3.1388.

43 On the importance of the printing press for the spread of this practice see Green, *Bombay Islam*, p. 149. Cf. a discussion of this practice in the Naqshbandī *ṭarīqa*, which otherwise is significantly different from the Niʿmatullāhiyya, and the controversy surrounding it in nineteenth- and twentieth-century India in Arthur F. Buehler, *Sufi Heirs of the Prophet: The Indian Naqshbandiyya and the Rise of the Mediating Sufi Shaykh* (Columbia, SC, 1998), pp. 134–8.

44 See Mahdī Kumpānī-zāriʿ, *Gunābādī wa tafsīr-i Bayān al-saʿāda* (Tehran, 1390 Sh./[2011]). See also Alessandro Cancian, 'Translation, Authority and Exegesis in Modern Iranian Sufism: Two Iranian Sufi Masters in Dialogue', *Journal of Persianate Studies* 7, no. 1 (2014), pp. 88–106; idem, *Sufism, Shiʿism and Qur'anic Exegesis in Early Modern Iran: Sulṭān ʿAlī Shāh Gunābādī and his Tafsīr Bayān al-Saʿāda* (forthcoming).

45 Namely, Q. 13:7: . . . *for every people is a guide* (*TS*, 5.2116) and Q. 27:20–40: *He said, 'O notables! Which of you will bring me her throne before they come unto me in submission?'* (*TS*, 7.3038) in which the agency of the transportation of the throne is attributed to ʿAlī.

46 In the order mentioned in the previous note.

47 For a readable contemporary example of this, see Muḥammad Sulṭān al-Wāʿiẓīn Shīrāzī, *Peshawar Nights: Convincing Shia-Sunni Dialogue* (Karachi, 1977). Thaʿlabī's references to the *ahl al-bayt* are still significant in contemporary intra-Islamic polemics, even affecting the way his works are edited. See in particular Walid A. Saleh, *The Formation of the Classical* Tafsīr *Tradition: The Qur'ān Commentary of al-Thaʿlabī (d. 427/1035)* (Boston, 2004), Appendix.

48 For example, in commenting upon Q. 13:7, . . . *for every people there is a guide*, Ṣafī begins by pointing out the agreement between the 'two sects' (*du firqa*) on the meaning of this Qur'anic phrase, which for those who are inclined towards 'outward' (*ẓāhir*) matters means that 'Alī is a worldly leader, and for those who are inclined towards 'inward' (*bāṭin*) matters means that he is a spiritual guide. See *TS*, 5.2116.

49 See, for example, Ṣafī's *tarjīʿ-band* (stanzaed poem) with the refrain 'For in truth, in the kingdom of being there is no king save 'Alī who is the friend of God'; Manṣūr Mushfiq, ed., *Dīwān-i Ṣafī 'Alī Shāh* (Tehran, 1379 Sh./[2000]), pp. 79–86.

50 *TS*, 5.2380.

51 Interesting examples include his reference to "Umar the Great' (*muʿaẓẓam*) making it unlawful for the inhabitants of Mecca to deny pilgrims access to their homes during the *ḥajj*, and his reference to 'Ā'isha as a 'shining sun' (*shams-i munīr*) in verses said to be revealed absolving her of what was calumniously attributed to her; see ibid., 6.2779 (Q. 22:25) and ibid., 6.2876 (Q. 24:26), respectively.

52 It is noteworthy that an important part of Ṣafī's life was spent in Bombay, which was home to a greater diversity of Muslims than Shiʿi Iran. However, the *Tafsīr* was written in Ṣafī's *khānaqā* in Tehran and not in Bombay, as his earlier *Zubdat al-asrār* was, so it would be more profitable to look for the influence of that diverse Islamic milieu in that earlier work and its treatment of the events of Karbala.

53 *TS*, 7.3302 (Q. 33:33). Shiʿis traditionally use these terms in this manner to distinguish between themselves and the more numerous Sunnis. However, in the Shiʿi-Sufi context the terms have an additional association since Sufis use them to distinguish themselves from those Muslims who confine their practice to the outward aspect of religion alone.

54 *TS*, 2.1049.

55 See, for example, *TS*, 2.726 (Q. 3:151) on being resolute (*'azm*) and *TS*, 2.905 (Q. 4:125) on generosity (*sikhāwat*).

56 *TS*, 6.2892–3. Commenting on these lines, Munajjimī states that this hadith is found in one of the most important Sunni commentaries, namely the *al-Durr al-Manthūr* of Jalāl al-Dīn Suyūṭī (d. 911/1505), for which he gives the chain of transmission (*isnād*). See *TS*, 6.2902.

57 *TS*, 8.3723–4.

58 See ibid., 5.2398.

59 Ibid., 6.2398.

60 On this latter topic, see Toshihiko Izutsu, *Ethico-Religious Concepts in the Qur'ān* (Montreal, 1966), pp. 156–77. Ṣafī presents a beautiful exposition on the stages of the spiritual path leading to *fanā'* (annihilation) and *baqā'* (subsistence), all of which must be traversed for a person's faith to be complete, in his commentary on Q. 9:112 (*The penitent, and the worshippers, and the celebrants of praise, and the wayfarers, and those who bow, and those who prostrate, and those who enjoin right, and those who forbid wrong, and those who maintain the limits set by God; and give glad tidings unto the believers*). Combined with the Shiʿi perspective on faith above, this elucidation of the relation between complete faith and *wilāya* is another area in

which Ṣafī's synthesis of Sufism and Shiʿism can be witnessed. See *TS*, 4.1704–5.

61 Ibid., 8.3719 (Q. 42:17).

62 Ibid., 2.982.

63 Ibid.

64 Q. 7:172 states, *And when thy Lord took from the Children of Adam, from their loins, their progeny and made them bear witness concerning themselves, 'Am I not* [*Alastu*] *your Lord?' they said, 'Yea, we bear witness' – lest you should say on the Day of Resurrection, 'Truly of this we were heedless'.* The covenant of Alast therefore represents the human relationship with God in pre-eternity, and the 'Day of Alast' is the moment in which this occurred. The fact that this moment is depicted in Sufi literature using imagery of music or intoxication indicates how particular Sufis have understood this pre-eternal moment. See Ashgar Seyed-Gohrab, 'Magic in Classical Persian Amatory Literature', *Iranian Studies* 32, no. 1 (1999), p. 95; Arthur John Arberry, 'Three Persian Poems', *Iran* 2 (1964), pp. 1–12; Gerhard Böwering, 'Ideas of Time in Persian Sufism', *Iran* 30 (1992), p. 82.

65 See *TS*, 2.1076–7 (Q. 5:67).

66 Ibid., 2.707.

67 Ibid.

68 Ibid.

69 Ibid., 2.707–8.

70 Ibid., 2.708.

71 For the *mathnawī* genre, I consider this formative period to extend from the composition of Ṣanāʿī's *Ḥadīqat al-ḥaqīqa* around 524/1130 to the completion of Rūmī's *Mathnawī* around 666/1268.

72 *TS*, 1.99 and 1.231.

73 Ibid., 4.1911 (Q. 12:6).

74 Ibid., 1.160.

75 Ibid., 10.4779 (Q. 97:4).

76 Ibid., 2.707 (Q. 3:125).

77 The formula is not always so straightforward, however. In more than one case, Ṣafī describes going beyond the duality of *farq* and *jamʿ*, returning to the world of daylight and sobriety whilst still utterly intoxicated. This is the state of the servant who has been given the responsibility to guide others on the path. See ibid., 6.2802 (Q. 22:58) and 9.4175 (Q. 58:12).

78 Ibid., 3.1298.

79 'Is this me, or have I come out from myself? / Having cast aside how and how many, I am in the how-less, / That Safi who just now was here, where is he? / He was speaking to us, where has he gone? / And the one who now speaks in his clothes, / The one who keeps his stature upright now, who is it?' (Ibid., 4.1934 [Q. 12:14]).

80 'I say that which he speaks to mine ear, / Of that which He speaks to my heart, I am silent.' (Ibid., 1.546 [Q. 2:253]); 'Neither tongue is at will, nor spirit in body, / Am I His confidant or is He me? / 'Tis not I who sayeth this, I have become "not", / I have sealed my lips and become an ocean's wave. / Now he pulls me to Himself, deep in the ocean, / Now he brings me forth, saying "Speak my secrets". / That is, He speaketh Himself from mine own lips, / What

are the lips? The lips of my [pronouncing] "... except" [God]. / I remain not. In me who is this speaker? / The ocean speaks, this is not "Ṣafī".' (Ibid., 6.2802 [Q. 22:58]).

81 'In this state the cry comes to my ear, / Awaken this drunken madman! / Return to him his state, / For his *tafsīr* is yet to be finished.' (Ibid., 10.4743 [Q. 94:3]). The theme of the journey towards God or towards unity, followed by a return to the world and multiplicity, is found in Sufism from its beginnings, particularly as a result of the influence of the image of the Prophet's celestial ascent. For early sources on this topic see Michael Sells, tr., ed. and intro., *Early Islamic Mysticism: Sufi, Qur'an, Mi'raj, Poetic and Theological Writings* (Mawhah, NJ, 1996), pp. 47–55, 242–50.

82 'I was illiterate, but from His own store / He expanded my breast beyond limitation. / So that the world might be filled with my gnosis, / That each learned man would be literate in my alphabet . . . / Delve now into this deep ocean, / I mean this *tafsīr*, if you are precise, / That thou might find the gift of the Real in totality, / To Safi, from this speech and explanation . . . / Were the whole of humanity to be gathered in resolution, / That they might bring a page of it into verse. / The intellect has no way of conceiving / That this might actually come into effect. / I have said this in thanks for the gift of the Bountiful, / Otherwise, what can one worthless bring into speech.' (*TS*, 3.1529–30 [Q. 7:206]); 'If thou have but a measure of knowledge, / There is nothing in the world so wondrous as the Qur'an. / After that wonder, wondrous is my *tafsīr*, / For from the Qur'an its composition hath come. / If thou seeth not that the Qur'an is miraculous, / It is meet that thou ponder a while this *tafsīr*. / Within this *tafsīr* see the Qur'an's miracle, / See this from God's grace and the aid of the *pīr*.' (Ibid., 5.2487–8 [Q. 18:24]).

83 This verse is referring to the Qur'anic term for the Prophet's proximity to God at the summit of the celestial ascent (*mi'rāj*): *within two bows' length or nearer* (Q. 53:9).

84 *TS*, 10.4743 (Q. 94:3).

10

Exegesis and the Place of Sufism in Nineteenth-Century Twelver Shiʿism: Sulṭān ʿAlī Shāh Gunābādī and his *Bayān al-saʿāda*

ALESSANDRO CANCIAN

THE PERIOD running from roughly the collapse of Safavid rule to the end of the Qajar dynasty and subsequent establishment of the Pahlavi monarchy (i.e. between 1722 and 1925), which is usually defined as 'early modern', was for Persia a time of momentous political and social turbulence. During this time, the country was plagued by invasions, internecine and dynastic wars, revolutions and revolts. Indeed, it was quite a dense and fertile ground for the historian interested in the political and social history of Iran, but it was also a time often and wrongly considered stagnant at the intellectual and religious levels. Recent scholarship has reversed this opinion,[1] and has started to show how thriving the intellectual environment was under the surface of political turmoil and undeniable material poverty.[2] It was during this time that the imposing spiritual synthesis of Sufism, philosophy and Shiʿism laid down under the Safavids by the School of Isfahan came to full maturation and shaped the emergent tradition of mysticism (*ʿirfān*).[3] *ʿIrfān* in turn defined, in many ways, other spiritual and intellectual traditions, thereby serving as the foundation for a significant fraction of the intellectual history of Qajar Iran. The theological–mystical tradition of the Shaykhīs, as well as its more rebellious offspring, the Bābī and Bahai movements, came into being at this time. Parallel to this landscape, the Uṣūlī camp of Twelver Shiʿism succeeded in establishing its own hegemony, though without preventing the defeated camp, the traditionist

Akhbārī school, from sowing the seeds of its intellectual legacy in large swaths of coeval Twelver Shiʿi theology and mysticism. However, while Uṣūlī Shiʿism was becoming synonymous with Twelver Shiʿism through the fine-tuning of the doctrine of the *marjaʿiyya* (the authority of the most learned of the jurists), Niʿmatullāhī Sufism had already made its return from India, where it had migrated in the tenth/fifteenth and eleventh/sixteenth centuries, and was undergoing an adaptive metamorphosis. It was turning from a charismatic and loosely Shiʿi order (*ṭariqa*) into a fully fledged Twelver Shiʿi mystical order: during the journey back, it began incorporating the philosophical tradition flourishing at the time as a result of the activities of the heavyweights of philosophy, such as Mullā Hādī Sabzawārī (d. 1873). While the intellectual landscape was thriving, however, the writing of Qur'anic commentaries was not enjoying the same vitality and health. The *tafsīr* tradition, with few remarkable exceptions, was in sharp decline, and had become repetitious and scholastic. It is here, at the intersection between a thriving intellectual and spiritual tradition and a stagnant exegetical one, that we can highlight the flourishing of a work that, among others, contributed to the revival of *tafsīr* writing in Iran. In the late nineteenth century, the master and leader of one branch of the Niʿmatullāhī order, Sulṭān ʿAlī Shāh Gunābādī (d. 1909), wrote a Qur'anic commentary that condensed into four large volumes the spirituality, theology and mysticism of the Sufi order that was named after him, the Gunābādiyya, which remains to date one of the most influential (if not *the* most influential) Sufi orders in the Persian-speaking world. The *tafsīr* was impactful when it was written and published, as well as in the following decades, but it was controversial due to its Sufi content and its not-entirely acceptable origin (Sufism was much frowned upon by many within the Twelver Shiʿi hierarchies, who looked upon it as a dangerous competitor to their authority), thus references to it were often only hinted at or omitted altogether.

It is only recently that Sulṭān ʿAlī Shāh's commentary, the *Bayān al-saʿāda fī maqāmāt al-ʿibāda*,[4] has started to be given the attention it deserves. The stigma of being a work written by a Sufi master of the most influential mystical order in Iran and Twelver Shiʿi scholar of unquestionable pedigree resulted in the ostracism of the work from the annals of Shiʿi *tafsīr* writing up until recent times. Until the late twentieth century, outside of Niʿmatullāhī circles, there was only scattered oral evidence of the diffusion of the *tafsīr*: the closed world of religious seminaries (sing. *ḥawza ʿilmiyya*) did not allow students and scholars to freely and openly associate themselves and their studies with Sufism in general, and with such a contested and controversial personality in particular. Although today we are not witnessing a full rehabilitation because a certain degree of discreetness remains, the mention of the commentary and of its author is no longer the unbreakable taboo that it used to be. What we can say is that, besides the extraordinary and obvious impact it had on Niʿmatullāhī Sufism, the *Bayān* is today a *tafsīr* very well known to anyone dealing with the exegesis of twentieth-century Iran, but its fame is far from being universal and widespread outside of specialist circles, unlike the *Mīzān*,[5] the *Namūna*,[6] or the *Tafsīr-i tasnīm*, the ongoing commentary by ʿAbd Allāh Jawādī Āmulī (b. 1933), for example.[7] Anecdotal evidence tells us of the delicateness of the matter.

In the following pages, I will place the *Bayān al-saʿāda* within the wider context of both the history of early modern Shiʿi Sufism and the history of exegesis in Shiʿism. I will highlight its importance in the positioning of Niʿmatullāhī Sufism within mainstream Uṣūlī Shiʿism and will also discuss its often neglected importance in the history of exegesis in Iran in the twentieth century.

Niʿmatullāhī Sufism and Twelver Shiʿism

The Gunābādiyya initiatic line (*silsila*), which originated with Sulṭān ʿAlī Shāh, is an offshoot of the Niʿmatullāhī order which dates back to the time of the celebrated poet and Sufi master Shāh Niʿmatullāh Walī (d. 834/1431), disciple of Shaykh ʿAbd Allāh Yāfiʿī (d. 769/1366–7) who was within the Qādirī lineage of initiation.[8] Shāh Niʿmatullāh Walī, originally from Aleppo, became active as a poet and Sufi master after settling in the area of Kirmān in Persia. His charisma resulted in a large following that became an independent mystical order known as the Niʿmatullāhiyya.[9] The masters of the order that came after Shāh Niʿmatullāh relocated to India when the Bahmanid ruler of the Deccan, Aḥmad Shāh Bahmānī (d. 839/1436), invited them to move to the subcontinent to provide spiritual patronage to his kingdom.[10] Even though Shāh Niʿmatullāh did not migrate there, his son and successor as the head of the order, Shāh Khalīlullāh (d. 859/1455), moved to Bidar in 835/1431, which was then the Bahmanid capital of the Deccan, thereby relocating the order to India. With the head and heart of the order permanently settled away from the motherland, Shāh Niʿmatullāh's heirs in Iran lost their edge, and the order there gradually declined into a 'moribund dynastic family tradition',[11] slowly receding from the history of Persian Sufism until its disappearance in the eleventh/seventeenth century. During this time, the order, now resident in the Deccan, entered into a close relationship with the Bahmanids, under whose rule it completed its Twelver Shiʿi turn.[12] From Hyderabad, the Niʿmatullāhī order headed back to Iran, where it spearheaded the renaissance of Sufism in the eighteenth and nineteenth centuries. As Leonard Lewisohn pointed out,[13] the history of modern Sufism in Iran began with the mission of Maʿṣūm ʿAlī Shāh (d. 1796) to Persia, which was inspired by Riḍā ʿAlī Shāh Dakkanī (d. 1799). The powerful, charismatic authority of the subsequent master, Nūr ʿAlī Shāh (d. 1797), then contributed to the reinforcement of the Niʿmatullāhī presence in its homeland.[14] Despite fierce opposition from the radical and already highly politicised exoteric clerics, Nūr ʿAlī Shāh was successful in gaining a large following, almost as if Sufism (*taṣawwuf*) was just smouldering under the ashes awaiting only a spark to set it ablaze anew. This renaissance, persisting despite clerical persecution[15] and the order's wavering relationship with the Zand and Qajar rulers and local governors,[16] bred more than a generation of charismatic masters whose influence shaped the subsequent spiritual character of the *ṭarīqa*.

The Niʿmatullāhī order went through internal vicissitudes and two subsequent schisms occurred, the Gunābādiyya being only one, albeit probably the most prominent, of the branches resulting from the split.[17] However, what is of interest here is how the formal adoption of Twelver Shiʿi doctrinal orthodoxy was reflected in the works and doctrines of the masters of this, which found itself operating simultaneously within the Uṣūlī Twelver Shiʿi hierarchy and in the tradition of classical Persian Sufism.

Works by the Niʿmatullāhī order's dignitaries have proceeded along an irregular path in terms of their formal adherence to the models of Twelver Shiʿi literature. In some cases, it is only the fact that the authors' religious affiliation is known that allows us to ascribe their work to that genre of literature. Such is the case with Nūr ʿAlī Shāh's major work, *Jannāt al-wiṣāl*,[18] where no reference is made to any core Shiʿi doctrine or tenet (of course we are talking about Uṣūlī doctrines having currency at the time, not general Imāmī tendencies).[19] The whole spiritual, semantic and doctrinal universe Nūr ʿAlī Shāh seems to be referring to is that of classical Sufism, and no Shiʿi colouring is noticeable, although references to a seminal nucleus of what would later become a fully fledged version of the Shiʿi Sufi nineteenth-century notion of the *quṭb* are made in his minor works.[20] What has been termed by Oliver Scharbrodt as the 'Shiʿitisation of Sufi *vilāyat*'[21] underwent a significant advancement in the work of Nūr ʿAlī's successor, Muẓaffar ʿAlī Shāh (d. 1800). While Muẓaffar seems to push Niʿmatullāhī doctrine in the direction of a more solid adherence to the Twelver notion of the imam, and his allegiance to the mainstream exoteric jurisprudence surfaces more distinctively, still his Uṣūlism seems to be only suggested, as shown in his take on the famous hadith that identifies the *ʿulamāʾ* as the heirs of the prophets. The master interprets it as referring to the sacred intuitive science passed down by esoteric means, rather than to exoteric juridical knowledge. Despite this concern with distinguishing mere exoteric knowledge from spiritual knowledge entrusted by means of inner instruction, the vocabulary used by Muẓaffar betrays a doctrinal inspiration that is by now fully imamocentric. The identification of the Sufi's perfect man[22] with the imam and the former's full manifestation in the historical personalities of the twelve imams are entirely accomplished. Hence the reformulation of the Sufi notion of the *quṭb*: the *quṭb* functions as the special representative (*nāʾib-i khass*) of the Hidden Imam. This accommodation allows the Niʿmatullāhīs to preserve both the Sufi doctrine of the *quṭb* (albeit in a new historicised fashion, which makes it rather exclusivist) and the Twelver Shiʿi formal orthodoxy.

The progressive integration of the Niʿmatullāhī Sufi doctrine with Twelver Shiʿism continued with Muẓaffar's successors Ḥusayn ʿAlī Shāh (d. 1818) and Majdhūb ʿAlī Shāh (d. 1823). Both erudite *ʿulamāʾ*, they were completely at ease within the rank and file of the exoteric Imāmī clerical establishment and were able to speak the *ʿulamāʾ*'s language. Majdhūb ʿAlī Shāh expounds the mystical understanding of the Imāmī creed, continuously referring to mainstream Twelver literature and hadiths, in keeping with the style that had become prevalent throughout the Safavid era. It is perhaps the first complete and articulated attempt by a Niʿmatullāhī master to define what a Sufi is from an unambiguous Imāmī Shiʿi standpoint. According to the idea that 'the real Sufi is the Shiʿi', Majdhūb, probably out of the need to denounce anti-Shiʿi tendencies circulating within some Sunni *ṭarīqa*s, goes as far as to vehemently attack such a well-established order as the Naqshbandiyya.[23]

By the time Sulṭān ʿAlī Shāh acceded to the *quṭbiyya*, the order's integration into the exoteric environment of Uṣūlī Shiʿism was fully realised, despite fierce opposition from the literalist *ʿulamāʾ*. The Niʿmatullāhī's writings are now far from just being Sufi literature with a Shiʿi colouring. What we have now is a completely new language of an already mature Shiʿi Sufism, able to appeal to mystical oriented and devout Twelver Shiʿis, in which the charismatic mode of expression of the first masters can be safely reinstated.

Shiʿi *Tafsīr* in Eighteenth- and Nineteenth-Century Iran

Reference works on Shiʿi *tafsīr* in Iran exhibit a dearth of information about exegesis in the eighteenth and early nineteenth centuries. It is as if after Safavid times Shiʿi scholars stopped writing *tafsīr*, only to resume it in the twentieth century. Notice is taken of some names, but no serious study has been undertaken so far. Secondary sources hardly take account of important works like the *Bayān al-saʿāda* or the *tafsīr* of Ṣafī ʿAlī Shāh (d. 1899).

If we look at the centuries preceding the *Bayān*, we find Shiʿi commentaries booming in the Safavid era in response to the demand for a theologically orthodox framework for the newly formed state.

This generated works of exegesis that were preaching in tone and largely apologetic in content; examples include *Tarjumat al-khawāṣṣ* by ʿAlī b. Ḥusayn Zawwāraʾī (d. *c.* late tenth/sixteenth century) and *Minhāj al-ṣādiqīn* by Fatḥ Allāh Kāshānī (d. 988/1580).[24] Most of the works written at this time were in Persian (the reason for this should be analysed separately). This thrust gained momentum both in quality and in quantity under Shāh Sulaymān (r. 1076–1105/1666–94). It was a time dominated by a heavy reliance on Hadith literature (*tafsīr riwāʾī*), consistent with the prominence of Akhbārism. During this period, overtly Akhbārī commentaries were composed, such as *Burhān* by Hāshim al-Baḥrānī and *Nūr al-thaqalayn* by ʿAbd ʿAlī b. Jumʿa Ḥuwayzī.[25] Along with these works, a number of marginalia on past commentaries were produced.

Tafsīr writing declined after the fall of the Safavids, reflecting the difficulty faced by scholars in Iran and the situation of political chaos following the instability caused by the Afghan invasion (1722–9). With few exceptions, no really remarkable commentaries were written through the Afshārid, Zand and early Qajar eras (1729 to mid-nineteenth century), although more research on this is needed. Among the few works worth noting are *al-Wajīz* by ʿAlī b. Abī Jāmiʿ ʿĀmilī (d. 1723–3),[26] which circulated in manuscript form for decades among clerical circles[27] before its recent publication; *ʿUrwat al-muttaqīn* by Muḥammad Ashraf Warnūsfādarānī (d. 1135/1722–3), on the 'Throne Verse' (*āyat al-kursī*; Q. 2:255), in Persian;[28] *al-Baḥr al-mawwāj* by Fāḍil Hindī (d. 1725), which was composed in 1702–3 in Isfahan and is an eclectic commentary with material from exegesis, theology, Hadith and philosophy, both Shiʿi and Sunni; *Manāhil al-taḥqīq* by Muḥammad Hāshim Shīrāzī (d. 1785), who succeeded Quṭb al-Dīn Nayrīzī as the head of the Dhahabī order;[29] works with marginalia, selections of older commentaries and even simple rearrangements of the verses of the Qur'an based on juridical subject matter, as, for example, in *Tafsīr āyāt al-aḥkām-i nādirī*, donated by Nādir Shāh to the shrine of the eighth imam ʿAlī al-Riḍā (d. 202/818) in 1733.

Among the few remarkable *tafsīr*s of the early nineteenth century, one should count the *Tafsīr-i Shubbar* by ʿAbd Allāh Shubbar (d. 1826).[30] Written in Arabic, it circulated as marginalia of the

Qur'an, which it explained in a very simple fashion, and it is still published in several editions in Iran.[31] Among the Persian *tafsīrs* from the Qajar period worth mentioning are *Tuḥfat al-Khāqān*[32] by Nawwāb Mīrzā Muḥammad Bāqir b. Muḥammad Lāhījānī (d. 1921), a commentary arranged according to subject matter under the headings *'Qiṣaṣ'*, *'Aḥkām'*, *'Ma'ārīf'*, *'Mawā'iẓ'* and *'Mawā'īd'*, which was commissioned by Fatḥ 'Alī Shah (d. 1834) in 1814 and completed in 1816; and *Baḥr al-ma'ārif* by Aḥmad b. Muḥammad Kāẓim Ashkiwarī (d. late eighteenth century), written in 1871 and dedicated to Muḥammad-Taqī Barāghānī.[33] The end of the nineteenth century is the time when reformist thought came to prominence. In this period, besides those who kept clinging to the classical styles of exegesis, there were reformist laymen and reformist-minded clerics, like Jamāl al-Dīn Afghānī (or Asadabādī, d. 1897) and 'Abd al-Raḥīm Ṭalibuf (d. 1911), who sought in the Qur'an a buttress for their agenda for social and political reform. The two strands of exegesis – classical and modernist/reformist – seemed to proceed virtually separately. No trace of the urge towards social reform is to be found anywhere in the *Bayān*, although the shift from the emphasis on the transmitted (*naqlī*) approach (in this case, one that is strictly hadith-based) to a more intellectual (*'aqlī*) one is reflected in it.

There was a sort of revival in *tafsīr* writing at the turn of the nineteenth century. Traditional circles continued the Safavid heritage, with such works as *Jawāmi' al-khayrāt fī tafsīr al-āyāt* by Ḥabīb al-Dīn Qummī (d. 1940) and *al-Tafsīr al-kabīr* by Ḥājjī Bajistānī (d. 1949). Other commentaries were published in classical fashion but with reformist content. Examples of these which were written with no reference to traditional sources are *Tarjumat al-Qur'ān fī sharā'iṭ al-īmān* by Muḥammad Taqī Qazwīnī (d. 1914) and *al-Qur'ān wa'l-'aql* by Nūr al-Dīn Arākī (d. 1923); examples of works using Qur'anic material to support constitutionalism are *Iḥyā' al-milla* by Ḥusayn Ahramī Būshihrī and *Bayān-i ma'ānī-yi salṭanat-i mashrūṭa* by 'Imād al-'Ulāmā' Khalkhālī, both of which were written in 1907–8, and *Kashf al-murād min al-mashrūta wa'l-istibdād* by Muḥammad Ḥusayn Tabrīzī, written in 1908–9.[34]

The *Tafsīr Bayān al-saʿāda* and its Features

The *Bayān al-saʿāda fī maqāmāt al-ʿibāda* was completed in 1893 by the eponymous master of the Gunābādī branch of the Nīʿmatullāhī order, Ḥājj Mullā Sulṭān Muḥammad Baydukhtī Gunābādī (d. 1909), whose initiatic name was Sulṭān ʿAlī Shāh. The *tafsīr* was edited by Riḍā Ṭihrānī and ʿAbbās ʿAlī Kaywān Qazwīnī, and was published through the efforts of Muḥammad Ḥasan Khaṭīb-bāshī Ṭihrānī, Muḥammad Ḥusayn Khān Sar-rishta-dār Iṣfahānī and Ghulām-Riḍā Khān Tafaḍḍulī Muṣaddiq al-Sulṭān in 1896.[35] The commentary was met with a certain amount of enthusiasm soon after its first edition was published, and due to the fame of its author it was immediately widely circulated in the learning centres of Iran. This fair success was probably among the reasons why the author was accused of plagiarism from the very beginning, echoes of which have reverberated in recent scholarship and crept into some of the secondary literature.[36] The range of the accusations was wide: that Sulṭān ʿAlī Shāh took an old manuscript from a library in Isfahan, deleted the author's name and put his own instead; or that he copied verbatim from Sabzawārī's thought; or that, as reported in Āqā Buzurg al-Ṭihrānī's *al-Dharīʿa*,[37] he copied from ʿAlī b. Aḥmad Mahāʾimī Kūkanī Nawāʾitī's (d. 835/1431–2) marginalia to ʿAbd Allāh b. ʿUmar Bayḍawī's (d. 685/1286) *Asrār al-tanzīl*,[38] some relevant passages which are reported in *Ṣubḥat al-marjān* (written in 1763–4) by Ghulām-ʿAlī Āzād Bilgrāmī (d. 1200/1785).[39]

As far as its content, style and positioning in the history of Qur'anic exegesis is concerned, the *Bayān al-saʿāda* is a medium-length commentary written from an entirely Sufi–Shiʿi viewpoint (we will see below in detail the import and meaning of this). It bears the signs of the late Safavid and Qajar times, with respect to the theological and intellectual debates that animated Twelver Shiʿism in that period, particularly with regard to the Akhbārī/Uṣūlī diatribe. Although showing a moderate Akhbārī leaning, the author of the *Bayān* unambiguously declares an extra-scriptural inspiration, which is not structurally connected with the Hadith corpus. This inspiration, which is really the original contribution of Sulṭān ʿAlī Shāh, is expressed in the form of 'allusions' (*ishārāt*, talwīḥāt) to the intimate meaning and subtleties (*laṭā'if*) of both the sacred text and the traditions (*akhbār*). It is indeed due to the abrupt revelation of such inspirations that the author ascribes the decision to write the commentary,[40] so that the revealed secrets would not be dispersed and forgotten. All in all, Sulṭān ʿAlī Shāh's approach to the use of hadith is flexible; while continuing the trend initiated in Safavid times, when the revival of hadith studies brought the use of traditions in religious literature centre stage, he did not refrain from employing Sunni hadiths when useful to illustrate points of doctrine, contrary to what one would expect from a pure Akhbārī approach.

The peculiar synthesis of the doctrines of classical Sufi tradition and the newly formulated vocabulary of premodern Shiʿi Sufism, along with its positioning within the framework of Shiʿi exegetical literature, sets the *Bayān* a world apart from other Shiʿi *tafsīr* literature. This fusion, at the same time, makes the *Bayān* an important work in the revival of exegesis in early modern Shiʿi Iran,[41] in that it combines some features of the pre-Buwayhid hadith-based commentaries (before the fourth/tenth century) and some typical tracts of the classical mystical *tafsīr*s, adding a fair amount of original speculation, all framed in an intellectual synthesis of Twelver Shiʿism and Sufism that reached maturation with Sulṭān ʿAlī Shāh himself.

The *Bayān* opens with a lengthy introduction that represents the hermeneutical manifesto of the entire work. The first six chapters of the introduction are devoted to the exposition of the Twelver Shiʿi creed, the discussion of the virtues of knowledge from a Sufi standpoint, the Qur'an and its recitation, the technicalities of exegetical activity and the dangers entailed in interpretation carried out without due qualifications. After establishing the permissibility of interpreting the Qur'an in Chapter 7, Chapter 8 addresses the crucial notion of the relationship between the outer (*ẓāhir*) and the inner (*bāṭin*), and it is through this polarisation that the four levels of the text gain their articulation; these four levels are expression (*ʿibāra*), allusion (*ishāra*), subtleties (*laṭā'if*) and inner realities (*ḥaqā'iq*), respectively associated with ordinary people, the elite, the friends of God and the prophets. Sulṭān ʿAlī Shah then concludes the introduction by solving the problem of the corruption of the text of the Qur'an (*taḥrīf*) in a moderate fashion. His perspective is similar to the stance taken by Muḥsin Fayḍ al-Kāshānī (d. 1091/1679),[42] whose introduction to his own *tafsīr* offers many parallels with the *Bayān*. According to Sulṭān ʿAlī Shah, the Book might well have been corrupted, but its actual version corresponds to the text that God, through his providence, had in any case entrusted to men, and it is with this *vulgata* that one has to faithfully work.

The overall structure of the *Bayān* is that of a treatise: the Qur'anic text is included in a stream of comprehensive discourse that is meant to reveal the connection of the verses through their meaning. The discourse is arranged by topic, highlighted by the words *taḥqīq* (verification), *bayān* (exposition) or *ishāra* (allusion).[43] It is this, rather than the single verses, that constitutes the internal partition of the *tafsīr*.

When Sulṭān ʿAlī Shāh wrote the *Bayān al-saʿāda*, nearly one century had passed since organised Sufism had returned to the central areas of Iran. It reappeared not as a marginal element, but as an important and legitimate voice in the religious discourse of late eighteenth- and early nineteenth-century Twelver Shiʿism. The religious establishment saw Twelver Shiʿi Sufism as a threat to their absolute and exclusive authority over Iranians' religiosity, and their reaction proved to be harsh. The right of Twelver Shiʿi Sufism to stand centre stage in Shiʿism had to be reaffirmed continuously, and Sulṭān ʿAlī Shāh's affirmative act of writing a Qur'anic commentary that encompassed both the Twelver Shiʿi doctrine and classical Persian Sufism was part and parcel of this process of legitimation. While, as we have seen, few remarkable commentaries seem to have been written and circulated in the Shiʿi centres of Iran or Iraq (or India) between the fall of the Safavids and the last decades of the nineteenth century, *tafsīr* as a genre had not lost its prestige among the learned. Writing a Qur'anic commentary was, and still is, quite an achievement, for the range of topics that needs to be mastered by the author is tremendous: lexical, grammatical, juridical, historical, philosophical, and so on and so forth. Many *ʿulamā'* had continued, during the early nineteenth century, to compose marginalia, commentaries (either complete or of a limited number of suras or even verses), both in Persian and in Arabic, in poetry[44] and in prose. However, most of these exegetical undertakings do not have much originality and reflect a sort of tiredness of exegetical thought. For instance, repetition of comments found in Safavid and pre-Safavid commentaries was the norm, and there is little evidence of original *tafsīr*s being widely circulated in religious circles. A cursory glance at the relevant entries in Āqā Buzurg's *Dharīʿa* testify to a situation where, of the many cited works, there were only a few, or even single, copies available; most copies were not actually seen by the author. Among the few remarkable exegetical works of the period, the *Bayān al-saʿāda* and the *tafsīr* by Ṣafī ʿAlī Shāh no doubt stand out as among the most influential. If the early twentieth century saw a revival in Qur'anic commentary writing, it is likely that the relatively wide circulation of both played some role in this. It is of course the need for exegetical responses to the new challenges posed by modernity and the collapse of Qajar rule that sparked a new wave of exegetical activity in the twentieth century, as we can see parallel phenomena in the rest of the Muslim world. The *Bayān* is to be considered, in some respects, a document representing the birth of a fully fledged and conscious Twelver Shiʿi Sufism; it certainly appeared as a fresh approach to the subject in nineteenth-century Shiʿi exegesis. Though the *Bayān* did not, perhaps, succeed in fostering an acceptance and approval of Sufism amongst the whole clerical body (or at least, whether or not it succeeded is a matter that depends on how we define or measure success), it provided the order with doctrinal standing, solidity and authoritativeness. These effects were perceivable throughout the twentieth century and continue well into the twenty-first.

Conclusion

Although the importance of *Bayān al-saʿāda* is undeniable, one should not overestimate the impact it made on twentieth-century Iran outside the Gunābādī order. If considered from the angle of the history of Shiʿi exegesis, it no doubt represented a welcome novelty in a landscape of commentary writing that had been stagnating for far more than a century. Repetition and tiresome reuse of preceding material was the norm in nineteenth-century Shiʿi centres of learning, and very few complete *tafsīr*s were being written at this time. The appearance of a full Qur'anic commentary that was as innovative, original and specific as the *Bayān* was a truly unusual event. The specialist exegetical knowledge and the Sufi element of the commentary prevented the work from being widely accepted or exerting its impact beyond Gunābādī circles or those *ʿulamāʾ* who were partial to mystical exegesis. To this, one should add that at the turn of the nineteenth century and throughout the twentieth century and beyond, *tafsīr* writing in Iran has decidedly gone down the path of the social interpretation of the Qur'an, marginalising the traditional approach in order to seek the response of a wider readership. A perfunctory glance at the general introductions to the history of Shiʿi exegesis that have appeared over the past decades confirms this fact. Even though the *Bayān*'s contribution in the history of Shiʿi *tafsīr* writing has been noted,[45] it is still not even mentioned in introductory books on Qur'anic exegesis.[46] The last few years have seen the production of a number of works that signal that the *Bayān* is generating much more interest than it used to, and the commentary's importance is now recognised even outside the circles of the exegetes (*mufassirūn*) themselves. Provided that a reasonable weighing of the proportions involved is not lost, it is safe to say that the *Bayān* was and is read much more than is actually acknowledged or recognised.[47]

As noted in the chapter, the *Bayān* had some success in addressing the Twelver Shiʿi scholarly elite. The author's choice of Arabic to write a Qur'anic commentary that would mainly reproduce the order's doctrine and later be expounded in other books may have been directed by the need to gain credit with the *ʿulamāʾ*. There have been cases of *ʿulamāʾ* being attracted to Sulṭān ʿAlī Shāh through reading his *tafsīr*. Emblematic of this is Asadullāh Gulpāygānī, later known as Darwīsh Nāṣir ʿAlī (d. 1947), who felt the urge to meet Sulṭān ʿAlī Shāh after reading the *Bayān al-saʿāda* while residing in Karbala.[48] Gunābādī sources record some early instances of reception of the *Bayān* among the scholarly community in Iran and elsewhere. According to these sources, in addition to winning over Āqā

Buzurg Ṭihrānī, who eventually recanted his uncomplimentary comments about the *Bayān* and exhibited appreciation for the work, the *Bayān* succeeded in breaking through the enmity of anti-Sufi scholars and was received positively by some remarkable *ʿulamāʾ*. One that is mentioned by Gunābādī sources is Ḥājj Āqā Muḥsin ʿIrāqī (d. 1907), a mujtahid from the city of Arāk, and one of the most outstanding local madrasa teachers (he taught philosophy, *uṣūl* and *tafsīr*). He is believed to have praised the *Bayān al-saʿāda*, and is said to have remarked that 'the commentary of Sulṭān is the sultan of commentaries' (*tafsīr al-Sulṭān sulṭān al-tafāsīr*).[49] Other *ʿulamāʾ* of the time who are credited by Gunābādī sources with praising the *Bayān* are the renowned gnostic (*ʿārif*) resident of the Madrasa Ṣadr in Isfahan, Muḥammad Kāshī (d. 1914), and the notable gnostic ʿAlī Simnānī (d. 1914).[50]

Though not easy to verify, it seems that the *Bayān* was circulated among the Shiʿi scholars of Syria.[51] This was probably due to the fact that the stigma attached to Sulṭān ʿAlī Shāh in Iran did not have much bearing there. In any case, the mere fact that it was a Sufi work seems to have been sufficient reason for it to be ostracised in Iran.

Whatever the reception of the commentary in the years immediately following its first edition, one has to go carefully through the subsequent *tafsīr* literature to find references to *Bayān al-saʿāda*. Among the *tafsīrs* that occasionally refer to *Bayān* are *Anwār al-ʿirfān fī tafsīr al-Qurʾān* by Abūʾl-Faḍl Dāwarpanāh,[52] *Tafsīr al-kāshif* by the Lebanese Muḥammad Jawād Mughniyya (d. 1904),[53] *Tafsīr-i rawshan* by Ḥasan Muṣṭafawī (d. 2005),[54] and *al-Furqān fī tafsīr al-Qurʾān* by Muḥammad Ṣādiqī Ṭihrānī.[55] A more extensive use, albeit still dispersed among other sources, is made in more mystical-oriented commentaries, or commentaries with a pronounced *ʿirfān* leaning. Such is the case of the *tafsīr* by Ibrāhīm ʿĀmilī,[56] and the *Tafsir al-Qurʾān al-karīm* by Muṣṭafā Khumaynī (d. 1977),[57] Ruhollah Khomeini's son. Both commentaries report numerous quotes from Sulṭān ʿAlī Shāh's commentary. Khumaynī's is replete with references from the classical tradition of Sufi exegesis, as he draws generously from Sahl al-Tustarī (d. 283/896), Abūʾl-Qāsim al-Qushayrī (d. 376/986), ʿAbd al-Raḥmān al-Sulamī (d. 500/1106) and Ṣadr al-Dīn al-Qunawī (d. 673/1274), in addition to the Ṣadrian tradition. In it, the *Bayān* is directly quoted twenty-two times, but its impact is felt throughout.[58] Though he did not approve of the Sufi approach of the commentary, he nevertheless used some of its philosophical points.[59] According to Muḥammad ʿAlī Ayyāzī, other admirers of Sulṭān ʿAlī Shāh were Murtaḍāʾ Muṭahharī (d. 1979), who was a keen reader of the *Bayān* and of the *Wilāyat-nāma*, a comprehensive treatise on the Shiʿi–Sufi notion of *wilāya* (the exercise of authority). Ḥusayn Ṭihrānī (d. 1995), a pupil of Muḥammad Ḥusayn Ṭabāṭabāʾī (d. 1981), said, after reading the *Bayān* and being questioned about the authenticity of it, that 'whoever has written it, he is one of the friends of God (*awliyāʾ Allāh*)'.[60]

Today, Jawādī Āmulī's *Tafsīr-i tasnīm* is an example of a commentary that, as has been suggested, keeps one eye on the *Bayān* and draws from it abundantly.[61] This is a monumental work that will comprise some eighty volumes when completed.[62] The *Tasnīm*, that is declaredly based on Ṭabāṭabāʾī's take on the methodology of the so-called 'interpretation of the Qur'an through the Qur'an' (*tafsīr-i Qurʾān ba-Qurʾān*), is probably the most ambitious and comprehensive exercise in Qur'anic exegesis occurring in Iran today and, in light of the intellectual calibre of the author and the size of the project, it will certainly be considered one of the most important commentaries of the early twenty-first century. In a few instances he also considers the position of Sulṭān ʿAlī Shāh more reliable than that of Ṭabāṭabāʾī.[63] Jawādī Āmulī is well acquainted with Gunābādī literature and does not refrain from referring to Sulṭān ʿAlī Shāh's commentary as an authoritative source, though he does criticise it, in a very respectful way, where he deems it appropriate.[64]

NOTES

1 See, for example, the recent collection of essays in Denis Hermann and Sabrina Mervin, eds, *Shiʿi Trends and Dynamics in Modern Times (XVIIIth–XXth Centuries)/Courants et dynamiques chiites à l'époque moderne (XVIIIe–XXe siècles)* (Beirut, 2010).

2 See, for example, Nikkie R. Keddie, 'The Economic History of Iran, 1800–1914, and its Political Impact: An Overview', *Iranian Studies* 5, nos. 2–3 (1972), pp. 58–78.

3 See the recent work by Ata Anzali, 'Safavid Shiʿism, the Eclipse of Sufism and the Emergence of 'Irfān' (Unpublished PhD dissertation, Rice University, 2012); idem, *'Mysticism' in Iran: The Safavid Roots of a Modern Concept* (Columbia, 2017).

4 Sulṭān Muḥammad Sulṭān ʿAlī Shāh Gunābādī, *Bayān al-saʿāda fī maqāmāt al-ʿibāda* (Tehran, 1344 Sh./1965–6).

5 Muḥammad Ḥusayn Ṭabāṭabāʾī, *al-Mīzān fī tafsīr al-Qurʾān* (Beirut, 1970–74).

6 Nāṣir Makārim Shīrāzī, *Tafsīr-i namūna* (Tehran, 1362–74 Sh./1983–95).

7 ʿAbd Allāh Jawādī Āmulī, *Tafsīr-i tasnīm* (Qum, 1380 Sh./2001–2). More on this towards the end of the chapter.

8 On Shāh Niʿmatullāh Walī's life, see Jean Aubin, *Matériaux pour la biographie de Shah Niʿmatullah Wali* (Tehran, 1956). See also the account in Nasrollah Pourjavady and Peter Lamborn Wilson, *Kings of Love: The Poetry and History of the Niʿmatullāhī Sufi Order* (Tehran, 1978), pp. 13–36; Terry Graham, 'Shāh Niʿmatullāh Walī: Founder of the Niʿmatullāhī Sufi Order', in Leonard Lewisohn, ed., *The Heritage of Sufism, Vol. II: The Legacy of Medieval Persian Sufism (1150–1500)* (Oxford, 1999), pp. 173–90.

9 On the history of the order, see Hamid Algar and J. Burton-Page, 'Niʿmat-Allāhiyya', *EI*^{2}, vol. VIII, pp. 44–8; Pourjavady and Lamborn Wilson, *Kings of Love*.

10 Pourjavadi and Lamborn Wilson, *Kings of Love*, pp. 27–9.

11 Terry Graham, 'The Niʿmat'ullāhī Order under Safavid Suppression and in Indian Exile', in Leonard Lewisohn and David Morgan eds, *The Heritage of Sufism, Vol. III: Late Classical Persianate Sufism (1501–1750)* (Oxford, 1999), p. 178.

12 Although the order became Twelver Shiʿi in nature, in the Deccan the masters of the order continued to be known as Qādirī Sufis or Qādirī-Kirmānīs. See Graham, 'The Niʿmat'ullāhī Order', p. 174. Little is known about the doctrinal history and mystical activity of the masters of the order from this time until the second half of the eleventh/seventeenth century, to the extent that, of the six masters between Mīr Kamāl al-Dīn ʿAṭiyyatullāh (d. after 914/1508) and Mīr Maḥmūd Dakkanī (d. 1100/1689), almost nothing has come down to us but the names. These six masters were Burhān al-Dīn Khalīlullāh II, Shams al-Dīn Muḥammad, Ḥabīb al-Dīn Muḥibbullāh II, Shams al-Dīn Muḥibbullāh II, Kamāl al-Dīn ʿAṭiyyatullāh II, Shams al-Dīn Muḥammad III. See Mīrzā Muḥammad Sulṭānī Gunābādī, *Rahbarān-i ṭarīqat wa ʿirfān* (Tehran, 1379 Sh./2000–2001), p. 196. On the crucial years before the order's return to Iran, see Fabrizio Speziale, 'À propos du renouveau *Niʿmatullāhī*: Le centre de Hyderabad au cours de la première modernité', *Studia Iranica* 42, no. 1 (2013), pp. 91–118.

13 Leonard Lewisohn, 'An Introduction to the History of Modern Persian Sufism, Part I: The Niʿmatullāhī Order: Persecution, Revival and Schism', *Bulletin of the School of Oriental and African Studies* 61, no. 3 (1998), p. 440.

14 Asadullāh Īzadgushasb Gulpāygānī, *Nūr al-abṣār: Dar sharḥ-i ḥāl-i yagāna-ʿārif-i kāmil wa shāʿir-i fāḍil maʿrūf wa mashhūr-i mutaʾakhkhirīn mawlānā Muḥammad ʿAlī 'Nūr ʿAlī Shāh' al-awwal-i Iṣfahānī* (Tehran, 1322 Sh./1943–4).

15 Maʿṣūm ʿAlī Shāh and Nūr ʿAlī Shāh were both assassinated by fanatical clerics. See Muḥammad Maʿṣūm Shīrāzī (Maʿṣūm ʿAlī Shāh), *Ṭarāʾiq al-ḥaqāʾiq* (Tehran, 1382 Sh./2003–4), vol. III, pp. 174–5.

16 This relationship fluctuated between patronage and persecution. See Lewisohn, 'An Introduction', pp. 442–4.

17 As a result of the first noteworthy schism, which occurred at Majdhūb ʿAlī Shāh's death in 1823, the order split into three branches. The two lesser branches became known as the Shamsiyya and the Kawthariyya (see Algar and Burton-Page, 'Niʿmat-Allāhiyya'). The Shamsiyya, despite its small following, produced one of the most renowned Iranian mystics of the nineteenth/twentieth century, Ḥusayn Shams al-ʿUrafā (d. 1935). (For more on him, see ʿAbd al-Ḥujjat Balāghī, *Maqālāt al-ḥunafā fī maqāmāt-i Shams al-ʿUrafā'* [Tehran, 1369–71 Sh./1990–93]). Despite mounting clerical opposition, the Niʿmatullāhī order faced a time of relative material improvement when Muḥammad Shāh (r. 1834–48) acceded to the throne. The shah himself was supportive of the Sufis. In fact, his grand vizier, Mīrzā Āqāsī (d. 1848), was a Sufi who was proactively involved in improving the material conditions of the Sufis in Qajar Persia, and was not just the shah's spiritual master, but, to some extent, a social reformer (see Abbas Amanat, 'Āqāsī', *EIr*, vol. II, pp. 183–8). In 1861, after the death of Raḥmat ʿAlī Shāh, the master of the main branch of the order, another dispute concerning the leadership of the order led to a second schism, whereby the Niʿmatullāhiyya divided into the following branches: the Munawwarʿalīshāhī, the Ṣafīʿalīshāhī and the Gunābādī, the latter being named after Gunābād, the town in Khorasan from whence the masters of the branch after 1872 hailed (see Lewisohn, 'An Introduction', pp. 449–50).

18 Nūr ʿAlī Shāh, *Jannāt al-wiṣāl*, ed. Jawād Nūrbakhsh (Tehran, 1348/1969–70).

19 See Michel de Miras, *Le method spirituelle d'un maître du Soufisme iranien: Nur Ali-Shah* (Paris, 1974).

20 Oliver Scharbrodt, 'The *Quṭb* as Special Representative of the Hidden Imam: The Conflation of Shiʿi and Sufi *Vilāyat* in the Niʿmatullāhī Order', in Denis Hermann and Sabrina Mervin, eds, *Shiʿi Trends and Dynamics in Modern Times (XVIIIth–XXth Centuries)/Courants et dynamiques chiites à l'époque moderne (XVIIIe–XXe siècles)* (Beirut, 2010), pp. 33–49.

21 Ibid, p. 44.

22 The 'perfect man' is the man who, having progressed through all the stations of the mystical path, assumes the cosmological role of intermediary between the visible and the invisible. See Masataka Takeshita, *Ibn ʿArabī's Theory of the Perfect Man and its Place in the History of Islamic Thought* (Tokyo, 1987).

23 Muḥammad Jaʿfar Majdhūb ʿAlī Shāh Kabūdarāhangī, *Mir'at al-ḥaqq* (Tehran, 1383 Sh./2004–5), pp. 127–52.

24 ʿAlī b. Ḥusayn Zawwāra'ī, *Tarjumat al-khawāṣṣ* (Tehran, 1394 Sh./2015–16); Fatḥ Allāh Kāshānī, *Minhāj al-ṣādiqīn fī ilzām al-mukhālifīn* (Tehran, 1346 Sh./1967–8).

25 Hāshim b. Sulaymān al-Baḥrānī, *al-Burhān fī tafsīr al-Qur'ān* (Beirut, 1999); ʿAbd ʿAlī b. Jumʿa al-Ḥuwayzī, *Tafsīr Nūr al-thaqalayn* (Beirut, 2015).

26 ʿAlī b. Abī Jāmiʿ ʿĀmilī, *al-Wajīz fī tafsīr al-Qur'ān al-ʿazīz* (Qum, 1413/1993).

27 ʿAqīqī Bakhshāyishī, *Tabaqāt-i mufassirān-i shīʿa* (Qum, 1371 Sh./1992–3), vol. III, p. 162.

28 Muḥammad Ashraf Warnūsfādarānī, *ʿUrwat al-muttaqīn dar sharḥ-i āyat al-kursī* (Isfahan, 1369/1948–9).

29 Muḥammad Hāshim Darwīsh Shīrāzī, *Manāhil al-taḥqīq*, ed. Muḥammad Yūsuf Nayyirī (Shiraz, 2003).

30 'Abd Allāh Shubbar, *Tafsīr-i Shubbar* (Qum, 1387 Sh./2008).

31 The original title was *al-Wajīz*. Its author was also responsible of writing two other *tafsīrs*, the *Jawhar al-thamīn fī tafsīr al-kitāb al-mubīn* and the *Ṣafwat al-tafāsīr*. See Muḥammad 'Alī Ayyāzī, *Sayr-i taṭawwur-i tafāsīr-i shī'a* (Tehran, 1385 Sh./2006), pp. 159–62.

32 See Aḥmad Munzawī, *Fihrist-i nuska-hā-yi khaṭṭī-yi fārsī* (Tehran, 1969), vol. I, p. 10; Charles Ambrose Storey, *Persian Literature: A Bio-bibliographical Survey, Vol. II, Part I* (London, 1935), p. 1203.

33 Munzawī, *Fihrist*, p. 7.

34 These treatises, among others, are published in Ghulām-Ḥusayn Zargarī-Nijād, ed., *Rasā'il-i mashrūṭiyyat* (Tehran, 1374 Sh./1995).

35 Sulṭān 'Alī Shāh Gunābādī, *Bayān al-sa'āda fī maqāmāt al-'ibāda*, ed. Riḍā Ṭihrānī and 'Abbās 'Alī Kaywān Qazwīnī, lithograph (Tehran, 1314/1896).

36 See, for instance, references to the work in Muḥammad Shafī'i, *Mufassirān-i Shi'a* (Shiraz, 1349 Sh./1970). Also, Hamid Algar's entry, 'Gonābādī Order', in the *EIr* mentions the *Bayān al-sa'āda* as the commentary Sulṭān 'Alī Shāh 'claimed to have written'. As I have demonstrated elsewhere (Alessandro Cancian, *Sufism, Shi'ism and Qur'anic Exegesis in Early Modern Iran: Sulṭān 'Alī Shāh Gunābādī and his Tafsīr Bayān al-Sa'āda*, forthcoming), the least far-fetched of the plagiarism hypotheses (that the *Bayān* was copied from Nawā'itī's *tafsīr* [see further in the chapter]), does not stand up on even a perfunctory comparative reading of the two works, as the resemblance is limited to a few pages out of thousands.

37 Āqā Buzurg al-Ṭihrānī, *al-Dharī'a ilā tasānif al-shī'a*, 3rd edn (Beirut, 1403/1983), vol. III, pp. 181–2. Although, an account that is not possible to confirm has Āqā Buzurg recanting his position on the *Bayān al-sa'āda* expressed in the *Dharī'a* (see Sulṭān Ḥusayn Tabanda Gunābādī [Riḍā 'Ālī Shāh], *Nābigha-yi 'ilm wa 'irfān dar qarn-i chahārdahum: sharḥ-i ḥāl-i marḥūm Ḥājj Mullā Sulṭān Muḥammad Gunābādi Sulṭān 'Alī Shāh* [Tehran, 1384 Sh./2005–6], p. 236). Additionally, Āqā Buzurg mistakes the date of Sulṭān 'Alī Shāh's death, establishing it as 1320/1902. Also, Āqā Buzurg's *Ṭabaqāt i'lām al-shī'a* attributes Nūr 'Alī Shāh's *Dhū'l-fiqār* to Sulṭān 'Alī Shāh (via Riḍā 'Alī Shāh, *Nābigha*, p. 557). In contemporary sources, imprecision and inaccuracies about Sulṭān 'Alī Shāh abound.

38 'Alī b. Aḥmad Mahā'imī, *Tafsīr al-Mahā'imī al-musammā Tabṣīr al-Raḥmān wa taysīr al-Mannān bi-ba'ḍi mā yushīru ilā i'jāz al-Qur'ān*, ed. Aḥmad Farīd al-Miziyādī (Beirut, 2011), vol. II, p. 135.

39 Ghulām-'Alī Āzād Bilgrāmī, *Subḥat al-marjān fī āthār Hindustān* (Aligarh, 1976), vol. I, pp. 97–101. On Sulṭān 'Alī Shāh's use of Bayḍawī's glosses on specific matters related to the 'aspects' (*wujūh*) of the Qur'anic text, we have the personal testimony of Muḥammad Ma'ṣūm Shīrāzī 'Ma'ṣūm 'Alī Shāh' (d. 1344/1926), who spent nearly ten months with the learning circle of the Sulṭān in Gunābād. In his *Ṭarā'iq al-ḥaqā'iq*, he reports how Sulṭān 'Alī Shāh would rely upon Bayḍawī's *Anwār al-tanzīl* and elaborate upon it (Muḥammad Ma'ṣūm Shīrāzī 'Ma'ṣūm 'Alī Shāh', *Ṭarā'iq al-ḥaqā'iq* (Tehran, 1382 Sh./2003–4), vol. III, pp. 540–541).

40 Sulṭān 'Alī Shāh, *Bayān*, vol. I, p. 2.

41 Largely understudied, if not neglected altogether, it is only recently that the *Bayān* has started to be given the attention it deserves. Among the studies produced on it, aside from the present chapter and the forthcoming monograph referred to above (Cancian, *Sufism, Shiʿism and Qur'anic Exegesis in Early Modern Iran*), one should mention ʿAlī Ghaffārzāda, 'Naqd wa barrasī-yi mabānī wa ruykard-hā-yi Sulṭān Muḥammad Gunābādī dar tafsīr "Bayān al-saʿāda fī maqāmāt al-ʿibāda"' (Unpublished PhD dissertation, University of Qum, 1390 Sh./2011); Ḥamīda Nīkrān and Shahrām Ṣaḥrā'ī, *Mabānī'yi ta'wīl-i āyāt al-aḥkām dar tafsīr Bayān al-saʿāda fī maqāmāt al-ʿibāda, az ālim-i rabbānī wa ʿārif-i ṣamadānī Ḥājj Mullā Ṣulṭān Muḥammad Gunābādi Sulṭān ʿAlī Shāh* (Mashhad, 1393 Sh./2014–15) (this is a reworking of a doctoral dissertation by Ḥamīda Nīkrān, 'Bar-rasī-yi abānī'yi ta'wīl-i āyāt al-aḥkām dar tafsīr Bayān al-saʿāda-yi Sulṭān ʿAlī Shāh Gunābādī' [Rāzī University, 1390 Sh./2011–12]); Mahdī Kumpānī-zāriʿ, *Gunābādī wa tafsīr-i Bayān al-saʿāda* (Tehran, 1390 Sh./2011); ʿAbd al-ʿAẓīm Bāstānī Pārīzī, *Tarjuma wa tawḍīḥ-i tafsīr-i sharīf-i Bayān al-saʿāda fī maqāmāt al-ʿibāda* (Qum, 1386 Sh./2007–8).

42 Muḥsin Fayḍ al-Kāshānī, *al-Ṣāfī fī tafsīr kalam Allāh al-wāfī* (Beirut, 1399/1979), vol. I, pp. 15–79. Fayḍ's openness to the possibility that 'the Qur'an that we hold in our hands' may not be the full version revealed to Muhammad is tempered by the traditional injunction to rely on God's providence, which set the Book as a guidance. Fayḍ's not entirely straightforward standing on the matter has been noted by Todd Lawson, 'Akhbārī Shīʿī Approaches to *Tafsīr*', in Gerald R. Hawting and Abdul-Kader A. Shareef, eds, *Approaches to the Qur'ān* (London, 1993), pp. 173–210, esp. pp. 183 and 186–7. See also Mahmoud Ayoub, 'The Speaking Qur'ān and the Silent Qur'ān: A Study of the Principles and Development of Imāmī Shīʿī *Tafsīr*', in Andrew Rippin, ed., *Approaches to the History of the Interpretation of the Qur'ān* (Oxford, 1988), pp. 177–98.

43 For example: *taḥqīq marātib al-qalb wa iṭlāqātihi wa taḥqīq katm al-qalb wa'l-baṣar* (Sulṭān ʿAlī Shāh, *Bayān*, vol. I, p. 54).

44 As with the case of *Tafsīr-i Basmal* by ʿAlī Akbar Nawwāb (d. 1263/1847), whose pen name (*takhalluṣ*) was Basmal. See Āqā Buzurg Ṭihrānī, *Dharīʿa*, vol. IV, p. 236.

45 For example, see Muḥammad Shafīʿī and Faḍl Allāh Ṣalawātī, *Tafsīr wa mufassirān-i shīʿa* (Tehran, 1391 Sh./2012), p. 322. Likewise, Muḥammad ʿAlī Ayyāzī, *Shinākht-nāma-yi tafāsīr: Nigāhī ijmālī ba 130 tafsīr-i barjasta az mufassirān-i shīʿa wa ahl al-sunnat* (Rasht, 1378/1999–2000), pp. 51–2.

46 Although familiar with the *Bayān*, Aḥmad Pākatchī does not mention it in his *Majmūʿa-yi dars guftār-hā-yi dar bāra-yi tārīkh-i tafsīr-i Qur'ān-i karīm* (Tehran, 1391 Sh./2012–13). Part of this chapter is based on insights provided by Dr Pākatchī, to whom I am grateful, in a private conversation held at the Imām-i Ṣādiq University in Tehran, March 2014.

47 That the *Bayān* is still a controversial piece of literature is attested, for example, by the way it is treated (or not treated) in the collections of exegetical literature compiled in Iran today. One illuminating case is provided by two rival digital collections of Imāmī works produced by two different institutes in Qum – the Nūr Institute and the Markaz al-Muʿjam al-Fiqhī. The first includes the *Bayān*

while the second does not, denoting a definite decision on the acceptability of the work in Shiʿi literature.

48 Riḍā ʿAlī Shāh, *Nābigha*, p. 413.

49 Ibid., p. 221.

50 An account that is impossible to confirm is reported in Riḍā ʿAlī Shāh, *Nābigha*, p. 226.

51 The *Nābigha* reports evidence from a letter written in 1377 Sh./1998–9 by a Shiʿi scholar of Latakya, Muḥammad Ḥaydar, that testified to the circulation of the *Bayān al-saʿāda* among the few Shiʿi scholars of Syria later in the twentieth century.

52 Abū'l-Faḍl Dāwarpanāh, *Anwār al-ʿirfān fī tafsīr al-Qur'ān* (Tehran, 1366 Sh./ 1987–8), vol. IX, p. 536.

53 Muḥammad Jawād Mughniyya, *Tafsīr al-kāshif* (Beirut, 2005), vol. I, p. 337.

54 Ḥasan Muṣṭafawī, *Tafsīr-i rawshan* (Tehran, 1380 Sh./2001–2), vol. XI, p. 159.

55 Muḥammad Ṣādiqī Ṭihrānī, *al-Furqān fī tafsīr al-Qur'ān* (Qum, 1397/1977). This only reports some traditions from the *Bayān*; see Ghaffārzāda, 'Naqd', p. 103, n. 4.

56 Ibrāhīm ʿĀmilī, *Tafsīr-i ʿĀmilī* (Tehran, 1360 Sh./1981–2). On this commentary, see Muḥammad ʿAlī Ayyāzī, 'Ibrāhīm Muwaththiq ʿĀmilī mufassir-i gum-nām', *Bayyināt* 13 (1376 Sh./1997–8), pp. 36–45. This was subsequently published with minor changes on the author's website, http://www.ayazi.net/index.php/2012-07-08-07-13-32/2012-10-28-14-32-04/2012-12-23-09-50-52/55-2013-01-14-06-05-56 (accessed 13 May 2014; link no longer available).

57 Muṣṭafā Khumaynī [Khomeini], *Tafsīr al-Qur'ān al-karīm* (Tehran, 1391 Sh./2012–13). On this *tafsīr*, see Muḥammad ʿAlī Ayyāzī, 'Girāyash-hā-yi ʿaqlānī dar tafsīr al-Qur'ān al-karīm-i Muṣṭafā Khumaynī', *Bayyināt* 15 (1376 Sh./1997–8), pp. 92–112 (reproduced, with some amendments, under the same title on the author's website, http://www.ayazi.net/index.php/2012-07-08-07-13-32/2012-10-28-14-32-04/2012-12-23-09-50-52/140-2013-07-03-05-45-01 (accessed 13 May 2014; link no longer available). See also Akbar Thaqafiyān, *Shahīd Muṣṭafā Khumaynī wa tafsīrash* (Tehran, 1391 Sh./2012–13).

58 See Ghaffārzāda, 'Naqd', p. 103.

59 Notably, the 'unity of being' (*waḥdat al-wujūd*). See Khumaynī, *Tafsīr al-Qur'ān al-karīm*, vol. II, p. 300.

60 Personal communication with Ṭihrānī, March 2014.

61 Ghaffārzāda, 'Naqd', p. 104.

62 Thirty-one volumes have been published so far by the publishing house associated with him, Isrāʿ. The final number of volumes has been estimated by its chief editor, ʿAlī Islāmī (see http://www.ibna.ir/vdcji8ex.uqea8zsffu.html).

63 Jawādī Āmulī, *Tafsīr-i tasnīm*, vol V, p. 685, with regard to the 'aspects of the Arabic suffix system (*iʿrāb*)'.

64 Another contemporary Shiʿi scholar who makes no mystery of his appreciation of the *Bayān* is Ḥasanzāda Āmulī (b. 1928). He has, on many occasions, urged his audience to refer to the *Bayān*, which he considers the most authoritative source of Qur'anic mystical exegesis.

11

In the Company of the Qur'an by Muḥyī al-Dīn Ilāhī Ghomshei*

LEONARD LEWISOHN

Introduction

THE CELEBRATED contemporary Iranian mystical theologian Ḥusayn Muḥyī al-Dīn Ilāhī Qumsha'ī (henceforth Ghomshei, b. 1940)[1] hails from a distinguished family of religious scholars. His father, Mahdī Ilāhī Qumsha'ī (d. 1973), who was known as Ḥakīm ['Sage'] Qumsha'ī, was himself a leading theosopher of his time and one of the first professors to teach in the Faculty of Theology at the University of Tehran. His monumental compendium of poetry (*dīwān*) is one of the most significant collections of Persian mystical poetry to have been written in the last century.[2] Ḥakīm Qumsha'ī was a student of two of the greatest masters of mystical philosophy (*ḥikma*) of the early twentieth century – Adīb Nayshābūrī (d. 1936)[3] and Āqā Buzurg Khurāsānī (d. 1936)[4] – in Ṭūs.[5] In his autobiography, he relates that Āqā Buzurg had been a student of the philosopher Āqā Muḥammad Riḍā Qumsha'ī (d. 1888),[6] who was in turn a student of the foremost Persian mystical philosopher of the nineteenth century, Ḥājj Mullā Hādī Sabzawārī (d. 1873). Ḥakīm Qumsha'ī regarded both his teachers (Adīb and Āqā Buzurg) as endowed with extra-ordinary mystical accomplishments, describing them as adepts in 'higher states of consciousness, spiritual stations, dervish frenzy, and the passion of the antinomian mystics (*aḥwāl wa maqāmat-i 'irfānī*

* I would like to thank my friend Terry Graham for his careful copy-editing of an earlier version of this essay and Dr Alessandro Cancian for his learned editorial comments and suggested changes to several passages.

wa shūr-i darwīshī wa qalandarī)'.[7] The spiritual tradition to which Ghomshei belongs directly derived from his father, who was his main teacher in Shi'i theosophy (*'irfān*), which is transmitted largely as an oral tradition[8] with no formal initiatic affiliation, in contrast to the spiritual chains (*silsilas*) of the orders of Sufism.[9]

In his formal academic studies, Ghomshei received a BA in Islamic Theology and Philosophy in 1961 and a PhD in Islamic Theology and Philosophy in 1965 from Tehran University. Following the collapse of the Iranian Pahlavi dynasty in 1979 and the subsequent *jacquerie* of the *'ulamā'* under the leadership of Ruhollah Khomeini (in power 1979–89), Ghomshei was appointed Director of the National Library of Iran, a position he held for a year (1981–2).[10] Over the next three decades, videos of his widely popular public lectures were regularly broadcast on Iranian television, where his stellar abilities as a public lecturer and orator on Islamic philosophy, theology and Persian literature earned him national popularity and renown.[11] His skill in presentation was such that he appealed to both the religiously inclined and those who were more secularly oriented but had a taste for the culture and poetry of Persian mysticism when eloquently expressed.

Ghomshei has also published a number of books on the great poets of Iran, such as 'Aṭṭār (d. 618/1221), Rūmī (d. 672/1273), Sa'dī (d. *c.* 691/1292), Maḥmūd Shabistarī (d. *c.* 720/1320) and Ḥāfiẓ (d. 791/1389), as well as on a host of related subjects. Some of his works bear mentioning here:

- *Selections from the 'Conference of the Birds'* by 'Aṭṭār, featuring a long introduction and commentary on difficult words and verses from the classic poem.[12]
- *365 Days in the Company of Rūmī*, a collection of selected passages from the *Mathnawī* and *Dīwān-i Shams* with commentary on each passage.[13]
- *Selections from Rūmī's 'Discourses'*, an abridgement with commentary.[14]
- *365 Days with Sa'dī*, the best anthology of this great Persian romantic poet in print.[15]
- An edition of Shabistarī's *Garden of Mystery* with a short commentary.[16]

- A finely calligraphed, lavishly illustrated edition of the *Dīwān* of Ḥāfiẓ, preceded by a long introduction, followed by an excellent appendix, and featuring a glossary of technical terms.[17]
- *In the Realm of Gold: 365 Days with English Literature*, an anthology of English literature accompanied by a Persian translation of the selected texts, reprinted several times since its publication in 2007.[18]
- *A Treasury of the Familiar: 365 Days with Persian Poetry*, a large anthology (982 pages) of Persian poetry, featuring a 128-page introduction and 55-page glossary of literary terms.[19]

Ghomshei is an accomplished prose stylist and literary essayist in Persian, whose *Collected Essays*, devoted to some of the major classical Persian mystics and poets, has appeared in many editions since its original publication in 1997.[20] Due to his professional background as official Translator of Legal Texts for the Iranian Ministry of Foreign Affairs (1965–79), he has published a number of books in the field of translation studies, such as *A Study of Islamic Texts in English Translation*,[21] and a Persian translation with Khusraw Shayasta of Philippa Stewart's *Shakespeare and his Theatre* (1992).[22] In collaboration with Sayyid Aḥmad Bihishtī Shīrāzī, he served as editor of *Alchemy* (*Kīmiyā*), a respected journal on literature, art and mysticism, which was published in Tehran for the better part of a decade.[23]

In the Company of the Qur'an: Exegetical Approach and Methodology

Amongst his prolific publications, the most popular book to date written by Ghomshei is his *365 Days in the Company of the Qur'an*.[24] It is an exegesis of 365 passages from the Qur'an, with the original Arabic text featured alongside Persian and English translations (by Yusuf Ali), with abundant commentary on each passage richly filling the 950 pages of this voluminous work. Rather than attempting to explain each and every verse of every sura, for each of the 365 days of the year those verses that had particular relevance or resonance for the author are selected for citation and represented in commentary. Since its initial publication in 2011 in a small print-run of only 2,000 copies, the work has been published in twelve editions and, by 2015, had sold over 24,000 copies. Its popularity can be attributed to several factors.

To begin with, the author's reputation precedes him.[25] A charismatic and beloved public speaker, he is often stopped for autographs.[26] He has been a household name in Iran for a good three decades. His frequent appearances on television and the eloquence of his extemporaneous public lectures often attract thousands of listeners. His in-depth understanding of Persian and Arabic literature, his phenomenal memory and his mastery of Islamic philosophy and Sufism make him a formidable and charismatic speaker. As an orator on classical subjects he is as venerated and beloved as the great classical singer Muḥammad Riḍā Shajariyān in the eyes of many Iranians. His books and recordings (both CD and DVD) are featured in shops throughout Iran.

Furthermore, *In the Company of the Qur'an* is a highly sophisticated work of Persian literature, literary criticism, theology, mystical philosophy and scriptural exegesis that offers appealing and sometimes highly original interpretations of Islam's holy missal in the light of classical Persian mystical literature and Sufi poetry. This exegesis of the Qur'an uses Persian Sufi prose and verse to bring forth the hidden gems of the scripture and make them accessible for all to contemplate.

If this mode of scriptural exegesis appears démodé today, it has a venerable pedigree with respect to both the history of Biblical exegesis through English poetry[27] and the history of Persian literature, poetry having been used from the very earliest days to interpret the Islamic scripture, with Qur'anic issues and points of exegesis traditionally encapsulated in Persian verse.[28] The Persianate societies of Iran, Tajikistan, Afghanistan and Persian-speaking parts of India still remain intensely bardic civilisations in which blacksmiths, taxi drivers, masons and farmers still sing the ghazals of Sanā'ī (d. 525/1131) and Rūmī as they work. Exactly the same Persian tongue – by and large – is declaimed today from lecterns in classrooms and pulpits in mosques, and broadcast on radio and television, as was spoken in the bazaars and madrasas of fourteenth-century Shiraz by Ḥāfiẓ. The lines of Rūmī's and Sa'dī's poetry still adorn conversations everywhere, whether amongst university professors in literature departments or the beau monde of café society. Threading through the milieus of modern-day society, their verses feed the repertoire of pop singers in cabarets and discothèques and of rap singers stirring the underground music scene.[29]

Apropos of this time-honoured poetic tradition of scriptural exegesis, Ghomshei inaugurates his extensive introduction to *In the Company of the Qur'an* with an ornate, highly poetic exordium in praise of the Prophet laced with citations from Sanā'ī, Niẓāmī (d. 605/1209), Rūmī, Saʿdī, Ḥāfiẓ, Shabistarī, Jāmī (d. 897/1492) and other classical Persian poets.[30] To adumbrate his exegetical approach and methodology, his exordium is followed by a section devoted to various poets' and philosophers' relationship to the Qur'an. These include Firdawsī (d. 411/1020) (pp. xlvi–xlix), Sanā'ī (pp. xlix–lii), Niẓāmī (pp. liii–lv), ʿAṭṭār (pp. lv–lviii), Rūmī (pp. lviii–lx), Saʿdī (pp. lx–lxii), Ḥāfiẓ (pp. lxiii–lxviii), Ibn ʿArabī (d. 638/1240) (pp. lxviii–lxxv) and Naṣīr al-Dīn Ṭūsī (pp. lxxv–lxxviii), the verse or prose of each of whom he cites.

The next section, 'The Tale of the One' (Dāstān-i aḥad),[31] presents the metaphysical assumptions underlying Ghomshei's commentary. He ramifies the well-known Islamic tripartite typology of Divine Unity (*tawḥīd*) into (a) Unity of the Divine Essence (*tawḥīd-i dhātī*), (b) Unity of the Divine Attributes (*tawḥīd-i ṣifatī*) and (c) Unity of the Divine Acts (*tawḥīd-i afʿālī*). This tripartite theory of *tawḥīd* is then expounded in terms of the philosophy of the Unity of Being (*waḥdat al-wujūd*), according to which Being *qua* God's Being is explained as a unitary divine substance, while everything else constitutes His theophanies.

The Qur'anic text which is explicated as the expression of *tawḥīd-i dhātī* is *Whithersoever ye turn, there is the presence of Allah* (Q. 2:115).[32] God's Being encompasses the dimensions of *the First and the Last, the Evident and the Immanent* (Q. 57:3), all together perceived as a unitary substance sustaining all manifestations or accidents. The principle of *tawḥīd-i ṣifatī* means that all God's Attributes, such as Knowledge, Will, Beauty and Goodness, are contained in the One and Unique Divine Essence. Lastly, at the degree of *tawḥīd-i afʿālī*, all powers, works and effects in creation are apprehended *sub specie aeternitatis* as effected and determined by the One Creator, according to the dictum: 'There is no strength and power except through God' (*lā ḥawl wa lā quwwat illā bi'llāh*).[33] In this context, Ghomshei brings in a particularly appropriate reference to the connection between 'Aḥad' ('the One', the surname for God) and 'Aḥmad' in the Qur'anic verse: *when thou threwest (a handful of dust), it was not thy act, but Allah's* (Q. 8:17).

Based on these metaphysical propositions, Ghomshei thus affirms that there is only one Lover and one Beloved, for all other lovers and beloveds are actually and ultimately manifestations of Him, given that 'there is no dweller but Him in the house' (*laysa fī'l-dār ghayra hū diyyār*) as the Sufi adage attests.[34] According to this erotic theology, 'Adam and Eve are theophanies of that same Love that the One has for His Infinite Beauty.'[35] Eve represents the Divine Feminine, the divine Beloved who is a theophanic apparition of beauty (*tajallī-yi jamāl*) of the Divine for man (Adam) on earth. He cites various quotations from Ḥāfiẓ and Ibn Fāriḍ in support of this viewpoint, basing his argument on the Qur'anic verse beloved to Sufis: *a people whom He will love* (*yuhibbūhum*) *as they will love Him* (*yuhibbūnahu*) . . . (Q. 5:54). The love of man for woman is theo-erotic, insofar as man is a theophanic receptacle (*maẓhar*) for the verse *and they love Him* (ibid.). Likewise, the esoteric meaning of *a people whom He loves* is the love of woman (Eve) for man (Adam).

The love between the sexes is therefore nothing but a reflection, on the human level, of the internal operation of God's own love in respect of divine affairs (*shu'ūnāt-i dhātiyya-yi khʷīsh*).[36] The author then embellishes this theo-erotic doctrine with gems of quotations from the verse of Saʿdī, Rūmī, Shabistarī and Hātif Iṣfahānī (d. 1783). While the wider context of this doctrine belongs, metaphysically speaking, to the realm of divine Unity, in which 'all is one', in the realm of plurality and multiplicity, one must take account of temporal conditions pertaining to number and division where, as Jāmī states:

Existence has myriad degrees
and each of these myriad decrees

and rules one must observe. Neglect them not,
else you will become a godless apostate.[37]

Another brief section on prophetology follows (pp. xl–xlv), where Ghomshei outlines his doctrine of the relationship between the One (*aḥad*) and the Prophet (Aḥmad). The poetry of Shabistarī and Niẓāmī is adduced to illustrate the idea that the Prophet is the first manifestation of divine Unity in the realm of plurality. The degree of the Prophet Muhammad, he writes, is that of 'Cosmic Consciousness', alluding to the famous book (1905) with this title by Richard Maurice Burke,[38] who had described the Prophet's experiences as characteristic of the cosmic mind. He interprets the night ascension (*miʿrāj*) of the Prophet as (citing Shabistarī's well-known verses to this effect)[39] 'a journey from the creature to the Creator, from part to the Universal whole, from plurality to Unity, or, in the words of the Persian mystics, from the soul (*nafs*), which is essentially multiple and manifold, to Love, which is that Unity that permeates the entire universe'.[40] At the end of his exposition of prophetology, verses from Niẓāmī and an Arabic passage from the *Fuṣūs al-ḥikam* of the philosopher Abū Naṣr Muḥammad al-Fārābī (d. 339/950) are quoted as vivid support for this mystical interpretation of the Prophet's *miʿrāj*.

The keystone of Ghomshei's introduction comes in a vital segment of thirty pages (pp. xlvi–lxxvii) where he clarifies the approach adopted throughout the rest of the book, discussing the views of the Qur'an given by some of the greatest Persian poets, philosophers and writers. Beginning with the *Shāh-nāma* of Firdawsī, he cites key verses where the Sage of Ṭūs had extolled the Qur'an, before proceeding to Sanā'ī, citing verses from his *Ḥadīqa* and from his *qaṣīdas* in praise of the Qur'an. He carries on in like manner with Niẓāmī, ʿAṭṭār, Rūmī, Saʿdī, Ḥāfiẓ and, finally, the *Fuṣūs al-ḥikam* of Ibn ʿArabī.

Ghomshei's hermeneutical approach to the testimony which the poets give to his subject, the meaning of the Qur'an, is best epitomised in his treatment of the poetry of Ḥāfiẓ. Though Ḥāfiẓ hardly ever mentions the Prophet Muhammad by name, there are scores of allusions to and indications of (*ishārāt wa talmīḥāt*) him, as the author demonstrates.[41] There are even more allusions to the book of the Qur'an, while scriptural tales and characters are threaded throughout his *Dīwān*.[42]

At the end of this section, Ghomshei offers a short citation from the *Nāṣirīan Ethics* (*Akhlāq-i Nāṣirī*) of Naṣīr al-Dīn Ṭūsī (d. 672/1273), demonstrating how the great Shi'i philosopher's treatise on philosophical ethics is predicated on the wisdom of the Qur'an. In prefacing the description of Ṭūsī's work, the author tells us how the 'silken strands of the sacred verses and phrases of the Qur'an' have become reinterpreted in 'the poetry and prose of the Persian-speaking gnostics, poets and theosophers', illustrating how the 'four streams of the Qur'anic paradise – water, milk, honey and wine – flow through the groves and jasmine-gardens of Persian culture, which itself is paradise on earth'.[43] Ghomshei's exegetical approach thus involves interpretation of the Arabic of the Qur'an through the medium of the mystical literature of Persia, since 'This Tigris River of [Qur'anic] Inspiration' flows through all of Persian literature, as the verse of Sa'dī attests:

Your words and lore are all
  The rage and fashion of the day,
Cascading round the globe.
  The Tigris never flowed so smooth
As your well-worn phrases' waves.[44]

Following this section Ghomshei briefly cites some of the favourable opinions about the Prophet Muhammad voiced by a number of notable Western and Eastern writers, including Goethe, Edward Gibbon, Mahatma Gandhi, Tennyson, George Bernard Shaw, Washington Irving, R.W. Emerson, Thomas Carlyle, Victor Hugo and, more recently, the literary critic Harold Bloom.[45] He finishes this section with a 'Friendly Word to Certain Intellectuals', where he addresses those Iranians (and by implication anyone of this school of thought) who make a modernist critique of the Prophet and the Qur'an, who denigrate the Prophet as a fraud or see the Qur'an as an incitement to aggression. He concedes that much of this negative point of view has been fed by the aggressive fundamentalism which has arisen amongst the Muslims of today and needs to be dealt with.[46]

Selections from *In the Company of the Qur'an*

For reasons of space it is obviously impossible to survey all the ideas presented in the 365 passages of this work. Thus, in the following pages I will provide an analytical introduction, followed by a translation of only three different passages from *In the Company of the Qur'an* to give a taste of its style and an insight into its significance as a work of Qur'anic exegesis.

Selection 1 (Q. 16:96): Ontology, philosophical ethics and classical Persian poetry

In the selection below, an exegesis of Q. 16:96, we encounter one of the leitmotifs of Ghomshei's thought: the Platonic Forms or Ideas. According to this theory, everything that is beautiful is so by its participation in the transcendental Form of 'the Beautiful'.[47] Everything that is good, likewise, is so by its participation in the transcendental Form of 'the Good', while the plurality of everything that is known is ultimately only understood and known through the invariability of the Real (*al-ḥaqq*), that is, through the mystical participation of the human knower with – via theophany of – the unchanging divine Name: 'the Knower' (*al-ʿalīm*).[48] This Islamic doctrine of the Platonic Forms constitutes the basis of Ghomshei's epistemology, ontology, ethics and philosophy of life.

In the final paragraph of the selection below, the importance and influence of *Nāṣirīan Ethics* on Ghomshei's philosophy of religion is revealed. He refers to the soul's acquisition of habitual characteristics or virtues by dint of constant practice and ascetic effort, which was one of Ṭūsī's key ethical theories. To acquire virtue requires an ascetic endeavour to inculcate a certain ethical quality within oneself and so transform it into a permanent 'habit of the soul' or 'psychological trait' (*malaka-yi nafsānī*). As Ṭūsī states in the *Akhlāq-i Nāṣirī*,[49] 'Such a psychological trait (*malaka*) then becomes a quality of the soul, a quality which has become its essential disposition (*khulq*), and the reason it can belong to the soul are two things: one, through its own nature, and the other by dint of habit (*'āda*).'[50]

After an extensive exposition of the debate between the proponents of nature and nurture, Ṭūsī comes out in support of the latter group, stating: 'It has often been seen how children and youths by means of education and association with people of good disposition or through social intercourse with them were able to acquire that disposition (*khulq*) for themselves, even though previously they had an entirely different disposition.'[51] Reviewing the moral theories of the Stoics and Galen and others, Ṭūsī finally stresses that he is opposed to the theory that states that human dispositions are 'natural' in their origin, asserting definitively that 'There is no such thing as a [purely] natural disposition (*hīch khulqī ṭabī'ī nabuwad*). The reason for this is that if human dispositions had been placed there by Nature, then they would be permanent and innate, and not able to be changed, whereas children's and youths' dispositions can indeed be changed.'[52] It is therefore necessary that parents in the first instance send their children to a preceptor to give them a general education in the Divine Law (*nāmūs-i ilāhī*). Once they reach the age of reason and discernment, they should then be sent to a teacher specialising in the science of philosophy (*ḥikma*), 'so they can realise all the degrees of perfection'.[53] Ultimately, the student, 'whether by choice or force, will be restrained to follow the ways of laudable morality and acceptable habits until these become ingrained as permanent virtues within him'.[54]

The technical terminology and most of the theories and ideas utilised by Ghomshei in this passage ultimately derive from Ṭūsī's *Akhlāq-i Nāṣirī*, as the above précis proves. Ghomshei's exegesis of this passage from the Qur'an is also very much indebted to classical Persian Sufism of the Age of Rūmī and Sa'dī, making his choice of poetic quotations from that period historically, intellectually and philosophically consistent with Ṭūṣī's ethical philosophy, which belongs to the same epoch.[55] By retaining its focus on the still living tradition of classical Persian mystical and theosophical thought, his commentary demonstrates how the Qur'an may be interpreted in the light of traditional Persian mystical poetry and ethical philosophy.

Ghomshei's interpretation of Q. 16:96

> *What is with you must vanish: what is with Allah will endure. And We will certainly bestow, on those who patiently persevere, their reward according to the best of their actions.* (Q. 16:96)

Since all the goods, possessions and pleasures of this world are ephemeral, transient and continually vanishing away into nothingness, the best deed one can do is to transform whatever is perishable and transient into that which is permanent and everlasting. To put this alchemy into practice, a person must sacrifice all they have to God. That is to say, one should spend all one has in way of raising oneself up into the realm of the Good (*khūbī*), the Joyous (*shādī*), the Knowing (*dānā'ī*) and the Beautiful (*zībā'ī*), which itself embraces and encompasses all kinds of good and pious charitable deeds. Having bequeathed all you own to God, you will find the eternal imperishable realm is already there within you, for nothing is ever lost in God's bosom. Rather, in God everything is always on the increase, for His realm is one of effusive grace, unending growth, constant burgeoning and bounty.

This transformation of the perishable into the eternal is not confined simply to the doing of good deeds, the practice of charitable works, or acts of generosity and altruistic giving. Rather, whenever a person devotes all his work to God, vowing to himself that he will not desert the path of the Beloved and seek only His goodwill and pleasure, and whenever he puts this vow into practice, that transformation immediately takes place. Henceforth, all he does will partake of eternity and never pass away. No good thing will ever pass him by, nor need he fear [the consequences of] his past [misdeeds]:

> If all the days of life flit by
> so what? Let them all pass away.
> May you remain, the one, the only:
> You, who are beyond compare.
>
> – Rūmī[56]

Whoever sells all his goods and wherewithal to that Rich Buyer Who is essentially Wealthy never will need to fear loss, since all he's given away will be returned to him, redoubled many times over. This is God's promise. The truly affluent person in the world is one who has no wealth of his own, considering himself to be a divine employee acting as God's agent and vicegerent in the world. Therefore, he never experiences any worry about being waylaid by the wiles of brigands or malefactors, nor anxiety about destruction through flood or storm, or fear of suffering loss due to economic depression or stagnation of the marketplace. His only concern is how best to make a worthy contribution of his services, whether this be to add further some good work or to fight with devils and demons who lead men astray . . .

Don't plight your faith and trust
  on any pettifogging slippery friend
    who is just a double-dealing villain.
Since good and bad both pass away
  all joy belongs to him who strikes
    the ball of Virtue in the net of play.
Go send ahead of death some serenity:
  some sprig of joy, for after your cortège
    no one will send you flowers to the crypt.

– Saʿdī[57]

Since even our good works in this world are perishable and ephemeral, it is necessary to learn how to transform the impermanent and transient into what's everlasting and eternal during this very lifetime. The right way to do this is to try to act in such a way that all our deeds are changed into permanently habitual characteristics innately within us, our works becoming instilled within our souls as 'virtues', a part of our spiritual makeup and eternal soul. Acts of generosity are extremely good, but they must be all transformed into the permanent disposition of our souls; in other words, generosity must become something innate within us, a virtue accompanying us during the voyage into the life hereafter. Likewise, suppression of anger must be transformed into [the virtue of] calm self-possession and great-heartedness. And so on and so forth: [other charitable acts such as] service to the poor and needy, or visitation to the sick, and, after all, our entire life, must be transformed into the very substance of divine love, so that, as in Ḥāfiẓ's words:

> I laid bare to my accoutred, veteran heart
> All the world that's here below and all the next.
> All that's mortal, ephemeral, dead, it confessed.
> 'But your love ever lasts: it shall always exist.'[58]

So it all behoves us to remain among accidental and nonessential things, for 'when you reach what is substantial, you will be freed of anxiety over cessation of existence'.[59]

Selection 2 (Q. 51:21): Self-knowledge, the platonic forms and Islamic ecumenism

In his commentary on Q. 51:21, Ghomshei ventures into the speculative metaphysics of the school of Muḥyī al-Dīn Ibn al-ʿArabī (d. 638/1240) and the Illuminationist (*ishrāqī*) theosophy of Shihāb al-Dīn Yaḥyā Suhrawardī (d. 587/1191) in an attempt to expound various abstruse aspects of the metaphysical thought of classical Sufism. Although this Qur'anic verse (cited below) only consists of four brief Arabic words, Ghomshei's exegesis spans four densely argued pages.

He begins his analysis with classic verses from Rūmī's *Mathnawī* which suggest a view similar to that of the Irish philosopher George Berkeley (d. 1753). According to the immaterialist theory of matter advocated by Berkeley, sensible objects are ontologically present only in the mind of God. Our ideas derived from the senses are passive; they flow through us, but the actual source we derive them from is God.[60] The Sufi mystic can actually perceive the flow of this stream of divine consciousness through the 'Eye of the Heart, which of course is not the physical organ, but the subtle organ of supra-natural perception (*oculus cordis*)'.[61] Thereby, one apprehends the revelation of God within oneself while simultaneously seeing God's reflection outside in the mirror of natural phenomenon. In this respect, while the real world is contemplated within the heart, the external world appears merely as a shadow that leaves faint traces or *āthār* (*vegtigia deo*) in the imagination of the 'real realm', which is that of the heart. Self-knowledge, in essence, therefore requires the same sort of Sufi intuition elaborated by Rūmī in the verses cited below.

According to this epistemic methodology, to 'know thyself' or know the 'self' is not so much a knowledge of physical functions but rather (because the real self is ultimately not the body but the soul, one is most true to oneself when one decreases one's physical involvements, when one is not 'dragged down by the body'[62]) a process of ascent by *philo-sophia* – love of wisdom – up to Intellectual Beauty. There is a therapeutic aspect of self-knowing according to Ghomshei, for the practice of self-recovery is a kind of salvation which leads our soul to its true nature, recalling Plotinus' views in this respect.[63] One thus recovers and knows one's 'self' in proportion to one's love of wisdom, a view famously advanced by Plato.[64]

To 'know thyself' therefore involves a mystical ascent to the three key divine Forms or Ideas: Beauty (*zībā'ī*), Knowledge (*dānā'ī*) and Goodness (*nīkū'ī*), leading to a realisation of the immortality of the soul in God's imperishable Being through direct knowledge of these divine attributes (which are also Platonic Forms). One cannot know oneself – much less know God – unless one is a lover of beauty, a seeker of knowledge, or a student of virtue striving to obtain goodness of character. Thus, these three pursuits, which are respectively erotic, noetic and ethical, are the *sine qua non* of self-knowledge. Love of these qualities, and the Platonic Forms from which they derive, constitute the 'Leitmotifs', the guiding sentiments and line of ascent for the soul in its progress from the ethical to the noetic back to the One.[65] As we have seen in the last selection, the theory of the divine Forms of Beauty, Knowledge and Goodness is a central theme that permeates the text of Ghomshei's *In the Company of the Qur'an*.

The reality of the human soul (*nafs*) is best grasped by one who understands the hadith: 'He who knows himself (*nafs*) knows his Lord.' According to this theory of mystical epistemology, the key to realisation of the immortality of the soul and imperishability of one's higher self is to be found through a process of contemplative introspection that leads us ultimately to cognisance of God's Being.

Introspection, Ghomshei argues, causes one to look within oneself, whence, transcending our physical being, one realises that one's temporal existence partakes of a universal divine Being that cannot perish. Anxiety over death here vanishes.[66] Ghomshei quotes a verse by Shabistarī to illustrate the idea that True Being is eternal, imperishable and unchanging in contrast to the unreal existence of the temporal, sentient realm which remains forever non-existent, save for that illumination – theophanic revelation and manifestation (*tajallī*) – of Being within it, which is ultimately its sole *raison d'être*.[67]

Ghomshei's interpretation of Q. 51:21

As also in your own selves: Will ye not then see? (Q. 51:21)

This verse comprises the pith of the most important and perennial doctrines of philosophy expressed in different languages and by various cultures. The verse was summed up by the famous epigram 'Know thyself', inscribed over the lintel of the oracle of Delphi in ancient Greece.

The source-spring of all the transcendental knowledge known to humanity is within. In reality, whatever is outside of man is merely a reflection of those interior effects (*āthār-i darūn*), the light of which is cast upon the exterior world, as Mawlānā in the *Mathnawī* elucidates:

Once in a garden, as the Sufis do,
A Sufi laid his head upon his knee,
And seeking spiritual expansion, delved
So deep in meditation, he seemed asleep.
A busybody by his lethargic form
Was bored and cried, 'What's all this somnolence?
Look up and see these leafy vines and trees,
This vernal sward, these signs of God's designs!
Hear God's command to "contemplate and gaze"
– So look upon these signs of divine mercy!'

The Sufi said: 'You say they are "signs"? Those "signs"
Are in the heart. This is your gluttony!
What is outside merely are the "signs of the signs".

This garden and greenery you see
Are in the soul's deepest essence, yet
Outside, like water in a flowing brook
The garden's likeness is reflected there.
It's but the garden's phantom that you see
Cascading by grace of the water there.
They are gardens in the heart and orchards there
All full of fruit, whose image is
Reflected on this water, earth and air.'[68]

It is being mindful of ourselves that allows us, first of all, to gain an awareness of the substance of our individual being, which then communicates to us that we are something else besides this physical body. This is because whenever we apprehend the essential substance of our individual being, we have no cognisance of our body and physical frame.

Second of all, we are led to understand that this self-essence, this individual being pertains to the category of *being* (*hastī*), insofar as we apprehend our *being* before anything else, without anything intervening between. If, in the words of Descartes, we were to 'think' or to 'doubt', that itself is a sign of our *being*, for if *being* did not exist, neither could thought nor meditation ever occur. Once we understand that the essence of our self belongs to the category of *being*, it becomes self-evident to our reason that *being* (*hastī*) can never be transformed into *non-being* (*'adam*). Therefore, we will never enter *non-being*, just as we never originated from *non-being*. In the words of Shaykh Maḥmūd Shabistarī:

For non-being to become existent is truly impossible;
Real being, in regard to existence, is immutable.[69]

Neither *being* can become *non-being*, nor *non-being* become *being*. Therefore, insofar as we do exist, we always have existed and always will exist. All fear and anxiety about perishing upon death should then vanish from our hearts.

Now, when we contemplate our souls once again, we soon discover that we are not endowed with all the characteristics we would like to have. There are many accomplishments and arts we admire and find that others possess, but which we lack, and whereupon this introspection, we find ourselves to be lacking and incomplete. Yet we only grasp this imperfection by means of cognisance of perfection, which appears to us in three different aspects: Beauty (*zībā'ī*), Knowledge (*dānā'ī*) and Goodness (*nīkū'ī*).

Love of these three angels belongs to our innate disposition. It is this selfsame love which, if not blocked by barriers such as forgetfulness, pride and ambition for social status and place, will bear us aloft towards perfection. Our entire life thus will naturally become a process of spiritual ascension and moral advancement (*sayr wa sulūk*) – a progression from imperfection to perfection. If one be asked, 'Who are you?' one may answer, 'I am a pilgrim, a traveller, going from the town of imperfection and privation to the city of perfection and complete fulfilment.' This perfection consists basically of four things.

Firstly, there is Physical Perfection (*kamāl-i jismānī*) that consists of keeping the body in perfect physical shape, so that our physical frame is harmonious and not ugly and misshapen. Although having a beautiful countenance is itself very good, that is not within everyone's capacity to control. What is of foremost importance is preserving one's inward purity (*pākīzigī*) and maintaining a happy, smiling and cheerful complexion (*gushāda-rū'ī*). All human beings are obliged to be of pure nature and maintain a smiling, cheerful complexion.

Secondly, there is Knowledge (*dānā'ī*), something we all search for from cradle to grave. We all want to increase our knowledge of the mysteries of the world, and we all venerate sages endowed with wisdom.

Thirdly, Beauty is our beloved. But beauty is both inward and outward, both for ourselves and for others. We are all pilgrims travelling on the road to the City of Beauty, so we must strive to instil every aspect of our lives with beauty: we must strive to speak beautifully, walk beautifully and move beautifully. We must endeavour to fill every aspect of our surroundings with beauty. We must strive hard to keep beautiful company and endeavour to have friends whose conversation bears witness to beauty.

Fourthly, we all seek Goodness, which is a quality originating from within the heart that enables us to discern good from evil, beauty from ugliness, and allows us to approach the former and avoid the latter . . . If asked what we hope to attain by this pursuit of Goodness, our reply is: 'In our hearts we have the conviction that good must result from good, and that the consequences of bad deeds are bad. If we travel towards Beauty, Knowledge and Goodness, we will certainly not end up encountering ugliness, ignorance, evil and corruption.'

If, again, we are asked 'What place do religion and faith have in this quest for perfection?' we would reply: 'Love for Beauty, Knowledge and Goodness is one and the same as love for God and also identical with love of all high principles and ideals.'[70]

Selection 3 (Q. 33:59): Woman and the veil of fire

An aside about the *ḥijāb*

A Charm invests a face
Imperfectly beheld –
The Lady dare not lift her Veil
For fear it be dispelled

But peers beyond her mesh –
And wishes – and denies –
Lest Interview – annul a want
That Image – satisfies.
– Emily Dickinson[71]

It is interesting that in his commentary on *Sūrat al-Aḥzāb* (Q. 33), out of all the references in this important chapter to the veil and women, Ghomshei did not specifically select the so-called *ḥijāb* verses (Q. 33:32–3) therein for commentary. The latter had mandated the wives of the Prophet to *make not a dazzling display, like that of the former Times of Ignorance* and to *stay quietly in your houses.* Nor does he refer to Q. 33:53, in which the believers are commanded never to request anything from the Prophet's wives except from *before a screen* (*min warāʾ ḥijāb*),[72] a verse which, when misinterpreted decades later by Muslim scholars as being relevant to *all* believing Muslim females, effectively led to the exclusion of women from public life throughout most of the Muslim world for centuries.[73] As Barbara Stowasser and Fatima Mernissi point out, this *ḥijāb* imposed on the Prophet's wives was primarily considered a confirmation of their elite status on the one hand, and on the other, served as a protective device against the sexualisation of attacks on the Prophet[74] by his enemies.[75]

Instead Ghomshei chose to comment on the 'Mantle Verse' (Q. 33:59) that decreed a general 'clothing law' for Muslim women to observe outside their houses. 'This piece of legislation differed from the *hijab* of 33:53 in two ways,' writes Barbara Stowasser: 'Firstly, it concerned individual female appearance when outside of the home, not seclusion within it; and secondly, it applied to all Muslim women, not just the Prophet's wives.'[76]

It is worth stressing here that nowhere in the Qur'an is the *ḥijāb qua* veil – that is, in any of the forms promulgated by conservatives in many Muslim countries today – ever mentioned in the Muslim holy book, and particularly, in none of these passages in this sura 'is there any specific mention of veiling the face, only of a more general covering'.[77] In fact, the only thing clear about the amorphous term *ḥijāb* is that it refers to some sort of barrier or curtain,[78] broadly indicating 'the notion of concealing garments that women wear outside their homes in keeping with an Islamic ethic of modesty'.[79] During the time of the Prophet, neither segregation of the sexes nor veiling of women existed, so the parochial, chauvinistic view that all Muslim women have been forever mandated by the Qur'an to wear a headscarf or veil themselves outside their homes is not only historically inaccurate but Qur'anically unjustified.[80]

This debatable doctrine, which is the result of a historically situated interpretation by a patriarchal juridical class, is not based on the insights of the revelation but is the product of the prejudices of their medieval education which led them to interpret the universe in terms of the Arabian tribal mores in the provincial circle with which they happened to be familiar.[81] Given the complete lack of textual evidence for any edict dictating that women must wear the headscarf or veil in the Qur'an,[82] many progressive Muslim scholars today no longer consider wearing it religiously obligatory at all.[83]

After the expansion of Islam beyond the borders of Arabia, we know practically nothing about the precise stages of the historical development of the female *ḥijāb*.[84] From its inception, the term was polyvalent and possessed multiple meanings. There was never any general consensus by the Muslim *'ulamā'* on exactly what the *ḥijāb* actually was or was not, nor was there any precise definition of which parts of the female body it was supposed to cover or not; each juridical school (*madhhab*) concocted their own interpretation of the scope of the veil. During the time of the Prophet – and specifically during the year 5/626 when this verse was revealed – 'it is certain that this custom [of veiling, referring to Q. 33:59] was very little observed in Medina'.[85]

Having myself witnessed a few years ago Muslim women sitting decked out in sensationally coloured African headscarves, yet topless from the waist up, counting their prayer beads on the front steps of the central mosque of Porto Novo, Benin, Ghomshei's observation that different societies have interpreted the meaning of the *ḥijāb* differently according to place and circumstance makes but common sense in the contemporary world.[86] His interpretation of Q. 33:59 was penned in a land where the wearing of the *ḥijāb* has been forcibly imposed on females throughout all public spaces. According to laws enacted since 1979 by the new religious elite of Iran, any woman whose clothing is deemed insufficiently conservative can be legally stopped in the street by the morality police (*kumita*) and carted off to prison.[87] Ghomshei's commentary on this verse was evidently penned in protest against this absolutist, puritanical ethic, and shatters a number of key political and social taboos.

Among other things, by focusing on the psycho-spiritual significance of the *ḥijāb* in the broader philosophical context of male–female relations, Ghomshei bypasses and thus removes the stigma of the *maḥram/nāmaḥram* paradigm by which the sexes are usually strictly segregated from each other in Iran today.[88] In this fashion, the author's exegesis of the 'Mantle Verse' effectively ignores the conservative sharia-centric discourse that has been traditionally used by mullahs the Muslim world over, from Mecca to Samarqand and Tehran to Kuala Lumpur, to advocate a strict sexual apartheid and maintain segregation of the sexes.

In the Company of the Qur'an *by Muḥyī al-Dīn Ilāhī Ghomshei*

Ghomshei's interpretation of Q. 33:59

> *O Prophet! Tell thy wives and daughters, and the believing women, that they should cast their outer garments over their persons (when abroad): that is most convenient, that they should be known (as such) and not molested. And Allah is Oft-Forgiving, Most Merciful.* (Q. 33:59)

How marvellous is this heaven-sent attire [Q. 7:26] and raiment that has been bequeathed by God as a boon to humankind, who has placed within it countless graces and subtleties, from which women in particular obtain such complete benefit! In the first place, it protects their dignity and gives them security so that they do not become the targets of unwelcome sexual advances and molestation from those who are not their intimate associates, that is to say, from those who have forsaken the inner sanctum of humanity. In this manner, God wishes women to appear in society so that their outer appearance may testify both to their captivating and endearing qualities (*maḥbūbiyāt*) and to their purity and chastity (*pākdāmanī*), lest anyone be incited to trespass into their private space and molest them.

However, it is possible for different societies in different days and ages to apply in different ways the precise bounds and laws required to obtain this end (*ḥudūd-i iḥrāz īn maqsūd*). Understanding these (boundaries and limits) is up to the true scholars (*dānishmandān-i ḥaqīqī*) and speculative thinkers of Islam (*ṣāḥib-naẓarān-i islāmī*) who exert themselves to pass independent judgement (*ijtihād*) so as to make suggestions about how women and girls, in various times, places and circumstances, on the basis of the universal divine message (*payām-i kullī-yi āyāt-i ilāhī*), may choose the most appropriate way to protect themselves from becoming the target of molestation.

In the *Mathnawī*, Mawlānā strikes the following beautiful simile (*tamthīl*) in order to better illustrate the circumstances of the male–female relationship. His simile is that [firstly] if woman may be compared to a fire capable of warming up the being of man, and [secondly] if lust (*shahwat*) can be compared to water – which, subject to certain conditions, can either extinguish or heat up that fire – then [thirdly] it must be said that if the fire and water confront each other without any veil intervening between them, the water of lust will simply extinguish the fire without receiving any warmth from it. However, if a pot or kettle is suspended between the [female] fire and the [lusty] water, the fire will effectively warm the water up and the water will not extinguish the fire. In Rūmī's words:

The water vanquishes the fire by shock,
  but fire will make it boil up in the pot.
And when a cauldron comes between the two,
  it makes the water vanish in thin air.[89]

Therefore, her veil and garments perform two basic services for woman. One is to render her inviolable to molestation from persons who are not her intimate associates, that is, from those who are strangers to the sanctum of love (*ḥarīm-i maḥabbat*). Chilly weather, scorching sunrays, dust storms, foggy mists and smog are likewise inimical to the flesh, so everybody – and especially women who are closer than men to the realm of all that is gentle and subtle (*'ālam-i laṭāfat*) – are advised to cover themselves up when confronted with such inclement weather conditions. Besides, a woman's allure and appeal (*maḥbūbiyat-i zan*) loses some of its lustre and mystique and becomes less attractive through overexposure and excessive familiarity. Therefore, for women, certain limitations must be kept intact so that both these special distinctions may be accorded them. In the words of Sa'dī:

You expose yourself to view, but then
You draw back and turn away: you fan
My own flames yet keep your sales hot.[90]

The term 'thin air' (*hawā'*) in Rūmī's verse above also connotes 'passionate love' (*'ishq*). The gist of the idea [in these verses] is that due to the presence of that veil, the [= female] fire [when placed under the pot of water = male lust] generates 'passionate love' which also connotes 'thin air' (*hawā'*). Therefore [to extend and expound the simile], if men and women are totally segregated from one another – water set apart to one side and fire set apart on the other – no warmth or love between the two sexes will ever be generated. On the other hand, if the sexes sit beside one another without any veil and limitation between them imposed at all, again, neither passionate love nor warm steam will be generated.

However, if men and women are permitted to freely frequent each other's company, to associate and sit next to each other in various social settings such as universities, art exhibitions, musical concerts and theatres, with the veil of the woman's alluring fascination, chastity and ethical obligations (*maḥbūbiyyat wa pākdāmanī wa taʿahhud-i akhlāqī*) between them preserved, both of the sexes then will be able to take maximum advantage of the grace of each other's being. Becoming acquainted with one another in such secure and unproblematic public spaces is particularly advantageous for the purpose of selecting a spouse, and will be effective in replacing the old-fashioned method of acquaintance between the sexes, which is parental matchmaking.[91]

Conclusion

In the three selections offered above from Ghomshei's *In the Company of the Qur'an*, the freshness and beauty of his interpretations of the Qur'an demonstrate how and why a major thinker's engagement with *studia humanitatis* and *studia adabiyya* of Muslim spirituality has succeeded in making Islam's ancient scripture accessible, attractive and comprehensible to a wide readership in contemporary Iran. Ghomshei's mystical commentary is clearly intended to provide general spiritual guidance (*irshād*)[92] to modern Iranians from all walks of life.

Ghomshei's frequent use of Persian poetry for exegetical purposes and constant citation of poetic texts full of metaphors of profane love are all part of a Sufi interpretative tradition that can be traced back to such mystical exegetes as Khwāja ʿAbd Allāh Anṣārī (d. 481/1089) and his disciple Rashīd al-Dīn Maybudī (d. 520/1126) a millennium ago.[93] However, he does not limit himself to Perso-Islamic poets and writers, and one finds throughout his commentary constant reference to the greats of classical and modern Western literature, such as

Shakespeare, Victor Hugo, Walt Whitman, Emily Dickinson, Emerson and Dostoyevsky, who illuminate his commentary.

His 'conversation' or 'keeping company' (*suḥbat*) with the Islamic scripture conveys to the reader many hidden spiritual meanings apprehended both through his own interior unveiling (*kashf*)[94] and the oral transmission of esoteric wisdom that he received from the tradition of mystical exegesis (*tafsīr-i ʿirfānī*) bequeathed him by his father, one of the major exegetes of the Qur'an in twentieth-century Iran (see above). In this respect, the key original observations broached by the author in each of the selections translated above merit highlighting here.

In the first passage, Ghomshei's commentary on Q. 16:96, it is clear that the Islamic doctrine of Platonic Forms has been used by him to create a cosmopolitan theory of religion that is simultaneously modern and traditional, at once grounded in classical Islamic theology and of universal relevance.

In the second passage, his interpretation of Q. 51:21, notwithstanding the metaphysical abstruseness of the subject, Ghomshei utilises common language expressions and a simple vocabulary, making his commentary easily graspable by anybody with even a cursory acquaintance with the vocabulary of Sufi mysticism. The Platonic lexicon of the Goodness, Beauty and Knowledge also allows him to escape from the orthodox Sunni position, maintained by the likes of Abū Ḥāmid al-Ghazālī (d. 505/1111), that nothing is good for any other reason than God ordained it so. On the contrary, he maintains, to love the Platonic Ideas is not only to love God, but to become a Muslim in the deepest sense of the word. At the same time, anyone who is not a Muslim, denominationally speaking, yet truly loves these Ideas and makes them the key principles of his life effectively becomes, for all practical purposes, an 'honorary Muslim'. The knowledge obtained from contemplative introspection is primary and self-sufficient, present in all those who live morally, act reasonably and intuit correctly, regardless of their exoteric religious affiliation. According to this Sufi epistemology of private revelation, the specifically 'Islamic' form of revelation is understood to be something supplementary to humankind's universal ecumenical consciousness.[95]

By adjudicating in the third passage, his interpretation of Q. 33:59, that different societies must be free to interpret and different scholars allowed the liberty to exercise *ijtihād* about the precise meaning and scope of the veil according to the exigencies of time, place and circumstance, Ghomshei effectively establishes the religious relativity – and hence ultimate spiritual insignificance – of the juridical level of gender discourse, as his citation of those key verses from Rūmī's *Mathnawī*, known as the 'Qur'an in Persian', on male–female sexual relations transmutes that nomocentric juridical discourse into an erotocentric poetic discourse. Apropos of arguing why the mingling of the sexes is socially and spiritually necessary to modern-day society, Ghomshei transforms and effectively sublimates a religious 'tradition of misogyny'[96] based on sex prejudice and the veiling of women into a faith based on unveiling the divine through vision of woman as an epiphany of the Eternal Feminine.

In sum, throughout *In the Company of the Qur'an*, the author shows himself to be one of those rare scholars who is thoroughly grounded in the Islamic tradition yet also able to engage in modernity in a sophisticated, thoughtful and extremely original way.[97]

NOTES

1 His surname is spelled Qumsha'ī in Persian but Ghomshei in his English writings, which is the spelling adopted here.

2 More or less totally ignored by literary historians to date, it was only recently published by a mainstream publisher in a popular edition: *Dīwān-i Ḥakīm Mahdī Ilāhī Qumsha'ī*, edited with an introduction by Ḥusayn Ilāhī Qumsha'ī (Tehran, 1377 Sh./1998). The *Dīwān* features 566 lyric poems (ghazals), 74 odes (*qaṣīdas*), 75 formulaic poems (*rubā'iyyāt*), as well as quite a few poems in other forms, such as those with rhyming couplets (*mathnawī*), four-line stanzaic poems (*murabba'*), etc. Ḥakīm Qumsha'ī authored a number of philosophical works, the best known of which are his *Ḥikmat-i ilāhī-yi khāṣṣ wa 'āmm*, ed. Hurmuz Būshahrpūr (Tehran, 1379 Sh./2000–2001) and a translation and commentary on the *Fuṣūṣ al-ḥikam* of Abū Naṣr Muḥammad al-Fārābī. He also composed a translation of the Qur'an into Persian, with marginal notes, called *Tarjuma-yi Qur'ān-i karīm* (Qum, 1390 Sh./2011). It is currently the most popularly referred to translation used by contemporary Persian speakers. Due to its comprehensive coverage of previous commentaries, it has been dubbed the 'epitome of exegeses' (*khulāṣat al-tafāsīr*).

However, it is probably worth noting that this translation has been recently prohibited by the Ministry of Culture and Islamic Guidance, according to this report: http://www.hamshahrionline.ir/details/321028/Thoughts/religion.

3 See Muḥammad Riḍā Nāṣirī, Adīb Nayshābūrī, Shaykh Muḥammad Taqī, Farzand-i Mīrzā Asadullāh', in idem, ed., *Athar-āfarīnān: Zindīgīnāma-yi nāmāwarān farhang-i Īrān* (Tehran, 1384 Sh./2005), vol. I, pp. 222–3.

4 See Muḥammad Riḍā Naṣīrī, 'Āqā Buzurg Ḥakīm, Āqā Mīrzā 'Askarī Shahīdī Mashhadī', in *Athar-āfarīnān*, vol. I, p. 45.

5 Ilāhī Qumsha'ī, *Dīwān-i Ḥakīm Mahdī Ilāhī Qumsha'ī*, introduction, pp. 9–11.

6 See Muḥammad Riḍā Naṣīrī, 'Qumsha'ī-yi Iṣfahānī, Muḥammad Riḍā Farzand-i Abū'l-Qāsim', in *Athar-āfarīnān*, vol. IV, p. 366.

7 See Ilāhī Qumsha'ī, *Dīwān-i Ḥakīm Mahdī Ilāhī Qumsha'ī*, introduction, p. 13.

8 Recalling his experience during the 1960s of attending Ḥakīm Qumsha'ī's private classes on Sufi texts in Tehran, Seyyed Hossein Nasr recounts: 'The reality of the oral tradition constitutes the reason why the line of transmission of traditional Islamic philosophy is nearly as important as the *silsila*s of the Sufis. In the latter case, the *baraka* [blessing] and initiatory power are transmitted which alone allow the soul to ascend to the higher levels of being, while in the former it is an oral teaching which is the necessary concomitant to the written text, a complement without which the text does not reveal all of its meaning save in exceptional cases'. See Seyyed Hossein Nasr, 'Oral Transmission and the Book in Islamic Education: The Spoken and the Written Word', *Journal of Islamic Studies* 3, no. 1 (1992), pp. 10–11.

9 The reference here is to the Persian Sufi orders such as the Ni'matullāhiyya or Dhahabiyya. The Shi'i oral tradition shares most of the ethical principles and mystical practices of Sufism. On the Iranian Sufi orders, see Leonard Lewisohn, 'An Introduction to the History of Modern Persian Sufism, Part I: The Ni'matullāhī Order. Persecution, Revival and Schism', *Bulletin of the School of Oriental and African Studies* 61, no. 3 (1998), pp. 437–64, and idem, 'An Introduction to the History of Modern Persian Sufism, Part II: A Socio-cultural Profile of Sufism, from the Dhahabī Revival to the Present Day', *Bulletin of the School of Oriental and African Studies* 62, no. 1 (1999), pp. 36–59.

10 Portions of the present biographical account are derived from my conversations with Ghomshei himself over the course of more than two decades. For further information on him, see his official website: http://www.drelahighomshei.com/e21.aspx.

11 Almost all the major and minor bookshops in Iran currently stock many of Ghomshei's audio cassettes and CDs, as well as videos of his popular public lectures.

12 Ḥusayn Muḥyī al-Dīn Ilāhī Qumsha'ī [Ghomshei], *Guzīda-yi Manṭiq al-ṭayr (Haft shahr-i 'ishq): Talkhīṣ, muqaddama wa sharḥ*, 2nd edn (Tehran, 1377 Sh./1998).

13 Idem, *365 rūz dar suḥbat-i Mawlānā* (Tehran, 1386 Sh./2007).

14 Idem, *Guzīda-yi Fīhi mā fīhi, Maqālāt-i Mawlānā: Talkhīṣ, muqaddama wa sharḥ* (Tehran, 1366 Sh./1987).

15 Idem, *365 rūz bā Sa'dī* (Tehran, 1381 Sh./2002).

16 Maḥmūd Shabistarī, *Gulshan-i rāz (bāgh-i dil)*, ed. Mahdī Ilāhī Qumsha'ī (Tehran, 1377 Sh./1998).

17 Ḥāfiẓ, *Dīwān-i Ḥāfiẓ: Muqaddama, taṣḥīḥ wa sharḥ*, ed. Mahdī Ilāhī Qumsha'ī (Tehran, 1382 Sh./2003).
18 Ḥusayn Muḥyī al-Dīn Ilāhī Qumsha'ī [Ghomshei], *Dar qalamraw-i zarrīn: 365 rūz bā adabiyāt-i inglīsī* (Tehran, 1386 Sh./2007).
19 Idem, *365 rūz dar ṣuḥbat-i shā'irān-i pārsīgū* (Tehran, 1392 Sh./2013).
20 Idem, *Maqālāt*, 1st edn (Tehran, 1376 Sh./1997). In a personal communication (in 2014) he told me that this work currently appears in ten editions and has sold over 20,000 copies.
21 Idem, *Barrasī-yi tarjuma shuda mutun-i islāmī* (Tehran, 1390 Sh./2011–12).
22 For details on this and other publications, see http://www.drelahighomshei.com/e21.aspx.
23 Ḥusayn Muḥyī al-Dīn Ilāhī Qumsha'ī [Ghomshei] and Aḥmad Bihishtī Shīrāzī, eds, *Kīmiyā: Daftarī dar adabiyāt wa hunar wa 'irfān* (Tehran, 1377–82 Sh./1998–2003), 5 volumes. Each volume varied between 200 and 600 pages.
24 Idem, *Dar suḥbat-i Qur'ān: 365 rūz bā Qur'ān* (Tehran, 1390 Sh./2011).
25 A word on his popularity is in order here. There are some in the academic community, both inside and outside Iran, who make the assumption that artistic meaning belongs only to a privileged elite, and that knowledge should be privatised and confined to just one class of society. Largely fuelled by envy, they deride Ghomshei's significance because he caters to the masses as a literary critic, anthologist, orator, writer, theologian and thinker. Very few scholars in the field of either Persian literature or Islamic studies in Iran have written bestsellers. Certainly none of them enjoy the immense respect and popular recognition from both the elite and the general masses that he does. His popularity spans the entire breadth of Iranian society: he is equally popular among taxi drivers, janitors, café waiters, housewives and gardeners as he is among wealthy international businessmen, college professors, secular intellectuals, pious mullahs, writers, classical musicians and avant-garde artists. I observed how ubiquitous his popularity throughout Iran actually was during the summer of 2005 when I accompanied him as a guest on a lecture tour to several cities in Iran. Outside the famous Qur'an Gate of Shiraz, a highway patrol officer pulled our car over for a major offence (one female in the car had exposed too much of her hair beneath her headscarf!). However, seeing Ghomshei in the passenger seat, the officer immediately smiled and professed himself to be an ardent fan of his lectures before waving us on without another word. Taking a promenade around Maydān-i Shāh in Isfahan (the largest and most beautiful public square in Iran), I saw him mobbed by hundreds of school children who were eager to take a photograph with him or get his autograph, which he dutifully obliged. At the shops in Maydān – where the vendors are notorious for their rapaciousness – the Isfahani shopkeepers miraculously refused to take payment from him. 'We are,' they professed, 'your devoted admirers' (*irādatmand-i shumā hastīm*). On an Iran Air flight from Tehran to Tabriz, a stewardess made her way up the aisle, single plastic teacup and saucer teetering in her hand, towards Ghomshei's seat, where she sat down beside him and plied him with questions on spiritual and metaphysical matters for the next hour until we landed. In Tabriz, after attending a banquet in his honour hosted by the governor of the Province of Azerbaijan, we drove two hours north to the remote village of Shabistar in a cavalcade led by the governor, where both of us had been invited by the town's mayor to give lectures

on the mystical poem *Gulshan-i rāz* written by the Sufi poet Shabistarī. The streets leading to the venue were filled with schoolgirls holding bouquets of white flowers to present to him. Our lectures were delivered in the town hall auditorium beside the poet's refurbished mausoleum; though there was seating for five hundred, there were over a thousand souls present, and more chairs were placed on the high street outside the hall so the public could hear our discourse over loudspeakers. Following his lecture, Ghomshei was mobbed for his autograph and not allowed to exit until he had signed the programme booklet of every member of the audience. In Nishapur, we were invited to dine with a prominent businessman in a local garden outside the city; on arriving there, we found some five hundred cars parked outside its gates; unbeknownst to him, Ghomshei had been billed as the guest speaker for an audience of a thousand people to celebrate Iran's 'National Day of Industry'. Clearly, Ghomshei's learned yet highly vernacular approach to Persian culture and literature fulfils a social and spiritual need among the populace. In Iran, a devotee's relationship with God is largely expressed through poetical discourse as well as myths and stories. Ghomshei's ecumenical ability to relate Muslim religious experiences and Sufi mystical expressions within a wide social context, his profound understanding of both the masters of the Persian poetic canon (in particular, Firdawsī, Niẓāmī, Rūmī, Sa'dī, Ḥāfiẓ, Jāmī, etc.) and the learned of the mystical philosophical tradition (Ibn 'Arabī, Naṣīr al-Dīn Ṭūsī, Mullā Ṣadrā, etc.), and his countering of the dogmatic theological Shi'ism of the turbaned clerical elite of Iran with his own sophisticated cosmopolitan religious pluralism are key reasons for his widespread popularity.

26 Being a fine calligrapher as well, these autographs by Ghomshei are collected and treasured as works of art.

27 On the tradition of Biblical exegesis through English poetry, see Robert Atwan and Laurance Wieder, eds, *Chapters into Verse: Poetry in English Inspired by the Bible. Vol. I: Genesis to Malachi*; *Vol. II: Gospels to Revelation* (Oxford, 1993). A similar anthology of Persian verse devoted to poetic exegesis of the Qur'an might easily run into many volumes.

28 See Alice Hunsberger, ed., *Pearls of Persia: The Philosophical Poetry of Nāṣir-i Khusraw* (London, 2012), pp. xvii–xxi.

29 See, for instance, the rock group Nahal-e Heyat and Mike Ghazavi's performance of Ḥāfiẓ's lyrics at https://www.youtube.com/watch?v=ZOBl2zO67uM; Mohsen Namjoo's modernist folk-rock rendition ('Zadeh Hafez') of a Ḥāfiẓ ghazal: https://www.youtube.com/watch?v=cvI9ZRVh5XA. See also Laudan Nooshin's discussion of Iranian underground music (*rock-i zīr-zamīnī*) in her 'Underground, Overground: Rock Music and Youth Discourses in Iran', *Iranian Studies* 38, no. 3 (2005), p. 478.

30 Ilāhī Ghomshei, *Dar suḥbat-i Qur'ān*. The exordium is from pp. xxvi–xxxii; the entire introduction is from pp. xxvi–xc.

31 Ibid., pp. xxxii–xxxix.

32 All translations of the Qur'an in this chapter are taken from Yusuf Ali.

33 Ilāhī Ghomshei, *Dar suḥbat-i Qur'ān*, p. xxxv.

34 On which, see Bāqir Ṣadr-niyā, ed., *Farhang-i mā'thūrāt-i mutūn-i 'irfānī (mushtamal ba aḥādīth, aqwāl wa amthāl-i mutūn-i 'irfānī-yi fārsī)* (Tehran, 1380 Sh./2001), p. 449.

35 Ilāhī Ghomshei, *Dar suḥbat-i Qur'ān*, p. xxxvii.

36 Ibid., introduction, p. xxxviii.
37 Ibid. From Jāmī's *Lawā'iḥ*, in A'lākhān Afṣaḥzād, Muḥammad Jān 'Umarūf and Abū Bakr Ẓuhūr al-Dīn, eds, *Bahāristān wa rasā'il-i Jāmī* (Tehran, 1379 Sh./ 2000), p. 462. My translation.
38 Richard Maurice Burke, *Cosmic Consciousness: A Study in the Evolution of the Human Mind* (Secaucus, NJ, 1973).
39 *Gulshan-i rāz* in Maḥmūd Shabistarī, *Majmū'a-i āthār-i Shaykh Maḥmūd Shabistarī*, ed. Ṣamad Muwaḥḥid (Tehran, 1365 Sh./1986), p. 67, vv. 8–9.
40 Ilāhī Ghomshei, *Dar suḥbat-i Qur'ān*, introduction, p. xlii.
41 Ibid., introduction, p. lxv.
42 Ibid., pp. lxvi–lxviii.
43 Ibid, p. lxxv.
44 Ibid.
45 Ibid., pp. lxxviii–lxxxvi.
46 Ibid., p. lxxxvii.
47 See Plato's *Symposium*, ed. M.C. Howatson and Frisbee C.C. Sheffield, tr. M.C. Howatson (Cambridge, 2008), 197b and 203c–212b.
48 See Plato's *Republic*, tr. Robin Waterfield (Oxford, 2008), V, 477a 3; X, 596a.
49 For the whole passage, see Naṣīr al-Dīn al-Ṭūsī, *Akhlāq-i Nāṣirī*, ed. Mujtabā Mīnuwī (Tehran, 1360 Sh./1981), pp. 101–6.
50 Ibid., p. 101.
51 Ibid., p. 102.
52 Ibid., pp. 104–5.
53 Ṭūsī, *Akhlāq-i Nāṣirī*, pp. 105–6.
54 Ibid., p. 106.
55 Although Ḥāfiẓ belongs to the fourteenth century, he remains a poetic and philosophic heir of the previous age.
56 Jalāl al-Dīn Rūmī, *The Mathnawí of Jalálu'ddín Rúmí*, tr. and ed. Reynold A. Nicholson (London, 1925–40), vol. I, 16 (my translation).
57 Sa'dī, *Kulliyāt-i Sa'dī*, ed. Muḥammad 'Alī Furūghī (Tehran, 1363 Sh./1984), *Gulīstān*, p. 31 (my translation).
58 Ḥāfiẓ, *Dīwān-i Khwāja Shams al-Dīn Muḥammad Ḥāfiẓ*, ed. Parvīz Nātil Khānlarī (Tehran, 1359 Sh./1980), ghazal 49, line 5 (my translation).
59 Ilāhī Ghomshei, *Dar suḥbat-i Qur'ān*, pp. 378–9. The quote in this last line is from Rūmī's *Fīhi mā fīhi*.
60 Robert McKim, 'Berkeley, George', *Encyclopedia of Philosophy*, 2nd edn, ed. Donald Borchert (New York, 2006), vol. I, pp. 573–88, esp. p. 580.
61 On which, see Frithjof Schuon, *The Eye of the Heart: Metaphysics, Cosmology, Spiritual Life* (Bloomington, IN, 1997), pp. 3–13.
62 See Plato, *Phaedo*, 79c 6–8, cited by Laura Westra, 'Self-Knowing in Plato, Plotinus and Avicenna', in Parviz Morewedge, ed., *Neoplatonism and Islamic Thought* (Albany, NY, 1992), p. 91.
63 Westra, 'Self-Knowing in Plato, Plotinus and Avicenna', p. 95.
64 See Plato, *Phaedo*, 115c, cited in ibid., p. 90.
65 Ghomshei's views here are quite close to Plotinus's; see Westra, 'Self-Knowing in Plato, Plotinus and Avicenna', pp. 98–102.
66 Many of the ideas in this passage are present in Ibn 'Arabī's *Futūḥāt* as well. See William C. Chittick's discussion of chapter 267 (The Soul) of the *Futūḥāt* in

The Self-Disclosure of God: Principles of Ibn 'Arabī's Cosmology (Albany, NY, 1992), 'Self and Soul', pp. 269–74.

67 Muḥammad Lāhījī, *Mafātīḥ al-'ijāz fī sharḥ-i Gulshan-i rāz*, ed. Muḥammad Riḍā Barzgār Khāliqī and 'Iffat Karbāsī (Tehran, 1371 Sh./1992), v. 706, pp. 486–7.

68 Rūmī, *The Mathnawí of Jalálu'ddín Rúmí*, vol. IV, pp. 1358–65 (my translation).

69 *Gulshan-i rāz* in Shabistarī, *Majmū'a-i āthār-i Shaykh Maḥmūd Shabistarī*, v. 704. Translation by Robert Darr, *The Garden of Mystery (Gulshan-i raz)* (Sausalito, CA, 1998), p. 83.

70 Ilāhī Ghomshei, *Dar suḥbat-i Qur'ān*, p. 713. Italics mine.

71 Emily Dickinson, *The Complete Poems of Emily Dickinson*, ed. Thomas Johnson (Toronto, 1961), no. 421.

72 For an interpretation of early Muslim exegetes' view of these verses, see Barbara Freyer Stowasser, *Women in the Qur'an: Traditions, and Interpretations* (Oxford, 1994), pp. 90–91.

73 Wiebke Walther, *Women in Islam: From Medieval to Modern Times*, tr. C.S.V. Salt (Princeton, NJ, 1993), p. 71. Scholars such as Fatima Mernissi have argued that the veil aims to subjugate women and delegitimise their presence in society, effectively depriving them of full citizenship on every level: emotional–psychological, economical and political. See Fatima Mernissi, *Islam and Democracy: Fear of the Modern World*, tr. Mary Jo Lakeland (London, 1993), pp. 164–5. The same point is also made even more forcefully in her autobiography: *Dreams of Trespass: Tales of a Harem Girlhood* (New York, 1994).

74 Referring to Q. 24:11–26.

75 Stowasser, *Women in the Qur'an*, p. 91, citing Mernissi, *Beyond the Veil: Male-Female Dynamics in Muslim Society* (Cambridge, MA, 1975), pp. 85ff., 162ff. For a thorough account of the historical reasons and social conditions behind the revelation of Q. 33:53, see Fatima Mernissi, *The Veil and the Male Elite*, tr. Mary Jo Lakeland (New York, 1991), chapter 10: 'The *Hijab* Descends on Medina', pp. 180–88.

76 Stowasser, *Women in the Qur'an*, p. 91.

77 Walther, *Women in Islam*, p. 70.

78 For an in-depth analysis of the history of the term *ḥijāb* and its various meanings throughout history, see Barbara Freyer Stowasser, 'The *Hijab:* How a Curtain Became an Institution and a Cultural Symbol', in Asma Afsaruddin and A.H. Mathias Zahniser, eds, *Humanism, Culture, and Language in the Near East: Studies in Honor of Georg Krotkoff* (Winona Lake, IN, 1997), pp. 87–104; and Mernissi, *The Veil and the Male Elite*, chapter 5: 'The *Hijab*, the Veil', pp. 85–101.

79 Sa'diyya Shaikh, 'Transforming Feminisms: Islam, Women, and Gender Justice', in Omid Safi, ed., *Progressive Muslims on Justice, Gender and Pluralism* (Oxford, 2003), p. 152.

80 'The Qur'an advocates neither the veil nor segregation of the sexes: rather it insists on sexual modesty. It is also certain on historical grounds that there was no veil in the Prophet's time, nor was there any segregation of the sexes in the sense that Muslim societies later developed it. In fact, the Qur'anic statements on modesty imply that neither veil nor segregation of the sexes existed. If there

had been segregation of the sexes, there would have been no point in asking the sexes to behave with modesty.' Fazlur Rahman, 'Status of Women in the Qur'an', in Guity Nashat, ed., *Women and Revolution in Iran* (Boulder, CO, 1983), p. 40.

81 See Mernissi, *The Veil and the Male Elite*, pp. 85–101, 185–95.

82 'Contrary to widely held opinion, veiling is nowhere enjoined in the Qur'an, which has just two passages that discuss women's dress. One calls on Muslim women to draw their cloaks (*jalaliyah*) tightly about them when they go abroad so that they may be recognised and not annoyed; the other tells believing women to cover their bosoms and hide their ornaments (*zinah*). The latter was later often interpreted, usually on the basis of supposed traditions from the Prophet, to mean covering all but the hands, feet, and perhaps the face, though some interpreters said this too should be covered. This interpretation, which became widespread, is improbable; if the Qur'an had wanted this much covered, why would it have referred specifically to the bosom? . . . Also, the widespread interpretation of *zinah* to cover hair, neck, forearms, and so on is linguistically farfetched.' Nahid Yeganeh and Nikki R. Keddie, 'Sexuality and Shi'i Social Protest in Iran', in Juan R.I. Cole and Nikki R. Keddie, eds, *Shi'ism and Social Protest* (New Haven, 1986), p. 113.

83 The Lebanese female scholar Naẓīra Zayn al-Dīn wrote a number of books in the 1920s advocating the religious illegitimacy of the *ḥijāb*. See Nazira Zain-ed-Din, 'Unveiling and Veiling: On the Liberation of the Woman and Social Renewal in the Islamic World', in Margot Badran and Miriam Cooke, eds, *Opening the Gates: A Century of Arab Feminist Writing* (Bloomington, IN, 1990), pp. 270–76. She was followed by the Egyptian intellectual Muḥammad Aḥmad Khalafullāh, who maintained that the Qur'an never prescribed a particular Islamic dress code and argued that the dress norms described in Q. 33:59 were of time-specific, not absolute, validity because the verse was revealed to reform public conduct in the early Medinan community. Muḥammad Aḥmad Khalafullāh, *Dirāsat fi'l-nuẓūm wa'l-tashrī'āt al-islāmiyya* (Cairo, 1977), pp. 189–99, cited in Stowasser, 'The *Hijab*', p. 103. For more recent debates on this issue, see Amina Wadud, *Inside the Gender Jihad: Women's Reform in Islam* (Oxford, 2006), chapter 7, pp. 217–53; and Bouthaina Shaaban, 'The Muted Voices of Women Interpreters', in Mahnaz Afkhami, ed., *Faith and Freedom: Women's Human Rights in the Muslim World* (Syracuse, NY, 1995), pp. 68–73.

84 Stowasser, *Women in the Qur'an*, p. 93.

85 J. Chelhod, "Ḥidjāb', *EI*[2], vol. III, p. 359.

86 To my Beninese friends who were with me (which included the mosque's imam), the only surprising thing after encountering a topless woman on the step of the mosque was when I averted my gaze in shock.

87 For lengthy discussions of the persecution and harassment of women by Iran's morality police, see Pardis Mahdavi, *Passionate Uprisings: Iran's Sexual Revolution* (Stanford, CA, 2009), index, s.v. 'morality police'.

88 'Islamic law conceives of gender relationships within the two categories of lawful, *maḥram*, and unlawful, *nāmaḥram*. Men and women must not associate freely with each other unless their relationship is prescribed either by blood or marriage. A *maḥram* relationship is formed either through blood or

marriage . . . Any gender relationships outside these two *maḥram* categories are unlawful, *nāmaḥram*: women have to veil and rules of segregation apply.' Shahla Haeri, *Law of Desire: Temporary Marriage in Shi'i Iran* (Syracuse, NY, 1989), p. 76.

89 Jalāl al-Dīn Rūmī, *Rumi: Spiritual Verses, The First Book of the Masnavi-ye ma'navi*, tr. Alan Williams (London, 2006), p. 228.

90 Sa'dī, *Kulliyāt-i Sa'dī*, p. 644 (my translation).

91 Ghomshei, *Dar suḥbat-i Qur'ān*, pp. 605–6.

92 See Annabel Keeler, *Sufi Hermeneutics: The Qur'an Commentary of Rashīd al-Dīn Maybudī* (Oxford, 2006), pp. 74–9 (section titled 'Mystical Commentary as *irshād*').

93 Ibid., p. 94. Maybudī authored the Sufi Qur'an commentary in Persian: *Kashf al-asrār wa 'uddat al-abrār*, ed. 'Alī Aṣghar Ḥikmat (Tehran, 1952–60).

94 On the role played by *kashf* (mystical unveiling) in traditional Sufi interpretations of the Qur'an, see Nicholas Heer, 'Abū Ḥamīd al-Ghazālī's Esoteric Exegesis of the Koran', in Leonard Lewisohn, ed., *The Heritage of Sufism, Vol. 1: Classical Persian Sufism from its Origins to Rumi* (Oxford, 1999), pp. 246–50 ('The Science of Disclosure'); Keeler, *Sufi Hermeneutics*, pp. 48–9.

95 For a comprehensive discussion of the various theological positions historically held by different schools on this debate in Islam, see Kevin A. Reinhart, *Before Revelation: The Boundaries of Muslim Moral Thought* (Albany, NY, 1995), pp. 177–84.

96 This phrase pays homage to Mernissi's two brilliant chapters (3 and 4) entitled 'A Tradition of Misogyny [1 and 2]', *The Veil and the Male Elite*, pp. 49–84.

97 For similar approaches, see Kecia Ali, *Sexual Ethics and Islam: Feminist Reflections on Qur'an, Hadith, and Jurisprudence* (Oxford, 2006).

SECTION III

The Arts, Material Culture and Everyday Life

12

A Contemporary Illustrated Qur'an: Zenderoudi's Illustrations of Grosjean's Translation (1972)

ALICE BOMBARDIER

A FRENCH VERSION of the Qur'an translated by the poet Jean Grosjean (d. 2006), with an introduction by Jacques Berque (d. 1995), a Professor at Collège de France, was published by Le Club du Livre in Paris in 1972 in a luxurious two-volume set.[1] In that same year, this Qur'an was elected by UNESCO as 'The Most Beautiful Book of the Year'.[2] This scarcely known but visually impressive Qur'an deserves to be rediscovered, as it represents a unique contribution to the Qur'anic illustrative tradition. Also for its connections with other trends in the history of Iranian art, popular religion and the visual aspect of the Book, the work deserves a primary place in the landscape of the contemporary reception of the Qur'an, and as such merits scholarly attention.

Closely studying this particular edition of the Qur'anic text, and especially its illustrations, remains a delicate issue. The French translation has obviously not the same sacredness as the original, but the invitation to illustrate it still represented a weighty assignment for an artist bred in a Muslim society. In this particular work, while drawing on various artistic skills he had developed throughout his career, the artist Charles-Hossein Zenderoudi[3] (b. 1937 in Tehran, now based in France) exhibits a pictorial style that evokes Sufi symbolism, the heritage of religious miniature painting and the tradition of Qur'anic illumination. The result is an outstanding illustrative contribution that is characterised by its hybridity.

This attempt by the artist to adapt sacred art to artistic modernity is particularly innovative in the context of Islamic art, and can be considered a rare initiative.[4] Through the lens of art history, a diachronic study of the visual ingredients and the original context that led to this Qur'an and its exceptional illustrations will be conducted. I will explore the various phases of Zenderoudi's career to better understand this contemporary Qur'an and its multi-faceted artistic dimension.

The Creative Trigger: Pilgrimage

Notwithstanding Zenderoudi's insistence not to be associated with any specific school or artistic trend, he has, time and again, been named among the leading figures of the Saqqākhāna trend.[5] His painting entitled *K+L+32+H+4*, *Mon père et moi* (My Father and I),[6] was deemed to be the originator of the Saqqākhāna trend by the Iranian art critic and journalist Karīm Imāmī (d. 2005).[7] In Iran, the Saqqākhāna artistic trend was commonly considered, between the years 1957 and 1964, to be a form of Iranian-Shiʿi folk art, as it combined the contemporary language of art and talismanic and votive Shiʿi folk symbols with semi-figurative or abstract shapes. It is for this reason that the trend was named after the traditional water dispensers that are installed for public drinking in Iranian cities. The Persian word *saqqākhāna* indicates a niche with a water fountain, which is generally decorated with the portrait of an imam and other votive elements (candles, padlocks, pieces of rag, popular images, mirror shards and draperies) usually connected with the martyrdom of Ḥusayn (d. 60/680) in Karbala. From 1964 onwards, some of the Saqqākhāna artists, including Zenderoudi, mainly used handwritten letters as the primary matrix of their artworks.[8]

It appears that Zenderoudi is the only Saqqākhāna artist to have illustrated a Qur'an. No detailed critical analysis of these illustrations has been conducted so far, nor has the substantial relationship between sacred aesthetics and the Saqqākhāna artistic trend been examined. Indeed, these Qur'anic illustrations have not even been included in the corpus and definition of the Saqqākhāna artistic trend, although we notice at first glance when we open this 1972 edition of the Qur'an that the painter, in many of the thirty-two serigraphies, put aside the pure calligraphic style he had been practising since 1964 to partly return to some of the original visual features of Saqqākhāna's artistic phase. Before detailing the iconography and the style of these colourful illustrations, I will firstly examine the literary and intellectual context from which the Saqqākhāna trend originated, then the links it developed with holy places and the Qur'anic visual tradition.

The art history scholar Hamid Keshmirshekan highlighted in one of his founding articles that criticism of the West and nativist or nationalist debates spread among the Iranian elite since the 1940s and 1950s had an influence on the young Saqqākhāna artists that should not be underestimated. According to him, the common trait of these intellectual movements was 'to encourage Iranians to discover their identity, tradition and national roots'.[9] He related these underlying, prevailing discourses to the term *gharbzadigī* (often translated as 'Westoxication'), a concept first coined in the 1940s by Aḥmad Fardīd (d. 1994), a philosopher at Tehran University,[10] and reused in 1962 by Jalāl Āl-i Aḥmad (d. 1969) who published that year his famous essay bearing the same title.[11]

Also relevant to the ethos of the Saqqākhāna trend is Jalāl Āl-i Aḥmad's short story entitled 'Ziyārat' (The Pilgrimage), which was successfully re-edited several times.[12] The story itself is presumably autobiographical and focuses almost exclusively on the narrator's personal feelings in the midst of a solemn Shi'i experience: the pilgrimage to the shrine of the third imam, Ḥusayn, in Karbala in Iraq. Jalāl Āl-i Aḥmad provided detailed sketches of daily life on the road to this shrine: the preparations, the solicitude of his entourage, the stages of the journey by bus, the stops at little coffee shops, the meeting of humble people and the intense emotions in the sepulchre. He also wrote about the perspective of the festivities once he had returned from pilgrimage and musings on his own death. He livened up his narrative with the description of anthropological features, traditional customs and religious rites, as can be seen, for example, in his description of a rite performed in support of the Qur'an in order to ensure divine blessing: 'Three times I passed beneath the Qur'an, the water and the flour, and the third time I kissed the Qur'an and laid it against my forehead. My relatives, breathing out their prayers and holy phrases, filled the air with an odour of mosque and sanctuary.'[13] Jalāl Āl-i Aḥmad quoted, many times, religious or social invocations. He explains: 'I had to repeat to all [the passers-by] the formula: "I too need your prayers." Some of them who were among my closest friends would not let go of me till they had whispered the call to prayer in my ears or quoted appropriate texts from the Qur'an to escort me on my way.'[14] Jalāl Āl-i Aḥmad also reported the popular atmosphere around the shrine and the deference shown by people towards the mullahs' songs:

> Unlike the country folk who frequent these places and talk of nothing but their cows and their donkeys, or who has just died, or of the parties they have been having for mourning or merriment, these men were silent, listening intently to a mullah who had just arrived from a nearby village in anticipation of the coming Moharram mourning days. He was chanting in a clear fresh voice a *rowzeh* on 'The Departure of the Caravan of the Family of the Mantle'.[15]

The critic Buzurg ʿAlawī likened Jalāl Āl-i Aḥmad in this short story to a photographer who could convey the whole complex emotional world of ordinary people by the careful selection and arrangement of ordinary snapshots.[16] Many visual ingredients of the Saqqākhāna works are present in this story: constant 'prayers', breathed out by the narrator's relatives, recited in the sepulchre;[17] 'flat-woven rugs' or 'matting made of rice stalks' on which people sat;[18] home-made architecture from 'matting' and 'straw';[19] the 'bloodstained banner of those beloved sons of Fatemeh';[20] the 'sepulchre's cool silver grill-work';[21] the 'bit of cloth' tied to the doors and walls of the sepulchre;[22] the 'padlocks' attached to the edges of the sepulchre;[23] the 'sacred dust and earth of the sepulchre';[24] and the omnipresent 'figures and inscriptions'.[25]

The Qur'an, specifically, is often quoted in this short story, especially in a poignant paragraph on the 'Arabic words' that Jalāl Āl-i Aḥmad had noticed everywhere in the holy place; and 'everything', as the story says, 'was absorbed by their power'.[26] Echoing some

Saqqākhāna compositions striated with calligraphic ornaments, he wrote:

> Words from the Koran echoed and re-echoed beneath the lofty domes. Those Arabic words poured out like rain and charged the whole place with holiness. On doors and walls, on the friezes, on the glasswork of the ceiling which reflected in countless broken fragments the images of that vast crowd, on the front and backs of Holy Books, on the prayer books in men's hands, on the threshold of the sepulchre and all around it, on the great silver padlocks of the Shrine – everywhere those Arabic words were inscribed in thousands of designs and figures and scrolls, on wood and tile, on brick, on silver, on gold: everything was absorbed by their power.[27]

Religion never ceased to play an important role in Jalāl Āl-i Aḥmad's imagination. Zenderoudi was immersed in this literary and intellectual context. In the late 1950s, the young Zenderoudi studied in a newly founded secondary school in Tehran specifically dedicated to the rediscovery of ancient and traditional Persian artistic practices, the Boys' Secondary Art School of the Country (Hunaristān-i Hunar-hā-yi Zībā-yi Kishwar).[28] As soon as he began to study, he initiated the creation of a huge linocut printed on linen entitled *Who is this Hossein the World is Crazy About?*[29] This work devoted to the martyrdom of Ḥusayn in Karbala shows how early Zenderoudi tapped into the older tradition of art inspired by the events of Karbala. This new inspiration had also been conveyed by Zenderoudi's visits to places of pilgrimage.

Places of pilgrimage were perhaps not sufficiently emphasised as a major source of inspiration for some Saqqākhāna artists, although they were an artistic trigger for leading artists such as Zenderoudi and the sculptor Parwīz Tanāwulī (Parviz Tanavoli) (b. 1937). They both drew inspiration in the late 1950s from personal journeys with an initiatory value. As reported by Imāmī in the *Saqqākhāna Exhibition Catalogue* of 1977, they followed the same way of 'returning to the self' (according to the terminology of the Iranian revolutionary and social thinker ʿAlī Sharīʿatī [d. 1977]) by visiting the sepulchre of Shāh ʿAbd al-ʿAẓīm in the city of Rayy in the late 1950s.[30] They were captivated by religious posters on the surrounding stalls, ancient seals or talismanic images, so they brought these objects to their workshops. Tanāwulī related that in 1961, during the months following Zenderoudi's first exhibition, which was held at Kabūd Gallery (a workshop and a gallery managed by him), the two artists purchased a new stock of religious images and prayer cards. Following the pilgrimage to the source of popular faith, Zenderoudi had drawn a draft stemming from these religious images on wrapping paper. Surrounded by calligraphic letters, this draft represented the holy pattern of the hand, meaning both the *panja-yi panj-tan*, the hand of Ḥazrat Fāṭima symbolising through the five fingers the *ahl al-kisā'* (the Prophet, his daughter Fāṭima, her husband ʿAlī, and their sons Ḥasan and Ḥusayn), and the hand of ʿAbbās (another son of Fāṭima and ʿAlī), which typically appears in processions during the sacred month of Muḥarram.[31]

During these visits to shrines, Zenderoudi noticed (and collected) the same accessories and testimonies of popular religiosity as Jalāl Āl-i Aḥmad's narrator. Moreover, they both experienced a 'shift' by being spectators of the intense faith filling the places of pilgrimage. The artist perpetuated this experience in his artworks by taking with him relics and drawing inspiration from them. However, if Jalāl Āl-i Aḥmad's narrator often referred to Qur'anic customs and quoted precise Arabic words or Qur'anic short passages, Zenderoudi mostly recreated in his first artworks the aspect of the religious folk accessories he had gathered, without focusing on their Qur'anic content. He did not give a readable appearance to the Qur'anic citations of the collected amulets or talismanic prayers from which he drew inspiration, even while he kept calligraphic traces in his works' structure. He, rather, recreated an identifiable traditional, religious or talismanic atmosphere. In an interview given to *Ferdowsi Magazine* in 1970 in Tehran, Zenderoudi specified that he had been primarily influenced by occult and magic spells, of which he wanted to convey the erratic and multiform ornamentation (mixed letters, signs and numbers).[32]

The visual ingredients of the Saqqākhāna style evoked in Jalāl Āl-i Aḥmad's story reminds us that the process of making a pilgrimage was an important source of inspiration, a trigger for some leading Saqqākhāna artists. This specific context, as well as the personal commitment to rediscover Shiʿi roots, influenced these Saqqākhāna artists. However, even if they wanted to imbue their artworks with a religious atmosphere, they mostly did not connect themselves with the Qur'anic visual tradition. In the next stages of this study, continuing from the perspective of the artworks, I will explore the creative stages of Zenderoudi's painting up until 1977, the eve of the Islamic Revolution (although it continues after). This will highlight the artistic apparatus he gathered in 1972 and which he brought to bear in the Grosjean Qur'an.[33]

Shi'i Folk Art and Magic Inspiration (1957–1962)

In 1977, Karīm Imāmī attested to the Saqqākhāna style being visible in one of the very first works of Zenderoudi. He said:

> There is no doubt that Saqqākhāna painting began with Zenderoudi. I saw one of his works in a friend's home. It was a simple sketch showing a Karbala martyr whose head and hands were cut off. It was embellished with diminutive writing like that used in spells. He had written whatever he wanted; some were serious and some were not. Years later, I also saw another one of his works that belonged to the early Saqqākhāna era. It was a huge linocut work that portrayed, step by step, the events of Karbala.[34]

As mentioned by Imāmī, the first appearance of the Saqqākhāna artistic style coincides with the creation by Zenderoudi of a series of sketches that illustrated events of Ḥusayn's martyrdom in Karbala. This linocut – *Who is this Hossein the World is Crazy About?* – then merged some of these drafts to form a broad composition. The artist had begun to create this linocut when registering in 1957 at the Boys' Secondary Art School of the Country and ended it after completing his three-year training there. This work manifests his early interest in Shiʿi folk topics and seems to be the result of several sources of inspiration. On the one hand, it is done in the style of a traditional coffeehouse painting (*naqqāshi-yi qahwahkhāna*), inspired by the *parda*, the fabric scroll rolled out by storytellers to narrate popular stories in traditional coffeehouses. The linocut represents scenes from the martyrdom of Ḥusayn, very similar to those shown on canvases or coffeehouse backdrops from the nineteenth and early twentieth centuries. On the other hand, it is affiliated with *parcham* wall hangings, which are used to decorate assembly halls during the months of Muḥarram and Ṣafar. It has been suggested that these wall hangings are 'visual elegies, narrating sacred history and expressing popular piety',[35] and that the eponymous sentence of the artwork, 'Who is this Hossein the World is Crazy About?' (repeated in Persian along some of the borders of the linocut), may be connected to this elegiac poetry. The sentence can be recognised as a line from the famous twelve-stanza elegy (*tarkīb-band*) by Muḥtasham Kāshānī (d. 996/1587), which is used for different ritual purposes, such as in the lamentation poetry (*rawḍa khānī* and *nawḥa*) in today's Iran.[36] Visually, especially from the point of view of the calligraphic inscriptions, the linocut can be associated with a specific *parcham* quoting other lines of Kāshānī's twelve-stanza elegy, presented in 1959 as an offering to a ritual assembly hall.[37]

Between 1957 and 1961, Zenderoudi still wavered between a more classical style and the style of his first Saqqākhāna artworks. In 1960, he presented at the Second Tehran Biennial an impressionist painting of a young girl.[38] The same year, he also painted, in a figurative manner, Rostam (the principal hero of the Iranian epic, the *Shāh-nāma*) and the dragon.[39] In parallel, the artist created his first Saqqākhāna paintings: *Lock*, *c.* 1959, an ink and tempera painting on paper which showed padlocks on a grillwork, resembling the votive locks clasped on the grillwork of the tombs in shrines or of the *saqqākhāna* fountains.[40] The calligraphic frieze framing the painting was in the manner of his above-mentioned founding linocut. Indeed, Zenderoudi's first Saqqākhāna paintings seem to be characterised by this shared framing calligraphic frieze. An intense ornamentation had also appeared, which decorated the inside of the padlocks or of the railings. Miniature symbols of the holy hand *panja-yi panj-tan* were visible inside the central lock.

The same pattern of the hand was the main representation of another early work dating *c.* 1959, *The Hand*, which constituted a new creative stage for Zenderoudi.[41] The texture-producing ornamentation in this work, and others henceforth, was significantly influenced by popular amulets, as exemplified by the new recurring pattern of the magical square, a constant feature of Arabic or Persian amulets. In magical squares, each cell is filled with a number or a letter and the sum of each horizontal, vertical or diagonal line must be the same.[42] Numbers, along with calligraphic patterns, became more and more present in the artist's work.

Zenderoudi's next artwork, *Sun and Lion*, created *c.* 1960, now combined numerology, decorative patterns and mostly illegible calligraphic forms.[43] The motif of the lion and the sun is an historical symbol of the former Iranian monarchy. In nineteenth-century Iran, it became the national symbol of the Qajar rulers, where the lion often brandished Dhū'l-Faqār, the split sword of ʿAlī. In the painting, the lion is brandishing this sword, a reference to ʿAlī. The lion is also an important figure on Muslim talismans.[44] The texture-producing ornamentation of the work contains magical squares. When comparing this painting with popular amulets including figural representations, similarities clearly appear. Thus, a brass arm amulet in the collection of the British Museum, dating from the mid-nineteenth century, also represents a lion whose body is made up of a 4 x 4 magical square. A sun with the upper part of a face is behind the lion. Except for the area with the magical square and sun, the rest of the armlet is entirely covered with all fifteen verses of *Sūrat al-Shams* (Q. 91), which is not the case in the painting.[45] Further examples of amulets with this motif of the lion and sun were published by Tanāwulī in 2007,[46] who also commented on the general signification of the archaic and mythological symbol of the lion that appeared in the Sassanid civilisation with a human face.[47]

In September 1960, Zenderoudi joined the Centre of Decorative Arts (Hunarkada-yi Hunar-hā-yi Tazʿīnī) in Tehran. That same year, the French government awarded him a scholarship to attend the École des Beaux-Arts in Paris. In spite of his time spent in Paris in 1961, Iranian/Shiʿi-inspired iconography became more and more present in his work.

Zenderoudi's artwork of recognition, *K+L+32+H+4, Mon père et moi*, was awarded the Imperial Prize at the Third Tehran Biennial in 1962. It depicted schematic bodies geometrically assembled and scattered with alphabetic characters or numbers. This human aspect is typical of the talismanic symbolism of shapes, whose overall geometrical nature does not prevent the work from getting close to figuration.[48] The human aspect of the geometric shapes in the painting was enhanced by hands appearing at the top of the rectangles or feet designed at the bottom. Inside the circles, which could be related to the sun, human features were also drawn. The rectangles or circles are tinged with red, green, ochre and sometimes light blue, which are colours associated with Shiʿi mourning. Imāmī wrote that this painting, inspired by Shiʿi places of pilgrimage, had a religious atmosphere, but to his eyes not in the distinguished, solemn and wise way of Iranian mosques, but rather in the intimate and familiar manner of the popular *saqqākhāna* fountains.[49]

Explorations of Mosque Architecture (1962–1964)

Despite Imāmī's comments, after 1962 mosque architecture became more and more a subject of inspiration for Zenderoudi. A religious content linked to mosque architecture could already be seen in the previous figurative works of the artist. In *Over the Green Dome* painted in 1960,[50] Zenderoudi had represented in a rather impressionist way an imposing mosque with turquoise tilework, two minarets and a large multicoloured bird flying above, which may be a peacock or a representation of the Sīmurgh, the mythical bird of Persia. In Islam, the glorious vision of the peacock with its magnificent tail indicates variously the universe, the full moon, the sun or the zenith.[51] In Islamic iconography, the peacock, whose tail was described as adorning Burāq, the horse ridden by the Prophet on his journey to the otherworld, may refer to the *miʿrāj*, the ascension of the Prophet to heaven. A peacock-like creature is also usually associated with the bird flying above the head of Solomon as he is holding court.[52]

Two works very similar to *Over the Green Dome* were painted by Zenderoudi in 1962, but this time in a Saqqākhāna, semi-abstract style: *Bird and Tower* and *BM+55+A*. The persistent interest that the artist expressed for patterns derived from mosque architecture and this specific composition show how far he could also draw inspiration, both in his early figurative works and at the turn of the Saqqākhāna era, from formal religion.

If mosque architecture was explored several times by Zenderoudi, another Saqqākhāna artist, Farāmarz Pīlārām (d. 1982), created a series of works similar in composition in 1962, entitled *Mosques of Isfahan*. In Pīlārām's paintings, architectural fragments of mosques, especially minarets, were merged to create geometric hybrid beings.[53]

Through the consecutive analysis of these artworks, it appears that the Qur'an had not directly been referenced in early Saqqākhāna paintings, even if the sacred text was often present on the original religious accessories – amulets, talismanic discs, astrolabes, metal plates on which prayers were etched – from which Zenderoudi, Tanāwulī or Pīlārām drew inspiration. The Qur'an may have indirectly been referred to through the general but indistinct use of calligraphic forms that Zenderoudi also presented as inspired by 'spells'.[54] However, the early and recurrent evocations of mosque architecture that I have highlighted above show that, alongside the Shi'i folk art that had hitherto been characteristic of the Saqqākhāna trend, the scholarly and solemn symbolism of mosques was gradually but systematically explored.

In his early Saqqākhāna works of the late 1950s, Zenderoudi had firstly referred to Shi'i iconography through representations of the Passion of Ḥusayn in Karbala or the pattern of the armed lion symbolising 'Alī. Then, he had also used magical or talismanic signs and religious props in general. From the outset, a tendency to present numbers calligraphy, stemming from Zenderoudi's interest in numerology, was particularly present in his paintings and could be considered, compared to the work of other Saqqākhāna artists from the calligraphic branch of the trend, a distinctive feature of his practice of calligraphy. Symbols of the holy hand or of animals were often mobilised to enhance the humanised aspects of the schematic bodies built through geometric forms. These humanised shapes, caught between geometric abstraction and the insinuation of the real, had been inspired by the specific mystical iconography of talismans. Besides Shi'i folk art and occult signs or magic semi-figurations, Zenderoudi was inspired by religious architecture, not only architectural elements from the popular *saqqākhāna* fountains like grillwork and locks, but also the formal sacred architecture of mosques. Indeed, minarets, domes or calligraphic friezes were recurrent features of Zenderoudi's as well as other Saqqākhāna artists' works in 1962. In 1966, Zenderoudi pursued the course of this inspiration and presented other similar works entitled *Minarets*[55] and *Domes*[56] at the Fifth Tehran Biennial.

Through the 'School of Letters' (1964 onwards)

From 1964 onwards, Zenderoudi's work began to change, becoming more linear and abstract in style. On entering this phase, the artist's work became mostly based on visual effects made up of Persian alphabetical characters, sometimes establishing a connection with Lettrism or Op Art (a style of art that creates optical illusions). His taste for texture-producing ornamentation almost completely vanished. Only an inclination towards the shapes of calligraphic letters persisted. In 1966 in Tehran, *Ferdowsi Magazine* wrote: 'In Zenderoudi's latest paintings, letters have turned to cardiographs and cellular and microscopic creatures.'[57] By 'cardiographs', the art critic is referring to the pulsating rhythm captured on heart-rate metres, which he connects with the punctuated aspect of some of the artist's calligraphic compositions.

Zenderoudi's calligraphic work could be considered to belong to the 'School of Letters' (*al-madrasa al-ḥurūfiyya* in Arabic),[58] an art movement which began at that time to spread through the Middle East and Pakistan. Iraqi artists had been the first promoters of this calligraphic art. It has been suggested that characters from the Arabic alphabet had started to appear as soon as the late 1940s in the work of two Iraqi artists, Jamīl Hamūdī (d. 2003) and Madīha ʿUmar (d. 2005).[59] It was also in the mid-1960s that another Iraqi artist, Shākir Ḥasan al-Saʿīd (d. 2004), generalised this notion of art based on calligraphy. In 1971, he founded the group al-Buʿd al-Wāḥid (The Unique Dimension), promoting the single creating mode of the line, the 1-D relief of the script, and published an art manifesto in 1973.[60] In 1974, during a congress of Arab artists, Saʿīd created the League of the Hurūfiyyūn Artists (the artists of the calligraphic letter).[61] Even if direct contact between Zenderoudi and these artists has not been identified, Zenderoudi seems to have touched upon this new approach. In 1970, he painted a calligraphic composition inspired by an Arabic 'poetic image' or 'image of the word'.[62] Arabic poetry often favoured visual effects from the combination of letters, the most famous being the combining of the letters *alif* and *lām* to express the idea of two interlaced bodies.[63] Zenderoudi's 1970 work entitled *LA+LA+LAM*,[64] which is based on these two specific letters, recreated this enlacing visual image highly regarded by Sufi poets.

From this period, Zenderoudi also employed more simple supports, mostly canvases, less fabric (except silkscreens) and stopped using wood. He experimented with a black and white period before 1976. During an interview conducted in 1973, when asked if he was conveying a specific point in his new calligraphic paintings, Zenderoudi had said: 'Yes, in a series of new works . . . I portrayed the Black September event [the massacre of Palestinians]. The canvas contained a series of the letter Heh, each resembling a human head.'[65]

Finally, around the mid-1970s, Zenderoudi refocused on numbers and made a series of works entitled *Numbers* (1976)[66] and *Calculations* (1977).[67] This period was marked by an arithmetical script that served no aesthetic purpose, the numerals, rather, defining space and movement like in mathematics. It is in this context that the artist undertook an illustration of the Qur'an.

The Multifaceted Edition of the Grosjean Qur'an

By 1964, Zenderoudi had made, for the first time, an allusion to Qur'anic sacred art. That year, in a work entitled *A Passage to Water*,[68] the artist had employed Kufic calligraphy. *Sokhan Monthly Magazine* in Iran, which published this information, also commented on this painting: '[Zenderoudi] unveils a mysterious world on his canvases and uses calligraphy and occultism. His interest in illumination, calligraphy and embellishment is indicative of his delicate and decisive skills, portraying a world of cipher and sarcasm that makes us hang in a state of query and expectancy.'[69] The same year, a work with an identical pattern[70] was presented with another title, *The Blue Hole*,[71] at the Fourth Tehran Biennial. It appears that the artist reused the composition of these previous, related works in two illustrations of the Grosjean Qur'an in 1972. Indeed, Illustration (Ill.) I.1 is very close to this concentric assemblage of forms and Kufic letters, while Ill.II.6 is based almost exactly on the same pattern.

Other explorations of Qur'anic calligraphy remain less known until the 1970s, when Zenderoudi participated in several exhibitions of the Salon d'Art Sacré in Paris.[72] It is during this period, in 1972, that Zenderoudi illustrated Grosjean's translation of the Qur'an. I now dedicate a detailed analysis to this impressive edition and to Zenderoudi's illustrative work, which is quite overlooked in the career of the artist, although a selection of the prints was exhibited from 15 December 1995 to 3 February 1996 in Châteauroux in France.[73]

The Qur'an on which the following analysis is based is an original 1972 edition numbered 910/3624 and comprises four volumes in two slipcases. The first casing comprises the illustrated Qur'an in two volumes, while the second is devoted to a re-edition of the Ibn al-Bawwāb (d. *c.* 412/1022) manuscript (facsimile)[74] with a brief commented volume of D. S. Rice (d. 1962).[75] This is a luxury edition with sophisticated packaging. The design may have a diplomatic dimension, as several issues of this edition of the Qur'an were numbered differently to be specifically sent not only to subscribers of the Club du Livre edition but also to religious authorities, French politicians or presidents of Islamic countries.[76] The origin of this book project has still to be investigated. It has not been possible for me to determine if it came about partly at the request of the French state seeking to reactivate its links with Muslim countries in the framework of Francophonie.

The two volumes of the Qur'an contain thirty-two, one-page, independently printed polychrome illustrations, sixteen in each volume, and black-and-white illuminations framing the sura headings, which mainly consist of arabesques or repetitive calligraphic letters assembled in geometric frames. The sixteen original illustrations in each of the two volumes comprise two duplicated serigraphies which are similar in both volumes, placed double-paged at the beginning and at the end of the two books. The other illustrations are inserted among the suras. Some of them are similar in aspect and colour, and seem to be pairs across the two volumes.[77]

Table 1: Location of illustrations within the suras in Grosjean's original edition of the Qur'an (1972) numbered 910/3624

Volume I		**Volume II**	
Ill.I.0		Ill.II.0	
Ill.I.1.	Sura 1. *L'entrée* [*The Start*]	Ill.II.1.	Sura 20. *Tâ hâ*
Ill.I.2.	Sura 2. *La vache* [*The Cow*]	Ill.II.2.	Sura 24. *La lumière* [*The Light*]
Ill.I.3.	Sura 2. *La vache* [*The Cow*]	Ill.II.3.	Sura 25. *Le critère* [*The Criterion*]
Ill.I.4.	Sura 3. *La famille d'Amram* [*The Family of Amram*]	Ill.II.4.	Sura 27. *Les fourmis* [*The Ants*]
Ill.I.5.	Sura 4. *Les femmes* [*The Women*]	Ill.II.5.	Sura 29. *L'araignée* [*The Spider*]
Ill.I.6.	Sura 5. *La table servie* [The Poured Table]	Ill.II.6.	Sura 36. *Yâ sîn*
Ill.I.7.	Sura 6. *Les troupeaux* [*The Herds*]	Ill.II.7.	Sura 39. *Les groupes* [*The Groups*]
Ill.I.8.	Sura 6. *Les troupeaux* [*The Herds*]	Ill.II.8.	Sura 43. *Les ornements* [*The Ornaments*]
Ill.I.9.	Sura 7. *Les franges* [*The Fringes*]	Ill.II.9.	Sura 50. *Qâf*
Ill.I.10.	Sura 9. *L'immunité* [*The Immunity*]	Ill.II.10.	Sura 57. *Le fer* [*The Iron*]
Ill.I.11.	Sura 10. *Jonas*	Ill.II.11.	Sura 71. *Noé* [Noah]
Ill.I.12.	Sura 14. *Abraham*	Ill.II.12.	Sura 75. *La résurrection* [*The Resurrection*]
Ill.I.13.	Sura 16. *Les abeilles* [*The Bees*]	Ill.II.13.	Sura 80. *Il s'est renfrogné* [*He Scowled*]
Ill.I.14.	Sura 18. *La caverne* [*The Cavern*]	Ill.II.14.	Sura 89. *Le tremblement de terre* [*The Earthquake*]
Ill.I.15		Ill.II.15	

Ill.: Illustration; I or II: volume number; 0, 1, 2 . . . : numbers assigned by Alice Bombardier to each illustration; the suras are titled according to the name given in the Grosjean Qur'an.

As far as iconography is concerned, the work combines some aspects of the Saqqākhāna phase of Zenderoudi's career with other visual explorations: of traditional Qur'anic illumination, Sufi symbolism, miniature painting and, seemingly, even Christian art. In the coloured paintings, the artist seems to have harboured sentiments from the religious visual tradition developed in Persian miniature painting, as evidenced by the title he gave on his website to his most famous illustration of this Qur'an, *Le Prophète sur le Cheval Volant* (The Prophet on the Flying Horse)[78] (Ill.I.3) (the only illustration he gave a precise title to), which seems to be a contribution to the representations of the *miʿrāj*. Furthermore, even if some non-religious characteristics of his Saqqākhāna style remain present and contribute a singular aspect to this Qur'an, the artist also borrowed several components from Sufi symbolism and from traditional Qur'anic illumination.

What is striking at first sight in this work are the two illustrations, Ill.I.11 in Q. 10 (*Jonas*) and Ill.II.13 in Q. 80 (*He Scowled*), where we can clearly distinguish a schematic human body structure through a geometric assemblage of intensively ornamented blocks. In the noteworthy illustration that the artist entitled *The Prophet on the Flying Horse* (Ill.I.3), rectangles also outline the silhouette of an animal and a rider. These semi-figurative schemes of bodies contrast with the traditional aesthetics of the Qur'an, which is imbued with strictly non-figurative rules, especially regarding human or animal forms. Yet, as we have seen previously, it is very representative of Zenderoudi's work from his Saqqākhāna phase. The artist appears to have been at that time influenced by the visual effects, sometimes close to human figuration, developed in the mystical iconography of talismans.

The influence of Zenderoudi's Saqqākhāna style is clear in almost half of the illustrations, characterised by written forms of alphabetical characters, small arabesques and abstract shapes drawn in the background as texture-producing material for the squares, triangles, rectangles and circles assembled at various levels. This multiform ornamentation lines the illustrations in their entirety and provides a connective layout. The shapes of numbers are present in a column of Ill.II.14, which is similar to an astronomy table. The illustration *The Prophet on the Flying Horse* (Ill.I.3) even reminds us in some ways, through the polyped geometric assemblage, of the artist's seminal work from the Third Tehran Biennial in 1962, *K+L+32+H+4, Mon père et moi*, which alluded to two characters. Nevertheless, other visual ingredients of this period, like specific Shiʿi or folk symbols, are absent.

The artist's calligraphic phase also influenced his Qur'an illustrations. In 1972, Zenderoudi was mostly creating free calligraphic paintings with letters, often in *nastaʿlīq* script, covering the canvas in repetitive movements and playing with perspective and vision. The connective texture made up by little drawings, letters and arabesques in the background had almost disappeared and was often replaced by plain colours, as, for example, in the work entitled *Arbab* (1972),[79] which is very similar to Ill.I.2.

Steeped in these two artistic phases, Zenderoudi's illustrations of the Qur'an have also the particularity of being imbued with Sufi symbolism. As mentioned before, in the work *LA+LA+LAM* (1970), the artist had already explored some Sufi-inspired poetic images. In the Qur'an illustrations, a recurrent use of simple geometric forms and pictograms whose assemblage is based on symbolism often found in Sufi thought can also be distinguished. In Ill.II.2, Zenderoudi reproduced a concentric symbol alluding to the cosmos and Islamic architecture. This circular scheme is present in several other illustrations, especially in the background of I.3 or as a component in I.1, II.3 and II.7. Zenderoudi often plays with the optical illusions generated by this concentric representation. A centrifugal movement also prevails at the heart of Ill.I.7 and conveys a powerful effect of infinitude.

The echo of Persian miniature painting and old manuscripts is also noticeable in the Qur'an illustrations. The introductive illustration in the two volumes of the Qur'an shows colophon-shaped medallions. Most importantly, the painting *The Prophet on the Flying Horse* shows itself to be affiliated with the illustrated autonomous tales of the ascension of the Prophet (*miʿrāj-nāma*). Around the sixteenth century, the representations of the *miʿrāj* became an artistic leitmotiv which evoked an ecstatic movement, a vision of the afterlife and the proximity of God.[80] The images of the *miʿrāj* evolved from an historical dimension to a more generic one, used by the mystics who wanted to describe some of their spiritual experiences.[81] This is why images of the *miʿrāj* tended to be used like visual praises. *The Prophet on the Flying Horse* in the Grosjean Qur'an may operate like a blazon of the visionary experience. The scene appears in a pared-down style, limited to geometric forms, schematic lines and a dense calligraphic ornamentation. The flying horse, Burāq, is condensed in a few rectangles: his head as a trident, his peacock tail as a large rectangle and the legs as seven blocks. Two little geometric forms seem to symbolise the wings on his back. The figure of the Prophet may be represented through two right-angled rectangles on the back of Burāq. The spiral of the ascension is suggested by the concentric arrangement of red and yellow shades.

Besides the influence of *miʿrāj-nāma* manuscripts, a few illustrations evoke themes present in astronomical manuscripts. Illustrations II.7 and II.11, for example, have circles linked by curved lines that suggest patterns of constellations. Placed at the end of the second volume, the table which corresponds to Ill.II.14 refers to astronomic grids from manuals of astronomy like the *Zik-i Shāhryār* from the Sassanid era, and serves as a synthetic visual conclusion.[82]

One other noteworthy aspect of Zenderoudi's illustrations is their connection with Qur'anic sacred art. This connection is created through the frequent use of Kufic script, which is the style of the first efforts by calligraphers to give the Qur'an an artistic dimension. In some illustrations, Kufic script appears in a distinctive form with marked horizontal strokes, often very elongated, for example in Ill.I.1, or is stylised to the point of becoming, in some places, like hieroglyphs (for example in Ill.I.6; I.7; I.10; II.2; II.4; II.9). A grave procession of hieroglyphs, sometimes very close to cuneiform script, is visible in Ill.I.7 and II.9. Vertical or bent shapes of Persian Kufic script, also called Eastern Kufic script, which was developed in Persia at the end of the fourth/tenth century, are even identifiable in Ill.II.5. The Kufic parent script is the most recurrent calligraphic style of this two-volume Qur'an and instils a strong connection with visual sacrament. This is not a script that the artist had often used in his career. It had occasionally been the case, for example, in 1964, in the aforementioned works entitled *A Passage to Water* or *The Blue Hole.*

Even though the calligraphic elements still bear a decorative function in most of the places of these Qur'anic illustrations, they are not entirely limited to a personalised pseudo-script of signs. This is an important difference from Zenderoudi's previous artistic phases, where the calligraphic works basically carried no meaning. On the contrary, in Ill.I.3, *The Prophet on the Flying Horse*, a few words like '*kitāb*' (book) or '*Allāh*', can be deciphered on the concentric lines of the background, although the overall aspect of the writing remains cryptic.

Gold, as well, is not a colour that Zenderoudi had favoured throughout his career, except in a few of his early Saqqākhāna works, but the artist used it here, significantly strengthening the ties with the art of Qur'anic illumination. Gold is present as a background or ornamental colour in ten of the thirty-two illustrations of this Qur'an. It is often used in association with blue, which is the dominant colour. By the middle of the fourth/tenth century, blue had been given a marked precedence over both green and red in Qur'anic illuminations.[83]

Another significant attempt to get closer to traditional models of Qur'anic art is the inclusion of shapes derived from Qur'anic illuminations. A complex palmette or rosace occupies the centre of Ill.II.10: a tile-inspired octagonal shape is surrounded by circles bearing calligraphic forms and then connected by petals. In Ill.I.4, a radiant central twelve-pointed star, which could be related to a solar palmette, goes along with twelve circles (symbolising Zodiac signs or the whole constellation) linked by concentric calligraphic lines.[84] A plurality of microcosms is here represented by calligraphic or geometric ornamental units. Circles, concentric bands, as many solar symbols, appear in several illustrations.[85] These comments on the palmette could be linked to Ill.II.8, which shows this time an arboreal shape, a tree with three branches running through its central pillar (merging the aspect of a human silhouette as the form bears two ends at the bottom) inside a solar circle.[86] A tree with green leaves is also suggested in Ill.I.14.[87]

Conclusion

Through the study of the intellectual and literary context, and then of the various stages of Zenderoudi's career, it appears that from 1964 onwards, his work lost its Iranian-Shi'i folk specificity and became closer in style to that of the Eastern calligraphic School of Letters. From then on, undertaking a parallel career in Europe, the artist drew inspiration from a variety of trends, both Western and Eastern. Many comparisons have been made by art critics with Western art movements like Op Art, Lettrism, Hypergraphism or even Pop Art. This Western reading of Zenderoudi's work must not eclipse the influence of neighbouring Middle-Eastern countries such as Iraq and Pakistan, where similar experiments (which remained in the shadows in the West until the last decade) were undertaken by artists who had even gone a step further by theorising their calligraphic practice in the form of manifestos (as the Iraqi Shākir Ḥasan al-Saʿīd did through the al-Buʿd al-Wāḥid art group and manifesto).

Despite the diversification of the artist's inspiration, his initial Saqqākhāna style surfaced in 1972 on the occasion of his illustrative contribution to Grosjean's French translation of the Qur'an. Through the detailed analysis of its illustrations, I showed how hybrid, multifaceted and polymorphous the artist's style was. This illustrative work is therefore a unique contribution to Zenderoudi's career. It combines at the same time rectangular Kufic, Persian Kufic and *nastaʿlīq* calligraphic scripts. It juxtaposes or merges Sufi symbolism, Islamic patterns, even pre-Islamic and magic inspiration. It borrows components from Qur'anic sacred art (palmettes or rosaces, blue or golden colours, arboreal or solar shapes, centrifugal movements) but simultaneously breaks with the most fundamental Qur'anic sacred rule by introducing in a stylised manner schematic silhouettes of human beings or animals. Inspired by talismanic mystical iconography, these silhouettes may realign the figural with transcendence in a postmodern approach. Moreover, in his artistic quest, Zenderoudi seems to have intertwined Islamic with Christian sacred aesthetics, raising trees as crosses or applying Persian calligraphy on backgrounds scattered with stained-glass effects. Thus, one could easily overlook some of the work of this eminent artist of the Saqqākhāna trend by not considering the dialogue that Zenderoudi engaged in – and maintained throughout his career after the publication of the Grosjean Qur'an – with the sacred. Indeed, Zenderoudi's contribution to the Qur'an was followed by other illustration projects highly imbued with religious or spiritual values. In 1980, Zenderoudi illustrated three books published in Tehran: *Shams-i Tabrīzī* by Mawlana (Rūmī), *Maʿrifat al-rūḥ* and *Asār al-ḥaqq* by Nūr ʿAlī Ilāhī, a spiritual thinker, musician and jurist.[88] In 1988, the book *Hafez: Dance of Life* published in Washington DC, which he also illustrated, was well received by book reviewers.[89]

The formal religious aspect is not what is currently emphasised by art historians in the definition of the Saqqākhāna artistic trend. Certainly, most of the Saqqākhāna artists created more secular-oriented artworks than those produced by artists such as Muḥammad Iḥṣā'ī (b. 1939) or Riḍā Māfī (d. 1982), who, from 1965 to 1966 in Tehran, started the 'calligraphy-painting' artistic trend, named Naqqāshīkhaṭṭ. Unlike Saqqākhāna artists, who were mostly painters, the Naqqāshīkhaṭṭ artists had specific training in calligraphy. From the beginning, they further underlined the sacred or literary aspects of calligraphy, as evidenced by Iḥṣā'ī's calligraphic painting entitled *Lā ilāha illā'llāh* exhibited in 1979 at the Ḥusayniyya 'Irshād' in Tehran,[90] or by his work entitled *Allāh*[91] (with '*Allāh*' distinctly inscribed on it) created in 1995. By contrast, the Saqqākhāna artists from the calligraphic branch of the trend concentrated their efforts on exploring the visual nature of religious and graphic elements, remodelling *ad infinitum* the geometry of their personalised alphabet.

It is also true that the recent success of the Saqqākhāna trend in the international art market and the attempts to raise a national art school in Iran strengthened the Iranian-Shiʿi features of the trend more than the formal Islamic aspects of its creations. However, some aspects exist as shown in this study. Even if the Qur'anic text had not explicitly been quoted in early Saqqākhāna artworks, the scholarly and solemn symbolism of mosque architecture constituted, from very early on, an artistic cornerstone of the Saqqākhāna trend, despite the pioneering analysis of Imāmī that was imbued with popular religiosity. Most importantly, the publication of this largely unrecognised Qur'an in 1972 allows us to partly connect some of the Saqqākhāna inspiration to sacred art. Paradoxically, this work even questions how sacred art could be understood and considered in the contemporary era. This is why, in the end, I want to ask, would this attempt to adapt Islamic sacred art to artistic modernity would still be publishable today?[92]

I would point out that a similar initiative was taken exactly at the same time in the Christian context, as a Bible illustrated by Salvador Dalí was published in Paris the same year, in 1972, by Denoël Édition.[93] Dalí also took great pleasure in exploring art in myriad forms. For that reason, he produced illustrations, often pen and ink drawings, for the major printers, publishers and advertising agencies of his time, disseminating his work to the widest possible audience. In 1972, reaffirming his faith in Catholicism, he created forty full-page colour plates for a new translation of the Bible. Semi-figurative or totally abstract, these illustrations reflect, according to Bernard Durand, not only Dalí's fascination with the great mystics but also his anxiety about death and the afterlife.[94] While the artistic treatment of the Bible had to meet, throughout the centuries, the requirements of the established Catholicism, Dalí operated a free reading of the sacred text in his illustrations,[95] and, especially, expressed his intimate feelings through them. Similarly, in the 1972 edition of the Grosjean Qur'an, Zenderoudi seems to have freed himself from the illustrative tradition of the Qur'an. Yet, a close observation of his work allows us to detect the presence of numerous references to the sacred.

NOTES

1 Jean Grosjean, tr., *Le Coran*, 2 vols, intro. Jacques Berque, illus. Charles-Hossein Zenderoudi, printed in 3,624 issues by Firmin-Didot and Saint Augustin Press in Bruges, dir. Philippe Lebaud, Jacques Cornulier, Jean-François Fouquereau, Adrien Frutiger and Bruno Pfaffi (Paris, 1972). Published with a facsimile of Ibn al-Bawwāb's manuscript and a commentary by D.S. Rice. Only the Qur'an was republished in 1979 both in a black-and-white simplified format and again in a coloured two-volume set with a leather binding and hardcover. Other black-and-white simplified formats were published in 1988 and 1994. Finally in 2001, it was published in paperback.

2 Ruyin Pakbaz, Yaghub Emdadian and Tooka Maleki, *Pioneers of Iranian Modern Art: Charles-Hossein Zenderoudi* (Tehran, 2001), p. 42.

3 The name is spelled according to the wishes of the artist.

4 Another example of an attempt to adapt sacred art to artistic modernity is seen in the Qur'an being published in the form of a comic strip. For more on this, see n. 92.

5 In this study, the term 'trend' is preferred to 'movement' or 'art school', considering firstly the rather heterogeneous aspect of the Saqqākhāna creations, and secondly, that the Saqqākhāna artists worked, for the most part, separately and did not form a real band even when working on the benches of their common schools in Tehran, the Boys' Secondary Art School of the Country (Hunaristān-i Hunar-hā-yi Zībā-yi Kishwar) and the Centre of Decorative Arts (Hunarkada-yi Hunar-hā-yi Taz'īnī).

6 Charles-Hossein Zenderoudi, *K+L+32+H+4. Mon père et moi*, 1962, felt pen and coloured ink on paper mounted on wood board, 89 x 58 cm, collection of MoMA in New York. See image on the artist's website, www.zenderoudi.com/english/K+L+32+H+4.html, and the website of the Modern Museum of Art (MoMA) Collection, https://www.moma.org/collection/works/36253?locale=en.

7 Imāmī was also a professor of English at the Centre of Decorative Arts in Tehran. See his foreword in the catalogue of the Saqqākhāna exhibition held in 1977 at the opening of the Tehran Museum of Contemporary Art (TMoCA): Karīm Imāmī, 'Nigāhī dubāra ba maktab-i Saqqākhāna', *Saqqākhāna Exhibition Catalogue* (Tehran, 1977), n.p.

8 It is necessary to specify that, from its inception in 1957, the Saqqākhāna artistic trend was split into two main branches. The first included artists such as Parwīz Tanāwulī (Parviz Tanavoli), Charles-Hossein Zenderoudi, Farāmarz Pīlārām, Manṣūr Qandrīz and Mas'ūd 'Arabshāhī, who attempted to find common ground between Western art, especially abstraction, and Iranian religious folk art. They created abstract works based on the geometric or ornamental potential of calligraphy and/or on pre-Islamic or Islamic shapes. From 1964 onwards, most of them overall produced strictly calligraphic compositions. The second branch gathered together artists such as Ṣādiq Tabrīzī, Nāṣir Uwaysī and Jāza Ṭabāṭabā'ī, who mainly drew their inspiration from miniature or Qajar paintings and created more figurative works. The term 'Saqqākhāna' was later generalised to refer to the works of Iranian artists who used, as a starting point for their creations, traditional or popular patterns, religious symbols, calligraphy or raw material (soil, sand, etc.). On these distinctions, see Hamid Keshmirshekan, 'Neo-Traditionalism and Modern Iranian Painting: The *Saqqa-khaneh* School in the 1960s', *Iranian Studies* 38, no. 4 (2005), pp. 607–30.

9 Ibid., p. 628.

10 See Aḥmad Fardīd, *Dīdār-i farrahī wa futūḥāt-i ākhar al-zamān* (Tehran, 2002). On Aḥmad Fardīd, see Ehsan Manzinani, 'La réception de Heidegger en Iran: Le cas de Ahmad Fardid (1910–1994). L'examen critique d'une lecture et ses implications' (Unpublished PhD dissertation, Sorbonne Nouvelle-Paris 3, 2008).

11 Jalāl Āl-i Aḥmad, *Gharbzadigī* (Tehran, 2001). Discourses pronounced later by ʿAlī Sharīʿatī (d. 1977) seem also relevant. Indeed, the criticism of the early champions of the popular, religious and national values had, in the 1970s, their most vibrant and influential second life through Sharīʿatī, who wrote, for example, in his book entitled *The Return to the Self. Vol. IV: Collected Works* (Tehran, 1978) that the rediscovery of popular Shiʿi roots was primordial. For an overview of these discourses, see Mehrzad Boroujerdi, *Iranian Intellectuals and the West: The Tormented Triumph of Nativism* (New York, 1996).

12 'Ziyārat' was Āl-i Aḥmad's first published short story, appearing in March 1945 in the monthly magazine *Sokhan*. Having enjoyed immediate critical success, it was republished at the end of the year in Āl-i Aḥmad's first collection of short stories, *Dīd wa bāzdīd* (The Exchange of Visits). A first English translation of this short story was made by Henry D.G. Law, titled 'The Pilgrimage', in *Life and Letters* 62, no. 148 (December 1949), pp. 202–209. Another translation was later published as 'The Pilgrimage' in Michael C. Hillman, comp. and ed., *Iranian Society: An Anthology of the Writings by Jalal Al-e Ahmad* (Lexington, KY, 1982), pp. 34–42.

13 Āl-i Aḥmad, 'The Pilgrimage', p. 34.

14 Ibid., p. 35.

15 Ibid., pp. 37–8.

16 Buzurg ʿAlawī, *Geschichte und Entwicklung der modernen persischen Literatur* (Berlin, 1964), p. 221.

17 Āl-i Aḥmad, 'The Pilgrimage', pp. 35 and 38.

18 Ibid., p. 37.

19 Ibid., p. 37.

20 Ibid., p. 38.

21 Ibid.

22 Ibid.

23 Ibid., p. 40.

24 Ibid.

25 Ibid., p. 41.

26 Ibid.

27 Ibid., pp. 40–41.

28 Pakbaz, Emdadian and Maleki, *Pioneers of Iranian Modern Art*, p. 33.

29 Charles-Hossein Zenderoudi, *Who is this Hossein the World is Crazy About?* 1957–1960, linocut printed on linen, 229 x 149 cm. See the British Museum's online collection (number 2011, 6034.1). A conference entitled 'Who is this Hossein the World is Crazy About? The work of Charles-Hossein Zenderoudi' was organised at the British Museum on 12 May 2013.

30 Imāmī, 'Nigāhī dubāra', n.p.

31 Pakbaz, Emdadian and Maleki, *Pioneers of Iranian Modern Art*, p. 35.

32 'Hossein Zenderoudi', *Ferdowsi Magazine* 984, October 1970, quoted in Pakbaz, Emdadian and Maleki, *Pioneers of Iranian Modern Art*, p. 40.

33 What follows is based on my individual assessment of the work in question. Before completing this study, I personally contacted Charles-Hossein Zenderoudi, submitting some questions about his work. In an email, the artist communicated his unwillingness to answer the questions. Some of the concerns he expressed in the email have been incorporated in this chapter, and

therefore inform my study nonetheless. This chapter is mainly based on the observation of the artist's work, especially on the illustrated Qur'an published in 1972, and on the work of other Saqqākhāna artists, but it by no means represents an attempt on my part to associate Zenderoudi with any specific school of confession.

34 Imāmī, 'Nigāhī dubāra', n.p.

35 Ingvild Flaskerud, *Visualizing Belief and Piety in Iranian Shiism* (London, 2010), p. 90.

36 Ibid., p. 94.

37 This *parcham* was photographed in 2000 by Ingvild Flaskerud in a private courtyard during commemorative rituals during Muḥarram. See ibid., Fig. 23 and the comments on pp. 93–4.

38 Zenderoudi, *Portrait*, 1960, oil on canvas, 45 x 29 cm. See *Catalogue of the Second Tehran Biennial* (Tehran, 1960), p. 87.

39 Zenderoudi, *Rostam and the Dragon*, 1960, oil on canvas, 130 x 48 cm, artist's collection; Pakbaz, Emdadian and Maleki, *Pioneers of Iranian Modern Art*, p. 102.

40 Zenderoudi, *Locks*, *c.* 1959, ink and tempera on paper, 49 x 36 cm. See the Grey Art Gallery website, https://greyartgallery.nyu.edu/artworks/lock-2/.

41 Zenderoudi, *The Hand*, *c.* 1959, paper collage with ink, watercolour, gold and silver paint, 70 x 46 cm. See the Grey Art Gallery website, https://greyartgallery.nyu.edu/artworks/the-hand-2/.

42 Venetia Porter, *Arabic and Persian Seals and Amulets in the British Museum* (London, 2011), p. 166.

43 Zenderoudi, *Sun and Lion*, *c.* 1960, ink, watercolour and gold paint on paper mounted on board, 115 x 155 cm. See the Grey Art Gallery website, https://greyartgallery.nyu.edu/artworks/sun-and-lion-2/.

44 Shaker Laibi, *Soufisme et art visuel: Iconographie du sacré* (Paris, 1998), pp. 38–40.

45 Porter, *Arabic and Persian Seals*, p. 168 (Item A119).

46 Parwīz Tanāwulī, *Tālism* (Tehran, 2007), p. 70.

47 About the lion's representations, see Parviz Tanavoli [Parwīz Tanāwulī], *Lion Rugs: The Lion in the Art and Culture of Iran* (New York, 1985).

48 According to Shaker Laibi, the mystical iconography of talismans, maintaining a relationship with the iconic tradition of the oldest mysticism, often recreated rather explicit visual assemblages to the point of approaching, even vaguely, a kind of human or animal figuration. See Laibi, *Soufisme et art visuel*, pp. 15–33.

49 Imāmī, 'Nigāhī dubāra', n.p.

50 Zenderoudi, *Over the Green Dome*, 1960, oil on canvas, 124 x 48 cm, artist's collection; Pakbaz, Emdadian and Maleki, *Pioneers of Iranian Modern Art*, p. 101.

51 Porter, *Arabic and Persian Seals*, p. 6.

52 Ibid.

53 Farāmarz Pīlārām, *Mosques of Isfahan (B)*, *c.* 1962, ink, watercolour, gold and silver paint on paper, 116 x 88 cm. See the Grey Art Gallery website, https://greyartgallery.nyu.edu/artworks/mosques-of-isfahan-b-2/. The artist created three works in the series *Mosques of Isfahan* and one related painting entitled *Village Mosque* (1962). All are in the Abby Weed Grey Collection of Modern

Asian and Middle Eastern Art, now housed at the Grey Art Gallery, New York University.

54 'Hossein Zenderoudi', *Ferdowsi Magazine* 984, October 1970, quoted in Pakbaz, Emdadian and Maleki, *Pioneers of Iranian Modern Art*, p. 40.

55 Zenderoudi, *Minarets*, 1966, watercolour, 149 x 97 cm. See *Catalogue of the Fifth Tehran Biennial* (Tehran, 1966), p. 133.

56 Zenderoudi, *Domes*, 1966, watercolour, 97 x 86 cm. Reported by Pakbaz, Emdadian and Maleki, *Pioneers of Iranian Modern Art*, p. 38.

57 P.N., 'Strong Techniques Give Zenderoudi's Work an International Recognition', *Ferdowsi Magazine* 803 (1966), quoted in Pakbaz, Emdadian and Maleki, *Pioneers of Iranian Modern Art*, p. 38.

58 See Sheila S. Blair, *Islamic Calligraphy* (Edinburgh, 2006), p. 589.

59 Silvia Naef, *L'art de l'écriture arabe: Passé et présent* (Geneva, 1993), p. 39.

60 Shākir Ḥasan al-Saʿīd, *al-bayyanāt al-fanniyya fīl-ʿIrāq* (The Art Manifestos in Iraq) (Baghdad, 1973), quoted in Naef, *L'art de l'écriture arabe*, pp. 56–61.

61 Naef, *L'art de l'écriture arabe*, pp. 56–61.

62 Terms coined by Erica Dodd, 'The Image of the Word: Notes on the Religious Iconography of Islam', *Berytus* 18 (1969), pp. 35–62.

63 Naef, *L'art de l'écriture arabe*, p. 30.

64 Zenderoudi, *LA+LA+LAM*, 1970, acrylic on canvas, 97 x 195 cm, TMoCA's collection; Pakbaz, Emdadian and Maleki, *Pioneers of Iranian Modern Art*, p. 86.

65 Manutshehr Atashi, 'Interview', *Tamasha Magazine*, January 1974, quoted in Pakbaz, Emdadian and Maleki, *Pioneers of Iranian Modern Art*, p. 43.

66 Zenderoudi, *Numbers*, 1976, acrylic and coloured ink on canvas, 129 x 96 cm, TMoCA collection; Pakbaz, Emdadian and Maleki, *Pioneers of Iranian Modern Art*, p. 71.

67 Zenderoudi, *Calculations*, 1977, coloured ink on canvas, 100 x 73 cm, TMoCA collection; Pakbaz, Emdadian and Maleki, *Pioneers of Iranian Modern Art*, p. 69. Other untitled works in the same style can be seen on pp. 72–3.

68 Zenderoudi, *A Passage to Water*, 1964, oil on canvas, 170 x 170 cm; Pakbaz, Emdadian and Maleki, *Pioneers of Iranian Modern Art*, pp. 37 and 120–21.

69 *Sokhan Monthly Magazine* 14, nos. 8–9 (April 1964), p. 847, quoted in Pakbaz, Emdadian and Maleki, *Pioneers of Iranian Modern Art*, p. 37.

70 The black and white prints do not allow us to check if the colours were also similar.

71 Zenderoudi, *The Blue Hole*, 170 x 170 cm. See *Catalogue of the Fourth Tehran Biennial* (Tehran, 1964), p. 141.

72 Zenderoudi participated in the Salon d'Art Sacré in Paris in 1970, 1971, 1973 and 1976; Pakbaz, Emdadian and Maleki, *Pioneers of Iranian Modern Art*, pp. 40 and 43.

73 An exhibition catalogue has been published: *Ecrits célestes: Exposition d'Hossein Zenderoudi, Châteauroux, Médiathèque Equinoxe* (Châteauroux, 1996), mentioned in Pakbaz, Emdadian and Maleki, *Pioneers of Iranian Modern Art*, p. 47.

74 Janine Sourdel and Dominique Sourdel, 'Ibn al-Bawwāb', *Dictionnaire historique de l'islam* (Paris, 2004), p. 363. The added manuscript of Ibn al-Bawwāb, a famous eleventh-century Arab calligrapher and illuminator, indubitably added value to the work of Zenderoudi, who is linked to the scholarly tradition of Arabic calligraphy, especially Qur'anic calligraphy. Indeed, Ibn al-Bawwāb, who

was a copyist in Baghdad and the Fars, is known for having signed the first issue of the Qur'an written in Arabic cursive calligraphy.

75 David Storm Rice, born in Vienna and educated in Haifa and Paris, was a researcher in Islamic archaeology and art. His PhD, 'Études sur les villages araméens de l'Anti-Liban' (University of Paris, 1939), was about the dialects and customs of the three Aramaic-speaking villages of the Anti-Lebanon. He studied and authenticated manuscripts of the Qur'an. See his monograph on one of the oldest complete version of the Qur'an (391/1001), which is signed by Ibn al-Bawwāb: David Storm Rice, *The Unique Ibn al-Bawwāb Manuscript in the Chester Beatty Library* (Dublin, 1955); Wiet Gaston, Review of *The Unique Ibn al-Bawwāb Manuscript in the Chester Beatty Library*, by D.S. Rice, *Syria: Archéologie, art et histoire* 32, nos. 3–4 (1955), pp. 365–7.

76 The editorial inscription on the last page of this illustrated Qur'an reads: 'Two issues marked A and B were published with two original gouaches and six drawings by Hossein Zenderoudi, six drawings by Adrian Frutiger, twenty signed serigraphies on vellum of Lana Paper Mill, the successive prints for two serigraphies, thirteen drawings on vellum of Arches by Hossein Zenderoudi and seven compositions on vellum of Arches by Adrian Frutiger; issues numbered 1 to 60 were printed on vellum of Hollande Van Gelder with one original gouache of Hossein Zenderoudi, twenty signed serigraphies on vellum of Lana Paper Mill, the successive prints for two serigraphies, thirteen drawings on vellum of Arches by Hossein Zenderoudi and seven compositions on vellum of Arches by Adrian Frutiger; issues 61 to 373 were printed on vellum of Hollande Van Gelder with twenty signed serigraphies on vellum of Lana Paper Mill, the successive prints for two serigraphies, thirteen drawings on vellum of Arches by Hossein Zenderoudi and seven compositions on vellum of Arches by Adrian Frutiger; issues 374 to 1623 were printed on a paper "pure thread" from Lana Paper Mill; issues 1624 to 3624 were printed on vellum of Lana Paper Mill; issues I to MMCC for libraries and bibliophiles; issues marked 0 for religious authorities, presidents of State, André Malraux, the French National Library and museums.'

77 This is the case for illustrations I.1 and II.6; I.5 and II.5; I.13 and II.1; I.6 and II.9; I.11 and II.13; and, to a lesser extent, inside one volume: II.7 and II.11.

78 See http://www.zenderoudi.com/english/LE%20PROPHETE%20SUR%20LE%20CHEVAL%20VOLANT.html.

79 Zenderoudi, *Arbab*, 1972, acrylic on canvas, 130 x 195 cm, artist's collection; Pakbaz, Emdadian and Maleki, *Pioneers of Iranian Modern Art*, p. 82.

80 Christiane Gruber, 'L'ascension du Prophète Mohammad dans la peinture et la littérature islamique', *Luqman* 20, no. 1 (2004), p. 71.

81 Ibid., p. 67.

82 Denise Aigle, 'L'histoire sous forme graphique, en arabe, persan et turc ottoman: Origines et fonctions', *Bulletin d'Études Orientales* 58 (2009), pp. 11–49.

83 Martin Lings, *The Quranic Art of Calligraphy and Illumination* (London, 1976), p. 76.

84 Martin Lings wrote about the symbolism of the sun in the Qur'an: 'Another symbol which expresses both perfection and infinitude, and which is intimately, though not apparently, related to the "tree," is the rayed sun. Again and again the Qur'an refers to itself as light or as being radiant with light, and many

periods of Qur'an illumination can give us examples of marginal verse counts inscribed in circles whose circumferences are rayed or scalloped. The solar roundels, *shamsa* or "little sun" is used also of stellar ornaments, and occasionally replace the rosettes which divide the verses, and the rosettes themselves are often made luminous with gold.' (Ibid., p. 74).

85 See Ills.I.1; I.5; I.9; I.12; II.2; II.3; II.4; II.6; II.7; II.8; II.10; II.11; II.12.

86 Martin Lings also commented on the combination of the symbol of the sun with this of the tree: 'Sometimes the symbolism of light is directly combined with that of the tree, as when a solar roundel figures inside the *Sura* palmette, or when the palmette itself is rounded and rayed, with its lobe replaced by an outward pointing finial.' Lings, *The Quranic Art*, p. 74.

87 My personal interpretation would also link some illustrations of this Qur'an to Christian sacred art. This publication of a French-translated Qur'an was aimed at French bibliophiles, but also at those in religious, political and diplomatic circles in order to contribute to the prestige of France and the French language. Visual elements that can be associated with Christian imagery appear along with Islamic ones. (The translator, Jean Grosjean was a Catholic priest from 1939 to 1950 and had previously translated the Gospels.) Thus, the tree in Ill.II.8 may be related to a three-branched cross. The composition of the background in illustrations I.8, I.13 and II.1 is also visually similar to the stained-glass windows ornamenting churches.

88 Mawlana, *Shams-i Tabrīzī*, illus. Zenderoudi (Tehran, 1980); Nūr ʿAlī Ilāhī, *Maʿrifat al-rūḥ*, illus. Zenderoudi (Tehran, 1980); idem, *Asār al-ḥaqq*, illus. Zenderoudi (Tehran, 1980).

89 *Hafez: Dance of Life*, illus. Zenderoudi, tr. M. Boylan (Washington DC, 1988).

90 Hossein Khosrojerdi, 'The Islamic Revolution in Contemporary Iranian Art', *Tavoos* (1999), p. 91.

91 Muḥammad Iḥṣā'ī, *Allāh*, 1995, oil on canvas, 90 x 60 cm. See Alice Bombardier, 'La peinture iranienne au XXème siècle (1911–2009): Historique, courants esthétiques et voix d'artistes. Contribution à l'étude des enjeux de l'art en Iran à l'époque contemporaine', Unpublished PhD dissertation, EHESS Paris/University of Geneva, 2012, p. 308.

92 In 1989, a Qur'an in the shape of a comic strip was also published in France: Youssef Seddik, *Si le Coran m'était conté*, 3 vols (Paris, 1989). The author respected the religious rule of non-figuration of the sacred: whenever the speech bubble came from the mouth of the Prophet or one of his Companions, the character was out of range or suggested by a pool of light. However, this did not prevent many Islamic authorities in the Maghreb and the Middle East from condemning these comic strips. The Organisation of Islamic Cooperation called them *bidʿa* (a dangerous innovation) in an official statement relayed by the media of all Muslim countries, except those of Iran and Turkey. The author ceased the publication after the third volume.

93 *La Bible de Jérusalem*, illus. Salvador Dalí (Paris, 1972).

94 Bernard Durand, *Dalí et Dieu: Un rendez-vous manqué?* (Barcelona, 2008).

95 Before Dalí, Marc Chagall also published, in 1956, innovative illustrations of the biblical text: *Bible*, with 105 etchings by Marc Chagall (Paris, 1956).

13

Women, the Qur'an and the Power of Calligraphy in Contemporary Iran

ANNA VANZAN

'And to think that when I tried to elaborate upon calligraphy as a young painter, in the 1950s in Iran, I was told that calligraphy (*khaṭṭniwīsī*) was a virus to kill!'

– Mansoureh Hosseini

THE ABOVE epigraph is by Mansoureh Hosseini (Manṣūra Ḥusaynī, d. 2012), one of the first Iranian artists to combine an extensive use of calligraphy with abstract painting from as early as the 1950s.[1] Today, in Iran (as well as in many other Islamic countries), calligraphy is more fashionable than ever; as far as techniques are concerned, many artists mainly rely on tradition as both a point of reference and a point of departure for new explorations, while the sources of inspiration for the majority of them continue to be both Persian poetry and the Qur'an.

As in many other artistic fields in Iran, the presence of women in the field of calligraphy is remarkable in spite of the apparent restrictions placed on them in the cultural sphere, and to date there are several hundred female calligraphers in the Islamic Republic of Iran.[2] Only a few women are exclusively involved in elaborating prayers and passages from the Qur'an, and have gained public recognition in exhibitions sponsored by the government; most of them display a more variegated production.

But what is the reason for the increasing female presence in the art of calligraphy, which historically has been dominated by men? Is it simply a matter of women becoming more involved in spreading a spiritual message, with this arising from their growing desire to have more visibility in the field of religious activities? Do female calligraphers believe that this presence will grant them more religious authority? To answer these questions, I met with and interviewed many female calligraphers in Iran in 2014 and 2015, and here present the findings of this research.

The Historical Frame

Women's presence in calligraphy (the premier form of Muslim art) in the Islamic world dates back to the start of its civilisation. *Tadhkiras* (bio-bibliographical collections on the lives of important persons) and treatises on calligraphy testify to a prosperous female activity in this field of Islamic art,[3] and Persianate countries were particularly generous in enriching this artistic branch with a wealth of female calligraphers.[4] As a whole, the history of women's presence in Islamic calligraphy is still to be written, but in the last few years interest in the topic has increased, and the increasing number of works that cast new light on the genderised aspect of calligraphy in Middle Eastern societies is a testament to this. Most of these works underline the difficulties in reconstructing a proper history of the female presence in calligraphy, because so far we have only scattered references to women's calligraphic activity. David Simonowitz ascribes the phenomenon to the 'hesitance of male authors in traditional Middle Eastern societies to draw attention to women and their histories'.[5]

In reality, however, evidence of women's contribution to calligraphy is abundant, although it comes to us in an oblique way, as is the case with almost every aspect of Middle Eastern women's life, at least until the modern era. Thus, our knowledge about female calligraphers comes from passing references to them in such sources as *tadhkiras* that give information on poets and the literati, collections of hadiths, genealogical reconstructions of illustrious Muslim families, biographies of Sufi saints, and so on. To collect these scattered nuggets of information in order to write a monograph on the history of female calligraphers in the Middle East is a very demanding task, and, as far as I know, no one has yet embarked on this project. In any case, articles on the topic, catalogues in exhibitions of calligraphy and the personal commitment of female calligraphers are emerging as valid aids in expanding our knowledge of the subject.

In Iran, the presence of women in calligraphy is attested from as early as the beginning of the fifth/eleventh,[6] although most women were involved in other artistic activities, such as composing poetry or music. Among the earliest women whose works have survived today is Pādshāh Khātūn (fl. *c.* early seventh/thirteenth century), who alternated her lyrical compositions with transcriptions of the Qur'an and other books.[7] After the tenth/sixteenth century, the Muslim world in general saw a considerable weakening of calligraphy production by women,[8] but this was not the case in Iran, where female calligraphers prospered throughout the Safavid era (1501–1736), with a decline occurring only at the end of the dynasty. Some of the Safavid ladies rivalled the men in terms of their outstanding artistic abilities; this was the case, for example, with Gawhar Shād Khātūn (fl. *c.* first half of the eleventh/seventeenth century), who belonged to a family of calligraphers (her father was the famous calligrapher Mīr ʿImād Qazwīnī) and whose prowess in the *nastaʿlīq* script (one of the main scripts used in Persian calligraphy)[9] secured her fame as the best calligrapher during the time of Shāh ʿAbbās (996–1038/1588–1629).[10]

During the Qajar epoch (1797–1925), female calligraphers thrived; 'calligraphy was regarded in aristocratic families as an appropriate accomplishment for girls',[11] so much so that we find numerous expert female calligraphers not only in the harems (*andarūns*) of Fatḥ ʿAlī Shāh (r. 1797–1834) and Nāṣir al-Dīn Shāh (r. 1848–96), but also in the *andarūn*s of the upper classes. The result is that there are a number of samples of women's calligraphic production from the nineteenth and twentieth centuries which are now preserved in the museums of Qum (Fāṭima Maʿṣūma's museum) and Tehran (in the Niyāwarān and Gulistān palace libraries), and also abroad, in Istanbul and in Saint Petersburg.[12] Women engaged in many calligraphic styles; though they had a preference for *nastaʿlīq*, they would also practice *naskh*, *thuluth* and *shikasta*. The level of their skill is apparent in specimens of Qur'an manuscripts (whether full text or containing only some suras), in collections of poetry or lyrical fragments, and in *farmāns* (mandates). Nowadays, we can admire manuscripts copied by Umm al-Salma (better known as Gilīn Khānum), one of Fatḥ ʿAlī Shāh's daughters; Mahd ʿUliyā, who was Nāṣir al-Dīn Shāh's mother; Māh Sharaf Kurdistānī, the daughter of the governor of Kurdistan, who lived during the turn of the nineteenth century; and by other women.[13] The closer we get to the beginning of the twentieth century, the more visible the presence of educated women in calligraphy. These ladies were highly accomplished in a variety of arts, but predominantly so in calligraphy and literature combined.[14]

Calligraphy and Power

Women often mastered calligraphy through their own efforts and taught other would-be-calligraphers.[15] That their teaching was not confined within the harem's walls and that there was virtually no impediment for women to teach men is proven at least as early as the fourth/tenth century. For example, Qāḍī Aḥmad b. Mīr Munshī al-Ḥusaynī (fl. *c.* late tenth/sixteenth century) informs us that when Ibn Muqla (d. *c.* 327/939 or 328//940), the inventor of the six styles of writing, passed away in his hometown of Baghdad, it was his daughter who transmitted her father's outstanding art to a male pupil.[16] No legal statutes actually dictated that women could not practice calligraphy as an 'official' profession.

It is true that calligraphy and power were (and still are) closely intertwined, and that power was held in patriarchal hands. Most Muslim rulers learnt calligraphy, as it was one among many ways that they could assert their prestige and claim legitimacy. Calligraphy was the visual affirmation of the power of Islam, and by practising it a ruler could exalt and reinforce his role as the authorised instrument of God's will. This link between calligraphy and power could lead to the supposition that women – traditionally kept on the periphery of power – would have been banned from practising calligraphy, at least on an official level. Quite the contrary is true, however, and it is demonstrated that women functioned as officers in the administration of the royal chancelleries. As early as the third/ninth century, many women were engaged as calligraphers for any kind of transaction in the imperial *dīwān*s (imperial offices) of Baghdad.[17] In Fatimid Cairo, the wife and daughter of the famous jurist and Qur'an reader Ibn al-Hati'a al-Fāsī (d. 561/1165) prospered, thanks to their prowess in copying both religious and literary books.[18] Again, these morsels of evidence are scattered in a multitude of heterogeneous sources and documents.

In Iran, perhaps the most famous example of a female *munshī* (secretary) is represented by Ḍiyā' al-Salṭana (Shāh Begum; d. 1873), another daughter of Fatḥ ʿAlī Shāh, who was placed in charge of editing the royal edicts.[19] She was also devoted to religious literature, and the Ḥaḍrat-i Maʿṣūma Library in Qum preserves a copy of a Qur'an in Ḍiyā' al-Salṭana's beautiful handwriting, which alternated *naskh* and *riqāʿ* styles. Naturally, she was also a poetess and a literata.[20]

Another crucial issue about 'calligraphy and power' comes to the fore when we consider the social standing of these female calligraphers. Needless to say, up to modern times, all these ladies belonged to either the royal circles or the upper segments of society: only a small number of women in the Middle East were educated and therefore had access to calligraphy and other cultural activities. I argue that women could only reach their elevated positions in society because they were the daughters, sisters, wives or mothers of some outstanding male personality. For the Shiʿa, in particular, women were important because they established this religious group's claims to legitimacy as descendants of the Prophet through his daughter Fāṭima (d. 11/632). Consequently, we can hypothesise that the increased activity of women in calligraphy in Iran witnessed in the Safavid period was also due to the process of legitimacy-building by the Shiʿi state, which was started and consolidated in that era.[21]

Thus, it is proven that women could access calligraphy and mould it to produce not only symbols of secular power (letters and edicts), but also the Islamic symbol par excellence, that is, the Qur'an. This fact can be added to the large portfolio of findings that counteract the common discourse in the West about the lack of material culture production by women in Muslim societies; nevertheless, it does prompt some questions about the discrepancy between the 'power of words' which ladies were granted and the withholding of power they suffered in another arena, notably in the juridical sphere. Perhaps it was deemed suitable for women to have access to the 'highest form of divinity'[22] because of the nature of calligraphy and its intrinsic characteristics. First, calligraphy is a silent activity to be practised in private and it does not require the calligrapher to be publicly exposed. Second, calligraphy was regulated by an elaborate set of rules that did not allow any freedom. To become a calligrapher implied strict physical and psychological discipline under the close supervision of a master, a long and intensive period of training, and the adherence to a set of conventions. In the past, pupils first had to learn how to sit properly and hold their pen, then they would study the measurements of the letters and, finally, they could start to copy the first lines of their manuscript.[23]

Calligraphers were supposed to copy, reproduce and imitate: in other words, they could not create. Both men and women were co-opted to perpetrate and preserve the tradition and the beauty of Islamic culture through calligraphy, which was considered to be one of the highest expressions of moral virtue. However, if we look at the essence of the Islamic message expressed by calligraphy – the Qur'an – we can conclude that men were allowed to write *tafsīr* while women were permitted to merely repeat and transmit religious knowledge. Ladies were not supposed to contribute any original or interpretive insight about the holy text.

Paradoxically, in spite of restrictions curbing female activities, there still resounded the voice of the 'orthodox' who were critical of women's learning activities, even though they consisted of ordinary acts of repetition and worship. However, the aim of these restrictions was not only to curtail women's access to positions of religious and political authority, but probably to prevent women from producing when they were considered to be unclean, such as during certain times of the month or when pregnant, for example, as calligraphers were expected to be in a state of ritual purity when they worked. Nevertheless, the role of female calligraphers remained important, accredited and deeply intertwined with religion.

In Iran, for example, the most accredited *mullā-bajī*s (religious instructresses) in the Qajar harems were both accomplished calligraphers and instructors of the Qur'an.[24] In order to be deemed professional calligraphers (*khaṭṭāṭs*), women and men had to study intensively under a master's direction in order to obtain their *ijāza* (i.e. the authorisation to sign the papers using their own name).[25] In this respect, calligraphy shares a further link with religious disciplines, such Hadith, *tafsīr* and even fiqh.[26] A calligrapher, in fact, 'is not merely an artist mastering a skill but a religious scholar with the role of passing on the Islamic faith'.[27] That said, it does not mean that copying the Qur'an was an act of hermeneutics or that it implied a rereading of the holy book; it was indeed an act of merely copying and reproducing, that is, an act of devotion that conferred upon the calligrapher many blessings from God. And this understanding has been maintained up to our age.

Calligraphy and the Islamic Republic: Continuity and Change

Predictably, traditional reproductions of the Qur'an had a renaissance after the Islamic Revolution (1979). Though calligraphy had never gone out of fashion in Iran, it experienced a rebirth in the late 1960s/early 1970s, when artists such as Muḥammad Iḥsā'ī, Riḍā Māfī, Ṣādiq Tabrīzī and Charles-Hossein Zenderoudi, to name just a few, began to explore new ways of using calligraphy in art. Some of these artists were promoters of the Saqqākhāna artistic trend born in the 1950s, the aim of which was to counteract the rampant Westernisation of Iranian art with a production based on local culture and iconography.[28] However, though Saqqākhāna and calligraphy were deeply rooted in the Islamic religion and culture, they both were also utilised by artists because of their Iranian-ness, their national character, their folkloristic core and even their links with the pre-Islamic past. The Saqqākhāna painters and their forerunner – who, I would like to stress, was a woman, that is, Mansoureh Hosseini – can be considered the founders of *naqqāshī khaṭṭ*, a combination of calligraphy and painting that, over the past few decades, has become more and more popular among artists in Iran and has exhibited a notable growth in female practitioners, as we will see.

With the advent of the Islamic Republic, traditional calligraphy was given a boost. The Iranian Society of Calligraphers (Anjuman-i Khushniwīsān-i Īrān), founded in 1950, flourished and even opened branches in the major Iranian towns.[29] Through the years, the Anjumans have organised courses on calligraphy, and attendance is necessary if members wish to be granted the *ijāza*. The Society of Calligraphers has expanded its activities by promoting exhibitions inside and outside the country's borders.

The Internet also testifies to the increased popularity of calligraphy, with several websites dedicated to this art. They advertise the calligraphers' activities, upcoming exhibits, and competitions and conferences in Iran and abroad. One of the more interesting websites, Azīzīhonar,[30] was launched in 2009 and claims to get more than 2,500 hits per day. It lists past and contemporary calligraphers according to their epoch (*khushniwīsān-i qudamā'*, *khushniwīsān-i muʿāṣir*), location (as they belong to different Iranian towns) and even gender, offering a list of fourteen contemporary female calligraphers. There is no statement about the criteria used to select male and female calligraphers for inclusion on the website. Interestingly, each profile contains not only biographical information (curriculum vitae, participation in exhibitions and the like), but also samples of the works and the photo of the artists (women included). The calligraphic specimens produced by women who are listed in Azīzīhonar are quite 'classic' in style and content. They are mostly *nastaʿlīq* pieces reproducing extracts from the Qur'an, mainly *Sūrat al-Fātiḥa* (Q. 1), the *basmala* (invocations to ʿAlī b. Abī Ṭālib [d. 40/661] and his wife Fāṭima) and verses from classical Persian poetry. Though these fourteen artists represent only the tip of the huge iceberg of female calligraphers, their production inspires some considerations.

In post-revolution Iran, the Qur'an is not solely a holy text, and the reading of the Qur'an carries social, political, ideological and cultural implications. This resonates with and suits female calligraphers in Iran, who hold a variety of positions in this respect. Many of them simply continue the ancient art of reproducing Qur'anic *āyāt* (verses) according to the various styles, most of them also intermingling this production with creations from Persian classical poetry. Others, however, totally avoid using verses from the Qur'an in their work. Yet, this fact should not lead us to make trite categorisations of female calligraphers as either 'religious' or 'non-religious'. It is true that some calligraphers are more religiously traditional in their celebration of the Muslim holy book, but it is also correct to say that many others regularly use seemingly secular texts of classical Persian literature that are, in fact, deeply imbued with Islamic mysticism and spirituality. In this respect, one of the most frequently utilised and beloved books seems to be the *Mathnawī-yi maʿnawī* by Jalāl al-Dīn Rūmī (d. 671/1273), which is permeated with Qur'anic meanings and references, so much so that Nūr al-Dīn Jāmī (d. 897/1492) referred to it as 'the Qur'an in Persian'.[31]

Predictably, it was the traditional reproductions of the Qur'an that first saw a renaissance after the revolution, and many women contributed to this trend. While many artists reproduce the Qur'an because they deeply believe in the religious message, it is also true that the artists who do so achieve the greatest visibility. In July 2011, for instance, Tehran Municipality, in collaboration with Tehran City Beautification Organisation (Sāzimān-i Zībāsāzī-yi Shahr-i Tihrān) and the Imam Reza Islamic Studies Institute, arranged a ten-day exhibition of 160 works of calligraphy, illumination and calligraphic painting inspired by the Qur'an, created by female artists and hosted by the Barg Gallery in Tehran. At the opening, the Tehran City Beautification Organisation's managing director Sayyid Muḥammad Jawād Shūshtarī highlighted the future opportunities for artists who utilised the Qur'an in their works by pointing out that Tehran Municipality had 'several galleries in the city and [declaring that] officials could negotiate with gallery owners to hold Qur'anic exhibitions in a number of them'.[32] The office for Women's Affairs of Tehran Municipality (Idāra-yi Kull-i Umūr-i Bānuwān-i Sahrdārī-yi Tihrān), inaugurated by Mahmoud Ahmadinejad in 2005, organises an annual festival-cum-prize for female calligraphers whose source of inspiration and subject matter is the Qur'an.[33]

This encouragement of women to become actively involved with the Qur'an from an artistic angle seems to be a kind of compensation for the correspondent disincentive faced by women in the religious fields. For although female seminaries have been opened and are well attended, women cannot easily reach the highest ranks of the clerical hierarchy – only a few of them have been able to achieve the title of mujtahid.[34] Not to speak of the fact that women involved in new gender-friendly interpretations of the Qur'an (such as those who are labelled 'Islamic feminists' and those who adhere to the Nawandīsh-i Dīnī movement) do not find favour with the clerical authorities.[35] In other words, women are encouraged to approach the Qur'an only in a passive way, using *taqlīd* (unquestioned acceptance of it) rather than *ijtihād* (applying independent reasoning), thus, even in the artistic field they are supposed to merely reproduce the holy book's *āyāt* without adding their own personal reading.

However, it is well known that in present-day Iran contestation of the 'imposed-from-above' religious system occurs. This is so, for example, at the private Qur'anic meetings in which women engage in their personal *ijtihād* and practice a gender-based exegesis.[36] The women who throng these *jalasa*s (gatherings) cannot be defined as 'irreligious' – quite the contrary. They consider themselves true believers, though they might also be animated by the same gender-friendly approaches to the Qur'an as the 'Islamic feminists'. By the same token, in the arts the Qur'an can be approached either in a traditional and uncompromising way or in an indirect way that combines faith and resistance. Some examples will clarify this point.

The New Female Calligraphers

I have met a number of female calligraphers in Iran, most of whom do not use the Qur'an in their works regularly, but rather Persian literature, from which they copy verses by both classical (e.g. Ḥāfiẓ, d. 792/1390, and Sa'dī, d. 691/1292) and modern poets (e.g. Suhrāb Sipihrī, d. 1980). For example, Nasrīn Purhamrang, based in Rasht, likes to use the Persian translation of the poems composed by foreign poets like William Blake and Paul Éluard.[37] Many of them combine calligraphy (*khaṭṭniwīsī*, also known as *khushniwīsī*) with other artistic activities, that is, they are poets, musicians, painters, and so on. Most started their career at an early age under a parent's supervision, and all followed a four-year course of study at an officially recognised Anjuman-i Khushniwīsān in order to get their diploma. In fact, according to the statistics provided by the various Anjumans, eighty per cent of students who enrol in calligraphy courses are women.[38] If this data is surprising, its 'gender-oriented' interpretation is also very interesting. According to one source, women attend these courses because they have 'comparatively . . . more free time for artistic dedication',[39] but Maliḥa Ṣabūrī, a calligrapher, writer and teacher at the Anjuman-i Khushniwīsān-i Tihrān, suggests that it is because women have discovered a new interest in the arts, and because they love to be engaged in learning and teaching at 'an institute of superior education'.[40] Ṣabūrī also notes that it is possible to make a living from calligraphy and art, and she is the proof of this, as for the past twenty-two years she has managed to maintain herself and her two children with the income from her artistic activities.

Calligraphy can be a viable (financial and otherwise) profession for women, as it had been for men in the past. And, as in the past, where scribes had to comply with a precise set of rules that included ensuring they looked after their physical well-being so that they would be able to give their best performance, female calligraphers today also seem to stick to a disciplined way of life, taking physical exercise on a regular basis. Maryam Jawānbakht, who is a young physician and a calligrapher as well, confirms the need for exercise, saying 'it is important to cultivate strength in the arm in order to have a good hand'.[41] Ṣabūrī, for example, adheres to this practice; she gets up every day at 5:30 a.m. to attend her yoga class, while other calligraphers practice aerobics and/or go to meditation classes. In fact, yoga and meditation appear frequently in the routine of these artists and indicate a new approach to spirituality and religion.[42]

As I mentioned above, Rūmī's *Mathnawī-yi maʿnawī*[43] is one of the favourite sources of inspiration for female artists, and the majority of them seem to prefer it to the Qur'an as an artistic chest of motifs. Sufism has been growing in popularity in post-revolution

Iran, though officials and conservative Shiʿi clerics say it is a deviation from Islam. Moreover, in the last thirty-five years Sufism has resumed some of its vocational dimensions, offering spiritual and emotional shelter from the difficult political situation. It is no secret that many Iranians live in their country as if they were exiled and that many more cope with difficulties by carving out alternative forms of spirituality. Therefore, we witness the resurgence of Sufism there not as an organised movement (*ṭarīqa*), but as a manifestation of religion that is informal and personal and is identified with the inner spiritual life. This new Sufism is found imbued in many contemporary artists, and it is particularly evident in female calligraphers, whose main source of inspiration is Rūmī's 'Persian' Qur'an. Some artists told me that initially they were drawn into calligraphy by Rūmī's poetry and by the desire to express and elucidate its meaning through a graphic rendition of his words.

Maryam Shīrīnlū, an internationally renowned artist who uses letters as a form of expression, speaks of her desire to increase people's awareness (*āgāhī*) of the relationship between calligraphy and philosophical issues. She does not have any traditional training in calligraphy and claims she is not a calligrapher at all. She holds a BA in graphic design and painting obtained in the United States, but when she returned to Iran, after twelve years of studying and living abroad, she developed such a fondness for Persian writing and mystical poetry that she decided to devote her life to a new form of art, using 'script as a bold uncontrolled form of writing to . . . convey [her] understanding of the fundamental truths hidden in mystical Persian poetry'.[44] Her art, though, cannot be defined as merely educational or illustrative of mystical poetry, because she also uses the letters, as she explains, 'as a form of expression, often illegible, also sometimes without specific meaning, but usually illustrating mystical poems'.[45] However, she usually gives the original texts beside the painting or behind the canvas.

Shīrīnlū mainly draws her calligraphic motifs from poetic verses and seems more concerned with the inner meaning of mystical poetry, its *bāṭin*, rather than with its apparent meaning, its *ẓāhir*. It is particularly telling that, in defining her personal, inner and artistic research, she quotes a famous ghazal by Rūmī that often appears in her paintings:

> I tried to find Him on the Christian cross,
> but He was not there;
> I went to the Temple of the Hindus and to the old pagoda,
> but I could not find a trace of Him anywhere.
> I searched the mountains and the valleys
> but neither in the heights nor in the depths was I able to find Him.
> I went to the Ka'ba in Mecca,
> but He was not there either.
> I questioned the scholars and philosophers,
> but He was beyond their understanding.
> I then looked into my heart
> and it was there where He dwelled that I saw him;
> He was nowhere else to be found.[46]

According to Shīrīnlū, the increasing favour enjoyed by calligraphy in Iran, as well as by other traditional activities such as music, poetry, handicrafts and the like, is due to Iranians rediscovering their roots. Other artists have confirmed this trend, too, and they have all referred to a strong feeling of 'Iranian-ness' which permeates their activities. With regard to this point, I found particularly revealing one of Shīrīnlū's paintings, in which she matches the *basmala* with verses from the *Shāh-nāma*, the Iranian poem par excellence, the symbol of Iranians' pride in and attachment to their homeland. This can be understood as a way of combining Iran and Islam, or of 'Persianising' Islam, a process of transformation that Iranians have been undergoing for about fourteen centuries, but that had been interrupted by the revolution and its aftermath, when the state tried to control the society through its version of Islam and even to Arabise the country and its citizens.

By the same token, it is interesting to note that all my Iranian interlocutors (men included) always spoke of *khaṭṭ-i fārsī* (Persian calligraphy) and never of *khaṭṭ-i ʿarabī* (Arabic calligraphy), even when they referred to the reproduction of the Qur'an. In this way, they implicitly stressed the sense of national pride for an art they consider to be a product of the Persian genius, rather than for any 'Islamic' and Arabic heritage.[47] In a recent interview published on another website devoted to calligraphy, Noqṭa-alif, master calligrapher Ilāha Khātamī asks fellow calligraphers to dedicate more care to the art of calligraphy, as it is 'our national art and a component of Iranian people's cultural identity cards'.[48]

Calligraphy is a distinctive component of Persian culture and part of the national heritage. Iranians even consider it a symbol of their superiority, for it serves as evidence of the way they seized the idea and the form of the script from the Arabs and refined it according to Persian tastes. The embeddedness of calligraphy in the culture seems to be the main reason that so many Iranians are driven to perform calligraphy, and its main consequence is that most artists prefer to write in *nastaʿlīq* rather than in *naskh* and to copy verses of lyrics or even quotations from Persian prose rather than from Qur'anic verses.

There is no doubt that the reluctance by the artists to reproduce the Qur'an and to instead adopt its 'Persian version' (i.e. the *Mathnawī-yi maʿnawī*) is a form of resistance, a way to protest not against the holy book per se, but against the imposition of religion as a system of the state.[49] By the same token, we can speculate that women's minimal use of the Qur'an in calligraphy can be interpreted as a form of protest. Moreover, it is also true that the practice of yoga and meditation, and the reappraisal of the Zoroastrian faith are now part of a new syncretic credo that is spreading, especially among the youth of the upper classes. This shows Iranians' need for a type of spirituality and religious formula that is free from political manipulation.[50]

In the variegated world of *khaṭṭniwīsī*, I came across a few calligraphers who declared they started calligraphy only to be able to reproduce the Qur'an, but they did not elaborate upon this choice. Their unsubstantiated assertion was, therefore, of scarce interest for my investigation. Only one of them (who wishes to remain anonymous) declared that she learnt calligraphy because of its primary importance in preserving God's word. Doubtlessly, because the Qur'an is the very heart of Islam and calligraphy is the highest form of Islamic art, she pursues her art with the belief that it is the most perfect expression of the Divine.

A New Hybrid Practice

Eventually, during my period of research in Iran, I met an artist who interestingly combines different styles and techniques of calligraphy: Azra Aghighi Bakshayeshi (ʿAdhrā ʿAqīqī Bakhshāyishī).

Aghighi Bakshayeshi (born in Qum in 1968) is devoted to *naqqāshī khaṭṭ*. *Naqqāshī khaṭṭ* is the Persian way of continuing an ancient art while evolving it by developing different styles and techniques. There are more than sixty female artists in Iran who employ this technique, but Aghighi Bakshayeshi is one of the most famous ones. She followed what seems to be the usual route in order to become a calligrapher, that is, she started at an early age at home (her mother comes from a family of very famous calligraphers), then she became the pupil of one of the leading masters (*ustād*s), and finally she got her licence from an Anjuman. Now, her signature is a brand,[51] as she says, and she has two assistants who are learning from her. Aghighi Bakshayeshi professes to be a true believer and indicates that she was encouraged to become a scholar of Islamic Studies by her father (now deceased), who was a cleric. In her large paintings on canvas, she uses both Kufic and *nastaʿlīq* styles and quotes equally from Persian poetry and from the Qur'an: she maintains that she draws much energy from the holy book because she believes in it. For the same reason, she regularly and often recites the ninety-nine names of God. But although she is inspired by religion (especially by early Islamic writings), religion is not at the heart of her practice:

> It is not my intention to pass [my religious inspirations] on to the viewer. I think my religious feelings in my work reveal my inner feelings. For me, these are very personal. I am delighted viewers appreciate my work and hope they can see that it is a contemporary artistic work. I am trying to show the viewer that my artistic inspiration continues to be part of a rich heritage from the golden treasure of Middle Eastern culture.[52]

In addition, Aghighi Bakshayeshi believes that viewers do not need to understand the meaning of the calligraphic letters and words to gain access to the core of her art; in fact, she says that not understanding the words is exactly what she wants from her audience:

> When viewers do not understand the meaning they are not reading the letters. I am looking for viewers who are seeing and not reading. These writings are whispers in my mind that do not mean too much, like a meditation. Sometimes they could be poetry, prayers, or just a conversation. I am not trying to convey spirituality with my writings. Speaking only one language creates a barrier between me and the viewer if they do not speak the same language. I am hoping to reach out to a broader audience with my art as a universal message.[53]

However, when she employs verses from the Qur'an, Aghighi Bakshayeshi would rather use the short ones 'that immediately give you the meaning'; in saying this, she shows me a big canvas hanging on the wall of her studio, in which prayer proceeds spiral-like until it becomes a tiny and unreadable sign. It is a real, written representation of *dhikr* (the devotional act of remembering God's name) that confirms the artist's Sufi soul.

Nevertheless, Aghighi Bakshayeshi is not someone who has retired from an active life to pursue a Sufi lifestyle of pure contemplation; quite the contrary. Her engagement is particularly evident in the book she published some years ago, an impressive anthology of biographical data and samples of calligraphy by about three hundred female calligraphers throughout the republic.[54] She says she wanted to bring attention to women in the field of calligraphy, so she launched a call for the submission of works by any woman who was interested in being listed in this modern version of a *tadhkira*. Aghighi Bakshayeshi did not have the money to publish the book and had to ask the bank for a loan. When the book was available, she called the calligraphers in the listing and requested that they both buy the book and advertise it.

According to Aghighi Bakshayeshi, only forty per cent of the women listed in her book would occasionally turn to the Qur'an for inspiration; the remaining sixty per cent would rather rely on Persian poetry. She maintains that this is not the result of any contestation of the holy book on their part, because 'all female calligraphers are believers; secular female calligraphers do not exist'.[55] She herself says she would use Qur'anic verses in only thirty per cent of her productions, with the rest of them inspired by Persian poetry, in particular by Rūmī. 'I am interested in God's beauty and in the beauty He has created', she states. She confirms her pantheistic love for beauty by affirming that she is an admirer of the works of Shirin Neshat, whose exhibition in Iran is prohibited by the local authorities because they are considered to be subversive.

Neshat is Iran's most internationally acclaimed female artist, who became famous for her use of calligraphy that excludes the Qur'an.[56] However, the images that Neshat uses are strongly linked to Islamic culture, primarily because calligraphy is the most recognisable Islamic art form.[57] The elegance of the Arabic/Persian/Islamic alphabet is the immediate imprint of a civilisation deeply imbued with faith, but this does not hinder the creation of a hybrid space in which tradition and modernity can coexist, as Iranian artists prove.

Final Remarks

'*Al-islām karāmat al-mar'āt*' (Islam is the honour of women)[58] is a statement that seems to reiterate the attitude of the Iranian religious authorities towards women. In theory, the authorities state that the Islamic Republic, which is based on Islamic principles (*in primis*, on the Qur'an), fully respects women's rights, and thus they do not see the requirement for any discussion about the need to improve women's social, cultural and legal position in the country. This rhetoric is maintained in every sphere of Iranian life, including the artistic one, with the same problems and results. If in the social, cultural and legal arena women suffer from discrimination and disadvantages often because of a patriarchal interpretation of the Qur'an, in the arts, and in particular in calligraphy, they likewise face the same restrictions and limitations: they are encouraged to interact with the holy book, but not to bring their knowledge of the Qur'an to bear in their works, so as not to challenge the *status quo*. Proof of this attitude was visible in two calligraphy exhibitions held in Tehran during the summer of 2013: the first one, organised by the Museum of Contemporary Art, exhibited the work of a large selection of calligraphers from all over the country but did not host a single female artist; the second one, at the Art Gallery in the Pārk-i Millat complex, displayed just one work signed by a woman. However, we cannot be sure that women were deliberately excluded from these exhibitions. The fact that, at the same time, the office for the Women's Affairs of Tehran Municipality launched a call for the seventh exhibition of female calligraphers inspired by the Qur'an is further proof of the gender apartheid pursued by the Iranian authorities; this kind of exhibition is more a ghettoisation than an attempt to integrate women's art into the mainstream.

Nevertheless, Iranian women have persevered in their efforts to carve out a space for themselves in difficult situations. While many of them have become theologians and are engaged in a new hermeneutic of the Qur'an, one in which they strongly believe they have the right to read and interpret the Qur'an as they please, others are convinced that they have the right to practice religion as they like. All this despite authorities and political systems building an arbitrary wall between Islamic and non-Islamic practices. Things in Iran are continuously changing and forms of religiosity or non-religiosity are being reshaped not only by the practices of the state, but, above all, by the practices of the people. Women's use of the Qur'an and other sources in their calligraphy enhances their claim that Islam allows space for change and for an expression of cultural diversity while maintaining its principles.

NOTES

1 Mansoureh Hosseini, personal communication with author, June 2011.

2 *Fars News Agency*, http://www.farsnews.com/newstext.php?nn=13920713000492. We might infer from the many websites dedicated to calligraphy that there are four times as many male practitioners in Iran as there are female.

3 See David Simonowitz, 'A Modern Master of Islamic Calligraphy and Her Peers', *Journal of Middle East Women's Studies* 6, no. 1 (2010), pp. 75–102.

4 There are several books on the history of calligraphers in Iran. In particular, see Mahdī Bayānī, *Aḥwāl wa Āthār-i khushniwīsān* (Tehran, 1363 Sh./1984).

5 Simonowitz, 'A Modern Master of Islamic Calligraphy', p. 76.

6 Rafī'ī Mihrābādī, *Khaṭṭ wa khaṭṭāṭān* (Tehran, 1345 Sh./1966), p. 81.

7 Muḥammad Ḥasan Rajabī, *Mashāhīr-i zanān-i īrānī wa pārsī-guy, az āghāz tā mashrūṭa* (Tehran, 1374 Sh./1995), pp. 41–2.

8 Betül İpşirli Argit and Salim Ayduz, 'Jewels of Muslim Calligraphy: Book Review of "Female Calligraphers: Past and Present", by Hilal Kazan', http://www.muslimheritage.com/article/jewels-muslim-calligraphy-book-review-%E2%80%9Cfemale-calligraphers-past-present-hilal-kazan%E2%80%9D.

9 Gawhar Shād Khātūn used the *nastaʿlīq* script to copy, among other books, *Gulistān* [The Rose Garden] by Saʿdī, considered to be the most notable prose book in Persian.

10 Rajabī, *Mashāhīr-i zanān*, p. 200.

11 Badr ol-Moluk Bàmdàd, *From Darkness into Light: Women's Emancipation in Iran*, ed. and tr. Frank Ronald Charles Bagley (New York, 1977), p. 19.

12 Mu'assisa-yi Muṭāliʿāt-i Tārīkh-i Muʿāṣir-i Īrān [Institute for Iranian Contemporary Historical Studies], http://www.iichs.org/srcfiles/printdoc.asp?id=421&doc_cat=9. There are also many samples of calligraphy by women in private collections; for a selection, see www.qajarwomen.org.

13 Rajabī, *Mashāhīr-i zanān*, pp. 217–19.

14 Also, the presence of female calligraphers in the modern Ottoman world is particularly well attested; see Simonowitz, 'A Modern Master of Islamic Calligraphy', pp. 79–80.

15 Bàmdàd, *From Darkness into Light*, p. 20.

16 Qāḍī Aḥmad b. Mīr Munshī al-Ḥusaynī, *Calligraphers and Painters*, tr. from the Persian by Vladimir Minorsky (Washington, DC, 1959), p. 56. In Qazwīn, Qāḍī Aḥmad served princess Parī-Khān (d. 983/1576), who was an influential figure of the Safavid state and the daughter of Shāh Ṭahmāsp (r. 930–84/1524–76); ibid., p. 14.

17 Ṣalāḥ al-Dīn al-Munajjid, 'Women's Roles in the Art of Arabic Calligraphy', in George N. Atiyeh, ed., *The Book in the Islamic World: The Written Word and Communication in the Middle East* (Albany, NY, 1995), p. 144.

18 Delia Cortese and Simonetta Calderini, *Women and the Fatimids in the World of Islam* (Edinburgh, 2006), p. 207.

19 Mīrzā Aḥmad Khān ʿAṣad al-Dawla, *Tārīkh-i ʿAṣadī* (Tehran, 1376 Sh./1997), p. 175.

20 Rajabī, *Mashāhīr-i zanān*, pp. 146–7.

21 However, some scholars maintain that the Safavid period saw a progressive marginalisation of women because Shiʿi Islam became the state religion. See this point of view from an Iranian perspective in Mitra Jahandide and Shahab Khaefi, 'Women's Status during the Safavid Period', in Vladimir Vasek, ed., *Recent Researches in Social Science, Digital Convergence, Manufacturing and Tourism: International Conference on Social Science, Social Economy and Digital Convergence* ([Athens], 2011), pp. 137–42.

22 Huda al-Tamimi, 'Islam, Calligraphy and Gender: An Overview on the Role of Women Calligraphers in Islam', *IRS Cultural Heritage* 13, no. 2 (2013), p. 28.

23 On the aspirant calligrapher's complete routine, see Annemarie Schimmel, *Calligraphy and Islamic Culture* (New York, 1984), chapter 2.

24 Bàmdàd, *From Darkness into Light*, p. 20.

25 Schimmel, *Calligraphy and Islamic Culture*, p. 47.

26 As a matter of fact, many female calligraphers were also Hadith scholars; see Muḥammad Zubayr Ṣiddīqī, *Ḥadīth Literature: Its Origin, Development and Special Features* (Cambridge, 1993), pp. 117–23.

27 Tamimi, 'Islam, Calligraphy and Gender', p. 28.
28 For more on the Saqqākhāna artistic trend, see Alice Bombardier's article in this volume, chapter 12.
29 For more information on the Society, see Persian Wikipedia: https://fa.wikipedia.org/wiki.
30 http://www.azizihonar.com/fa/.
31 Seyyed Hossein Nasr, 'Foreword', in Seyyed Ghahreman Safavi and Simon Weightman, *Rūmī's Mystical Design: Reading the Mathnawī, Book One* (Albany, NY, 2009), p. x.
32 From Abna agency, http://abna.co/data.asp?lang=3&Id=252190 (webpage no longer available).
33 The seventh session of the festival was held in Mordād 1392 Sh./August 2013.
34 See Keiko Sakurai, 'Shi'ite Women's Seminaries (*howzeh-ye 'elmiyyeh-ye khahran*) in Iran: Possibilities and Limitations', *Iranian Studies* 45, no. 6 (2012), pp. 727–44.
35 See Anna Vanzan, *Le donne di Allah: Viaggio nei femminismi islamici* (Milan, 2012), chapter 2.
36 See, among others, Arzoo Osanloo, *The Politics of Women's Rights in Iran* (Princeton, NJ, 2009), chapter 3.
37 Nasrīn Purhamrang, personal communication with author, June 2013.
38 Maryam Ala Amjadi, 'Moving Ahead in Curves: The Art of Calligraphy', *Tehran Times*, 28 February 2012, http://www.tehrantimes.com/life-style/95917-moving-ahead-in-curves-the-art-of-calligraphy-in-iran (accessed June 2014; link no longer available).
39 Ibid. However, it is not clear if this statement belongs to the interviewer or to the interviewee.
40 Maliḥa Ṣabūrī, personal conversation with author, Tehran, June 2013.
41 Maryam Jawānbakht, personal conversation with author, Tehran, June 2013.
42 During the discussion at the colloquium 'Approaches to the Qur'an in Contemporary Iran' held at the Institute of Ismaili Studies, London, 2–4 September 2013 (which served as the basis for the present volume), Niloofar Haeri pointed out that in present-day Iran women use breathing techniques from yoga when performing prayer (*namāz*) (albeit unconscious of this connection to yoga, I would add).
43 Jalāl al-Dīn Rūmī, *The Mathnawí of Jalálud'dín Rúmí*, ed. Reynold A. Nicholson (London, 1982).
44 Maryam Shīrīnlū, personal conversation with the author, Tehran, June 2013.
45 Ibid.
46 Ibid.
47 A similar remark about the patriotic aspect of Persian calligraphers is made by Vlad Atanasiu in 'The President and the Calligrapher: Arabic Calligraphy and its Political Use', in *Studies in Architecture, History and Culture: Papers Presented by the 2003–2004 AKPIA@MIT Visiting Fellows* (Cambridge, MA, 2006), p. 14.
48 'Kushniwīsī parcham-i jahānī-yi hunar-i māst', 6 Bahman 1392 Sh./26 January 2014, http://www.noghtealef.com/index.php/fa/mosahebe/192-elahekhatami.
49 I would like to note here Dr Mohammad Mesbahi's remark, made during his presentation at the colloquium 'Approaches to the Qur'an in Contemporary

Iran', when, in his position as Director of the Islamic College in London, he stated that in post-revolution Iran children do not learn the Qur'an well because it is forced on them.

50 This new approach to Zoroastrianism is not devoid of some naivety, as many people turn to the ancient Iranian faith because of its supposed democratic stance. (It is also a way of advertising one's status in society, as Zoroastrianism's aristocratic and exclusive character is well known.) As an example, during the 2012 to 2013 international exhibition at the Tehran National Museum, the Cyrus Cylinder – the document of the Achaemenian king's declaration of tolerance towards all his subjects and testament to Ancient Persia's religious tolerance – provoked a stir among young Iranians, with many adopting a replica of the cylinder as a personal charm.

51 Azra Aghighi Bakshayeshi, personal conversation with author, Tehran, June 2013.

52 http://www.kashyahildebrand.org/zurich/bakhshayeshi/bakhshayeshi002.html. I am quoting from an interview between Aghighi Bakshayeshi and the Kashya Hildebrand Gallery, Zurich, as it partly resumes the conversation I had with the artist.

53 Ibid.

54 'Adhrā 'Aqīqī Bakhshāyishī [Azra Aghighi Bakshayeshi], *Zanān-i khushniwīs* (Tehran 1388 Sh./2009).

55 Aghighi Bakshayeshi, personal conversation with the author, Tehran, June 2013.

56 Neshat's decision to not use the Qur'an in her work deserves more analysis. In my opinion, her choice reflects a response to several issues that reverberate with other artists from the Middle East and North Africa in general. While some do decide to employ the Qur'an in their work as a declaration that women's oppression in Muslim countries does not stem from the original message of Islam (i.e. the Qur'an), others, such as Neshat, prefer to give voice to local literata (such as Forugh Farrakhzād) to express local women's protest. The absence of the Qur'an from Neshat's art might, additionally, be due to her desire not to offend the religious sensibility of Muslims who would accept the depiction, in her photos, of profane lyrics on the hands, but would surely reject the depiction of Qur'anic suras on the human body's most despised part, such as the feet.

57 This also explains why many artists from the Middle East and North Africa use calligraphy; they do so in order to achieve international visibility. They sometimes even present their art as Orientalism in reverse – using a combination of calligraphy and naked women's bodies in their work, for instance. See Barbad Golshiri. 'For they Know What They Do Know', *E-Flux* 9 (September 2009), http://www.e-flux.com/journal/for-they-know-what-they-do-know/#_ftnref17.

58 Quoted in Haifaa Khalafallah, 'Muslim Women: Public Authority, Scriptures and "Islamic Law"', in Amira El-Azhary Sonbol, ed., *Beyond the Exotic: Women's Histories in Islamic Societies* (Cairo, 2006), p. 37.

14

The Divine Word on the Screen: Imaging the Qur'an in Iranian Cinema*

NACIM PAK-SHIRAZ

THE VAST financial support available for the production of 'preferred' films in Iran has led to the recent emergence of a genre that can loosely be referred to as the 'religious epic' within Iranian cinema. Whilst the genre has had a long history in Western cinema, it is a new development within Iranian cinema. Much has been written on the Biblical epic within Western cinema, particularly Hollywood cinema, but no academic attention has been paid to films that derive their narratives from the Qur'an. Indeed, even the term 'Qur'anic epic' did not exist as a conceptual category until recently.[1] Academic attention to Iranian cinema both inside and outside Iran has largely concentrated on art-house films, with little discussion of commercial cinema[2] and nothing at all on epic or Qur'anic films.

Studies of the Qur'an, on the other hand, have so far mainly focused on its textual analysis within strictly theological and jurisprudential fields. In studying the Qur'an and the arts, the usual approach, as Oleg Grabar argues, focuses either on what the Qur'an receives from the society that adorns it or what it gives to objects, buildings and the arts more generally. A third approach, little explored and which Grabar calls the hermeneutics of the Qur'an for the arts, 'explains why visual creativity became what it is within Islamic culture' and has the potential to lead us into the 'cultural context and rhetorical forms which surrounded [the works of art], and thus into a deeper understanding of whatever constitutes the particular genius and the many facets of Islamic art'.[3]

* This research was supported by a grant from the Carnegie Trust for the Universities of Scotland.

No study has thus far examined how cinema has been employed as a new medium for engaging with the Qur'an. My research aims to initiate this debate within both film studies and Islamic studies. I have already investigated the emergence of the Qur'anic epic as a genre in Iranian cinema and examined the challenges of negotiating the balance between religious authenticity and dramatic effectiveness in creating Iranian religious epics.[4] In this chapter, I will analyse the first Iranian Qur'anic epic, *The Kingdom of Solomon* (*Mulk-i Sulayman*, Shahriar Bahrani, 2010),[5] to investigate the active partnership between theologians and filmmakers in creating an authentic interpretation of the Qur'anic discourse.

I will first provide an overview of the production of the film and locate my study within earlier depictions of Solomon, including Islamic manuscript illustrations, medieval commentaries and Hollywood representations. I will then explore how the film claims to provide a contemporary reading of Solomon's story by emphasising the centrality of the Qur'an as a resource, allowing it to rectify what it deems contradictory to the scripture in earlier narratives. Next, I will examine how the film claims to have attained a religious function – not as an attempt to simply retell ancient religious history but, more importantly, to present an image of the future. Finally, I will evaluate the Shi'i elements embedded within the film, particularly in the characterisation of Solomon and the challenges to his authority as a parallel to 'Alī, the first Shi'i imam.

The Kingdom of Solomon is the first 'big-production' film to have secured the largest funding in the history of Iranian cinema at the time of its making.[6] The film was also first on a number of other fronts. In an unprecedented move, the budget for the film was approved by and obtained from the Majlis, the Iranian parliament. Being one of the first Iranian films to employ large-scale digital and computer-generated images (DGI and CGI), the special effects for *The Kingdom of Solomon* were outsourced to Hong Kong. Furthermore, the production team prided itself on being the first to have produced a film in which the Qur'an was central to the filmic narrative, and to have thereby created a truly Qur'anic film.

A number of research groups – including the Taha Qur'anic Research Group, headed by Ḥujjat al-Islām Saeed Isfahanian, and a historical research group – were employed for the making of this film. Isfahanian explained to me that it was important to arrive at the main text of the story of Solomon, and so they began with the Qur'an.[7] This research began about two years before the shooting of the film. The twenty or so members of the Qur'anic research group alone ranged from high-standing clerics, who acted as consultants on the project, to divinity students from the Universities of Tehran and Imam Ṣādiq, who worked as research assistants on the film. Moreover, this collaboration extended beyond the research period. At the request of Mojtaba Faravardeh (the producer) and Shahriar Bahrani (the director), Isfahanian was also present as a consultant during filming. The film's official website included an overview of this extensive research in eleven documents amounting to about one hundred pages; however, these have since been taken down.[8] Bahrani also emphasised the meticulousness of both the underpinning research and the artistic value of the film. The screenplay was revised thirty-nine times and reduced from 150 pages to sixty pages to remove the narrative's heavy reliance on dialogue and better utilise the medium's artistic potential in conveying its message.[9] The film was nominated in nine categories at the 28th Fajr International Film Festival in 2010 and won five awards.[10]

Earlier Depictions of Solomon

When Iranian cinema became serious about making religious epics, it had to consider the audience's familiarity with these stories. In creating a Qur'anic epic on Solomon, Iranian filmmakers were faced with the challenge of not only producing something new but also negotiating the pre-existing narratives and images that informed the ideas and expectations of many of their viewers. Culturally, these ranged from the more traditional, such as Qur'anic references, narratives of the classical period of Islam and medieval illustrations, to the more popular, such as Iranian folklore and twentieth-century Hollywood productions of biblical epics. In this section I will highlight some of these earlier narratives and images to identify common tropes through which Solomon has been imagined.

Illustrations of Solomon in painting

In early Muslim depictions of Solomon, certain imagery and motifs dominate these representations, providing us with an insight into how earlier artists and patrons had imagined him. In researching these depictions, I examined twelve representations of Solomon across six centuries (Table 1). These included one contemporary miniature painting by the acclaimed artist Mahmoud Farshchian entitled *The Queen of Sheba Visits Solomon* and eleven illustrations from the eight manuscripts written in Persian listed below:

1. *Miʿrāj-nāma* (unknown artist, 839/1436, Herat)[11]
2. Tīmūrid manuscript (unknown artist, late ninth/fifteenth century, Persia)[12]
3. Firdawsī's *Shāh-nāma* (unknown artist, *c.* 946–56/1540–50, Shiraz)[13]
4. Firdawsī's *Shāh-nāma* (unknown artist, *c.* 946–56/1540–50, Shiraz)[14]
5. Firdawsī's *Shāh-nāma* (unknown artist, tenth/sixteenth century, Shiraz)[15]
6. Firdawsī's *Shāh-nāma* (unknown artist, c. 1575–90, Shiraz)[16]
7. Miniature painting pasted on an album leaf (Shaykh Riḍā ʿAbbāsī, 1074/1664, Isfahan)[17]
8. *Dīwān* of Ḥāfiẓ (unknown artist, 1796, Kashmir)[18]

All twelve illustrations depict Solomon with a halo, a clear reference to his position as the prophet-king. He is always depicted on a throne, unless he is in the company of other prophets, as in the *Miʿrāj-nāma*, where he is standing in front of the Prophet Muhammad, or sitting on the floor, as in one of the illustrations from the *Dīwān* of Ḥāfiẓ, with the prophets Joseph and Jacob. He also is not depicted on a throne in the twentieth-century miniature *The Queen of Sheba Visits Solomon*. When Solomon is not depicted with other prophets, the jinns are the most recurring image accompanying him. The expanse of his kingdom and power is reflected in the diversity of races and cultures present in his court, depicted through the different skin colours, headgear and robes of the courtiers. Except in the *Miʿrāj-nāma* and two of the illustrations in the *Dīwān*, animals and birds are included in all of the manuscripts, alluding to Solomon's gift of comprehending the speech of birds and animals. Eight of the twelve illustrations include angels, emphasising the strength of his retinue and power. As such, these depictions underscore Solomon's prophethood and his unique powers over the natural and supernatural worlds.

Solomon's encounter with Bilqīs, the Queen of Sheba, captured the imagination of many of the artists illustrating Solomon. Three of the four sixteenth-century manuscripts of the *Shāh-nāma* include elaborate paintings of Solomon and Bilqīs. Each has a double-paged frontispiece depicting the monarchs on separate pages, sitting on their thrones. Angels, jinns, mythical birds and animals surround them. In all three illustrations, only the Sīmurgh (mythical bird) is depicted with Solomon, but many angels accompany Bilqīs, including an angel flying towards her holding a halo in two of these manuscripts. Farshchian's twentieth-century painting includes all of the above imagery and motifs but brings Solomon and Bilqīs onto the same page, with Bilqīs holding out a flower to Solomon and a hoopoe hovering between them. A rainbow of mythical creatures, Sīmurghs, translucent angels, people of different races, harp-playing jinns, demons, wild beasts, deer and peacocks surround the lovers. The fluid brush strokes coupled with the smiles on the faces of all these disparate characters create the harmony, unity and love that the artist intends to illustrate. Like many of the earlier depictions of Solomon, Farshchian highlights the extraordinary, the glamour and the power of Solomon, and his love story with Bilqīs. These are recurring elements within the story of Solomon. Interestingly, there are no depictions of the popular concept of his 'flying carpet' or any other flying objects in these paintings that would refer to Solomon's control of the wind. In one of the *Dīwān* paintings, his throne is carried by demons.

Although the *Shāh-nāma* itself does not carry the story of Solomon, it is illustrated as frontispieces in three of the manuscripts discussed above, and scholars have drawn links between the *Shāh-nāma* and Solomon. Some argue that with the coming of Islam, pre-Islamic Iranian myths were appropriated into the new religious narrative. Fāṭima Mudarrisī, for example, compares the characteristics and

Table 1: Details of imagery in the illustrations of Solomon

Manuscript/ Painting	Artist	Date	Place	Jinn and demons	Sīmurgh	Angels	Animals	Bilqīs	Solomon with halo	Birds	Throne	People of different nations and stations
Miʿrāj-nāma	Unknown artist	839/1436	Herat	No	No	Gabriel	Burāq	No	Yes	No	No	No. David and Prophet Muhammad
Tīmūrid manuscript	Unknown artist	late ninth/ fifteenth century	Persia	Yes	Yes	Yes	Mythical and real	No	Yes	Mythical and real	Yes	People wearing different types of headgear and robes, and having different skin colours
Firdawsī's *Shāh-nāma* (David Collection)	Unknown artist	*c.* 946–56/ 1540–50	Shiraz	Yes	Yes	Yes	Mythical and real	Solomon and Bilqīs on separate thrones and pages	Yes	Yes	Yes	Homogenous in each court but different from each other
Firdawsī's *Shāh-nāma* (Sotheby's)	Unknown artist	*c.* 946–56/ 1540–50	Shiraz	Yes	Yes	Yes	Yes	Solomon and Bilqīs on separate thrones and pages	Yes	Yes	Yes	People wearing different types of headgear and robes, and having different hairstyles
Firdawsī's *Shāh-nāma* (Sotheby's)	Unknown artist	tenth/ sixteenth century	Shiraz	Yes	Yes	Yes	Many varieties of mythical and real	Solomon and Bilqīs on separate thrones and pages	Yes	Mythical and real	Yes	People wearing different types of headgear and robes, and having different hairstyles
Firdawsī's *Shāh-nāma* (Harvard Art Museums)	Unknown artist	*c.* 982–98/ 1575–90	Shiraz	Yes	Yes	Yes	Mythical and real	No	Yes	Mythical and real	Yes	Not visible

Miniature painting, pasted on album leaf (David Collection)	Shaykh Riḍā ʿAbbāsī	1074/1664	Isfahan	Yes	No	Yes	Only one monkey	No	Yes	Only one to the left of the throne	Yes	Indians, Europeans, and people of various tribes wearing different types of headgear and robes, and having different hairstyles
Dīwān of Ḥāfiẓ, fol.43a (Walters MS)	Unknown artist	1796	Kashmir	No	No	No	No	No	Yes	No	Yes	Three courtiers and one servant
Dīwān of Ḥāfiẓ, fol. 84a (Walters MS)	Unknown artist	1796	Kashmir	Yes	No	No	No	No	Yes	Hoopoe	Yes	One servant and two subordinates
Dīwān of Ḥāfiẓ, fol. 125a (Walters MS)	Unknown artist	1796	Kashmir	Yes	No	No	No	No	Yes	Hoopoe and doves	Yes	No
Dīwān of Ḥāfiẓ, fol. 192a (Walters MS)	Unknown artist	1796	Kashmir	Yes	No	No	No	No	Yes	No	No. Solomon seated at the same level as the other two prophets	Prophets Jacob and Joseph and two subordinates
The Queen of Sheba Visits Solomon	Mahmoud Farshchian	20th century	Tehran	Yes	Yes	Yes	Yes	Yes	No	Mythical and real with hoopoe in the middle	Court but no throne	People wearing different types of headgear and robes, and having different hairstyles

narratives surrounding the mythical ancient Iranian king Jamshīd with those of the Islamic prophet Solomon.[19] Tracing fourteen similarities between the two figures, Mudarrisī concludes that when the Iranians encountered the Muslim narratives of the glory and magnificence of Solomon, many understood Solomon and Jamshīd to have been one and the same figure. Consequently, some Iranian-Islamic texts attributed Solomon's characteristics to Jamshīd and vice-versa.[20]

Solomon in Ṭabarī and Hollywood

To recreate the filmic image and narrative of Solomon, contemporary Iranian imagination drew not only from the Iranian-Islamic tradition but also upon the Western genre of religious epics. While they had inherited the Muslim heritage of narrating stories of the prophets, they also found themselves largely bound by the Western cinematic codes and conventions of the epic genre. One of *The Kingdom of Solomon*'s significant aims, therefore, was to rectify these pre-existing images within both Western and Muslim narratives. As such, one of the eleven documents of the Taha Qur'anic Research Group was dedicated to listing the discrepancies between the Islamic and non-Islamic sources on Solomon. These comprised no less than twenty-six topics. Here, I will locate *The Kingdom of Solomon* within some of these pre-existing narratives and highlight its focus on a contemporary retelling of this ancient story. These narratives include two Western epics on Solomon, the cinematic film *Solomon and Sheba* (King Vidor, 1959) and the television movie *Solomon* (Roger Young, 1997), as well as the traditional Islamic narratives of Solomon found in the work of Persian historian Abū Jaʿfar Muḥammad Ṭabarī (d. 310/923).

Solomon and Sheba centres around the romance between the title characters. It begins with the appointment of Solomon as David's heir and ends with Solomon regaining his throne from his brother Adonijah (who had defected to the Pharaoh) and with the Queen of Sheba's 'conversion' and return to her realm. The film has been criticised for 'its irreverent and irrelevant digressions from the biblical text and its inevitable concentration on a vapid romantic plot'.[21] *Solomon*, on the other hand, is a part of the *Bible Collection* miniseries and so it presents a more 'authentic' depiction. This movie also starts with the rivalry of the two brothers but ends with the disintegration of Solomon's kingdom soon after his death.

The romance with Sheba drives the plot of *Solomon and Sheba*, with only very brief references to Solomon's many harem wives. *Solomon*, however, includes a series of the king's marriages and his many children from these unions, a reference to the biblical account of his 700 wives and 300 concubines. Sheba is only introduced in the second half of the film. Solomon's mother, Bathsheba, is far more developed in *Solomon*, and particularly for her role in securing Solomon's succession, than in *Solomon and Sheba*, where she appears briefly as a passive character with a marginal role.

In the Islamic context, the *qiṣaṣ al-anbiyā'* is a valuable source for filling in the gaps in the narratives on the Muslim prophets. The *qiṣaṣ al-anbiyā'*, 'the "legends of the pre-Islamic prophets", is the title of several works relating the lives of the prophets of the Old Testament, the story of Jesus, and some other events [in] which pious heroes or enemies of God are involved'.[22] Equally, *Ta'rīkh al-rusul wa'l-mulūk* by Ṭabarī is one of the most influential works informing Muslim understanding of the lives of the pre-Islamic prophets. As Clifford Edmund Bosworth notes, 'In form it is a universal history, dealing firstly with the Creation, the Old Testament patriarchs and prophets, the rulers of ancient Israel and of the ancient Persians, and the culmination of the prophets before Muhammad, Jesus, before arriving at the history of the Persian Sāsānids.'[23]

Stories of Solomon in these early sources are surrounded with romance going back to his conception. Unlike the Judaeo-Christian sources which recount David's adultery with Bathsheba,[24] traditional Muslim sources have commuted his transgression from adultery to lusting after Uriah's wife. Thus, according to these sources, David ensures that his commander, Uriah, is sent to battles that would not see his return, allowing David to marry the commander's widow, Bathsheba.[25] The Qur'anic reference used in the sources to refer to this episode is itself very brief, with no direct reference to David's transgression but to his greed, for which he ultimately repents and is forgiven by God.[26]

Ṭabarī emphasises the magnitude of Solomon's kingdom in a number of places: 'It is said that there were only three kings (in all of history) who ruled over the entire earth and all its people. Nimrod b. Arghu, Dhū'l-Qarnayn, and Solomon b. David.'[27] Just as the Taha Qur'anic Research Group refers to the Qur'an to narrate the story of Solomon, so too does Ṭabarī intersperse his history of Solomon with Qur'anic verses, thereby underlining the authenticity of his chronicles. These sources, however, expand and dramatise the Qur'anic verses. Ṭabarī narrates accounts of Solomon's army, claimed to be one hundred parasangs long, with each quarter comprising humans, jinns, wild animals and birds.[28] Solomon's 'flying object' was pieces of wood put together that could hold all of the above and more, carried by the wind, which was subservient to Solomon, a reference to Q. 38:36 (*Then We subjected the wind to his power, to flow gently to his order, Whithersoever he willed*).[29] A slight switch in the numbers of wives and concubines of the Israelite sources turns them into three hundred wives and seven hundred concubines.[30]

The details that Ṭabarī draws from different sources allow him to fill the silences in the Qur'an, which does not concern itself with providing comprehensive narratives of the prophets.[31] As such, a whole chapter is dedicated to the story of Solomon and Bilqīs, with rich details such as the divine memory-wipe of everyone but Solomon after Bilqīs blasphemously challenges him to state God's colour.[32] The manipulation of time and space in this narrative are reminiscent of sci-fi films, an irresistible if anachronistic reading. Another entertaining detail is the origin of the first depilatory paste, made by the demons at the order of Solomon, who was keen to marry Bilqīs but was nonetheless repulsed after seeing the reflection of her extremely hairy legs.[33] The wrath of God upon Solomon and the subsequent loss of his kingdom is the result of the idolatry of one his wives. But this only lasts for forty days, the same length as the wife's worship of her father's statue, which she had placed in Solomon's palace. Unlike in *Solomon and Sheba*, where Bilqīs/Sheba is the idolatrous wife, the wife in Ṭabarī's narration is the daughter of a powerful king whom Solomon had defeated and killed.[34] The connection between Ṭabarī's narrative and the Qur'an, however, becomes quite tenuous for these episodes, and Qur'anic quotes to support the storyline are few and far between.

Contemporary Interpretation of the Qur'an through Filmic Discourses

The Kingdom of Solomon provides an alternative narrative to the dominant understanding of the story of Solomon. In doing so, it counters not only religious understandings about a prophet perceived to have been miscast in earlier sacred texts but also challenges what it sees as the misuse of this narrative in the global political sphere. According to the consultant cleric Isfahanian, this fresh approach to the Qur'an and Solomon, devoid of any preconditioned ideas based on the Judaeo-Christian traditions, or even stemming from their own *ḥawza* (Shiʿi seminary) or popular tales, provided the research group with a new perspective on Solomon. The Qur'an, Isfahanian said, is not a storybook and therefore does not dramatise events. Rather, it is a book for 'recognising signs' (*āya shināsī*). Studying it, he continued, reveals that the Qur'an focuses on three main stages of Solomon's kingship: his initial ordinary realm, its elevation after his prayer for an unrivalled kingdom, and the testing period in-between. This explains the film's emphasis on the various challenges to Solomon's kingdom rather than the usual focus on the romance between him and the Queen of Sheba. Accordingly, and despite the fact that the most sequential Qur'anic verses on Solomon relate to the Queen of Sheba (in *Sūrat al-Naml*, Q. 27), the events of their encounter are deferred to the final part of the trilogy.[35]

Isfahanian distinguishes this film's approach to the creation of the narrative from that of other Iranian religious films. According to him, there are three different approaches to the making of religious films. The first is a historical approach. In this approach the films are made by filmmakers and producers who are believers but who rely on history rather than the Qur'an in creating their narratives, resulting in films that are not 'bona fide religious films'. The two television series *Imam Ali* (Davud Mirbaqeri, 1997) and *The Loneliest Warrior* (*Tanhātarīn Sardār*, Mehdi Fakhimzadeh, 1997) are examples of such films.[36] Isfahanian argues that these films have a 'historical' rather than a 'religious' fabric. In the second approach, there is a move away from the dominance of history over religious texts. For Isfahanian, these films attains more depth because of this, though some of them, he says, have been more successful than others. He cites, for example, the television series *Saint Mary* (*Maryam-i muqaddas*, Shahriar Bahrani, 2002), which he believes has achieved more depth than *Joseph the Prophet* (*Yūsuf-i payāmbar*, Farajollah Salahshoor, 2008) due to its reliance on the Qur'an. The third approach is a new wave within Iranian religious cinema, which starts with *The Kingdom of Solomon*. It is a rewriting of history that comes from the depths of the Qur'an, with other sources being secondary to it. Nonetheless, when the research groups created the six-metre-long timeline from Adam to Jesus in preparation for the writing and filming of *The Kingdom of Solomon*, sources other than the Qur'an were not ignored either. The research groups incorporated information not only from traditional sources but also from the latest scientific approaches, including developments in DNA research, and from archaeological findings. However, the film maintains the centrality of the Qur'an, and as such claims to be a departure from dominant ideas about Solomon, not simply within the West but also within Muslim societies, which have also drawn much of their ideas about Solomon from Judaeo-Christian texts.

The film's producer Faravardeh, who also worked with the screenwriting team, explained in our meeting in August 2013 that even though they had aimed to arrive at the origins of the narrative, they recognised that the film was still limited to being an account from their understanding of the Qur'an: 'What we do claim is that our resource is the Qur'an. The artist therefore engages with the Qur'an through the medium of film.' *The Kingdom of Solomon*, he continued, is not a religious or historical film, but 'a Qur'anic film because it is based on the Qur'an'. Were they to claim that *The Kingdom of Solomon* is a historical film, Faravardeh believed that many would disagree with them. This is not because the film's narrative is ahistorical but because the bulk of the available sources rely heavily on Judaeo-Christian sources, which contradict the Qur'an and, therefore, the film's historicity.

Isfahanian is in support of artists using their imagination based on their understanding of the Qur'an and other religious texts. Religious imagination, he argues, has to happen within a particular framework, which is not necessarily limiting. In fact, when appropriately equipped 'it enables you to soar to the heavens. Only those who rely on their ego are limited.' For Faravardeh, *The Kingdom of Solomon* does not claim to be the most perfect or complete narrative on Solomon but the result of a group of filmic artists' understanding of the Qur'an. Even the *tafsir*s (Qur'anic exegeses), he contended, are a result of the imagination of those thinkers based on their understanding of the sources. However, many great scholars including Ali Khamenei (b. 1939), ʿAbd Allāh Jawādī Āmulī (b. 1933) and Jaʿfar Sobhani (b. 1929) had watched this film. None of them reproached the filmmakers for using the Isrāʾīliyyāt sources (Judaeo-Christian traditions including narratives of the prophets). The next section will examine both the continuities and discontinuities of these earlier portrayals in *The Kingdom of Solomon*.

Rectifying the Narratives on Solomon

In discussing the foundational theories of *The Kingdom of Solomon*, the Taha group argues that it is imperative to rely on 'authentic texts' to understand the events surrounding Solomon's life because of alterations in the 'sacred texts of certain religions'.[37] Even though they are not named, the reference to the other two monotheistic traditions that share the figure of Solomon in their religious texts is clear. As such, right from the beginning, the research group establishes its departure from the Judaeo-Christian narratives on this prophet. This concern about the alteration of earlier sacred texts is a recurrent theme within the film. The discussion concludes that we need to refer to the Qur'an because it is the 'most authentic, genuine, comprehensive religious, ethical and historical text that is accepted not only amongst all religious groups within Islam but also the unbiased of the world'.[38] Invoking the *ḥadīth al-thaqalayn*, the research group further emphasises that after the Qur'an, the words of the authentic hadiths of the divine guides (*hādiyān-i ilāhī*), that is, the imams and *ahl al-bayt* (the People of the House), equally demand our reflection, and so 'by God's command we are to obey his Prophet's bidding as evident in verse 7 of chapter 59', which reads: *So take what the Messenger assigns to you, and deny yourselves that which he withholds from you.*[39] My examination of the sources across all the documents revealed a strong reliance on accounts related from the twelve Ithnāʿasharī imams.

As discussed in the previous section, one of the predominant motifs in the illustrations of Solomon is his throne, which emphasises his position as the prophet-king. This stress on his kingship is given prominence in *The Kingdom of Solomon*, as the title itself attests, and it is also the case in the background documents prepared by the Qur'anic research group which were of such importance in creating the filmic narrative. In studying the concept of kingship, the research group boasted of having undertaken a comprehensive study of 442 volumes of hadith across 187 titles, as well as 1,010 volumes in 205 titles of *tafsīr* from both Shiʿi and more general sources.

The Taha group's study revealed that the Qur'an uses four different terms to refer to kingship: *dawlat*, *imārat*, derivatives from the root of *ḥakama*, and derivatives from the root of *malaka*.[40] They further expand on each of these terms with examples from Qur'anic verses.[41] After having studied all 1,452 sources, the group claims to have found no reference to *dawlat*, *ḥukūmat* or *imārat* in reference to Solomon. Only *mulk* and its derivatives were used in reference to the kingship of Solomon. The Qur'an, according to this study, speaks of gracing four divine kingships: those of Joseph, Saul (Ṭālūt), David and Solomon.[42] Solomon becomes the focus of the film, Faravardeh explained, because, of all the divinely approved kingdoms in the Qur'an, it is Solomon's that is the most complete and precise.

In other words, it was the focus on kingship that led to the selection of the story of Solomon rather than the selection of the story of Solomon that led to the focus on kingship. Interestingly, in referring to Solomon's kingship, the Taha group also used the Persian word '*pādishāhī*'. This is a term that the Islamic Republic often used pejoratively and synonymously with *ṭāghūt* (non-Islamic forms of governance)[43] to attribute tyranny and injustice to earlier Iranian kingships from whose domination it claimed to have freed Iranians. In the discussions regarding Solomon, however, *pādishāhī* becomes a religious imperative. Even as the kingdoms of the prophets are studied in the context of Qur'anic verses and the sayings of the imams, no mention is made of the rulership of the imams themselves, other than in a brief footnote stating that the discussion of the rulership of the Prophet should be undertaken together with the analysis of the kingdom of the *ahl al-bayt* at the end of time. Although the link between the worldly and spiritual authority of Solomon and that of the *wilāyat-i faqīh* (guardianship of the jurist) is not directly referenced, it is easily deduced. The Taha group's use of resources is further revealing, as it includes texts by the mujtahid Mulla Aḥmad Narāqī (d. 1831), who lived during Fatḥ ʿAlī Shāh Qājār's reign (r. 1797–1834). It was he who proposed the concept of *wilāyat-i faqīh*, and the leadership of the clergy. Here, though, he is quoted to substantiate arguments regarding the three different worlds – *jabarūt* (which is free of matter, form and time), *malakūt* (which is free of matter and time) and *mulk* (which is the world of matter) – and not directly or necessarily on *wilāyat-i faqīh*.[44]

From the very beginning, *The Kingdom of Solomon* establishes Solomon's loving relationship with his wife, Miriam, who is expecting their first child. Unlike the Western versions, Solomon is clearly in a monogamous relationship – there are no references to other wives or a harem for that matter. Even though God has granted his prayer for an unprecedented kingdom, Solomon leads a modest life with his mother, wife and extended family as an ordinary man in their living quarters at the court. In all three films under discussion, Solomon asks for divine help to rule wisely: in *Solomon and Sheba*, he asks for 'an understanding heart' and 'discerning judgement'; in *Solomon*, he asks for the ability to rule justly; and in *The Kingdom of Solomon*, he asks for an unparalleled kingdom. In all three, too, he builds a temple, though it is destroyed in *Solomon and Sheba* because of God's wrath at Solomon for attending the pagan rituals of Sheba. Whereas the Biblical series of *Solomon* emphasises the role of his mother by presenting Bathsheba as a shrewd politician who secures Solomon's succession, in *Solomon and Sheba* she plays a marginal role, appearing only at David's deathbed and then very briefly in some background shots. *The Kingdom of Solomon*, however, is keen to portray her as a pious woman by Solomon's side who takes a pivotal role in times of crisis. As Faravardeh emphasised, one of the film's aims was to rectify the existing misconceptions about her in Western literature and Muslim tradition. Both refer to her adulterous relationship with David, resulting in Solomon's illegitimacy. In *The Kingdom of Solomon*, when Solomon and his brothers are away fighting the enemy, Bathsheba heads the family and leads the people of Jerusalem to calm during the unrest. When the kingdom comes under the attack of the Jewish tribes, she takes up arms to defend it alongside other warriors. In their documentation, the Taha group emphasises the significance of her role in Solomon's education after his father's death and refers to her as the 'hidden teacher' (*muʿālim-i pinhānī*).[45] There is, therefore, a stark difference in this depiction of Solomon's mother compared to the usual narratives of lust and betrayal that surround her.

For Isfahanian, the Qur'anic film counters the Judaeo-Christian texts, which stripped Solomon of his prophethood and rendered him an illegitimate child. Outside of the Qur'an, Solomon is a diminished figure. Instead of focusing on his rulership in its entirety, attention is placed on the later part of his reign and that of the Queen of Sheba. Solomon has been misunderstood and remains unknown to most. This misperception, according to Isfahanian, is not limited to Western narratives. Even the research communities of Iranian society, he said, do not know Solomon as he is and the film, therefore, strives to rectify this.

Unlike Jewish accounts and Western films which depict Solomon's rivalry with his brothers, particularly with his brother Adonijah, in *The Kingdom of Solomon* they are Solomon's greatest allies. Indeed, Isfahanian asserted, since the starting point had been the Qur'an, 'falsifications in the Judaeo-Christian texts could be easily contradicted, such as the enmity of Solomon's brothers towards him'. He explained that the previous scriptures were right about Solomon having brothers, but as Q. 34:13 demonstrates, there was no animosity between them. Indeed, where the Qur'an says '*Work ye, sons of David, with thanks!*' this is a reference to a practical gratefulness and to the fact that the brothers were working for him. As such, Isfahanian continued, the Qur'anic film rectifies the prevailing narratives about Solomon and his brothers.

As with the manuscript illustrations, while the jinns and demons are depicted in *The Kingdom of Solomon*, they have no place in the Western films. Although religious iconography is far more prevalent in the Judaeo-Christian tradition than in Islam, Solomon's relationship with the supernatural, such as with the demons, is not depicted in the classical Judaeo-Christian period. Sarit Shalev-Eyni notes that, apart from the fourteenth-century manuscript of *The Tripartite Mahzor* produced in the south of Germany, 'almost no depictions of Solomon and the demons exist outside the Islamic domain' and, equally, even though these 'Islamic legends . . . are firmly rooted in earlier Jewish sources, the visual representations produced between the thirteenth and sixteenth centuries have no earlier pictorial sources in Jewish or Christian art'.[46]

In *The Kingdom of Solomon* the jinns possess people, and the only way to fight them is through piety and obedience. The supporting documents of the film state that, even though the jinns had always existed, their impact was catastrophic during Solomon's time. What made that time different from other periods is the physical appearance of the jinns on earth, 'a theory which resolves many of the questions that may appear regarding the jinns and their existence across time'.[47] The documents then make reference to a number of Qur'anic verses in support of this argument, including Q. 2:102, Q. 21:82, Q. 34:12–13 and Q. 38:36–8.[48] As such, the film reinforces the Muslim narratives regarding the existence of demons and jinns.

The Religious Function of the Film

In *The Kingdom of Solomon*, the emphasis is on authenticity, not simply in terms of its use of historical sources but in its accentuation of the Qur'an as the only authoritative source. The filmmakers thus claim that because they synthesised a wide range of sources and repackaged it in an accessible format, they have produced the most authentic narrative on Solomon. Audiences, therefore, do not need to go through the thousand volumes that they had to.[49] The researchers, including the Taha Qur'anic Research Group, were not simply consulted but actively involved with the scriptwriting and engaged throughout the filming process to ensure the authenticity of the final product. The claim to authenticity was the starting point of the film, with the dramatic effectiveness relying heavily on the visual effects it employed.

This conviction extends to the religious role of the film itself. Of course, this function is not unique to the Qur'anic epic. The father of the biblical epic, Cecil B. DeMille, maintained that 'he had embraced a religious purpose, to show the truths of the Bible, when he made *The Ten Commandments* in 1956'.[50] I was intrigued to know whether Isfahanian considered the viewing of the film a religious act. His response was an emphatic yes; in his view, watching *The Kingdom of Solomon* was by far the most powerful tool for conveying the Qur'an to an audience. He said:

> I may read the verses on Solomon once and have a particular take on them but later become distanced from them. But then I may sit and watch 110 minutes of film and in this 110 minutes I do not just see a verse but tens of verses . . . I'm not hearing tens of verses that I may forget, I'm not reading tens of verses which I may forget after a few months, I'm *seeing* these tens of verses. More importantly, those who have created this film have discovered the relationship between these verses, they have come to live in this atmosphere, to find out the mystery of the verses and see their relationships with each other. Thus, a lasting sense will be transmitted to me . . . It can be far more influential than reading the Qur'an tens of times.

Isfahanian averred that the closer the film is to the Qur'an, the more it becomes an image of the Qur'an. As such, 'watching it is worship, working towards it is worship, and its influence is religious'. Isfahanian commented on how the film had improved the understanding and ritual practices of friends and relatives:

> In the year that *Saint Mary* was released, we had a meeting with the Supreme Leader. He said, 'I had read *Sūrat Maryam* over 1,000 times, I had taught it, discussed it, but when I saw the film I

understood aspects that I had not before.' Why is this? It is a characteristic of art. When the various elements are scattered, the understanding of it becomes difficult. If they are put together in an artistic way, of course in full loyalty to the text, there are things that get discovered that the interpreter of the Qur'an says that he had not discovered in reading the verses, in discussing them or teaching them. It is a huge deal that an interpreter and the religious leader of a country says this out of humility. It says a lot about the religious influence of art.

Depicting the Future of the World

The importance of Solomon is not simply that his was a perfect kingdom in the past or that it is relevant today; rather, it is that it provides a model for the future. This finding emerged from my study of the Qur'anic research group's documents and was reinforced during my fieldwork in Iran. As one of the documents clearly states, the example of Solomon illustrates that politics and religion can exist side by side and that this type of divine religion can shoulder the responsibilities of managing society.[51] There is hope, it says, that we can learn from the most distinctive state (*ḥukūmat*) described by the Qur'an to strengthen the principles/foundations (*mabānī*) of the Islamic Republic.[52]

In our own discussion, Faravardeh stated that *The Kingdom of Solomon* was a contribution to Shi'i Islam and served as an alternative to the West's presentation of its own utopian vision of the future. He continued:

> After a very long time, a religious and Shi'i government has finally appeared – imperfect as it may be. The film is a reflection on how a centrally governed world or a rulership should be. Instead of presenting our own model, which would be derived either from the Greek traditions or from Muslim philosophers and theologians (*mutakallimīn*), all of whom present their own understanding of religion and religious rule, we have gone to the origins. The imams did not have their own rule, and when they did, they were killed by despots. Whenever the imams were asked

about when they would rule, the response was 'Towards the end of time'.

Faravardeh also commented that the Qur'anic narratives about the prophets were not simply stories within the Qur'an but guides providing us with a vision and understanding of the future; it was thus imperative for the film to access and present this understanding. According to him, the West not only dominates the writing of history but also pronouncements about the future. These, however, are 'their understanding of the historical facts, which ... are directed by their liberal-democrat policies and presented to societies'. Through various fields, including film, he continued, the West is trying to portray and predict the future. Contrary to my expectation that he was referring to Western sci-fi films, Faravardeh illustrated his point by citing examples from films such as *The Chronicles of Narnia*, *Harry Potter*, *Avatar* and *Lord of the Rings*. These examples revealed a concern not with projections about the impact of scientific developments on the nature and quality of human life, but with Western definitions of the supernatural dimension in the world. As such, these kinds of films were considered far more serious contenders to the Shi'i religious notions of the mystical and of the future of the world. For Faravardeh, the stories in the Qur'an, including that of Solomon, provide a glimpse of the future. The filmmakers focused on Solomon because, of the four divinely approved kingdoms in the Qur'an, Solomon's was the most complete and precise. It is the story of a prophet who strived to create a divine kingdom and to maintain justice and equality.[53] Accordingly, for Faravardeh, Solomon's rule about 3,000 years ago is the model of leadership that should be striven towards and obtained at the end of time, a point not obvious in an ordinary viewing of the film *The Kingdom of Solomon*.

In the documents, the research group observes that from the beginning of the history of humanity, kingship and leadership have been desired by many, but 'many who upon reaching it or wishing for it ended up in the depths of hell'. It comments on 'how few there are of those who have endeavoured to accomplish the divine aims', and points to Solomon as 'one of the few in the latter group'.[54] According to the analysis within the document, after being appointed as prophet and messenger of God, the divinely appointed king wanted to clearly demonstrate the establishment of a divine kingdom.[55] In Faravardeh's own words:

> You can say that Solomon was born in 950 BC, but Solomon's kingdom was not just something relevant to that period alone . . . The Qur'an tells the story of Solomon to allow us to understand the future . . . We do not claim our version to be the most perfect but we do claim that this is our understanding of the Qur'an and that the Qur'an narrated this story so that we would be presented with the events of the end of time and have a version of the end of time.

Furthermore, according to Isfahanian, the film sends an international message that Solomon is not exclusively an Israelite, but a prophet who belongs to Muslims too: 'in fact, of the 6,236 Qur'anic verses, nearly 950 are about Moses and the Israelite prophets and kings, which means that they belong to us and are relevant to us as Muslims.' He went on:

> It is essential for humanity to look at Solomon in this age. His story demonstrates a shared sacred tradition that can encourage dialogue rather than the prevailing tension between religious groups. However, Solomon is used as the foundation of an oppressive state. Israel states that they are celebrating the third millennium anniversary of his rule to legitimate their claim to the land. However, Solomon was not prepared even to step on ants and was a righteous man.

Clearly, the film's political message is as important as its religious narrative, if not more so. Nonetheless, the film is framed as an alternative to aggression and as a means of dialogue that allows the establishment/filmmakers to highlight commonality over difference.

Shi'i Elements within *The Kingdom of Solomon*

The film's Qur'anic perspective of Solomon is informed by a Shi'i understanding of the Qur'an and other sources. As Faravardeh previously noted, Shi'i Islam has contributed significantly to the reporting and historiography of the past and has presented accounts of the future; *The Kingdom of Solomon* is, in its own way, part of this contribution by Shiʿi Islam. However, the film is not simply a Shiʿi reading of the Qur'anic narrative. In fact, the very construction of the character and life of Solomon in the film closely resembles that of ʿAlī, who was not only the cousin and son-in-law of the Prophet but the first Shiʿi imam and the fourth Muslim caliph. As such, the film is not simply a Shiʿi reading of the Qur'anic narrative as it transposes the figure of ʿAlī into that of Solomon. The main challenge for the filmmakers was refraining from using sources other than the preferred Shiʿi narratives.

The plot in *The Kingdom of Solomon* revolves around the dissension within Solomon's kingdom. In Western filmic tradition, tribal objections to Solomon and the sundering of their unity is the result of Solomon's associations with his pagan wives and his allowing them to hold their sacred rites within his kingdom, and, in some narratives, such as in *Solomon and Sheba*, even going so far as to participate in them. This ultimately incurs the wrath of God, who destroys the temple Solomon had built for Him. In the Iranian film, the tribes are led by corrupt Jewish rabbis who collaborate with magicians and do not shy away from using evil to achieve their goals. When Solomon warns them of the threat of the demons and jinns and asks for their help, they challenge his claims to have heard the voice of God, not only proclaiming that none of the Jewish tribes believe in his prophethood, but also dismissing David's Psalms. Furthermore, they admonish him for claiming to be able to create God's kingdom on earth or to go to war against jinns and demons.

The conflict within the kingdom reflects the dissension within the early Muslim community on matters of leadership and authority. The challenges to Solomon's kingdom parallels much of the opposition faced by ʿAlī. The dismissal of Solomon's spiritual and political role as his people's legitimate leader mirrors the challenges posed to ʿAlī's leadership of the Muslim community after the death of the Prophet. ʿAlī, too, had lacked the support of the majority of the ruling class, being thrice bypassed before finally taking over a turbulent community. In *The Kingdom of Solomon*, the complaints of the Jewish tribe about David having appointed a nine-year-old as his heir is strikingly similar to the narrative in Muslim tradition of the child ʿAlī being the first male to publicly acknowledge Muhammad's mission and recognise his prophethood.[56] Like ʿAlī, Solomon is left with only a few loyal companions.

One of the documents prepared by the Taha research group listed all the Qur'anic verses referring either directly or indirectly to Solomon and his prophethood in order to build a picture of his life.[57] Even though there is great emphasis on the primacy of the Qur'an as the film's key resource, the dearth of its references to Solomon's life story has enabled the filmmakers to be creative in their reading of the story. When I questioned Faravardeh about the basis for the animosity of the Jews towards Solomon, which I did not think was referenced in the Qur'an, he cited Q. 2:101–3 and explained that 'they' in Q. 2:102 refers to the Jews: *They followed what the evil ones gave out (falsely) against the power of Solomon: the blasphemers Were not Solomon, but the evil ones, teaching men Magic, and such things as came down at Babylon to the angels Harut and Marut.* He argued that as it was the Jews who lived there during Solomon's time, the reference to 'they' in the Qur'anic verse is clearly to them.

Throughout the film, Solomon's enemies employ sorcery to do evil, and Solomon condemns a rabbi's defence of usury as accepted practice within the Torah, pointing to it as evidence of the falsification of the sacred Book. The invocation of the concept of *taḥrīf* here is obvious.[58] Solomon also foretells what is to unfold on the Jerusalem stone, including the night journey of the Prophet (*miʿrāj*) and the victory of the Mahdī at the end of time. In this way, he is not simply a Jewish prophet but a Muslim one with added Shiʿi resonances.

Miriam and Solomon's relationship in the film is comparable to the one between ʿAlī and his wife Fāṭima, the daughter of the Prophet. Even though Solomon's polygamous marriage is well-recorded, the film depicts him in a monogamous relationship with Miriam just as ʿAlī remained monogamous until the death of Fāṭima. Moreover, the death of Miriam also resembles that of Fāṭima. According to popular Shiʿi belief, Fāṭima's death was a result of the injuries she sustained to her ribs whilst pregnant. This occurred when ʿUmar b. al-Khaṭṭāb (r. 13–23/634–44), the second caliph, pushed the door to her home into her side while trying to force ʿAlī to come out and pledge allegiance to Abū Bakr (r. 11–13/632–4), who became the first caliph and whose claim to such a title ʿAlī and Fāṭima initially disputed. In *The Kingdom of Solomon*, Yazar, the chief rabbi, uses magic to kill the pregnant Miriam in an effort to pressure Solomon into abdicating the throne. Unlike the Western films, there are no scenes of Solomon enjoying his harem; instead we see his pain at losing Miriam.

The dissension led by the chief rabbi in Jerusalem against Solomon and his men also closely parallels an important historical event during the caliphate of ʿAlī and arguably led to "ʿAlī's undoing'.[59] In the film, when Solomon's soldiers rise up against the opposing group led by the dissenting tribes and are about to defeat them, Yazar holds up the Torah and asks if the soldiers are going to fight the word of God. Just as Solomon's men put down their weapons, Yazar's men attack them. Similarly, during the battle of Ṣiffīn, Muʿāwiyya led the Syrian army against ʿAlī and 'when it seemed . . . that ʿAlī was gaining the upper hand, some Syrians held up the copies of the Qurʾān on their lances, an indication that they were ready for arbitration'.[60]

Another example is the inclusion of *illiyyā* or the *nūr* (light) of ʿAlī in the film. Isfahanian stated that according to various Sunni and Shiʿi texts, some humans are special and existed as light before the physical creation of the world. From the Qur'an, he continued, we know that one of these lights is ʿAlī, known as *illiyyān*. The proof, however, is a particular interpretation of Q. 2:31–2 regarding the teaching of names to Adam. That which was beyond the understanding of the angels, Isfahanian argued, was the name of the light. In the film, along with the appearance of the heavenly light as divine aid, Solomon is bestowed with the power to control demons and jinns through this light which gets embedded in his ring. It is after this period that the demons and jinns begin to materialise, emerging out of the bodies of Solomon's enemies as in *Alien* (Ridley Scott, 1979) and its sequels, complete with screeching and accompanying goo. This Iranian Islamic cinematic imagination of devils has thus ultimately relied on previous Western images of horror and evil incarnate.

Whilst the film intimates these parallels between Solomon and ʿAlī, the Taha group establishes a far more direct link, expanding ʿAlī's relationship not just with Solomon but with the monotheistic prophets at large. A sixteen-page document titled ʿAmīr al-muʾminīn ʿAlī, muʿallim-i anbiyā'' outlines how ʿAlī accompanied the prophets in non-material form and was their educator. It cites Hādī Sabzawārī's *Sharḥ-i duʿā'-i Ṣabāḥ*, attributing the following to ʿAlī: 'I accompanied all the prophets unseen and accompanied the Prophet in a visible form.'[61]

ʿAlī's role as an educator of prophets is further emphasised with reference to *khuṭba taṭanjiyya* (a gnostic sermon attributed to ʿAlī) from *Mashāriq al-Anwār*, and *ʿAlī wa Khuṭab-i Nādira*: 'We accompanied Adam and Noah and Moses and Jesus and David and Solomon and we were with them and amongst them and with the prophets. Thus all of them are towards us and take steps within us, and through us (are granted eminence and grace).'[62] The Taha research group further argues that the connection of the prophets with the *ahl al-bayt* is a serious matter that is mentioned in scriptures, narratives and historical texts. Strangely, however, the document continues, its enormity has led to it being ignored and at times even denied.[63] These associations have been referred to in a veiled manner, such as through references to the 'Holy Spirit' and its support of the army of the prophets, and discussions regarding *illiyyā*.[64] In the document there is a quote from *Biḥar al-anwār*. This is a work which was written by the Shiʿi scholar Muḥammad Bāqir Majlisī (d. 1700) and is considered to be 'one of the most extensive collections of Imamite hadith . . . [comprising] 111 volumes in the printed edition'.[65] The quote appears under the heading "Alī as the Teacher of Solomon', and it reads:

> I am the one who carried Noah in his ark on my Creator's command, I am the one who took Jonah out of the fish's belly with God's permission, I am the one who parted the sea for Moses on my Creator's command, I am the one who took Ibrāhīm out of

> the fire by God's permission, I am the one who with God's permission runs the rivers' waters, opens its springs, plants its trees . . . and I am Khiẓr, that knower of Moses, and the teacher of Solomon, the son of David.[66]

'Alī's elevated status is not substantiated solely through Shi'i sources. For example, the document invokes an old manuscript of the *Zabūr* (the Psalms) 'that is with Ahzān Allāh Damishqī, the leader of the Christians' and quoted in *al-Haram* magazine:

> Obedience to his eminence who is called Illī is obligatory and obedience to him rectifies all the deeds of the world and religion. That great personality is also referred to as 'Ḥadār'. He is the helper of the lonely and the lion of all lions. His strength and power are great and his birth shall be in 'Ka'āba'. It is obligatory for everyone to rely on him and to be obedient to him like a slave. Whoever has an ear will hear, whoever has an intellect and intelligence will understand, whoever has a brain and a heart will see him, for as the time passes he will not return.[67]

The document also references non-religious sources, such as an archaeological find in Russia reported in the *London Weekly Mirror* magazine in an article titled "Alī and the Prophets', p. 43, 1 February 1954. The accompanying footnote reads: 'In 1951 a group of Russian mining experts found an ancient piece of wood with inscriptions on it. On 27 February 1953 a committee of 7 archaeologists began studying this piece of wood and after 8 months declared that this was from Noah's ark.'[68] A number of online news articles cite this magazine article almost verbatim.[69] This is a translation of the inscription from the find, rendered in Persian on the sixteen-page document titled 'Amīr al-mu'minīn 'Alī, mu'allim-i anbiyā':

> Oh my God, my helper,
>
> In your kindness and mercy and for the sake of the Holy essences, Muhammad and Illiyyā and Shabar and Shabīr and Fāṭima, hold my hand, these five holy persons who are higher than anyone else and to whom respect is obligatory, and all the world has been erected for them. Oh God! Through their names help me. You can guide everyone to the right path.

The Shiʿi reading of Solomon and his kingdom, both subtle and apparent in the film, was certainly a challenge to one of its other ambitions – reaching a global audience. When I asked the producer about maintaining the balance between a universal outlook and a Shiʿi outlook in the film to boost its marketing potential and appeal to a wide audience, he paused for a long time before laughing out loud, saying: 'The reality is that we are Shiʿi guys and even though we have that universal outlook, we also have our own Shiʿi approach to events and stand by it. This is our belief. Fundamentally, we are making these films to say these things. There are some parts of it that some may not understand, but it doesn't matter.'

Conclusion

The Qur'anic film in Iranian cinema is an ambitious project aiming to achieve a number of social, religious and political objectives. What is rare and refreshing about the approach of this developing genre is that it is unapologetic and confident in deriving its narrative from sacred sources rather than trying to validate itself by claiming historical authenticity.

The Kingdom of Solomon attempts to wrest control of the monotheistic prophets away from what its producers perceive to be a Judaeo-Christian monopoly on the subject. This includes the West's influence on the Islamic narratives, which have in turn informed popular Muslim understandings of the figure of Solomon, not least regarding Solomon's mother and the focus on his harem. In part, the film aims to rectify these narratives by offering up its own version, which it claims to derive independently from the depths of the Qur'an. *The Kingdom of Solomon*, therefore, seeks to replace the popular texts that shape people's understanding of the Qur'anic stories, particularly that of the laity who do not study the Qur'an in a scholarly fashion. Equally, it wants to present an authentic and original text devoid of any contamination, as its producers see it, by untrustworthy sources and, as such, compete with existing Muslim scholarly work. In providing an understanding of the Qur'an, the film strives to offer its own Shiʿi interpretation whilst maintaining its universal appeal to both Sunni-majority Muslim societies and non-Muslim societies. However, these objectives are secondary to the political undercurrents of the film. On the one hand, it emphasises perfect leadership as a combination of religious authority and political power – a reference to the concept of *wilāyat-i faqīh*. On the other hand, it aims to discredit perceived Jewish political claims to the figure of Solomon and reclaim him as a Muslim prophet, situating him within a continued chain of prophets and imams.

This research on the Qur'anic epic also demonstrated the clergy's participation in the productions of sacred history outside of their usual framework. This suggests an evolution of both the delivery of Shiʿi religious discourse and the Iranian cinema industry. The religious strata who had initially condemned cinema as a corrupting agent within Iranian society are now at the forefront of employing it, not only as an educational tool, as Ruhollah Khomeini (d. 1989) had proposed in the early days of the Iranian Revolution, but also as an effective religious discourse that competes with the traditional religious discourses. This formerly Western medium has now not only been validated as a medium of relating religious content but has also been elevated to having a religious function – in the right hands.

This epic's very focus on the *kingdom* of Solomon is also a departure from popular Muslim and non-Muslim narratives of Solomon. Creating a religious epic meant working within the demands of the cinematic genre. For instance, the genre's demand for entertainment in this film is met through the implementation of digital effects outsourced to Hong Kong studios. Yet, its real emphasis is the reconstruction of 'true' history with a clear political message. Even in the context of scholarly Muslim interpretations of the Qur'an's narration of events surrounding the prophets' lives, the film aims to distance itself from merely telling a story. In other words, it is a departure from approaches such as *qiṣaṣ al-anbiyāʾ*, which are not presented as visions of the future. Finally, if *The Kingdom of Solomon* is also partly a reaction to Western films divining or attempting to exercise control over the future of humanity, as Faravardeh implied, then it is also a kind of epic that is different from biblical films, where such futurism is entirely absent. Even as both biblical and Qur'anic epics focus on stories shared with the Old Testament, Qur'anic films such as *The Kingdom of Solomon* offer not only a Muslim version of these stories but also a fascinating new development in the epic genre itself.

NOTES

1 Nacim Pak-Shiraz, 'The Qur'anic Epic in Iranian Cinema', *Journal of Religion and Film* 20, no. 1 (2016), pp. 1–25.

2 See, however, Nacim Pak-Shiraz, 'Imagining the Diaspora in the New Millennium Comedies of Iranian Cinema', *Iranian Studies* 46, no. 2 (2013), pp. 165–84; eadem, 'Comedy in Iranian Cinema', in Parviz Jahed, ed., *Directory of World Cinema: Iran 2* (Chicago, IL, 2017), pp. 262–70.

3 Oleg Grabar, 'The Qur'an as a Source of Artistic Inspiration', in Fahmida Suleman, ed., *Word of God, Art of Man: The Qur'an and its Creative Expressions* (Oxford, 2007), p. 38.

4 Pak-Shiraz, 'The Qur'anic Epic'.

5 Shahriar Bahrani, *The Kingdom of Solomon* (*Mulk-i Sulayman*) (Iran, 2010), www.kingdomofsolomon.com (accessed 26 August 2015; link no longer available).

6 Majid Majidi's *Muḥammad Rasūl Allāh* (*Muhammad: The Messenger of God*) (Iran, 2015), however, has since trumped all previous Iranian productions in terms of both scale and investment; see Nacim Pak-Shiraz, 'Representing Muhammad on Screen' (forthcoming).

7 Unless otherwise stated, all references to Saeed Isfahanian and, later in the chapter, Mojtaba Faravardeh (the film's producer) are from my interviews with them in August 2013.

8 See http://kingdomofsolomon.com. I had downloaded these resources on 11 January 2013 but they are no longer available online. They were titled as follows:

1.1. Survey of verses referring to Prophet Solomon in the Qur'an (Iḥṣāy-i kulli-yi ayāt-i marbūṭ bi Sulaymān dar Qur'ān)
1.2. The chronological order of the Qur'anic verses referring to Solomon and the reasons for it (Taqaddum wa ta'khur zamānī āyāt-i Sulaymān wa addilih-yi ān)
1.3. The foundational theories on the Kingdom of Solomon (Mabānī nazarī mabḥath-i mulk-i Sulaymān)
1.4. The countenance of Satan (Chihrih-yi Shayṭān)
1.5. Reasons for the physical appearance of the jinns and the devils in the time of Solomon (Dalā'il mādī shudan-i jin wa shayāṭīn dar zamān-i Sulaymān)
1.6. Comparison of the discussions on Solomon in Islam and other sacred books (Muqāyisih-i mabāḥith-i Ḥaẓrat Sulaymān dar Islām wa 'ahdayn)

1.7. The importance of engaging with the story of Solomon in contemporary times (Ḍarūrat pardākhtan bi mājarāh-yi Sulaymān dar īn zamān)
1.8. Amīr al-Mu'minīn 'Alī, the teacher of the prophets (Amīr al-mu'minīn 'Alī, mu'allim-i anbiyā')
1.9. A brief survey of the story of Solomon in the Qur'an (Nigāhi ijmālī bi dāstān-i Sulaymān dar Qur'ān)
1.10. Why is Jerusalem called *illiyyā*? (Chirā Bayt al-Muqaddas '*illiyyā*' nāmīdih shudih?)
1.11. The worlds and their chronological order (in the thought of Mullā Mehdī Narāqī and Mullā Aḥmad Narāqī) ('Awālim wa taqaddum wa ta'khkhur ān [dar andīshih-i Mullā Mehdī wa Mullā Aḥmad Narāqī])

9 Tabnak News Site, http://www.tabnak.ir/fa/pages/?cid=127239.

10 The film won awards in the categories of Best Music, Best Sound Effects, Best Visual Effects, Best Make-up and Best Supporting Actor; see http://www.fajrfilmfestival.com/default.aspx?p=cntpage&txtid=6002 (accessed 20 January 2013; link no longer working). Curiously, although all other sources point to the prize for Best Sound Effects being awarded to *The Kingdom of Solomon*, this is no longer listed on the festival's official website.

11 *Mi'rāj-nāma*, translated by Richard Pevear as *The Miraculous Journey of Mahomet*, with introduction and commentaries by Marie Rose Séguy, reproduced from the illuminated manuscript *Supplément Turc 190* belonging to the Bibliothèque Nationale, Paris (New York, 1977).

12 'An Illustrated and Illuminated Leaf: Suleyman and his Court with the Jinns, Birds and Animals, Persia, Tīmurid, Late 15th Century', Sotheby's, http://www.sothebys.com/en/auctions/ecatalogue/2012/arts-of-the-islamic-world-2012/lot.68.lotnum.html.

13 'Solomon and Bilqis Enthroned', The David Collection, Inv. no. 83b/2006 and 83a/2006, http://www.davidmus.dk/en/collections/islamic/dynasties/safavids/art/83a-b-2006.

14 'Sulayman and Bilqis Enthroned with Courtiers, Animals, Birds and Jinns: Illustrated Double-page Frontispiece from a Manuscript of Persian Poetry, Safavid, Shiraz School, circa 1540–50', Sotheby's, http://www.sothebys.com/en/auctions/ecatalogue/lot.27.html/2009/arts-of-the-islamic-world-l09721.

15 'An Illustrated and Illuminated Double Page from a Manuscript of Firdausi's Shahnameh: Suleyman and Bilqis Enthroned with Courtiers, Animals, Birds and Jinns, and the Illuminated Opening of the Baysunghuri Preface, Persia, Safavid, Shiraz, 16th century', Sotheby's, http://www.sothebys.com/en/auctions/ecatalogue/2014/arts-islamic-world-l14220/lot.11.html.

16 'Solomon Enthroned with Angels, Beasts, and Demons', Harvard Art Museums/Arthur M. Sackler Museum, The Norma Jean Calderwood Collection of Islamic Art, Accession Year 2002 Object Number 2002.50.37, http://www.harvardartmuseums.org/collections/object/143112?position=0.

17 'The Judgment of Solomon', The David Collection, Inv. no. 162/2006, http://www.davidmus.dk/en/collections/islamic/materials/miniatures/art/162-2006.

18 *Dīwān-i Ḥāfiẓ*, Walters MS. W.636, http://www.thedigitalwalters.org/Data/WaltersManuscripts/html/W636/description.html. This eighteenth-century collection of poems (*dīwāns*) contains forty-eight illustrations, four of which

are of Solomon. Its illustrations differ in detail and scale from the other six manuscripts and the contemporary painting, which are larger, more delicate, more detailed and have more characters and images.

19 Fāṭima Mudarrisī, 'Uṣṭūra-yi Jamshīd bā nigāhī bi sarguzasht-i Sulaymān-i Nabī', *Majalla-yi dānishkada-i adabiyyāt 'ulūm insānī* 2, no. 1 (1385 Sh./2006), pp. 9–35.

20 Ibid., p. 33.

21 Jon Solomon, *The Ancient World in the Cinema*, revised and expanded edn (New Haven, CT, 2001), p. 171.

22 Tilman Nagel, 'Ḳiṣaṣ al-Anbiyā'', *EI*[2], vol. V, pp. 180–81.

23 Clifford E. Bosworth, 'al-Ṭabarī', *EI*[2], vol. X, pp. 11–15.

24 'So David sent messengers, and took her; and she came to him, and he lay with her' (2 Samuel 11:4, Revised Standard Version of the Bible).

25 Abū Ja'far Muḥammad b. Jarīr al-Ṭabarī, *Ta'rīkh al-rusul wa'l-mulūk*, tr. and annot. William M. Brinner as *The History of al-Ṭabarī*, vol. III: *The Children of Israel* (Albany, NY, 1991), pp. 144–50.

26 *When they entered the presence of David, and he was terrified of them, they said: 'Fear not: We are two disputants, one of whom has wronged the other: Decide now between us with truth, and treat us not with injustice, but guide us to the even Path. 'This man is my brother: He has nine and ninety ewes, and I have (but) one: Yet he says "commit her to my care," and is (moreover) harsh to me in speech'. (David) said: 'He has undoubtedly wronged thee in demanding thy (single) ewe to be added to his (flock of) ewes: truly many are the partners (in business) who wrong each other: Not so do those who believe and work deeds of righteousness, and how few are they?' . . . and David gathered that We had tried him: he asked forgiveness of his Lord, fell down, bowing (in prostration), and turned (to Allah in repentance). So We forgave him this (lapse): he enjoyed, indeed, a Near Approach to Us, and a beautiful place of (Final) Return* (Q. 38:22–5).

27 Ṭabarī, *Ta'rīkh*, vol. II, pp. 49–50.

28 Ṭabarī, *Ta'rīkh*, vol. III, p. 154.

29 Ibid., p. 153.

30 Ibid., p. 154.

31 The only exception being the story of Joseph, with the eponymous *Sūrat Yūsuf* (Q. 12) of the Qur'an being entirely dedicated to this prophet.

32 Ṭabarī, *Ta'rīkh*, vol. III, pp. 161–2.

33 Ibid., pp. 162–3.

34 Ibid., pp. 166–7.

35 Interview with Faravardeh, August 2013.

36 These two television series were based on the lives of the first and second Shi'i imams respectively. For details on the making of *Imam Ali* and the director's efforts to maintain the balance between religious authenticity and dramatic effectiveness, see Pak-Shiraz, 'The Qur'anic Epic'.

37 Taha Qur'anic Research Group, 'Mabānī nazarī mabḥath-i mulk-i Sulaymān', p. 1.

38 Ibid.

39 The quote, 'by God's command . . .' is taken from ibid., p. 2. All translations of the Qur'an in this chapter are from Yusuf Ali.

40 In 'Mabānī nazarī mabḥath-i mulk-i Sulaymān', p. 3, the Taha research group states that the four terms referencing kingship in the sayings of the imams are: *dawlat*, *imārat*, *ḥukūmat* and *mulk*. An illustrative example is provided for each of them: (a) *Dawlat*: Citing the fifth Twelver imam, Muḥammad al-Bāqir (d. 114/733), from p. 472 of Muḥammad b. al-Ḥasan al-Tūsī's *al-Ghaybat*: 'Our government is the last of the governments. And there will never be a government established unless others before us have ruled as kings; this is because when they see our ways/conduct (*sīra*) they do not say if we ruled we would have conducted ourselves in their ways; and this is the word of God that the end belongs to the people of piety.' Also, from *Imalī Sudūq*, p. 489, Ja'far al-Ṣādiq (d. 148/765), the sixth Twelver imam: 'For all people there is a *dawlat* for which they are waiting; our government shall appear at the end of this long period.' (b) *Imārat*: From *Nahjul Balāgha*, *khuṭba* 40, p. 82, 'Alī b. Abī Ṭālib (d. 40/661), the first Twelver imam: 'People have no option other than to have an *'amīr*; he is either a righteous person or he is sinful (*fājir*).' (c) *Ḥukūmat*: From *Tafsīr kanz jami'l fawā'id wa ta'wīl al-āyāt al-zāhīra*, p. 763, Ḥasan, the second Twelver imam (d. 50/670): '[on judgement day] God has the permission of our *ḥukūmat*.' (d) *Mulk*: From *Kafī*, vol. I, p. 471, Bāqir: 'O people, which way are you hastening towards? Which way has been decided for you? God has guided the first of you with us and the last of you will also be taken to the end by us. If for you there is a short rule here in this world, for us there is a long rule in the future, and after our *mulk* [royal power] and *pādishāhī* [rulership], there is no other *mulk*, as we are the people of the end; God has said that the end is for the people of piety.'

41 The root of the word '*dawla*' appears only two times: (a) *Such days (of varying fortunes) We give to men and men by turns* (*nudāwilha*) . . . (Q. 3:140); (b) *What Allah has bestowed on His Messenger (and taken away) from the people of the townships – belongs to Allah – to His Messenger and to kindred and orphans, the needy and the wayfarer; In order that it may not (merely) make a circuit* (*dawla*) *between the wealthy among you* (Q. 59:7). The root of the word '*imāra*' appears just once: *Then when they opened their baggage, they found their stock-in-trade had been returned to them. They said: 'O our father! What (more) can we desire? This our stock-in-trade has been returned to us: so we shall get (more) food (namīru) for our family . . .* (Q. 12:65).

For the derivatives of the letters *ḥ-k-m*, there are 210 instances in 189 verses. Of these, three verses refer to the *ḥukm* of Solomon: Q. 6:89, Q. 21:78 and 79. Interestingly, the term *ḥukūmat* is not used in any of these verses.

For the derivatives of *m-l-k*, there are 114 instances in 102 verses which include: (a) twenty instances of *malik* and other similar terms such as *al-malik*, *malika*, *malīk*, *al-mulūk*, *mulūka*, *mālik*, *mālikun*; (b) forty-nine instances of *mulk* and other similar terms: *al-mulk*, *bi'l-mulk*, *bi-mulkinā*, *mulkā*, *mulkihī*; (c) forty-five instances of other derivatives of *m-l-k* which include *amlak*, *tamalluk*, *tamallukuhum*. Taha Qur'anic Research Group, 'Mabānī nazarī mabḥath-i mulk-i Sulaymān', p. 5.

42 Only one verse is identified in reference to the kingdom of Joseph (Q. 12:101), and three verses to that of Saul (Q. 2:246, 247 and 248).

43 See Ruhollah Khomeini, *Wilāyat-i faqīh*, tr. Hamid Algar as *Governance of the Jurist* (*Velayat-e faqeeh*): *Islamic Government* (Tehran, 2006), p. 23.

44 Taha Qur'anic Research Group, "Awālim wa taqaddum wa ta'khkhur ān', p. 6.
45 Taha Qur'anic Research Group, 'Nigāhi ijmālī bi dāstān-i Sulaymān dar Qur'ān', p. 1.
46 Sarit Shalev-Eyni, 'Solomon, his Demons and Jongleurs: The Meeting of Islamic, Judaic and Christian Culture', *al-Masāq: Journal of the Medieval Mediterranean* 18, no. 2 (2006), p. 150.
47 Taha Qur'anic Research Group, 'Dalā'il mādī shudan-i jin wa shayāṭīn dar zamān-i Sulaymān', p. 3.
48 Ibid., pp. 1–16.
49 Ibid., p. 13.
50 See Constantine Santas, *The Epic in Film: From Myth to Blockbuster* (Lanham, MD, 2008), p. 74, where Santas refers to the 'Special Features' in *The Ten Commandments*, DVD Disc two (Paramount Pictures, 2006).
51 Taha Qur'anic Research Group, 'Nigāhi ijmālī bi dāstān-i Sulaymān dar Qur'ān', p. 2.
52 Ibid.
53 Taha Qur'anic Research Group, 'Mabānī nazarī mabḥath-i mulk-i Sulaymān', p. 2.
54 Ibid., p. 3.
55 Ibid., p. 2.
56 Despite disagreements between Sunni and Shi'i sources placing 'Alī as either the second or third Muslim convert, most early sources refer to him as the second convert, after the Prophet's first wife Khadīja, and between the ages of nine and eleven at the time. See Robert M. Gleave, ''Alī b. Abī Ṭālib', *EI THREE* (Brill Online).
57 Taha Qur'anic Research Group, 'Iḥṣāy-i kulli-yi ayāt-i marbūṭ bi Sulaymān dar Qur'ān', pp. 1–8.
58 *Taḥrīf* is commonly understood 'amongst Muslim authors, especially from the 5th/11th century up to modern times', as a concept 'which accused Jews and Christians of having deliberately falsified the text of their own respective Scriptures'. See Hava Lazarus-Yafeh, 'Taḥrīf', *EI*[2], vol. X, pp. 111–12.
59 Gleave, "Alī b. Abī Ṭālib', *EI THREE* (Brill Online).
60 Ibid.
61 Taha Qur'anic Research Group, 'Amīr al-mu'minīn 'Alī, mu'allim-i anbiyā'', p. 4.
62 Ibid.
63 Ibid., p. 3.
64 Ibid.
65 Brunner, Rainer, 'Majlesi, Moḥammad-Bāqer', *Encyclopaedia Iranica*, http://www.iranicaonline.org/articles/majlesi-mohammad-baqer, accessed 4 October 2018.
66 Taha Qur'anic Research Group, 'Amīr al-mu'minīn 'Alī, mu'allim-i anbiyā'', p. 8.
67 Ibid., p. 7. This issue of *al-Haram* magazine is cited as being published in Cairo, Dhū'l-Qa'da 1374/[July 1955]. However, I was unable to locate this publication in any leading library database.
68 Ibid., p. 5, n. 3. I was also unable to locate this text. I would like to thank Shenxiao Tong for his help in trying to identify this and the previously cited resource.

69 For example, see https://www.facebook.com/notes/moula-ali-as-mushkil-kusha/ahl-ul-bayt-as-and-prophet-as-noahs-ark/10150535314231328; http://muslimvillage.com/forums/topic/45517-prophet-noah-pbuh-invokes-allah-with-blessed-names/ (link no longer available; accessed 26 August 2015) and http://www.ya-hussain.com/int_coll/int_coll_net/noahsark.htm (link no longer available; accessed 29 January 2016).

15

Notes on Ritual Prayer in Iran: *Qunūt* Choices among a Group of Shi'i Women

NILOOFAR HAERI

My central goal in this chapter is to describe some of the sources of variation in the performance of ritual prayer (*namāz*; Arabic, *ṣalāt*) among a group of Shi'a women living in Tehran (see below).[1] The act of *namāz* is generally performed five times a day: at dawn, at noon, in the afternoon, in the evening and at night. While it is well-known that the Shi'a combine the noon and afternoon prayers, and the evening and night prayers, hence praying three times a day, some women in this study did, at times, perform each prayer separately. They would leave their prayer rug open all day and return to it when they were ready to perform the second of the two prayers. This was not considered an unusual act among them. Each period of *namāz* is made up of prayer cycles or *rak'āts* – the dawn has two, the evening has three and the rest all have four *rak'āts*. A *rak'āt* is composed of suras or 'chapters' from the Qur'an. Every *namāz* begins with *Sūrat al-Fātiḥa* (Q. 1; called *al-Ḥamd* by the Iranians), the only obligatory chapter. After that, theoretically, any other can be chosen from the Qur'an and recited. However, in practice, there are a number of suras that have become standard choices, such as *Sūrat al-Ikhlāṣ* (or *Tawḥīḍ*, Q. 112), which seems to be chosen by most people. There are two sources of variation in *namāz* that I have observed, one having to do with the individual's experience and the other with practice.

There is a prevalent view of *namāz* as a ritual that does not change from one performance to another, nor from one reciter to the next.

This view might have arisen because most studies have been concerned with what Iranians call *namāz-i jamāʿat* or congregational prayer.[2] The question of individual creativity and variation by the performer does not come up in Friday prayers, for example, since worshippers must follow the prayer leader. None of the women (or men) that I talked to about their experiences of praying claim any authorship of *namāz*. They all agree that each *namāz* performed at different times of the day has, as it were, a script composed largely of suras from the Qur'an with the obligatory *Fātiḥa*. *Namāz* also has its customary rules (*ādāb*), and my interlocutors try to follow these as best as they can: they must memorise the verses, the order of the suras and the relevant body postures. These they learned from their parents or teachers. The performance of the ablutions, wearing clean and modest clothes and standing on clean ground, often provided by their own prayer rug, are widely shared practices with respect to the appropriate etiquette of *namāz*. Yet, here, there is inevitably a certain amount of variation. Some women believe if you have just taken a shower, there is no need for ablutions. Some wear veils while others choose a white loose scarf; some put a small amount of make-up on, taking the view that 'God loves beauty', while some do not. Also, upon talking to individuals about their performance of *namāz*, I found that people do not have a uniform understanding of what the *ādāb* of *namāz* are, how best to perform it and which suras to choose. Furthermore, there is no uniformity with respect to the reasons people pray, beyond it being a requirement of their religion.

On the level of experience, individuals describe differences in the course of a day (and over a lifetime) each time the prayer is recited. Differences exist across individuals, depending on their age (e.g. the *namāz* of an eighteen-year-old is not the same as that of a sixty-year-old), the length of time they have been performing *namāz*, their degree of literacy, the channels through which they learned about religion, their particular life conditions and so on. As one woman told me, 'I am not the same person today as I was yesterday, so my *namāz* is not the same either.' Were it the case that differences between reciters failed to translate into any differences in the individual's practice and experience of *namāz*, were it the case that there was no space in which the reciter could 'own' *namāz* in any specific iteration of it in time and space, that is, if they could not in any way be creative, then indeed every performance of *namāz* would be like every other.

There are performances of *namāz* where the reciter manages to arrive at feelings of closeness and intimacy with God – where a union (*waṣl*) is achieved – and there are those which fail to achieve that. The women I spoke to described both. Some spoke of times when, upon finishing their prayer, they felt light and happy and close to God, while others told me, for example, 'I am not satisfied with my praying these days. I can't concentrate, I can't make a connection.' What I found in my research is that the potential to create a connection to the Divine is not primarily due to matters of doctrinal belief.

In Persian, the expressions *ḥuḍūr-i qalb* (presence of the heart) and *khulūṣ* (sincerity, purity) are used to describe a *namāz* performance in which the reciter feels absorbed in the act, fully focused and free of extraneous thoughts about the surrounding world.[3] *Ḥuḍūr-i qalb* is crucial to the individual's experience of the prayer, and it depends on the individual being able to achieve a profound level of concentration (*tamarkuz*). Those whom I talked to about *namāz* mentioned the constant and formidable struggle to achieve *tamarkuz* due to their mind wandering, or forgetting which *rak'āt* they were performing and how many were left. In handbooks on *namāz* and on the websites of almost all religious leaders there are sections devoted to *shakkiyyāt-i namāz* (doubts on the correct performance of *namāz*), indicating what a common problem this is.[4] Individuals may doubt, for example, whether they have performed the prosternation or not, and mistakenly perform two; or they may recite the profession of faith (*tashahhud*) in the third *rak'āt* instead of in the fourth. However, the problem of concentration is larger than simply forgetting the number of *rak'āt*s that are left, or the number of prostrations, for the aim is to be free of thoughts other than those that are relevant during the act of prayer.

The need to concentrate leads people to develop techniques for better concentration. For success in concentration, it seems to matter little how fervently the reciter believes certain doctrinal matters of religion or exactly what the contours of their beliefs are. Many of the women in this study told me one of the reasons they do not like praying at the mosque is that they are far less able to concentrate. In response to my question about what conditions promoted *tamarkuz* for them, they replied that they needed to be alone in their own rooms, and they would turn off the radio or television to try to limit distracting sounds, close the door and draw the curtains. When they stood to pray, they would not immediately launch into prayer, but would pause, take a breath and gather their thoughts. In addition to all of these, they found that being particularly 'thirsty' (*tishna*) to talk to God for whatever reason helped their concentration. In short, as exhibited by this example, *tamarkuz* was a necessary condition for arriving at *khulūṣ*.

I have so far spoken on the individual's experience resulting in variations in *namāz*. Now I would like to move to practice. The question that interests me here is whether there is variability in the practice of *namāz*, or any other ritual (*'ibādāt*) for that matter, and, if so, where this variability comes from and what its sources are.

In the struggle to attain concentration, the women in this study sought to perform *namāz* in ways that prevented it from becoming routine (*rūtīn nabāyad bisha*). These ways, ideas, practices and choices helped them to arrive at a presence in the course of the prayer. The prevalent view of repetition in the social sciences is that it precludes creativity – that is, the individual practising the act of repetition is thought to be simply replicating it, not bringing anything new to it. However, even a brief consideration of acts of repetition in other realms proves this false. In the playing of a musical instrument, for example, it is clear that those who master a piece of music through repetition do so while creating their own version of it – they bring their own interpretation to the notes, even though they have not written them. Pure repetition, therefore, does not seem possible given that our individuality comes to be interwoven in what we do and given an imponderable number of contexts that keep changing at each iteration. This is so, too, with the practice of *namāz*.

In the context of our discussions, I argue that some of the women in this study do manage to create a certain individual presence in their *namāz* though they may have repeated this performance for decades. I have described in detail elsewhere the quality of this presence based on the women's descriptions of their experience.[5] In this chapter, however, I would like to elaborate on a part of this creative *ḥuḍūr* which stems from the recitation of the *qunūt*. *Qunūt* literally means obedience, but I am using it here in the sense in which it is most often used, that is, to refer to the inclusion of any desired prayer within the formula of the *namāz*. I argue that the women's use of *qunūt* brings individuality and variability to their performance of *namāz*. Before making specific arguments on this point, I will say something about the women who were the interlocutors in this research.

The Women and their Religious Activities

The women that I worked with in Tehran were middle-class, well-educated and women mostly in their sixties. Almost half were born and raised in other parts of Iran but had ended up living in the capital. Depending on various factors including availability, I have had many more conversations with some of these women than with others. I interviewed around twenty-five women in total. However, over the years, I have also talked to and observed a larger group of Muslim women and men. Therefore, while I mostly rely on the views and statements of the smaller group, I also draw on a larger set of interlocutors and a longer time span. I cannot, therefore, claim either a broad or a profound understanding of the particularities of the ideas, thoughts and practices of ordinary Muslims. I would argue, however, that this group's approach to Islam is fairly representative of professional, middle-class women who have gone to university and pursued economic independence.

Upon finishing high school, some of the women pursued further education at teacher training colleges and/or universities where they specialised in fields such as psychology, literature and language. They held long-term jobs as high school teachers (mostly in public schools, but also a few in private schools), headmistresses, editors of dictionaries and other similar posts requiring linguistic and cultural expertise; they are retired now and receive pensions. Most of the women engaged in extensive and systematic charity work. This presented them with a wide network of friends and acquaintances in several parts of Iran, with whose families they became intimately familiar. This is important to note because class issues, such as how relations across class lines may influence religious practice, need further study and are not easily predictable.

After the revolution of 1979, there emerged a reflexive turn in Iranian society. People developed an interest in becoming more knowledgeable about Iran's history, religion, poetry, music, philosophy, art and so on, resulting in a great demand for classes in any number of subjects. The women in my group took classes throughout the year, the most regular being Qur'an and poetry classes. The Qur'an classes were generally conducted all-year round and one could join at any time. Many were offered in people's homes (and these required a personal introduction), though there were also many provided at neighbourhood cultural centres or *farhangsarās*. Poetry classes were also popular, such as those on Ḥāfiẓ (d. 792/1390), Rūmī (d. 671/1273), Saʿadī (d. *c.* 689/1291), Firdawsī (d. 411/1020) to name a few. At the time of my fieldwork, a number of the women were attending classes devoted to Rūmī's *Mathnawī*, though they had also been to ones on Ḥāfiẓ, Niẓāmī (d. 605/1209) and other poets. Some of the women in this group came from religious families in which scholarly knowledge of Islam was highly valued. One consequence of being from such families is that they learned from their parents and other family members how to pray and how to read the Qur'an and other religious texts, including those of the Shiʿi imams.

The question of channels of learning is important because how and from whom one learns to pray – whether from family members, teachers, religious figures or authors of books and manuals – has implications for structures of authority and the variability and creativity that an individual brings to the performance of *namāz* and other rituals. Formal figures and institutions of authority are not automatically sought out by believers. For example, in childhood, one learns from kin, neighbours and friends. Those who have learned about their religion through kinship networks engage in variation without worrying about first getting authorisation from a leader or *marja*ʿ. The kind of pedagogical process that one experiences with family, friends' families, teachers, classes, manuals, books and combinations thereof can make a fundamental difference both to the ways in which rituals come to be embodied and in the legitimacy of variation and sources of authority. To learn to pray from a kinship network is to learn variability because inevitably there are individual differences that are explicitly commented on and discussed. One hears people say, for example, 'my grandmother told me . . .', 'I like to say *subhān Allāh* three times when I go into *sujūd* but your grandfather preferred *yā laṭīf* . . .' and so on.

The Use of *Qunūt*

Let me now return to the topic of variation, individuality, creativity and the relevance of these to the way in which the Qur'an is negotiated in today's Iran. As mentioned earlier, *namāz* is made up of suras from the Qur'an. For example, the first sura in the dawn prayer, as with all other prayers, is *Sūrat al-Fātiḥa*, the opening chapter of the Qur'an. This is often followed by *Surat al-Ikhlāṣ*. In the second *rak*ʿ*āt*, one can repeat the same suras or choose, for example, some of the shorter suras towards the end of the Qur'an, such as *Sūrat al-Falaq* (Q. 113), *Sūrat al-Nās* (Q. 114), *Sūrat al-*ʿ*Aṣr* (Q. 103) or *Sūrat al-Fatḥ* (Q. 48).

One of the main sites of potential creativity in *namāz* is the *qunūt*. Within the structure of each prayer, in particular that of the dawn prayer, there is a non-obligatory act that is favoured (*mustaḥabb*) and that is the *qunūt*. According to Ayatollah Taqī Mudarrisī (b. 1945), *qunūt* is a special *du*ʿ*ā*ʾ which must be performed in the following manner: hands must be raised and held in front of the face with 'the palms . . . facing the sky and the back of the hands, the earth'.[6] Generally, in the second *rak*ʿ*āt* of the dawn prayer, after the recitation of the second sura, the *qunūt* may be performed. Those who feel inclined to do so will raise both hands while standing and tell God what they want. In speaking to God at this time, they are able, if they wish, to go beyond the words of the Qur'an (which they had previously been reciting) and use their own words. The content of what is said during the *qunūt* can vary greatly: sometimes a few verses of a sura are spoken, or the worshipper may talk to God in Persian, or recite a prayer (*duʿā*ʾ) or even a few verses of poetry (see more on this later). So the *qunūt* provides another opportunity for introducing variability in *namāz*.

The women in this study all liked to include the *qunūt* in their worship. Some described it as 'talking to God, having an intimate conversation (*rāz u niyāz*) with God', as being 'a chance to tell God what was in [their] heart', and to 'tell [Him] how great it was that [He] was there so I could talk to [Him] (*niyāyish*)'. Some elaborated on the hand gesture, explaining that 'we hold our hands like that so that light is guided into our hearts'. A usual response was that in the *qunūt* you get to say what was 'left over' to tell God. A few told me that they rarely changed what they said in the *qunūt*: they seemed to treat it as a fixed part of the prayer. They said, for example, three times '*Allāhu akbar*' or '*Allāhumma ṣalli ʿalā Muḥammad wa āl-i Muḥammad*' or '*rabbanā aʿaṭinā fīʾl-dunyā ḥasana wa fīʾl-ākhirati ḥasana* . . .' However, quite a few also said that they chose different texts or simply spoke to God in Persian. At times, they did not know exactly what the source of the *duʿā*ʾ or the phrase was, but they had learned it from their father, mother, relative or friend, and that memory made the *duʿā*ʾ particularly meaningful; in saying that particular *duʿā*ʾ, they felt that they were memorialising the person. So one very crucial source of variation is what one learns from individuals, especially those with whom one has had a positive emotional bond, such as parents and grandparents. Members of different generations also show the accumulation of various practices of their ancestors and many of these keep getting passed on to younger generations.

There was a question about whether the *qunūt* should be recited in Persian or Arabic. This issue is addressed by religious leaders, as can be seen from a glance at their respective websites, and there is variability in their responses about whether it is acceptable to recite the *qunūt* in Persian. Some say that to be sure of the acceptance of prayer (*iḥtiyāṭ*), people should first say the *qunūt* in Arabic and then follow it with what they want to say in Persian. One leader, Muḥsin Qarāʾatī, when asked whether it was acceptable to recite the *qunūt* in Persian, replied: 'God does not have a [specific] code [i.e. language]; [His] code is that of love.'[7] Hence, for him, any language is acceptable. Ayatollah ʿAlī al-Sīstānī says, 'The use of *duʿā'* in Persian does not render *namāz* void [*bāṭil*].'[8]

A prevalent view of *qunūt* and one that I frequently heard is that it is a Shiʿi innovation. The idea is that Sunnis do not have *qunūt*. In my experience, some Iranian Sunni Arabs (in Qeshm Island) do include it and as John Bowen argues in his book on Indonesia, the question of whether to include the *qunūt* was a subject of debate.[9] Also, as Najam Haidar has shown in *The Origins of the Shīʿa*,[10] it existed at the time of the Prophet and was used by him to curse enemy tribes or pray to God for allies. Hence the idea that this is an exclusively Shiʿi practice does not seem accurate. The idea of the *qunūt* is articulated in these terms by both laypeople and clerics in these terms: 'to tell God that which is still left for you to say beyond the suras that you are reciting'. It is an occasion to speak directly from the heart.

A few people said that at times they recited a line of poetry from Rūmī, Ḥāfiẓ and others. One person said that she saw on television a cleric (*rūḥānī*) – she did not remember his name – who told the audience he chose verses of Ḥāfiẓ for his *qunūt*. I had not heard or read about this being done before. Perhaps, then, the *qunūt* is emerging as a site where, not just individual creativity, but the neighbourliness of prayer and poetry are realised. However, at the moment, it does not seem to be just any kind of poetry that is being used, but almost exclusively mystical poetry from Ḥāfiẓ and Rūmī. Gnostic (*ʿirfān*) poetry appears to be creating a presence in *namāz* for some people, but the phenomenon itself is quite interesting and can have important implications for the ways in which the experience and practice of *namāz* can be inflected by sources outside the Qur'an.

Conclusion

I will summarise here the sources of variability in the *qunūt* that I have examined in this chapter. Spontaneous *duʿā*'s in Persian are themselves a source of variation, because what is conveyed to God can vary depending on the particular mood and circumstances of the reciter. It is clear that the form and content of what is said in the *qunūt* when it is in Persian and related to the conditions of the reciter can change from one *namāz* to another. For those who have learned a *duʿā'* or a verse from family members, the source of variation is that family member. The Qur'an itself is a source of variation, in that many different verses can be chosen. *Duʿā'* books such as *Mafātīḥ al-jinān* (Keys to the Heavens) offer different kinds of *qunūt*, though I never came across anyone who had actually used one of these texts. And finally, it seems that mystical poetry is entering the prayer through *qunūt*, as some people recite verses from Rūmī and Ḥāfiẓ. It is clear that there is far more variability than we are used to thinking exists in the recitation of *namāz*. The variability points to sources that lie also outside of the Qur'an, an outcome that becomes clearer with fieldwork among ordinary believers.

Perhaps it is worth ending with a related but more question. Do reciters approach the suras of the Qur'an differently when they recite them within *namāz* compared to when they read the Qur'an for other purposes, outside of rituals? Specifically, is one approach dominated by hermeneutic attempts while the other, in the performance of *namāz*, enters experiential realms that are less concerned with interpretation and understanding? My tentative answer is that depending on the conditions under which *namāz* is performed and the text of the Qur'an is read, an element of hermeneutics can be present in both situations. The women in this group go back and forth between the performance of *namāz* and attending regular Qur'an classes in which the meanings of each verse may be debated at great length. Given such engagement offered by the weekly classes, it is difficult to imagine that their performance of *namāz* is left entirely untouched by the hermeneutic approach. I hope to return to these and similar questions in future work on prayer.

NOTES

1 These observations stem from fieldwork that I conducted in Iran between 2008 and 2013.

2 David Parkin, 'Inside and Outside the Mosque: A Master Trope', in David Parkin and Stephen Headley, eds, *Islamic Prayer across the Indian Ocean: Inside and Outside the Mosque* (Richmond, 2000), pp. 1–22.

3 See Marion Holmes Katz, *Prayer in Islamic Thought and Practice* (Cambridge, 2013), p. 44.

4 See the website of an ayatollah, Makārim Shīrāzī, which deals with these problems: http://portal.anhar.ir/node/640#gsc.tab=0.

5 Niloofar Haeri, 'The Private Performance of *Salat* Prayers: Time, Repetition, and Meaning', *Anthropological Quarterly* 86, no. 1, pp. 5–34.

6 See Taqī Mudarrisī's website, http://www.almodarresi.com/Persian/fbook/42/pl0tx6xz.htm (link no longer active; accessed 25 September 2010). There are many other websites that discuss the *qunūt.*

7 See Hujjat al-Islām Qarā'atī's website, http://www.gharaati.ir/show.php?page=darsha&id=80&query=%D9%82%D9%86%D9%88%D8%AA&exact. (His assertion about the code of God being that of love has been removed.)

8 See 'Alī al-Sīstānī's website, http://www.sistani.org/index.php?p=827020&id=1003&perpage=6#13590.

9 John R. Bowen, *Muslims through Discourse: Religion and Ritual in Gayo Society* (Princeton, NJ, 1993), p. 69.

10 Najam Haidar, *The Origins of the Shī'a: Identity, Ritual and Sacred Space in Eighth-Century Kūfa* (New York, 2011), pp. 99–101 and 109.

16

Twelver Shi'i Women's Appropriation of the Qur'an in Contemporary Iran

INGVILD FLASKERUD

WESTERN SCHOLARSHIP on the Qur'an and its exegesis has in recent years developed a pluralistic understanding of the critical exposition of this fundamental text in Islam. Such scholarship sees Muslim exegetes as engaged readers who bring their experience to the text, and views their interpretations as being influenced by the specific sociocultural, political and historical conditions in which they live.[1] As such, the study of exegesis is perceived to offer information about the text's interpreters, the intellectual discourses built around the text and the context framing such activities rather than revealing any meaning intrinsic to the Qur'anic text. Some Western scholars even suggest that the Qur'an itself can be read as an exegetic exposition.[2] Also the ethnographically informed research on Muslim communities has in recent years increasingly turned to the study of Islamic texts and intellectual debates. While this type of research takes an interest in the works and activities of Muslim scholars, attention is also given to how ordinary people interpret religious texts, whether in written or oral forms, and what they do with them.[3] Contemporary research on the Qur'an is thus directed at discovering how texts are produced, transmitted, read and reread, while also exploring the social implications of people's engagements with those texts in their everyday life. A similar reorientation can be observed in sociologically and anthropologically informed studies which enquire into how people practise their religion, how circumstances in people's everyday lives shape their religious belief and practice, and, conversely, how religion influences their daily life.[4]

Nevertheless, Mahmoud Ayoub's comment made over thirty years ago, pointing out Western scholars' scant attention to the Qur'an's function in the lives of Muslims, is still appropriate.[5] Admittedly, the use of passages of Qur'anic text for protective, curative and salvific purposes is well documented, as can be perceived through examinations of literary sources such as Hadith literature, theological and juridical treaties, and prayer manuals, as well as studies of material culture, with respect to objects known as charms, amulets and talismans.[6] Also ethnographic research focusing on recitation practices suggest it is not uncommon for Muslims to recite parts of the Qur'an or the entire text in order to benefit from its protective or beneficial powers in ritual events. In Iran, for example, *Sūrat al-Anʿām* (Q. 6), which is held to be abundant with grace, is recited in the collective ritual called *khatm-i anʿam*, to promote the prosperity of the ritual's host. Sometimes, such rituals are held on a weekly basis to sustain prosperity.[7] Another popular ritual held for the same purpose among Muslims, but which involves the recitation of the entire Qur'an, is the 'sealing of the Qur'an' (*khatam al-Qurʾān*).[8] Nevertheless, more research is necessary in order to develop our understanding of how the Qur'an is appropriated to function as a positive asset in people's lives.

In the following, I explore the multiple ways that the women of a local Twelver Shiʿa community in Shiraz proceeded in order to put to work the power they perceived to be embedded in the Quran. The discussion is based on field-research conducted between 1999 and 2003 when I attended Qur'an classes as well as liturgical rituals including the celebration of birthdays (*mawlūd*) and commemorative rituals (*mātam majlis*) hosted in a ritual location called the *zaynabiyya*.[9] Exploring two events that I observed in 2001, I examine how the Qur'an's efficacious power was communicated to people, what its beneficial effects were perceived to be, how its power was authenticated, how it was put to use and which skills were considered necessary in order to appropriate its power. The first event I discuss is a Qur'an class and the second is a ritual in which three liturgical times were conflated: 1) Ramadan, the month of fasting; 2) *laylat al-qadr* (The Night of Power); and 3) the commemoration of the death of ʿAlī b. Abī Ṭālib (d. 40/661), the

Prophet's cousin and son-in-law. Most students in the Qur'an class attended the ritual while not all ritual participants attended the Qur'an class. However, as they were hosted in the same location under the guardianship of one family, the two events represent a continuum in how the Qur'an is appropriated within a broader informal network of women.

The Qur'an Class

The Qur'an class held in the *zaynabiyya* was organised by the guardian of this place of ritual. She was a middle-aged widow who, with assistance from the women in her family, ran the *zaynabiyya*, which had been donated by her late husband as an endowment (*waqf*).[10] Classes were scheduled for Sunday afternoons and the students belonged to an informal network of women who regularly visited the location for rituals of commemoration and celebration. The women came from households of diverse economic means. Some were wives of rich bazar merchants, others were widows with children trying hard to make ends meet as unskilled labourers. What united them was their affection for this particular ritual hall which specialised in hosting rituals rather than sermons. On the particular afternoon discussed here – Sunday, 4 November 2001 (18 Shaʿbān) – twenty-two women between the age of twenty-five and seventy were present, and some had brought their youngest children. The students sat in a circle on the carpeted floor and many kept a booklet containing a selection of Qur'an chapters open in front of them. The teacher sat among the students on the floor, equipped with a copy of the Qur'an, collections of *tafsīr* (exegesis) and a notebook. Tea was served and a few elder women smoked the hookah.

Before the establishment of the Islamic Republic of Iran in 1979, women had few opportunities for obtaining formal religious education. Many received training in the family, and tutoring varied according to the teacher's skills and the purpose of the training.[11] Some women were taught Qur'an recitation and exegetic traditions by scholarly, educated fathers. These women would sometimes later act as reciters, lecturers and teachers for other women. In addition, mothers or other female relatives passed on ritual performance skills, such as the recitation of stories (*rawḍa*) and lamentations (*nawḥa*), to younger women who aspired to become ritual leaders (*maddāḥ*) in women-only gatherings.[12] Typically, such forms of private tutoring did not offer a formal certificate.[13] Another option was for the women to enrol in small, private religious schools called *maktabs*.[14] While such forms of religious transmission still take place, the state has, since the early 1980s, institutionalised the religious education of women. Formal educational programmes now cover a number of fields and are offered at different levels.[15] At a basic level, religious education is targeted towards raising women's moral standards, whereas more advanced courses offer women the professional skills to become teachers and preachers. In official female seminaries, such as the Jamīʿat al-Zahrā, students are also trained to convey and propagate the officially recognised understanding of Islam.[16] The graduates take up positions in educational institutions and act as teachers and preachers at informal gatherings for women.

The Qur'an class discussed here is an example of such informal gatherings and, typical of a practice noted also by Azam Torab in South Tehran, the guardian was free to choose which teachers to invite to conduct the classes.[17] In this case, the guardian had made arrangements with a woman who acted as one of several leaders at rituals hosted in the *zaynabiyya*. The teacher was in her mid-forties and had trained for five years at the Dār al-Qur'ān in Shiraz, an institute established by Ruhollah Khomeini after the revolution.[18] Upon completing her exams, she had received a certificate authorising her to call herself 'teacher' (*murabbī* or *muʿallim*), and to teach Arabic pronunciation and Qur'an recitation, give advice in appropriate and commendable ritual performance, and offer Qur'an commentaries according to exegetic texts she had studied. In particular, her education included studies on the treatise on the practical laws (*risāla ʿamaliyya*) of Khomeini, her chosen source of emulation (*marjaʿ al-taqlīd*) in these matters.[19] When this study was being conducted, she had already been teaching for five years. The teacher and students in the informal Qur'an class had thus known each other for some years.

The students' competence in reading the Qur'an varied. Women in their mid-thirties and younger could read and recite many verses from the Qur'an, as this was part of the public school curriculum. Older women, though familiar with the text, were not necessarily able to read or recite it. Therefore, some students attended the class to practice Arabic pronunciation and learn to recite the Qur'an in a fluent manner, while a core group of attendants aspired to succeed in memorising either parts or all of the text.[20] The method used for training and memorising was to have students listen to taped recordings of the renowned reciter (*murattil*) Shahriyār Parhīzkār cantillating the Qur'an according to the intoned technique of recitation (*tartīl*). After listening to the taped recording of a particular verse, the women took turns in reciting it. They imitated the style of recitation and rehearsed Arabic diction under the supervision of the teacher, who used a small portable blackboard to explain the differences between Arabic and Persian phonology.[21] This particular educational setting, with its slow and repetitive reading of passages of the text, gave older illiterate women the opportunity to memorise Qur'an passages through auditive training. Some women, moreover, attended classes primarily to hear the Word of God being spoken as the Qur'an was recited to them. Reciting as well as listening to recitation were considered meritorious, and both activities allowed women to engage as pious subjects. Apart from familiarising themselves with the Qur'anic text, students saw the class as an opportunity to learn from the teacher's guidelines (*aḥkām*) on ritual practices and to discuss, within a religious framework, problems they faced in everyday life. In the following, I demonstrate how the teacher introduced the students to the protective qualities associated with the Qur'anic texts they recited.

Teaching the protective power of the Qur'an

After a session of reciting and memorising Qur'an verses, the teacher translated the verses from Arabic into Persian and elaborated on their protective powers. Her choice of topics was based on first-hand knowledge of the needs of her audience.[22] She explained: 'There are four chapters in the Qur'an which begin with the imperative "Say" (*qul*), and they are called the Four Declarations (*chahār qul*). These chapters are very useful when you are in need of protection.' The teacher here referred to four short chapters to be found towards the end of the Qur'an: *Sūrat al-Kāfirūn* (Q. 109), *Sūrat al-Ikhlāṣ* (Q. 112), *Sūrat al-Falaq* (Q. 113) and *Sūrat al-Nās* (Q. 114). Notably, none of the Qur'an verses recited for protection referred to in this study say 'I protect thee'. In *Sūrat al-Kāfirūn*, believers are advised to avoid disbelief (*shirk*) and are called upon to distance themselves from the faith held by non-Muslims. *Sūrat al-Ikhlāṣ* affirms the most important dogma in Islam, the unicity (*tawḥīd*) of God. In the next two suras, *Sūrat al-Falaq* and *Sūrat al-Nās*, people are encouraged to seek refuge from evil and witchcraft in God. The use of these verses for protection in matters of this world as well as in the afterlife is widespread in the Muslim world.[23]

The central topics in the teacher's exposition were the manner in which these chapters could work, in keeping with Twelver Shi'i tradition, as protective forces, when to use them and what to do in order to make them work.[24] The illustrating examples she gave were of a general nature, and had to do with making a trip or seeking protection from evil, such as evil perpetrated by jealous people or those who talk behind people's backs. At this point one of the students interrupted to supply an example of what she saw as a threat specifically faced by women in today's society. She pointed to the danger posed by women who lured other women's husbands away from the family, a threat she had experienced. The teacher acknowledged the danger and again advised the women to read the 'Four Declarations' to protect themselves.[25] Nevertheless, the topic was not dropped, as the conversation among the students turned into a discussion on witchcraft and how some women use their beauty to manipulate those around them, in particular men. After listening attentively, the teacher confirmed that several suras in the Qur'an speak about the workings of the *jinn* – *Sūrat al-Naml* (Q. 27), *Sūrat al-Aḥqāf* (Q. 46), *Sūrat al-Raḥmān* (Q. 55) and *Sūrat al-Jin* (Q. 72) in particular. She warned that human beings might be influenced by bad spirits but did not elaborate on the spirits' intervention in the life of humans, even when a student concluded that bad women operate in connection with evil spirits. Instead, she reminded them of human beings' ability to practice self-control and emphasised that if women acted in a morally acceptable way, society would be safe. As this is not always the case, she concluded, the women should first and foremost put their trust in God in order to be safe.

Thus directing the attention back to the Qur'anic text, the teacher next read the Throne Verse (*āyat al-kursī*, Q. 2:255). She explained that this verse was also beneficial to recite when in need of protection. Several students agreed. One commented that she read the verse every time she got behind the wheel of her car, and she had never experienced an accident. Another declared that she read the verse aloud in her house in order to protect it, and there had never been any burglary. The teacher welcomed these accounts and took the opportunity to share a story about a critical moment in her own life. According to her story, she always read the Throne Verse to protect her children before leaving them alone at home while she was at work. Once, she returned home from a lecture to find that the water pipe had burst and the flood caused the electricity to spark at the fuses. The children were small and helpless. However, the fire brigade arrived and saved them. She described their rescue as being 'a miracle' that was clearly promoted by her having read the protective verse before leaving the house.

Authenticating the protective powers of the Qur'an

In the authentication of the protective powers of the Qur'an, the teacher did not refer to sources outside the Qur'an, such as hadiths, the *faḍā'il al-Qur'ān* (virtues of the Qur'an), or other religious scholarly texts.[26] Instead, when the informal setting of the class motivated students to make comments and share experiences, the instruction was transformed into a colloquial exchange of first-hand experiences affecting the women's emotional, social and financial situation. Such everyday experiences functioned as sources for authenticating the protective powers of the Qur'an. This interactive and dialogical style of teaching stands in sharp contrast to the monologist style of teaching noted by Zahra Kamalkhani in Shiraz in the early 1990s.[27]

As such, the colloquial, dialogic style also functioned as a mode of authorisation in which the students were given, and took, the authority to individually interpret and practice Islam within the realm of their everyday needs and experiences.[28] The exchange in the present case did, nevertheless, represent a challenge for the teacher, in that it brought to the surface a widespread belief in the evil eye, witchcraft and spirits. In fact, upon visiting the homes of several of the students, I had observed samples of the eye-shaped glass amulets in white, and dark and light blue, typically used to divert the evil eye (Persian, *chashm naẓar* or *naẓar ghurbānī*). Moreover, I had witnessed some of the women letting smoke produced by burning seeds from *ispand* fill their homes to chase away the evil eye.[29] This act of purification was also performed in locations I attended during rituals of commemoration in Muḥarram, including the *zaynabiyya*.[30] These are only some of the many methods used in Iran for protective and therapeutic purposes.[31] The teacher avoided making reference to such beliefs and practices, and to the rich literature available on how to secure protection from various dangers, since in modernist Twelver Shiʿi theology these are viewed as bordering on magic, sorcery and witchcraft, which are considered tantamount to *shirk*, in the sense that the source of power is held to be independent and autonomous from God.[32]

The teacher also avoided venturing into discourses which could easily have become politicised. One could argue that the matrimonial worries raised by some of the students were directly connected to the post-revolutionary government's liberalisation of men's right to polygamy and the granting of men's unlimited rights to divorce, compared with women's restricted rights.[33] The Family Law, which deals with divorce, polygamy, temporary marriage and child custody, has been a highly contentious issue in Iran and has been debated on theological, legal and political grounds. In fact, the exchange in the class carried subtle political undertones of Khomeinist and post-revolutionary gender discourses in which women's sexuality is perceived to have tremendous power over men, an idea which has provided a strong argument for segregating the sexes and forcing women to veil in public.[34] When I talked to some of the younger students after class I learned that they were upset by the teacher's remarks on women's moral behaviour. In their view, the idea that women were to blame for husbands being unfaithful or leaving their family belonged to the past. In the present age, they argued, one would expect a man to exercise some self-discipline and give priority to his family. Instead, the problem was embedded in the way the society was structured, with little contact between men and women in general. When I asked why these opinions had not been voiced in class, they argued that the topic was beyond religious leaders' professional competence. Despite the critique, I think it is fair to say that the teacher indirectly acknowledged her limited competence in discussing legal and social matters when she repeatedly referred to the Qur'an as a trustworthy source to secure and improve life. Moreover, she tailored her teaching to suit her host's objective to provide guidance in the use of the Qur'an, rather than present a sermon.

The power of the spoken word

The *chahār qul* and the *āyat al-kursī* were presented by the authorised Qur'an teacher as useful for those in need of protection. This idea that the Qur'anic text, both in its oral and written form, has beneficial powers is widespread among Muslims.[35] Additional verses attributed with such power are, for example, Q. 65:3; Q. 61:13, also called the Victory Verse (*Help from God and a speedy victory*); the Seven Verses, which is a selection of verses from different chapters of the Qur'an; and the verses of *Sūrat Yā Sīn* (Q. 36).[36] These and other Qur'an verses might be voiced in various speech events with the expectation of bringing about specific effects. In anthropology, such speech events are known as spells, prayers and supplications. The examination of performative utterances in the study of rituals has been inspired by John L. Austin's theorising on speech performance.[37] Particularly useful has been his distinction between doing something *in* saying something, which he calls an illocutionary act, and doing something *by* saying something, which he calls a perlocutionary act.[38] In such literature, prayers, spells and magic are defined as illocutionary utterances – that is, words paraphrased as acts – since pronouncing them is to perform the very act they speak about, as in the case of, for example, the words spoken in the Christian baptismal rite, 'I baptise thee in the name of the Father . . .'[39] In the present case, however, I suggest that the performance of Qur'an verses functions as a perlocutionary speech act. The reciter performing the verses invokes God's protection *by* reciting His words. The difference is one of authority. In illocutionary speech acts the agency rests with the speaker. In the present case, agency rests with God, while the speaker, by the speech act, activates the power embedded in the Word of God. The training during the Qur'an class – rehearsing pronunciation and recitation, and memorising the Word – enabled the women to perfect the skills necessary to invoke God's protection *by* recitation, not to perform or control such power *in* recitation.

The embodiment of the Qur'anic text as an oral performative skill managed by lay believers stresses using the text in speech acts. Such logocentrism differs from the widespread practice of *duʿāʾ niwīsī*, the writing of Qur'an passages on amulets and talismans as supplication for good luck and protection of the carrier against misfortune. The distinction between amulet and talisman in ethnological and anthropological studies of Muslim practices is blurred. However, an amulet is sometimes seen to be an object worn on an everyday basis, for example as a pendant or as a belt clasp.[40] A talisman, on the other hand, denotes something used occasionally, for a special purpose, for example, talismanic shirts used in warfare.[41] In addition to wearing an amulet or a talisman, protective and curative strategies are often held to be strengthened by accompanying actions, such as fasting for a number of days.[42] Islamic discussions concerning the legitimate and illegitimate use of spells typically revolve around the use of objects as transporters of effects, and objects as the cause of effects. The teacher's emphasis on the oral performance of the text held an implicit caution against objectifying the Word. Following her instruction, the power to protect was held to be intrinsic to the Word of God and could be released or summoned by uttering the words, unaided by gestures or by the use of objects. The teacher's position could be interpreted as an attempt to discipline the students' use of material objects inscribed with Qur'anic texts, which was not uncommon in the community researched here. For example, the child of one of the students wore an amulet inscribed with the *āyat al-kursī*, and over the pulpit in the *zaynabiyya* hung a banner inscribed with the Victory Verse; wall-hangings imprinted with the *chahār qul* are normally available for purchase in the bazaar. From my conversation with the child's mother and with owners of wall-hangings, it is clear that the amulet and the calligraphic wall-hanging were perceived as mediums and not as powerful objects in themselves.

The Ritual Event

On the 20th of Ramadan (Thursday, 6 December 2001), a ritual event was staged in the *zaynabiyya*, during which three liturgical times conflated: the time of fasting, the time of *laylat al-qadr* and the time of mourning the martyrdom of ʿAlī b. Abī Ṭālib. The ritual performance involved the recitation of the entire Qur'an, and in the following sections I examine how the recitation interacted with other liturgical elements used by ritual performers to produce an efficacious effect. The attendees included students from the Qur'an class referred to above and women from the larger informal network associated with this ritual location. The programme started at 4:00 p.m. and ran through the night until the dawn prayer, when the women took their *suḥūr* meal before the beginning of a new day of fasting. The month of fasting is commonly held to be a time for contemplating the Word of God. People throughout the Muslim world come together to recite the Qur'an, and each sentence read is generally held to be worth the equivalence of reading the whole book during any other month. The *laylat al-qadr* is held by tradition to be particularly powerful and beneficial. According to the Qur'an (Q. 2:185), Ramadan is the month in which the Qur'an was revealed to Muhammad, *laylat al-qadr* being night in which the first revelation happened (Q. 97:1–5).[43] Its date is not specified in the Qur'an, and both Sunni and Shiʿi sources are not univocal about the exact date, but Twelver Shiʿis typically celebrate *laylat al-qadr* on the 19th, 20th or 21st of Ramadan.[44] During these nights, people gather for collective readings of the whole text until the break of dawn. The guardian of the *zaynabiyya* had organised full-length readings of the Qur'an on all three nights. I attended the reading that took place on the 21st, which is also the date when 'Alī died in 41/661. Three teachers had been invited to guide the women through the Qur'an recitation and to give short lectures on how to perform the fast. In addition, four *maddāḥ* were invited, and they took turns to lead the ritual commemorating 'Alī. In the following section, I describe how the women combined the three liturgical moments during this evening to make it a beneficial moment.

Beneficial moments: Ramadan, *laylat al-qadr* and commemorating the death of ʿAlī

Women started arriving at the *zaynabiyya* in the late afternoon and gathered in small groups on the carpeted floor. Under the supervision of the three teachers, each group read different sections of the Qur'an simultaneously, a method applied to enable, collectively, the complete reading the Qur'an before dawn.[45] After school and working hours the attendance increased, and by 11:00 p.m. there were about a hundred women present. In between sessions of Qur'an recitation, the teachers gave short lectures about the beneficial circumstances for devotion provided by Ramadan. While the teachers in their lectures focused on Ramadan, the guardian's decoration of the *zaynabiyya* emphasised the commemorative aspects of the ritual event.[46] The pulpit was covered in black and green fabrics, the colours of mourning and of Islam, respectively.[47] In addition to the black, green and red wall-hangings presenting calligraphic embroideries, decorating the walls were portraits of 'Alī, as he is imagined to have looked.[48] On the floor in front of the pulpit was placed a proxy of 'Alī's sarcophagus in Najaf, Iraq. The proxy shrine consisted of a short, rectangular table covered by a black cloth inscribed with golden calligraphy and decorated with a black turban (which symbolically pointed to 'Alī), a book stand (*raḥl*) holding a Qur'an, two green candles, a jar with rosewater and a vase with red plastic roses; this arrangement imitated decorations of shrines (*imamzadeh*) in Iran. The women's black dress code further enhanced the sad atmosphere of mourning.

It was, however, close to midnight before ritual commemoration was brought to the forefront. Women gathered in a circle around the proxy grave to perform a rite of commemoration known in Persian as *sina-zanī*, which involves slapping one's chest and face.[49] The rite was accompanied by two *maddāḥ*s reciting *nawḥa*, while many women wept. The lamentation rite lasted for about thirty minutes. Apparently, the commemoration of ʿAlī is not always included in women-only rituals during *laylat al-qadr*. Torab noted, for example, the absence of such rites in the ceremonies she attended in Tehran in the early 1990s. Learning that the dirge for ʿAlī dominated the men's ceremonies at the local mosques in town, she speculates whether this practice represents gender differences in ritual performance.[50] However, in light of my observations, such gendered differences are not consistently adopted throughout Iran.

From midnight until dawn the programme alternated between the women, under the teachers' supervision, collectively reciting the Qur'an and the *maddāḥ*s presenting supplications. First, two *maddāḥ*s shared the task of reciting the supplication *jawshan kabīr* (the large steel plate) from the Twelver Shiʿi prayer manual *Mafātīḥ al-Jinān* (Keys to Heaven) compiled by the religious scholar ʿAbbās b. Muḥammad Riḍā Qummī (d. 1940).[51] The supplication is often read on *laylat al-qadr*, and some of the women kept a copy of the book open in front of them while reading; others listened with their eyes closed. Hands were held out in prayer. Simultaneously, tea was served. Before the recitation began, a teacher gave a short lecture on the usefulness of reciting this prayer. According to the fourth imam, al-Sajjād (d. 95/713), she informed them, the supplication had been brought to Muhammad by Gabriel during a war he had been fighting. Muhammad's armour was heavy, and Gabriel said: 'God sends you regards. Take off your coat of mail and recite this *duʿā'*. It will protect you and your nation.' The supplication, the teacher explained, worked as a 'coat of mail' (*jawshan* or *jushn*). In accordance with the advice offered by Qummī in *Mafātīḥ al-Jinān*, the teacher elaborated on the beneficial qualities of reciting the supplication during Ramadan and *laylat al-qadr* and underlined that God has promised the reciters protection from the punitive fires of the afterlife and entry to Paradise. She authenticated the efficacy of the *du'ā'* with a reference to a report (*riwāya*) from Ḥusayn (d. 61/680), who said that his father, 'Alī, asked to have the supplication written on his burial shroud (*kafan*) so that he would be protected from the flames of the afterlife.[52] The teacher from the Qur'an class next read the supplication of Abū Ḥamza Thumālī. Abū Ḥamza Thumālī is said to have been a close companion of al-Sajjād, and he recounted that the imam read this prayer during most nights of Ramadan. In the prayer, the supplicant praises God for His generosity and mercifulness, admits to his/her sins, asks forgiveness, and calls for help and redemption. When the teacher had completed reciting this rather long supplication, she let her students recite Qur'an verses until 2:00 a.m.

After completing the recitation of the Qur'an, the women returned to presenting supplications, but this time addressing 'Alī as an intercessor. A teacher explained to her audience that tonight was the night of worship and prayer, the night of 'Alī, and the night when God would register the good deeds for the future (the Day of Judgement). She encouraged the women to seize this opportunity to present a supplication to 'Alī 'if you have any problems in your house, if there are sick members in your family, or for whatever reasons you came here tonight'. To assist the individual request for help, she read a prayer, asking God to guide them to Him and to 'Alī. She encouraged the women to turn their hearts towards the imam and read a poem about his compassion and generosity. After focusing in this manner on the possibility for seeking help in matters of this world, she turned to the topic of redemption. She reminded the women that on *laylat al-qadr* the door to mercy was open, and it was a good occasion for asking forgiveness on behalf of the dead. In order to enhance their prayers, she read a poem in which 'Alī was addressed as a mediator: 'Tonight I came because of your love, Mawlānā. If I am guilty, please don't refuse me tonight but help me, by God.' The teacher underlined 'Alī's mediating role by telling a story about al-Sajjād confirming 'Alī's nearness to God, and explained his power to intervene on behalf of human beings on the Day of Judgement. She then recited a *rawḍa* on 'Alī's death, during which many women sat with the chador covering their heads, crying. Finally, the teacher read a supplication directed to ʿAlī, acknowledging the injustice he suffered, and asked his intercession.

At around 3:00 a.m., the women turned towards the direction of prayer (the *qibla*) and placed the Qur'an on their heads, thereby using the Qur'an as a mediator.[53] A ritual leader recited a prayer: 'God, although I am guilty, I put the Qur'an between me and you as a mediator.'[54] The gesture was further accompanied by a prayer invoking the names of God and the *panj-tan* (the five holy members of the Prophet's family – Muhammad, Fāṭima, ʿAlī, Ḥasan and Ḥusayn).[55] The rite was followed by a sequence of supplications addressed to the Twelve Shiʿi imams, and the ritual event was concluded by the dawn prayer. It was then time to eat before the fast would begin again. A tablecloth was laid on the floor and *suḥūr* was served. After first consuming hot water, tea and dates, the women enjoyed rice and lentils with chicken. Around 4:00 a.m. they all returned home through the quiet, desolated streets of Shiraz.

Performing *thaqalayn*: Bringing the Qur'an to life

On this particular night, the women had gathered to fast, to celebrate *laylat al-qadr* and to mourn the death of ʿAlī. The occasion was considered imbued with beneficial potential, a time when the gates to heaven were open, sins would be forgiven and one could ask for protection, mediation, healing and redemption. Qur'an recitation took up most of the time, and the text, in being recited, was held to be beneficial for the women and their families. The Qur'an was also used as a mediator in a very tactile manner when the women turned towards the *qibla* and placed the book on their heads. Supplications were also performed to mediate God's mercy. One set of supplications (*jawshan al-kabīr* and the one of Abū Ḥamza Thumālī) addressed God as the granter of protection and redemption. Another set of supplications were addressed to members of the People of the House (*ahl al-bayt*), who were asked to act as mediators. In particular, by acknowledging ʿAlī's sufferings and deprivation through their ritual performance, the women hoped to invoke his intercession.

Such reliance on the *ahl al-bayt* did not, I suggest, undermine the unique status of the Qur'an. Rather, in their practice, the women enacted theological discourses regarding the concepts of the *thaqalayn* and mediation (*shafāʿa*). According to the hadith on *thaqalayn* (two precious things), as recounted by Sunni and Shiʿi sources, Prophet Muhammad told his followers he would leave behind 'two precious things': 'The Book of God' and 'The People of the House'.[56] He supposedly asserted that as long as they clung to these two, they would never go astray.[57] Following Twelver Shiʿi theology, ʿAlī and the *ahl al-bayt*, together with the Qur'an, are the true sources of authoritative knowledge.[58] Twelver Shiʿi theological discourse also contends that the imams are bestowed with the power to act as intercessors (*shāfiʿ*) when a devotee seeks favourable introduction to God (*wasīla*). The prayers, supplications and poems performed by the women in the ritual are, I suggest, enactments of these central aspects of Twelver Shiʿa theology. The women turned to the Qur'an and *ahl al-bayt* for protection and mediation, simultaneously following and appropriating the theology of the *thaqalayn* and mediation.

Appropriating the Qur'an as an Efficacious Text

The main objective in this study has been to explore how the Qur'an is appropriated to function as an efficacious text for the benefit of people. The analysis has focused on how the notion of the Qur'an as an efficacious power is communicated to people, what its beneficial effects are perceived to be, how its power is authenticated, how it is put to use and which skills are perceived to be necessary in order to appropriate the text's power.

In the Qur'an class discussed in this chapter, students were instructed in how to use short Qur'an verses, the Four Declarations (*chahār qul*) and *āyat al-kursī* for protection in their everyday lives, for example, as a safeguard against accidents or slander. In such everyday situations, often characterised by time constraints and sudden turns of events, protection could be called upon by the individual's performance of a single verse. The ritual performed during Ramadan, celebrating *laylat al-qadr* and commemorating the death of ʿAlī b. Abī Ṭālib, instead provided a unique beneficial moment for asking for help, forgiveness and redemption, and this was done by those who contributed in the collective effort to recite the whole Qur'an under the guidance of teachers and *maddāḥ*s. In both of these situations, the Qur'an's efficacious power was brought to life in a perlocutionary speech act, that is, through the participants invoking God's protection by reciting his words. Pronunciation and memorisation were the skills necessary to appropriate the Qur'an, and these skills had been honed during the class where the women had been trained to invoke God's protection *by* recitation, not to perform or control such power *in* recitation.

Brian Stock speaks of religious communities as 'textual communities' that come to understand their identities through the mediation of written texts, which often are interpreted for them by key individuals.[59] However, I would suggest that the local informal network of women introduced in the present study should instead be perceived as a 'performative community'. In the ritual performance, the Qur'an was recited in constellation with other texts, such as supplications mediated or authorised by the imams. By situating the Qur'an in a 'textual complex',[60] the women appropriated and embodied central Twelver Shiʿa theological expositions about the relationship between the Qur'an and the *ahl al-bayt*, as it is laid out in theological expositions of *thaqalayn*. The significance of performativity, understood as an act of accomplishment and fulfilment, was also expressed by the Persian-speaking interlocutors in their local vernacular comments about *laylat al-qadr* as 'the night of bringing the Qur'an to life' (*laylat al-ahya*). Aesthetic manipulations of the ritual location to create an atmosphere of mourning for ʿAlī was an additional performative element in the women's effort to bring the text to life.

Performativity was also a crucial aspect of authenticating the Qur'anic text as an efficacious power. The trained teacher's instructions about the beneficial power of the Qur'an carried formal authority. The students did not, however, adopt a transmitted interpretation of the text's power, but discussed the text's usefulness while trying to understand the parameters of its influence, with its protective qualities tested against their personal experiences. The text's authenticity as a protective resource derived precisely from its ability to provide solutions to everyday concerns. The discussion in class thus offered a particular way of looking at the Qur'an, namely to see it as an efficacious text. Understood in this way, the Qur'an's protective power was available to anyone, to be called upon by religious experts as well as ordinary people, whenever they thought it necessary. While its power to work rested with the will of God, the memorisation of the text and knowledge about when to use it gave women some sort of agency, in that they knew how to protect themselves and those close to them in certain situations. In this capacity, the Qur'an had a central place in the lives of the women in this study.

NOTES

1 Michael Mumisa, 'Towards an African Qur'anic Hermeneutics', *Journal of Qur'anic Studies* 4, no. 1 (2002), pp. 61–76; Walid Saleh, *The Formation of the Classical* Tafsīr *Tradition: The Qur'ān Commentary of al-Thaʿlabī (d. 427/1035)* (Leiden, 2004).

2 Angelika Neuwirth, 'The House of Abraham and the House of Amram: Genealogy, Patriarchal Authority and Exegetical Professionalism', in Angelika Neuwirth, Nicolai Sinai and Michael Marx, eds, *The Qur'ān in Context: Historical and Literary Investigations into the Qur'ānic Milieu* (Leiden, 2011), pp. 499–532.

3 See Richard T. Antoun, *Muslim Preacher in the Modern World: A Jordanian Case Study in Comparative Perspective* (Princeton, NJ, 1989); John R. Bowen, *Muslims through Discourse: Religion and Ritual in Gayo Society* (Princeton, NJ, 1993); Michael Lambek, *Knowledge and Practice in Mayotte: Local Discourses of Islam, Sorcery, and Spirit Possession* (Toronto, 1993); Fadwa El Guindi, *Veil: Modesty, Privacy and Resistance* (Oxford, 1999); Charles Hirschkind, *The Ethical Soundscape: Cassette Sermons and Islamic Counterpublics* (New York, 2006).

4 See, for example, Nancy T. Ammerman, ed., *Everyday Religion: Observing Modern Religious Lives* (Oxford, 2007); Meredith B. McGuire, *Lived Religion: Faith and Practice in Everyday Life* (Oxford, 2008); Baudouin Dupret *et al.*, eds, *Ethnographies of Islam: Ritual Performances and Everyday Practice* (Edinburgh, 2012); Nathal M. Dessing *et al.*, eds, *Everyday Lived Islam in Europe* (Farnham, 2013).

5 Mahmoud Ayoub, *The Qur'an and Its Interpreters, Volume I* (Albany, NY, 1984), p. 16.

6 See, for example, Rudolf Kriss and Hubert Kriss-Heinrich, *Volksglaube in Bereich des Islam, Vol. II: Amulette, Zauberformeln und Beschwörungen* (Wiesbaden, 1962), pp. 1–58; Ayoub, *The Qur'an and Its Interpreters*; Mahmoud Omidsalar, 'Charms', *EIr*, vol. V (1992), pp. 385–8; Constance E. Padwick, *Muslim Devotions: A Study of Prayer-Manuals in Common Use* (Oxford, 1997); Fahmida Suleman, ed., *Word of God, Art of Man: The Qur'an and its Creative Expressions* (Oxford, 2007); Faegheh Shirazi, *Velvet Jihad: Muslim Women's Quiet Resistance to Islamic Fundamentalism* (Gainesville, FL, 2009); Jürgen Wasim Frembgen, ed., *The Aura of Alif: The Art of Writing in Islam* (Munich, 2010).

7 Azam Torab, *Performing Islam: Gender and Ritual in Iran* (Leiden, 2007), pp. 85–6.

8 Ibid., p. 234; Pnina Werbner, '"Sealing the Koran": Offering and Sacrifice among Pakistani Labour Migrants', *Cultural Dynamics* 1, no. 1 (1988), pp. 77–97.

9 The research was generously funded by the Norwegian Research Council. For a discussion of the rituals occurring in the *zaynabiyya*, see Ingvild Flaskerud, '"Oh, My Heart is Sad. It is Moharram, the Month of Zaynab": The Role of Aesthetics and Women's Mourning Ceremonies in Shiraz', in Kamran Scot Aghaie, ed., *The Women of Karbala: Ritual Performance and Symbolic Discourses in Modern Shi'i Islam* (Austin, TX, 2005), pp. 65–91; eadem, *Visualizing Belief and Piety in Iranian Shiism* (London, 2010). The existence of such ritual locations in Twelver Shi'a communities is widespread. Typically, they are named after the Prophet's grandson, Ḥusayn, i.e. *ḥusayniyya*; his mother Fāṭima al-Zahrā', i.e. *fāṭimiyya*; his brother Ḥasan, i.e. *ḥasaniyya*; or, as in the case discussed here, his sister Zaynab.

10 The location had been available to women in need of a place to host religious instruction, offer ex-votive meals and celebrate religious holidays. However, during the presidency of Mahmoud Ahmadinejad (2005–13) the state confiscated many such endowments and the *zaynabiyya* was taken over by the government in 2010. The activities hosted in the ritual hall are now government controlled and only men can attend. The female network affiliated with the locality is partly dissolved. (Personal communication with a local ritual expert in 2014.)

11 This information was gathered from interviews with ritual leaders in Shiraz between 2000 and 2003. For an overview of women's religious education before and after the establishment of the Islamic Republic, see also Mary Elaine Hegland, 'Gender and Religion in the Middle East and South Asia: Women's Voices Rising', in Margaret L. Meriwether and Judith E. Tucker, eds, *A Social History of Women and Gender in the Modern Middle East* (Berkeley, CA, 1999), pp. 177–212.

12 *Rawḍa* and *nawḥa* are genres of devotional literature which draw on collections of martyrdom narratives known as *maqtal* literature and on lamentation poetry known as *marāthī*. *Rawḍa* and *nawḥa* are communicated to large audiences orally during ritual performances. During the ritual called *rawḍa-khānī*, an elocutionist (*rawḍa-khān*) recites stories from the lives of the imams and of the members of their families and supporters, typically focusing on dramatic moments in their lives. Listeners respond with lamentations and sometimes flagellation. The *nawḥa* deals with the call to go to Karbala, the arrival at the plains, and the battle and its aftermath, and is intended to stir the feelings of the listeners and engage them in the performance. It is a form of responsorial song, with worshippers presenting stylised answers to the lead singer's lines. *Rawḍa* and *nawḥa* are reproduced in books and pamphlets sold in religious bookstores and are available in public libraries. For more on this, see Peter Chelkowski, 'From *maqatil* Literature to Drama', *al-Serat* 12 (1986), pp. 227–64; Lynda Clarke, 'Some Examples of Elegy on Imam Husayn', *al-Serat* 12 (1986), pp. 13–28; Flaskerud, *Visualizing Belief and Piety in Iranian Shiism*, pp. 6, 210–16.

13 Personal communication with female ritual leaders in Shiraz between 2000 and 2003.

14 Keiko Sakurai, 'Shi'ite Women's Seminaries (*howzeh-ye 'elmiyyeh-ye khahran*) in Iran: Possibilities and Limitations', *Iranian Studies* 45, no. 6 (2012), p. 729.

15 Azam Torab, 'The Politicization of Women's Religious Circles in Post-revolutionary Iran', in Sarah Ansari and Vanessa Martin, eds, *Women, Religion and Culture in Iran* (Richmond, 2002), pp. 143–68; Sakurai, 'Shi'ite Women's Seminaries', pp. 727–44. For similar developments in Pakistan, and for contacts between Pakistan and Iran when it comes to the religious education of women, see Mariam Abou Zahab, 'Between Pakistan and Qom: Shi'i Women's Madrasas and New Transnational Networks', in Farish A. Noor, Yoginder Sikand and Martin van Bruinessen, eds, *The Madrasa in Asia: Political Activism and Transnational Linkages* (Amsterdam, 2008), pp. 123–40.

16 Though in principle the education required to be a mujtahid (an independent interpreter of Islamic law) has never been denied at the female seminaries, the official seminars have not yet been successful in producing a female mujtahid. Nevertheless, a few women have risen to the rank, but without being recognised as formal members of the religious hierarchy. See Sakurai, 'Shi'ite Women's Seminaries', p. 740.

17 Torab, *Performing Islam*, p. 32.

18 There exist several different forms of Qur'an education and classes in Iran. The Dār al-Qur'ān is run by the state and the education is free, but the students have to pay for their learning material. In addition, there are associations such as the Ma'had-i Qur'ān-i Karīm, which are non-governmental institutes funded by donation.

19 In general, a *risāla 'amaliyya* or *risāliyya* presents a mujtahid's opinion on issues regarding rules about how to pray and live as a Muslim (*aḥkām*).

20 The training to become a Qur'an reciter (*ḥāfiẓ*) followed a certain procedure. The Qur'an is divided into thirty parts. When a student had learned to recite by heart the first part, she was rewarded with a box of thirty tapes of the Qur'an. When the student had learned to recite parts 1–3, she received a recorder; parts 1–7, a golden coin; parts 1–15, a certificate on interpreting the Qur'an, called *Tafsīr-nāma*. Upon memorising part 30, the award was three golden coins and a pilgrimage (*ziyārat*) to a shrine.

21 For a different, rather sensuous approach to teaching Qur'an recitation that underlines the 'pleasing transformative effect' of recitation (*hāl dādan*), see Torab, *Performing Islam*, pp. 235–6.

22 Personal communication with the teacher.

23 See, for example, how the recitation of some of these verses is central to funerals in Gayo, Indonesia, as discussed by Bowen, *Muslims through Discourse*, pp. 262–8.

24 The Prophet is said to have used the verses from *Sūrat al-Falaq* and *Sūrat al-Nās*, known as the 'verses for seeking refuge from evil', to protect himself from bewitchment. Tewfik Canaan, 'The Decipherment of Arabic Talismans', *Berytus* 5 (1937), p. 75. There is also a tradition which says that Ḥusayn apparently wore these two verses around his neck before he was martyred.

25 Because they open with the term 'say' (*qul*), John R. Bowen suggests these four suras are a kind of call (*daʿwa*) to Muslims, reminding them of the basis of their religion; see John R. Bowen, *A New Anthropology of Islam* (Cambridge, 2012), p. 113. My suggestion that the texts are protective devices does not undermine Bowen's analysis, but rather underscores his point that Islamic belief and practice are always localised. In fact, Bowen has noted that in Indonesia, *Sūrat al-Ikhlāṣ* is recited as part of the congregational prayer, for meditation and to achieve a practical end.

26 The literary genre called the *faḍāʾil al-Qurʾān* developed in the early part of the third/ninth century. Two prominent Shiʿi scholars of the fourth/tenth century credited with *faḍāʾil al-Qurʾān* works are the Qur'an exegete ʿAlī b. Ibrāhīm al-Qummī (d. after 307/919) and Abū Jaʿfar Muḥammad al-Kulaynī (d. 329/941). The literature talks about the merits of the Qur'an and its properties – the merit of reciting it, listening to its recital, following its precepts, memorising it and transmitting it – and about the intercession of the Qur'an on behalf of its 'patron' (*ṣāḥib*) on the Day of Judgement. See, for example, Asma Afsaruddin, 'The Excellences of the Qurʾān: Textual Sacrality and the Organization of Early Islamic Society', *Journal of the American Oriental Society* 122, no. 1 (2002), pp. 1–24; Travis Zadeh, 'An Ingestible Scripture: Qurʾānic Erasure and the Limits of "Popular" Religion', in Benjamin J. Fleming and Richard D. Mann, eds, *Material Culture and Asian Religions: Text, Image, Object* (London, 2014), pp. 97–119.

27 Zahra Kamalkhani, *Women's Islam: Religious Practice among Women in Today's Iran* (London, 1998), pp. 55–6, 59.

28 The study of Muslim religious authority has in recent years attracted more attention. The main approach seems to focus on the reproduction or transmission of authoritative ideas. See, for example, Gudrun Krämer and Sabine Schmidtke, eds, *Speaking for Islam: Religious Authorities in Muslim Societies* (Leiden, 2014).

29 *Ispand* in Persian is also known as *esfand daneh*; in Latin, *peganum harmala*. *Peganum harmala* is a perennial shrub with fleshy, spikey leaves, growing up to one metre tall. Its small, brown seeds contain harmine and other harmala alkaloids. It is one of the plants speculated to be the Soma, or Haoma, of ancient Persia.

30 Flaskerud, *Visualizing Belief and Piety in Iranian Shiism*, p. 216.

31 Upon review of publications she had purchased in Tehran in 2004, shortly after the present field research was conducted, Faegheh Shirazi observed that geomancy, numerology, witchcraft and sorcery were used as beneficial strategies. See Shirazi, *Velvet Jihad*, pp. 62–71.

32 For this definition of *shirk*, see Jaʿfar Sobhani, *Doctrines of Shiʿi Islam: A Compendium of Imami Beliefs and Practices*, tr. and ed. Reza Shah-Kazemi (London, 2001), p. 155.

33 Janet Afary, *Sexual Politics in Modern Iran* (Cambridge, 2009). In 1982 an amendment was added to the 1979 Family Law which made it possible for women to insert stipulations against polygamy in the marriage contract.

34 Afsaneh Najmabadi, 'Hazards of Modernity and Morality: Women, State and Ideology in Contemporary Iran', in Deniz Kandiyoti, ed., *Women, Islam and the State* (London, 1991), pp. 48–76.

35 See Padwick, *Muslim Devotions*, pp. 116–17.
36 The Seven Verses comprise Q. 9:51, Q. 10:107, Q. 11:6, 56, Q. 29:6, Q. 35:2 and Q. 39:38. For a description and discussion of how these verses are used by Muslims in Gayo, see Bowen, *Muslims through Discourse*, p. 96.
37 Partly inspired by John L. Austin's *How to do Things with Words* (Oxford, 1962), Stanley Tambiah theorised rituals as performances; see Stanley Tambiah, 'A Performative Approach to Ritual', *Proceedings of the British Academy* 65 (1981), pp. 113–69. For a discussion of Austin's and Tambiah's contributions to ritual studies, see Ursula Rao, 'Ritual in Society', in Jens Kreinath, Jan Snoek and Michael Stausberg, eds, *Theorizing Rituals: Issues, Topics, Approaches, Concepts* (Leiden, 2006), pp. 143–60, and Robert A. Yelle, *Semiotics of Religion: Signs of the Sacred in History* (London, 2013), pp. 25–7.
38 See Yelle, *Semiotics of Religion*, p. 15.
39 Jørgen Podemann Sørensen, 'Efficacy', in *Theorizing Rituals*, p. 525.
40 Frembgen, *The Aura of Alif*, p. 28, figs. 14 a–c.
41 Patricia L. Baker, *Islam and the Religious Arts* (London, 2004), p. 191.
42 Ibid., p. 193.
43 'Laylat al-qadr', *Shorter Encyclopaedia of Islam* (Leiden, 1974), pp. 468–9.
44 Among the Sunnis, *laylat al-qadr* is celebrated on the 21st, 23rd, 25th, 27th or 29th.
45 The Qur'an is divided into 114 chapters varying in length between 3 and 286 verses. In order to be able to recite the text in its entirety over a particular period of time, it has been divided into thirty equal parts (*ajzā'*); see Ayoub, *The Qur'an and Its Interpreters*, p. 14. The women in the ritual event divided each of these parts into subparts. After having together completed reciting one part they continued to the next.
46 For a discussion on the use of decorative programmes in ritual assembly halls in Iran in modern times, see Flaskerud, *Visualizing Belief and Piety in Iranian Shiism*.
47 See Baker, *Islam and the Religious Arts*, p. 222; Flaskerud, *Visualizing Belief and Piety in Iranian Shiism*, pp. 199–230; Annemarie Schimmel, *Deciphering the Signs of God: A Phenomenological Approach to Islam* (Albany, NY, 1994), p. 16.
48 Local viewers do not perceive these images to be authentic and are aware of their imaginary nature. In this case, the legitimacy of the image is based on the iconography's ability to visually portray a person whom Muslim viewers will recognise as representing or standing for ʿAlī. See Flaskerud, *Visualizing Belief and Piety in Iranian Shiism*, pp. 21–78.
49 For a more detailed description of commemorative rituals in this community, see Ingvild Flaskerud, '"Oh, My Heart is Sad"', pp. 65–91.
50 See Torab, *Performing Islam*, pp. 239.
51 ʿAbbās b. Muḥammad Riḍā Qummī, *Mafātīḥ al-Jinān* (Tehran, 1381 Sh./2001). The prayer manual includes selected chapters from the Qur'an, supplications and pilgrimage prayers, and advice on when to perform the prayers and prayer etiquette. The manual has been translated into many languages, and is commonly found in Twelver Shiʿi households. It is also available online.
52 This information is also found in the introduction to *duʿā' jawshan kabīr* in the *Mafātīḥ al-Jinān*.

53 Another practice common in this environment, and elsewhere in Iran, is to walk under the Qur'an three times to secure protection before setting out on a journey.

54 In this community it was common practice for individuals to place the Qur'an on their head when asking God's forgiveness after having committed a sin. They accompanied the ritual by reciting *Sūrat al-Tawba* (Q. 9).

55 In Persian the *panj-tan* refer to the 'Holy Five' who are believed to be purified by God and endowed with the spiritual authority to guide Muslims. In Arabic they are referred to as the 'People of the Cloak' (*ahl al-kisā'*). The concept originates with a hadith in which Muhammad is said to have brought these members of his family under his cloak and the Qur'anic verse Q. 33:33 was revealed.

56 Moojan Momen, *An Introduction to Shiʿi Islam: The History and Doctrines of Twelver Shiʿism* (New Haven, CT, 1985), pp. 16–17. According to some traditions, the *thaqalayn* was presented at Ghadīr Khumm during Muhammad's last pilgrimage to Mecca in 11/632. To the Twelver Shiʿas, the hadith is held to be one of the proofs validating their claim that Muhammad appointed ʿAlī b. Abī Ṭālib to be his successor.

57 The *thaqalayn* is thus fundamental to the theory of the imamate. The sixth imam, Jaʿfar al-Ṣādiq (d. 148/765), was instrumental in developing the notion that the world was in permanent need of a divinely guided imam who could act as the authoritative teacher in all religious matters. See Said Amir Arjomand, *The Shadow of God and the Hidden Imam* (Chicago, IL, 1987), p. 35.

58 This interpretation is supported by Q. 4:59: *O ye who believe! Obey God and obey the Apostle and those vested with authority from among you*. Qur'an translation taken from *The Holy Qur'an*, tr. S.V. Mir Ahmed Ali (New York, 1988).

59 Brian Stock, *The Implications of Literacy: Written Language and Models of Interpretation in the Eleventh and Twelfth Centuries* (Princeton, NJ, 1983), pp. 88–150, paraphrased in C. Annette Grisé, 'The Textual Community of Syon Abbey', *Florilegium* 19 (2002), p. 149.

60 I here draw on Burkhard Gladigow's theorising about 'ritual complex'; see Burkhard Gladigow, 'Complexity', in *Theorizing Rituals*, pp. 483–94.

17

The Qur'an as an Aesthetical Model in Music? The Case of Muḥammad Riḍā Shajariyān between the Qur'an and *radīf*

GIOVANNI DE ZORZI

For Leonard and Jane

Any reader who has ever been immersed in the soundscape of any given region of the Muslim world, crossed as it is five times a day by the call to prayer (*adhān*) and other defining sounds of Muslim devotion, will be well aware of the sonic nature of the Qur'an. In order to fully appreciate the meaning of the following remarks, the reader should ideally be able to stop the inner and outer dialogue, to be silent (a requirement stated in Q. 7:204[1]) and to listen. In the following pages, I will look at how the 'sonic nature' of the Qur'an may have influenced, even unconsciously, poetry, singing and instrumental music. This will prepare the ground for a discussion of the situation in twentieth- and twenty-first-century Iran, particularly regarding our focus on the key figure of the Iranian singer Muḥammad Riḍā Shajariyān (b. 1940), who was at ease with both art repertory (*radīf*) and Qur'anic cantillation.

Notes on the Sonic Nature of the Qur'an

In Islam, more than in other spiritual cultures, the sonic, vibrational, nature of the Qur'an is fundamental. In fact, this is immanent in the very term itself, for, as is well known, '*qur'ān*' means 'recitation' or 'reading', and not at all 'scripture'.[2] Apart from the term itself, the Qur'an's sonic nature is evident if we meditate on the history of its transmission: according to Islamic belief, the Qur'an had been revealed orally, sonically, through the archangel Gabriel to the Prophet, who received it mostly aurally, through listening.[3] In a second phase, the Prophet recited the revelations to his followers and Companions, who memorised it. Only in a third phase did the period of oral/aural transmission come to an end when the revelation was fixed in a written form and canonised *c.* 26/647.[4] Afterwards, the Qur'an was transmitted to the next generations both verbally and in script form, but, in fact, the oral form had superseded the written one because all the written texts of the scripture were compiled from the oral transmissions passed down by the transmitters (sing. *ḥāfiẓ*) and reciters (sing. *qārī*) of the Qur'an.

'Giving Voice to the Sacred Text': On Some Technical Terms

The centrality of the Qur'an in the intellectual activity of the early Muslims gave rise to a range of Qur'anic sciences which attempted to cover the multiple ways and modes of understanding the holy Book. Among them is *ʿilm al-tajwīd* (the science of Qur'anic recitation),[5] a term that derives from the verb *jawwada*, which, very significantly, means 'to make better', 'to embellish', 'to beautify'. Yet, as F.M. Denny points out, *tajwīd* is a general umbrella term for the 'art of reciting the Qur'an', and encompasses more specific terms like *qirāʾa* (recitation, recital) or *tilāwa* (to follow, to read/to read out loud).

In Q. 73:4 we find the verse *wa rattil al-Qurʾān tartīlan* (*and recite the Qur'an by means of* tartīl).[6] The meaning of the term *tartīl* poses many problems for reciters, commentators and translators; however, here, I will adopt the etic/emic dichotomy from the field of anthropology.[7] Using an etic approach, I define *tartīl* as Qur'anic 'cantillation', employing the term ethnomusicologists use for the analogous vocal renditions of other sacred texts; while, from an 'emic' point of view, I refer to ʿAlī b. Abī Ṭālib (d. 40/660), son-in-law of the Prophet and the fourth caliph/first imam, who, in answer to a question about the meaning of our problematic term, replied that *tartīl* means the 'excellent rendering of the consonant sounds and knowledge of the pauses' (*tajwīd al-ḥurūf wa maʿrifat al-wuqūf*). This latter, concise definition influenced from its birth *ʿilm al-tajwīd*, which developed by examining the phonetic 'places of articulation' (*makhārij*) of the consonants and vowels in the human body (the breast, throat, tongue, lips and nose) as well as the art of the pauses (*waqf*, pl. *wuqūf*). The rules of *ʿilm al-tajwīd* were transmitted orally/aurally among Qur'anic reciters, from master to disciple, as we will see, but, at the same time, were also codified in a written corpus of technical literature.

Through the centuries, particular styles of recitation/cantillation also developed. These were the plain *murattal* (term that derives from *tartīl*) style and the slower-paced but highly embellished *mujawwad* style, which often employs musical modes (*maqāmāt*) and a way of reciting the Qur'an melodiously (*taghannī*).[8]

Towards a Musicological Description of Qur'anic Cantillation

Qur'anic cantillation can be described in musicological terms as a succession of variable phrases of unequal length that are separated by eloquent pauses, and in which the declamatory aspect has priority over the melodic one. More particularly, in the embellished styles of cantillation, where the melodic and melismatic aspects acquire greater importance, the reciter tries to cantillate each verse in such a way as to avoid repetition; this is achieved through a more-or-less conscious use of codified secular musical modes (*maqāmāt*) with their characteristic melodic formulae types.

Regarding the elusive topic of the silences and pauses, we must recognise that it is rather difficult to deal with such an enormous theme, which ranges from the basic activity of breathing[9] to the highest peaks of aesthetic.[10] In Qur'anic cantillation, such pauses have an enormous importance – already alluded to in the saying attributed to ʿAlī – because they affect the meaning and the balance of the entire Qur'anic verse. Apart from rhetoric, we should note the emotional aspects of such silences and pauses, which can be filled with inexpressible and unutterable meanings and often elicit deep sighs and crying from the audience.

Outside of the strict environment of Qur'anic recitation, the application of 'Alī's *ma'rifat al-wuqūf* had a subtler impact on the aesthetic of all the 'arts of sound' which came to life in the vast world of Islam: the pervasive and omnipresent Qur'anic cantillation, with its eloquent pauses and silences, may have affected singers and musicians, even unconsciously. Such effects are clearly detectable in unmetered vocal (and instrumental) genres.

The Qur'an as a Base for the Unmetered Genres

In the Arab, Ottoman–Turkish and Persian classical and folk music traditions, there is a clear distinction between genres characterised by ethnomusicologists as being 'unmetered' or having a 'free rhythm' and genres that are 'metered' or 'rhythmed'. As an example, such a distinction is very clear in Turkey, where the folk vocal repertoire is traditionally divided between *uzun hava* ('long air') and *kırık hava* ('broken air'). The *uzun hava* is part of a larger family of 'free-rhythm' vocal genres, which include the *özen küi* among the Tatars, the *uzun küi* among the Bashkiri, the *ut dun* among the Kalmuks and the *urtyn duu* among the Mongols. The 'length' or 'fracture' of singing does not depend on the length or the brevity of the melodic line, but, rather, on the text being 'unmetered' or 'metered', and therefore 'broken' or 'fragmented' into rhythmic modules and based on rhythmic cycles.

In any given unmetered piece, performers are free from formal constraints and rhythmic rules: they can take their time, using rallentando, or go faster, using accelerando, and employ all the expressive devices to render their feelings related to the text without time constraints. Yet, the fact that performers are free from rhythmic constraints does not mean that they are free from the text's formal constraints: if a piece is unmetered, this does not mean that it does not have its own set of inner rhythmic rules of development, which basically derive from the versification. In Arab, Persian, Ottoman–Turkish and Central Asian classical traditions, poetry is measured according to a system (*arūḍ*) considered 'quantitative' because it is composed of syllables of unequal length – brief and long.[11]

As is well known, the Qur'an is not poetry, yet its rhymed prose (*saj*ʿ) constitutes the above-quoted 'set of inner rhythmic rules of development' that influence vocal performance. The pauses, silences, spaces and modulations are the tools that Qur'an reciters or readers use in order to translate the inner rhythmic values of the text. Apart from such values, the argument in the text and the meanings of the text influence the performer: for example, a passage that contains a reflection on Hell cannot be rendered in a joyous way. In short, the Qur'an in itself influences the vocalists during their unmetered performances. It is not unusual to see reciters having to stop because they have become overwhelmed by the emotion that the Qur'an provokes in them.

The unmetered vocal genres of sung poetry have a central place in all Islamic music cultures; such genres are paralleled by unmetered, free-rhythm, mostly improvised instrumental genres. It suffices to reflect on the examples of the classical vocal genres, such as the Persian *ghazal*, the Ottoman *gazel* or the Uzbek–Tajik *katta ashula* and their instrumental counterparts in the suite of unmetered *gushe*s in Persian classical repertoire (*radīf*) or the *taqsīm* for the Arab and Ottoman–Turkish traditions: for all these vocal and instrumental genres we can suppose a common aesthetical root, that is, the pervasive cantillation of the Qur'an.

Apart from the formal considerations, many singers and musicians knew by heart large tracts of the Qur'an and its rhyme resulting from *saj*ʿ. In the Persian *radīf*, which is modelled on poetry, many pure melodies cannot be understood if separated from the text that inspired the composer. The poems of Saʿdī (d. 691/1292), Rūmī (672/1273) and Ḥāfiẓ (791/1389 or 792/1390), for example, have deeply influenced the rhythmic sense of Persian musicians. At the same time, on the topic of the aesthetical proximity between the instrumental and the vocal, we should remember that a good performance is said to have made the instrument 'speak' or 'sing'.

The Art of the *Ḥāfiẓ* and the *Qārī*

Through the centuries, there emerged key figures who were experts in the cantillation of the Qur'an. These were called *qārī*, and when they knew by heart all the text, *ḥāfiẓ* (preserver): the *qārī* and the *ḥāfiẓ* were from the very first times key figures in the transmission of the Qur'an, before it was fixed in written form. But, from our musical perspective, they were, and are, first and foremost trained *mujawwids* who know how to use the voice with great technical artistry due to their understanding of the highly elaborate rules of *ʿilm al-tajwīd*.

Many of the great singers from the world of Islam had a solid upbringing as religious singers and often were, at the same time, great repositories for and transmitters of the huge oral repertoire of classical music which, though secular, was very often based on mystical poetry. Such an upbringing in religious singing, which was simultaneously musical and spiritual, was common among many great stars of the Islamic world. The Egyptian diva Umm Kulthum (d. 1975), the Turkish *ḥāfiẓ* and Mevlevi dervish Kani Karaca (d. 2004) and the standard bearer of the Uzbek–Tajik art music tradition (*shash maqom*), Jurabeg Nabiev (b. 1941), all come to mind. As far as early modern Iran is concerned, we should remember the examples of Iqbāl Sulṭān Ādhar (d. 1971), Ghulām-Ḥusayn Banān (d. 1986) and the great Muḥammad Riḍā Shajariyān (b. 1940), who is universally acclaimed as Iran's greatest living singer.

Muḥammad Riḍā Shajariyān between Qur'an and *Radīf*

Muḥammad Riḍā Shajariyān seems representative of the tradition of great vocalists of *radīf* who received an upbringing as religious singers. In the following pages, I will outline episodes from his life and works; these are intended just as a small sample of this musical tradition in twentieth-century Iran, yet are capable of reflecting the whole tradition that preceded him.

Shajariyān was born 23 September 1940 in Mashhad and started singing at the age of five under the supervision of his father, himself a *qārī*.[12] At the age of twelve, unbeknownst to his father, he began studying *radīf*. He launched his singing career in 1959 at the local radio station in Mashhad, and by 1966 he had moved to the National Iranian Radio Organisation in Tehran, where he rose to prominence with his distinctively rich vocal timbre and technical mastery.

His main teachers were *radīf* masters 'Abd Allāh Dawāmī (d. 1981), Ismā'īl Mihrtāsh (d. 1980), Nūr 'Alī Būrūmand (d. 1977), Aḥmad 'Ibādī (d. 1993) and Farāmarz Pāywar (d. 2009). He also learned the vocal styles of singers from previous generations, Riḍā Qulī Mīrzā Ẓillī (dates unknown), Farīburz Manūchihrī (dates unknown), Qamar Mulūk Wazīrī (d. 1959), Iqbāl Ādhar (d. 1971) and Tāj Iṣfahānī (d. 1981), though he always declared his love for the style of Ghulām-Ḥusayn Banān (d. 1986).

As an example of the proximity between instrumental and vocal styles discussed above, it seems worthy of note that Shajariyān was not only influenced by vocalists, but also by instrumentalists. In a lecture he gave on 2 March 2012 at California State University, Sacramento, Shajariyān said that the playing style he tried to mimic the most with his own singing style was that of Jalīl Shāhnāz (d. 2013), the legendary musician whose instrument was the Iranian long-necked lute (*tār*). Shajariyān performed regularly on Iranian Radio between 1966 and 1986, and many of the broadcasts were subsequently released as commercial recordings. He also appeared frequently on national television between 1971 and 1976. Since 1977, he has performed with many ensembles, giving concerts in Europe, North America and Asia, and has recorded albums with them. His work as a singer reflects his extensive knowledge of classical Iranian poetry.

A man of many talents, Shajariyān as well as being a singer is also a musician (he plays the hammered zither known as the *sanṭūr*), calligrapher and, recently, creator of new musical instruments.[13] He also taught at the University of Tehran from 1977 to 1979, and then returned there in 1990. His interest in the regional music of Iran dates from his earliest musical experiences in Khorasan, the region where he was born and raised, and he has carried out much research into the various types of folk music in Iran. He is very popular and commands great respect in Iran where he is generally regarded as the foremost classical vocalist of the post-revolutionary period.

To illustrate Shajariyān's ease in performing both Persian art music (*radīf*) and Qur'an cantillation, I would now like to discuss here just one recording among Shajariyān's vast collection of secular art music recordings which merges the two. It is his beautiful unmetered singing of a *ghazal* of Ḥāfiẓ, performed in duo with the *santūr* maestro Parviz Meshkatian (d. 2009). It is found on the CD titled *Iran. Mohammad Reza Shadjarian: Musique classique persane*,[14] which was recorded live at the Théâtre de la Ville, Paris, 30 October 1989. The vocal, free-rhythm episode is found on track 2 at the heart of the suite based on the mode *āwāz-i Afshārī*.[15] After a long, composed and metered instrumental prelude (*pīsh darāmad*), brilliantly and lively performed by the ensemble composed of the *santūr* (hammered zither), *barbat* (short necked lute), *tār* (long-necked lute), *ney haftband* (rim-blown flute) and *zarb* (goblet drum, also called *tumbak*), there is a carefully spaced long solo introduction on the *santūr* by the late Meshkatian. Shajariyān enters the performance (with great inspiration) only at 2′53″, and there begins an intense dialogue between the voice and the accompanying instrument on three traditional *gushe*s (corners) selected from the vast repertoire of the traditional suite in *āwāz-i Afshārī*; these *gushe*s are known by their evocative titles, *Jameh darān* (heart rending), *Dād* (lamentation) and *Mūyeh* (wailing). Operatively, in a suite, the singer himself chooses the poem, normally from the masterworks of Persian poets. Here, Shajariyān sings the verses he has chosen from Ḥāfiẓ in a way that makes use of the expressive devices of traditional Persian classical singing, above all the ornamental vocal technique *taḥrīr* of the *bulbulī* type, which requires rapid alternation between vocal registers resonating in the breast and the head. It is very important to note that in Persian classical music, the difference between a classical singer and a non-classical singer lies precisely in his/her capability to interpret unmetered genres, which are often based on classical poetry, and to be able to freely interpret the text using improvised embellishments, melismas, pauses and – crucially – *taḥrīr*. The expressive devices used in traditional singing could be compared to the tools of the art of rhetoric, which allows the orator to improvise; in this light, then, Shajariyān's use of long and eloquent pauses filled by the comments and the 'answers' of the *santūr* add a deep resonance to the passionate verses of Ḥāfiẓ's *ghazal*. After this unmetered episode, the suite starts again with a *chahār mezrāb* performed by the ensemble, but we will leave it here to its pursuance and to the closing enthusiastic applause of the Théâtre de la Ville's audience.

At the end of the 1990s, after a forty-year singing career (twenty of them in the period of the Islamic republic), Shajariyān released a two-volume CD of Qur'anic cantillation dedicated to the memory of his beloved father, who had just passed away, entitled *Bi-yād-i pidar* (In Memory of my Father).[16] Followers and fans knew vaguely that Shajariyān had received a religious education but the liner notes explain how he was trained as a *qārī* by his father, to whom he pays posthumous tribute. Here, Shajariyān, known for his skill in the Persian modal system (*dastgāh*), recites and modulates through the Arab modes (*maqām*) with just as great a degree of mastery and elegance. In *Bi-yād-i pidar*, there is the usual introductory *basmala* formula, always cantillated *recto tono* in the low register (with a long pause, a theme discussed above, between *aʿūdhu bi'llāhi min al-shayṭān al-rajīm* and the *basmala*). Shajariyān selects a single passage from a long sura[17] and cantillates it in a slow *mujawwad* style, with long pauses (even inside a single verse), modulations through the modes, ascensions in the high register – as, for example, in *Sūrat al-Anʿām* (Q. 6) from 5′34″ to 7′14″ arriving between 7′18″ and 9′03″ to what would be called a peak (*ʿawj*) in secular music – and descents to the lower register.

Yet, from this same CD, I would like to draw the attention of the reader/listener to the only original and new track entitled 'Dooaye Rabana' ('Duʿā-yi rabbanā'), which is the second track of *Bi-yād-i pidar*, volume II.[18] This is a free invocation (*duʿā*) that Shajariyān composed *ex novo* by assembling different verses from the Qur'an with the word *rabana* (Our Lord). The invocation begins in the high register and displays, throughout the tune, the burning intensity of Shajariyān's feelings. Here, the interpretation does not follow the prescriptions of *qirāʾa* but, rather, Shajariyān's inspiration. The result stands as a masterpiece. It seems highly significant that 'Duʿā-yi rabbanā' had enormous success, and that until recently, in Iran it was listened to at the close of the day of fasting (*ṣawm*) during the end of Ramadan until it was prohibited and censored. The reason for this is that, in 2010, Shajariyān openly and frankly criticised the Islamic republic. As stated by the *Guardian*:

> But at sunset on Wednesday, the first day of Ramadan in Iran, the thirsty and hungry faithful waiting for Iftar were disappointed not to hear *Rabana* from the state-owned Islamic Republic of Iran Broadcasting (IRIB). In fact, the IRIB stopped airing the prayer when Shajarian made clear he was siding with the Opposition Green Movement and gave an interview to BBC Persian criticising the Islamic republic for its crackdown on music and dissent.[19]

However, eight years after, in a country with millions of private accounts to social media and to the web, the IRIB ban has been bypassed and 'Dooaye Rabana' ('Du'ā-yi rabbanā'), with its heartfelt invocations from the Qur'an, continues to close Iranian days of Ramadan.

Conclusions

The term 'cantillation', in the terminology of ethnomusicology, seems appropriate for defining the vocal rendering of the Qur'an. Such a vocal rendering can be considered neither music (*musīqī*) nor singing (*ṣawt*, *ghinā'*) even if it can be performed 'melodiously' (*taghannī*). The Qur'an, then, cannot be adapted to musical modes nor 'stretched' to rhythms, as stated many centuries ago by the great al-Ghazālī (d. 505/1111), and therefore, it should be defined as a practice that is somewhere between singing and recitation, and which is deemed 'other' than music. Yet, even if not musical, the cantillation of the Qur'an, so pervasive throughout Iran, embedded itself as an ideal model in the consciousness of musicians, and thereby influenced their performances. Such an influence on vocalists and musicians is clearly detectable in the unmetered forms of music, both vocal (*āwāz*) and instrumental (*taqsīm*).

The Qur'an is not poetry at all, but the rhymed nature of its *saj'* creates a 'set of inner rhythmic rules of development' that influence vocal performance, as happens with poetic texts; this, in turn, affects the use of pauses, silences, spaces and modulations. Conversely, all these traits have influenced the performance of poetry in music.

Finally, adopting a more sociocultural approach, it is important to note how many great singers were often also specialists in the cantillation of the Qur'an. Comparisons between the executions of classical/secular repertoire and religious/Qur'anic cantillation derive from this human factor.

This is the case, for example, with the great Muḥammad Riḍā Shajariyān, who can be viewed as the present link in a very ancient chain of masters versed both in Qur'anic cantillation and in secular singing.

NOTES

1 By virtue of this verse, musicians facing a noisy audience sometimes begin their performance with the recitation of the Qur'an in order to quieten the audience. Oral communication by world-renowned *ney* (flute) soloist, Kudsi Erguner (b. 1952).

2 A.T. Welch, R. Paret and J.D. Pearson, 'al-Ḳur'ān', *EI*[2], vol. V, p. 400.

3 For a general survey, see Daniel Madigan, 'Revelation and Inspiration', *EQ*, vol. IV, pp. 437–48. See also Arthur Jeffery, 'The Qur'ān as Scripture', *Muslim World* 40, nos. 1–4 (1950), pp. 41–55, 106–34, 185–206 and 257–75; idem, *The Qur'ān as Scripture* (New York, 1952).

4 For a general survey, see John Burton, 'The Collection of the Qur'ān', *EQ*, vol. I, pp. 351–61.

5 F.M. Denny, 'Tad̲jwīd', *EI*[2], vol. 10, pp. 72–5.

6 The translations of the Qur'an are my own.

7 In anthropology, the terms etic and emic refer to two kinds of viewpoints: *Etic* is from outside, from the perspective of the observer, while *emic* is from within the social group, from the perspective of the subject.

8 *Taghannī* derives from the term *ghinā'* (song, singing), which nowadays has negative connotations among the *'ulamā'*. Yet the term *ghinā'* has a long and noble history that seems worthy of note: the term *musīqī* (music) arrived in Islamic culture between the third/ninth and fourth/tenth centuries as a calque from the Greek *mousiké*. In his *Kitāb al-Mūsīqī al-kabīr* (Great Book of Music), Abū Naṣr Muḥammad al-Fārābī (d. 339/950) affirms that before 'music' the original Arabic terms and concepts were rather *ṣawt* (vocal expressions) and *ghinā'* (song, singing), combining poetry and singing. Over time, the term *ghinā'* became a synonym for secular music and, moreover, in nineteenth-century Persia, came to designate a light urban genre of music associated with troupes of dancers. On the process by which *ghinā'* came to be associated with secular music and performances, see Muḥammad Taqī Dānishpazhūh, *Namuna'i az fihrist-i āthār-i dānishmandān-i īrānī wa islāmī dar ghinā' wa mūsīqī* (Tehran, 1355 Sh./1976). On the *'ulamā'*'s opposition to *ghinā'*, see Andrew Newman, 'Clerical Perceptions of Sufi Practices in Late Seventeenth-Century Persia: Arguments over the Permissibility of Singing (*Ghinā'*)', in Leonard Lewisohn and David Morgan, eds, *The Heritage of Sufism. Vol. III: Late Classical Persianate Sufism (1501–1750)* (Oxford, 1999), pp. 135–64.

9 Both in music and in poetry, the pause is connected with the taking of a breath.

This, of course, is a fundamental issue for the vocalist (Qur'anic or otherwise), the vocal ensemble or the wind instrument player, but is an extremely important feature also in the performance of any given ensemble which has to 'breathe together'. In prosody, we should remember the caesura, which is a break in the flow of sound in the middle of a line of verse, often caused by the ending of a word within a foot.

10 It is interesting to note here that in traditional Japanese music it is the *ma* (silence or pause) that gives meaning to sound. See Luciana Galliano and Chie Wada, eds, *Ma: La sensibilità estetica giapponese* (Torino, 2004).

11 It seems worthy of note, by the way, that the different combinations of brief and long seem to have given life to the many measured, rhythmic cycles (*iqāʾt*) that we find in Islamic music cultures.

12 Nooshin Laudan, 'Shajariān, Mohammed Rezā', in Stanley Sadie, ed., *The New Grove Dictionary of Music and Musicians* (London, 2001–2), vol. XXIII, p. 191; https://en.wikipedia.org/wiki/Mohammad-Reza_Shajarian.

13 See 'Shajarian Calls Upon Musicians to Create New Instruments', *Payvand*, http://www.payvand.com/news/11/may/1089.html.

14 Muḥammad Riḍā Shajariyān, *Iran. Mohammad Reza Shadjarian: Musique classique persane* (Paris, Ocora Radio France, 1990, CD: C 559097).

15 For more on the *āwāz-i Afshārī* and the use of *āwāz* in general in Shajariyān's work, see Rob Simms and Amir Koushkani, *The Art of Avaz and Mohammad Reza Shajarian: Foundations and Contexts* (Lanham, MD, Lexington Books, 2012). – Ed.

16 I would like to thank my friend Mehdi Jaghouri, musicophile and passionate Shajariyān fan, for kindly lending me a copy of the difficult-to-find two-volume CD.

17 Much like the singer's selection of a poetic text in a traditional art music suite.

18 The tune, with English translation of the text, can be found on YouTube, https://www.youtube.com/watch?v=YCRb92fbMOs.

19 See Saeed Kamali Dehghan, 'Iran Listens for Mohammad-Reza Shajarian, the Lost Voice of Ramadan', 10 July 2013, https://www.theguardian.com/world/2013/jul/10/ramadan-mohammed-rez-shajarian-iran.

Bibliography

This is a comprehensive bibliography of the sources used for the articles in this volume. Authors have often used different editions of the same primary source; these are listed in the same entry, separated by a semicolon. When different editions have the same title, this title has not been repeated in the entry. Variant titles are listed after the semicolon. Entries which can be considered both a primary and a secondary source appear under both categories.

Each bibliographic entry is followed by the initials of the author who has used it, in square brackets, as follows: Introduction: Alessandro Cancian [AC – Intr.]; Chapter 1: Seyfeddin Kara [SK]; Chapter 2: Sajjad Rizvi [SR]; Chapter 3: Liyakat Takim [LT]; Chapter 4: Neguin Yavari [NY]; Chapter 5: Banafsheh Madaninejad [BM]; Chapter 6: Yaser Mirdamadi [YM]; Chapter 7: Reza Tabandeh [RT]; Chapter 8: Rainer Brunner [RB]; Chapter 9: Nicholas Boylston [NB]; Chapter 10: Alessandro Cancian [AC]; Chapter 11: Leonard Lewisohn [LL]; Chapter 12: Alice Bombardier [AB]; Chapter 13: Anna Vanzan [AV]; Chapter 14: Nacim Pak-Shiraz [NPS]; Chapter 15: Niloofar Haeri [NH]; Chapter 16: Ingvild Flaskerud [IF]; Chapter 17: Giovanni De Zorzi [GZ].

Manuscripts

Hamadānī, Muḥammad Riḍā. *Irshād al-muḍillīn fī ithbāt khātam al-nabī'īn*. MS, Āstan Quds-i Raḍawī, Mashhad. [RT]

Hidāyat, Riḍā Qulī Khān. *Uṣūl al-fuṣūl*. MS 22920, Kitābkhāna-yi Majlis Shūrā-yi Islāmī, Tehran. [RT]

——. *Uṣūl al-fuṣūl*. MS 57B, registration number 56326, Bū ʿAlī Sīnā University Library, Hamadān. [RT]

Khū'ī, Muḥammad Taqī. *Ādāb al-musāfirīn*. MS 2409, Kitābkhāna-yi Dānishgāh-i Tihrān, Tehran. [RT]

Nūrī, ʿAlī. *Ḥujjat al-islām*. MS IR10-23243, Majlis Library, Tehran. [RT]

Film and Music

Bahrani, Shahriar, dir. *Mulk-i Sulayman* (*The Kingdom of Solomon*). Iran, Farabi Cinema Foundation, 2010. [NPS]

——, dir. *Maryam-i muqaddas* (*Saint Mary*). Iran, 2002. [NPS]

Fakhimzadeh, Mehdi, dir. *Tanhātarīn Sardār* (*The Loneliest Warrior*). Iran, 1997. [NPS]

Majidi, Majid, dir. *Muḥammad Rasūl Allāh* (*Muhammad: The Messenger of God*). Iran, Nourtaban Film Industry, 2015. [NPS]

Mirbaqeri, Davud, dir. *Imām 'Alī* (*Imam Ali*). Iran, 1997. [NPS]

Salahshoor, Farajollah, dir. *Yūsuf-i payāmbar* (*Joseph the Prophet*). Iran, 2002. [NPS]

Scott, Ridley, dir. *Alien*. USA, Twentieth-Century Fox, 1979. [NPS]

Shajariyān, Muḥammad Riḍā. *Bi-yād-i pidar*, 2 vols. [Iran,] 1358 Sh./1979–80 and 1361 Sh./1982–3. [GZ]

——. *Iran. Mohammad Reza Shadjarian: Musique classique persane*. Paris, Ocora Radio France, 1990, CD: C 559097. [GZ]

Vidor, King, dir. *Solomon and Sheba*. USA, Edward Small Productions, 1959. [NPS]

Young, Roger, dir. *Solomon*. UK/Czech Republic/France/Italy/Germany/USA, 1997. [NPS]

Primary Sources

Al-ʿAbd: ʿAbd-i khudā Muḥammad Taqī Bahjat. Tehran, Muʾassasa-yi Farhangī-yi Shams al-Shumūs, 1390 Sh./2011. [SR]

Abou El-Fadl, Khaled. *Speaking in God's Name: Islamic Law, Authority and Women*. Oxford, Oneworld, 2001. [BM]

Afṣaḥzād, Aʿlākhān, Muḥammad Jān ʿUmarūf and Abū Bakr Ẓuhūr al-Dīn, eds. *Bahāristān wa rasāʾil-i Jāmī*. Tehran, Nashr-i Mīrāth-i Maktūb, 1379 Sh./2000. [LL]

Agamben, Giorgio. *What is an Apparatus and Other Essays*, tr. David Kishik and Stefan Pedatella. Stanford, CA, Stanford University Press, 2009. [SR]

ʿAlī, ʿAbd al-Raḥīm Muḥammad. *Shaykh al-bāḥithīn Āqā Buzurg al-Ṭihrānī: Ḥayātuhu wa āthāruhu (1875–1970)*. Najaf, Maṭbaʿat al-Nuʿmān, 1970. [RB]

ʿAmilī, ʿAlī b. Abī Jāmīʿ. *al-Wajīz fī tafsīr al-Qurʾān al-ʿazīz*. Qum, Dār al-Qurʾān al-Karīm, 1413/1993. [AC]

al-ʿĀmilī, Bahāʾ al-Dīn. *Miftāḥ al-falāḥ*, ed. Ḥasanzāda Āmulī. Tehran, Intishārāt-i Ḥikmat, 1366 Sh./1987. [SR]

ʿĀmilī, Ibrāhīm. *Bahjat al-ʿārifīn*. Beirut, Dār al-Maḥajja al-Bayḍāʾ, 2007. [SR]

——. *Tafsīr-i ʿĀmilī*. Tehran, Ṣadūq, 1360 Sh./1981–2. [AC]

al-ʿĀmilī, Jaʿfar Murtaḍā. *Ḥaqāʾiq hāmma ḥawl al-Qurʾān al-karīm*, 2nd edn. Beirut, Dār al-Ṣafwa, 1413/1992. [RB]

al-ʿĀmilī, Muḥammad b. al-Ḥasan al-Ḥurr. *Tafṣīl wasāʾil al-shīʿa*. *See* al-Nūrī al-Ṭabrisī, Mīrzā Ḥusayn b. Taqī, *Mustadrak al-wasāʾil*. [RB]

al-Amīn, Muḥsin. *Naqḍ al-washīʿa aw al-shīʿa bayn al-ḥaqāʾiq waʾl-awhām*. Beirut, Maṭbaʿat al-Inṣāf, 2001 (1st edn 1951). [RB]

Āmulī, Ḥaydar. *Jāmiʿ al-asrār wa manbaʿ al-anwār*, ed. Henry Corbin and Osman Yahya. Tehran, Intishārāt-i ʿIlmī wa Farhangī, 1384 Sh./2005. [RT]

ʿAqīqī Bakhshāyishī, ʿAdhrā [Azra Aghighi Bakshayeshi]. *Zanān-i khushniwīs*. Tehran, Kalhur, 1388 Sh./2009. [AV]

Asad, Muḥammad Samīʿullāh. *Qurʾān-i manẓūm maʿ farhang wa tafsīr*. Calcutta, 2004. [NB]

Asad, Talal, Wendy Brown, Judith P. Butler and Saba Mahmood. *Is Critique Secular? Blasphemy, Injury, and Free Speech*. New York, Fordham University Press, 2013. [BM]

ʿAṣad al-Dawla, Mīrzā Aḥmad Khān. *Tārīkh-i ʿAṣadī*. Tehran, Nashr-i ʿElm, 1376 Sh./1997. [AV]

Āṣif, Muḥammad Hāshim ('Rustam al-Ḥukamā"). *Rustam al-tawārikh*. Tehran, Chāpkhāna-yi Sipihr, 1352 Sh./1973. [RT]

ʿAṭash: Nā-gufta-hā-yi az sayr-i tawḥīdī-yi kāmil-i ʿaẓīm ḥaḍrat-i Āyatullāh Sayyid ʿAlī Qāḍī Ṭabāṭabāʾī. Tehran, Muʾassasa-yi Farhangī-yi Shams al-Shumūs, 1383 Sh./2004. [SR]

al-ʿAyyāshī, Abū Nāḍr al-Samarqandī. *Tafsīr*, ed. Muḥammad al-Kāẓim, 2 vols. Beirut, Manshūrāt al-Aʿlamī, 1991. [SR]

Bahārī Hamadānī, Shaykh Muḥammad. *Tadhkira al-muttaqīn*. Tehran, 1361 Sh./1982; collected in *Tadhkirat al-muttaqīn fī ādāb al-sayr waʾl-sulūk*, tr. Ḥusayn Kūrānī. Qum, Intishārāt-i Madīn, 2006. [AC – Intr.] [SR]

'Baḥr al-ʿUlūm', Sayyid Mahdī Ṭabāṭabāʾī (attrib.). *Risāla-yi sayr wa sulūk*, With commentary by Muḥammad Ḥusayn Ṭabāṭabāʾī, ed. Sayyid Muḥammad Ḥusayn Ḥusaynī-yi Ṭihrānī. Mashhad, Intishārāt-i ʿAllāma Ṭabāṭabāʾī, 1416/1995. Translated by Tawus Raja as *Treatise on Spiritual Journeying and Wayfaring*. Chicago, IL, Kazi Publications, 2013. [AC – Intr.] [SR]

al-Baḥrānī, Hāshim b. Sulaymān. *al-Burhān fī tafsīr al-Qurʾān*. Beirut, Muʾassasat al-Aʿlamī liʾl-Maṭbūʿāt, 1999. [AC]

al-Balāghī al-Najafī, Muḥammad Jawād. *Ālāʾ al-raḥmān fī tafsīr al-Qurʾān*, 2 vols. Ṣaydā, Maṭbaʿat al-ʿIrfān, 1933. [RB]

Bāqir al-Ṣadr, Muḥammad. *Durūs fī ʿilm al-uṣūl*, 3 vols. Beirut, Dār al-Kitāb al-Lubnānī, 1978. [LT]

Baqlī, Ruzbihān. *Sharḥ-i shaṭḥiyyāt*. Tehran, Intishārāt-i Ṭahūrī, 2003. [RT]

Bayānī, Mahdī. *Aḥwāl wa Āthār-i khushniwīsān*, 4 vols. Tehran, 1363 Sh./1984. [AV]

Baydāwī, ʿAbd Allāh and Maḥmūd Iṣfahānī. *Nature, Man and God in Medieval Islam: ʿAbd Allah Baydawi's Text, Tawaliʿ al-Anwar min Mataliʿ al-Anzar, along with Mahmud Isfahani's Commentary, Mataliʿ al-Anzar, Sharh Tawaliʿ al-Anwar*, tr. Edwin Elliott Calverley and James W. Pollock, 2 vols. Leiden, Brill, 2002. [YM]

Bible, with etchings by Marc Chagall. Paris, Tériade, 1956. [AB]

La Bible de Jérusalem, illus. Salvador Dalí. Paris, Denoël, 1972. [AB]

Bilgrāmī, Ghulām-ʿAlī Āzād. *Subḥat al-marjān fī āthār Hindustān*, 2 vols. Aligarh, Maʿhad al-Dirāsāt al-Islāmiyya Jāmiʿat ʿAligarh al-Islāmiyya, 1976. [AC]

Bujnūrdī, Muḥammad Mūsawī. *Majmūʿa-yi maqālāt-i fiqhī, ḥuqūqī wa ijtimāʿī*, 8 vols. Tehran, Intishārāt-i Pajūhishkada-yi Imām Khumaynī wa Inqilāb-i Islāmī, 2002. [LT]

Le Coran, 2 vols, tr. Jean Grosjean, intro. Jacques Berque, illus. Charles-Hossein Zenderoudi, printed by Firmin-Didot and Saint Augustin Press in Bruges, dir. Philippe Lebaud, Jacques Cornulier, Jean-François Fouquereau, Adrien Frutiger and Bruno Pfaffi. Paris, Le Club du Livre, 1972 (Published with a facsimile of Ibn al-Bawwāb's manuscript and a commentary by D.S. Rice); Paris, Philippe Lebaud, 1979; tr. Jean

Grosjean. Paris, Philippe Lebaud, 1988; tr. Jean Grosjean. Paris, Félin, 1994; Paris, Le Seuil, 2001. [AB]

Darwīsh Shīrāzī, Muḥammad Hāshim. *Manāhil al-taḥqīq*, ed. Muḥammad Yūsuf Nayyirī. Shiraz, Daryā-yi Nūr, 2003. [AC]

Derricotte, Toi. *The Black Notebooks: An Interior Journey*. New York, Norton, 1997. [BM]

Dickinson, Emily. *The Complete Poems of Emily Dickinson*, ed. Thomas Johnson. Toronto, Little, Brown, 1961. [LL]

al-Dijwī, Yūsuf b. Aḥmad. *al-Jawāb al-munīf fī'l-radd 'alā mudda'ī'l-taḥrīf fī'l-kitāb al-sharīf*. Cairo, Maṭba'at al-Nahḍa al-Adabiyya, 1913. [RB]

Dilshuda. Tehran, Mu'assasa-yi Farhangī-yi Shams al-Shumūs, 1386 Sh./2007. [SR]

Dīwānbaygī Shīrāzī, Aḥmad. *Ḥadīqat al-shu'arā*, ed. 'Abd al-Ḥusayn Nawā'ī, 3 vols. Tehran, Zarrīn, 1364 Sh./1985. [RT]

Faḍlallāh, Muḥammad Ḥusayn. *Min waḥy al-Qur'ān*, 24 vols. Beirut, Dār al-Malāk, 1998. [RB]

Fanā'ī, Abū'l-Qāsim [Abolghasem Fanaei]. *Akhlāq-i dīnshināsī*, 2nd edn. Tehran, Nashr-i Nigāh-i Mu'āṣir, 1392 Sh./2013–14. [BM]

——. *Dīn dar tarāzū-yi akhlāq*, 2nd edn. Tehran, Mu'assasa-yi Farhangī-yi Sirāṭ, 2013–14. [BM]

Fī madrasat al-Shaykh al-Bahjat, 2 vols. Beirut, Dār al-Anām, 2005. [SR]

Gawhar, Ghaws Muhammad. *Manẓūm Sindhī Tafsīr*. Kotli Kabir, 2005. [NB].

al-Ḥaddād, Sayyid 'Alī. *al-'Ārif fī riḥāb al-qudsiyya*. Beirut, Manshūrāt al-Riḍā, 2007. [SR]

Hafez: Dance of Life, illus. Charles-Hossein Zenderoudi, tr. Michael Boylan. Washington DC, Mage Publishers, 1988. [AB]

Ḥāfiẓ. *Dīwān-i Ḥāfiẓ: Muqaddama, taṣḥīḥ wa sharḥ*, ed. Mahdī Ilāhī Qumsha'ī. Tehran, Intishārāt-i Payk-i 'Ulūm, 1382 Sh./2003. [LL]

——. *Dīwān-i Khwāja Shams al-Dīn Muḥammad Ḥāfiẓ*, ed. Parvīz Nātil Khānlarī. Tehran, Khawārazmī, 1359 Sh./1980. [LL]

al-Ḥakīm, Muḥammad Taqī. *al-Uṣūl al-'āmma li'l-fiqh al-muqāran*, 2nd edn. Beirut, Dār al-Andalus, 1979 (1st edn 1963). [RB]

Hamadānī, 'Abd al-Ṣamad. *Baḥr al-ma'ārif*, ed. Ḥasan Ustād-Walī, 3 vols. Tehran, Intishārāt-i Ḥikmat, 1416/1995. [SR]

Hamadānī, Muḥammad Riḍā. *Miftāḥ al-nubuwwa*. Tehran, 1961. [RT]

al-Ḥasanī, Hāshim Ma'rūf. *Dirāsāt fī'l-kāfī li'l-Kulaynī wa'l-ṣaḥīḥ li'l-Bukhārī*. Ṣūr, Maṭba'at Ṣūr al-Ḥadītha, 1388/1968. [RB]

Hāshimī Rafsanjānī, 'Alī Akbar. *Mardumsālārī az dīdgāh-i Hāshimī*, ed. Mihrdād Siyāwushī-Far. Tehran, I'tidāl Gustarān-i Fardā, 2015. [NY]

al-Hibri, Azizah. 'Muslim Women's Rights in the Global Village: Challenges and Opportunities', *Journal of Law and Religion* 15, nos. 1–2 (2000–2001), pp. 37–66. [BM]

Hidāyat, Riḍā Qulī Khān. *Tadhkira-yi Rīyāḍ al-'ārifīn*. Tehran, Institute for Humanities and Cultural Studies, 1385 Sh./2007. [RT]

Hidayatullah, Aysha. *Feminist Edges of the Qur'an*. New York, Oxford University Press, 2013. [BM]

Hujwīrī, Abū'l-Ḥasan 'Alī b. 'Uthmān. *Kashf al-maḥjūb*, ed. Maḥmūd 'Ābidī. Tehran, Soroush, 1384 Sh./2005. [RT]

Ḥusayn ʿAlī Shāh Iṣfahānī, Muḥammad Ḥusayn. *Radd-i pādrī*. Tehran, Ḥaqīqat, 1387 Sh./2008. [AC – Intr.] [RT]

Ḥusaynī Nasab, Riḍā. *Dar Tarīqi waḥdat-i islāmī: Pāsukh ba 35 pursish ka pīrāmūn-i īn hadaf maṭraḥ mīkardand*. Qum, Dabīr-khāna-yi Dāʾimī-yi Kungra-yi Jahānī-yi Qadāsat was Amniyyat-i Ḥaram, 1366 Sh./1988. [RB]

Ḥusaynī Ṭihrānī, Sayyid Muḥammad Ḥusayn. *Mihr-i tābān: Yādnāma wa muṣāḥibāt-i tilmīdh wa ʿallāma*. Mashhad, Intishārāt-i ʿAllāma Ṭabāṭabāʾī, 1418/1997. [SR]

——. *Mihr-i tābnāk*. Mashhad, Intishārāt-i ʿAllāma-yi Ṭabāṭabāʾī, 1375 Sh./ 1996 [SR]

——. *Nafahāt-i uns: Insān-i kāmil dar farhang-i shīʿa*. Tehran, Intishārāt-i ʿAllāma-yi Ṭabāṭabāʾī, 1395 Sh./2016. [SR]

——. *Nūr-i mujarrad*, 2 vols. Mashhad, Intishārāt-i ʿAllāma-yi Ṭabāṭabāʾī, 2015. [SR]

——. *Risāla-yi Lubb al-lubāb dar sayr wa sulūk-i uliʾl-albāb*. Mashhad, Intishārāt-i ʿAllāma-yi Ṭabāṭabāʾī, 1375 Sh./1996. Translated by Mohammad H. Faghfoory as *Kernel of the Kernel: Concerning the Wayfaring and Spiritual Journey of the People of Intellect*. Albany, State University of New York Press, 2003. [SR]

——. *Rūḥ-i mujarrad*. Mashhad, Intishārāt-i ʿAllāma Ṭabāṭabāʾī, 1416/1995. [SR]

——, ed. *Tawḥīd-i ʿilmī wa ʿaynī dar makātib-i ḥikmī wa ʿirfānī-yi Ḥājj Sayyid Aḥmad Karbalāʾī wa Ḥājj Shaykh Muḥammad Ḥusayn Iṣfahānī Kumpānī bā ḍamīma-yi tadhyīlāt wa muḥākamāt-i Ḥājj Sayyid Muḥammad Ḥusayn Ṭabāṭabāʾī*. Tehran, Intishārāt-i Ḥikmat, 1410/1989. [SR]

al-Ḥuwayzī, ʿAbd ʿAlī b. Jumʿa. *Tafsīr Nūr al-thaqalayn*. Beirut, Dār al-Maḥajjat al-Bayḍāʾ, 2015. [AC]

Ibn Sīnā, Abū ʿAlī. *al-Najāt fīʾl-manṭiq waʾl-ilāhiyyāt*, ed. ʿAbd al-Raḥmān ʿUmayara, 2 vols. Beirut, Dār al-Jayl, 1992. [YM]

Ibrāhīm, ʿIzz al-Dīn. *Mawqif ʿulamāʾ al-muslimīn min al-shīʿa waʾl-thawra al-islāmiyya*. Tehran, 1406/1986. [RB]

Ilāhī, Nūr ʿAlī. *Asār al-ḥaqq*, illus. Charles-Hossein Zenderoudi. Tehran, 1980. [AB]

——. *Maʿrifat al-rūḥ*, illus. Charles-Hossein Zenderoudi. Tehran, 1980. [AB]

Ilāhī Qumshaʾī [Ghomshei], Ḥusayn Muḥyī al-Dīn. *Barrasī-yi tarjuma shuda mutun-i islāmī*. Tehran, Sāzmān-i Muṭālaʿa wa Tadwīn Kutub-i ʿUlūm-i Insānī-yi Dānishgāh-hā, 1390 Sh./2011–12. [LL]

——. *Dar qalamraw-i zarrīn: 365 rūz bā adabiyāt-i inglīsī*. Tehran, Sukhan 1386 Sh./2007. [LL]

——. *Dar suḥbat-i Qurʾān: 365 rūz bā Qurʾān*. Tehran, Sukhan, 1390 Sh./2011. [LL]

——. *Guzīda-yi Fīhi mā fīhi, Maqālāt-i Mawlānā: Talkhīṣ, muqaddama wa sharḥ*. Tehran, Intishārāt-i ʿIlmī wa Farhangī, 1366 Sh./1987. [LL]

——. *Guzīda-yi Manṭiq al-ṭayr (Haft shahr-i ʿishq): Talkhīṣ, muqaddama wa sharḥ*, 2nd edn. Tehran, Intishārāt-i ʿIlmī wa Farhangī, 1377 Sh./1998. [LL]

——. *Maqālāt*, 1st edn. Tehran, Rawzana, 1376 Sh./1997. [LL]

——. *365 rūz bā Saʿdī*. Tehran, Sukhan, 1381 Sh./2002. [LL]

——. *365 rūz dar suḥbat-i Mawlānā*. Tehran, Sukhan, 1386 Sh./2007. [LL]

——. *365 rūz dar ṣuḥbat-i shāʿirān-i pārsīgū*. Tehran, Sukhan, 1392 Sh./2013. [LL]

—— and Aḥmad Bihishtī Shīrāzī, eds. *Kīmiyā: Daftarī dar adabiyāt wa hunar wa ʿirfān*, 5 vols. Tehran, Rawzana, 1377–82 Sh./1998–2003. [LL]

Ilāhī Qumshaʾī, Mahdī. *Dīwān-i Ḥakīm Mahdī Ilāhī Qumshaʾī*, edited with an introduction by Ḥusayn Ilāhī Qumshaʾī. Tehran, Rawzana, 1377 Sh./ 1998. [LL]

——. *Ḥikmat-i ilāhī-yi khāṣṣ wa ʿāmm*, ed. Hurmuz Būshahrpūr. Tehran, Rawzana, 1379 Sh./2000–2001. [LL]

——. *Tarjuma-yi Qurʾān-i karīm*. Qum, Fāṭima al-Zahrāʾ, 1390 Sh./2011. [LL]

Ilāhiyya: Sharḥ-i aḥwāl-i ʿārif-i ilāhī Āyatullāh Sayyid Muḥammad Ḥasan Ilāhī Ṭabāṭabāʾī. Tehran, Muʾassasa-yi Farhangī-yi Shams al-Shumūs, 1386 Sh./2007. [SR]

Iʿtimād al-Salṭana. *al-Maʾāthir waʾl-āthār*, ed. Īraj Afshār. Tehran, Intishārāt-i Asāṭīr, 1363 Sh./1984. [SR]

Īzadgushasb Gulpāygānī, Asadullāh. *Nūr al-abṣār: Dar sharḥ-i ḥāl-i yagāna-ʿārif-i kāmil wa shāʿir-i fāḍil maʿrūf wa mashhūr-i mutaʾakhkhirīn mawlānā Muḥammad ʿAlī ʿNūr ʿAlī Shāhʾ al-awwal-i Iṣfahānī*. Tehran, 1322 Sh./1943–4. [AC] [RT]

Jaʿfariyān, Rasūl. ʻA Study of Sunnī and Shīʿī Traditions Concerning Taḥrīfʼ, *al-Tawḥīd* 6, no. 4 (Rajab–Ramaḍān 1409/1988), pp. 34–42. [RB]

——. *Ukdhūbat taḥrīf al-Qurʾān bayn al-shīʿa waʾl-sunna*. N.p., Mumaththiliyyat al-Imām al-Qāʾid al-Sayyid Khaminaʾī fīʾl-Ḥajj, 1413/1992–3 (1st edn 1985). [RB]

Jawādī Āmulī, ʿAbd Allāh. *Qurʾān dar Qurʾān*, 10th edn, 2 vols. Qum, Markaz-i Nashr-i Isrāʾ, 2011. [SK]

——. *Tafsīr-i tasnīm*, 34 vols. Qum, Markaz-i Nashr-i Isrāʾ, 1380 Sh./2001–2. [AC] [AC - Intr.]; *Tasnīm*, 8th edn, 24 vols. Qum, Markaz-i Nashr-i Isrāʾ, 2009. [SK]

Jeffery, Arthur. *Materials for the History of the Text of the Qurʾān: The Old Codices*. Leiden, Brill, 1937. [RB]

Kabūdarāhangī, Muḥammad Jaʿfar. *Rasāʾil-i Majdhūbīyya*. Tehran, Ḥaqīqat, 1377 Sh./1998. [RT]

Kadivar, Mohsen. ʻAz Islām-i tārikhī ba Islām-i maʿnawīʼ, in *Ḥaqq al-nās: Islām wa huqūq-i bashar*. Tehran, Intishārāt-i Kawīr, 2008, pp. 15–34. [BM]

Kāshānī, Fatḥ Allāh. *Minhāj al-ṣādiqīn fī ilzām al-mukhālifīn*. Tehran, Kitābfurushī-yi Islāmiyya, 1346 Sh./1967–8. [AC]

al-Kāshānī, Muḥsin Fayḍ. *Kalimāt-i maknūna*, ed. ʿAlī-Riḍā Aṣgharī. Tehran, Madrasa-yi Muṭahharī, 1387 Sh./2008. [SR]

——. *Minhāj al-najāt*, ed. Ghālib Ḥasan Shābandar. Beirut, Maṭbaʿa Mahdiyya, 1987. [SR]

——. *al-Ṣāfī fī tafsīr kalam Allāh al-wāfī*, 5 vols. Beirut, Muʾassasat al-Aʿlamī liʾl-Maṭbūʿāt, 1399/1979. [AC]

al-Khaṭīb, Muḥibb al-Dīn. *al-Khuṭūṭ al-ʿarīḍa liʾl-usus allatī qāma ʿalayhā dīn al-shīʿa al-imāmiyya al-ithnā ʿashariyya*, 10th edn. Cairo, Maṭbaʿat al-Salafiyya, 1982 (1st edn, Jeddah, 1961). [RB] al-Khoei, Yūsuf [also al-Kho'i, Yousif]. 'Abū'l-Qāsim al-Ḫū'ī', *Oriente Moderno* New Series, 18 (79), no. 2 (1999), pp. 491–500. [RB]

al-Kho'i, Yousif [also al-Khoei, Yūsuf]. 'Grand Ayatollah Abu al-Qassim al-Kho'i: Political Thought and Positions', in Faleh Abdul-Jabar, ed., *Ayatollahs, Sufis and Ideologues: State, Religion and Social Movements in Iraq*. London, Saqi Books, 2002, pp. 223–30. [RB]

Khomeini, Ruhollah. *Islam and Revolution: Writings and Declarations of Imam Khomeini (1941–1980)*, tr. and annot. Hamid Algar. Berkeley, CA, Mizan Press, 1981. [NY].

——. *Kashf al-asrār*. Qum, Intishārāt-i Āzādī, *c.* 1980. [RB]

——. *The Mystery of Prayer: The Ascension of the Wayfarers and the Prayer of the Gnostics*, tr. Sayyid Amjad Naqawi. Leiden, Brill, 2015. [SR]

——. *Taḥrīr al-wasīla*. Beirut, Dar al-Kutub al-Islamiyya, 1981, vol. I, pp. 472–6, via Cook, *Commanding Right and Forbidding Wrong in Islamic Thought*, p. 534. [NY]

——. *Wilāyat-i faqīh*. Translated by Hamid Algar as *Governance of the Jurist (Velayat-e faqeeh): Islamic Government*. Tehran, The Institute for Compilation and Publication of Imam Khomeini's Works, 2006. [NPS]

Khosrokhavar, Farhad. 'The New Intellectuals in Iran', *Social Compass* 51, no. 2 (2004), pp. 191–202. [BM]

al-Khū'ī, Abū'l-Qāsim. *al-Bayān fī tafsīr al-Qur'ān*. Najaf, al-Maṭbaʿa al-ʿIlmiyya fī'l-Najaf, 1375/1955–6. Translated and introduced by Abdulaziz A. Sachedina as *The Prolegomena to the Qur'an*. Oxford, Oxford University Press, 1998. [RB]

Khumaynī [Khomeini], Muṣṭafā. *Tafsīr al-Qur'ān al-karīm*, 4 vols. Tehran, Intishārāt-i ʿUrūj, 1391 Sh./2012–13. [AC]

Khurramshāhī, Bahā' al-Dīn. *Qur'ān-pazhūhī: Haftād baḥth wa taḥqīq-i qur'ānī*. Tehran, Markaz-i Nashr-i Farhangī-yi Mashriq, 1372 Sh./1994. [RB]

al-Kulaynī, Abū Jaʿfar Muḥammad b. Yaʿqūb. *Uṣūl min al-Kāfī*. Tehran, Mu'assisa-yi Taḥqiqātī wa Intishārātī Nūr, 1358 Sh./1979. [RT]; *Uṣūl al-Kāfī*, 2 vols, ed. Muḥammad Jawād al-Faqīh and Yūsuf al-Biqāʿī. Beirut, Dār al-Aḍwā', 1413/1992. [RB]; *al-Kāfī,* 8 vols. Qum, Dār al-Ḥadīth, 2005. [SR]

Lāhīji, Muḥammad. *Mafātīḥ al-ʿijāz fī sharḥ-i Gulshan-i rāz*, ed. Muḥammad Riḍā Barzgār Khāliqī and ʿIffat Karbāsī. Tehran, Zawwār, 1371 Sh./1992. [LL]

Mahā'imī, ʿAlī b. Aḥmad. *Tafsīr al-Mahā'imī al-musammā Tabṣīr al-Raḥmān wa taysīr al-Mannān bi-baʿḍi mā yushīru ilā iʿjāz al-Qur'ān*, ed. Aḥmad Farīd al-Miziyādī, 3 vols. Beirut, Kitāb Nashirūn, 2011. [AC]

Mahrīzī, Mahdī. *Mas'alat al-mar'a: Dirāsāt fī tajdīd al-fikr al-dīnī*. Beirut, Binaya al-Sabah, 2008. [LT]

Majd, Umīd. *Qur'ān-i Majīd yā Tarjuma-yi Manẓūm* (*Qur'ān-nāma*). Tehran, Intishārāt-i Umīd Majd, 1376 Sh./[1997]. [NB]

Majdhūb ʿAlī Shāh Kabūdarāhangī, Muḥammad Jaʿfar. *Mir'at al-ḥaqq*. Tehran, Ḥaqīqat, 1383 Sh./2004–5. [AC]

Majlisī, Muḥammad Bāqir. *Biḥār al-anwār*, 110 vols. Beirut, Mu'assasat al-Wafā', 1983. [SR]

Makārim Shīrāzī, Nāṣir. *Tafsīr-i namūna*, 27 vols. Tehran, Dār al-Kitāb al-Islāmī, 1362–74 Sh./1983–95. [AC] [AC - Intr.]

Malakī Tabrīzī, Mīrzā Jawād. *Risāla-yi liqā' Allāh*, ed. Sayyid Aḥmad Fihrī. Tehran, Nahḍat-i Zanān-i Musalmān, 1360 Sh./1981. [SR]

Malekian, Mostafa. *Rāhī ba Rahā'ī: Jastārhā-yī dar ʿaqlānīyyat wa maʿnawīyyat*, 2nd edn. Tehran, Nashr-i Nigāh-i Muʿāṣir, 2002–3. [BM]

Maʿrifat, Muḥammad Hādī. *Ṣiyānat al-Qur'ān min al-taḥrīf*. Qum, Dār al-Qur'ān al-Karīm, 1410/1990. [RB]

Martyn, Henry. *Mīzān al-ḥaqq*. N.p., 1833. [AC - Intr.] [RT]

Maʿṣūm ʿAlī Shāh. *See* Shīrāzī, Muḥammad Maʿṣūm.

Mawlana. *Shams-i Tabrīzī*, *See* Rūmī.

Maybudī, Rashīd al-Dīn. *Kashf al-asrār wa ʿuddat al-abrār*, 10 vols, ed. ʿAlī Aṣghar Ḥikmat. Tehran, Intishārāt-i Dānishgāhī, 1952–60. [LL]

Mihrābādī, Rafīʿī. *Khaṭṭ wa khaṭṭāṭān*. Tehran, Amīr Kabīr, 1345 Sh./1966. [AV]

Mīlānī, ʿAlī al-Ḥusaynī. *al-Taḥqīq fī nafy al-taḥrīf ʿan al-Qur'ān al-sharīf*. Qum, Dār al-Qur'ān al-Karīm, 1410/1990. [RB]

Miʿrāj-nāma, translated by Richard Pevear as *The Miraculous Journey of Mahomet*, with introduction and commentaries by Marie Rose Séguy, reproduced from the illuminated manuscript *Supplément Turc 190* belonging to the Bibliothèque Nationale, Paris. New York, George Braziller, 1977. [NPS]

Mīrzā Ghulām Ḥasan Beg, ʿĀrif and ʿAbd al-Raḥmān Wār. *ʿIrfān-i Qur'ān: Tarjumah, Tafsīr o Manẓūm-i Jaqhar Rukūʿ ba-Zabān-i Kashmīrī*. Srīnagar, Iqrā', 2004. [NB].

Miṣbāḥ Yazdī, Muḥammad Taqī. *Jān-hā fadā-yi dīn*, ed. Muḥammad Mahdī Nādirī Qumī. Qum, Instītū-yi Āmūzishī wa Pazhūhishī-i Imām Khumaynī, 2004. [NY]

Miyān, Muḥammad Ismāʿīl. *Tafsīr-i Qur'ān Jān-i islām nūr-i īmān manẓūm ba-zubān-e panjābī*. Gujarat, 1955. [NB].

Modarressi, Hossein. 'Early Debates on the Integrity of the Qur'ān: A Brief Survey', *Studia Islamica* 77 (1993), pp. 5–39. [RB]

Moosa, Ebrahim. 'Arabic and Islamic Hermeneutics', in Jeff Malpas and Hans-Helmuth Gander, eds, *The Routledge Companion to Hermeneutics*. London, Routledge, 2015, pp. 707–21. [BM]

Mughniyya, Muḥammad Jawād. *al-Tafsīr al-kāshif*, 7 vols. Beirut, Dār al-Anwār, 1978. [RB]; 2 vols. Beirut, Dār al-Kitāb al-Islāmī, 2005. [AC]

Āl Muḥsin, ʿAlī. *Kashf al-ḥaqā'iq: Radd ʿalā 'Hādhihi naṣīḥatī ilā kull shīʿī'*. Beirut, Dār al-Ṣafwa, 1416/1995. [RB]

Mullā Ṣadrā. *al-Ḥikmat al-mutaʿāliyya fī'l-asfār al-ʿaqliyya al-arbaʿa*, annotated by Muḥammad Ḥusayn Ṭabāṭabā'ī, 9 vols. Beirut, Dār Iḥyā' al-Turāth al-ʿArabī, 1990. [YM]

Munajjimī, ʿAlī Riḍā. *See* Ṣafī ʿAlī Shāh, Mirzā Ḥasan Iṣfahānī. *Tafsīr-i Ṣafī*. [NB]

Mūsawī Masqaṭī, Sayyid Taqī. *Qudwat al-ʿārifīn*. Beirut, Dār al-Maḥajja al-Bayḍā', 2007. [SR]

Mushfiq, Manṣūr, ed. *Dīwān-i Ṣafī ʿAlī Shāh*. Tehran, 1379 Sh./[2000]. [NB]

Muṣṭafawī, Ḥasan. *Tafsīr-i rawshan*, 16 vols. Tehran, Markaz-i Nashr-i Kitāb, 1380 Sh./2001–2. [AC] al-Muẓaffar, Muḥammad Riḍā. *Uṣūl al-fiqh*, 2 vols. Beirut, Muassasat al-Aʿlamī, 1990. [SK]

Narāqī, Aḥmad b. Muḥammad Mahdī. *Sayf al-umma wa burhān al-milla*. Qum, Center for Revival of Islamic Heritage; Academy of Islamic Sciences and Culture, 2006. [RT]

Naẓīr, Ḥakīm Naẓīr Aḥmad. *Ṣūrah-i Kahf da Panjābī vich Tarjamah te Ohdi Manẓūm Tafsīr Aṣḥāb-i Kahf*. Sharqpur, 1992. [NB]

Nūr ʿAlī Shāh, Mullā Muḥammad ʿAlī. *Dīwān*, ed. Jawād Nūrbakhsh. Tehran, Intishārāt Yaldā Qalam, 1381 Sh./2002. [RT]

——. *Jannāt al-wiṣāl*, ed. Jawād Nūrbakhsh, 2 vols. Tehran, Khāniqāh-i Niʿmatullāhī, 1348 Sh./1969–70. [AC]

Nūrbakhsh, Jawād. *Tafsīr-i Manẓūm-i Ṣūra-hā-yi al-Ḥujurāt wa Qāf wa al-Ḥashr. Ba Inḍimām-i Sharḥ-i Manẓūm-i Khuṭba-hā-yi Mūʾminīn wa Muttaqīn-i Ḥaḍrat-i ʿAlī ʿalayhi al-salām*. Tehran, Ṣāḥib Athar, 1994. [NB]

al-Nūrī al-Ṭabrisī, Mīrzā Ḥusayn b. Taqī. *Faṣl al-khiṭāb fī taḥrīf Kitāb Rabb al-arbāb*, lithograph. Tehran, 1298/1881; Cairo, Dār Nūn, 2010 [partial edn]; Iḥsān Ilāhī Ẓahīr, ed., *al-Shīʿa waʾl-Qurʾān*, 3rd edn. Lahore, Idārat Tarjumān al-Sunna, 1983, pp. 136–344 [partial edn]. [RB] [AC - Intr.]

——. *Mustadrak al-wasāʾil* [A continuation of ʿĀmilī's *Tafṣīl wasāʾil al-shīʿa*], lithograph. Tehran, 1311–21/1893–1903. [RB]

Plato. *Republic*, tr. Robin Waterfield. Oxford, Oxford University Press, 2008. [LL]

——. *Symposium*, ed. M.C. Howatson and Frisbee C.C. Sheffield, tr. M.C. Howatson. Cambridge, Cambridge University Press, 2008. [LL]

Plotinus. *The Enneads*, tr. Stephen Mackenna. London, Penguin, 1991. [SR]

Qāḍī, Sayyid ʿAlī. *Sharḥ-i duʿāʾ-yi simāt*. Tehran, Muʾassasa-yi Farhangī-yi Shams al-Shumūs, 1387 Sh./2008. [SR]

al-Qafārī, Nāṣir b. ʿAbd Allāh b. ʿAlī. *Uṣūl madhhab al-shīʿa al-imāmiyya al-ithnā ʿashariyya: ʿArḍ wa naqd*, 3 vols. Riyadh, Jāmiʿat al-Imām Muḥammad Ibn Saʿūd al-Islāmiyya, 1414/1993. [RB]

Qānūn-i asāsī-i Jumhūrī-i Islāmī-i Īrān. Tehran, Azhang, 1990. [NY]

Qaragūzluw, Muḥammad b. ʿAbd Allāh. *Abḥāthʾi ʿashara*. Tehran, Intishārāt-i Ḥaqīqat, 1385 Sh./2007. [RT]

Qazwīnī, Muḥammad Ḥasan. *Kashf al-ghitāʾ ʿan wujūh marāsim al-ihtidāʾ fī ʿilm al-akhlāq*, ed. Muḥsin Aḥmadī. Qum, Muʾtamar al-Mawlā Mahdī al-Narāqī, 1380 Sh./2001. [SR]

Qummī, Abbās b. Muḥammad Riḍā. *Mafātīḥ al-Jinān*. Tehran, 1381 Sh./2001. [IF]

al-Qummī, Abū Jaʿfar al-Ṣaffār. *Baṣāʾir al-darajāt*, edited under the supervision of Sayyid Muḥammad Abṭaḥī, 2 vols. Qum, Madrasat al-Imām al-Mahdī, 2010. [SR]

The Qurʾan, tr. Abdullah Yusuf Ali as *The Holy Qurʾan*. Ware, Wordsworth Editions, 2000. [LL] [BM] [NPS] [RT] [NY]

——, tr. Arthur J. Arberry as *The Koran Interpreted: A Translation*. New York, Touchstone, 1996. [RB]

——. tr. S.V. Mir Ahmed Ali as *The Holy Qurʾan*. New York, Elmhurst, 1988. [IF]

——, tr. Saheeh International as *The Qurʾan*. Jeddah, al-Muntada al-Islami Trust, 2012. [LT]

——, ed. and tr. Seyyed Hossein Nasr, Caner Dagli, Maria Massi Dakake, Joseph Lumbard and Mohammed Rustom as *The Study Quran: A New Translation and Commentary*. New York, HarperOne, 2015. [NB]

——. *See also Le Coran*.

al-Qushayrī, Abū'l-Qāsim. *Risāla Qushayriyya*, tr. Abū ʿAlī Aḥmad ʿUthmānī. Tehran, Intishārāt-i ʿIlmī wa Farhangī, 1361 Sh./1982. [RT]

al-Raḍawī, Murtaḍā. *al-Burhān ʿalā ʿadam taḥrīf al-Qur'ān*. Beirut, al-Irshād li'l-Ṭibāʿa wa'l-Nashr, 1411/1991. [RB]

Rahman, Fazlur. *Islam and Modernity: Transformation of an Intellectual Tradition*. Chicago, IL, University of Chicago Press, 1982. [BM]

Rajabī, Muḥammad Ḥasan. *Mashāhīr-i zanān-i īrānī wa pārsī-guy, az āghāz tā mashrūṭa*. Tehran, Surūsh, 1374 Sh./1995. [AV]

Rashīd Riḍā, Muḥammad. *al-Sunna wa'l-shīʿa aw al-wahhābiyya wa'l-rāfiḍa*. Cairo, Maṭbaʿat al-Manār, 1928. [RB]

Razavi, Shahra. 'Islamic Politics, Human Rights and Women's Claims for Equality in Iran', *Third World Quarterly* 27, no. 7 (2006), pp. 1223–37. [BM]

al-Rāzī, Fakhr al-Dīn. *Mafātīh al-ghayb*, 32 vols. Beirut, Dār al-Fikr, 1981. [SK]

Ridgeon, Lloyd. 'Iranian Intellectuals (1997–2007)', *British Journal of Middle Eastern Studies* 34, no. 3 (2007), pp. 261–5. [BM]

Rūmī, Jalāl al-Dīn. *The Mathnawí of Jalálu'ddín Rúmí*, 6 vols, ed. and tr. Reynold Nicholson. London, Luzac, 1925–40. [NB] [LL]; ed. Reynold A. Nicholson. London, Luzac, 1982. [AV]; tr. Reynold A. Nicholson. Reprint. Istanbul, Konya Metropolitan Municipality, 2004. [RT]

——. *Rumi: Spiritual Verses, The First Book of the Masnavi-ye maʿnavi*, tr. Alan Williams. London, Penguin Books, 2006. [LL]

——. *Shams-i Tabrīzī*, illus. Charles-Hossein Zenderoudi. Tehran, 1980. [AB]

Saʿdī. *Kulliyāt-i Saʿdī*, ed. Muḥammad ʿAlī Furūghī. Tehran, Amīr Kabīr, 1363 Sh./1984. [LL]

Ṣādiqī Ṭihrānī, Muḥammad. *al-Furqān fī tafsīr al-Qur'ān*, 30 vols. Qum, Shukrāna, 1392 Sh./2013. [AC]

Ṣafī ʿAlī Shāh, Ḥasan Iṣfahānī. *Baḥr al-ḥaqā'iq; bi-inḍimām-i Mīzān al-maʿrifa*. Tehran, Kitābkhānān-i Sanā'ī, 1363 Sh./[1985]. [NB]

——. *Tafsīr-i Ṣafī*. Lithographic edn, Tehran, 1308/1890; Lithographic edn, Tehran, 1318 Sh./1939; ed. Ḥāmid Nājī Iṣfahānī. Isfahan, 1383 Sh./2004; ed. ʿAlī Riḍā Munajjimī, *Sharḥ-i jāmiʿ-i tafsīr-i ʿirfānī wa manẓūm-i Qur'ān-i Ṣafī*, 10 vols. Tehran, Abā Ṣāliḥ, 1385 Sh./2006–7; ed. Bihrūz Thirwatiyān. Tehran, Nashr-i Bayn al-Milal, 1393 Sh./2014. [NB] [AC – Intr.]

——. *Zubdat al-asrār*. Tehran, Bungāh-i Maṭbūʿātī-i Ṣafī ʿAlī-Shāh, 1341 Sh./1963. [NB]

Sālūs, ʿAlī Aḥmad. *Bayn al-shīʿa wa'l-sunna: Dirāsa muqārina fī'l-tafsīr wa uṣūlihi*. Cairo, Dār al-Iʿtiṣām, 1989. [RB]

——. *Maʿa al-shīʿa al-ithnā ʿashariyya fī'l-uṣūl wa'l-furūʿ: Mawsūʿa shāmila*, 4 vols. al-Dawḥa, Dār al-Thaqāfa, 1417/1997. [RB]

Sanā'ī, Abū'l-Majd. *Dīwān ḥakīm Abū'l-Majdūd b. Ādam Sanā'ī Ghaznawī*, ed. Muḥammad Taqī Mudarris Raḍawī. Tehran, Intishārāt-ī Sanā'ī, 1380 Sh./2006. [RT]

——. *Ḥadīqat al-ḥaqīqa*, ed. Mudarris Riḍawī. Tehran, Intishārāt-i Dānishgāh Tihrān, 1387 Sh./2008. [NB]

Ṣāniʿī, Yūsuf. *Wujūb ṭalāq al-khulʿ ʿalā al-rajul*. Qum, Muʾassasat Fiqh al-Thaqalayn al-Thaqafiyya, n.d. [LT]

The Sayings of Muhammad, tr. Neal Robinson. London, Gerald Duckworth, 2003. [RT]

al-Sayyārī, Aḥmad b. Muḥammad. *Revelation and Falsification: The Kitāb al-Qirāʾāt of Aḥmad b. Muḥammad al-Sayyārī*, Critical Edition with an Introduction and Notes by Etan Kohlberg and Mohammad Ali Amir-Moezzi. Leiden, Brill, 2009. [RB]

Shabistarī, Maḥmūd. *Gulshan-i rāz (bāgh-i dil)*, ed. Mahdī Ilāhī Qumshaʾī. Tehran, Intishārāt-i ʿIlmī wa Farhangī, 1377 Sh./1998. [LL]

——. *Majmūʿa-i āthār-i Shaykh Maḥmūd Shabistarī*, ed. Ṣamad Muwaḥḥid. Tehran, Ṭahūrī, 1365 Sh./1986. [LL]

al-Shahrastānī, Hibat al-Dīn. 'Tanzīh-i muṣḥaf-i sharīf az naskh wa naqṣ wa taḥrīf', in idem, *Kitāb Tanzīh al-tanzīl mushtamal bar sa bakhsh wa yak khātima*. Tehran, Chāpkhāna-yi Ḥaydarī, 1331 Sh./1951–52, pp. 5–79. [RB]

Shaydā. Tehran, Muʾassasa-yi Farhangī-yi Shams al-Shumūs, 1389 Sh./2010. [SR]

Shīrāzī, Muḥammad Maʿṣūm [Maʿṣūm ʿAlī Shāh]. *Ṭarāʾiq al-ḥaqāʾiq*, 3 vols. Tehran, Sanāʾī, 1966. [RT]; *Ṭarāʾiq al-ḥaqāʾiq*, ed. Muḥammad Jaʿfar Maḥjūb, 3 vols. Tehran, Intishārāt-i Sanāʾī, 1966. [SR]; Tehran, Sanāʾī, 1382 Sh./2003–4. [AC] [AC - Intr.]

Shīrāzī, Muḥammad Sulṭān al-Wāʿiẓīn. *Peshawar Nights: Convincing Shia-Sunni Dialogue*. Karachi, Peermahomed Ebrahim Trust, 1977. [NB]

Shīrwānī, Zayn al-ʿĀbidīn (Mast ʿAlī Shāh). *Bustān al-sīyāḥa*. Tehran, Ḥaqīqat, 2010. [RT]

——. *Ḥadāʾiq al-siyāḥa*. Tehran, Sāzmān-i Chāp-i Danishgāh, 1348 Sh./1969. [RT]

Shubbar, ʿAbd Allāh. *Tafsīr-i Shubbar*. Qum, Muʾassasa-yi Farhangī wa Iṭṭilāʿ-Rasānī Tibiyān, 1387 Sh./2008. [AC]

Sobhani, Jaʿfar [also Subḥānī, Jaʿfar]. *Doctrines of Shiʿi Islam: A Compendium of Imami Beliefs and Practices*, tr. and ed. Reza Shah-Kazemi. London, I.B. Tauris, 2001. [RB] [IF]

Soroush, Abdolkarim. *Expansion of the Prophetic Experience: Essays on Historicity, Contingency and Plurality in Religion*. Leiden, Brill, 2009. [BM]

——. *Qabḍ wa basṭ-i tiʾūrīkī-yi sharīʿat: Naẓarīya-yi takāmul-i dīnī*. Muʾassasa-yi Farhangī-yi Ṣirāt, 1994; 8th edn. Tehran, Sirāṭ, 1999–2000. [BM]

——. *Reason, Freedom, and Democracy in Islam: Essential Writings of Abdolkarim Soroush*, tr. Mahmoud Sadri and Ahmad Sadri. Oxford, Oxford University Press, 2002. [BM]

Soroush Dabbagh. *Dar Bāb-i Rawshanfikrī-yi Dīnī wa Akhlāq*. Tehran, Intishārāt-i Ṣirāṭ, 2009. [BM]

Sulṭān ʿAlī Shāh Gunābādī, Sulṭān Muḥammad. *Bayān al-saʿāda fī maqāmāt al-ʿibāda*, ed. Riḍā Ṭihrānī and ʿAbbās ʿAlī Kaywān Qazwīnī, lithograph. Tehran, 1314/1896. [AC] [AC - Intr.]; 4 vols. Tehran, Maṭbaʿa Dānishgāh-i Tihrān, 1344 Sh./1965–6. [AC]

Sulṭānī Gunābādī, Mīrzā Muḥammad. *Rahbarān-i ṭarīqat wa ʿirfān*. Tehran, Ḥaqīqat, 1379 Sh./2000–2001. [AC]

Tabanda Gunābādī (Riḍā ʿĀlī Shāh), Sulṭān Ḥusayn. *Nābigha-yi ʿilm wa ʿirfān dar qarn-i chahārdahum: sharḥ-i ḥāl-i marḥūm Ḥājj Mullā Sulṭān Muḥammad Gunābādi Sulṭān ʿAlī Shāh*. Tehran, Ḥaqīqat, 1384 Sh./2005–6. [AC]

al-Ṭabarī, Abū Jaʿfar Muḥammad b. Jarīr. *Taʾrīkh al-rusul waʾl-mulūk*. Translated and annotated by William M. Brinner as *The History of al-Ṭabarī*, vol. II: *Prophets and Patriarchs*. Albany, State University of New York Press, 1987; vol. III: *The Children of Israel*. Albany, State University of New York Press, 1991. [NPS]

Ṭabaṭabāʾī, Muḥammad Ḥusayn. *Majmūʿat al-rasāʾil*. Qum, Bustān-i Kitāb, 1387 Sh./2008. [SR]

——. *al-Mīzān fī tafsīr al-Qurʾān*, 20 vols. Beirut, Muʾassasat al-Aʿlamī lʾil-Maṭbūʿāt, 1970–74. [AC] [AC - Intr.]; 1411/1991. [RB]; 2nd edn, 20 vols. Qum, Ismāʿīliyyān, 1993. Vols. 1–24 translated by Sayyid Saeed Akhtar Rizvi and Sayyid Akhtar Rizvi as *al-Mīzān: An Exegesis of the Qurʾan*. Tehran, World Organization for Islamic Services, 1983; vols. 25–40, translated by Tawus Raja, edited by Amina Inloes. Australia, Tawheed Institute Australia, 2018. [SK]

——. *Qurʾān dar islām*. Tehran, Dār al-Kutub al-Islāmī, 1974. Edited and translated into English by Seyyed Hossein Nasr, *The Qurʾan in Islam*. London, Zahra Publications, 1987. [SK]

——. *Risālat al-walāya*, in *Yādnāma-yi mufassir-i kabīr ustād ʿallāma-yi sayyid Muḥammad Ḥusayn Ṭabāṭabāʾī*. Qum, Intishārāt-i Shafaq, 1361 Sh./1982, pp. 251–305. [AC – Intr.] [SR]

——. *Tafsīr al-Mīzān*, Persian tr. by Nāṣir Makārim Shīrāzī. Qum, Intishārāt-i Jāmiʿ-yi Muddarisīn Ḥawzih ʿIlmiyya, 1364 Sh./1985. [RT]

——. ʻZindagī-yi manʼ, in *Marzubān-i waḥī wa khirad: Yādnāma-yi marḥūm ʿallāma-yi sayyid Muḥammad Ḥusayn Ṭabāṭabāʾī*. Qum, Bustān-i Kitāb, 1381 Sh./2002, pp. 39–47. [SR]

al-Ṭabrisī, al-Faḍl b. al-Ḥasan. *Majmaʿ al-bayān fī tafsīr al-Qurʾān*, 10 vols. Beirut, Dār al-ʿUlūm, 2005. [RB]

Tājzāda, Muṣṭafā. ʻAmr bi maʿrūf, taʿāwun wa taḥazzubʼ, *Yās-i naw*, 8 Tīr 1382 Sh./30 June 2003; reprinted in Muṣṭafā Tājzāda, *Jawāmiʿ-i musalmān, dimukrāsī wa Bin Lādin*, ed. Muḥammad Turkamān. Tehran, Dhikr, 2004, pp. 200–202. [NY]

Taylor, Charles. *A Secular Age*. Cambridge, MA, The Belknap Press of Harvard University Press, 2007. [BM]

al-Ṭihrānī, Āqā Buzurg. *al-Dharīʿa ilā taṣānīf al-shīʿa*, 25 vols. Beirut, Dār al-Aḍwāʾ, 1983. [RB]; 26 vols. Qum, 1408/1987. [RT]

Ṭihrānī, Muḥammad Ṣādiqī. *al-Furqān fī tafsīr al-Qurʾān*, 30 vols. Beirut, Muʾssasat al-Aʿlamī, 1397/1977. [AC]

al-Tirmidhī, Abū ʿĪsā Muḥammad b. ʿĪsā. *Jāmiʿ al-Tirmidhī*, ed. Ḥāfiẓ Abū Ṭāhir Zubayr ʿAlī Zaʾī, 6 vols. Riyadh, Darussalam, 2007. [SK]

Tunikābunī, Muḥammad b. Sulaymān. *Qiṣaṣ al-ʿulamāʾ*. Tehran, Intishārāt-i ʿIlmī Farhangī, 1383 Sh./2004. [RT]

al-Ṭūsī, Abū Naṣr al-Sarrāj. *Kitāb al-Lumaʿ fīʾl-taṣawwuf*, tr. Mihdī Maḥabbatī. Tehran, Intishārāt-i Asāṭīr, 1383 Sh./2004. [RT]

Ṭūsī, Muḥammad b. Ḥasan. *al-Tibyān fī tafsīr al-Qur'ān*, 10 vols. Beirut, Dār Iḥyā' al-Turāth al-ʿArabī, n.d. [RT]

al-Ṭūsī, Naṣīr al-Dīn. *Akhlāq-i Nāṣirī*, ed. Mujtabā Mīnuwī. Tehran, Khwārazmī, 1360 Sh./1981. [LL]

Wadud, Amina. *Inside the Gender Jihad: Women's Reform in Islam*. London, Oneworld, 2006. [BM]

Warnūsfādarānī, Muḥammad Ashraf. *ʿUrwat al-muttaqīn dar sharḥ-i āyat al-kursī*. Isfahan, Bungāh-i Maṭbūʿātī-yi Furūzān, 1369/1948–9. [AC]

Ẓahīr, Iḥsān Ilāhī. *al-Shīʿa wa'l-Qur'ān*, 3rd edn. *See* al-Nūrī al-Ṭabrisī, Mīrzā Ḥusayn b. Taqī. *Faṣl al-khiṭāb fī taḥrīf Kitāb Rabb al-arbāb*. [RB]

Zawwāra'ī, ʿAlī b. Ḥusayn. *Tarjumat al-khawāṣṣ*. Tehran, Shirkat-i Intishārāt-i ʿIlmī wa Farhangī, 1394 Sh./2015–16. [AC]

Secondary Sources

Abdul Kadir, Mohd Najib, Abur Hamdi Usman, Mohd Akil Muhamed Ali, Mohd Arif Nazri, Ahamad Asmadi Sakat and Bayu Taufiq Possumah. '*Al-Mizan Fi Tafsir Al-Quran*: A Review on Al-Tabataba'i's Philosophical Exegesis', *The Social Sciences* (*Medwell Journals*) 10, no. 3 (2015), pp. 325–32. [SK]

Abou Zahab, Mariam. 'Between Pakistan and Qom: Shiʿi Women's Madrasas and New Transnational Networks', in Farish A. Noor, Yoginder Sikand and Martin van Bruinessen, eds, *The Madrasa in Asia: Political Activism and Transnational Linkages*. Amsterdam, Amsterdam University Press, 2008, pp. 123–40. [IF]

Abrahamian, Ervand. *Iran: Between Two Revolutions*. Princeton, NJ, Princeton University Press, 1982. [NY]

Abrahamov, Binyamin, ed and tr. *Anthropomorphism and Interpretation of the Qur'ān in the Theology of al-Qāsim ibn Ibrāhīm: Kitāb al-Mustarshid*. Leiden, Brill, 1996. [SK]

Adang, Camilla. *Muslim Writers on Judaism and the Hebrew Bible: From Ibn Rabban to Ibn Hazm*. Leiden, Brill, 1996. [RB]

Afary, Janet. *Sexual Politics in Modern Iran*. Cambridge, Cambridge University Press, 2009. [IF]

Afsaruddin, Asma. 'The Excellences of the Qur'ān: Textual Sacrality and the Organization of Early Islamic Society', *Journal of the American Oriental Society* 122, no. 1 (2002), pp. 1–24. [IF]

Ahmed, Shahab. *What is Islam? The Importance of Being Islamic*. Princeton, NJ, Princeton University Press, 2015. [SR]

Aigle, Denise. 'L'histoire sous forme graphique, en arabe, persan et turc ottoman: Origines et fonctions', *Bulletin d'Études Orientales* 58 (2009), pp. 11–49. [AB]

Akhavi, Shahrough. 'The Thought and Role of Ayatollah Hossein'ali Montazeri in the Politics of Post-1979 Iran', *Iranian Studies* 41, no. 5 (2008), pp. 645–66. [NY]

ʿAlawī, Buzurg. *Geschichte und Entwicklung der modernen persischen Literatur*. Berlin, Akademie-Verlag, 1964. [AB]

Algar, Hamid. *Religion and State in Iran*. Los Angeles, CA, University of California Press, 1969. [RT]

——. "Allāma Sayyid Muḥammad Ḥusayn Ṭabāṭabā'ī: Philosopher, Exegete, and Gnostic', *Journal of Islamic Studies* 17 (2006), pp. 326–51. [RB] [SR]

Āl-i Aḥmad, Jalāl. 'Ziyārat', *Sokhan*, March 1945; republished in idem, *Dīd wa bāzdīd*. Tehran, 1945; translated by Henry D.G. Law as 'The Pilgrimage', *Life and Letters* 62, no. 148 (December 1949), pp. 202–9; translated as 'The Pilgrimage', in Michael C. Hillman, comp. and ed., *Iranian Society: An Anthology of the Writings by Jalal Al-e Ahmad*. Lexington, KY, Mazda Publishers, 1982, pp. 34–42. [AB]

——. *Gharbzadigī*. Tehran, Intishārāt-i Ferdows, 2001 (1st edition 1962). [AB]

Ali, Kecia. *Sexual Ethics and Islam: Feminist Reflections on Qur'an, Hadith, and Jurisprudence*. Oxford, Oneworld, 2006. [LL]

Alston, William P. 'Realism and the Christian Faith', *International Journal for Philosophy of Religion* 38, no. 1/3 (1995), pp. 37–60. [YM]

Amanat, Abbas. *Resurrection and Renewal: The Making of the Babi Movement in Iran, 1844–1850*. Ithaca, NY, Cornell University Press, 1989. [RT]

——. '*Mujtahids* and Missionaries: Shī'ī Responses to Christian Polemics in the Early Qajar Period', in Robert Gleave, ed., *Religion and Society in Qajar Iran*. London, RoutledgeCurzon, 2005, pp. 247–69. [RT]

al-Amīn, Sayyid Muḥsin. *A'yān al-shī'a*, 10 vols. Beirut, Dār al-Ta'ārruf, 1986. [SR]

Amir-Moezzi, Mohammad Ali. *The Divine Guide in Early Shi'ism: The Sources of Esotericism in Islam*, tr. David Streight. Albany, State University of New York Press, 1994. [RT]

——. *Le Coran silencieux et le Coran parlant: Sources scripturaires de l'islam entre histoire et ferveur*. Paris, CNRS, 2011. [SR]

——. *The Spirituality of Shi'i Islam*. London, I.B. Tauris, 2011. [RT]

——. 'Al-Šayḫ al-Mufīd (m. 413/1022) et la question de la falsification du Coran', in Daniel De Smet and Mohammad Ali Amir-Moezzi, eds, *Controverses sur les écritures canoniques de l'Islam*. Paris, Éditions du Cerf, 2014, pp. 199–229. [RB]

—— and Hassan Ansari. 'Muḥammad b. Ya'qūb al-Kulaynī (m. 328 ou 329/939–40 ou 940–41) et son *Kitāb al-Kāfī*: Une introduction', *Studia Iranica* 38 (2009), pp. 191–247. [RB]

Ammerman, Nancy T., ed. *Everyday Religion: Observing Modern Religious Lives*. Oxford, Oxford University Press, 2007. [IF]

Āmulī, Ḥasanzāda. 'Nigarishī-yi kūtāh bih zindagī-yi ustād', in *Yādnāma-yi ustad 'Allāma Ṭabāṭabā'ī*. Qum, Intishārāt-i Shafaq, 1361 Sh./1982, pp. 76–116. [SR]

——. *Dar āsimān-i ma'rifat: Tadhkira-yi awḥadī az 'ālimān-i rabbānī*. Qum, Intishārāt-i Ishrāq, 1375 Sh./1996. [SR]

Antoun, Richard T. *Muslim Preacher in the Modern World: A Jordanian Case Study in Comparative Perspective*. Princeton, NJ, Princeton University Press, 1989. [IF]

Anūsha, Ḥasan. 'Pādrī', *Da'irat al-ma'ārif-i tashayu', Vol. VI*. Tehran, Intishārāt-i Dā'irat al-Ma'ārif-i Tashayyu', 1996. [RT]

Anzali, Ata. 'Safavid Shiʿism, the Eclipse of Sufism and the Emergence of 'Irfān'. Unpublished PhD dissertation, Rice University, 2012. [AC] [SR] [RT]

——. *'Mysticism' in Iran: The Safavid Roots of a Modern Concept*. Columbia, University of South Carolina Press, 2017. [AC]

Appiah, Kwame Anthony. *Thinking It Through: An Introduction to Contemporary Philosophy*. Oxford, Oxford University Press, 2003. [YM]

Arberry, Arthur John. 'Three Persian Poems', *Iran* 2 (1964), pp. 1–12. [NB]

Ardeli, Wara. *Henry Martyn*, tr. Soheil Azari. Tehran, Nūr Jahān, 1962. [RT]

Arjomand, Said [Saïd] Amir. *The Shadow of God and the Hidden Imam*. Chicago, IL, University of Chicago Press, 1987. [IF]

——. 'The Consolation of Theology: Absence of the Imam and Tradition from Chiliasm to Law in Shiʿism', *Journal of Religion* 76 (1996), pp. 548–71. [RB]

Arkoun, Mohammed. 'Introduction: An Assessment of and Perspectives on the Study of the Qur'an', in Andrew Rippin, ed., *The Qur'an: Style and Contents*. Aldershot, Ashgate, 2001, pp. 297–332. [SK]

Asad, Talal. *On the Idea of an Anthropology of Islam*. Washington, DC, Center for Contemporary Arab Studies, Georgetown University, 1986. [SR]

Atanasiu, Vlad. 'The President and the Calligrapher: Arabic Calligraphy and its Political Use', in *Studies in Architecture, History and Culture: Papers Presented by the 2003–2004 AKPIA@MIT Visiting Fellows*. Cambridge, MA, Aga Khan Program for Islamic Architecture at the MIT, 2006, pp. 7–20. [AV]

Atwan, Robert and Laurance Wieder, eds. *Chapters into Verse: Poetry in English Inspired by the Bible. Vol. I: Genesis to Malachi*; *Vol. II: Gospels to Revelation*. Oxford, Oxford University Press, 1993. [LL]

Aubin, Jean. *Matériaux pour la biographie de Shah Niʿmatullah Wali*. Tehran, Département d'Iranologie de l'Institut Franco-Iranien, 1956. [AC]

Austin, John L. *How to do Things with Words*. Oxford, Clarendon Press, 1962. [IF]

Austin, Ralph J.W. 'The Sophianic Feminine in the Work of Ibn 'Arabī and Rumi', in Leonard Lewisohn, ed., *The Heritage of Sufism, Vol. II: The Legacy of Medieval Persian Sufism (1150–1500)*. Oxford, Oneworld, 1999, pp. 233–45. [RT]

Awsī, ʿAlī. *al-Ṭabāṭabāʾī wa manhajuhu fī tafsīrihi al-Mīzān*. Tehran, Muʿāwiniyya al-Riʾāsa liʾl-ʿAlāqāt al-Dawliyya fī Munaẓẓamat al-Aʿlām al-Islāmī, 1405/1985. [RB]; Tehran, Muʿāwanat al-Riyāsa liʾl-ʿAlāqāt al-Duwaliyya, 1986. [SR]

Ayoub, Mahmoud. *The Qur'an and its Interpreters, Volume I*. Albany, State University of New York Press, 1984. [IF] [SK] [RT]

——. 'The Speaking Qur'ān and the Silent Qur'ān: A Study of the Principles and Development of Imāmī Shīʿī *Tafsīr*', in Andrew Rippin, ed., *Approaches to the History of the Interpretation of the Qur'ān*. Oxford, Oxford University Press, 1988, pp. 177–98. [AC] [SK]

——. 'Literary Exegesis of the Qur'ān: The Case of al-Sharīf al-Raḍī', in Issa J. Boullata, ed., *Literary Structures of Religious Meaning in the Qur'ān*. Richmond, Curzon, 2000, pp. 292–309. [SK]

——. *Islam: Faith and History*. London, Oneworld, 2012. [LT]

Ayyāzī, Muḥammad ʿAlī. ʻGirāyash-hā-yi ʿaqlānī dar tafsīr al-Qurʾān al-karīm-i Muṣṭafā Khumaynī', *Bayyināt* 15 (1376 Sh./1997–8), pp. 92–112. [AC]

——. ʻIbrāhīm Muwaththiq ʿĀmilī mufassir-i gum-nām', *Bayyināt* 13 (1376 Sh./1997–8), pp. 36–45. [AC]

——. *Sayr-i taṭawwur-i tafāsīr-i shīʿa*. Tehran, Dānishgāh-i Āzād-i Islāmī, 1385 Sh./2006. [AC]

——. *Shinākht-nāma-yi tafāsīr: Nigāhī ijmālī ba 130 tafsīr-i barjasta az mufassirān-i shīʿa wa ahl al-sunnat*. Rasht, Intishārāt-i Kitāb-i Mubīn, 1378 Sh./1999–2000. [AC]

Badrī, Maḥmūd. *Uswat al-ʿārifīn*. Qum, Maktabat Fadak, 1382 Sh./2003. [SR]

Baker, Patricia L. *Islam and the Religious Arts*. London, Continuum, 2004. [IF]

Bakhshāyishī, ʿAqīqī. *Tabaqāt-i mufassirān-i shīʿa*, 5 vols. Qum, Nashr-i Nawīd-i Islām, 1371/1992–3. [AC]

Bakhtiari, Bahman and Augustus Richard Norton. ʻVoices within Islam: Four Perspectives on Tolerance and Diversity', *Current History* (2005), pp. 37–45. [BM]

Balāghī, ʿAbd al-Ḥujjat. *Maqālāt al-ḥunafā fī maqāmāt-i Shams al-ʿUrafā*, 2 vols. Tehran, Chāpkhāna-yi Maẓāhirī, 1369–71 Sh./1990–93. [AC]

Bàmdàd, Badr ol-Moluk. *From Darkness into Light: Women's Emancipation in Iran*, ed. and tr. Frank Ronald Charles. New York, Exposition Press, 1977. [AV]

Bāqirī Bīd-i Hindī, Nāṣir. ʻMufassir wa ḥakīm-i ilāhī', *Nūr al-ʿIlm* 3, no. 9 (Āzar 1368 Sh./1989), pp. 45–79. [SR]

Barq, ʿAṭā Karīm. *Justujū dar aḥwāl wa āthār-i Ṣafī ʿAlī Shāh*. Tehran, Ibn Sīnā, 1352 Sh./1973. [NB]

Bāstānī Pārīzī, ʿAbd al-ʿAẓīm. *Tarjuma wa tawḍīḥ-i tafsīr-i sharīf-i Bayān al-saʿāda fī maqāmāt al-ʿibāda*. Qum, Nashr-i Ārāsta, 1386 Sh./2007–8. [AC]

Bauer, Karen, ed. *Aims, Methods and Contexts of Qur'anic Exegesis (2nd/8th–9th/15th C.)*. Oxford, Oxford University Press in association with the Institute of Ismaili Studies, 2013. Qur'anic Studies Series 9. [SR]

Bint al-Shati'. *The Wives of the Prophet*, tr. Matti Moosa and D. Nicholas Ranson. New Jersey, Gorgias Press, 2006. [RT]

El-Bizri, Nader. ʻGod: Essence and Attributes', in Tim Winter, ed., *The Cambridge Companion to Classical Islamic Theology*. Cambridge, Cambridge University Press, 2008, pp. 121–40. [SK]

Blair, Sheila S. *Islamic Calligraphy*. Edinburgh, Edinburgh University Press, 2006. [AB]

Bombardier, Alice. ʻLa peinture iranienne au XXème siècle (1911–2009): Historique, courants esthétiques et voix d'artistes. Contribution à l'étude des enjeux de l'art en Iran à l'époque contemporaine'. Unpublished PhD dissertation, EHESS Paris/University of Geneva, 2012. [AB]

Bonaud, Christian. *L'Imam Khomeyni, un gnostique méconnu du XXe siècle: Métaphysique et théologie dans les oeuvres philosophiques et spirituelles de l'Imam Khomeyni*. Beirut, Al-Bouraq, 1997.

Boroujerdi, Mehrzad. *Iranian Intellectuals and the West: The Tormented Triumph of Nativism*. New York, Syracuse University Press, 1996. [AB]

Bowen, John R. *Muslims through Discourse: Religion and Ritual in Gayo Society*. Princeton, NJ, Princeton University Press, 1993. [IF] [NH]

——. *A New Anthropology of Islam*. Cambridge, Cambridge University Press, 2012. [IF]

Böwering, Gerhard. 'Ideas of Time in Persian Sufism', *Iran* 30 (1992), pp. 77–89. [NB]

Brown, Daniel. 'The Triumph of Scripturalism: The Doctrine of Naskh and its Modern Critics', in Earle H. Waugh and Frederick M. Denny, eds, *The Shaping of an American Islamic Discourse: A Memorial to Fazlur Rahman*. Atlanta, GA, Scholars Press, 1998, pp. 49–66. [RB]

Brumberg, Daniel. *Reinventing Khomeini: The Struggle for Reform in Iran*. Chicago, IL, University of Chicago Press, 2001. [AC - Intr.]; 2003. [NY]

Brunner, Rainer. *Die Schia und die Koranfälschung*. Würzburg, Ergon, 2001. [RB]

——. *Islamic Ecumenism in the 20th Century: The Azhar and Shiism between Rapprochement and Restraint*. Leiden, Brill, 2004. [RB]

Buehler, Arthur F. *Sufi Heirs of the Prophet: The Indian Naqshbandiyya and the Rise of the Mediating Sufi Shaykh*. Columbia, University of South Carolina Press, 1998. [NB]

Burke, Richard Maurice. *Cosmic Consciousness: A Study in the Evolution of the Human Mind*. Secaucus, NJ, Citadel Press, 1973. [LL]

Burton, John. *The Collection of the Qur'ān*. Cambridge, Cambridge University Press, 1977. [RB]

——. *The Sources of Islamic Law: Islamic Theories of Abrogation*. Edinburgh, Edinburgh University Press, 1990. [RB]

Canaan, Tewfick. 'The Decipherment of Arabic Talismans', *Berytus* 5 (1937), pp. 69–110. Reprinted in Emilie Savage-Smith, ed. *Magic and Divination in Early Islam: The Formation of the Classical Islamic World*. Aldershot, Ashgate, 2004, pp. 125–78. [IF]

Cancian, Alessandro. *Sufism, Shi'ism and Qur'anic Exegesis in Early Modern Iran: Sulṭān 'Alī Shāh Gunābādī and his Tafsīr Bayān al-Sa'āda*, forthcoming. [NB] [AC]

——. 'Translation, Authority and Exegesis in Modern Iranian Sufism: Two Iranian Sufi Masters in Dialogue', *Journal of Persianate Studies* 7, no. 1 (2014), pp. 88–106. [NB]

Catalogue of the Second Tehran Biennial. Tehran, General Administration of Fine Arts, 1960. [AB]

Catalogue of the Third Tehran Biennial. Tehran, General Administration of Fine Arts, 1962. [AB]

Catalogue of the Fourth Tehran Biennial. Tehran, General Administration of Fine Arts, 1964. [AB]

Catalogue of the Fifth Tehran Biennial. Tehran, Ministry of Culture and Arts and Ethnographical Museum, 1966. [AB]

Chejne, Anwar G. 'Mu'ammar Ibn 'Abbād al-Sulamī, a Leading Mu'tazilite of the Eighth–Ninth Centuries', *Muslim World* 51, no. 4 (1961), pp. 311–20. [YM]

Chelkowski, Peter. 'From *maqatil* Literature to Drama', *al-Serat* 12 (1986), pp. 227–64. [IF]

Chittick, William C. *The Self-Disclosure of God: Principles of Ibn 'Arabī's Cosmology*. Albany, State University of New York Press, 1992. [LL]

——. *Imaginal Worlds: Ibn al-'Arabī and the Problem of Religious Diversity*. Albany, State University of New York, 1994. [NB]

——. 'Time, Space, and the Objectivity of Ethical Norms: The Teachings of Ibn al-'Arabī', *Islamic Studies* 39, no. 4 (2000), pp. 581–96. [NB]

——. *Divine Love: Islamic Literature and the Path to God*. New Haven, CT, Yale University Press, 2013. [NB]

Chodkiewicz, Michel. *An Ocean without Shore: Ibn Arabī, the Book, and the Law*. Albany, State University of New York Press, 1993. [NB]

Clarke, Lynda. 'Some Examples of Elegy on Imam Husayn', *al-Serat* 12 (1986), pp. 13–28. [IF]

Cook, Michael. *Commanding Right and Forbidding Wrong in Islamic Thought*. Cambridge, Cambridge University Press, 2000. [NY]

Corbin, Henry. *History of Islamic Philosophy*. Abingdon, Routledge, 2014. Originally published as *Histoire de la philosophie islamique*. Paris, Gallimard, 1964. [SK]

——. *La philosophie iranienne islamique aux XVIIe et XVIIIe siècles*. Paris, Buchet/Chastel, 1981. [SR]

Corboz, Elvire. *Guardians of Shi'ism: Sacred Authority and Transnational Networks*. Edinburgh, Edinburgh University Press, 2015. [RB]

Cortese, Delia and Simonetta Calderini. *Women and the Fatimids in the World of Islam*. Edinburgh, Edinburgh University Press, 2006. [AV]

Cronin, Stephanie. *Reformers and Revolutionaries in Modern Iran: New Perspectives on the Iranian Left*. London, RoutledgeCurzon, 2004. [NY]

Cupitt, Don. *Mysticism after Modernity*. Malden, Blackwell, 1998. [YM]

Dabashi, Hamid. *Authority in Islam: From the Rise of Muhammad to the Establishment of the Umayyads*. New York, Transaction Publishers, 1989. [SR]

——. *Theology of Discontent: The Ideological Foundations of the Islamic Revolution in Iran*. New York, New York University Press, 1993. [RB] [SR]

Dānishpazhūh, Muḥammad Taqī. *Namuna'i az fihrist-i āthār-i dānish-mandān-i īrānī wa islāmī dar ghinā' wa mūsīqī*. Tehran, Idāra-yi Kull Nigārish-i Wizārat-i Farhang wa Hunar, 1355 Sh./1976. [GZ]

Dāwarpanāh, Abū'l-Faḍl. *Anwār al-'irfān fī tafsīr al-Qur'ān*, 16 vols. Tehran, Kitābkhāna-yi Ṣadr, 1366 Sh./1987–8. [AC]

Dessing, Nathal M., Nadia Jeldtoft, Jørgen S. Nielsen and Linda Woodhead, eds. *Everyday Lived Islam in Europe*. Farnham, Ashgate, 2013. [IF]

Dodd, Erica. 'The Image of the Word: Notes on the Religious Iconography of Islam', *Berytus* 18 (1969), pp. 35–62. [AB]

Doostdar, Alireza. 'Fantasies of Reason: Science, Superstition, and the Supernatural in Iran'. Unpublished PhD dissertation, Harvard University, 2012. [SR]

Dupret, Baudouin, Thomas Pierret, Paulo G. Pinot and Kathryn Spellman-Poots, eds. *Ethnographies of Islam: Ritual Performances and Everyday Practices*. Edinburgh, Edinburgh University Press, 2012. [IF]

Durand, Bernard. *Dalí et Dieu: Un rendez-vous manqué?* Barcelona, Mediterrania, 2008. [AB]

Ehteshami, Amin and Sajjad Rizvi. 'Beyond the Letter: Explanation (*tafsīr*) versus Adaptation (*taṭbīq*) in Ṭabāṭabā'ī's *al-Mīzān*', in Annabel Keeler and Sajjad Rizvi, eds, *The Spirit and the Letter: Approaches to the Esoteric Interpretation of the Qur'an*. Oxford, Oxford University Press in association with the Institute of Ismaili Studies, 2016, pp. 443–73. Qur'anic Studies Series 15. [SR]

Elder, John. *Tārīkh-i mīssiyūn Āmrīkā'ī dar Īrān*, tr. Suhayl Āzarī. Tehran, Nūr Jahān, 1956. [RT]

Elias, Jamal. *Aisha's Cushion: Religious Art, Perception, and Practice in Islam*. Cambridge, MA, Harvard University Press, 2012. [SR]

Elias, Norbert. *The Civilizing Process*, tr. Benjamin Jephcott. Oxford, Blackwell, 1994. [SR]

Elmi, Mohammad Jafar. 'An Objective Approach to Revelation: S.M.Ḥ. Ṭabāṭabā'ī's Method of Interpreting the Qur'ān'. Unpublished PhD dissertation, University of Birmingham, 2002. [SK]

——. 'The Views of Ṭabāṭabā'ī on Traditions (*Aḥādīth*) and Occasions of Revelation (*Asbāb al-Nuzūl*) in Interpreting the Qur'an', *Journal of Shi'a Islamic Studies* 1 (2008), pp. 57–84. [RB]

Eltantawi, Sarah. 'Ṭūsī Did Not "Opt Out": Shiite Jurisprudence and the Solidification of the Stoning Punishment in the Islamic Legal Tradition', in Alireza Korangy, Wheeler M. Thackston, Roy P. Mottahedeh and William Granara, eds, *Essays in Islamic Philology, History, and Philosophy*. Berlin, De Gruyter, 2016, pp. 312–32. [RB]

Ende, Werner. 'Der amtsmüde Ayatollah', in Gebhard J. Selz, ed., *Festschrift für Burkhart Kienast: Zu seinem 70. Geburtstage dargebracht von Freunden, Schülern und Kollegen*. Münster, Ugarit-Verlag, 2003, pp. 51–63. [RB]

van Ess, Josef. *Theologie und Gesellschaft im 2. und 3. Jahrhundert Hidschra: Eine Geschichte des religiösen Denkens im frühen Islam*, 6 vols. Berlin, de Gruyter, 1991–7. [RB]

Fakhry, Majid. *A History of Islamic Philosophy*, 3rd edn. New York, Columbia University Press, 2004. [YM]

Faqīh, Shubbar. *al-Dalāla al-qur'āniyya fī fikr Muḥammad Ḥusayn Ṭabāṭabā'ī*. Beirut, Dār al-Hādī, 2008. [SR]

Fardīd, Aḥmad. *Dīdār-i farrahī wa futūḥāt-i ākhar al-zamān*. Tehran, Mu'assasa-i Farhangī Pažūhišī Čāp wa Našr-i Naẓar, 2002. [AB]

Farzām, Ḥamīd. *Taḥqīq dar aḥwāl wa naqd-i athār wa afkār-i Shāh Ni'matullāh Walī*. Tehran, Soroush, 2000. [RT]

Fischer, Michael M.J. and Mehdi Abedi. *Debating Muslims: Cultural Dialogues in Postmodernity and Tradition*. Madison, University of Wisconsin Press, 1990. [SR]

Flaskerud, Ingvild. '"Oh, My Heart is Sad. It is Moharram, the Month of Zaynab": The Role of Aesthetics and Women's Mourning Ceremonies in Shiraz', in Kamran Scot Aghaie, ed., *The Women of Karbala: Ritual Performance and Symbolic Discourses in Modern Shi'i Islam*. Austin, University of Texas Press, 2005, pp. 65–91. [IF]

——. *Visualizing Belief and Piety in Iranian Shiism*. London, Continuum, 2010. [AB] [IF]

Foucault, Michel. *Power/Knowledge: Selected Interviews and Other Writings, 1972–1977*, ed. Colin Gordon, tr. Colin Gordon, Leo Marshall, John Mepham and Kate Soper. New York, Pantheon Books, 1980. [SR]

Frembgen, Jürgen Wasim, ed. *The Aura of Alif: The Art of Writing in Islam*. Munich, Prestel, 2010. [IF]

Freyer Stowasser, Barbara. *Women in the Qur'an: Traditions, and Interpretations*. Oxford, Oxford University Press, 1994. [LL]

——. 'The *Hijab:* How a Curtain Became an Institution and a Cultural Symbol', in Asma Afsaruddin and A.H. Mathias Zahniser, eds, *Humanism, Culture, and Language in the Near East: Studies in Honor of Georg Krotkoff*. Winona Lake, IN, Eisenbrauns, 1997, pp. 87–104. [LL]

Furūzānfar, Badīʿ al-Zamān. *Sukhan wa sukhanwarān*. Tehran, Zawwār, 1387 Sh./2008–9. [AC – Intr.]

Galliano, Luciana and Chie Wada, eds. *Ma: La sensibilità estetica giapponese*. Torino, Angolo Manzoni, 2004. [GZ]

van Gelder, Geert Jan and Marlé Hammond, eds. *Takhyīl: The Imaginary in Classical Arabic Poetics*. Cambridge, Gibb Memorial Trust, 2009. [SR]

Ghaemmaghami, Omid. 'Arresting the Eschaton: Mirza Husayn Tabarsi Nuri (d. 1902) and the Babi and Baha'i Religions', *Journal of Religious History* 36, no. 4 (2012), pp. 486–98. [RB]

Ghaffārzāda, ʿAlī. 'Naqd wa barrasī-yi mabānī wa ruykard-hā-yi Sulṭān Muḥammad Gunābādī dar tafsīr "Bayān al-saʿāda fī maqāmāt al-ʿibāda"'. Unpublished PhD dissertation, University of Qum, 1390 Sh./2011. [AC]

Ghamari-Tabrizi, Behrooz. *Islam and Dissent in Postrevolutionary Iran: Abdolkarim Soroush, Religious Politics and Democratic Reform*. London, I.B. Tauris, 2008. [BM]

Ghobadzadeh, Naser. *Religious Secularity: A Theological Challenge to the Islamic State*. New York, Oxford University Press, 2014. [LT]

Gladigow, Burkhard. 'Complexity', in Jens Kreinath, Jan Snoek and Michael Stausberg, eds, *Theorizing Rituals: Issues, Topics, Approaches, Concepts*. Leiden, Brill, 2006, pp. 483–94. [IF]

Gleave, Robert. *Inevitable Doubt: Two Theories of Shīʿī Jurisprudence*. Leiden, Brill, 2000 [LT]

——. 'Modern Šīʿī Discussions of *Ḫabar al-wāḥid*: Ṣādr, Ḫumaynī and Ḫū'ī', *Oriente Moderno* New Series, 21 (82), no. 1 (2002), pp. 179–94. [RB]

——. 'Political Aspects of Modern Shiʿi Legal Discussions: Khumayni and Khu'i on *ijtihâd* and *qada*", *Mediterranean Politics* 7 (2002), pp. 96–116. [RB]

——. *Scripturalist Islam: The History and Doctrines of the Akhbārī Shīʿī School*. Leiden, Brill, 2007. [RB] [SK]

Gonzalez, Valerie. *Beauty and Islam: Aesthetics in Islamic Art and Architecture*. London, I.B. Tauris in association with the Institute of Ismaili Studies, 2001. [SR]

Görke, Andreas and Johanna Pink, eds. *Tafsīr and Islamic Intellectual History: Exploring the Boundaries of a Genre*. Oxford, Oxford University Press in association with the Institute of Ismaili Studies, 2014. Qur'anic Studies Series 12. [AC – Intr.]

Gorski, Philip, David Kyuman Kim, John Torpey and Jonathan VanAntwerpen, eds. *The Post-Secular in Question: Religion in*

Contemporary Society. New York, New York University Press, 2012. [BM]

Grabar, Oleg. 'The Qur'an as a Source of Artistic Inspiration', in Fahmida Suleman, ed., *Word of God, Art of Man: The Qur'an and its Creative Expressions*. Oxford, Oxford University Press in association with the Institute of Ismaili Studies, 2007, pp. 27–39. Qur'anic Studies Series 4. [NPS]

Graham, Terry. 'The Niʿmat'ullāhī Order under Safavid Suppression and in Indian Exile', in Leonard Lewisohn and David Morgan, eds, *The Heritage of Sufism, Vol III: Late Classical Persianate Sufism (1501–1750)*. Oxford, Oneworld, 1999, pp. 165–200. [AC]

——. 'Shāh Niʿmatullāh Walī: Founder of the Niʿmatullāhī Sufi Order', in Leonard Lewisohn, ed., *The Heritage of Sufism, Vol. II: The Legacy of Medieval Persian Sufism (1150–1500)*. Oxford, Oneworld, 1999, pp. 173–90. [AC] [RT]

Gramlich, Richard. *Die schiitischen Derwischorden Persiens. Erster Teil: Die Affiliationen*. Wiesbaden, Franz Steiner, 1965. [SR]

Green, Nile. 'A Persian Sufi in British India: The Travels of Mīrzā Ḥasan Ṣafī ʿAlī Shāh (1251/1835–1316/1899)', *Iran* 42 (2004), pp. 201–18. [NB]

——, intro. and tr. 'A Persian Sufi in the Age of Printing: Mirza Hasan Safi ʿAli Shah (1835–99)', in Lloyd Ridgeon, ed., *Religion and Politics in Modern Iran: A Reader*. London, I.B. Tauris, 2005, pp. 99–112. [NB]

——. *Bombay Islam: The Religious Economy of the West Indian Ocean, 1840–1915*. Cambridge, Cambridge University Press, 2011. [NB]

Grisé, C. Annette. 'The Textual Community of Syon Abbey', *Florilegium* 19 (2002), pp. 149–62. [IF]

Gruber, Christiane. 'L'ascension du Prophète Mohammad dans la peinture et la littérature islamique', *Luqman* 20, no. 1 (2004), pp. 55–79. [AB]

El Guindi, Fadwa. *Veil: Modesty, Privacy and Resistance*. Oxford, Berg, 1999. [IF]

Gulī Zawwāra, Ghulām-Riḍā. *Jurʿa-hā-yi jānbakhsh: Farāz-hā-yi az zindagī-yi ʿAllāma Ṭabāṭabāʾī wa asātīd wa shāgirdān-i ān mufassir-i ʿālī-qadr*. Qum, Intishārāt-i Ḥuḍūr, 1375 Sh./1996. [SR]

Haeri, Niloofar. 'The Private Performance of *Salat* Prayers: Time, Repetition, and Meaning', *Anthropological Quarterly* 86, no. 1, pp. 5–34. [NH]

Haeri, Shahla. *Law of Desire: Temporary Marriage in Shiʿi Iran*. Syracuse, NY, Syracuse University Press, 1989. [LL]

Haidar, Najam. *The Origins of the Shīʿa: Identity, Ritual and Sacred Space in Eighth-Century Kūfa*. New York, Cambridge University Press, 2011. [NH]

Ḥāʾirī, ʿAbd al-Hādī. *Nakhustīn rūyārūyī-i andīshihgarān-i Īrān*. Tehran, Amīr Kabīr, 1367 Sh./1988. [RT]

Hamza, Feras and Sajjad Rizvi, with Farhana Mayer, eds. *An Anthology of Qur'anic Commentaries, Volume I: On the Nature of the Divine*. Oxford, Oxford University Press in association with the Institute of Ismaili Studies, 2008. Qur'anic Studies Series 5. [SR]

Ḥaqīqat, ʿAbd al-Rafīʿ. *Tārīkh-i ʿirfān wa ʿurafāʾ-yi Īrānī*. Tehran, Intishārāt-i Iṭṭilāʿāt, 1370 Sh./1991. [SR]

——. *Tārīkh-i ʿirfān wa ʿārifān-i Īrānī*. Tehran, Kūmish, 1388 Sh./2009. [RT]

Ḥasanzāda, Ṣādiq. *Uswat al-ʿurafāʾ*. Qum, Intishārāt-i Ishrāq, 1424/2003. [SR]

——. *Ṭarīq-i ʿirfān: Tarjuma wa sharḥ-i risālat al-walāya*. Qum, Intishārāt-i Ishrāq, 1383 Sh./2004. [SR]

Hāshimiyān, Hādī and Sayyid Muḥammad Ṣafavī. *Daryā-yi ʿirfān: Sharḥ-i ḥāl-i Āyatullāh Sayyid ʿAlī Qāḍī Ṭabāṭabāʾī*. Qum, Intishārāt-i Ṭāhā, 1382 Sh./2003. [SR]

Hawting, Gerald R. *The Idea of Idolatry and the Emergence of Islam: From Polemic to History*. Cambridge, Cambridge University Press, 1999. [SK]

al-Ḥaydarī, Sayyid Kamāl. *Uṣūl al-tafsīr wa'l-ta'wīl: Muqārana manhajiyya bayn ārāʾ al-Ṭabāṭabāʾī wa abraz al-mufassirīn*. Beirut, Muʾassasat al-Taʾrīkh al-ʿArabī, 2006. [SR]

Heer, Nicholas. 'Abū Ḥamīd al-Ghazālī's Esoteric Exegesis of the Koran', in Leonard Lewisohn, ed., *The Heritage of Sufism, Vol. I: Classical Persian Sufism from its Origins to Rumi*. Oxford, Oneworld, 1999, pp. 235–58. [LL]

Heern, Zackery M. *The Emergence of Modern Shiʿism: Islamic Reform in Iraq and Iran*. London, Oneworld, 2015. [AC – Intr.] [SK]

Hegland, Mary Elaine. 'Gender and Religion in the Middle East and South Asia: Women's Voices Rising', in Margaret L. Meriwether and Judith E. Tucker, eds, *A Social History of Women and Gender in the Modern Middle East*. Berkeley, CA, Westview Press, 1999, pp. 177–212. [IF]

Heiler, Friedrich. *Erscheinungsformen und Wesen der Religion*. Stuttgart, Kohlhammer, 1961. [SR]

Hellot, Florence. 'The Western Missionaries in Azerbaijani Society (1835–1914)', in Robert Gleave, ed., *Religion and Society in Qajar Iran*. London, RoutledgeCurzon, 2005, pp. 270–92. [RT]

Hermann, Denis and Sabrina Mervin, eds. *Shiʿi Trends and Dynamics in Modern Times (XVIIIth–XXth Centuries)/Courants et dynamiques chiites à l'époque moderne (XVIIIe–XXe siècles)*. Beirut, Orient-Institut/Ergon-Verlag, 2010. [AC]

Hick, John. *An Interpretation of Religion: Human Responses to the Transcendent*, 2nd edn. New Haven, CT, Yale University Press, 2004. [YM]

Hirschkind, Charles. *The Ethical Soundscape: Cassette Sermons and Islamic Counterpublics*. New York, Columbia University Press, 2006. [IF]

—— and David Scott, eds. *Powers of the Secular Modern: Talal Asad and His Interlocutors*. Redwood, CA, Stanford University Press, 2006. [BM]

al-Ḥirz, ʿAbd al-Laṭīf. *Min al-ʿirfān ilā'l-dawla: al-taṣawwuf fī fikr al-imām al-Khumaynī wa'l-shahīd al-Ṣadr*. Beirut, Dār al-Fārābī, 2011. [SR]

Hodgson, Marshall G.S. *The Venture of Islam, Vol. I: The Classical Age of Islam*. Chicago, IL, University of Chicago Press, 1988; *Vol. II: The Expansion of Islam in the Middle Periods*. Chicago, IL, University of Chicago Press, 1977. [RT]

Humayūnī, Masʿūd. *Tārīkh-i silsila-yi ṭarīqa-yi Niʿmatullāhī*. Tehran, Maktab-i ʿIrfān-i Īrān, 1355 Sh./1976. [NB]

Hunsberger, Alice, ed. *Pearls of Persia: The Philosophical Poetry of Nāṣir-i Khusraw*. London, I.B. Tauris in association with the Institute of Ismaili Studies, 2012. [LL]

al-Ḥusaynī, Qāḍī Aḥmad b. Mīr Munshī. *Calligraphers and Painters*, tr. from the Persian by Vladimir Minorsky. Washington, DC, Freer Gallery of Art Occasional Papers, 1959. [AV]

Ibrāhīm, Ḥāṭim. *Qiṣaṣ al-ʿurafāʾ*. Beirut, Manshūrāt al-Fajr, 2008. [SR]
Imāmī, Karīm. 'Nigāhī dubāra ba maktab-i Saqqākhāna', *Saqqākhāna Exhibition Catalogue*. Tehran, Tehran Museum of Contemporary Art, 1977, n.p. [AB]
Izutsu, Toshihiko. *Ethico-Religious Concepts in the Qurʾān*. Montreal, McGill University Press, 1966. [NB]
——. *Sufism and Taoism: A Comparative Study of Key Philosophical Concepts*. Los Angeles, University of California Press, 1984. [RT]
Jahanbakhsh, Forough. *Islam, Democracy and Religious Modernism in Iran, 1953–2000: From Bazargan to Soroush*. Leiden, Brill, 2001. [YM]
Jahandide, Mitra and Shahab Khaefi. 'Women's Status during the Safavid Period', in Vladimir Vasek, ed., *Recent Researches in Social Science, Digital Convergence, Manufacturing and Tourism: International Conference on Social Science, Social Economy and Digital Convergence*. [Athens], World Scientific and Engineering Academy and Society Press, 2011, pp. 137–42. [AV]
Jahanpour, Farhang. 'Iran: The Rise and Fall of the Tudeh Party', *The World Today* 40, no. 4 (1984), pp. 152–9. [NY]
Jalāʾīpūr, Muḥammad Riḍā. 'Marḥala-yi baʿdī-yi rawshanfikrī-yi dīnī', *Mehrnamah Quarterly*, November 2011. [BM]
Jāmiʿī, ʿAlī Riḍā Masjid. *Pazhuhishī dar maʿārif imāmīyih*. Tehran, Wizārat-i Farhang wa Irshād-i Islāmī, 1380 Sh./2001. [RT]
Jawādī Āmulī, ʿAbd Allāh. *Shams al-waḥī-yi Tabrīzī: Sīra-yi ʿilmī-yi ʿAllāma Ṭabāṭabāʾī*. Qum, Markaz-i Nashr-i Isrāʾ, 1386 Sh./2007. [SR]
Jeffery, Arthur. 'The Qurʾān as Scripture', *Muslim World* 40, nos. 1–4 (1950), pp. 41–55, 106–34, 185–206 and 257–75. [GZ]
——. *The Qurʾān as Scripture*. New York, R. F. Moore, 1952. [GZ]
Kalmo, Hent and Quentin Skinner. 'Introduction: A Concept in Fragments', in idem, *Sovereignty in Fragments: The Past, Present and Future of a Contested Concept*. Cambridge, Cambridge University Press, 2010, pp. 1–25. [NY]
Kamalkhani, Zahra. *Women's Islam: Religious Practice among Women in Today's Iran*. London, Kegan Paul, 1998. [IF]
Karamustafa, Ahmet T. *Sufism: The Formative Period*. Berkeley, CA, University of California Press, 2007. [RT]
Karbāsīzāda Iṣfahānī, ʿAlī. *Ḥakīm-i mutaʾallih Bīdābādī*. Tehran, Pazhūhishgāh-i ʿUlūm-i Insānī wa Muṭālaʿāt-i Farhangī, 1381 Sh./2002. [SR]
Karimi-Nia, Morteza. 'Contemporary Qur'anic Studies in Iran and its Relationship with Qur'anic Studies in the West', *Journal of Qur'anic Studies* 14, no. 1 (2012), pp. 45–72. [AC – Intr.]
Kashmīrī, Mīrzā Muḥammad. *Takmilat Nujūm al-samāʾ*, 2 vols. Qum, Kitābkhāna-yi Āyatullāh Marʿashī Najafī, 1979. [SR]
Katz, Marion Holmes. *Prayer in Islamic Thought and Practice*. Cambridge, Cambridge University Press, 2013. [NH]
Kauz, Ralph. *Politische Parteien und Bevölkerung in Iran: Die Ḥezb-e Demukrāt-e Īrān und ihr Führer Qavāmo s-Salṭanä*. Berlin, Klaus Schwarz Verlag, 1995, pp. 154–95. [NY]
Keddie, Nikki R. *Religion and Rebellion in Iran: The Iranian Tobacco Protest of 1891–1892*. London, Cass, 1966. [RB]

——. 'The Economic History of Iran, 1800–1914, and its Political Impact: An Overview', *Iranian Studies* 5, nos. 2–3 (1972), pp. 58–78. [AC]

Keeler, Annabel. *Sufi Hermeneutics: The Qur'an Commentary of Rashīd al-Dīn Maybudī*. Oxford, Oxford University Press in association with the Institute of Ismaili Studies, 2006. Qur'anic Studies Series 3. [NB] [LL]

Kermani, Navid. *God is Beautiful: The Aesthetic Experience of the Quran*, tr. Tony Crawford. Cambridge, Polity Press, 2015. [SR]

Keshmirshekan, Hamid. 'Neo-Traditionalism and Modern Iranian Painting: The *Saqqa-khaneh* School in the 1960s', *Iranian Studies* 38, no. 4 (2005), pp. 607–30. [AB]

Khalafallah, Ahmad Muhammad. 'al-Fann al-qaṣaṣī fī'l-Qur'ān al-karīm'. Phd dissertation, Cairo University, 1947. Published as *al-Fann al-qaṣaṣī fī'l-Qur'ān al-karīm*. Cairo, Maktabat al-Nahda al-Miṣriyya, 1951. [BM]

Khalafallah, Haifaa. 'Muslim Women: Public Authority, Scriptures and "Islamic Law"', in Amira El-Azhary Sonbol, ed., *Beyond the Exotic: Women's Histories in Islamic Societies*. Cairo, American University in Cairo Press, 2006, pp. 37–49. [AV]

Khani, Mohammad Hassan. 'Political Parties in the Islamic Republic of Iran: A Short Review', *Iran Review* ONLINE (17 July 2012). [NY]

Khāwarī, Asadullāh. *Dhahabiyya: Taṣawwuf-i ʿamalī-āthāri adabī*. Tehran, Intishārāt-i Dānishgāh Tehran, 1362 Sh./1983. [RT]

al-Khoei, Yūsuf [also al-Kho'i, Yousif]. 'Abū'l-Qāsim al-Ḫū'ī', *Oriente Moderno* New Series, 18 (79), no. 2 (1999), pp. 491–500. [RB]

al-Kho'i, Yousif [also al-Khoei, Yūsuf]. 'Grand Ayatollah Abu al-Qassim al-Kho'i: Political Thought and Positions', in Faleh Abdul-Jabar, ed., *Ayatollahs, Sufis and Ideologues: State, Religion and Social Movements in Iraq*. London, Saqi Books, 2002, pp. 223–30. [RB]

Khomeini, Ruhollah. *Islam and Revolution: Writings and Declarations of Imam Khomeini (1941–1980)*, tr. and ed. Hamid Algar. Berkeley, CA, Mizan Press, 1981. [SR]

Khosrojerdi, Hossein. 'The Islamic Revolution in Contemporary Iranian Art', *Tavoos* (1999), pp. 91–3. [AB]

Khosrokhavar, Farhad. 'The New Intellectuals in Iran', *Social Compass* 51, no. 2 (2004), pp. 191–202. [YM]

Kinberg, Leah. '*Muḥkamāt* and *Mutashābihāt* (Koran 3/7): Implication of a Koranic Pair of Terms in Medieval Exegesis', *Studia Islamica* 35 (1988), pp. 143–72. [RB]

Kīyānī, Muḥsin. *Tārīkh-i khāniqāh dar Īrān*. Tehran, Ṭahūrī, 1369 Sh./1990. [RT]

Kohlberg, Etan. 'Some Notes on the Imāmite Attitude to the Qur'ān', in Samuel M. Stern, Albert H. Hourani and Vivian Brown, eds, *Islamic Philosophy and the Classical Tradition: Essays Presented by His Friends and Pupils to Richard Walzer on His Seventieth Birthday*. Oxford, Cassirer, 1972, pp. 209–24. [RB]

Koskenniemi, Martti. 'Conclusion: Vocabularies of Sovereignty – Powers of a Paradox', in Hent Kalmo and Quentin Skinner, eds, *Sovereignty in Fragments: The Past, Present and Future of a Contested Concept*. Cambridge, Cambridge University Press, 2010, pp. 222–42. [NY]

Krämer, Gudrun and Sabine Schmidtke, eds. *Speaking for Islam: Religious Authorities in Muslim Societies*. Leiden, Brill, 2014. [IF]

Kresse, Kai. *Philosophising in Mombasa: Knowledge, Islam and Intellectual Practice on the Swahili Coast*. Edinburgh, Edinburgh University Press for the International African Institute, 2007. [SR]

Kriss, Rudolf and Hubert Kriss-Heinrich. *Volksglaube in Bereich des Islam, Vol. II: Amulette, Zauberformeln und Beschwörungen*. Wiesbaden, Otto Harrassowitz, 1962. [IF]

Kumpānī-zāriʿ, Mahdī. *Gunābādī wa tafsīr-i Bayān al-saʿāda*. Tehran, Khāna-yi Chāp, 1390 Sh./2011. [NB] [AC]

Laibi, Shaker. *Soufisme et art visuel: Iconographie du sacré*. Paris, L'Harmattan, 1998. [AB]

Lambek, Michael. *Knowledge and Practice in Mayotte: Local Discourses of Islam, Sorcery, and Spirit Possession*. Toronto, University of Toronto Press, 1993. [IF]

Lawson, Todd. 'Akhbārī Shīʿī Approaches to *Tafsīr*', in Gerald R. Hawting and Abdul-Kader A. Shareef, eds, *Approaches to the Qur'ān*. London, Routledge, 1993, pp. 173–210. [AC] [SK]

Lewisohn, Leonard. 'An Introduction to the History of Modern Persian Sufism, Part I: The Niʿmatullāhī Order: Persecution, Revival and Schism', *Bulletin of the School of Oriental and African Studies* 61, no. 3 (1998), pp. 437–64. [NB] [AC] [LL] [RT]

——. 'An Introduction to the History of Modern Persian Sufism, Part II: A Socio-cultural Profile of Sufism, from the Dhahabī Revival to the Present Day', *Bulletin of the School of Oriental and African Studies* 62, no. 1 (1999), pp. 36–59. [LL] [RT]

Lings, Martin. *The Quranic Art of Calligraphy and Illumination*. London, World of Islam Festival Trust, 1976. [AB]

Litvak, Meir. *Shiʿi Scholars of Nineteenth-Century Iraq: The 'ulama' of Najaf and Karbala'*. Cambridge, Cambridge University Press, 1998. [RB]

Loeffler, Reinhold. *Islam in Practice: Religious Beliefs in a Persian Village*. Albany, State University of New York Press, 1988. [SR]

Lotman, Yuri. *Universe of the Mind: A Semiotic Theory of Culture*. Bloomington, Indiana University Press, 1990. [SR]

Luizard, Pierre-Jean. *La formation de l'Irak contemporain: Le rôle politique des ulémas chiites à la fin de la domination ottomane et au moment de la construction de l'état irakien*. Paris, Éditions du CNRS, 1991. [RB]

Mahdavi, Pardis. *Passionate Uprisings: Iran's Sexual Revolution*. Stanford, CA, Stanford University Press, 2009. [LL]

Malcolm, John. *The History of Persia: From the Most Early Period to the Present Time*, 2 vols. London, John Murray, 1815. [RT]

Mandaville, Peter. Review of *Islamic Political Thought: An Introduction*, edited by Gerhard Bowering, *Journal of Islamic Studies* 29, no. 3 (2018), pp. 476–8. [NY]

Manzinani, Ehsan. 'La réception de Heidegger en Iran: Le cas de Ahmad Fardid (1910–1994). L'examen critique d'une lecture et ses implications'. Unpublished Phd dissertation, Sorbonne Nouvelle-Paris 3, 2008. [AB]

Maʿrifat, Muḥammad Hādī. *Ṣiyānat al-Qurʾān min al-taḥrīf*. Qum, Dār al-Qurʾān al-Karīm, 1410/1990. [RB]
Martin, Vanessa. *Creating an Islamic State: Khomeini and the Making of a New Iran*. London, I.B. Tauris, 2003. [SR]
Masud, Muhammad Khalid and Armando Salvatore. 'Western Scholars of Islam on the Issue of Modernity', in Muhammad Khalid Masud, Armando Salvatore and Martin van Bruinessen, eds, *Islam and Modernity: Key Issues and Debates*. Edinburgh, Edinburgh University Press, 2009, pp. 36–53. [NY]
Matsunaga, Yasuyuki. 'Mohsen Kadivar: An Advocate of Postrevivalist Islam in Iran', *British Journal of Middle Eastern Studies* 34, no. 3 (2007), pp. 317–29. [BM]
Mavani, Hamid. 'Paradigm Shift in Twelver Shiʿi Legal Theory (*uṣūl al-fiqh*): Ayatullah Yusef Saanei', *Muslim World* 99, no. 2 (2009), pp. 335–55. [LT]
McAuliffe, Jane Dammen. 'Text and Textuality: Q. 3:7 as a Point of Intersection', in Issa J. Boullata, ed., *Literary Structures of Religious Meaning in the Qurʾān*. Richmond, Curzon, 2000, pp. 56–76. [SK]
——. *Qurʾānic Christians: An Analysis of Classical and Modern Exegesis*. Cambridge, Cambridge University Press, 2007. [NB]
——, Barry D. Walfish and Joseph W. Goering, eds. *With Reverence for the Word: Medieval Scriptural Exegesis in Judaism, Christianity, and Islam*. Oxford, Oxford University Press, 2003. [SR]
McDermott, Martin. *The Theology of al-Shaikh al-Mufīd (d. 413/1022)*. Beirut, Dar el-Machreq, 1978. [LT]
McGuire, Meredith. *Lived Religion: Faith and Practice in Everyday Life*. Oxford, Oxford University Press, 2008. [IF]
Medoff, Louis. 'Ijtihad and Renewal in Qur'anic Hermeneutics: An Analysis of Muḥammad Ḥusayn al-Ṭabāṭabāʾī's *al-Mīzān fī tafsīr al-Qurʾān*'. Unpublished PhD dissertation, University of California, Berkeley, 2007. [SR]
Mernissi, Fatema [also Fatima]. *Beyond the Veil: Male–Female Dynamics in Muslim Society*. Cambridge, MA, Schenkman, 1975. [LL]
——. *The Veil and the Male Elite*, tr. Mary Jo Lakeland. New York, Perseus Books, 1991. [LL]
——. *Islam and Democracy: Fear of the Modern World*, tr. Mary Jo Lakeland. London, Virago, 1993. [LL]
——. *Dreams of Trespass: Tales of a Harem Girlhood*. New York, Basic Books, 1994. [LL]
Metcalf, Barbara, ed. *Moral Conduct and Authority: The Place of* adab *in South Asian Islam*. Berkeley, University of California Press, 1984. [SR]
——, ed. *Islam in South Asia in Practice*. Princeton, NJ, Princeton University Press, 2009. [SR]
Michot, Yahya. 'Revelation', in Tim Winter, ed., *The Cambridge Companion to Classical Islamic Theology*. Cambridge, Cambridge University Press, 2008, pp. 180–96. [YM]
Mikāʾīlī, ʿAzīz. "Urafā'-yi muʿāṣir-i silsila-yi Jūlā', *Furūgh-i andīsha* 1 (1380 Sh./2001), pp. 47–54. [SR]

Mir-Hosseini, Ziba. *Islam and Gender: The Religious Debate in Contemporary Iran*. Princeton, NJ, Princeton University Press, 1999. [LT]

de Miras, Michel. *Le method spirituelle d'un maître du Soufisme iranien: Nur Ali-Shah*. Paris, Éditions du Sirac, 1974. [AC]

Modarressi, Hossein. 'Early Debates on the Integrity of the Qur'ān: A Brief Survey', *Studia Islamica* 77 (1993), pp. 5–39. [RB]

Mojaddedi, Jawid. 'Rūmī', in Andrew Rippin, ed., *The Blackwell Companion to the Qur'ān*. Malden, MA, Blackwell, 2006, pp. 362–72. [NB]

Mokhtari, Mohammad Hossein. 'The Exegesis of Tabatabaei and the Hermeneutics of Hirsch: A Comparative Study'. Unpublished PhD dissertation, Durham University, 2007. Available at Durham e-Theses Online, http://etheses.dur.ac.uk/2569/. [SK]

Momen, Moojan. *An Introduction to Shi'i Islam: The History and Doctrines of Twelver Shi'ism*. New Haven, CT, Yale University Press, 1985. [IF] [RT]

Moosa, Ebrahim. 'Arabic and Islamic Hermeneutics', in Jeff Malpas and Hans-Helmuth Gander, eds, *The Routledge Companion to Hermeneutics*. London, Routledge, 2015, pp. 707–21. [BM]

Moosa, Matti. *Extremist Shiites: The Ghulat Sects*. Syracuse, NY, Syracuse University Press, 1988. [RT]

Mottahedeh, Roy P. *The Mantle of the Prophet: Religion and Politics in Iran*. New York, Simon and Schuster, 1985. [AC – Intr.]

Moussawi, Ibrahim. *Shi'ism and the Democratisation Process in Iran: With a Focus on Wilayat al-Faqih*. London, Saqi Books, 2011. [NY]

Mudarrisī, Fāṭima. 'Uṣtūra-yi Jamshīd bā nigāhī bi sarguzasht-i Sulaymān-i Nabī', *Majalla-yi dānishkada-i adabīyāt 'ulūm insānī* 2, no. 1 (1385 Sh./2006), pp. 9–35. [NPS]

Mudarrissī Chahārdihī, Nūr al-Dīn. 'Silsila-yi kawthariyya', *Wahīd* 243 (1357 Sh./1978), pp. 41–2. [SR]

Muhaghegh-Damad, Seyyed Mostafa. 'The Role of Time and Social Welfare in the Modification of Legal Rulings', in Lynda Clarke, ed., *Shī'ite Heritage: Essays on Classical and Modern Traditions*. Binghamton, NY, Global, 2001, pp. 213–22. [LT]

Mumisa, Michael. 'Towards an African Qur'anic Hermeneutics', *Journal of Qur'anic Studies* 4, no. 1 (2002), pp. 61–76. [IF]

al-Munajjid, Ṣalāḥ al-Dīn. 'Women's Roles in the Art of Arabic Calligraphy', in George N. Atiyeh, ed., *The Book in the Islamic World: The Written Word and Communication in the Middle East*. Albany, State University of New York Press, 1995, pp. 141–8. [AV]

Munzawī, Aḥmad. *Fihrist-i nuska-hā-yi khaṭṭī-yi fārsī*, 6 vols. Tehran, Mu'assasa-yi Farhangī-yi Manṭaqa'ī, 1969. [AC]

Muṭahharī, Murtaḍā. *Yāddāsht-hāyi Ustād Muṭahharī, Vol. I*. Tehran, Ṣadrā, 1998. [NY]

——. *Āshnā'ī bā Qur'ān*. Tehran, Intishārāt-i Ṣadrā, 1381 Sh./2002. [RT]

——. *Khatm nubuwat*. Tehran, Intishārāt-i Ṣadrā, 1388 Sh./2009. [RT]

Naef, Silvia. *L'art de l'écriture arabe: Passé et présent*. Geneva, Slatkine, 1993. [AB]

Nafīsī, Saʿīd. *Tārīkh-i ijtimāʿī wa sīyāsī dar dawra-yi muāāṣir*, 2 vols. Tehran, Bunyād, 1354 Sh./1975. [RT]

Najīb Muḥammad, Ḥusayn. *Waṣāyā al-ʿurafā'*. Beirut, Manshūrāt al-Fajr, 2011. [SR]

Najmabadi, Afsaneh. 'Hazards of Modernity and Morality: Women, State and Ideology in Contemporary Iran', in Deniz Kandiyoti, ed., *Women, Islam and the State*. London, Macmillan, 1991, pp. 48–76. [IF]

Nāṣirī, Muḥammad Bāqir. *al-Durūʿ al-ḥaṣīna wa'l-kunūz al-dafīna*. Beirut, Dār al-Maḥajja al-Bayḍā', 2004. [SR]

Naṣīrī, Muḥammad Riḍā. 'Adīb Nayshābūrī, Shaykh Muḥammad Taqī, Farzand-i Mīrzā Asadullāh,' in idem, ed., *Athar-āfarīnān: Zindīgīnāma-yi nāmāwarān farhang-i Īrān*. Tehran, Amjuman-i Āthār wa Mafākhir-i Farhangī, 1384 Sh./2005, vol. I, pp. 222–3. [LL]

——. 'Āqā Buzurg Ḥakīm, Āqā Mīrzā 'Askarī Shahīdī Mashhadī', in idem, ed., *Athar-āfarīnān: Zindīgīnāma-yi nāmāwarān farhang-i Īrān*. Tehran, Amjuman-i Āthār wa Mafākhir-i Farhangī, 1384 Sh./2005, vol. I, p. 45. [LL]

——. 'Qumsha'ī-yi Iṣfahānī, Muḥammad Riḍā Farzand-i Abū'l-Qāsim', in *Athar-āfarīnān*: *Zindīgīnāma-yi nāmāwarān farhang-i Īrān*. Tehran, Amjuman-i Āthār wa Mafākhir-i Farhangī, 1384 Sh./2005, vol. IV, p. 366 [LL].

Nasr, Seyyed Hossein. *Islamic Art and Spirituality*. Albany, State University of New York Press, 1990. [NB]

——. 'Oral Transmission and the Book in Islamic Education: The Spoken and the Written Word', *Journal of Islamic Studies* 3, no. 1 (1992), pp. 1–14. [LL]

——. 'Foreword', in Seyyed Ghahreman Safavi and Simon Weightman, *Rūmī's Mystical Design: Reading the Mathnawī, Book One*. Albany, State University of New York Press, 2009, pp. vii–xi. [AV]

Nasr, Vali and Ali Gheissari. *Democracy in Iran: History and the Quest for Liberty*. Oxford, Oxford University Press, 2006. [YM]

Nehamas, Alexander. *The Art of Living: Socratic Reflections from Plato to Foucault*. Berkeley, University of California Press, 1998. [SR]

Nelson, Kristina. *The Art of Reciting the Qur'an*. Cairo, American University in Cairo Press, 2001. [SR]

Netton, Ian Richard. *Islam, Christianity and the Mystic Journey: A Comparative Exploration*. Edinburgh, Edinburgh University Press, 2011. [YM]

Neuwirth, Angelika. 'The House of Abraham and the House of Amram: Genealogy, Patriarchal Authority and Exegetical Professionalism', in Angelika Neuwirth, Nicolai Sinai and Michael Marx, eds, *The Qur'ān in Context: Historical and Literary Investigations into the Qur'ānic Milieu*. Leiden, Brill, 2011, pp. 499–532. [IF]

Newman, Andrew. 'The Development of Political Significance of the Rationalist (Uṣūlī) and Traditionalist (Akhbārī) Schools in Imāmī Shiʿī History from the Third/Ninth to the Tenth/Sixteenth Century A.D.' Unpublished PhD dissertation, University of California, Los Angeles, 1986. [SK]

——. 'Clerical Perceptions of Sufi Practices in Late Seventeenth-Century Persia: Arguments over the Permissibility of Singing (*Ghinā'*)', in Leonard Lewisohn and David Morgan, eds, *The Heritage of Sufism*.

Vol. III: Late Classical Persianate Sufism (1501–1750). Oxford, Oneworld, 1999, pp. 135–64. [GZ]

Nīkbakht, Raḥīm and Ṣamad Ismāʿīlzāda. *Zindagānī wa mubārizāt-i Āyatullāh Qāḍī Ṭabāṭabāʾī*. Tehran, Markaz-i Asnād-i Inqilāb-i Islāmī, 1380 Sh./2001. [SR]

Nīkrān, Ḥamīda and Shahrām Ṣaḥrāʾī. *Mabānīʾyi taʾwīl-i āyāt al-aḥkām dar tafsīr Bayān al-saʿāda fī maqāmāt al-ʿibāda, az ālim-i rabbānī wa ʿārif-i ṣamadānī Ḥājj Mullā Ṣulṭān Muḥammad Gunābādi Sulṭān ʿAlī Shāh*. Mashhad, Silsilat al-Riḍā, 1393 Sh./2014–15. (Reworking of a doctoral dissertation by Ḥamīda Nīkrān, 'Bar-rasī-yi abānīʾyi taʾwīl-i āyāt al-aḥkām dar tafsīr Bayān al-saʿāda-yi Sulṭān ʿAlī Shāh Gunābādī', Rāzī University, 1390 Sh./2011–12.) [AC]

Nithārī, Aḥmad. *Shamʿ-yi jamʿ: Sharḥ-i ḥāl-i Āyatullāh Mullā Ḥusayn Qulī Hamadānī*. Tehran, Kānūn-i Andīsha-yi Javān, 1375 Sh./1996. [SR]

Nooshin, Laudan. 'Underground, Overground: Rock Music and Youth Discourses in Iran', *Iranian Studies* 38, no. 3 (2005), pp. 463–94. [LL]

Nurbakhsh, Javad [Jawād Nūrbakhsh]. *Masters of the Path: A History of the Masters of the Nimatullahi Sufi Order*. New York, Khaniqahi-Nimatullahi, 1980. [RT]

Osanloo, Arzoo. *The Politics of Women's Rights in Iran*. Princeton, NJ, Princeton University Press, 2009. [AV]

Padwick, Constance E. *Muslim Devotions: A Study of Prayer-Manuals in Common Use*. Oxford, Oneworld, 1997. [IF]

Pak-Shiraz, Nacim. 'Imagining the Diaspora in the New Millennium Comedies of Iranian Cinema', *Iranian Studies* 46, no. 2 (2013), pp. 165–84. [NPS]

——. 'The Qur'anic Epic in Iranian Cinema', *Journal of Religion and Film* 20, no. 1 (2016), pp. 1–25. [NPS]

——. 'Comedy in Iranian Cinema', in Parviz Jahed, ed., *Directory of World Cinema: Iran 2*. Chicago, IL, Intellect, 2017, pp. 262–70. [NPS]

——. 'Representing Muhammad on Screen'. Forthcoming. [NPS]

Pākatchī, Aḥmad. *Majmūʿa-yi dars guftār-hā-yi dar bāra-yi tārīkh-i tafsīr-i Qurʾān-i karīm*. Tehran, Intishārāt-i Imām-i Ṣādiq, 1391 Sh./2012–13. [AC]

Pakbaz, Ruyin, Yaghub Emdadian and Tooka Maleki. *Pioneers of Iranian Modern Art: Charles-Hossein Zenderoudi*. Tehran, Tehran Museum of Contemporary Art/Mahriz, 2001. [AB]

Parkin, David. 'Inside and Outside the Mosque: A Master Trope', in David Parkin and Stephen Headley, eds. *Islamic Prayer across the Indian Ocean: Inside and Outside the Mosque*. Richmond, Curzon, 2000, pp. 1–22. [NH]

Pāzūkī, Shahrām. 'Taṣawwuf dar Īrān baʿd az qarn shishum', in *Tārīkh wa Jughrāfīyāy-i taṣawwuf*. Tehran, Nashr Kitāb Marjaʿ, 1388 Sh./2009, pp. 27–55. [RT]

Pocock, J.G.A. Review of *The History of Politics and the Politics of History*, by Quentin Skinner, *Common Knowledge* 10, no. 3 (2004), pp. 532–50. [NY]

Podemann Sørensen, Jørgen. 'Efficacy', in Jens Kreinath, Jan Snoek and Michael Stausberg, eds, *Theorizing Rituals: Issues, Topics, Approaches, Concepts*. Leiden, Brill, 2006, pp. 523–32. [IF]

Porter, Venetia. *Arabic and Persian Seals and Amulets in the British Museum*. London, British Museum, 2011. [AB]

Pourjavady, Nasrollah, ed. *Majmūʿih athār-i Abū ʿAbd al-Raḥmān Sulamī*. Tehran, Markaz-i Nashr-i Dānishgāhī, 1369 Sh./1990. [RT]

—— and Peter Lamborn Wilson. *Kings of Love: The Poetry and History of the Niʿmatullāhī Sufi Order*. Tehran, Imperial Iranian Academy of Philosophy, 1978. [AC] [RT]

Powers, David S. 'The Exegetical Genre *nāsikh al-Qurʾān wa mansūkhuhu*', in Andrew Rippin, ed., *Approaches to the History of the Interpretation of the Qurʾān*. Oxford, Clarendon Press, 1988, pp. 117–38. [RB]

Qāʾim-maqāmī, Sayyid ʿAbbās. 'Āthār wa afkār-i Ṣadr al-Dīn Kāshif Dizfūlī', *Kayhān-i andīsha* 38 (1992), pp. 77–93. [SR]

Qasim Zaman, Muhammad. *The Ulama in Contemporary Islam: Custodians of Change*. Princeton, NJ, Princeton University Press, 2002. [LT].

Quinn, Sholeh A. 'Rewriting Niʿmatu'llāhī History in Safavid Chronicles', in Leonard Lewisohn and David Morgan, eds, *Heritage of Sufism, Vol. III: Late Classical Persianate Sufism (1501–1750)*. Oxford, Oneworld, 1999, pp. 201–25. [RT]

Rādfar, Abū'l-Qāsim. 'Tarjuma-hā-yi Qur'ān-i Majīd bi Zabān-i Urdū', *Faṣl-nāma-yi Fadak* 1, no. 1 (1389 Sh./[2010], pp. 87–100. [NB]

Rahman, Fazlur. 'Status of Women in the Qur'an', in Guity Nashat, ed., *Women and Revolution in Iran*. Boulder, CO, Westview Press, 1983, pp. 37–54. [LL]

Rahnema, Ali. *An Islamic Utopian: A Political Biography of Ali Shariʿati*. London, I.B. Tauris, 2000. [YM]

Rakel, Eva. *Power, Islam, and Political Elite in Iran: A Study on the Iranian Political Elite from Khomeini to Ahmadinejad*. Leiden, Brill, 2008. [YM]

Rao, Ursula. 'Ritual in Society', in Jens Kreinath, Jan Snoek and Michael Stausberg, eds, *Theorizing Rituals: Issues, Topics, Approaches, Concepts*. Leiden, Brill, 2006, pp. 143–60. [IF]

Rayshahrī, Muḥammadī. *Kīmiyā-yi muḥabbat: Yādnāma-yi marḥūm shaykh Rajab ʿAlī Khayyāṭ*. Qum, Dār al-Ḥadīth, 1385 Sh./2006. [SR]

Razavi, Shahra. 'Islamic Politics, Human Rights and Women's Claims for Equality in Iran', *Third World Quarterly* 27, no. 7 (2006), pp. 1223–37. [BM]

Reinhart, Kevin A. *Before Revelation: The Boundaries of Muslim Moral Thought*. Albany, State University of New York Press, 1995. [LL]

Rezaei, Hassan. 'The Politics in Post-Revolution Iran: With Special Reference to Khatami's Presidency'. PhD dissertation, University of Pune, 2011. [NY]

Rice, David Storm. *The Unique Ibn al-Bawwāb Manuscript in the Chester Beatty Library*. Dublin, Emery Walker, 1955. [AB]

Ridgeon, Lloyd. 'Iranian Intellectuals (1997–2007)', *British Journal of Middle Eastern Studies* 34, no. 3 (2007), pp. 261–5. [BM]

Rippin, Andrew. 'The Exegetical Literature of Abrogation: Form and Content', in Gerald R. Hawting, Jawid Ahmad Mojaddedi and Alexander Samely, eds, *Studies in Islamic and Middle Eastern Texts and Traditions in Memory of Norman Calder*. Oxford, Oxford University Press, 2000, pp. 213–31. [RB]

Rizvi, Sajjad. 'Being (*wujūd*) and Sanctity (*wilāya*): Two Poles of Intellectual and Mystical Enquiry in Qajar Iran', in Robert Gleave, ed., *Religion and Society in Qajar Iran*. Abingdon, RoutledgeCurzon, 2005, pp. 113–26. [NB]

Royce, William Ronald. 'Mīr Maʿṣūm ʿAlī Shāh and the Niʿmat Allāhī Revival, 1776–77 to 1796–97: A Study of Sufism and Its Opponents in Late Eighteenth Century Iran'. Unpublished PhD dissertation, Princeton University, 1979. [RT]

Runzo, Joseph, ed. *Is God Real?* New York, Macmillan, 1993. [YM]

Sachedina, Abdulaziz A. 'Al-Khūʾī and the Twelver Shīʿites', in Abū al-Qāsim al-Mūsawī al-Khūʾī, *The Prolegomena to the Qurʾan*, tr. and intro. Abdulaziz A. Sachedina. Oxford, Oxford University Press, 1998, pp. 3–22. [RG]

Sādāt Ittifāghfar, Firishta and Ṣādiq Zībākalām. *Hāshimi bidūn-i rūtūsh: Panj sāl guftugū bā Hāshimī Rafsanjānī*. Tehran, Rawzana, 2008. [NY]

Sadeghi-Boroujerdi, Eskandar. *Revolution and its Discontents: Political Thought and Reform in Iran*. Cambridge, Cambridge University Press, 2019. [NY]

Saʿdiyya Shaikh. 'Transforming Feminisms: Islam, Women, and Gender Justice', in Omid Safi, ed., *Progressive Muslims on Justice, Gender and Pluralism*. Oxford, Oneworld, 2003, pp. 147–62. [LL]

al-Ṣadr, Sayyid al-Ḥasan. *Takmilat Amal al-āmil*, ed. ʿAbd al-Karīm Dabbāgh, 6 vols. Beirut, Dār al-Muʾarrikh al-ʿArabī, 2008. [SR]

Ṣadr-niyā, Bāqir, ed. *Farhang-i māʾthūrāt-i mutūn-i ʿirfānī (mushtamal ba aḥādīth, aqwāl wa amthāl-i mutūn-i ʿirfānī-yi fārsī)*. Tehran, Surūsh, 1380 Sh./2001. [LL]

Sadri, Mahmoud. 'Sacral Defense of Secularism: The Political Theologies of Soroush, Shabestari and Kadivar', *International Journal of Politics, Culture and Society* 15, no. 2 (2001), pp. 257–70. [BM] [YM]

Ṣadūqī Suhā, Manūchihr. *Tārīkh-i ḥukamāʾ wa ʿurafāʾ-yi mutaʾakhkhir az Ṣadr al-mutaʾallihīn*. Tehran, Anjuman-i Ḥikmat, 1980. [SR]

Sakurai, Keiko. 'Shiʿite Women's Seminaries (*howzeh-ye ʿelmiyyeh-ye khahran*) in Iran: Possibilities and Limitations', *Iranian Studies* 45, no. 6 (2012), pp. 727–44. [IF] [AV]

Saleh, Walid A. *The Formation of the Classical* Tafsīr *Tradition: The Qurʾān Commentary of al-Thaʿlabī (d. 427/1035)*. Boston, MA and Leiden, Brill, 2004. [NB] [IF]

Salvatore, Armando. 'The Sociology of Islam: Precedents and Perspectives', *Sociology of Islam* 1 (2013), pp. 7–13. [NY]

Samīʿī, Kaywān and Manūchihr Ṣadūqī. *Du Risāla dar Tārīkh-i jadīd-i taṣawwuf*. Tehran, Pāzhang, 1370 Sh./1991. [RT]

Ṣanʿatī, Riḍā. *Hāshimī dar sāl-i 88*. Tehran, Salman Farsi, 2011. [NY]

Santas, Constantine. *The Epic in Film: From Myth to Blockbuster*. Lanham, MD, Rowman and Littlefield, 2008. [NPS]

Scharbrodt, Oliver. 'The *Quṭb* as Special Representative of the Hidden Imam: The Conflation of Shiʿi and Sufi *Vilāyat* in the Niʿmatullāhī Order', in Denis Hermann and Sabrina Mervin, eds, *Shiʿi Trends and Dynamics in Modern Times (XVIIIth–XXth Centuries)/Courants et dynamiques chiites à l'époque moderne (XVIIIe–XXe siècles)*. Beirut, Orient-Institut/Ergon-Verlag, 2010, pp. 33–49. [AC]

Schimmel, Annemarie. *Mystical Dimensions of Islam*. Chapel Hill, University of North Carolina Press, 1975. [RT]

——. *Calligraphy and Islamic Culture*. New York, New York University Press, 1984. [AV]

——. *Deciphering the Signs of God: A Phenomenological Approach to Islam*. Albany, State University of New York Press, 1994. [IF]

Schleiermacher, Friedrich. 'The Hermeneutics: Outline of the 1819 Lectures', *New Literary History* 10, no. 1, Literary Hermeneutics (Autumn 1978), pp. 1–16. [BM]

Schulze, Reinhard. *A Modern History of the Islamic World*, tr. Azizeh Azodi. New York, New York University Press, 2002. [NY]

Schuon, Frithjof. *The Eye of the Heart: Metaphysics, Cosmology, Spiritual Life*. Bloomington, IN, World Wisdom, 1997. [LL]

Seddik, Youssef. *Si le Coran m'était conté*, 3 vols. Paris, Alef, 1989. [AB]

Seestani [Sīstānī], Syed Ali al-Husaini. *Islamic Laws: English Version of Taudhihul Masae'l*. London, World Federation, 1994. [LT]

Sells, Michael, tr., ed. and intro. *Early Islamic Mysticism: Sufi, Qur'an, Mi'raj, Poetic and Theological Writings*. Mawhah, NJ, Paulist Press, 1996. [NB] [RT]

Seyed-Gohrab, Ashgar. 'Magic in Classical Persian Amatory Literature', *Iranian Studies* 32, no. 1 (1999), pp. 71–97. [NB]

Shaaban, Bouthaina. 'The Muted Voices of Women Interpreters', in Mahnaz Afkhami, ed., *Faith and Freedom: Women's Human Rights in the Muslim World*. Syracuse, NY, Syracuse University Press, 1995, pp. 61–77. [LL]

Shaʿbānzāda, Bahman. *Tārīkh-i shafāhī-yi Madrasa-yi Ḥaqqānī*. Tehran, Markaz-i Asnād-i Inqilāb-i Islāmī, 2005. [NY]

Shabistarī, Maḥmūd. *The Garden of Mystery (Gulshan-i raz)*, tr. Robert Darr. Sausalito, CA, Real Impressions, 1998. [LL]

Shafīʿi, Muḥammad. *Mufassirān-i Shiʿa*. Shiraz, Dānishgāh-i Pahlawī, 1349 Sh./1970. [AC]

—— and Faḍl Allāh Ṣalawātī. *Tafsīr wa mufassirān-i shīʿa*. Tehran, Iṭṭilāʿāt, 1391 Sh./2012. [AC]

Shalev-Eyni, Sarit. 'Solomon, his Demons and Jongleurs: The Meeting of Islamic, Judaic and Christian Culture', *al-Masāq: Journal of the Medieval Mediterranean* 18, no. 2 (2006), pp. 145–60. [NPS]

Sharīʿatī, ʿAlī. *The Return to the Self, Vol. IV: Collected Works*. Tehran, Ḥusayniyya Irshād Press, 1978. [AB]

Shaykh, Maḥmūd. *Maktab-i akhlāqī-yi ʿirfānī-yi Najaf: Maktab-i ʿirfānī-yi Mullā Ḥusayn-qulī Hamadānī*. Tehran, Pazhūhishgāh-i Farhang wa Andīsha-yi Islāmī, 1395 Sh./2016. [SR]

Shirazi, Faegheh. *Velvet Jihad: Muslim Women's Quiet Resistance to Islamic Fundamentalism*. Gainesville, University Press of Florida, 2009. [IF]

Siavoshi, Sussan. *Montazeri: The Life and Times of Iran's Revolutionary Ayatollah*. Cambridge, Cambridge University Press, 2017. [NY]

Ṣiddīqī, Muḥammad Zubayr. *Ḥadīth Literature: Its Origin, Development and Special Features*. Cambridge, Islamic Texts Society, 1993. [AV]

Simms, Rob and Amir Koushkani. *The Art of Avaz and Mohammad Reza Shajarian: Foundations and Contexts*. Lanham, MD, Lexington Books, 2012. [GZ]

Simonowitz, David. 'A Modern Master of Islamic Calligraphy and Her Peers', *Journal of Middle East Women's Studies* 6, no. 1 (2010), pp. 75–102. [AV]

Sirriyeh, Elizabeth. 'Modern Muslim Interpretations of *Shirk*', *Religion* 20, no. 2 (1990), pp. 139–59. [SK]

Smith, George. *Henry Martyn, Saint and Scholar: First Modern Missionary to the Mohammedans, 1781–1812*. New York, The Taxton Press, n.d. [RT]

Solomon, Jon. *The Ancient World in the Cinema*, revised and expanded edn. New Haven, CT, Yale University Press, 2001. [NPS]

Soroush, Abdolkarim [also Abdulkarim]. *Naqdī wa dar-āmadī bar taḍādd-i diyāliktīkī: Bi-ḍamīma: Naqdī bar rawish-i shinākht*. Tehran, Ḥikmat, 1357 Sh./1978. [YM]

——. *Basṭ-i tajruba-yi nabawī*. Tehran, Ṣirāṭ, 1999. [YM]

——. *Ṣirāṭhā-yi mustaqīm*. Tehran, Ṣirāṭ, 1999. [YM]

——. *Nahād-i nā-ārām-i jahān*. Tehran, Ṣirāṭ, 1379 Sh./2000. [YM]

——. *Reason, Freedom, and Democracy in Islam: Essential Writings of Abdolkarim Soroush*, ed. Mahmoud Sadri and Ahmad Sadri. Oxford, Oxford University Press, 2000. [YM]

——. *The Expansion of Prophetic Experience: Essays on Historicity, Contingency and Plurality in Religion*, tr. Nilou Mobasser. Leiden, Brill, 2009. [YM]

Speziale, Fabrizio. 'À propos du renouveau *Niʿmatullāhī*: Le centre de Hyderabad au cours de la première modernité', *Studia Iranica* 42, no. 1 (2013), pp. 91–118. [AC]

Steigerwald, Diana. 'Twelver Shīʿī Ta'wīl', in Andrew Rippin, ed., *The Blackwell Companion to the Qur'ān*. Malden, MA, Blackwell, 2006, pp. 373–85. [SK]

Stewart, Devin J. *Islamic Legal Orthodoxy: Twelver Shiite Responses to the Sunni Legal System*. Salt Lake City, UT, University of Utah Press, 1998. [SK]

——. 'Islamic Juridical Hierarchies and the Office of *Marjaʿ al-taqlīd*', in Lynda Clarke, ed., *Shīʿite Heritage: Essays on Classical and Modern Traditions*. Binghamton, NY, Global Publications, 2001, pp. 137–58. [NY]

Stock, Brian. *The Implications of Literacy: Written Language and Models of Interpretation in the Eleventh and Twelfth Centuries*. Princeton, NJ, Princeton University Press, 1983. [IF]

Storey, Charles Ambrose. *Persian Literature: A Bio-bibliographical Survey, Vol. II, Part I*. London, Luzac, 1935. [AC]

Subḥānī, Jaʿfar. 'Naẓarī wa gudharī bar zindagānī-yi ustād', in *Yādnāma-yi ustad ʿAllāma Ṭabāṭabā'ī*. Qum, Intishārāt-i Shafaq, 1361 Sh./1982, pp. 45–74. [SR]

Suleman, Fahmida, ed. *Word of God, Art of Man: The Qur'an and its Creative Expressions*. Oxford, Oxford University Press in association with the Institute of Ismaili Studies, 2007. Qur'anic Studies Series 4. [IF]

Sulṭānī, Ḥājj Mīrzā Muḥammad Bāqir. *Rahbarān-i ṭarīqat wa ʿirfān*. Tehran, Mu'assisa Intishārātī Maḥbūb, 1371 Sh./1992. [RT]

Surūr, Ibrāhīm. *Sīrat al-ʿurafā'*. Beirut, Dār al-Kitāb al-ʿArabī, 2008. [SR]

Ṭabāṭabā'ī, Muḥammad Ḥusayn and Murtaḍā Muṭahharī. *Uṣūl-i falsafa wa rawish-i ri'ālīsm*, 3 vols. Tehran, Intishārāti Islāmī, n.d. [YM]

Tabrīzī, Ja'far Subḥānī. *Manshūr-i 'aqāyid imāmiyya: Sharḥī gūyā wa mustadal az 'aqāyid shī'a; athnā 'asharī dar yikṣad wa panjāh aṣl*. Qum, Mu'asasa-yi Imām Ṣādiq, 1385 Sh./2006. [RT]

Takeshita, Masataka. *Ibn 'Arabī's Theory of the Perfect Man and its Place in the History of Islamic Thought*. Tokyo, University of Foreign Studies, 1987. [AC]

Takeyh, Ray. *Guardians of the Revolution: Iran and the World in the Age of the Ayatollahs*. Oxford, Oxford University Press, 2009. [YM]

Takim, Liyakat. *The Heirs of the Prophet: Charisma and Religious Authority in Shi'ite Islam*. Albany, State University of New York Press, 2006. [LT]

——. *Shi'ism in America*. New York, New York University Press, 2009. [LT]

—— '*Ijtihad* and the Derivation of New Jurisprudence in Contemporary Shi'ism: The Rulings of Ayatollah Bujnurdi', in Carool Kersten and Susanne Olsson, eds, *Alternative Islamic Discourses and Religious Authority*. Farnham, Ashgate, 2013, pp. 17–34. [LT]

——. 'Maqāṣid al-Sharī'a in Contemporary Shī'ī Jurisprudence', in Adis Duderija, ed., *Maqasid al-Shari'a and Contemporary Reformist Muslim Thought: An Examination*. New York, Palgrave, 2014, pp. 101–25. [LT]

——. 'Customary Law as a Source of Legislation for Shi'i Law', *Studies in Religion/Sciences Religieuses* 47, no. 4 (2018), pp. 481–99. [LT]

Tambiah, Stanley. 'A Performative Approach to Ritual', *Proceedings of the British Academy* 65 (1981), pp. 113–69.

al-Tamimi, Huda. 'Islam, Calligraphy and Gender: An Overview on the Role of Women Calligraphers in Islam', *IRS Cultural Heritage* 13, no. 2 (2013), pp. 26–33. [AV]

Tanāwulī, Parwīz [Tanavoli, Parviz]. *Lion Rugs: The Lion in the Art and Culture of Iran*. New York, Trans Book, 1985. [AB]

——. *Tālism*. Tehran, Bon-Gah Publications, 2007. [AB]

Thaqafī, Murād. 'Aḥzāb wa junbish-hāyi Islāmī: Yik bastar wa dū rūyā'?' *Goft-o-gu* 67 (Tīr 1394 Sh./July 2015), pp. 105–25. [NY]

Thaqafiyān, Akbar. *Shahīd Muṣṭafā Khumaynī wa tafsīrash*. Tehran, Khāna-yi Kitāb, 1391 Sh./2012–13. [AC]

Thirwatiyān, Bihrūz. *Ṣafī 'Alī Shāh wa tafsīr-ash*. Tehran, Khāna-yi Kitāb, 1389 Sh./2010. [NB]

Ṭihrānī, Āqā Buzurg. *al-Dharī'a ilā taṣānīf al-shī'a*, 29 vols. Najaf, al-Maṭba'a al-Ḥaydariyya, 1978. [SR]; 3rd edn, 25 vols. Beirut, Dār al-Aḍwā', 1403/1983. [AC]

——. *Ṭabaqāt a'lām al-shī'a*, 19 vols. Beirut, Mu'assasat al-Maḥajja al-Bayḍā', 2009. [SR]

——. *Sarguzasht-i 'ārifān*. Tehran, Mīrāth-i Māndigār, 1393 Sh./2014. [SR]

Tomkins, Stephen. *John Wesley: A Biography*. Oxford, Lion Publishing, 2003. [RT]

Torab, Azam. 'The Politicization of Women's Religious Circles in Post-revolutionary Iran', in Sarah Ansari and Vanessa Martin, eds, *Women, Religion and Culture in Iran*. Richmond, Curzon, 2002, pp. 143–68. [IF]

——. *Performing Islam: Gender and Ritual in Iran*. Leiden, Brill, 2007. [IF]

Turner, Colin. *Islam without Allah? The Rise of Religious Externalism in Safavid Iran*. Richmond, Curzon, 2000. [SK]

al-Tustarī, Sahl. *Tafsīr al-Qur'ān al-'aẓīm*, ed. Muḥammad Jīrat Allāh. Cairo, Dār al-Thaqāfiyya li'l-Nashr, 2002. [SR]

Vahdat, Farzin. 'Religious Modernity in Iran: Dilemmas of Islamic Democracy in the Discourse of Mohammad Khatami', *Comparative Studies of South Asia, Africa and the Middle East* 25, no. 3 (2005), pp. 650–64. [BM]

Van Den Bos, Matthijs. *Mystic Regimes: Sufism and the State in Iran, from the Late Qajar Era to the Islamic Republic*. Leiden, Brill, 2002. [NB] [SR] [AV]

Vanzan, Anna. *Le donne di Allah: Viaggio nei femminismi islamici*. Milan, Mondadori, 2012. [AV]

Vikør, Knut S. 'The Shari'a and the Nation State: Who Can Codify Islamic Law', in Bjørn Olav Utvik and Knut S. Vikør, eds, *The Middle East in a Globalized World: Papers from the Fourth Nordic Conference on Middle Eastern Studies, Oslo, 1998*. London, Hurst, 2000, pp. 220–50. [NY]

Vogel, Frank E. 'The Public and Private in Saudi Arabia: Restrictions on the Powers of Committees for Ordering the Good and Forbidding the Evil', *Social Research: An International Quarterly of Social Sciences* 70, no. 3 (2003), pp. 749–68. [NY]

Wadud, Amina. *Inside the Gender Jihad: Women's Reform in Islam*. Oxford, Oneworld, 2006. [LL]

Walther, Wiebke. *Women in Islam: From Medieval to Modern Times*, tr. C.S.V. Salt. Princeton, NJ, Markus Wiener, 1993. [LL]

Ware, Rudolph T. *The Walking Qur'an: Islamic Education, Embodied Knowledge, and History in West Africa*. Chapel Hill, University of North Carolina Press, 2014. [SR]

Warner, Michael, Jonathan VanAntwerpen and Craig Calhoun, eds. *Varieties of Secularism in a Secular Age*. Cambridge, MA, Harvard University Press, 2013. [BM]

Waterfield, Robin. *Christians in Persia: Assyrians, Armenians, Roman Catholics and Protestants*. London, George Allen and Unwin, 1973. [RT]

Watt, W. Montgomery and Richard Bell. *Introduction to the Qur'an*. Edinburgh, Edinburgh University Press, 2003. [RT]

Werbner, Pnina. '"Sealing the Koran": Offering and Sacrifice among Pakistani Labour Migrants', *Cultural Dynamics* 1, no. 1 (1988), pp. 77–97. [IF]

Westra, Laura. 'Self-Knowing in Plato, Plotinus and Avicenna', in Parviz Morewedge, ed., *Neoplatonism and Islamic Thought*. Albany, State University of New York Press, 1992, pp. 89–110. [LL]

Wiet, Gaston. Review of *The Unique Ibn al-Bawwāb Manuscript in the Chester Beatty Library*, by D.S. Rice, *Syria: Archéologie, art et histoire* 32, nos. 3–4 (1955), pp. 365–7. [AB]

Wolfson, Harry Austryn. *The Philosophy of the Kalam*. Cambridge, MA, Harvard University Press, 1976. [YM]

Wright, Denis. *The English amongst the Persians: Imperial Lives in Nineteenth-Century Iran*. London, Heinemann, 1977. [RT]

Yavari, Neguin. '*Tafsīr* and the Mythology of Islamic Fundamentalism', in Andreas Görke and Johanna Pink, eds, *Tafsīr and Islamic Intellectual History: Exploring the Boundaries of a Genre*. Oxford, Oxford University

Press in association with the Institute of Ismaili Studies, 2014, pp. 289–319. Qur'anic Studies Series 12. [NY]

Yazdī, Muḥammadtaqī Miṣbāḥ. *Ma'ārif Qur'ān: Rāh wa rahnamāshināsī*, 8 vols in 2. Qum, Mu'asasa-yi Āmūzishī wa Pazhuhishī Imām Khomeini, 1386 Sh./2007. [RT]

Yeganeh, Nahid and Nikki R. Keddie. 'Sexuality and Shi'i Social Protest in Iran', in Juan R.I. Cole and Nikki R. Keddie, eds, *Shi'ism and Social Protest*. New Haven, Yale University Press, 1986, pp. 108–36. [LL]

Yelle, Robert. A. *Semiotics of Religion: Signs of the Sacred in History*. London, Bloomsbury, 2013. [IF]

Zadeh, Travis. *The Vernacular Qur'an: Translation and the Rise of Persian Exegesis*. Oxford, Oxford University Press in association with the Institute of Ismaili Studies, 2012. Qur'anic Studies Series 7. [NB] [AC - Intr.] [SR]

——. 'An Ingestible Scripture: Qur'ānic Erasure and the Limits of "Popular" Religion', in Benjamin J. Fleming and Richard D. Mann, eds, *Material Culture and Asian Religions: Text, Image, Object*. London, Routledge, 2014, pp. 97–119. [IF]

——. 'Persian Qur'anic Networks and the Writings of "an Iranian Lady", Nusrat Amin Khanum', in Suha Taji-Farouki, ed., *The Qur'an and its Readers Worldwide: Contemporary Commentaries and Translations*. Oxford, Oxford University Press in association with the Institute of Ismaili Studies, 2015, pp. 275–323. Qur'anic Studies Series 14. [AC - Intr.]

Zain-ed-Din, Nazira. 'Unveiling and Veiling: On the Liberation of the Woman and Social Renewal in the Islamic World', in Margot Badran and Miriam Cooke, eds, *Opening the Gates: A Century of Arab Feminist Writing*. Bloomington, Indiana University Press, 1990, pp. 270–76. [LL]

Zaman, Muhammad Qasim. 'The Sovereignty of God in Modern Islamic Thought', *Journal of the Royal Asiatic Society* 25, no. 3 (2015), pp. 389–418. [NY]

Zargarī-Nijād, Ghulām-Ḥusayn, ed. *Rasā'il-i mashrūṭiyyat*. Tehran, Kawīr, 1374 Sh./1995. [AC]

Ẓarīfīniyā, Ḥamīd Riḍā. *Kālbudshikāfī-yi jināh-hā-yi siyāsī-yi Iran*, intro. Muṣṭafā Tājzāda. Tehran, Āzādī-yi Andīsha, 1999. [NY]

Zarrīnkūb, 'Abd al-Ḥusayn. *Dunbāla-yi justujū dar taṣawwuf-i Īrān*. Tehran, Intishārāt-i Amīr Kabīr, 1362 Sh./1983. [RT]

Index of Qur'anic Citations

Index of Qur'anic Citations

Index of Qur'anic Citations

General Index

Page numbers in *italics* refer to illustrations and tables.

Eve 202, 296
evil eye (*chasm naẓar, naẓar ghurbānī*) 428
evil spirits 26, 426–7
  see also demons
excommunication (*takfīr*) 21, 188
exegesis *see* Qur'anic exegesis; *tafsīr*
exoteric exegesis 43, 59, 63, 188, 207, 209–10, 246, 250, 252, 261, 275–6
Expansion of the Prophetic Experience (Theory of the Qur'anic revelation, Abdolkarim Soroush) 136–9, 148n. 63, 154–7
  arguments for theory 157–9
  historical roots of theory 160–5
  implications of theory 176–8
  objections to theory 140–1, 157–60
  philosophical assessment and categorisation of theory 165–7
  religious critical realistic interpretation of revelation 166, 167, 169, 171–2, 174–6
  religious direct realistic interpretation of revelation 166, 167–8, 171
  religious non-realistic interpretation of revelation 166, 167, 169, 171, 175
  on role of God in revelation 154–7
  on role of Muhammad in revelation 154, 155
  updated version 179n. 24

faḍā'īl al-Qur'ān (literary genre) 441n. 26
Fadak garden 254
El-Fadl, Khaled Abou 124
Fajr International Film Festival 377
Fakhimzadeh, Mehdi 385
falsification of scripture (*taḥrīf*) 9–10, 225–7, 281, 397, 407n. 58
  Khū'ī on 233–5, 236, 237
  Nūrī on 227–31, 233, 234, 237
  Shahrastānī on 231–3, 234, 236, 237
  Ṭabāṭabā'ī on 235–7
Fanā'ī, Abū'l-Qāsim 7, 16n. 12, 123, 125, 126, 159
  on historically situating *tanzīl* process 132, 139–42
al-Fārābī, Abū Naṣr Muḥammad 455n. 8
  Fuṣūs al-ḥikam 297, 315n. 2
Farāhānī, Mīrzā Buzurg Qā'im-Maqām 199
Faravardeh, Mojtaba 377, 386, 387, 388, 390, 394–5, 402
Fardīd, Aḥmad 327
al-Fārisī, Salmān 56
Farrakhzād, Forugh 373n. 56
Farshchian, Mahmoud, *The Queen of Sheba Visits Solomon* 378, 379, *381*
Fasā'ī, Mīrzā Ibrāhīm 194
Fatḥ ʿAlī Shāh (Qajar ruler of Persia, r. 1797–1834) 201, 245, 355
  commissioning refutations of missionaries' doctrines 8, 192, 193, 198, 199, 200, 278
  and Niʿmatullāhīs 188, 189, 190, 191
Fāṭima Maʿṣūma Museum (Qum) 355
Fāṭima bt. Muḥammad 254, 255, 256, 330, 357, 397–8, 435
  hand of Fāṭima 330, 332
Fayḍ ʿAlī Shāh, Mullā ʿAbd al-Ḥusayn Ṭabasī 187, 188, 190
feminist exegesis, Western Muslim 123–4, 130
  method 123, 134
  problems in finding gender justice in Qur'an 124
feminist intellectuals, Muslim 7
feminists, Muslim 362
Ferdowsi Magazine 330, 336
film industry *see* cinema
fiqh see jurisprudence
Firdawsī 295, 414
  Shāh-nāma 1, 297, 365, 378, 379, *380*
'fixed' Qur'an 126, 130–2, 133, 134, 136, 142–3
forbidding wrong and commanding right *see amr bi'l-maʿrūf*
Foreign Policy (magazine) 150
formness of God 155–6, 157, 159–60
Foucault, Michel 46–7
Four Declarations (*chahār qul*) 425–6, 429, 431, 436
fragilization, mutual 129, 145n. 12
Fraternal Society (Anjuman-i Ukhuwwat) 246
Freedom Movement of Iran 148n. 64

Muṣṭafawī, Ḥasan, *Tafsīr-i rawshan* 284
mutaghayyir law (law subject to change) 134
Muṭahharī, Murtaḍā' 2, 92, 105, 106, 116–17, 151, 285
mutashābihāt (equivocal verses), *muḥkamāt* (unequivocal verses) vs 32–5
Muʿtazilī school 19, 161, 180n. 43
  on Qur'anic revelation 8, 131–2, 150, 162–4
muṭlaq (unconditional, jurisprudential concept) 26, 28
mutual prayer (*mubāhala*) 200–1
al-Muẓaffar, Muḥammad Riḍā, *Uṣūl al-fiqh* 29
Muẓaffar ʿAlī Shāh, Mīrzā Muḥammad Taqī 187–8, 275
mystical attractions 261–3, 269n. 77
mystical exegesis 251–2, 258–64
mystical seeker (*ʿārif*) 49
mystical union 65–6
mystical-ethical school of Najaf (*madrasa-yi akhlāqī-yi ʿirfānī-yi Najaf*) 53
mysticism (*ʿirfān*) 12, 48, 49, 50, 51–2, 53, 66–7, 271–3
  see also ṭarīqa

Nabiev, Jurabeg 450
Nādir Shāh 277
Nā'īnī, ʿAbd al-Wahāb (Pīr Nā'īn) 199–200
Nā'īnī, Mīrzā Ḥusayn 49, 58
Najaf 49, 53, 54, 58, 61
namāz see ritual prayer
namāz-i jamāʿat (congregational prayer) 410
Naqqāshīkhāṭṭ (calligraphy-painting) 345, 359, 367
Naqshbandī order 54, 61, 186, 276
Narāghī (Narāqī), Ārash 147n. 59, 158
Narāqī, ʿAllāma Aḥmad 199, 200
Narāqī, Mahdī, *Jāmiʿ al-saʿādāt* 73n. 76
Narāqī, Mullā Aḥmad 389
  Sayf al-umma 200
Nāṣir al-Dīn Shāh (Qajar ruler, r. 1848–96) 10, 245, 246, 355
naskh see abrogation
naskh (calligraphic style) 355, 357
naskh al-tilāwa dūn al-ḥukm (abrogation of wording of Qur'anic verse, but not its meaning) 230, 233, 234, 236
  see also abrogation
Nasr, Seyyed Hossein 145n. 14, 266n. 33, 316n. 8
nastaʿlīq (calligraphic style) 341, 344, 355, 360, 366, 367
National Iranian Radio Organisation (Tehran) 450
Nawā'itī, ʿAlī b. Aḥmad Mahā'imī Kūkanī 279, 288n. 36
nawḥa (lamentations) 424, 433, 439n. 12
Nayrīzī, Quṭb al-Dīn 277
Nayshābūrī, Adīb 291
naẓar ghurbānī see evil eye
al-Naẓẓām, Ibrāhīm 163, 164
negative (apophatic) theology 179n. 27
  on human cognitive faculties 161
  influence on revelation theory 161–2
  see also Muʿtazilī school
Neshat, Shirin 369, 373n. 56
Netton, Ian Richard 179n. 27
New Testament 194–5, 198, 199, 200, 202, 211, 234
  see also Bible
New Theology (Iranian Religious Intellectual Movement) 125, 126, 132
The Night of Power *see laylat al-qadr*
Niʿmatullāh Walī, Shāh 186, 251, 273
Niʿmatullāhī order 53, 57, 186–9, 199, 244, 253, 272, 273
  decline and revival 186, 274
  in India 186, 244–5, 272, 274, 286n. 12
  persecution by Twelver Shiʿis 187–9, 191, 192
  position within Uṣūlī/Twelver Shiʿism 273–6
  schisms 274, 287n. 17
Nimrod b. Arghu 384
Niyāwarān Palace (Tehran) 355
Niẓāmī Ganjawī 295, 297, 414
Noah 399, 400
Noqṭa-alif (website) 366
nubuwwa see prophethood

al-Ṭabrisī, al-Faḍl b. al-Ḥasan 226, 228, 255
al-Ṭabrisī, Mīrzā Ḥusayn b. Taqī al-Nūrī *see* al-Nūrī al-Ṭabrisī, Mīrzā Ḥusayn b. Tāqī
Tabriz 49, 51
Tabrīzī, Muḥammad Ḥusayn, *Kashf al-murād min al-mashrūta wa'l-istibdād* 278
Tabrīzī, Ṣādiq 347n. 8, 359
tadhkiras (bio-bibliographical collections) 354
tafsīr (genre of Qur'anic exegesis) 20
  in 18th and 19th century Iran 276–8
  decline and revival of tradition 272, 276, 277, 278, 281, 283
  ḥawza-based *tafsīr*s 3–4
  reasoning in 24, 26–7
  repetition and reuse of material in 279, 283
  verse form in 243, 247, 248
  see also Qur'anic exegesis
Tafsīr āyāt al-aḥkām-i nādirī 277
Tafsīr-i namūna (Nāṣir Makārim Shīrāzī) 2, 15n. 4, 273
Tafsīr-i Ṣafī (Ṣafī ʿAlī Shāh) 10, 11, 243, 245, 250–1, 276
  ʿAlī in 253, 256–8
  contents, context and style 246–50
  exoteric and esoteric exegesis in 250, 252
  inimitability of 263
  love of Household of Prophet in 255–7
  mystical attractions in 261–3
  ontological framework 251
  on sainthood 257–9, 263, 268n. 60
  Shiʿi–Sufi dimension of 252–8
  Sunni sources in 253–4
taghannī (melodious recital of Qur'an) 447, 454, 455n. 8
ṭāghūt (false idols) 112
Taha Qur'anic Research Group 376–7, 382, 384, 385, 387, 388, 389, 390, 392, 399
  'Amīr al-mu'minīn ʿAlī, muʿallim-i anbiyā" (Persian document) 399, 400
taḥrīf see falsification
taḥrīr (vocal technique) 452
tajwīd see cantillation
Tājzāda, Muṣṭafā 112, 118n. 1
  on commanding right and forbidding wrong 6–7, 101–2, 105–7, 115–17
takfīr see excommunication
ṭalāq see divorce
Ṭalibuf, ʿAbd al-Raḥīm 278
Ṭāliqānī, Maḥmūd 2, 144n. 1, 145n. 14
talismans 430–1
Talmud 197
Ṭālūt (Saul) 388
tamarkuz see concentration
Tanāwulī, Parwīz (Parviz Tanavoli, sculptor) 329–30, 333, 335, 347n. 8
Tanhā'ī-yi Laylā' (television show) 113
Tanhātarīn Sardār (television series) 385–6
tanzīl see revelation
taqiyya see dissimulation
ṭarīqa (Sufi order/school) 48, 53–9
  see also al-Mīzān fī tafsīr al-Qur'ān (Ṭabāṭabā'ī); Sufism
ṭarīqa-yi maʿrifat-i nafs (path of self-knowledge) 53
tartīl see cantillation; recitation of the Qur'an
Tasnīm (Jawādī Āmulī) 4, 5, 273, 285
  on apparent meaning of Qur'an 29, 30–1
  methodology 25–8, 35–6
  on reasoning 26–7
  on unequivocal vs equivocal Qur'anic verses 33, 34–5
Tatars 448
Tawheed Institute Australia 22
tawḥīd see Divine Unity
tawḥīdic paradigm 123
Taylor, Charles, Immanent Frame 125, 128–30
Tehran 245
  ritual prayer by women in 13–14, 409–18
Tehran Biennial 332, 333, 336, 338, 341
Tehran City Beautification Organisation (Sāzimān-i Zībāsāzī-yi Shahr-i Tihrān) 361
Tehran Municipality 361, 370

temporality, 'principle of materiality and temporality of every accidental being' (Mullā Ṣadrā Shīrāzī) 156
The Ten Commandments (film) 392
Tennyson 298
testimony, giving 80
al-Thaʿlabī, Abū Isḥāq 253
thaqalayn (two precious things) 435–6, 437, 443nn. 56 and 57
Théâtre de la Ville (Paris) 452, 453
Theory of the Qur'anic Revelation *see* Expansion of the Prophetic Experience
365 Days in the Company of the Qur'an see In the Company of the Qur'an
Throne Verse (*āyat al-kursī*, Q. 2:255) 277, 427, 429, 431, 436
Thumālī, Abū Ḥamza 434, 435
al-Ṭihranī, Āqā Buzurg 227, 229, 283–4, 288n. 37
  al-Dharīʿa 279, 282
  Ṭabaqāt iʿlām al-shīʿa 288n. 37
Ṭihrānī, Muḥammad Ḥasan Khaṭīb-bāshī 279
Ṭihrānī, Muḥammad Ḥusayn Ḥusaynī *see* Ḥusaynī Ṭihrānī, Muḥammad Ḥusayn
Ṭihrānī, Muḥammad Ṣādiqī, *al-Furqān fī tafsīr al-Qur'ān* 284
Ṭihrānī, Riḍā 279
Time (magazine) 150
Tīmūrid manuscript 378
Torab, Azam 424, 433
Torah 211–12, 397, 398
  see also Bible; New Testament; Old Testament
transcendence 64–5, 127, 129, 155, 160, 161, 170–1, 172, 262, 299
transformation
  of perishable into eternal 301–3
  'transformational parity' 173–4
Trinity 195, 212
The Tripartite Mahzor (fourteenth-century manuscript) 391
Tudeh Party 108, 109
al-Ṭūsī, Abū Naṣr al-Sarrāj 211
al-Ṭūsī, Muḥammad b. al-Ḥasan 33, 223n. 208
  al-Ghaybat 406n. 40
al-Ṭūsī, Muḥammad b. Jaʿfar 86, 226
Ṭūsī, Naṣīr al-Dīn 295
  Akhlāq-i Nāṣirī (*Nāṣirian Ethics*) 298, 299–300
al-Tustarī, Sahl 284
Twelver Shiʿism 8, 9, 11, 186
  on abrogation and falsification 225–38
  juridical schools 20
  place of women within 14
  position of Niʿmatullāhī order within 273–6
  Sufism in nineteenth century 271–3
  see also Akhbārism/Akhbārīs; Uṣūlism/Uṣūlīs

ʿUliyā, Mahd 356
al-ʿUlūm, Mahdī Baḥr *see* Baḥr al-ʿUlūm
ʿUmar, Madīha 336
ʿUmar b. al-Khaṭṭāb 230, 235, 254, 268n. 51, 398
Umayyad rulers 257
Umm Kulthum 450
Umm al-Salma 356
unconditional (*ʿām*, *muṭlaq*, jurisprudential concept) 26, 28
unequivocal Qur'anic verses, equivocal vs 32–5
UNESCO 325
The Unique Dimension *see* al-Buʿd al-Wāhid
Unity, Divine (*tawḥīd*) 34, 66, 295–7, 426
Unity of Being (*waḥdat al-wujūd*) 200, 251, 266n. 37, 295
unity of religions 202–3
universities, cooperation with *ḥawza* 3–4
University of Tehran 451
unmetered genres (music/poetry), Qur'an as base for 448–9
ʿuqalāʾ (people of intellect) 29–30, 31, 88–91
al-ʿUrafā, Ḥusayn Shams 287n. 17
Uriah the Hittite 383
uṣūl (pillars/unequivocal verses) 33, 34
uṣūl al-fiqh (principles of Islamic jurisprudence) 29, 30, 200
Uṣūlism/Uṣūlīs 213, 226